KT-558-076

050212
THE HENLEY COLLEGE LIBRARY
111295

Hands On C++

A Complete Self-Study Guide to C++

Alistair Stewart

DIGITAL SKILLS
Milton
Barr
Girvan
Ayrshire
KA26 9TY

www.digital-skills.co.uk

email : sales@digital-skills.co.uk

phone : 01465-861-638

Copyright © Alistair Stewart 1996 - 2004
All rights reserved

No part of this work may be reproduced or used in any form without written permission from the author.

First printed by DIGITAL SKILLS August 2002

Updated August 2004
Reprinted July 2006

Title : Hands On C++

ISBN : 1-874107-04-1

Other Titles by the same Author

Hands On Pascal
Hands On Java
Hands On XHTML
Hands On DarkBASIC Pro vol 1
Hands On DarkBASIC Pro vol 2

Table Of Contents

Introduction

Chapter 1 Background

Chapter 2 Starting C++

Chapter 3 Control Structures

Chapter 4 Functions

Chapter 5 Data Structures

Chapter 6 File Handling

Chapter 7 Tables

Chapter 8 Dynamic Linear Types

Chapter 9 Advanced Data Structures

Chapter 10 Borland Graphics

Chapter 11 Classes and Objects

Chapter 12 Class Relationships

Chapter 13 I/O Streams

Chapter 14 Handling Errors

INTRODUCTION

Learn by Doing

The only way to become a programming expert is to practice. No one ever learned any skill by simply reading. Hence, this is not a text book where you can sit back in a passive way slowly reading through each chapter; rather it is designed as a teaching package in which you will do most of the work. The tasks embedded in the text are included to test your understanding of what has gone before and as a method of discovering for yourself some of the subtler aspects and techniques of the language. It is therefore important that you tackle each task since they are designed to test your knowledge and develop your skill. In addition, many of the short programs developed in the early chapters of the book are used to construct a final project in the last section of the text.

Who this Publication is For

This book is designed for the following groups

- People new to programming who want to develop a high degree of skill in C++.
- People wanting to move on from C to C++.
- Students learning programming techniques using C or C++.
- Anyone requiring a practical introduction to object-oriented design and programming.

No previous knowledge of computers or programming is required since what follows assumes you are new to these topics.

This text is designed for independent self-study by students in the first year of a degree or HNC/D Computing course, professional programmers who wish to develop skills in the most popular object-oriented language, as well as any individual curious to discover the fascinating world of C++.

The Contents

Chapter 1 covers some background material including number systems and a simple program definition language.

Chapters 2 to 9 cover the conventional aspects of C and C++.

Chapter 10 covers Borland's graphics routines.

Chapters 11 to 14 deal with the object-oriented aspects of C++.

How To Get the Most out of this Package

Experience has shown that students derive most benefit from this material by approaching its study in an organised way. The following strategy for study is highly recommended:

1. Read a chapter or section through without taking notes or worrying too much about topics that are not immediately clear to you. This will give you an overview of the purpose of that chapter/section.

2. Re-read the chapter. This time take things slowly; make notes and summaries of the material you are reading (even if you understand the material, making notes helps to retain the facts in your long-term memory); re-read any parts you are unclear about.

3. Embedded in the material are a series of tasks. Do each task as you reach it. These are designed to test your knowledge and understanding of what has gone before. Do not be tempted to skip over them, promise to come back to them later, or to make only a half-hearted attempt at tackling them before looking up the answer (there are solutions at the end of each chapter). Once you have attempted a task, look at the solution given. Often there will be important points emphasised in the solution which will aid your understanding.

4. As you progress through the book go back and re-read earlier chapters since you will often get something new from them as your knowledge increases.

Language Syntax Diagrams

The text contains many syntax diagrams which give a visual representation of the format of various statements allowed in C++. These diagrams make no attempt to be complete but merely act as a guide to the format most likely to be used. The accompanying text and example should highlight the more complex options available.

Below is a typical diagram:

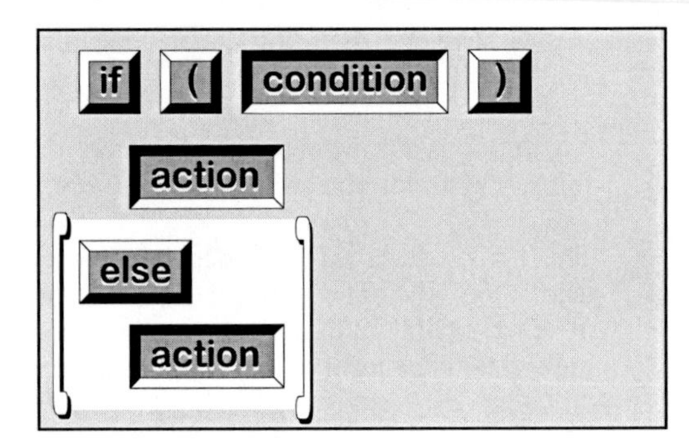

Each tile in the diagram holds a **token** of the statement.

Raised tiles represent fixed terms in the statement which must be entered exactly as shown.

Sunken tiles represent tokens whose exact value is decided by you, the programmer, but again these values must conform to some stated rule.

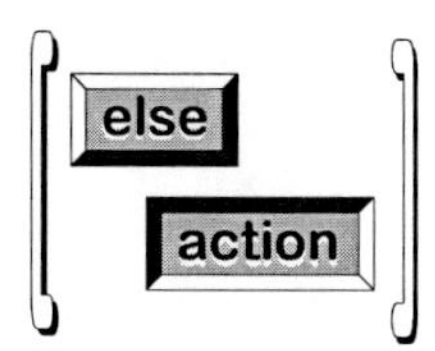

Items enclosed in parentheses may be omitted if not required.

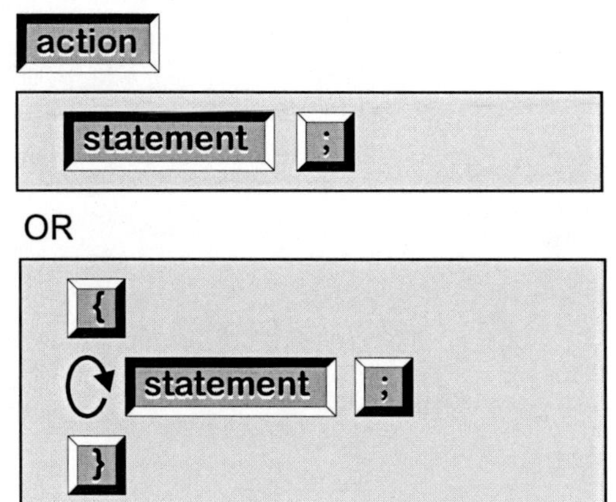

Some tiles will be given a diagram of their own in order to explain their meaning in more detail. For example, the token, **action**, given above is defined in more detail by the diagram shown overleaf.

This shows that action has two possible interpretations: either a single statement, or a series of statements enclosed in braces.

Where one or more tokens in a diagram may be repeated indefinitely, this is shown using the curved, arrowed line.

C++ makes use of three types of brackets: ( ), { }, and [ ]. Rather than use this informal term, the correct names for each is used throughout this text. These names are shown in the table below.

Symbol	Name
( )	Parentheses
{ }	Braces
[ ]	Brackets

CHAPTER 1

Background

This chapter covers the following topics:

Binary Numbers

Boolean Expressions

Character Codes

Converting Between Number Bases

Designing Algorithms

Floating Point Numbers

Hexadecimal Numbers

Octal Numbers

Program Structures

Stepwise Refinement

The Compilation Process

The Development Life Cycle

DESIGNING ALGORITHMS

Following Instructions

We're all used to following instructions: anything from fire evacuation procedures to how to assemble a flat-pack kitchen unit. Such a sequence of instructions is designed to allow us to perform some specific task. Sometimes the instructions we are carrying out are so familiar to us that we are not even aware of them; for example, driving a car requires us to perform various actions such as changing gear, pressing the brake or accelerator pedals, or turning the wheel. Other tasks, which are new to us, require a more deliberate adherence to the instructions given; for example, when we prepare a pre-packed meal from the freezer we are supplied with instructions such as:

```
Remove meal from carton
Remove lid
Preheat oven to 200°C
Place on baking tray in top half of oven
Leave for 35 minutes
```

A sequence of instructions designed to perform some specific task is known as an **algorithm**.

Every computer operates by following instructions. Such a set of instructions is known as a **computer program**.

The American spelling of program is used to differentiate a computer program from other types such as a TV programme.

Just as we may perform a great diversity of tasks by following a different set of instructions, so the computer can be made to carry out any task for which a program exists.

Computer programs are normally copied (or **loaded**) from a magnetic disk into the computer's memory and then executed (or **run**). Execution of a program involves the computer performing each instruction in the program one after the other. This it does at impressively high rates, possibly exceeding 200 million instructions per second (200 mips).

Depending on the program being run, the computer may act as a word processor, a database, a spreadsheet, a game, a musical instrument or one of many other possibilities.

Of course, as a programmer, you are required to design and write computer programs rather than use them.

Computer programs are written in a very formal style using a limited number of commands known to the computer. Like us, computers use many different languages; in this publication we use a relatively new programming language called C++.

Program Structures

Although programming is certainly complicated, there are only a few basic concepts and statements which you need to master before you are ready to start producing software. Luckily, the concepts are already familiar to you in everyday situations; all that is needed is to formalise their use to better suit a programming environment.

Sequence

The set of instructions from the frozen meal was given as:

```
Remove meal from carton
Remove lid
Preheat oven to 200°C
Place on baking tray in top half of oven
Leave for 35 minutes
```

This is an example of a **sequence** of instructions. In other words, instructions which are to be carried out one after another, beginning at the first and continuing, without omitting any, until the final one is completed.

> **TASK 1.1**
>
> Write down the set of instructions required to wash clothes in an automatic washing machine.

Binary Selection

Often a group of instructions in an algorithm should only be carried out when certain circumstances arise. For example, if we were producing a set of instructions to record a program on the video we might write:

```
Put a new tape in the machine if there isn't enough space on the
current tape.
```

Such a statement contains two components:

a condition : *there isn't enough space on the current tape*

and

an instruction : *put a new tape in the machine*

A condition is sometimes referred to as a **Boolean expression**

The instruction is only to be carried out if the condition is **true** and hence this is sometimes known as a **conditional instruction**. Although we could rewrite the above instruction in many different ways, when we produce a set of commands in a formal manner, as we are required to do here, then the following format is always used:

```
IF condition THEN
    conditional instructions (executed when condition is true)
ENDIF
```

Using this layout, the instruction to insert a new video tape would be written as:

```
IF there isn't enough space on the current tape THEN
    Put a new tape in the machine
ENDIF
```

Sometimes, there will be several instructions to be carried out when the condition specified is met. For example,

```
IF light bulb is not working THEN
    Switch off power
    Remove old bulb
    Insert new bulb
    Switch on
ENDIF
```

Of course, the conditional statement will almost certainly appear in a longer sequence of instructions. For example, the instructions for sitting an exam may be given as:

```
Write your name and class on the front sheet
When told to do so, turn over and read the exam paper
IF you have any questions THEN
    Raise your hand
    When the invigilator approaches you, ask any questions
ENDIF
Answer all questions in Section A of the paper
Answer only three questions from Section B
When you have finished, give your answer paper to the invigilator
Leave the room quietly
```

This longer sequence of instructions highlights the usefulness of the term **ENDIF** in separating the final conditional instruction, `When the invigilator approaches you, ask any questions`, from subsequent unconditional instructions.

> **TASK 1.2**
>
> Write a sequence of instructions to make a cup of tea. Start with the instruction `Fill kettle`, end with `Drink tea` and allow for options to add milk and sugar.

The **IF** structure is also used in an extended form to offer a choice between two alternative actions. For example, our earlier cooking instructions could give alternatives for using a conventional cooker or a microwave:

```
IF using a microwave THEN
    Place meal in microwave
    Set to HIGH
    Leave for 12 minutes
ELSE
    Preheat oven to 200°C
    Place on baking tray in top half of oven
    Leave for 35 minutes
ENDIF
```

If the condition is **true** then the statements following the term **THEN** are executed otherwise those following **ELSE** are carried out. The general form of this extended IF statement is:

```
IF condition THEN
    statements to be carried out when condition is true
ELSE
    statements to be carried out when condition is false
ENDIF
```

> **TASK 1.3**
>
> Write a set of instructions to write and post a letter. Start with `Write letter`, end with `Place letter in Post Box` and allow for the choice of sending by first or second class post.

Choosing between two alternative actions is called **binary selection**.

Multi-way Selection

Sometimes choosing from two alternatives is not enough. If our frozen food example gave separate instructions for gas and electric cookers as well as microwaves, we could use two **IF** statements to describe this:

```
IF using a microwave THEN
    Place meal in microwave
    Set to HIGH
    Leave for 12 minutes
ELSE
    IF using an electric oven THEN
        Preheat oven to 200°C
        Place on baking tray in top half of oven
        Leave for 35 minutes
    ELSE
        Preheat oven at gas mark 7
        Place on baking tray in bottom half of oven
        Leave for 40 minutes
    ENDIF
ENDIF
```

Where one IF statement occurs inside another IF statement this is termed **nested IFs.**

Although this is quite acceptable, it is rather difficult to follow. A better method would be to have labelled alternatives:

```
IF
    using microwave:
        Place meal in microwave
        Set to HIGH
        Leave for 12 minutes
    using an electric oven :
        Preheat oven to 200°C
        Place on baking tray in top half of oven
        Leave for 35 minutes
    using a gas oven:
        Preheat oven at gas mark 7
        Place in baking tray in bottom half of oven
        Leave for 40 minutes
ENDIF
```

Each option is explicitly named and only the one which is **true** will be carried out, the others will be ignored. Of course, we are not limited to merely three options; there can be as many as the situation requires.

TASK 1.4

Write a set of instructions to pay for items bought in a large store in which you have an account. Allow options to pay by cash, credit card, cheque or through your account. Start with *Find out total cost*, end with *Take purchases*. You should include statements such as *Hand over credit card*, *Sign authorisation slip*, *Give account number*, *Take change*, and *Show cheque card.*

When producing a program for a computer, all possibilities have to be taken into account. If we apply that approach to our instructions for cooking the meal, we have to allow for any other possible methods of preparing the meal. Since we cannot know exactly what other methods might be used (possibly portable gas stove, grilling etc.) we need an option which groups all the other possibilities together and supplies a set of instructions to deal with them.

```
IF
    using microwave:
        Place meal in microwave
        Set to HIGH
        Cook for 12 minutes
    using an electric oven :
        Preheat oven to 200°C
        Place on baking tray in top half of oven
        Cook for 35 minutes
    using a gas oven:
        Preheat oven at gas mark 7
        Place on baking tray in bottom half of oven
        Cook for 40 minutes
    ELSE:
        Heat meal until edible
ENDIF
```

The additional **ELSE:** option will be chosen only if none of the other options are applicable. This gives us the final form of:

```
IF
    condition 1 :
        statements to be carried out when condition 1 is met
    condition 2 :
        statements to be carried out when condition 2 is met
          .
          .
    condition x:
        statements to be carried out when condition x is met
    ELSE :
        statements to be carried out when none of the previous
        conditions are met
ENDIF
```

Choosing between several alternatives is known as **multi-way selection**.

Complex Conditions

Often the condition given in an **IF** statement is a complex one. For example, if a college only admits a student to a course when he has the academic qualifications and good references, then this can be described in our more formal style as:

```
IF student has sufficient qualifications AND has good references
THEN
    Admit student to course
ELSE
    Reject student
ENDIF
```

Note the use of the word **AND** in the above example. **AND** (called a **Boolean operator**) is one of the terms used to link simple conditions in order to produce a more complex one. The conditions on either side of the **AND** are called the **operands**. Both operands must be **true** for the overall condition to be **true**. We can generalise this to describe the **AND** operator as being used in the form:

```
condition 1   AND   condition 2
```

The result of the **AND** operator is determined using the following rules:

1. Determine the truth of condition 1
2. Determine the truth of condition 2
3. IF both conditions are **true** THEN
   the result is **true**
   ELSE
   the result is **false**
   ENDIF

The results of the **AND** operator are summarised in TABLE-1.1.

TABLE-1.1

The AND Operator

condition 1	condition 2	condition 1 AND condition 2
FALSE	FALSE	FALSE
FALSE	TRUE	FALSE
TRUE	FALSE	FALSE
TRUE	TRUE	TRUE

Simple conditions may also be linked by the Boolean operator **OR** as in the instruction:

```
IF it's raining OR it's cold THEN
    Put on coat
ENDIF
```

Like **AND**, the **OR** operator works on two operands:

```
condition 1   OR   condition 2
```

When **OR** is used, only one of the conditions involved needs to be **true** for the overall result to be **true**. Hence the results are determined by the following rules:

1. Determine the truth of condition 1
2. Determine the truth of condition 2
3. IF any of the conditions are **true** THEN
       the result is **true**
   ELSE
       the result is **false**
   ENDIF

The results of the **OR** operator are summarised in TABLE-1.2.

TABLE-1.2

The OR Operator

condition 1	condition 2	condition 1 OR condition 2
FALSE	FALSE	FALSE
FALSE	TRUE	TRUE
TRUE	FALSE	TRUE
TRUE	TRUE	TRUE

The final Boolean operator which can be used as part of a condition is **NOT**. This operator is used to negate the meaning of a condition. Hence ***NOT** over 21* has the opposite meaning from *over 21*; that is to say that if *over 21* is **true** then ***NOT** over 21* is **false**. Unlike **AND** and **OR**, **NOT** is used with a single operand:

```
NOT condition
```

The results of the **NOT** operator are summarised in TABLE-1.3.

TABLE-1.3 The NOT Operator

condition	NOT condition
FALSE	TRUE
TRUE	FALSE

Complex conditions are not limited to a single occurrence of a Boolean operator, hence it is valid to have the statement:

```
IF it's raining OR it's cold OR it's windy THEN
    Put on coat
ENDIF
```

In this situation, the final result is produced by first determining the truthfulness of each simple condition. If we assume it's a ***dry***, ***warm*** but ***windy*** day then the original expression can be reduced to:

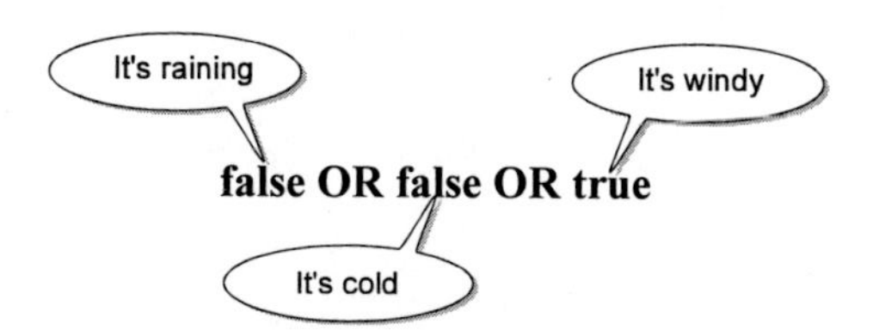

Next, the result from each Boolean operation is substituted. The left-most operator is dealt with first giving:

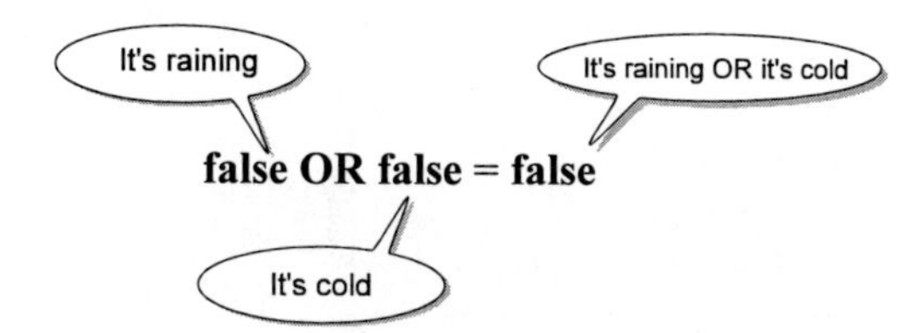

and replacing this result in the original expression gives:

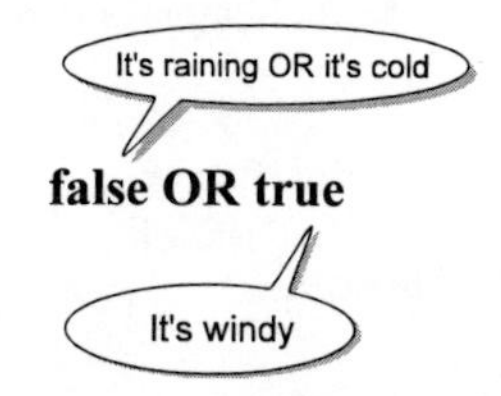

which has a result of:

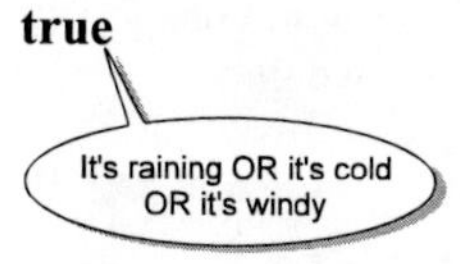

And, since the overall result is **true,** *Put on coat* is performed.

Finally, **AND**, **OR** and **NOT** operators may be used in any combination. For example, we might define people due to retire to be those which met the condition:

```
IF you are male AND aged over 65 OR
    you are female AND aged over 60
THEN
    You may retire
ENDIF
```

When various operators are used, **NOT** operations are performed first, followed by **AND** and finally **OR** operations. Where there is more than one identical operator these are calculated from left to right. In the above example, for a 53 year old female we get:

false AND false OR true AND false

Since there are no **NOT** operations, the **AND**s are determined first. Being more than one such operator, the left-most is handled first giving:

false OR true AND false

The second **AND** results in:

false OR false

which gives as a final result:

false

Boolean operator priority is summarised in TABLE-1.4.

TABLE-1.4

Boolean Operator Priority

Operator	Priority
NOT	Highest
AND	
OR	Lowest

Sometimes the priority of operators works against what we are trying to express. For example, if an insurance company wants to add an excess to the premium of people under 25 living in Glasgow, Manchester or London then we might be tempted to write:

```
IF living in Glasgow OR living in Manchester OR
    living in London AND under 25
THEN
    Add excess to premium
ENDIF
```

We would not expect a 26 year old living in Glasgow to pay the excess. But, if we look at the calculation for such a case, we get:

true OR false OR false AND false

the **AND** is calculated to give:

true OR false OR false

Next the left-most **OR** is reduced to give:

true OR false

Which finally reduces to **true**.

To achieve the correct results, we need the **OR** operations to be performed first and this can be done by giving the **OR** operators a higher priority than the **AND**.

Luckily, operator priority can be modified by the use of parentheses. Items in parentheses are always performed first. Rewriting the condition as:

```
IF (living in Glasgow OR living in Manchester OR
    living in London) AND under 25
THEN
    Add excess to premium
ENDIF
```

We now evaluate this as:

	(true	**OR**	**false**	**OR**	**false)**	**AND**	**false**
=	**(true**			**OR**	**false)**	**AND**	**false**
=	**true**					**AND**	**false**
=	**false**						

> **TASK 1.5**
>
> Write the expression for the conditions required in order for a laser printer to produce output. It will be necessary for the printer to be on-line and the toner should not be empty. There must also be paper in the main tray or in the auxiliary tray.

Iteration

There are certain circumstances in which it is necessary to perform the same sequence of instructions several times. For example, if a student sits three tests (each having a possible score of 100) and is given a pass only if his average mark for the tests is 50% or above, then we might describe the logic required in making such a decision as:

```
Set the total to zero
Read mark from test paper
Add mark to total
Read mark from test paper
Add mark to total
Read mark from test paper
Add mark to total
Calculate average as total divided by 3
IF average is not less than 50% THEN
    Student has passed
ELSE
    Student has failed
ENDIF
```

You can see from the above that two instructions,

```
Read mark from test paper
Add mark to total
```

are carried out three times; once for each test taken by the student. Not only does it seem rather time-consuming to have to write the same pair of instructions three times, but it would be worse if the student had sat 10 tests!

What is required is a structure which allows us to specify that a section of the instructions are to be repeated a fixed number of times. This is done using the **FOR..ENDFOR** structure:

```
FOR .. ENDFOR
```

Now the above can be rewritten as:

```
Set the total to zero
FOR 3 times DO
    Read mark from test paper
    Add mark to total
ENDFOR
Calculate average as total divided by 3
IF average is not less than 50% THEN
    Student has passed
ELSE
    Student has failed
ENDIF
```

The instructions between the terms **FOR** and **ENDFOR** are now carried out three times. Should the students have to sit 10 tests then all we need to do is rewrite the **FOR** statement as:

```
FOR 10 times DO
    Read mark from test paper
    Add mark to total
ENDFOR
```

The general form of this statement is:

```
FOR number of times required DO
    instructions to be repeated
ENDFOR
```

This structure is often referred to as a **loop structure** and the instructions to be repeated are known as the **loop body**.

TASK 1.6

Write a set of instructions to list the names of those students who achieve a score of less than 50% in an exam. There are exactly 20 students in the class. Your solution should contain the statements

```
Read mark and name
Add name to list of fails
IF mark is less than 50% THEN
```

REPEAT .. UNTIL

There are other circumstances in which, although we want to repeat instructions, the number of times we wish to do this cannot be specified. For example, if we were describing the action of playing a simple slot machine we might write:

```
Put coin in machine
Pull handle
IF you win THEN
    Collect winnings
ENDIF
Repeat the previous statements above until you want to stop
```

Although this describes exactly what is required, the final statement is too clumsy and informal. The instructions can be rewritten as:

```
REPEAT
    Put coin in machine
    Pull handle
    IF you win THEN
        Collect winnings
    ENDIF
UNTIL you want to stop
```

This is a better format since the start and end of the loop body are identified using the terms **REPEAT** and **UNTIL** respectively. The **UNTIL** statement also specifies the condition under which iteration is to stop; this is known as the **terminating condition**.

The general form of this structure is:

```
REPEAT
    loop body
UNTIL terminating condition
```

The terminating condition may use the Boolean operators **AND**, **OR** and **NOT** as well as parentheses, where necessary.

> **TASK 1.7**
>
> Write instructions to look through the articles in a magazine until one written by *Liz Herron* is found. Your solution should contain the instructions
> ```
> Find start of article
> Read the author's name
> ```

WHILE .. ENDWHILE

A final method of iteration, differing only subtly from the **REPEAT.. UNTIL** loop, is the **WHILE .. ENDWHILE** structure which has an **entry condition** at the start of the loop.

For example, when weighing out a half kilogram of individual wrapped sweets, most shopkeepers will empty out roughly the correct amount on to the scales and then add or remove individual sweets until the weight is correct. Using the WHILE structure to describe this action we get:

```
Empty approximately the correct weight of sweets on to the scale
WHILE the weight is incorrect DO
    IF the weight is over THEN
        Remove one sweet from scales
    ELSE
        Add one sweet to scales
    ENDIF
ENDWHILE
Place sweets in paper bag
```

The instruction between the **WHILE** and **ENDWHILE** will be carried out as long as the weight is incorrect. Once the weight is correct (that is, when the condition *weight is incorrect* is **false**) looping terminates and the statement following **ENDWHILE** is performed (*Place sweets in paper bag*).

In what way does this differ from the **REPEAT** statement? There are two differences:

1. The condition is given at the beginning of the loop.
2. Looping stops when the condition is **false**.

The main consequence of this is that it is possible to bypass the loop body of a **WHILE** structure entirely without ever carrying out any of the instructions it contains. If the shopkeeper gets lucky and empties the correct amount on to the scales at the beginning then the condition, *the weight is incorrect*, will be **false** and hence control jumps directly to *Place sweets in paper bag*. In contrast, since the condition is at the end of the loop, the loop body of a **REPEAT** structure must be carried out at least once.

If we try to replace the **WHILE** loop directly with a **REPEAT** loop we get:

```
Empty approximately the correct weight of sweets on to the scale
REPEAT
    IF the weight is over THEN
        Remove one sweet from scales
    ELSE
        Add one sweet to scales
    ENDIF
UNTIL the weight is correct
Place sweets in paper bag
```

Note that the condition has been reversed from that in the original description.

But this doesn't work properly since, if the correct amount is placed on the scales at the beginning, we nevertheless go inside the **REPEAT** loop, find *the weight is over* to be **false** (since the weight is correct), jump to **ELSE** and *Add one sweet to the scales;* but now the condition, *the weight is correct*, in the **UNTIL** statement is no longer **true** and hence we go back round the loop structure to the **IF** statement where the condition, *the weight is over*, is now **true** and hence we remove a sweet. At this point, by first adding then removing a sweet, we have returned to the correct weight so that the condition in the **UNTIL** statement (*the weight is correct*) is at last **true** and the loop is exited and the sweets placed in the bag.

Although the **REPEAT** loop has produced the correct result in the end, it generated some unnecessary actions.

TASK 1.8

A game involves throwing two dice. If the two values thrown are not the same, then the die showing the lower value must be rolled again as often as is necessary until both dice show the same value. Write a set of instructions to perform this game. Your solution should contain the statements

```
Roll both dice
```

and

```
Choose die with lower value
```

Infinite Loops

A potential problem with REPEAT and WHILE loops is, since they do not specify exactly how many times the loop body is to be executed, it is possible to set up a loop structure which will never terminate. For example, we might attempt to describe the logic of weighing sweets as:

```
Empty approximately the correct weight of sweets on to the scale
WHILE the weight is incorrect DO
    Remove sweet from scales
ENDWHILE
Place sweets in paper bag
```

The above logic is fine - as long as we don't put too few sweets on the scale at the beginning! Should that happen removing a sweet will only take us further from the goal of getting the correct weight of sweets. With no chance of the condition, *the weight is incorrect,* being **false**, iteration will continue forever (although it won't be possible to keep removing sweets). This is known as an **infinite loop** and should be avoided. You can guard against such loops by mentally checking that some activity within the loop body will eventually result in the loop being exited.

Data

Imagine we need to write down instructions for a trainee insurance salesman who sells car insurance policies by phone. The caller will supply details of the car, his age and the city in which he lives. The salesman will calculate the premium due, adding any excess where necessary, and tell the caller the cost. If the caller accepts the offer, the salesman will take additional personal details from the caller and fill out an application form which he then places in a *New Policies* tray on his desk. Our formal description of the operation might be:

```
Get details of car model, engine size, caller's age and city
Calculate premium as half the engine size in cc
IF (city is Glasgow OR Manchester OR London) AND
    age is under 25
THEN
    Calculate excess due as £50 for each year under 25
    Add excess to premium
ENDIF
Tell caller the amount of the premium
Ask if he wishes to accept the policy
IF policy accepted THEN
    Get caller's name, street, post code, phone number and car
    registration number
    Transfer details to policy form
    Get policy number from the top right hand of policy form
    Tell the policy number to caller
    Place form in New Policies tray
ENDIF
```

This example, and the previous test marks example, introduce the need to process facts and figures (known as **data**). In a computing environment most algorithms involve the processing of data. An item of data has two basic characteristics :

a name
and a value.

The name of a data item is a description of the type of information it represents. Hence *caller's name*, *caller's age* and *car registration number* are names of data items; *"Fred Bloggs"*, *27*, and *"M1 CKY"* are examples of the actual values which might be given to these data items.

Note that textual values are enclosed in double quotes while numeric values are not.

In programming, a data item is often referred to as a **variable**. This term arises from the fact that, although the name assigned to a data item cannot change, its value may vary.

TASK 1.9

List the names of five other data items in the insurance example above and give a possible value for each.

There are four basic operations which can be performed on data:

Input

The first involves obtaining a value for a data item. For example, the insurance salesman's instructions include *Get car model*. *Car model* is the name of a data item and the command requires the salesman to obtain a value which he may associate with that name from the caller. In a computer environment, the request to get a value for a data item requires the user of the computer to enter a value at the keyboard. We describe this as a value being **input** to a data item.

Calculation

The second operation involves calculating the value of a data item. For example, *Calculate premium as half the engine size in cc* produces a value for the data item *premium* by calculation. This calculation involves the value of another data item (*engine size*). If *engine size* had been given as 2000cc then *premium* would be £1000.00. Notice also that it is possible to modify the value of a data item; for instance, later in the algorithm we have the instruction *Add excess to premium*, which, for a 21 year-old living in London would result in an excess of £200.00 being added to *premium*; changing the value of that data item from £1000.00 to £1200.00. This is referred to as a **calculation operation**.

Comparison

The value of a data item may be compared against some other value. The insurance example compares the value given to *city* to see if it is equal to "Glasgow", "Manchester" or "London".

Output

The final operation is to disclose the value currently held in a data item. For example, the instruction, *Tell caller the amount of the premium*, is a request to state the value associated with the data item, *premium*. In a computer environment, the equivalent operation would normally involve displaying information on a screen or printing it on paper. This is called **output** of data.

TASK 1.10

Identify other input, calculation and output statements in the insurance premium example above.

When describing a calculation, it is common to use arithmetic operator symbols rather than English. Hence, instead of writing the word *subtract* we use the minus sign (-). A summary of the operators available are given in TABLE-1.5.

TABLE-1.5

Mathematical Operators

English	Symbol
Multiply	*
Divide	/
Add	+
Subtract	-

Like Boolean operators, mathematical operators are dealt with on a priority basis. Multiply and divide have the higher (and equal) priority; add and subtract, the lower.

As well as replacing the arithmetic operator words with symbols, the term, `calculate`, is often replaced by the shorter but more cryptic symbol, :=

Using this abbreviated form, the instruction:

```
Calculate premium as half the engine size in cc
```

becomes

```
premium := engine size in cc / 2
```

Read the symbol := as "is assigned the value".

Levels of Detail

Although we might write the instructions for setting a video to record a program as

```
Put new tape in video
Set timer details
```

this lacks enough detail for anyone unfamiliar with the operation of the machine. We could replace the first statement with

```
Press the eject button
IF there is a tape in the machine THEN
    Remove it
ENDIF
Place the new tape in the machine
```

and the second statement could be substituted by:

```
Switch to timer mode
Enter start time
Enter finish time
Select channel
```

This approach of starting with a less detailed sequence of instructions and then, where necessary, replacing each of these with more detailed instructions can be used to good effect when tackling long and complex problems. By using this technique, we are defining the original problem as an equivalent sequence of simpler tasks before going on to create a set of instructions for each of these simpler problems. This divide-and-conquer strategy is known as **stepwise refinement**.

The following is a fully worked example of this technique:

Problem:
Produce a wage slip for an hourly paid worker. The worker gets paid £5.60 per hour when working between 0900 and 1700 Monday to Friday. If he works on Saturdays or after 1700 during the working week, he is paid £8.40 per hour. Sunday working pays a rate of £11.20 per hour. He has to pay 9% of his gross wage to superannuation, 10% of the gross wage to National Insurance. Of the remainder, the first £80.00 is tax free and the remainder is taxed at 25%.

Outline Solution

```
1. Get details of hours worked
2. Calculate gross wage
3. Calculate deductions
4. Calculate net wage
5. Write details on to wage slip
```

This is termed a **LEVEL 1 solution.**

As a guideline we should aim for a LEVEL 1 solution with, at most, 20 statements - preferably significantly less.

Notice that each instruction has been numbered. This is merely to help with identification during the stepwise refinement process.

Before going any further, we must assure ourselves that this is a correct and full (though not detailed) description of all the steps required to tackle the original problem. If we are not happy with the solution then changes must be made before we go any further.

Next, we examine each statement in turn and determine if it should be described in more detail. Where this is necessary, rewrite the statement to be dealt with, and below it, give the more detailed version. For example, *Get details of hours worked* would be expanded thus:

```
1.  Get details of hours worked
    1.1 Get hours at basic rate
    1.2 Get hours at time-and-a-half
    1.3 Get hours at double time
```

The numbering of the new statement reflects that they are the detailed instructions pertaining to statement 1. Also note that the number system is not decimal fraction, so if there were to be many more statements they would be numbered 1.4, 1.5, 1.6, 1.7, 1.8, 1.9, 1.10, 1.11, etc.

It is important that these sets of more detailed instructions describe how to perform only the original task being examined - they must achieve no more and no less. Sometimes the detailed instructions will contain control structures such as IFs, WHILEs or FORs. Where this is the case, the whole structure must be included in the detailed instructions. That is to say, it is not possible to have, say, a FOR statement to start in the breakdown of statement 1 and the corresponding ENDFOR statement to appear in the breakdown of statement 2.

Having satisfied ourselves that the breakdown is correct, we proceed to the next statement from the original solution.

```
2.  Calculate gross wage
    2.1 Calculate gross wage as hours at basic rate * £5.60 +
        hours at time-and-a-half * £8.40 +
        hours at double time * £11.20
```

This time we haven't expanded into more statements but simply added detail to the original instruction.

The other statements expand as follows:

```
3.  Calculate deductions
    3.1 Calculate superannuation as 9% of gross wage
    3.2 Calculate national insurance as 10% of gross wage
    3.3 Calculate taxable pay as gross wage -
        (superannuation + national insurance + £80.00)
    3.4 IF taxable pay is greater than zero THEN
    3.5     Calculate tax due as 25% of taxable pay
    3.6 ELSE
    3.7     Set tax due to zero
    3.8 ENDIF
```

The **IF** statement allows for the possibility that the gross wage is not sufficient to incur tax.

Note that we have introduced a new data item, *taxable pay*, which although useful in arriving at *net wage* is not itself one of the data items required by the system. Such data items are called **temporary** or **local variables.**

```
4.  Calculate net wage
    4.1 Calculate net wage as gross wage -
        (superannuation + national insurance + tax due)
```

```
5.  Write details on to wage slip
    5.1 Write gross wage on payslip
    5.2 Write superannuation on wage slip
    5.3 Write national insurance on wage slip
    5.4 Write tax due on wage slip
    5.5 Write net wage on wage slip
```

Finally, we can describe the solution to the original problem in terms of the more detailed sequence of instructions:

```
1.1 Get hours at basic rate
1.2 Get hours at time-and-a-half
1.3 Get hours at double time
2.1 Calculate gross wage as hours at basic rate * £5.60
    + hours at time-and-a-half * £8.40
    + hours at double time * £11.20
3.1 Calculate superannuation as 9% of gross wage
3.2 Calculate national insurance as 10% of gross wage
3.3 Calculate taxable pay as gross wage -
    (superannuation + national insurance + £80.00)
3.4 IF taxable pay is greater than zero THEN
3.5     Calculate tax due as 25% of taxable pay
3.6 ELSE
3.7     Set tax due to zero
3.8 ENDIF
4.1 Calculate net wage as gross wage -
    (superannuation + national insurance + tax due)
5.1 Write gross wage on payslip
5.2 Write superannuation on wage slip
5.3 Write national insurance on wage slip
5.4 Write tax due on wage slip
5.5 Write net wage on wage slip
```

This is a LEVEL 2 solution. Note that a level 2 solution is produced by bringing together, in the correct order, the individual solutions of the LEVEL 1 instructions.

A Few Points to Note About Stepwise Refinement

For some more complex problems it may be necessary to repeat this process to more levels before sufficient details are achieved. That is, statements in LEVEL 2 may need to be given more detail in a LEVEL 3 breakdown.

Not all statements need to be broken down to a lower level. For example, a LEVEL 1 solution might contain the statement `FOR 10 times DO` which may be left unaltered in a LEVEL 2 solution.

TASK 1.11

An orders clerk for a mail order company takes orders over the telephone. Customers begin by stating the number of different items they wish to purchase. For each item the clerk requests the catalogue number, which if given incorrectly, will require to be restated (it is possible that an invalid number will be given several times before the customer finally gives a recognised value). The clerk also asks the quantity required before checking if the item is in stock. If the item is out of stock or there is insufficient quantity, the clerk will offer an alternative if one is available. The clerk adds available items to an order list. Once the call is complete, the order list is sent to the dispatches department.

Continued on next page

TASK 1.11 (continued)

A possible LEVEL 1 solution to this task is:

```
1.  Get number of items
2.  FOR each item DO
3.      Get order details
4.      Process item
5.  ENDFOR
6.  Send order to dispatches department
```

Write a LEVEL 2 solution which should include statements such as:

IF item in stock AND sufficient quantity THEN
WHILE catalogue number is invalid DO
Check for alternative
IF alternative acceptable THEN

Summary

- Computers can perform many tasks by executing different programs.
- An **algorithm** is a sequence of instructions that solves a specific problem.
- A **program** is a sequence of computer instructions which usually manipulates data and produces results.
- **Three control structures** are used in programs :
  Sequence;
  Selection;
  Iteration.
- A **sequence** is a list of instructions which are performed one after the other.
- **Selection** is performed using the IF statement.
- **There are three forms of IF statement:**

```
IF condition THEN
    instructions
ENDIF
```

```
IF condition THEN
    instructions
ELSE
    instructions
ENDIF
```

```
IF
    condition 1:
        instructions
    condition 2:
        instructions
        .
        .
    condition x :
        instructions
    ELSE:
        instructions
ENDIF
```

- **Iteration** is performed using one of three instructions:

```
FOR number of iterations required DO
    instructions
ENDFOR


REPEAT
    instructions
UNTIL condition


WHILE condition DO
    instructions
ENDWHILE
```

- **An infinite loop** may result from an incorrectly formed iteration.

- A **condition** is an expression which is either **true** or **false**.

- **Simple conditions can be linked** using **AND** or **OR** to produce a complex condition.

- **The meaning of a condition can be reversed** by adding the word **NOT**.

- **Data items** (or variables) hold the information used by the algorithm.

- **Data item values** may be:

  Input
  Calculated
  Compared
  or Output

- **Calculations** can be performed using the operators

Multiplication	*
Division	/
Addition	+
Subtraction	-

- **The symbol :=** is used to assign a value to a data item. Read this symbol as *is assigned the value.*

- In programming, a data item is referred to as a **variable**.

- The divide-and-conquer strategy of **stepwise refinement** can be used when creating an algorithm.

- **LEVEL 1 solution gives an overview** of the sub-tasks involved in carrying out the required operation.

- **LEVEL 2 gives a more detailed solution** by taking each sub-task from LEVEL 1 and, where necessary, giving a more detailed list of instructions required to perform that sub-task.

- **Further levels of detail** may be necessary when using stepwise refinement for complex problems.

- **Further refinement may not be required** for every statement.

■ The order of priority of operators are:

Operator	Meaning	Priority
*	Multiply	1
/	Divide	1
+	Add	2
-	Subtract	2
NOT		3
AND		4
OR		5
:=	Is assigned the value	6

Items of equal priority are evaluated from left to right.

■ The order of priority may be over-ridden using parentheses.

THE DEVELOPMENT LIFE CYCLE

Designing algorithms is only one stage in producing any significant piece of software. The stages involved depend on the approach used. However, generally, the following stages can be identified:

Statement of Requirements

This is a document, produced by those requiring the software, which specifies what the system is required to do.

Requirements Analysis

Since the statement of requirements is often brief, as well as containing contradictions, ambiguities and omissions, there is a need to examine the requirements in more detail, clearing up any outstanding problems. This activity is known as **requirements analysis**. The **System Specification** is the document produced as a result of the requirements analysis and is basically an organised, correct and full definition of the system to be developed.

System Design

This involves defining the structure and architecture of the system. Each component is described in terms of what task it is to perform. The **System Design Document** is the by-product of System Design stage and contains descriptions of each component of the system.

Detailed Design

Whereas Systems Design involves producing a description of what each component of the system must do, Detailed Design describes how each component functions; that is, it is in this stage of the development that the many algorithms of a system are specified. The processing to be performed may be described in Structured English or in a more computer program-like **program design language** (PDL) - sometimes referred to as **pseudocode**.

Implementation

Each component of the design must now be written in a form which can be understood by the computer. In other words, the program design language must be translated into a programming language. As the components are coded they must be tested for errors. This is called **unit testing**.

Tested units are then added to the system and the partially finished system is tested to ensure that the components integrate correctly into the system. This is called **integration testing.** The code produced during implementation will be listed for future reference. In addition, the programs are also retained in a form readable by the machine (probably held as files on a magnetic disk). The output produced by the programs during testing will be retained as evidence of the software's performance and correctness.

By this stage a complete working system has been produced. This system is then given to the customer who will perform his own set of tests on the software before accepting it. This is called **acceptance testing**.

Iterating the Development Cycle

At each stage it may be necessary to back-track to an earlier one. For example, in creating a System Specification, it may be necessary to return to the customer who requested the software and revise the Statement of Requirements, or problems found at the testing stage may require us to rethink the System Design.

This continual requirement to return to earlier stages in the life cycle makes the whole design process an iterative one, but excessive revision of earlier work and late detection of errors carried forward from earlier stages can add significantly to the time and costs involved in producing the software.

Validation and Verification

An obvious requirement which must be kept in mind while developing a system is that it meets the customer's requirements. The actions applied by the developer to ensure this is the case is known as **verification and validation**.

Verification ensures that the product of a given phase of the life cycle satisfies the document on which that phase is based. For example, the Systems Design document (the product of Systems Design activity) is checked to see that it satisfies the description given in the systems specification. To summarise, verification involves ensuring that the output of a given stage correctly reflects the input to that stage.

Validation, on the other hand, is the process of checking that a document or piece of software accurately reflects the requirements of the customer.

Maintenance

After delivery to the customer, further work is often required on the system. In fact, as much as 80% of the total time spent working on a system can take place during the maintenance phase.

Maintenance may be required because of errors which have remained undetected until the software was in operation. Such corrections are considered to be part of the original contract for the system.

Another reason for maintenance is caused by changes to the environment in which the software operates. For example, software which calculates monthly salary payments will require to be changed if a local income tax system is to be introduced.

Finally, a system may require maintenance because the customer wishes extra features to be added. For example, a store's stock control system may require an additional feature to give statistical details of sales.

The last two causes of maintenance are not considered to be part of the original contract and hence the customer will be charged for any changes made.

The maintenance period is from the date of delivery to the time when the software is replaced. This may be many years.

NUMBER SYSTEMS

Introduction

The counting system we use today is the decimal or, more correctly, the denary system. It uses ten different symbols (0,1,2,3,4,5,6,7,8,9) to represent any value. The number of digits used in a number system is known as the **base** or **radix** of the system. Hence denary is a base 10 system.

In our number system, the position of a digit affects the value. Hence, 19 and 91, although containing the same digits, represent two different values.

In primary school we are often taught the theory of numbers by the use of column headings:

Thousands *Hundreds* *Tens* *Units*

To represent a value, we merely write the required numeric symbol in each of the appropriate columns. For example, to write down the number seven hundred and thirteen we place a 7 in the Hundreds column, a 1 in the Tens column and a 3 in the Units column:

Hundreds	*Tens*	*Units*
7	1	3

A more mathematical heading for these columns would be

10^2 is simply short-hand for 10*10.

The result of raising any number to the power zero is 1.

10^2	10^1	10^0
7	1	3

Note that the column value is based on the number radix being used. Hence, for any number system (say, to the base R) the value of the columns can be written as

$$\ldots \quad R^4 \quad R^3 \quad R^2 \quad R^1 \quad R^0$$

The Binary System

The modern computer stores all the information it holds, be it instructions, numbers or text, as a sequence of number codes. But the number system used by the computer has a base of two rather than ten. This is the **binary system** where every value is represented by only two digits: 0 and 1. Columns in this system have the values:

$$\ldots \quad 2^7 \quad 2^6 \quad 2^5 \quad 2^4 \quad 2^3 \quad 2^2 \quad 2^1 \quad 2^0$$

which replacing the powers of two headings, gives the column values:

128 64 32 16 8 4 2 1

The binary digits, 0 and 1, are referred to as **bits** (short for **b**inary dig**its**). Values are most often stored in eight bit groups.

This collection of eight bits is called a **byte**.

Converting from Decimal to Binary

From this information we can begin to see how we might represent a decimal number, say 23, in binary. Since 23 can be constructed from the values 16 + 4 + 2 + 1, we simply need to place a 1 in each of those columns, filling all other columns with zeros. Using the standard eight bit grouping the decimal value 23 is represented as:

128	*64*	*32*	*16*	*8*	*4*	*2*	*1*
0	0	0	1	0	1	1	1

Generalising this approach, we can construct a simple algorithm to convert any decimal number to its binary equivalent:

```
Get positive decimal number
REPEAT
    Divide by 2, writing down integer part of the answer
    and whole number remainder
UNTIL the answer is zero
Write down the remainders in a line, last one first, from left
to right
```

The operation is shown in FIG-1.1.

FIG-1.1

Converting Decimal to Binary

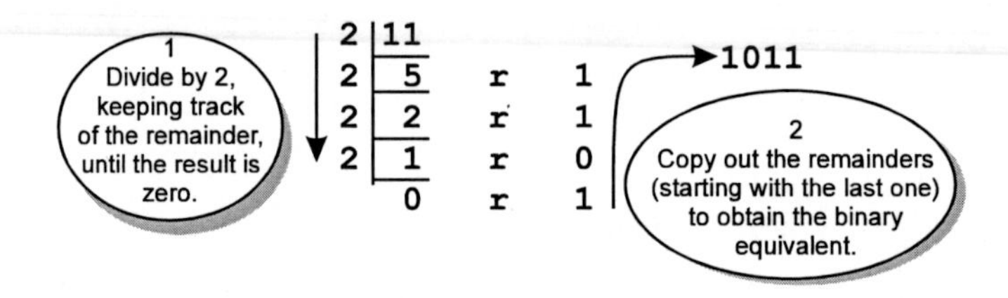

> **TASK 1.12**
>
> Convert the following numbers to 8-bit binary:
>
> 19
> 72
> 63

Binary to Decimal

To convert from binary to decimal, take the value of each column containing a one and add these values to arrive at the decimal equivalent. An example is shown in FIG-1.2.

FIG-1.2

Binary to Decimal Conversion

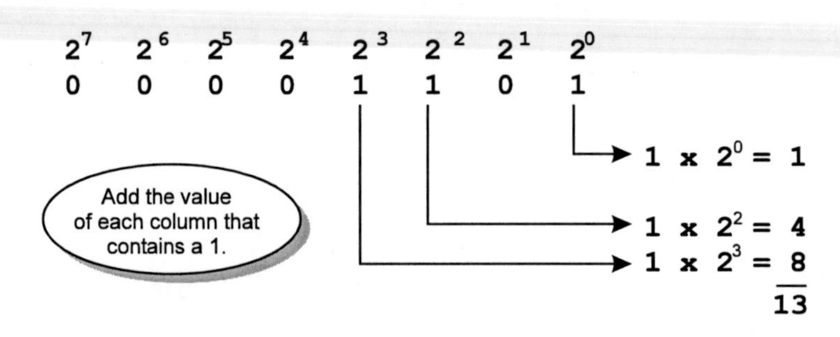

TASK 1.13

Convert the following binary values to decimal.

```
00101001
11111111
10101010
```

Converting Fractions

So far we have only looked at converting whole numbers (integers) but we also need to be able to represent decimal fractions in binary.

Decimal fractions have column values of

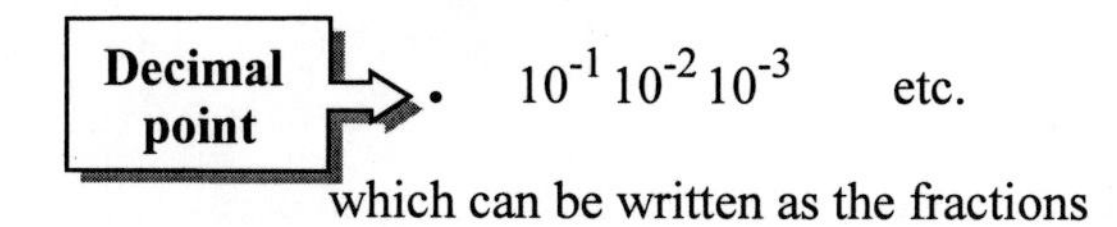

• $10^{-1}\,10^{-2}\,10^{-3}$ etc.

which can be written as the fractions

• $\frac{1}{10}\;\frac{1}{100}\;\frac{1}{1000}$

Binary fractions, on the other hand, have column values of

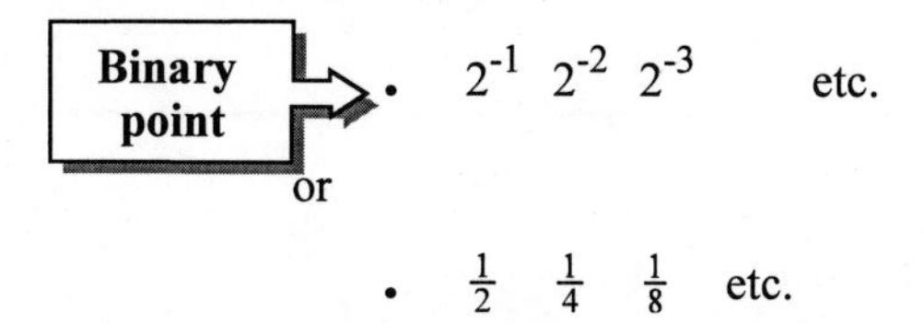

• $2^{-1}\;2^{-2}\;2^{-3}$ etc.

or

• $\frac{1}{2}\;\frac{1}{4}\;\frac{1}{8}$ etc.

To convert from a decimal fraction to the binary equivalent, the following algorithm can be employed:

```
Get decimal fraction
Set worked value to the decimal fraction
Write '.'
REPEAT
    Multiply worked value by 2
    Write down integer part of the result
    Remove the integer part from the worked value
UNTIL worked value is zero OR required degree of accuracy obtained
```

The first iteration of this operation is shown in FIG-1.3.

FIG-1.3

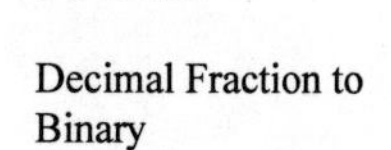

Decimal Fraction to Binary

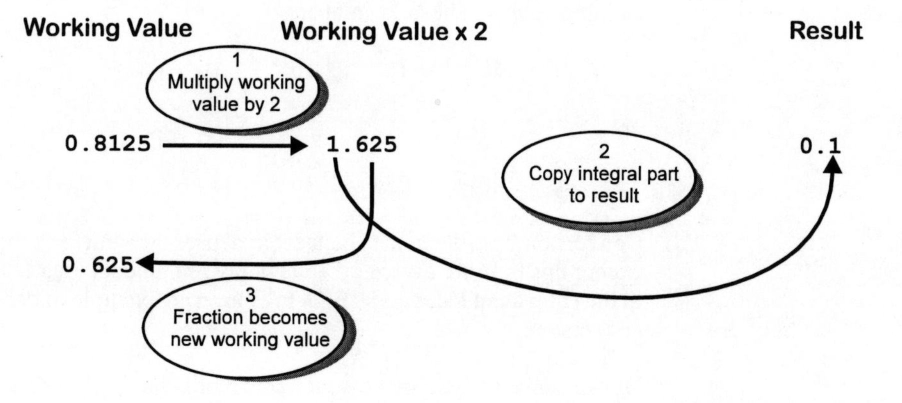

A full example of the conversion is shown below:

Value to be converted : 0.8125

Working value		*Working value x 2*	*Result*
			0.
0.8125	x 2	1.625	0.1
0.625	x 2	1.25	0.11
0.25	x 2	0.5	0.110
0.5	x 2	1.0	0.1101
0			

TASK 1.14

Convert the following decimal fractions to binary (stop after 6 binary places):

```
0.75
0.3125
0.38
```

Binary fractions to decimal present no problem since, like integers, it is simply a matter of adding the values of any column containing a 1.

To convert decimal numbers which contain a whole number and fraction part, such as 3.1415, simply split the number into its two parts, integer and fraction, and convert each separately.

TASK 1.15

1. Convert the binary value 0.01011 to decimal.

2. Convert the decimal value 12.625 to binary.

Hexadecimal

The hexadecimal system is another number system which is widely used in computing. It has a base of 16 which implies there are 16 different digits. However, since our own decimal system has only 10 digits, we are left with the problem of representing values between 10 and 15 (decimal) by a single digit. This is achieved by using the first 6 letters of the alphabet. Thus decimal 10 is represented by A, 11 by B and so on.

Column values in hexadecimal are

... 16^3 16^2 16^1 16^0

or

4096 256 16 1

Conversion from decimal to hexadecimal uses the same technique as that for binary, except this time we divide by 16 and any remainders greater than 9 are converted to the equivalent letter code. FIG-1.4 shows an example of decimal to hexadecimal conversion.

Hexadecimal to decimal uses the same method as with binary to decimal; only the column values are different (see FIG-1.5).

FIG-1.4

Decimal to Hexadecimal Conversion

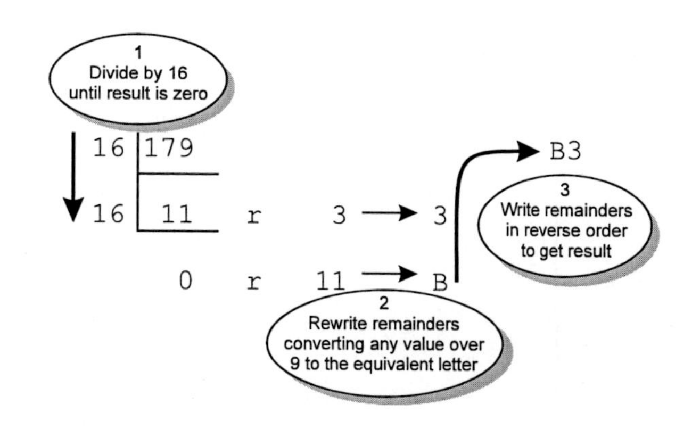

FIG-1.5

Hexadecimal to Decimal Conversion

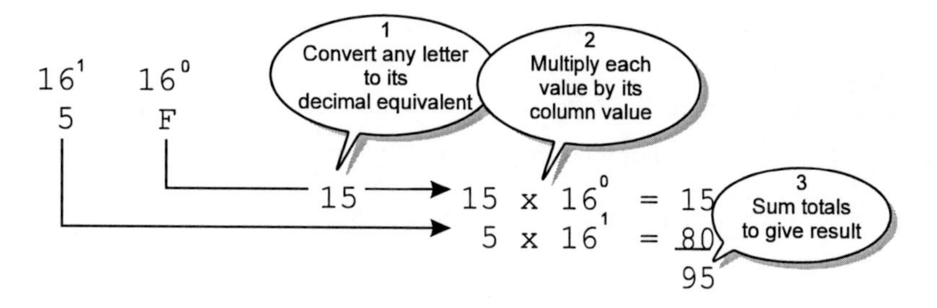

The most likely conversions when using hexadecimal are to and from binary. Four binary digits can range between 0000 and 1111 in value. Since this represents the values 0 to 15 we can use a single hexadecimal digit, 0 to F, to represent these four bits. Thus the contents of a single byte can be shown as two hexadecimal digits. The conversion technique is shown in FIG-1.6.

Conversion from hexadecimal to binary simply involves reversing this process as shown in FIG-1.7.

FIG-1.6

Binary to Hexadecimal Conversion

FIG-1.7

Hexadecimal to Binary Conversion

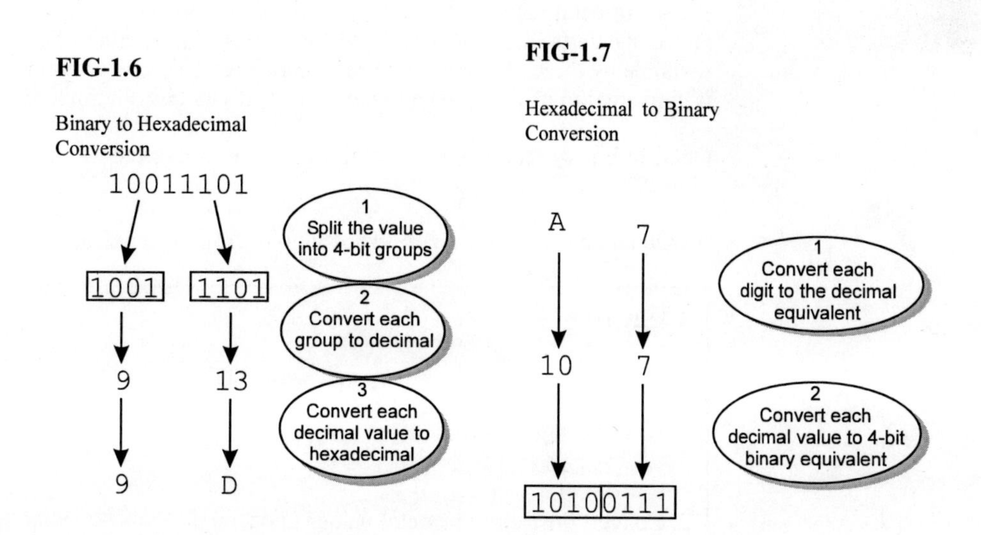

TASK 1.16

1. Convert the following binary values to hexadecimal:

```
01000111
11111111
11001011
```

2. Convert the following hexadecimal values to binary:

```
73
A2
FE
```

Octal

A final number system, which is useful in machines that use a 6 bit configuration rather than the more widespread 8 bit organisation, is **octal**. Octal is a base 8 numbering system using the digits 0 to 7.

Column values are

... 8^2 8^1 8^0

that is

... 64 8 1

Decimal to octal is achieved by continually dividing by 8 until a result of zero is arrived at and then copying out the remainders (last one being the most-significant).

Octal to decimal is performed by multiplying each digit in the octal value by its column value and summing these values.

Binary to octal requires the binary value to be split into groupings of three bits. Grouping starts from the right-hand side; where the number of bits is not exactly divisible by three, the left-most group may have only one or two bits. Each group is converted to its decimal equivalent; these digits give the final result.

Octal to binary requires each octal digit to be converted to exactly three binary digits.

It will not be necessary to convert octal to or from hexadecimal.

TASK 1.17

1. Convert the following binary values to octal:

```
  101001
10011100
11111111
```

2. Convert the following octal values to decimal:

```
 75
121
333
```

Identify a Number's Base

Where a piece of text may refer to several number systems it is usual to include a subscript giving the number base being represented. Hence the decimal value 77 would be written as

77_{10}

while the hexadecimal value 57 would be shown as

57_{16}

Negative Numbers

In an 8 bit byte we can store any binary value between 00000000 and 11111111 which, in decimal, is 0 to 255. But how are negative numbers, such as -17, stored?

Imagine we are sitting in a car whose current journey odometer is set to 0000. If we drive forward one mile then we will have a reading of 0001. If, on the other hand, we were to drive in reverse for one mile the reading would be 9999. Now, if we consider moving forward in the car as equivalent to moving up through the positive numbers while reversing is a movement through the negative range (as illustrated in FIG-1.8), then we can think of the reading on the odometer as a way of representing both positive and negative numbers (e.g. 0001 = +1; 9999 = -1). Some of the values are shown in TABLE-1.6.

FIG-1.8

Representing Positive and Negative Values on the Odometer

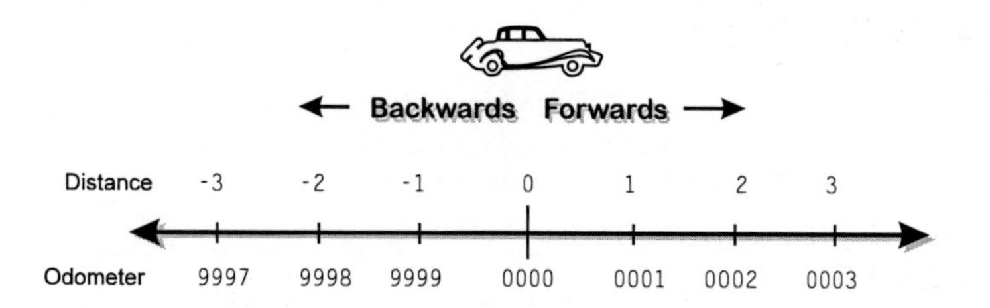

TABLE-1.6

Representation of Positive and Negative Values

Integer value	Reading
-3	9997
-2	9998
-1	9999
0	0000
1	0001
2	0002
3	0003

Of course, using this approach has a cost since the range of positive numbers we can represent has now been reduced, since readings such as 9996 no longer represent the value +9996 but rather -4. And what of the reading 5001? Does it represent the value +5001 or -4999? At some point on our readings we have to decide on a split between those which represent positive values and those which are negative. If we make the split half way (giving 5000 positive values - if zero is included; and 5000 negative values) we get the reading split as shown in TABLE-1.7.

TABLE-1.7

Negative and Positive Ranges

Reading	Integer value
0000	0
4999	4999
5000	-5000
9999	-1

This representation of negative values works rather well when performing arithmetic operations. For example, the subtraction:

47 -12

which can be rewritten as:

47 + (-12)

This is represented in our new system as:

0047 + (9988)

which, when added, gives:

0035

Remember, the odometer only has 4 digits, so the fifth digit (1) of the above addition is not stored in the result.

2's Complement

This same approach is used in binary where this method of representation is known as **2's complement**. With an 8 bit storage unit, values between -128 and +127 can be stored (as shown in TABLE-1.8)

TABLE-1.8

Negative and Positive Ranges

Byte	Integer value
00000000	0
01111111	127
10000000	-128
11111111	-1

Decimal to 2's Complement

We already have a technique for converting a positive whole number to its binary equivalent and this can be extended to find the 2's complement value for negative numbers. The algorithm required is:

```
Get negative value
Ignoring the sign, convert to binary using all bits
Starting at right hand digit
REPEAT
    Copy current digit into result
    Move to the next digit to the left
UNTIL digit copied is a 1
FOR each remaining digit DO
    Copy the opposite digit into the result
ENDFOR
```

Opposite digit means 1's are changed to zeros and vice versa.

For example, to find the 2's complement form of the value -68, we first find the binary representation of +68:

```
01000100
```

This example assumes the value is being stored in a single byte (8 bits).

Next copy every digit (from the right) unchanged up to and including the first 1:

```
        100
```

Finally, copy the remaining digits but changing 1's to 0's and vice versa:

```
10111100
```

Where a number is stored over 16 bits (2 bytes) this allows a larger range of values: -32,768 to 32,767 to be held, but the same 2's complement strategy is employed Hence, the value -68 would be stored in 16 bits as:

```
11111111 10111100
```

TASK 1.18

Convert the following values to 2's complement form in both 8 and 16 bit format:

```
  -3
 -42
-127
```

2's Complement to Decimal

Before converting a 2's complement value to decimal we must first decide if we are dealing with a negative value or a positive one. Looking back at TABLE-1.8 we can see that the left-most digit of all negative values is a 1 while it is 0 for positive values. Hence, where the left-most digit is a zero, conversion is achieved by following the same technique as that described earlier for positive binary values: add the values of each column containing a 1.

This means that, for negative values, we first convert the value to the equivalent positive value. Therefore, faced with the value

```
11001110
```

we begin by copying all the digits from the right up to and including the first 1

```
      10
```

and then changing each of the remaining digits:

```
00110010
```

This results in the positive form of the original number which can then be converted in the usual way. Obviously, a minus sign must be placed in front of the result:

```
        128 64  32  16   8   4   2   1
         0   0   1   1   0   0   1   0

    =   -(32 + 16 + 2)

    =   -50
```

To summarise, whole numbers are stored in a computer's memory as a binary pattern. The representation used may not allow for negative numbers (the storage format is said to be **unsigned** or **absolute**). Alternatively, by using 2's complement (or **signed** format), both positive and negative values may be stored. If a value is stored in a single byte, using unsigned format, any value between 0 and 255 can be represented while 2's complement will allow values in the range -128 to +127.

When presented with a binary value it is necessary to know which of the above storage formats is being used before converting the value to decimal. For example, 11111111 represents the value 255 in unsigned format and -1 in 2's complement form.

Floating Point Values

Real numbers (those with fractional parts) are stored in a different format. The format used within the computer is similar to that employed when writing numbers in scientific notation. Numbers such as 12.8 are said to be written in **fixed point format** but the same number can also be written as 1.28E1. This is **scientific** or **floating point** notation. Although it may look somewhat unfriendly, if you're unfamiliar with this form, it is simply a formula for the original number. Hence,

$$1.28 \times 10^1$$
$$= 1.28 \times 10$$
$$= 12.8$$

The value 365.249 would be written as 3.65249E2 which is:

$$3.65249 \times 10^2$$
$$= 3.65249 \times 100$$
$$= 365.249$$

The first part of the floating point number (e.g. 3.65249) is termed the **mantissa**; the second part following the letter E is the **exponent**. The exponent represents the power of ten by which the mantissa must be multiplied to give the value being represented. The mantissa is always shown as a value greater than or equal to one and less than ten. This is called the **normalised mantissa.**

For small numbers, such as 0.00013 the exponent will be negative:

0.00013
= 1.3E-4

For negative values, the mantissa is negative:

-6712.8
= -6.7128E3

Again conversion from fixed to floating point notation can be explained using a simple algorithm:

```
Get the fixed point value
The mantissa is the original number with the decimal point
 moved between the first and second non-zero digit
Add an 'E'
IF the original value was less than 1 THEN
    Place a minus sign in front of the exponent
ENDIF
The exponent is the number of places the decimal point
 had to be moved to change the original number into the
 normalised mantissa
```

TASK 1.19

Convert the following values to floating point notation:

```
123.98
  6.9
 -0.00000001
```

When using floating point notation within the computer, the following approach is employed:

```
Get decimal value
Convert it to binary
Create the mantissa by moving binary point to left of the most
 significant 1
The exponent is the number of places the point was moved
 (written in binary)
IF the binary point was moved to the right THEN
    The exponent is negative
ENDIF
```

For example:

```
46.375
```

converts to

```
101110.011
```

giving a mantissa of

```
.101110011
```

and an exponent of

```
110
```

This format is changed slightly in most software to optimise the storage requirements and the efficiency of the algorithms used for manipulating floating point values.

There are two main changes. When storing real numbers in binary form, the exponent is usually held as a positive value. This is achieved by adding some value to the correct exponent, which may well be negative. For example, if the exponent occupies 8 bits of the space allocated to a real value, this allows for a range of values from -128 to 127 when 2's complement form is being used. However, if we add 128 to the exponent once it has been calculated and hold the value in unsigned format, a range of 0 to 255 can be accommodated. This is called a **biased exponent**. The mantissa is also modified slightly by omitting the most significant digit when it is stored. Since the first digit of the mantissa must be a 1, there is little point in storing it, hence freeing 1 more bit to hold the remaining digits of the mantissa which results in slightly increased accuracy.

The storage format used is shown in FIG-1.9. The number of bits allocated to each component will depend on the implementation.

FIG-1.9

Floating Point Storage

Biased Exponent	Mantissa

TASK 1.20

Assuming floating point numbers are stored in 24 bits, the mantissa occupying 16 bits and the exponent 8 bits, show how the value 0.09375 would be stored. Assume an exponent with a bias value of 128.

Character Coding

As well as numbers, computers need to store characters. Since everything in the machine is stored in binary, this means that we need some coding system to represent these characters. This is much the same approach as employed in morse code where dots and dashes are used to represent letters.

ASCII stands for American Standard Code for Information Interchange

Although several coding methods are employed, originally the most universal one was the **ASCII** coding system. This uses a single byte (of which only 7 bits are used) to store a letter in upper or lower case, or a punctuation character. This allows 128 different characters. For example the code for 'A' is

```
01000001
```

This is also the binary equivalent of the decimal value 65 and in order to correctly interpret a binary pattern stored in the machine, the computer needs to be aware of the type of value the pattern represents (a number or a character).

The IBM extended character set is an extension of the ASCII coding which makes use of the eighth bit to allow an extra 128 characters. Some of these codes are used for special European characters, others allow for simple graphics characters.

A new coding system using 16 bits is currently being finalised. This allocates codes to the characters of many other languages used throughout the world. The new coding system is referred to as **unicode**.

The full IBM extended character set is shown in APPENDIX A.

Summary

- Computers store all data in **binary**.
- **Binary is a base 2 number system.**
- **Binary uses the digits 0 and 1.**
- **A binary digit** is often referred to as a **bit**.
- **Bits are most often organised into 8 bits**. 8 bits is known as a **byte**.
- **Decimal to binary** conversion of integer values is achieved by continually dividing by 2 until a result of zero is achieved. The remainders (last one being the most-significant digit) form the result.
- **Decimal to binary** conversion of fractions is achieved by continually multiplying the remaining fraction by 2 until a result of zero or the required accuracy is achieved. The integral part of each result forms the binary value.

- **Real decimal values greater than 1** are changed to binary by converting the integer and fractional parts separately.

- **Before converting from binary to decimal** it is necessary to know which format is being used: **unsigned** or **2's complement** format.

- **For positive values,** binary to decimal conversion is achieved by summing the value of each column containing a one.

- **For negative values,** binary to decimal conversion is achieved by first converting to the positive equivalent.

- **Hexadecimal is a base 16 number system** using the digits 0 to 9, A to F.

- **A single byte can be represented by** two hexadecimal digits.

- **Decimal to hexadecimal** conversion is achieved by continually dividing by 16 until a result of zero is achieved. Any remainder over 9 is converted to the equivalent hexadecimal letter (10 = A, 11 = B etc.). The remainders (last one being the most-significant digit) represent the result.

- **Hexadecimal to decimal** conversion is achieved by summing the value of each column containing a non-zero digit.

- **Binary to hexadecimal** conversion is achieved by grouping the binary value into 4 bit groups; converting each group to the decimal equivalent; converting each decimal value to the hexadecimal equivalent.

- **Hexadecimal to binary** conversion is achieved by converting each hexadecimal digit to the decimal equivalent; converting each decimal value to the equivalent 4 bit binary value.

- **Octal is a base 8 number system** using the digits 0 to 7.

- **Decimal to octal** conversion is achieved by continually dividing by 8 until a result of zero is achieved. The remainders (last one being the most-significant digit) represent the result.

- **Octal to decimal** conversion is achieved by summing the value of each column containing a non-zero digit.

- **Binary to octal** conversion is achieved by grouping the binary value into 3 bit groups; converting each group to the decimal equivalent.

- **Octal to binary** conversion is achieved by converting each octal digit to the equivalent 3 bit binary value.

- **The base of a value** can be shown as a subscript following the number.

- **Signed binary values** are held in 2's complement form.

- **Floating point values** are constructed from a mantissa and exponent.

- **Normalising a decimal mantissa** involves moving the decimal point until its value is not less than 1 and less than 10.

- **Normalising a binary mantissa** involves moving the binary point until the most significant 1 is to its immediate right.

- **The exponent represents** the number of places the mantissa's point must be moved to restore the original number. The exponent is negative if the point needs to be moved to the left.
- In the computer, **floating point values are often held with a biased exponent and the first 1 missing from the mantissa.**
- **The IBM extended character set** is used by most computers. This allows for 256 different characters and is an extension of ASCII.

THE COMPILATION PROCESS

Since computers are only capable of recognising and executing commands given in their own native processor instruction set (known as **machine code**) and since computer programs are normally written in other languages, the computer is required to perform a translation process to convert the original program code (known as the **source code**) into the equivalent sequence of machine code instructions (the **object code**) which can then be executed by the computer.

This operation is known as **compilation** and is performed by a piece of software called a **compiler**. Each compiler is designed to translate one specific source language, in this case C++.

Any practical compiler is more complex than this simplified model. For example, it is often the case that the source code which makes up the complete program is not held within a single file but is constructed from several files. In this situation, the compiler must first bring together the contents of each source file involved before beginning the main compilation process. This task is carried out by part of the compiler known as the **preprocessor**.

The term **function** is used here to mean pieces of program code which perform some specific operation. Hence a function may exist to calculate the cosine of an angle.

Most programs are unlikely to contain the source code for all the functions they require. More likely, a program will make use of existing functions which are available only in object code form. For example, a program may require to calculate the square root of some value, move the cursor to a new position on the screen, or open a disk file. A collection of such precompiled functions is held in a disk file known as a **library**. Although libraries are provided as part of the compiler package, the programmer is free to create a library of his own more specialised routines.

FIG-1.10

The Compilation Process

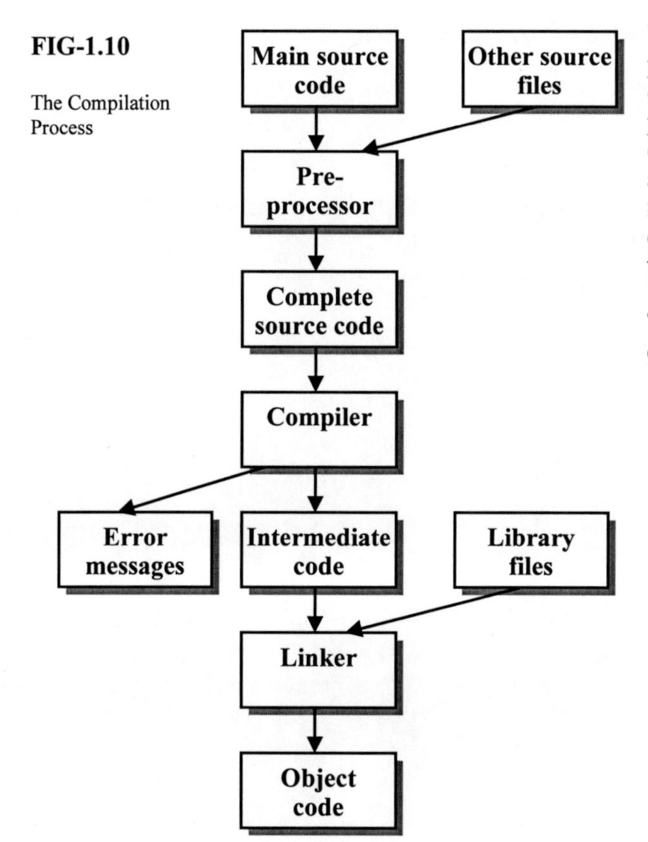

When the first stage of compilation takes place the source code is converted to object code, but where there is a call to a precompiled function held in other files the compiler merely makes a note of which additional functions it requires to insert in the final version of the program. These are embedded in the final source code by part of the compiler known as a **linker**.

This, more complete model of the compilation process is shown in FIG-1.10.

SELF-ASSESSMENT REVIEW

1. Name the three basic control structures.

2. A, B and C are Boolean expressions. A and B are **true** while C is **false**. What is the result of the compound expression:

   A **AND NOT**(B **OR** C) ?

3. Define the term **infinite loop**.

4. Using stepwise refinement, write the set of instructions necessary to place a music cassette in a personal stereo and to begin playing at tape counter position 312 on side B of the tape. Start by removing any tape which may already be in the machine; end with pressing the play button.

5. Convert the following values to binary

   103_{10}
   $8E_{16}$
   17_8

6. Convert the following unsigned binary values to decimal, hexadecimal and octal:

```
01000111
10001010
11001100
```

7. Convert the following signed values to decimal:

```
01110001
10001101
11101001
```

8. Convert the following value to binary floating point using an 8 bit exponent and 16 bit mantissa.

```
121.0783
```

SOLUTIONS TO TASKS

TASK 1.1

A possible solution is:

```
Open door of washing machine
Place clothes in washing machine
Put washing powder in powder tray
Close door
Choose required setting
When washing cycle complete, remove clothes
from machine
```

Of course, you will almost certainly have produced a solution which differs from the one above. But, as long as your logic is correct, (for example, it would be wrong to put the clothes in the machine before opening the door) then any solution is acceptable.
Remember to take a separate line for each instruction.

TASK 1.2

```
Fill kettle
Switch on kettle
Put tea in teapot
When water boils, pour into teapot
Wait for tea to infuse
Pour tea into cup
IF milk is required THEN
    Add milk
ENDIF
IF sugar is required THEN
    Add sugar
    Stir tea
ENDIF
Drink tea
```

Other solutions are possible but make sure the milk and sugar are dealt with by two separate IF statement, and that the ENDIF terms are included.

TASK 1.3

```
Write letter
Fold letter
Place letter in envelope
Seal envelope
Write address on envelope
IF sending first class THEN
    Stick first class stamp on envelope
ELSE
    Stick second class stamp on envelope
ENDIF
Take letter to post box
Post letter
```

Ensure you use an IF .. THEN .. ELSE structure when selecting the stamp.

TASK 1.4

```
Find out total cost
IF
    paying by cash:
        Give cashier sufficient money
        IF any change is due THEN
            Collect change
        ENDIF
    paying by cheque:
        Write out cheque
        Give cheque to cashier
        Show cheque card
    paying by credit card:
        Hand over credit card
        Sign authorisation slip
        Take back credit card
        Take credit transaction slip
    paying through account:
        Give account number
ENDIF
Take till receipt
Take purchases
```

TASK 1.5

```
printer on-line AND toner not empty AND (paper
in main tray OR paper in auxiliary tray)
```

TASK 1.6

```
FOR 20 times DO
    Read mark and name
    IF mark is less than 50% THEN
        Add name to list of fails
    ENDIF
ENDFOR
```

TASK 1.7

```
REPEAT
    Find start of next article
    Read author's name
UNTIL author's name is "Liz Herron"
```

TASK 1.8

```
Roll both dice
WHILE both dice are not equal DO
    Choose die with lower value
    Throw die
ENDWHILE
```

TASK 1.9

Possible data items are:

```
car model
engine size
city
premium
street
post code
phone number
policy number
```

TASK 1.10

Input statements:

```
Get caller's name, street, post code, phone
number and car registration number.

Get policy number from top right hand of policy
form
```

Calculation statements:

```
Calculate excess due as £50 for each year under
25

Add excess to premium
```

Output statements:

```
Give the policy number to caller
```

TASK 1.11

Only two statements need to be expanded to give more detail:

```
3. Get order details
4. Process item
```

Possible expansions are:

```
3. Get order details
    3.1 Get catalogue number
    3.2 WHILE catalogue number is invalid DO
    3.3     Tell customer number is invalid
    3.4     Get catalogue number again
    3.5 ENDWHILE
    3.6 Get quantity required

4.  Process order
    4.1 IF item in stock AND sufficient quantity THEN
    4.2     Add details to order list
    4.3 ELSE
    4.4     Check for alternative
    4.5     IF there is an alternative THEN
    4.6         Tell customer details of
                alternative
    4.7         IF alternative acceptable THEN
    4.8             Add alternative's details
                    to order list
    4.9         ENDIF
    4.10    ELSE
    4.11        Tell customer item not available
    4.12    ENDIF
    4.13 ENDIF
```

This gives a final LEVEL 2 algorithm of:

```
1.      Get number of items
2.      FOR each item DO
3.1         Get catalogue number
3.2         WHILE catalogue number is invalid DO
3.3             Tell customer number is invalid
3.4             Get catalogue number again
3.5         ENDWHILE
3.6         Get quantity required
4.1         IF item in stock AND sufficient quantity
            THEN
4.2             Add details to order list
4.3         ELSE
4.4             Check for alternative
4.5             IF there is an alternative THEN
4.6                 Tell customer details of
                    alternative
4.7                 IF alternative acceptable THEN
4.8                     Add alternative's details
                        to order list
4.9                 ENDIF
4.10             ELSE
4.11                Tell customer item not available
4.12            ENDIF
4.13        ENDIF
5       ENDFOR
6.      Send order to dispatches department
```

TASK 1.12

```
00010011

01001000

00111111
```

TASK 1.13

```
41

255

170
```

TASK 1.14

```
0.11
0.0101
0.011000
```

TASK 1.15

```
1.
0.34375

2.
1100.101
```

TASK 1.16

```
1.
    47
    FF
    CB

2.
    01110011
    10100010
    11111110
```

TASK 1.17

```
1.
    51
    234
    377

2.
    61
    81
    219
```

TASK 1.18

8 bits	16 bits
11111101	1111111111111101
11010110	1111111111010110
10000001	1111111110000001

TASK 1.19

```
1.2398E2

6.9E0

-1.0E-8
```

TASK 1.20

```
01111101 1000000000000000
```

Remember the most-significant 1 in the mantissa is omitted.

CHAPTER 2

Starting C++

This chapter covers the following topics:

A Brief History of C and C++

Arithmetic Operators

Assignment Operator

Basic Program Structure

cin

Comma Operator

Constants

cout

Increment & Decrement Operators

sizeof

Type Conversion

Variable Types & Storage

A BRIEF HISTORY OF C & C++

C was developed at the beginning of the 1970s by Dennis M Ritchie at AT&T Bell Laboratories in New Jersey. The language was an offspring of B which was itself based on a language called BCPL, developed by Martin Richard.

It was Ken Thompson who developed the operating system, UNIX, which was finally implemented in C on a PDP-11computer in 1973. In the early years, C was only available on UNIX-based systems.

C is a high-level language, developed as a tool for producing operating systems and other systems software. It has features which allow the programmer a level of control normally only possible when using assembly language.

C gives you almost absolute power over the machine, but it assumes that you know what you are doing! There is not much help in the way of run-time error checking: no overflow checking; no array subscript checking; no parameter passing checks.

An ANSI standard for C was adopted in 1990.

C++ was developed by Bjarne Stroustrup, again at AT&T, as an attempt to not only introduce object-oriented features, but also to improve and expand the basic language structures. Initially, called *C with Classes*, the name C++ (C plus plus) was coined by Rick Mascitti in 1983. Whether the name is a reference to the language's ++ operator or is derived from George Orwell's *1984* is unclear.

The new language, which is basically a super-set of C, took many of its features from the earlier object-oriented language Simula67 but other features come from languages such as Algol68, Clu, and Ada.

The first C++ translators simply changed the source program into the equivalent C code which was then compiled by a standard C compiler. Current C++ compilers translate directly to machine code.

C++ has been revised three times: in 1985 and 1990 and 1998.

The 1998 changes are not included in this text since they have not been implemented in the Borland product.

C++ : PROGRAM STRUCTURE

An Overview

Every C++ program is constructed from one or more functions. A function is a section of code designed to perform some specific task.

Before describing the basic elements of C++, we'll begin with a quick look at some code to give you the general structure of a simple C++ program. The program in LISTING-2.1 displays the message *Hello world* on the screen.

LISTING-2.1

A Simple C++ Program

```
#include <iostream.h>
void main( )
{
  cout<<"Hello world.\n";
}
```

An Explanation of the Code

The keywords of all C++ programs must be in lowercase.

A function prototype gives the name and parameter list of a function.

#include <iostream.h> — This is a preprocessor command which instructs the compiler to include at the beginning of the program the contents of the file *iostream.h*. Files with the extension *.h* are known as **header files** and generally contain constants and function prototypes. In this case *iostream.h* contains the prototype of the function cout which is used later in the code. Without this #include instruction, the compiler would signal an error when encountering cout in the program code.

void — Signifies that no value is returned by the function main which follows.

main — The name of the function. All C++ programs must contain a function called main.
Execution always begins with the main function.

( ) — Inside the parentheses any parameters passed to the program would be listed. The empty parentheses signify that no parameters are passed.

{ — Marks the beginning of a block of code. In this case the code for function main.

pronounced see-out

cout — The term cout is used to produce screen output.
The prototype of this command is included in the *iostream.h* file which must be included in any program using this function.

<< — The **output operator** (also known as the **insertion operator**) which is normally followed by the value to be output.

"Hello world.\n" — Is the argument of cout and is the text string to be displayed. Note that strings are enclosed in double quotes. *\n* represents the single character, **linefeed**, and has the effect of moving the cursor to the beginning of a new line after the message, *Hello world*, is displayed.

`;` The semi-colon ends a statement. Normally all statements in C++ must end with the semi-colon.

`}` Block terminator symbol. In this case, the end of the function `main`. **Note** that `}` is not followed by a semicolon.

The next program, (see LISTING-2.2) which inputs and sums two values, introduces program variables, comments, data input and calculations.

LISTING-2.2

Input, Variables and Assignment

```
#include <iostream.h>
void main( )
{
   int no1,no2,answer;

   /* Program adds two numbers */

   //   *** Read in two values
   cout<<"Enter two values\n";
   cin>>no1>>no2;

   //   *** Add values entered
   answer = no1 + no2;

   //   *** Display result
   cout<<"The sum of "<<no1<<" and "<<no2<<" is "
        <<answer<<"\n";
}
```

An Explanation of the Code

`int no1,no2,answer;` This defines the three variables, *no1*, *no2* and *answer* as integers.

`/* Program adds two numbers */`
This is a comment. Comments are enclosed between /* and */. Comments given in this format can span several lines of the program.

`//*** Read in two values` An alternative to /* .. */ is to use two forward slashes (//) which makes the remainder of the current line a comment. The RETURN character marks the end of the comment.

A RETURN character is added to the file every time you press the ENTER key.

`cin` The command `cin` accepts input from the keyboard. Like `cout`, the prototype for this routine is the *iostream.h* header file.

pronounced see-in

`>>` The **input** (or **extraction**) **operator** used with `cin`. Normally, followed by the input variable name.

`no1 >> no2` Specifies the variables in which the values input are to be stored. Hence the first value entered from the keyboard is stored in the variable *no1*; the second in *no2*. The >> operator is used to separate each item to be input.

```
cout<<"The sum of "<<no1<<" and " <<no2<<" is " <<answer<<"\n";
```

Outputs a combination of strings and variable values to the screen. Each item is separated from the next by << and the final string , *"\n"*, forces the cursor to move to a new line when output is complete.

PROGRAMMING EXERCISE 2.1

Type in and run both of the above programs.

In the second program, enter the values 4 and 2. The values should be entered separated by a space.

Summary

A simple C++ program has the following structure (see FIG-2.1).

FIG-2.1

Structure of a simple C++ program

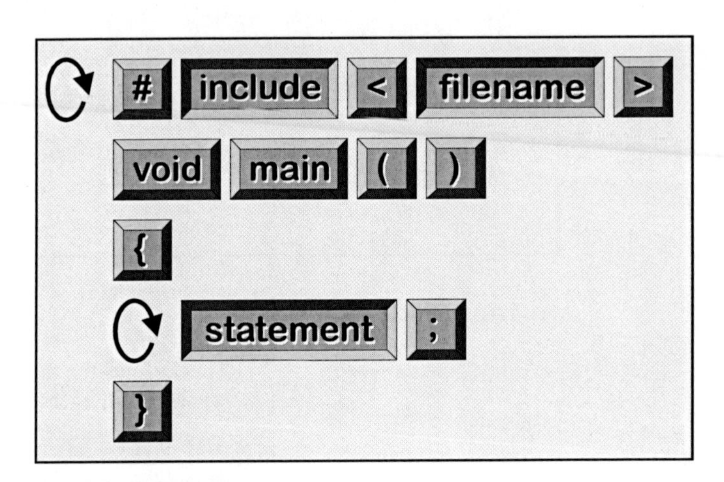

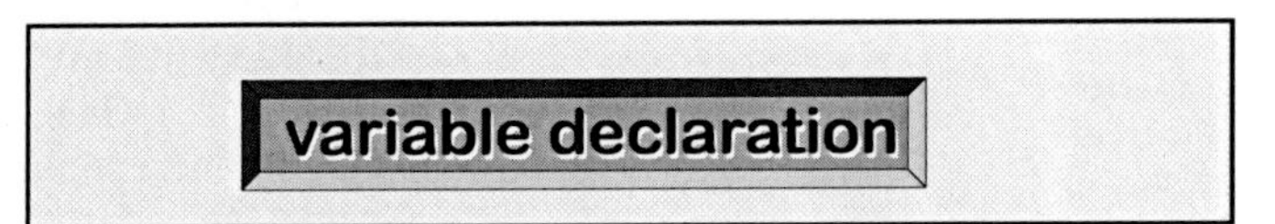

OR

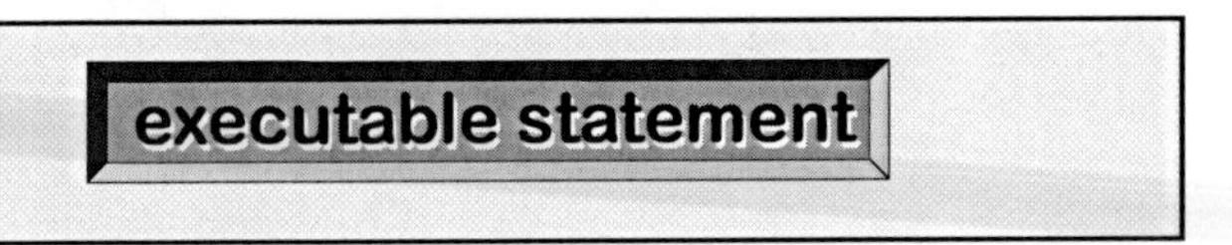

- All C++ terms must be entered in lowercase.

VARIABLES AND CONSTANTS

Variables

What is a Variable?

Almost everyone has had to fill in a form similar to the one shown in FIG-2.2. Each entry in the form has a boxed area in which we are required to enter information. Beside each box is a label (or name) giving us an indication of what information we are meant to place in that box. Each box differs in size and format depending on the type of information it is designed to hold. Hence the *address* box is long because it requires several lines of information whereas the *sex* box has sufficient space for only a single character ('M' or 'F') and the *date of birth* box contains two forward slash characters (/) to separate the day, month and year values.

FIG-2.2

Part of a Typical Form

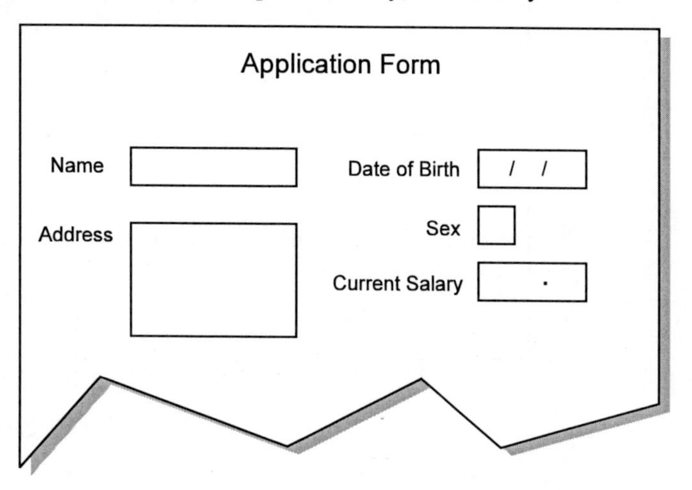

If a computer program requires to store similar information, then it too needs areas in which to hold that information (more commonly called **data**). However, in a program, data is stored in variables and, like the boxes on the form, variables need to be given names. LISTING-2.2 (on page 43) defined three variables: *no1*, *no2* and *answer*.

Variable Types

Just as the boxes in the form are designed with the type of value they are going to hold in mind (such as a date, single character, amount of money etc.), so the type of value a program variable is to hold must also be specified.

C++ recognises several types of values. Two value types are **integer** (whole numbers - positive or negative) and **real** (numbers containing fractional parts). The term `int` is used when defining integer variables; in LISTING-2.2 the three variables were defined as integers with the statement:

```
int no1, no2, answer;
```

The term `float` is short for floating-point which is the format used by the machine when storing real numbers.

Real values are defined using the term `float`. For example,

```
float angle, discount;
```

Naming Variables

Although there is no limit to the length of variable names, Borland C++ recognises only the first 32 characters of a variable name.

The name given to a variable in a C++ program must conform to the following rules:

- The first character must be a letter or an underscore (_).
- Subsequent characters can be a letter, underscore or numeric.
- Capital and lower case **ARE** significant (*NO* and *no* are different).
- A variable name must **NOT** be a keyword.

A **keyword** is a word recognised by C++ to have some specific meaning. A list of keywords is given in TABLE-2.1.

TABLE-2.1

C++ Keywords

C++ KEYWORDS				
asm	do	inline	return	union
auto	double	int	short	unsigned
break	else	interrupt	signed	virtual
case	enum	long	sizeof	void
catch	extern	near	static	volatile
cdecl	far	new	struct	while
char	float	operator	switch	
class	for	pascal	template	
const	friend	private	this	
continue	goto	protected	throw	
default	huge	public	try	
delete	if	register	typedef	

Your own compiler may have several more keywords; check your software's programming guide for details.

NOTE: All keywords are in lower case.

TASK 2.1

Indicate which of the following are invalid variable names:

```
no1
first_ans
3no
no_1
_result
try
final total
```

Memory Allocation

Computer memory is often organised in bytes with each byte being allocated a unique identifying value known as the **memory address**. This setup is shown in FIG-2.3.

A byte is enough memory to store a single character (e.g. the letter 'A' will occupy one byte of computer memory when stored) and consists of 8 bits.

FIG -2.3

Memory Organisation

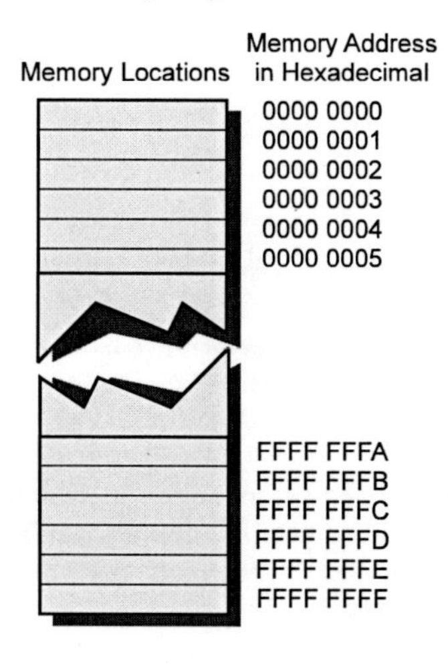

Every variable defined in a program is allocated its own space in the computer's memory. The amount of space, that is the number of bytes, allocated depends on the variable's type. This memory space will be used to store, in binary, any value placed in the variable by the program.

A single byte is not sufficient to store a reasonable range of numeric values and hence variables are normally allocated more than one byte.

We have already used type `int` variables which are used to store integer values. Most compilers now allocate four bytes to an `int` variable which, using 2's complement notation, allows values in the range -2,147,483,648 to 2,147,483,647 to be stored (although Borland C++ 4.5 uses two bytes). However, there are several variations on the basic type `int` which can hold a larger range of values; stores values in unsigned format; or occupies less storage space. For example, `unsigned int` variables also occupy four bytes but store only positive values in the range 0 to 4,294,967,295; `long int` and `unsigned long int` variables also occupy four bytes and hence are not different from `int` and `unsigned int`.

Single characters (e.g. 'A','?','$' etc.) are stored in `char` variables which are allocated a single byte in memory. Small integer values can also be held in `char` variables. It may seem strange that two different types of values can be stored in the same variable type but remember that all data is stored as a binary pattern; with `char` variables this binary pattern may be interpreted as the ASCII code for a character or as a binary numeric value.

TABLE-2.2 lists all the variable types available in Borland C++ along with the range of values which may be stored and the number of bytes allocated.

TABLE-2.2

C++ Variable Types in Borland C++

Note that in this implementation there is no difference between `int` and `short` types.

Variable type	Range of values	Number of bytes
Integer Types		
char	-128 to 127 or 0 to 255	1
signed char	-128 to 127	1
unsigned char	0 to 255	1
short int	-32,768 to 32,767	2
unsigned short int	0 to 65,535	2
int	-32,768 to 32,767	2
unsigned int	0 to 65,535	2
long int	-2,147,483,648 to 2,147,483,647	4
unsigned long int	0 to 4,294,967,295	4
Real Types		
float	$-3.4\times10^{+38}$ to $3.4\times10^{+38}$	4
double	$-1.7\times10^{+308}$ to $1.7\times10^{+308}$	8
long double	$-3.4\times10^{+4932}$ to $1.1\times10^{+4932}$	10

To summarise, every variable defined in a program has four characteristics associated with it:

- A name — e.g. no1
- A type — e.g. int
- A value — e.g. -17
- An address in memory — e.g. FFFF FFFD

Where the variable is allocated several bytes, the address associated with the variable is that of the first location allocated.

The term `int` may be omitted when used with the modifying terms `unsigned`, `short` and `long`; hence we can use `unsigned` instead of `unsigned int`.

The term `char` may be used without the preceding `signed` or `unsigned` in which case it is normal to assume `signed`, but you should check since this default can be changed. Although there is no difference in implementation between `char` and `signed char` types, C++ considers them to be separate types.

> **TASK 2.2**
>
> A C++ program uses two `int` and three `double` variables. State the total number of bytes allocated to these variables.

Storage Format

FIG-2.4

Variable Storage Formats

Each data type stores data in differing formats. The various layouts used are shown in FIG-2.4.

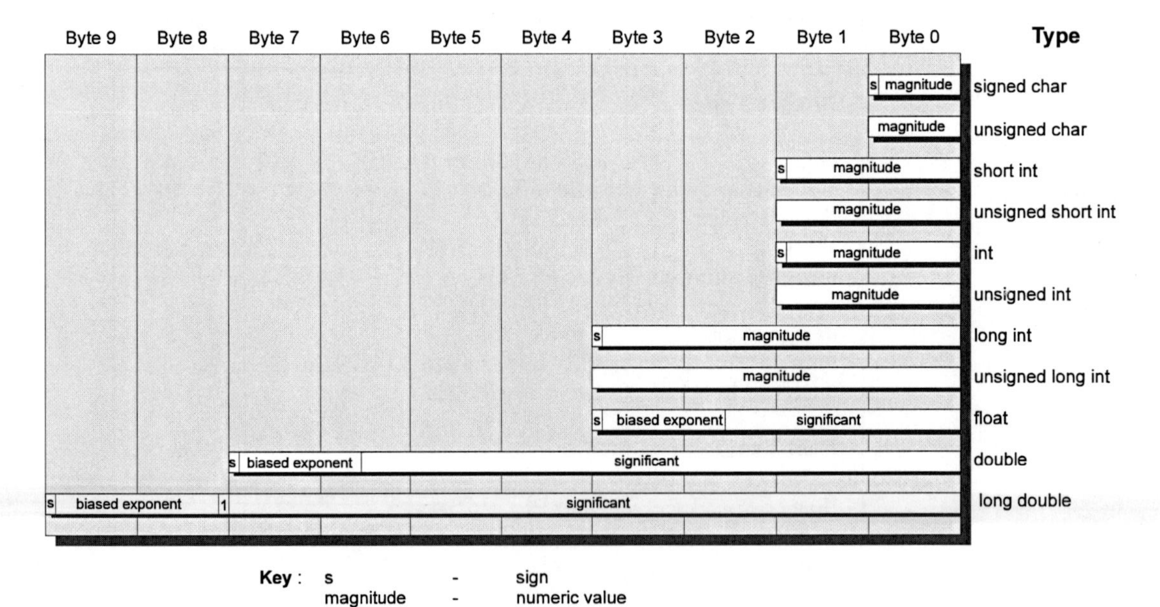

Negative integer values are stored in 2's complement form.

Constants

As well as variables, most programs make use of constants; that is, fixed numeric or non-numeric values. For example, a program might use the value 3.1415 when calculating the area of a circle, or the message "Enter name" as a prompt for the user to key in a value. 3.1415 is a **numeric constant**; "*Enter name*" is a **string constant**.

Numeric Constants

There are two main classes of numeric constants: integer and real.

Integer Constants

An integer constant in C++ is any non-negative whole number, hence 0, 7 and 124 are all examples of integer constants. Although integer values are, by default, assumed to be given in decimal (base 10), it is also possible to specify integer constants in hexadecimal (base 16) or octal (base 8). Hexadecimal values are preceded by 0x or 0X (zero X) whereas octal values are simply preceded by 0 (zero). Integer constants are held in `int`, `unsigned int`, `long` or `unsigned long` format depending on the value. For example, the following lines all represent the same numeric value :

```
65          (decimal)
0X41        (hexadecimal)
0101        (octal)
```

Normally, all integer constants are stored in 4 bytes (i.e. in `int` format).

> **TASK 2.3**
>
> What range of values would be stored in :
>
> a) `signed char` format?
> b) `unsigned char` format?
>
> Give the range for each in decimal, hexadecimal and octal.

Since `int` and `long` formats are identical in 32-bit versions of C++, adding the L serves no purpose in these cases.

It is possible to force an integer constant to occupy a `long` format, irrespective of its value, by terminating it with the letter L (for `long`). Hence 213L will be stored in `long` rather than `int` format. Where a constant with the suffix L is too large to be stored in `long` format, it is stored as `unsigned long int`.

It is also possible to force storage in an `unsigned` format by using the suffix U. Hence 213U will be stored as an `unsigned int` and 66000U, which is too large to be held in an `unsigned int`, will be stored as `unsigned long int`.

`unsigned long int` can be forced on any constant by ending with both U and L (e.g. 213UL).

U and L may be specified in upper or lower case and, when used together, may come in any order.

Various examples of integer constants and their storage requirements are given in TABLE-2.3.

TABLE-2.3

Constant Storage Requirements in Borland C++ version 4.5

	STORAGE REQUIREMENT			
	int	unsigned int	long	unsigned long
Decimal				
-32,768	X			
32,767	X			
32,768			X	
65,535			X	
-2,147,483,648			X	
2,147,483,647			X	
2,147,483,648				X
4,294,967,295				X
540L			X	
65,536L				X
540U		X		
65,536U				X
540UL				X
Hexadecimal				
0X0	X			
0X7FFF	X			
0X8000		X		
0XFFFF		X		
0X10000			X	
0X7FFFFFFF			X	
0X80000000				X
0XFFFFFFFF				X
0X2FFL			X	
0X80000000L				X
0X2FFU		X		
0X10000U				X
0X2FFUL				X
Octal				
00	X			
077777	X			
0100000		X		
0177777		X		
0200000			X	
017777777777			X	
020000000000				X
037777777777				X
0317L			X	
020000000000L				X
0317U		X		
0200000U				X
0317UL				X

Real Constants

Real values may be given in fixed or floating point notation. For example, we may use 3.1415 or 0.31415E01 to represent the approximate value of pi .

Irrespective of value, real constants default to `double` format storage. However, if the constant is terminated with the letter F (e.g. 3.1415F), then `float` format is employed; when ending with the letter L (e.g. 3.1415L) storage is in `long double` format.

F and L may be used in either upper or lower case.

Some examples of real constants and their storage requirements are shown in TABLE-2.4.

TABLE-2.4

Real constants

REAL CONSTANTS		
Fixed point Notation	Floating point Notation	Storage
-6.78	-0.678E01	double
-0.0005	-0.5E-03	double
0.0	0.0E00	double
0.003F	0.3E-02F	float
0.9L	0.9E00L	long double
1425.89	0.142589E04	double

Non-Numeric Constants

Non-numeric constants fall into two types: character and string.

Character Constants

A character constant is any single character and is normally shown enclosed in single quotes:

```
'a'
'*'
'9'
```

Character constants are stored in `char` format.

Some characters, such as **delete**, **newline** and **backspace** cannot be typed in directly. For example, we have already seen that the newline character is displayed using the code '\n'. Collectively these are known as the **escape codes** and can be specified by using the backslash character (\ ), followed by a second character. The full list of escape codes is shown in TABLE-2.5.

TABLE-2.5

Escape Codes

Escape Code	Meaning
\a	Alert (bell)
\b	Backspace
\f	Form feed
\n	Newline
\r	Return
\t	Horizontal tab
\v	Vertical tab
\\	Backslash
\'	Single quote
\"	Double quote
\?	Question mark
\0	Null Character

The Null character has an ASCII code of zero and is of special significance in C++

An upper case X may also be used when defining hexadecimal values

In addition, any character can be specified using the backslash character followed by the ASCII value of the required character in either octal or hexadecimal. Hence the letter 'A' may be specified as \101 in octal or \x41 in hexadecimal.

The general format for defining a character in terms of its ASCII code is:

Maximum value allowed: \377

ccc when using octal
where *ccc* represents one, two or three octal digits as required.

or

\x*hhh*... when using hexadecimal
where *hhh*... represents any number of hexadecimal digits.

The maximum value allowed is \xFF. Hence \x0003E is accepted; \x3A1 is not.

String Constants

A string is a collection of zero or more characters enclosed in double quotes. For example:

```
"This is a string."
```

An empty string (i.e. a string with zero characters) is depicted as two adjacent double quote characters

```
""
```

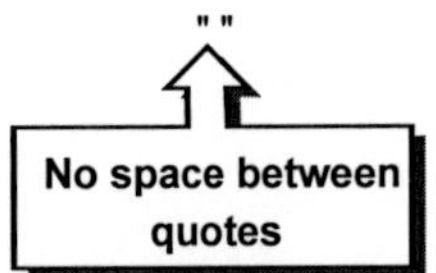

A string may contain escape characters. The string, *"How are you?"he said*, would be written as

```
"\"How are you\?\"he said"
```

Strings are stored as a sequence of characters, each character occupying a single byte. Since strings vary in the number of characters they contain, C++ adds a null character ('\0') to indicate the end of a string. Hence the string *Hello world* is stored as:

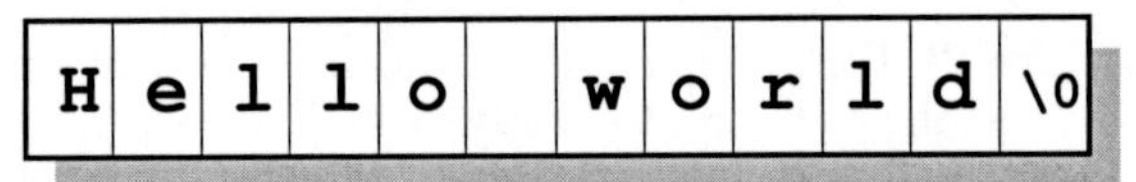

> **TASK 2.4**
>
> How many bytes would the string "*Enter name*" occupy?

The term **whitespace** is used to describe space, tab and newline characters.

String constants separated only by spaces, tabs or return characters are treated as a single string constant. Hence

```
"Al" "to"
"get"       "her"
```

is equivalent to

```
"Altogether".
```

Where it is necessary to split a string literal between two or more lines, the backslash character (\ ) acts as a continuation character. Hence

```
"This is a \
single string"
```

is equivalent to

```
"This is a single string"
```

Defining Variables

Every variable used in a C++ program must be explicitly defined. A variable definition begins with the variable type followed by the variable name and ends with a semi-colon. For example:

```
int                no;
float              square;
char               sex;
unsigned long int  total;
```

As well as using meaningful names, it is advisable to add a comment explaining the purpose of a variable:

```
unsigned long int  total;  //*** Number of phone calls ***
```

Where several variables of the same type are required, they can be defined in a single statement using commas to separate each item.

```
int x1,y1,x2,y2;   //*** Co-ordinates of rectangle ***
```

This can be split over several lines to allow comments to be added to each variable:

```
int
    x1,     //*** x ordinate of top left corner ***
    y1,     //*** y ordinate of top left corner ***
    x2,     //*** x ordinate of bottom right corner ***
    y2;     //*** y ordinate of bottom right corner ***
```

Often, in simple programs, variable definition will be done at the beginning of the code:

```
void main( )
{
    variables defined here
```

But, in fact, C++ allows variables to be defined anywhere in a program. The only restriction being that a variable must be defined before it is referenced by another C++ statement.

Initialising Variables

For exceptions, see storage classes in Chapter 5.

When a variable is allocated space in the computer's memory, the current contents of that area of memory normally remain unchanged. This means that any binary pattern which happens to be contained in the memory allocated, is subsequently taken to be the starting value assigned to that variable. For example, if a program were to begin with the statements

```
#include <iostream.h>
void main( )
{
    int no;
    cout << no;
```

some unpredictable value will be displayed by the `cout` command. Where no specific value has been assigned to a variable, it is said to be **uninitialised**. Although this is acceptable if the variable is subsequently given a value by a `cin` or assignment statement, where the variable is needed as a count or total, then the variable will require to be initialised.

Luckily, variables may be assigned a starting value in the definition statement. Hence we could ensure a count begins at zero with the definition

```
int count = 0;
```

Any value can be assigned by following the variable name by an equals sign and the value to be assigned. Character constant values given to `char` variables must be enclosed in single quotes:

```
char code = 'A';
```

Where several variables of the same type have to be given the same value, each can be assigned separately as in:

```
int count = 0, total = 0, subtotal = 0;
```

It is also possible to initialise variables using a previously defined variable, or an expression:

```
int no1 = 7;
int no2 = no1;
int no3 = no2*3;
```

It is also possible to assign an octal or hexadecimal value to a variable. For example:

```
int hexval = 0XA7;
int octval = 017;
```

Where the value assigned is not of the same type as the variable, C++ handles conversion automatically. Hence we might define a `char` variable to have an initial value of 'B' using either

```
char classify = 'B';
```

or

```
char classify = 66;
```

66 is the ASCII code for a capital 'B'.

The general format of a variable definition is shown in FIG-2.5.

FIG-2.5

Variable Definition

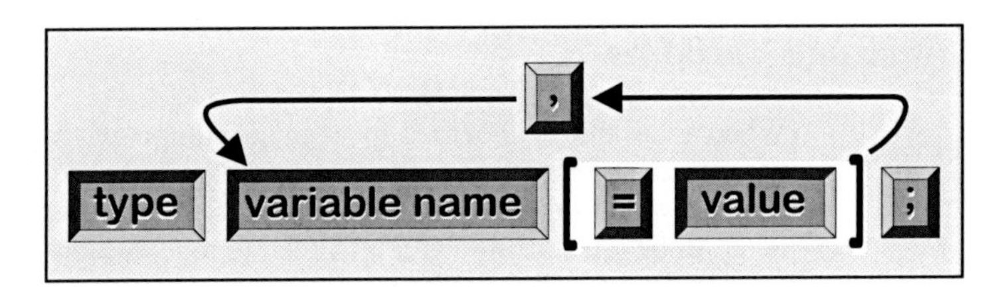

TASK 2.5

State which of the following definitions is invalid.

```
1. char no = 12;
2. int letter = "C";
3. float x = y = z = -6.812;
4. int no = 13, no2 = 0, no3 = 6;
5. int x = 0XAE, int y = 015;
```

Named Constants

A named constant allows us to associate an identifying name with a constant. So rather than write statements such as

```
tax_deduction = gross_wage * 0.25;
```

with its obscure reference to a tax rate of 25%, it is possible to define a variable constant for this value using

```
const float tax_rate = 0.25;
```

and then use this name, `tax_rate`, to create a more readable version of the original statement:

```
tax_deduction = gross_wage * tax_rate;
```

The value assigned to a named constant cannot be changed at a later point in a program.

A named constant can be assigned any constant value. For example:

```
const float tax_rate = 0.25;
const char delete_code = 'D';
```

The format of the `const` statement is shown in FIG-2.6.

FIG-2.6

`const` Definition

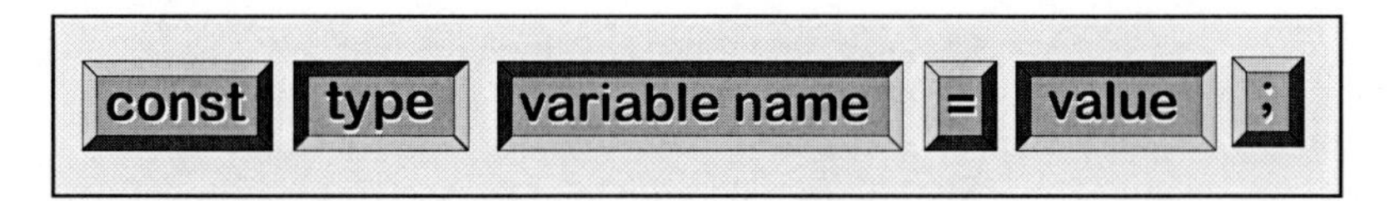

Once defined, one named constant may be used to assign a value to other named constants or normal variables defined later in the program:

```
const int dozen = 12;
const int months_in_year = dozen; //dozen's value assigned to
                                  //constant months_in_year

int no1 = dozen;                  //dozen's value assigned to
                                  //variable no1
```

TASK 2.6

Which of the following constant definition statements are invalid?

1. `const a = 6;`
2. `const int b = 3, c = 5;`
3. `const char letter;`
4. `const int a = 3; int b = 1;`
5. `const int no = 10+3;`

Summary

- **Variables are used to** hold values used or created by a program.

- **Variables have:** a name, a type and a value and are allocated an address in memory.

- **Variable names are constructed from** letters, numeric digits and the underscore character (_).

  They cannot begin with a numeric digit.

  They cannot be a C++ keyword.

- **The following types are available:**

```
char
signed char
unsigned char
int
unsigned int
long int
unsigned long int
float
double
long double
```

- `char` variables are implemented as `signed char` or `unsigned char` depending on the default setting of the compiler.

- **The initial value held by a variable** is undefined.

- **Each variable is allocated an area of computer memory** where its value is stored. The size of this area depends on the variable's type.

- **Variables can be defined at almost any point** in a C++ program.

- **Constants** are fixed values.

- **Constants can be** integer, real, character or string.

- **Integer constants can be specified in** decimal, hexadecimal or octal.
  Hexadecimal values begin with 0X (zero X) (e.g. `0X6F`).
  Octal values begin with 0 (zero) (e.g. `052`).
  Decimal values begin with any non-zero digit (e.g. `23`).

- **Integer constants are stored in** `int`, `unsigned`, `long` or `unsigned long` format depending on the magnitude of the value.

- **The storage format can be forced** to `long`/`unsigned long` by the suffix L (e.g. `12L`).

  The storage format can be forced to `unsigned int`/`unsigned long` by the suffix U (e.g. `12U`).

  The storage format can be forced to `unsigned long` by the suffix UL (e.g. `12UL`).

■ **Real constants are normally stored as** type `double`.

■ **Real constants can be stored as** type `float` by adding the suffix F. (e.g. `3.14F`)

Real constants can be stored as type `long double` by adding the suffix L. (e.g. `3.14L`)

■ **A character constant** is a single character enclosed in single quotes (e.g. `'A'`)

■ Certain characters, which cannot be entered directly from the keyboard have special methods of definition. These are called the **escape codes.** (e.g. `'\n'` - the newline character)

■ **A character can also be specified using \ X** followed by the character's code in hexadecimal. (e.g. `'\X41'`)

■ **A character can be specified using ** followed by the character's code in octal. (e.g. `'\102'`)

■ **String constants are enclosed in double quotes**. (e.g. `"This is a string""`)

■ **String values are stored with an additional, terminating null character, '\0'.**

■ **Escape codes may be embedded in strings**. (e.g. `"Line1\nLine2"`)

■ **Spaces, tabs and newline characters** are collectively known as **whitespace** characters.

■ **Individual strings separated only by whitespace characters** are treated as a single string constant.
(e.g. `"De"        "noun"        "ced"` is treated as *"Denounced"*)

■ **A string constant can also be split** over two or more lines by using the backslash character (\) as a continuation marker.

Subsequent lines of the string must begin in column 1

(e.g.
```
"Win\
dow\
s"
```
is treated as *"Windows"*)

■ **Variables may be initialised** (i.e. given a starting value) during definition. (e.g. `int count = 0;`)

■ **Named constants** allow names to be assigned to fixed values. (e.g. `const float pi = 3.1415;`)

■ **The value associated with a named constant** cannot be changed.

THE ASSIGNMENT OPERATORS

The = Operator

Although variables may be assigned values when they are defined, it is also possible to modify the value of a variable later in the program using the basic assignment operator (=). For example, assuming a program contains the definition

```
int no1 = 0;        //*** Initial value of zero ***
```

then the statement

```
no1 = 5;        //*** New value is 5 ***
```

changes the contents of the variable *no1* from zero to 5.

The assignment statement takes the form defined in FIG-2.7.

FIG-2.7

The Assignment Operator (=)

Execution of an assignment statement results in *value* being copied to the memory allocated to *variable name*. Any previous value held by *variable name* is lost.

value must be one of the following:

a constant,
another variable
or an expression

Constant

Where *value* is a constant, that fixed value is assigned to the variable. See LISTING-2.3 for examples.

LISTING-2.3

Assigning a Constant to a Variable

```
const float  pi = 3.1415;
int          no1,no2;
double       rno1, rno2;
char         letter;

no1     = 6;
no2     = -10;
rno1    = -4.891;
letter  = 'D';
rno2    = pi;
```

Variable

Alternatively, the value held in one variable can be copied into another. The contents of the right-hand variable are unaffected. See LISTING-2.4 for examples.

LISTING-2.4

Assigning the Value of a Variable to some other Variable

```
int       no1 = 12,no2;
float     rno1 = 13.008,rno2;
char      letter1 = 'G',letter2;

no2       = no1;
rno2      = rno1;
letter2   = letter1;
```

Expressions

An expression is usually, but not always, an arithmetic expression containing constants, variables and arithmetic operators. The arithmetic operators, with one exception, are those already described in Chapter 1:

	Addition	+
	Subtraction	-
	Multiplication	*
	Division	/
and	Remainder	%

Division

The effect of the division operator (/) in C++ is not always identical to its arithmetic counterpart: when used on two integer values the division operator supplies an integer result. Hence,

8/3 will give a result of 2

However, if any of the operands are real, the result is also real. For example,

8.0/3 will give a result of 2.67

Where one of the values involved is negative then the result is the smallest negative integer greater than the actual result. For instance,

-8/5
= -1

The Remainder Operator (%)

The remainder operator (%) is used to determine the integer remainder after division. For example,

9 % 5
= 4

since 5 divides into 9 once with a remainder of 4.

Where both values have the same sign, the result has that sign. Hence,

-8%-5
= -3

Where the two values have different signs, the result has the same sign as the first value.

Examples:

```
    -8 % 5              8 % -5
=   -3             =    3
```

The remainder operator may only be used with integer type values.

The remainder operator can also be used to perform the modulo operation. Remainder and modulo give the same result when the signs of both values are equal. However, when dealing with values of differing signs as in

-7 modulo 3

the mathematical operator gives a result of 2,

while in C++

-7 % 3

gives a result of -1.

We can ensure that the % operator is equivalent to modulo by using the following algorithm:

```
Calculate the remainder when value1 is divided by value2
Add value2 to the result
Calculate the remainder when the modified result is divided by
value2
```

This translates into C++ as

All variables in this example are defined as type `int`.

```
result         = value1 % value2;
modifiedresult = result + value2;
answer         = modifiedresult % value2;
```

and can be reduced to a single, though more cryptic, statement:

```
result = ((value1 % value2) + value2) % value2;
```

As in Structured English, the parentheses are used to modify the order of precedence of the operators

Using the division or remainder operator where the second operand is zero will result in an error.

TASK 2.7

Determine the values of the following expressions:

8 / 4	8 % 4
9 / 4	9 % 4
9 / 4.0	9 % 4.0
7 / 0	7 % 0
0 / 7	0 % 7
2 / 8	2 % 8
-11 / 3	-12 % 3
-15 / -6	-15 % -6
9 / -2	9 % -2

As with Structured English, an arithmetic expression can contain an unlimited number of operators in any order. Normal operator precedence applies with the remainder operator given the same priority as multiplication and division. Operator precedence is overridden by the use of parentheses - expressions in parentheses being evaluated first. For example, in the expression

```
(no1 + 6) / 10
```

the addition operation will be performed before that of division.

Where there is more than one set of parentheses in an expression, such as

```
(no1 + 6) / (no2 + 10)
```

then the contents of the left-most parentheses are evaluated first.

Where parentheses are nested, as in

```
((no1 + 6) * (12 - no3) + 1) / (no2 + 10)
```

the contents of the innermost parentheses are evaluated first. For the expression above, the terms are evaluated in the order:

1. `(no1 + 6)`
2. `(12 - no3)`
3. `((no1 + 6) * (12 - no3) + 1)`
4. `(no2 + 10)`
5. `((no1 + 6) * (12 - no3) + 1) / (no2 + 10)`

The arithmetic operators and their precedences are given in TABLE-2.6.

TABLE-2.6

Arithmetic Operators

Operator	Description	Priority
( )	parentheses	3
*	multiplication	2
/	division	2
%	remainder	2
+	addition	1
-	subtraction	1

LISTING-2.5 gives several examples of expressions used with the assignment operator.

LISTING-2.5

Assigning the Result of an Expression to a Variable

```
int      no1 = 4, no2 = 5, no3, ans;
float    rno1 = 1.56, rno2 = 7.8, rno3, result;

no3      =    no1 + no2;
rno3     =    rno1 - rno2;
no1      =    23 * no2;
rno2     =    rno3 / 12;
result   =    (rno1 + rno2) / rno3;
ans      =    ((no1 + 2) * 3 - 1) / (no3 - 2);
```

Automatic Type Conversion

So far, all the assignment examples have transferred values of the same type as the receiving variable. C++ will also allow assignment between differing types, conversion between the various types being performed automatically. Hence, we may do such things as copy an `int` value to a `float` or a `char` to an `unsigned long int`. Each transfer possibility is discussed below.

INTEGER to REAL

Any integer value can be transferred to a real variable. C++ automatically transforms the internal formats of the value involved from integer binary to floating point format. Some examples are given in LISTING-2.6.

LISTING-2.6

Transferring an Integer Value to a Real Variable

```
float        rno1, rno2;
double       dno1, dno2;
char         let1 = 'C';
int          no = 9;
long         lno = 357812;

rno1     =   12;          //*** Integer constant to float ***
no       =   -9;
rno2     =   no;          //*** int variable to float ***
dno1     =   let1;        //*** char to double ***
dno1     =   lno;         //*** long to double ***
```

REAL to INTEGER

Although a real value can be transferred to an integer, only the integral part will be copied over, any fraction being lost. Also, the integral part of the real value must lie within the range of values which the integer variable can accommodate, otherwise the transfer will give incorrect results. Likewise, attempting to assign a negative real number to an unsigned integer type will result in an error. Some examples are given in LISTING-2.7.

LISTING-2.7

Assigning a Real value to an Integer

```
int          no1, no2;
long int     lno1, lno2;
float        rno;
double       dno = 6789123.7623;
long double  ldno = 58152436738.12345

no1      =   12.78;       //*** Real constant to int ***
rno      =   3.89;
no2      =   rno;         //*** Real variable to int ***
lno1     =   dno;         //*** double to long int ***
lno2     =   ldno;        //*** long double to long int ***
```

CHARACTER to INTEGER

Since the character types (`char`, `unsigned char` and `signed char`) are a subclass of the integer types, it is natural that transfers to other integer types (`int`, `long int` etc.) should be allowed. When a character value is transferred to an `int` type the ASCII value of the character is placed in the integer variable. LISTING-2.8 gives some examples.

LISTING-2.8

Assigning a Character value to an Integer

```
int      no1, no2;
char     letter;

no1      =   'A';         /* Stores 65 (A is 65 in ASCII) */
letter   =   'B';         /* ASCII code for B is 66 */
no2      =   letter;      /* Stores 66 */
```

Originally ASCII character codes ranged from 0 to 127 giving binary values ranging between:

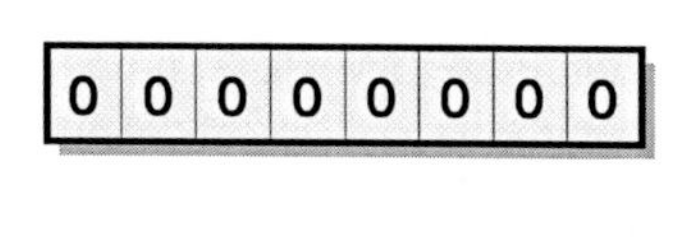

and

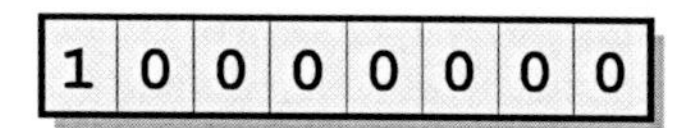

Any of these values are transferred to an `int` (or `long int`, etc.) by copying the contents of the `char` byte to the first byte of the `int` variable. This operation is shown in FIG-2.8.

FIG-2.8

Transferring a low value `char` to an `int`.

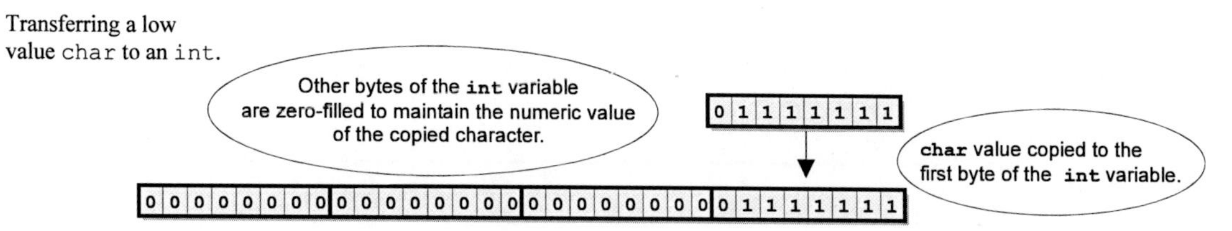

However, codes from 128 to 255 are sometimes used for an extended IBM character set. These have binary patterns in the range:

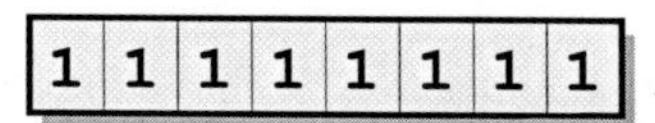

to

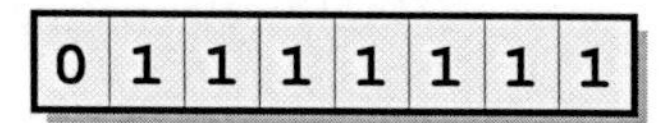

A problem arises when a character variable whose value lies in this range of values is transferred to an integer variable. How is the character's binary pattern to be interpreted? Is the original value in 2's complement form? If this is the case, it represents a negative number, the value of which can only be maintained by filling the most significant byte of the integer with 1's. For example, if a character contains the binary pattern 10111101 and this is assumed to be a 2's complement value (-67) then the character should be transferred, as shown below, to retain the same negative value (-67).

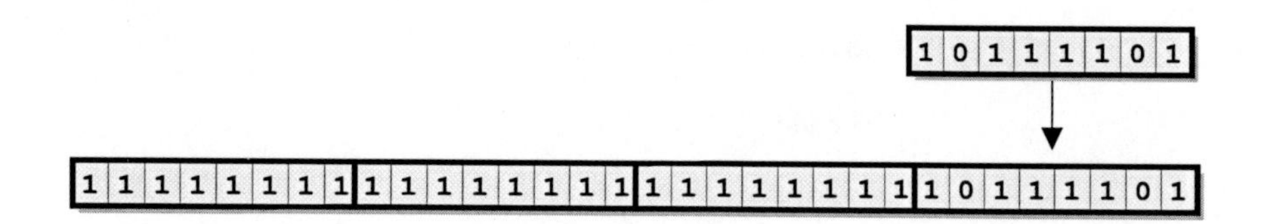

Alternatively, if the same pattern is assumed to be an unsigned value (189) then the transfer should give the result shown below.

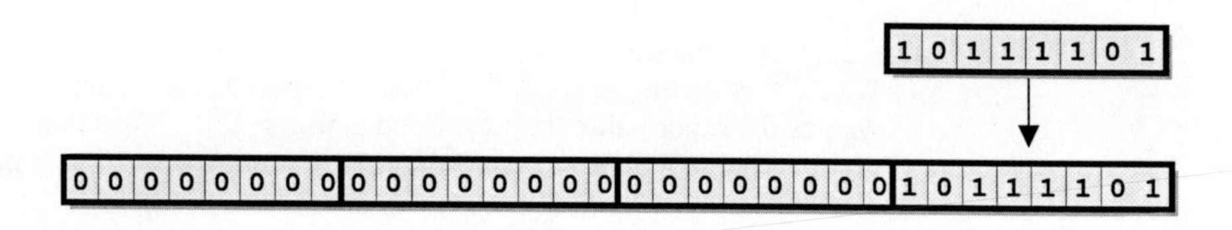

The transfer method used depends on how the character variable was defined. A `signed char` variable will be transferred using the first method while an `unsigned char` variable will be transferred using the second approach.

Defining a variable as type `char` will create either a `signed char`, or `unsigned char` variable depending on which default is set for your compiler.

TASK 2.8

Show the binary pattern in both variables immediately after execution of the following code:

```
int no;
signed char letter = '\X8A';

no = letter;
```

INTEGER to CHARACTER

An integer value can be copied into a character variable, but the following points should be noted:

An `unsigned char` cannot be given a negative value.

An integer value which is too large to be stored in 8 bits will give unpredictable results.

Some examples of integer to character transfers are given in LISTING-2.9.

LISTING-2.9

Assigning an Integer value to a Character

```
int  no;
unsigned char     uletter1,uletter2;
signed char       sletter1;

uletter1     =    67; //*** Equivalent to letter1 = 'B';***
no           =    68;
uletter2     =    no; //*** Equivalent to letter2 = 'C';***
sletter      =    -67; //*** -67 transfers the binary pattern
                       //    10111101 to sletter. This is the
                       //    pattern for ASCII character 189
```

Converting Expressions

The code

```
void main( )
{
    unsigned int    no1 = 34;
    long            answer;

    answer  =   no1 * 12.3;
```

contains three types in the final line: a `long` (*answer*), an `unsigned int` (*no1*) and a `double` (*12.3*). In order to evaluate any part of an expression, C++ requires the values associated with an operator (such as +, - , * etc.) to be of the same type. Where this is not the case, C++ converts one of the values involved to the same type as the other value. In the example above, this means that the `int` value (*no1*) is converted to a `double` before the multiplication operation is performed:

```
    34.0 * 12.3
=   418.2
```

Finally, this is converted to the same type as the receiving variable before being assigned. In the previous example this means that the `double` result is converted to a `long` (any fractional part being truncated) before being copied to *answer*, giving a result of:

answer = 418

The rules of conversion used when an expression contains differing types are summarised below:

```
IF expression contains char, unsigned char, signed char or
    short values
THEN
    Convert these to int
ENDIF
IF expression contains any unsigned short values THEN
    Convert these to unsigned int
ENDIF
FOR each arithmetic operation being performed DO
    IF
        either value is long double:
            Convert other to long double
        either value is double:
            Convert other to double
        either value is float:
            Convert other to float
        either value is unsigned long:
            Convert other to unsigned long
        either value is long:
            Convert other to long
        either value is unsigned int:
            Convert other to unsigned int
    ENDIF
    Perform operation storing result as same type as values
        involved
ENDFOR
```

TASK 2.9

For each line indicated in the code given below, state what type will be used when evaluating the expression.

```
void main( )
{
    char    cno1, cno2 = 65;
    int     no1, no2 = 1452;
    float   rno1, rno2 = 5.78;

    cno1    =   cno2 + 1;           line 1
    no1     =   no2 + 12U;          line 2
    rno1    =   rno2 + 0.5;         line 3
}
```

The consequences of this conversion rule mean that expressions which may appear strange are, in fact, quite acceptable. Hence we may have statements such as:

```
no1 =   'A' + 1;        // no1 =   66
no2 =   'C' - 'A';      // no2 =    2
```

Converting Different Sized Types

Copying a `long` value to a `short` variable or `double` to `float` are allowable, but it is your responsibility as programmer to ensure that the values being transferred are within the range acceptable to the receiving variable. For example, if a `long` value is copied into a `short` variable, only the contents of the lower 2 bytes will be copied over. See FIG-2.9.

FIG-2.9

Copying to a Shorter Type

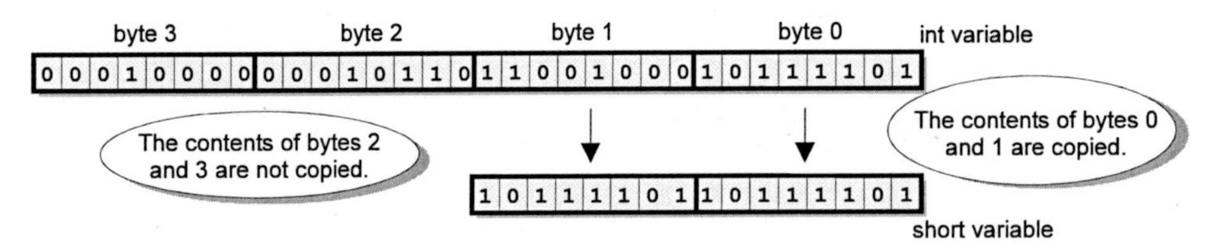

Insufficient storage space can also occur when C++ is calculating intermediate results in an expression. For example, in the 16-bit version of C++, where `int` values occupy only 16 bits, we would expect the statement

```
answer = (500 * 100)/25;
```

to return a result of 2000 but, unfortunately, the result will be quite different. Since all values involved in the expression are type `int`, all intermediate results will also be of type `int`. However, the first calculation, 500*100, gives a result (50,000) which is too large to be stored in the 16 bits allocated to an `int` value. Consequently, only the least-significant 16 bits of the product are retained and this is then divided by 25 giving a spurious result which is placed in the variable, *answer*.

This problem can be overcome by forcing one of the two values used in the multiplication to be stored in some format which can accommodate sufficiently large values:

```
answer = (500L * 100)/25;
```

Now the intermediate results will also be in `long` format before being converted to type `int` and copied to *answer*. The final value being less than 32,768 (i.e. occupying only the first 2 bytes of the `long` format), means that no significant bits will be lost in this transfer.

Arithmetic Assignment Operators:
+= -= *= /= %=

Two common instructions are adding to a count (e.g. counting cars passing a set of sensors) and adding to a total (e.g. adding the price of an item to the bill total). In Structured English we might write such statements as:

```
Add 1 to count
```

or

```
Add cost of item to total
```

Most programming languages would use statements such as:

```
count = count + 1;      // The new value of count is its current
                        // value plus one
```

and

```
total = total + cost;   // The new value of total is its current
                        // value plus cost
```

The above statements are also perfectly valid in C++ (assuming the variables have been defined appropriately), but the same effect can be achieved by the briefer, but slightly less readable:

```
count += 1;
```

and

```
total += cost;
```

The overall effect of the operator += is to add the value on the right hand side to the variable on the left.

All arithmetic operators can be used in this way. These new operators are referred to as **arithmetic assignment operators.**

Other arithmetic assignment operations are given in TABLE-2.7.

TABLE-2.7

Arithmetic Assignment Operators

Operator	Description	Example	Equivalence
+=	addition assignment	`no += 6;`	`no = no + 6;`
-=	subtraction assignment	`bal -= cash;`	`bal = bal-cash;`
*=	multiplication assignment	`ans *= 5;`	`ans = ans * 5;`
/=	division assignment	`half /= 2;`	`half = half/2;`
%=	remainder assignment	`rem %= no;`	`rem = rem % no;`

TASK 2.10

Using the arithmetic assignment operators, write the equivalent of the following statements:

1. `sum = sum + no;`
2. `count = count - 6;`
3. `answer = answer * (mark / 7);`
4. `dividend = dividend / (takings - costs);`
5. `total_remainder = total_remainder % (previous*current);`

The Increment And Decrement Operators

As we have already seen, we can add 1 to the value of a variable in one of two ways:

```
count = count + 1;
```

or

```
count += 1;
```

NOTE: It is from this operator that C++ gets its name since it is a language which is one generation later than C.

But C++ has an operator specifically designed to perform such an operation: ++. This **increment operator** adds 1 to (i.e. increments) the contents of a variable. Hence we may add one to *count* with the statement:

```
count++;
```

It is also permissible to place the increment operator before the variable involved:

```
++count;
```

In these examples, the position of the operator has no affect on the result. But the increment operator may be used as part of a longer statement or within an arithmetic expression. Hence we may write:

```
int ans, no = 6;
ans = no++;
```

This last statement has the effect of changing the value in both *ans* and *no*. But there are two possible ways of doing this:

Copy the value in *no* into *ans* (hence *ans* = 6) then increment *no* (*no* =7)

or

Increment *no* (*no* = 7) then copy the value of *no* into *ans* (*ans* = 7)

The position of the increment operator determines which of the two alternatives is used: when ++ follows the variable (e.g. `ans = no++;`), then incrementation happens last; when ++ comes before the variable, incrementation happens first.

These options are referred to as **post-incrementing** and **pre-incrementing** respectively.

TASK 2.11

Is the statement

```
ans = no++ ;
```

pre-incrementing or post-incrementing?

Write down the coding for the alternative incremental method.

A decrement operator (--) is also available to subtract 1 from a variable. This can also be used in a pre-incrementing and post-incrementing form and as part of a larger statement. This allows statements such as:

```
int ans, no = 6;

no--;               //*** no  = 5 ***
--no;               //*** no  = 4 ***
ans = no--;         //*** ans = 4 , no  = 3 ***
ans = --no;         //*** no  = 2 , ans = 2 ***
```

TASK 2.12

Write down the intermediate and final values produced by the following code:

```
int no1 = 1, no2 = 10, answer;

answer  = ++no1 + no2--;
answer  *= no1++;
```

There are many cases where the results obtained when using ++ and -- are undefined and differ from compiler to compiler, so if you are using these operators keep it simple. You will see some of the situations in which they are traditionally used, later in this text.

Multiple Assignment

If several variables are to be set to the same value, this can be done using a multiple assignment statement. As in the definition statement, it is possible to assign the same value to several variables in a single statement. For example:

```
no1 = no2 = no3 = 0;
letter1 = letter2 = 'F';
rno1 = rno2 = rno3 * 5;
```

The compiler evaluates the assignments from right to left. That is, in the first example, *no3* is given the value zero then *no2* is given the value held in *no3* then *no1* is given the value held in *no2*.

The Comma Operator ,

Like the addition (+) or subtraction (-) operators, the comma operator (,) acts on two values to return a single result. Hence we may write

```
5, 6
```

as part of some larger expression.

The result returned by this operator is that of the second argument in the term. Hence 5, 6 returns the value 6. This allows us to write statements such as

```
no = (5, 6);
```

which will assign the value 6 to the variable *no*. The parentheses are required because the comma operator has a lower priority than the assignment operator.

The values involved may be constants, variables or expressions. Hence, assuming the definition

```
int no,no1=8,no2=4;
```

then the following statements are valid

```
no = (no1, no2);            //*** no = 4  ***
no = (no1 - no2, no2 * 6); //*** no = 24 ***
```

We can go even further than this, with each term being an assignment statement in its own right:

```
no = (no1 = 17, no2 = 12); //*** no1=17,no2=12,no=12 ***
```

There's no obligation to actually assign the result produced by this operator to a variable, so we can write:

```
no1 = 17, no2 = 12;
```

This can be used as a device for allowing several separate instructions to be carried out as part of a single compound instruction. Therefore,

```
no1 = 17, no2 = 12;
```

is an alternative method of achieving the effect produced by the statements

```
no1 = 17;
no2 = 12;
```

The terms used with the comma operator are evaluated from left to right. In the next example the second expression's value is determined by that of the first:

```
no1 = 6 , no2 = 3 + no1;
```

no1 is set to 6, *no2* is set to 9 (3 + 6) and the value returned by the comma operator is 9.

TASK 2.13

Assuming the definitions:

```
int no1, no2, no3, no4, no5, no6;
```

List the final results of each of the following statements:.

```
no1 = (5, 8);
no3 = (no2 = 6, no1 + 4);
no6 = (no4 = no1, no5 = 3 + no4);
```

The comma operator may not seem to add much to the language, but, as we will see in later chapters, it can be used to good effect in combination with other statements.

Structured English Equivalents

TABLE-2.8 lists some Structured English statements and their C++ equivalent.

TABLE-2.8

Assignment Equivalents

Structured English	C++
Set total to zero	int total = 0;
Add 1 to count	count++;
Add mark to sum	sum += mark;
Calculate dividend as 10% of total	dividend = total * 0.1;
Calculate remaining ounces as remainder of (oz1 + oz2) divided by 16	remoz = (oz1 + oz2) % 16;

The `sizeof` Operator

The `sizeof` operator returns the number of bytes required to store a given type or variable. Hence the expression

```
sizeof(int)
```

will return the value 2 (since an `int` is stored in two bytes).

Alternatively, a variable name may be used as an operand:

```
float rno;

sizeof(rno)      // returns 4
```

`sizeof` can be used without parentheses, allowing expressions such as:

```
sizeof rno
```

The value returned from `sizeof` is stored in `unsigned int` format.

Summary

- **The assignment operator** is used to give a value to a variable.

  Any previous value held by the variable is overwritten by the new value.

- The simplest assignment has the form **`variable = value;`**

- **The value assigned** may be one of the following:

  a constant
  the value contained in some other variable
  the result of an expression

- **Arithmetic expressions** can use the operators:

*	Multiplication
/	Division
%	Remainder
+	Addition
-	Subtraction

- **The division operator** (/) returns an integer result when both values involved are integers, otherwise a real result is produced.

- **The remainder operation** (%) can only be used with two integer values.

- **Where the second operand is zero**, an error will occur when using the division or remainder operators (e.g. 8/0).

- **When evaluating expressions**, multiplication, division and remainder operations (*, / ,%) are performed before addition and subtraction (+, -).

  This rule is modified by the use of parentheses: expressions in parentheses being performed first.

- **All `short` and `char`** types are converted to type `int` before any expression is evaluated. Values of type `unsigned short` are converted to `unsigned int`.

- **Where the values used in an arithmetic operation are of mixed types** these are converted to compatible types before evaluation.

- **Assigning a value of a different type** to a variable will result in automatic conversion by C++.

- **When a character value is copied into an integer variable**, it is done in such a way as to retain the numeric value of the original character value.

  For character values greater than 127, this will be affected by the use of the terms `signed` and `unsigned` when defining the character variable.

- It is the programmer's responsibility to ensure that **the variable type being used is adequate to store the value to be placed in it.**

- **The arithmetic assignment operators** (`+=`, `-=`, `*=` , `/=` and `%=`) allow the receiving variable to be part of the right-hand-side expression without explicitly specifying it.

- **The increment operator,** ++, is used to add 1 to the value of a variable. When placed before the variable, the variable is incremented before the remainder of any expression is evaluated.

  When placed after the variable, any expression is evaluated before the variable is incremented.

- **The decrement operator,** `- -`, is used to reduce the value of a variable by one.

  Like ++, it may be placed before or after the variable to be decremented.

- As in definition, **several variables may be assigned the same value in a single statement.**
  (e.g. `no1 = no2 = no3 = 12;`)

- **The comma operator** (,) expects an expression on either side of it. Each is evaluated in turn (left then right). The value of the right expression is the value returned by this operation.
  (e.g. `no1 = (no2=4,no3=no2+2);`
  gives the results
  no1 = 6, *no2* = 4, *no3* = 6)

- **The** `sizeof` **operator** returns the storage requirements, in bytes, of a variable or type.

  (e.g.
```
int no1;
float x;

sizeof(no1)     returns 2
sizeof(float)   returns 4
```
)

BASIC INPUT/OUTPUT

It is rather difficult to think of any worthwhile program which is not going to require some input from the keyboard (or other device) and produce output on the screen or paper.

There are many ways of achieving such input and output in C++, but for the moment we will look only briefly at two of these.

cin

The `cin` (pronounced *see-in*) keyword allows a variable to be assigned a value entered from the keyboard. This obviously allows a program much more flexibility than the assignment statement, since the user can type in different values each time the program is used.

Instead of assigning the value 3 to the variable *month* in a statement such as:

```
month = 3;
```

`cin` can be used to allow a value for *month* to be entered at run time from the keyboard:

```
cin >> month;
```

Following the term `cin` is the *extraction* (or *input*) operator, >>, and the name of the variable in which the value is to be placed. We can interpret the above C++ statement as:

Get a value from the keyboard and insert it in the variable month.

When the computer executes this statement, it will wait patiently for a value to be entered at the keyboard. Once the *ENTER* key is pressed, the value keyed in is assigned to the variable specified. It is possible to enter more than one value at a time using `cin` by simply adding more >> symbols and variable names:

```
cin >> day >> month >> year;
```

This time three values may be entered. All three values should be keyed in (separated by spaces) before pressing *ENTER*.

The general format for the `cin` statement is given in FIG-2.10.

FIG-2.10

cin

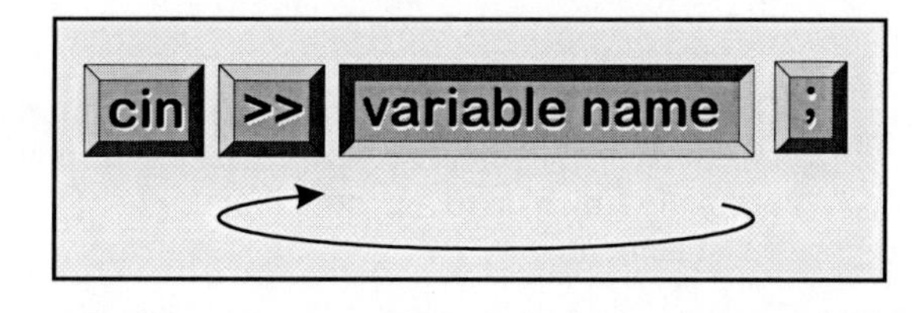

In general, it is best to have a separate `cin` statement for each value that is to be input.

At this stage, it will be up to the user of the program to ensure that the values entered are valid for the variables specified and for the logic of the program. Later we will look at ways which allow the program to check whether values entered are acceptable.

To use `cin`, your program must contain the preprocessor command

```
#include <iostream.h>
```

since this header file contains the definition of `cin` .

TASK 2.14

Identify the invalid commands in the following code:

```
#include <iostream.h>
void main()
{
    int no1, no2;
    float rno1, rno2;

    cin << no1;
    cin >> no1, no2;
    cin >> rno1 >> rno2;
    cin >> no1 >> rno1;
}
```

cout

The `cout` (see-out) command allows output to the computer screen.

The output value can be a constant as in:

```
cout << "Hello world"; // String Constant
```

or

```
cout << 17;            // Numeric constant
```

with `cout` being followed by the output operator, <<, and the data item to be displayed.

The contents of a variable can be displayed by specifying the variable's name:

```
#include <iostream.h>
void main ( )
{
    int no = 17;
    cout << no;
}
```

Output begins at the current cursor position and occupies as many character positions on the screen as is necessary to display the required value. The cursor will normally finish up to the immediate right of the last character output. For example, the statement

```
cout << "Hello world";
```

would produce the output shown in FIG-2.11.

FIG-2.11

Screen Output 1

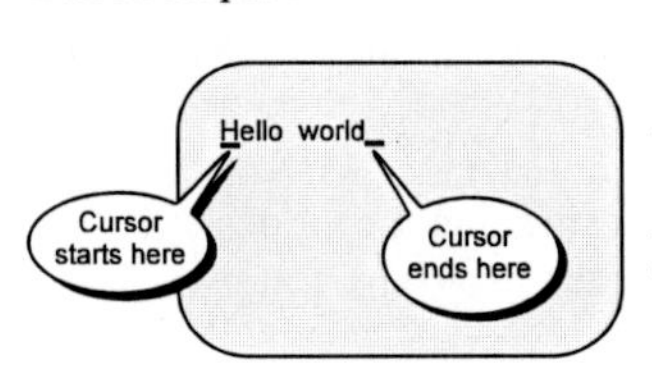

By adding a newline character to the end of the string as in

```
cout << "Hello world\n";
```

FIG-2.12

Screen Output 2

Hello world

Cursor starts here

Cursor ends here

the cursor would end up at the beginning of the next line (FIG-2.12).

The newline character ('\n') normally only moves the cursor vertically down. However, when used with cout it also moves the cursor to the left-hand edge of the line.

A vertical tab character ('\v') will force output on to a new line immediately below the current cursor position. Hence

```
cout << "Hello\vworld";
```

FIG-2.13

Screen Output 3

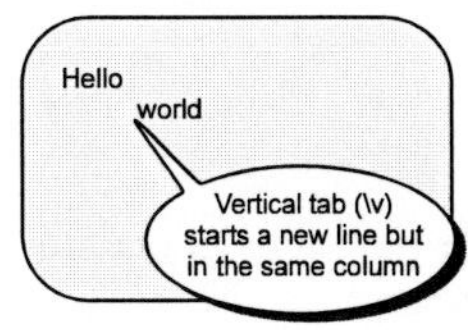

would produce the output shown in FIG-2.13.

The horizontal tab character ('\t') moves the cursor to the next tab position. These are normally at columns 10, 20, 30 etc. The output produced by the statement

```
cout << "Hello\tworld";
```

is shown in FIG-2.14.

FIG-2.14

Screen Output 4

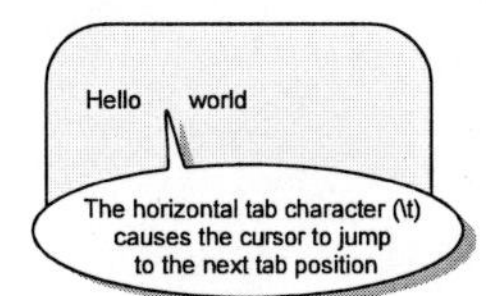

The cursor can be moved one space to the left using the backspace character ('\b'). To delete the character to the left of the cursor, the backspace character can be used in combination with a space :

```
cout << "\b \b";
```

The effect of this code can be described as:

```
backspace cursor
display space (hence removing previous at this
                position on the screen character)
backspace     (moves cursor to the immediate
                right of any remaining characters)
```

The computer can be made to sound what was once a mechanical bell, but has now been reduced to an electronic beep, by outputing the alert character ('\a'):

```
cout << '\a';
```

Outputting the alert character has no effect on the screen display or cursor position.

If more than one value is to be output in a single statement, then each value is preceded by an output operator. For example:

```
cout << "The result is " << answer << endl;
```

endl has the same effect as outputing the newline character '\n'

When using cout, the command #include <iostream.h> must be included in your program.

Formatting Output

cout will allow several values to be output in a single statement (each being separated from the previous one by the << operator. However, if we attempt to output more than one value at a time, such as in the code

```
#include <iostream.h>
void main( )
{
    int no1 = 123, no2 = 456, no3 = 789;

    cout << no1 << no2 << no3;
```

the result will appear to be a single very large value:

```
123456789
```

This is because *cout* makes no attempt to insert separating characters of its own. This leaves the programmer with solutions such as:

These are single space characters between each value. Where more spaces are required these should be enclosed in double quotes (") since more than one character would normally constitute a string.

```
cout << no1 << ' ' << no2 << ' ' << no3;
or
cout << no1 << '\t' << no2 << '\t' << no3;
```

An alternative approach is to force the output produced to occupy a specified number of character positions on the screen. This is achieved using the instruction `setw(n)` within the *cout* command, where *n* is the number of characters the output is to occupy on the screen. The `setw()` instruction must precede the value to be output:

```
cout<<setw(6) << no1;
```

Since *no1* only contains a three digit value (*123*), the first three positions allocated for the output are occupied by space characters, giving the display:

The character Δ is used here to represent a single space.

```
ΔΔΔ123
```

`setw()` must be used for each variable which is to be given a width. The width specified may be different in each case. Hence if we wish to output all three variables (*no1*, *no2* and *no3*) with a field width of 6, the the command would be

```
cout<<setw(6) << no1 << setw(6) << no2 << setw(6) << no3;
```

giving output of

```
ΔΔΔ123ΔΔΔ456ΔΔΔ789
```

The commands used to modify the format of the display are known as **manipulators**. In order to use manipulators such as `setw()`, the program must contain the statement:

```
#include <iomanip.h>
```

A second manipulator, `setprecision()`, allows us to specify the total number of digits to be displayed when outputting a real value. Again, this must be used with each real (`float`, `double`, `long double`) variable for which the default number of digits is to be overridden. Typically usage would be

The order of the `#include` commands is irrelevant.

```
#include <iomanip.h>
#include <iostream.h>
void main()
{
    float area = 317.93512, volume = 86.2191;
    cout << setprecision(5) << area << ' ' << setprecision(5)
         << volume;
```

which would produce the output:

Notice the use of automatic rounding in the output.

```
317.94 86.219
```

It is also possible to specify the base in which integer values are to be displayed. This allows hexadecimal and octal output as well as the default decimal. Use `hex` to produce hexadecimal output and `oct` for octal. Unlike the `setw()` instruction, `hex` and `oct` cause a permanent change to the number base used in the output, hence they need only be used each time the base is to be changed. To change back to

THE HENLEY COLLEGE LIBRARY

decimal output, use the instruction `dec`. The following statement displays the values of *no1* and *no2* in hexadecimal; *no3* in octal and then sets the base back to decimal for any subsequent output.

```
cout << hex << no1 << ' ' << no2 << ' ' << oct << no3 << dec;
```

Assuming *no1*= 123, *no2* = 456 and *no3* = 789, the output produced will be:

```
7B 1C8 1425
```

The general format for using `cout` is given in FIG-2.15.

FIG-2.15

cout

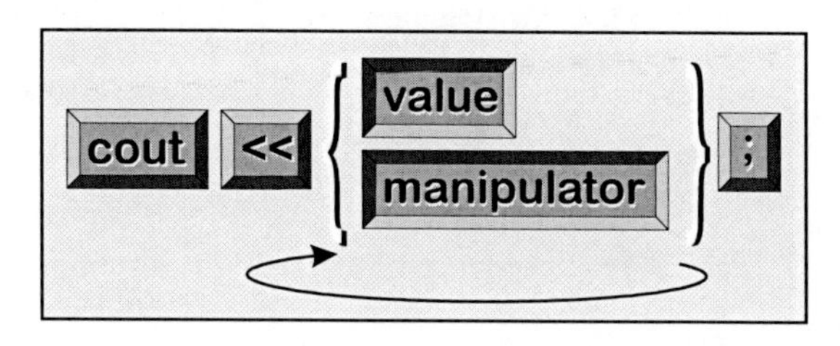

User Prompts

We have already seen that `cin` can be used to accept values from the keyboard. However, when a `cin` command is executed by the machine it simply sits and waits for a value to be entered. If the user of the program did not write the code, he is likely to be blissfully unaware of the fact that the program has stopped and is awaiting data entry! Good programming practice requires that the user be issued with a meaningful screen prompt. Hence rather than write

```
cin >> year;
```

a better approach would be:

```
cout << "\nPlease enter year ";
cin >> year;
```

Specify units of measurement where necessary:

```
cout << "\nEnter your height in metres ";
cin >> height;
```

It may also be appropriate to give a range of acceptable input values:

```
cout << "\n Enter a number between 1 and 12 ";
cin >> no;
```

TASK 2.15

Identify the errors in the following code:

```
void main()
{
    int no1 = 6, no2 = 3;
    float rno1 = 7.317, rno2 = -14.268;
    cout << rno1;
    cout << 'Value is ',no1;
    cout << "\nrno1 = "<<setprecision(3)<<rno1;
    cout << hex << rno2;
}
```

Clearing the Screen

A common requirement when producing output in DOS mode is to begin with an empty screen. In Borland C++ this is achieved by the statement

pronounced clear screen

```
clrscr( );
```

which clears the screen and moves the cursor to the top left corner of the screen.

This statement will normally appear in a program before any output statements. In order to use this statement your program must contain the `include` statement:

```
#include <conio.h>
```

Typical usage is shown in LISTING-2.10.

LISTING-2.10

Using clrscr( )

```
#include <conio.h>              //*** Needed for clrscr()
#include <iostream.h>           //*** Needed for cin and cout
void main( )
{
  int no1, no2, ans;

  //*** Clear the screen at start of program ***
  clrscr( );

  //*** Accept values from the keyboard ***
  cout << "Please enter a number between 1 and 100 ";
  cin >> no1;
  cout << "Please enter another number between 1 and 100 ";
  cin >> no2;

  //*** Calculate result ***
  ans = no1 / no2;

  //*** Clear screen before giving result ***
  clrscr( );
  cout << "\n\n"<<no1<<"/" << no2 << "=" << ans << '\n';
}
```

Calling *clrscr()* is unnecessary when creating a Windows application since an new, blank window is created automatically when the program runs.

Note that a single character can be specified as a character constant (single quotes) or a string (double quotes). Using characters is more efficient.

See Chapter 4 for more details on `clrscr()`.

Structured English Equivalents

TABLE-2.9 gives some Structured English input/output statements and their C++ equivalents.

TABLE-2.9

Assignment Equivalents

Structured English	C++
`Get age`	`cout << "Enter age ";` `cin >> age;`
`Display weight`	`cout <<"Weight is "<<setprecision(2)` `<<weight;`

`Get date`	`cout << "Enter date in form:\n\t\t"`
	`"dd mm yyyy :";`
	`cin >>day >> month >> year;`

`Display date`	`cout << setw(2)<<day<<'/'<<setw(2)` `<<month<<'/'<<year;`

How a `cout` Instruction is Evaluated

When output of more than one value is required, as in the statement

```
cout << no1 << no2;
```

the values to be output are determined on a right-to-left basis. In other words, the machine determines the value of *no2* and then the value of *no1* before displaying the value of *no1* and *no2* (this time, in the order expected) on the screen.

Most of the time, this method of operation is irrelevant to us and can be ignored. However, there are occasions when it is vital to know what's going on, otherwise you are going to get very confused about some of the results your program produces. For example, in the code fragment

```
int no = 5;

cout << ++no << --no;
```

we might expect to see the values 6 and 5 displayed; in fact, the result is 5 and 4. The reason for this should be clear: since the values in the `cout` statement are evaluated on a right-to-left basis, *no* is first decremented (giving 4) and then incremented (giving 5); finally, the values are displayed in the specified order.

As a general rule it is best to avoid such expressions in the `cout` statement since they can easily lead to confusion.

Summary

- `cin` allows the value assigned to a variable to be entered from the keyboard.
- `cout` displays constants or variable values on the screen.
- **The statement `#include <iostream.h>`** must be included in your program when using either `cin` or `cout`,
- **The escape characters** `'\n'` (new line), `'\t'` (horizontal tab) and `'\v'` (vertical tab) can be used within strings, or on their own, to position the cursor in a `cout` statement. `setprecision()` can be used with `cout` to define the number of decimal places to be displayed when printing a real number.
- **Move the cursor to the start of the next line** using the newline character (`'\n'`) or `endl` in a `cout` statement.
- **The statement `#include <iomanip.h>`** must be included at the start of any program using `setw()` or `setprecision()`.
- **`setw()` and `setprecision()`** must come before EVERY value on which it is to be used
- **`hex`, `oct` and `dec`** can be used to specify the number base employed when displaying integer values.

  Once a base has been specified, it continues to be used when displaying subsequent values.
- **`clrscr()`** can be used to clear the screen.

- **The statement** `#include <conio.h>` must be included at the start of any program using `clrscr()`.
- `setw()` can be used with `cout` to define the number of coluumns a value being displayed is to occupy.
- `setprecision()` can be used to define the number of digits used when displaying a real value.
- **Evaluation of the `cout` statement** is from right to left.

CASE STUDY

Most chapters in this book contain small case studies. These are an attempt to show how the statements covered in that chapter are used within a larger program. In addition, it is a chance to discuss some of the other aspects which go to make up a good approach to programming.

The Problem

The program to be installed in a new cash register allows the total due by the customer to be entered along with the amount offered in payment. The register then specifies the notes and coinage to be given in the change. For example, if £1.00 is offered for a purchase of £0.76 then the result would be COINAGE: 1x20p 2x2p.

Clarification

As a software designer, you will almost certainly be presented with problems which are not completely defined. That is, you will probably be able to find parts of the description which are ambiguous, unclear or do not describe what is to be done under unusual conditions.

With the cash register software, the problem lies in the rule to be used in determining which coinage is to be returned: we could give all of the change in 1p coins! Where software is being written for a customer you MUST get a ruling on such matters from the customer rather than make your own assumptions. In this case, we wish to give the highest value coinage possible in change. Also the largest note offered in change will be £5.

The Approach

Before getting involved with a detailed solution to any complex problem, it's worth taking some time to think, only in a very broad sense, the strategy to be used in tackling the problem.

Sometimes it is useful to take a few specific examples, work them through and see if their solutions suggest any general algorithm which might be applied to the problem.

Change Examples

Money Given	Cost	Change	Coinage							
			£5	£1	50p	20p	10p	5p	2p	1p
10.00	3.75	6.25	1	1	0	1	0	1	0	0
20.00	9.51	10.49	2	0	0	2	0	1	2	0

The strategy employed in solving these examples is to examine first the change figure, and then each column in turn, looking to see how often that column's value will divide into the change. We then remove the corresponding amount from the change and try the next column until no change remains.

The Algorithm

Our examples have given us an approach, and from that we developed a general strategy for solving the problem. The next stage is to change the informal explanation in the strategy above into the more formal style of Structured English:

```
1.  Get amount offered
2.  Get cost
3.  Calculate change as amount offered - cost
4.  Calculate £5 notes as number of times £5 goes into change
5.  Subtract the value of the £5 notes from the change
6.  Calculate £1 notes as the number of times £1 goes into change
7.  Subtract the value of the £1 notes from the change
8.  Calculate 50p coins as the number of times 50p goes into change
9.  Subtract the value of the 50p coins from the change
10. Calculate 20p coins as the number of times 20p goes into change
11. Subtract the value of the 20p coins from the change
12. Calculate 10p coins as the number of times 10p goes into change
13. Subtract the value of the 10p coins from the change
14. Calculate 5p coins as the number of times 5p goes into change
15. Subtract the value of the 5p coins from the change
16. Calculate 2p coins as the number of times 2p goes into change
17. Subtract the value of the 2p coins from the change
18. Calculate 1p coins as the number of times 1p goes into change
19. Display coinage
```

Next we need to check that the algorithm has no major flaws. This may be done by working our way though the algorithm using one of the examples we had calculated out earlier, to ensure it gives us the same results. This **dry run** should be done in a formal way so as to avoid mistakes when working through the algorithm. This can be achieved by creating a table to record each step and the latest value of all the variables involved. See TABLE-2.10.

TABLE-2.10

Dry Run

Statement	**Variables**										
	paid	cost	change	£5	£1	50p	20p	10p	5p	2p	1p
1	20.00										
2		9.51									
3			10.49								
4				2							
5			0.49								
6					0						
7			0.49								
8						0					
9			0.49								
10							2				
11			0.09								
12								0			
13			0.09								
14									1		
15			0.04								
16										2	
17			0.00								
18											0
19	Displays 2,0,0,2,0,1,2,0										

The Program

The program is created by converting each statement in the Structured English algorithm to the equivalent C++ statement. Depending on how much detail is given in the algorithm, one statement in Structured English may translate to one or more C++ statements. Where there are many occurrences of a single statement in the Structured English translating to several C++ statements, it is possible that the original Structured English needs to be broken down into more detail before attempting the translation.

When writing a program (rather than just short exercises) you should include documentary details in the program comments. These should list such things as the program title, author, date written, version number (which is updated each time a change is made), the equipment on which the program is to be run and the compiler used to create the executable version, etc. See LISTING-2.11 for the full code.

LISTING-2.11

Change (version 0.1)

```
// ************************************************
// * PROGRAM      : Change Calculator             *
// * AUTHOR       : Patricia Stamp                *
// * DATE         : 20/7/1994                     *
// * VERSION      : 0.1                           *
// * DESCRIPTION  : Calculates the change and coinage*
// *                due for a given purchase      *
// * HARDWARE     : PC Compatible.                *
// * SOURCE       : Turbo C++ v4.0                *
// ************************************************


#include <conio.h>
#include <iostream.h>
#include <iomanip.h>

void main()
{
  float    cash,         //*** Amount paid by customer
           cost,         //*** Total cost of items purchased
           change;       //*** Total change to be given
  int      pnds5,        //*** No. of £5 notes in change
           pnds1,        //*** No. of £1 notes in change
           pence50,      //*** No. of 50p coins in change
           pence20,      //*** No. of 20p coins in change
           pence10,      //*** No. of 10p coins in change
           pence5,       //*** No. of 5p coins in change
           pence2,       //*** No. of 2p coins in change
           pence1;       //*** No. of 1p coins in change

  // *** Enter cash and cost ***
  clrscr();
  cout << "\nEnter the amount paid : ";
  cin >> cash;
  cout << "\nEnter the cost : ";
  cin >> cost;

  // *** Calculate the change ***
  change = cash - cost;

  // *** Calculate coinage ***
  pnds5   = change/5;
  change -= pnds5*5;
  pnds1   = change;
  change -= pnds1;
```

Continued on next page

LISTING-2.11
(continued)

Change (version 0.1)

```
    pence50 = change/0.50;
    change -= pence50*0.50;
    pence20 = change/0.20;
    change -= pence20*0.20;
    pence10 = change/0.10;
    change -= pence10*0.10;
    pence5  = change/0.05;
    change -= pence5*0.05;
    pence2  = change/0.02;
    change -= pence2*0.02;
    pence1  = change/0.01;
    change -= pence1*0.01;

    // *** Display results ***
    clrscr();
    cout << "Change                     Coinage\n";
*   cout << "              £5   £1   50p  20p  10p  5p   2p"
*   "  1p\n\n";
    cout <<setw(5)<<(cash-cost)<<"         "<<pnds5<<"     "<<pnds1
    <<"    "<<pence50<<"    "<<pence20<<"    "<<pence10
    <<"    "<<pence5<<"    "<<pence2<<"    "<<pence1;
}
```

Note one of the `cout` commands (indicated by asterisks) contains a string too long to fit on a single line. Rather than use to separate `cout` commands, it is possible to break a string over two or more lines by splitting the string into two separate parts, each enclosed in double quotes. C++ will treat the two parts as one continuous string.

Testing

Every program must be tested. Testing attempts to highlight errors in a program. To test a piece of code, we need to devise a set of values to be used for any variables whose value needs to be input. This is called the **test data**. Next, we need to predict the effects such test data will have on the program's output. Where the output is text or numeric values, we need to determine what these values will be.

In this program we could use as test data the values we looked at earlier while deciding on the approach to be used. These values were:

Cash = 10.00; Cost = 3.75

When creating test data, our minimum aim is to ensure that the test data created will result in every line of code in the program being executed at least once. In this program we have a simple sequential structure, so our one set of test data will be sufficient to meet this requirement. However, in this case we'll go beyond the minimum requirements and use the second set of values :

Cash = 20.00; Cost = 9.51

In order to know if the program is behaving correctly, we have to predict in advance what results to expect from our test data. Therefore, the expected outputs for the test data must also be determined.

All this information is usually laid out in tabular form (TABLE-2.11).

TABLE-2.11

Test Data

TEST DATA		
Test Run	**Test Data**	**Expected Results**
1	cash = 10.00 cost = 3.75	pnds5 = 1 pnds1 = 1 pence50 = 0 pence20 = 1 pence10 = 0 pence5 = 1 pence2 = 0 pence1 = 0
2	cash = 20.00 cost = 9.51	pnds5 = 2 pnds1 = 0 pence50 = 0 pence20 = 2 pence10 = 0 pence5 = 1 pence2 = 2 pence1 = 0

PROGRAMMING EXERCISE 2.2

Type in the program above and run it using the test data given.

The Flaw

The results of the above exercise show the importance of testing. Even when the algorithm seems to be correct, problems can occur in the computer program. One possible problem is that the translation from Structured English to C++ has introduced an error. This time, however, the problem is a subtle one involving fractions and the binary system.

In the decimal system, we are quite familiar with values which cannot be expressed exactly. For example, one third can only be approximated as 0.33333 (taken to 5 decimal places). This is not a problem when dealing with money, since pence, which are expressed as a decimal fraction of a pound can all be represented exactly. Hence the change from our second set of test data can be represented exactly as the real number 10.49. Unfortunately, as with one third in decimal, binary cannot represent fractions such as 0.49 exactly. As the program extracts coinage values from the change figure, we arrive at a point where only 4p remains. This is expressed in decimal as 0.04 but again the binary representation is not exact. Were we to take the binary value held by the computer and convert it back to decimal we would have a value of 0.039998. If we attempt to divide this inaccurate figure by 0.02 to determine how many 2p pieces are in the change, we get a result of 1 rather than the 2 we are expecting. In fact, this highlights a major problem when computers are dealing with money : their inability to accurately represent fractions of a point in floating point notation, where such errors could be of critical importance.

One way to overcome this is to deal only with integers when handling money values. This can easily be achieved by converting all amounts of money into pence by multiplying by 100. This approach gives rise to the second version of the program given below (LISTING-2.12).

LISTING-2.12

Change (version 2)

```
// **************************************************
// * PROGRAM       : Change Calculator              *
// * AUTHOR        : Patricia Stamp                 *
// * DATE          : 20/7/1994                      *
// * VERSION       : 0.2                            *
// * DESCRIPTION   : Calculates the change and coinage*
//                   due for a given purchase       *
// * HARDWARE      : PC Compatible.                 *
// * SOURCE        : Turbo C++ v4.0                 *
// **************************************************

#include <conio.h>
#include <iostream.h>
#include <iomanip.h>

void main()
{
  float    cash,          //*** Amount paid by customer
           cost;          //*** Total cost of items purchased

  int      change,        //*** Total change to be given
           pnds5,         //*** No. of £5 notes in change
           pnds1,         //*** No. of £1 notes in change
           pence50,       //*** No. of 50p coins in change
           pence20,       //*** No. of 20p coins in change
           pence10,       //*** No. of 10p coins in change
           pence5,        //*** No. of 5p coins in change
           pence2,        //*** No. of 2p coins in change
           pence1;        //*** No. of 1p coins in change

  //*** Enter cash and cost ***
  clrscr();
  cout << "\nEnter the amount paid :";
  cin >> cash;
  cout << "\nEnter the cost : ";
  cin >> cost;
  //*** Calculate change in pence ***
  change = (cash - cost)*100+0.5;
  //*** Calculate coinage ***
  pnds5   = change/500;
  change -= pnds5*500;
  pnds1   = change/100;
  change -= pnds1*100;
  pence50 = change/50;
  change -= pence50 *50;
  pence20 = change/20;
  change -= pence20 *20;
  pence10 = change/10;
  change -= pence10 *10;
  pence5  = change/5;
  change -= pence5 *5;
  pence2  = change/2;
  change -= pence2 *2;
  pence1  = change;
  //*** Display results ***
  clrscr();
  cout << "Change                         Coinage\n";
  cout << "                  £5    £1    50p  20p  10p  5p    2p"
       "1p\n\n";
  cout << (cash-cost) << "          " << pnds5 << "     " << pnds1
  << "     " << pence50 << "     " << pence20 << "     " << pence10
  << "     " << pence5 << "     " << pence2 << "     " << pence1;
}
```

See NOTE below

Note that, in converting the change to pence, it is necessary to add 0.5; if the change (10.49) is stored inaccurately (say as 10.48998) then multiplication by 100 will result in the figure 1048.998, which if copied directly to *change* would give a result of 1048 (remembering that when a real value is copied to an integer the fraction is truncated - not rounded). However, by adding the 0.5 before transfer, we eliminate the effects of this inaccuracy (1048.998 +0.5 gives 1049.498 which transfers as 1049). Other changes include multiplying by 100 the value of each coin, since we are now working in pence; and updating the version number.

When any change is made to a program, all testing must be redone. This is necessary since the program modifications may have introduced new errors and hence it cannot be assumed that tests which had previously given correct results will continue to do so.

PROGRAMMING EXERCISE 2.3

Enter and test this new version of the program.

PROGRAMMING EXERCISE 2.4

1. Read in a decimal integer and display it. Include appropriate text.

2. Read in an integer value between 30 and 254. Display the value in decimal, octal, hexadecimal and the equivalent character.

3. Read in 4 values representing two weights given in pounds and ounces. Print the sum of the weights in pounds and ounces. There are 16 ounces to one pound.
   OUTLINE LOGIC:
   ```
   Get pounds and ounces of first weight (lbs1,oz1)
   Get pounds and ounces of second weight (lbs2,oz2)
   Calculate totaloz as oz1 + oz2
   Calculate carry as integer part of totaloz/16
   Calculate ouncessum as remainder of totaloz/16
   Calculate poundssum as lbs1 + lbs2 + carry
   Display poundssum and ouncessum
   ```

4. Read in a character. Print the character and also the preceding and succeeding characters in the ASCII set
   (e.g. if B is input, output would be A B C)

5. Read in two integer values (using variables *no1* and *no2*). Without using any other variables, swap the contents of *no1* and *no2*. For example, if *no1* = 5 and *no2* = 1 at the beginning of the program, at completion the contents of *no1* and *no2* should be 1 and 5 respectively.

6. Read in an alphabetic character in lower case and display the upper case version of the letter.
   HINT: Look at the ASCII codes for letters in APPENDIX A.

7. Input a value in centimetres and convert it to yards, feet and inches.

   There are 2.4cm to an inch; 12 inches in 1 foot and 3 feet in 1 yard.

Continued on next page

PROGRAMMING EXERCISE 2.4 (continued)

8. Zeller's Congruence is used to discover which day of the week a given date fell on.

   The formula is:

   $$d = ([2.6M-0.2] + D + Y + [Y/4] + [C/4] - 2C) \text{ modulo } 7$$

   where

d	is the day of the week (0 = Sunday, 1 = Monday...)
D	is the day of the month
M	is the month number (March = 1..December = 10 January and February are month 11 and 12 of the previous year)
C	is the 2 most significant digits of the year.
Y	is the 2 least significant digits of the year.
[*x*]	is the largest integer not greater than *x*.

   Thus for 28/2/1961

   D = 28
   M = 12
   C = 19
   Y = 60

   Write a program to accept a date as 3 integers and print out the day of the week on which it fell represented by a value between 0 and 6.
   OUTLINE LOGIC:

```
Get  day month and year
Calculate M as (month+9)modulo 12 + 1
Calculate CY as year - integer part of (M/11)
Calculate C as the integer part of (CY/100)
Calculate Y as the remainder of (CY/100)
Calculate temp as integer part of (2.6*M-0.2)
Calculate d as (temp + day + Y + integer part of (Y/4) +
          integer part of (C/4)-2*C)modulo 7
Display d
```

INVESTIGATION

The investigation section which appears in most chapters is designed to help you discover how a program reacts to unusual input or program code.

Short programs will be required for most of the situations suggested below.

1. Attempt to key in a non-numeric value to an `int` variable.

2. Attempt to key in a value too large to be held in the variable defined.

3. Write a `cin` statement to accept one `int` value followed by one `char` value. Enter both values with:
   a) a space between the two values entered;
   b) a comma between the two values entered;
   c) a tab between the two values entered;
   d) an ENTER character between the two values entered.

4. Use the remainder operator (%) with:
   a) real values.
   b) character values

5. Find out how real values are displayed when the `setprecision()` manipulator is not used.

6. Use horizontal tabs within a single `cout` statement to produce output which is too large to fit on a single line.

7. Use the backspace character (`'\b'`) when the cursor is already at the extreme left of the current line.

8. Use the `setw()` manipulator with a variable as an argument rather than a constant.

9. Attempt to display a string value enclosed in single quotes.

10. Use the comma operator to separate `cin` and `cout` statements. (e.g. `cin >> x, cout << x`)

11. Use a sequence of comma operators in a single statement. (e.g. `x=i=2,i++,i+3`)

12. Read in and display an integer value. When entering the value:
    a) use an integer value between 10 and 17.
    b) include a leading zero (i.e. 010 to 017).
    c) include the leading characters zero, 'X' (i.e. 0X10 to 0X17).
    d) use a value from 0X1A to 0XFF.

13. What will be displayed by the code fragment

```
int no = 5;

cout << no++ << no-- << endl;
```

SELF-ASSESSMENT REVIEW

1. State the purpose of *include* files.

2. How many real variable types are available in C++?

3. In what format is a variable of type `char` stored?

4. At what point in a program are variables defined?

5. What is the default format for real constants?

6. List the arithmetic operators available in C++.

7. State the results of each of the following calculations:

   7/6
   7/6.0
   -7/6
   8%3
   -9%4
   -9%-4

8. How many bytes would the string "`Mary\'s lambs`" occupy?

9. What is the result given to the variable, *ans*, in the following assignment?

```
ans = no = 4,no*3;
```

10. What is the final value of each variable in the expression:

```
no = -7;
ans = ++no*3;
```

11. Which escape character is required to move the cursor vertically down?

12. Define the term whitespace.

13. What is the effect of the term `endl` used in a `cout` statement?

14. What is the result of the expression `sizeof(long)`?

Solutions

TASK 2.1

3no	- cannot begin with a numeric digit.
try	- a reserved word.
final note	- no spaces are allowed.

TASK 2.2

28 bytes
2 int values at 2 bytes each = 4 bytes
3 double values at 8 bytes each = 24 bytes

TASK 2.3

signed char decimal : -128 to 127;
hexadecimal : 00 to FF; octal : 000 to 377
unsigned char decimal : 0 to 255;
hexadecimal : 00 to FF; octal : 000 to 377

TASK 2.4

11 bytes

TASK 2.5

1. Valid	12 will be converted to a char value automatically.
2. Invalid	Although a char value would be converted to int automatically, what we have here is a string (because of the double quotes) and this cannot be converted.
3. Inalid	Each assignment must be separated.
4. Valid	
5. Valid	

TASK 2.6

1. Invalid.	No type.
2. Invalid.	Only one variable allowed per const.
3. Invalid.	No value given.
4. Valid.	A const followed by a variable definition.
5. Valid.	Although the value is given as an arithmetic expression the result is a known constant.

TASK 2.7

2	0
2	1
2.25	invalid
invalid	invalid
0	0
0	2
-3	0
2	3
-4	1

TASK 2.8

```
letter          no
10001010        1111111110001010
```

TASK 2.9

LINE	TYPE
1	int
2	unsigned int
3	double

TASK 2.10

```
sum +=no;
count -=6;
answer *= mark/7;
divide /= takings-costs;
total_remainder %= previous*current;
```

TASK 2.11

post-incrementing.
ans = ++no;

TASK 2.12

no1	no2	answer
2	9	12
3		24

TASK 2.13

no1=8
no2=6 and no3=12
no4=8 and no5=11 and no6=11

TASK 2.14

```
cin << no1;  should be cin >> no1;
cin >> no1, no2; should be cin >> no1 >> no2;
```

TASK 2.15

```
    #include<iostream.h>
    #include<iomanip.h>
missing from program

    cout << 'Value is ',no1;
should be
    cout << "Value is "<<no1;

    cout << hex << rno2;
hex can only be used on integer values.
```

PROGRAMMING EXERCISE 2.4

```
1.

#include <iostream.h>
#include <conio.h>
void main()
{
    int no;

    // *** Clear screen ***
    clrscr();
    // *** Get value ***
    cout << "Please enter a value : ";
    cin >> no;
    // *** Display value entered ***
    cout << "The number entered was " << no;
}
```

2.
```
#include <iostream.h>
#include <conio.h>
void main()
{
    int no;
    char letter;

    // *** Clear screen ***
    clrscr();
    // *** Get value ***
    cout << "Please enter a value : ";
    cin >>no;
    // *** Copy to character variable for
    //      display ***
    letter = no;
    // *** Display required output ***
    cout <<"Decimal\tHex\tOctal\tChar\n";
    cout <<no<<'\t'<<hex<<no<<'\t'<<oct<<no
         <<'\t'<<dec<<letter;
}
```

3.
```
#include <iostream.h>
#include <conio.h>
void main()
{
     int
        lbs1,oz1,   // First weight
        lbs2,oz2,   // Second weight
        poundssum, ouncessum, //Total weight
        totaloz,    // Total of ounces part of
                    //  both weights
        carry;      // Carry from ounces column to
                    //  pounds

    // *** Clear screen ***
    clrscr();
    // *** Get weights ***
    cout << "Please enter first weight : ";
    cin >>lbs1 >>oz1;
    cout << "Please enter second weight : ";
    cin >>lbs2 >>oz2;
    // *** Add weights ***
    totaloz = oz1 + oz2;
    carry = totaloz/16;
    ouncessum = totaloz % 16;
    poundssum = lbs1 + lbs2 + carry;
    // *** Display total weight ***
    cout <<"Total weight is "<<poundssum
         <<" lbs "<<ouncessum<<" ozs";
 }
```

4.
```
#include <iostream.h>
#include <conio.h>
void main()
{
     char letter, previous, next;

    // *** Clear screen ***
    clrscr();
    // *** Get value ***
    cout << "Please enter a character : ";
    cin >>letter;
    // *** Determine previous and next characters ***
    previous = letter - 1;
    next = letter + 1;
    // *** Display characters ***
    cout <<previous<<letter<<next;
}
```

5.
```
#include <iostream.h>
#include <conio.h>
void main()
{
    int no1,no2;

    // *** Clear screen ***
    clrscr();
    // *** Get values ***
    cout << "Please enter first number : ";
    cin >>no1;
    cout << "Please enter second number : ";
    cin >>no2;
    // *** Swap contents ***
    no1 = no1 + no2;
    no2 = no1-no2;
    no1 = no1-no2;
    // *** Display contents ***
    cout <<"First variable now = "<<no1;
    cout <<"\nSecond variable now = "<<no2;
};
```

6.
```
#include <iostream.h>
#include <conio.h>
void main()
{
    char lowercaseletter,uppercaseletter;

    // *** Clear screen ***
    clrscr();
    // *** Get lower case letter ***
    cout << "Please enter lower case letter : ";
    cin >>lowercaseletter;
    // *** Determine upper case letter ***
    uppercaseletter = lowercaseletter - 32;
    // *** Display contents ***
    cout <<"Lower case = "<<lowercaseletter;
    cout <<"\nUpper case = "<<uppercaseletter;
 }
```

7.
```
#include <iostream.h>
#include <conio.h>
void main()
{
     int
        centimetres,         // Metric length
        yards,feet, inches, // Imperial length
        total_inches, total_feet;
                        // temporary variables

    // *** Clear screen ***
    clrscr();
    // *** Get distance ***
    cout << "Please enter length : ";
    cin >>centimetres;
    // *** Convert to imperial ***
    total_inches = (centimetres/2.4)+0.5;
    inches = total_inches%12;
    total_feet = total_inches/12;
    feet = total_feet%3;
    yards = total_feet/3;
    // *** Display result ***
    cout <<centimetres<<"cm = "<<yards
         <<" yards "<<feet<<" feet "
         <<inches<<" inches";
}
```

8.
```
#include <iostream.h>
#include <conio.h>
void main()
{
     int
        day,month,year, // Date to be converted
                        // to day of week
        M,CY,C,Y,       // Modified date values
        temp,            // temporary variable
        d;              // Day of week on
                        // which date falls
                        // 0 = Sunday,
                        // 1 = Monday etc.

    // *** Clear screen ***
    clrscr();
    // *** Get date ***
    cout<<"Please enter a date"
         " in the form xx xx xxxx : ";
    cin>>day>>month>>year;
    // *** Determine modified version of date ***
    M = (month + 9) % 12 + 1;
    CY = year - M/11;
    C = CY/100;
    Y = CY%100;
    temp = 2.6*M-0.2;
    d = ((temp + day + Y + Y/4 + C/4 - 2*C)
       % 7+7)%7;
    // *** Display results ***
    cout <<day<<'/'<<month<<'/'<<year
         <<" is a "<<d<<endl;
}
```

CHAPTER 3
Control Structures

This chapter covers the following topics:

Binary Selection (if .. else)

Boolean Operators (&& || !)

Compound Statements

Conditional Assignment Operator

Debugging

Iteration (while, do..while, for)

Jump Statements (break, continue, goto)

Lifetime, Scope & Visibility

Multiway Selection (switch)

Nested Loops

Operator Precedence

Relational Operators

White Box Testing

SELECTION

Binary Selection

Binary selection allows us to choose between two alternative actions within a program. In Structured English, the simplest form of binary selection is implemented using the form:

See Chapter 1 for a fuller explanation of Structured English.

```
IF condition THEN
    statement
        .
    statement
ENDIF
```

C++ also uses an `if` statement to implement binary selection. The simplest form of this statement is:

```
if (expression)
    statement;
```

where

`expression`
: is any term which can be reduced to a **true** or **false** value.

`statement`
: is any executable C++ statement. If `expression` evaluates to **true**, then `statement` will be executed otherwise `statement` will be bypassed.

Expression

The expression may be a Boolean one in which the relationship between two quantities is compared. For example, the expression `no < 0` will be **true** if the contents of the variable *no* is less than zero (i.e. negative). Boolean expressions have the general form:

value1 relational operator *value2*

where

value1 and *value2*
: may be constants, variables or expressions.

relational operator
: is one of the operators given in TABLE-3.1.

If *value1* and *value2* are of different types, automatic conversion takes place before the expression is evaluated.

TABLE-3.1

Relational Operators

Relational Operators	
Symbol	**Meaning**
	Greater than
>=	Greater than or equal to
<	Less than
<=	Less than or equal to
==	Equal to
!=	Not equal to

TASK 3.1

Assuming the following definitions:

```
int     no1, no2, no3;
char    let1, let2;
```

Which of the following are NOT valid Boolean expressions.

1. `no1 < no2`
2. `let1 = let2`
3. `let2 >= no3`
4. `no1 * 2 == no3 / 4`
5. `let1 != 65`

TABLE-3.2 shows some Structured English IF statements and the equivalent C++ code.

TABLE-3.2

Simple C++ if Statements

Structured English	C++ Code

IF *no* is negative THEN
Make *no* positive
ENDIF
	`if(no < 0)`
	`no = -no;`

IF *day* is zero THEN
Display "Sunday"
ENDIF
	`if(day == 0)`
	`cout << "Sunday";`

IF *value* is even THEN
Subtract 1 from *value*
ENDIF
	`if(value % 2 == 0)`
	`value--;`

C++ is very flexible in what it considers to be an acceptable expression. As well as Boolean expressions, any other expression which is capable of being reduced to a single integer value can be used. For example:

```
int no1 = 6, no2 = 2;
if(no1 - no2)
    cout << "Not equal\n";
```

At first sight this may seem to contain an expression, `(no1 - no2)`, which cannot be reduced to a **true** or **false** value. To understand why this is an acceptable C++ statement, it is necessary to understand how the language determines the Boolean value of any expression. When presented with any expression, C++ reduces the expression to a single numeric value. Once this has been done, the result is considered to be **false** if the final value of the expression is zero, otherwise the result is considered to be **true**.

So, in the example above, the expression *(no1 - no2)* is evaluated as (6 - 2). The result, 4, being non-zero is considered to be **true** and hence the statement `cout << "Not equal\n"` is executed.

Various examples of expressions and their **true** or **false** values are given in TABLE-3.3.

TABLE-3.3

Examples of **true/false** Expressions

Expressions	
TRUE	FALSE
1 2 -1 'A' '\12' 5*6 12.5	0 5-5 3*2-6 'A'-65 '\0' 12%2 0.0

Therefore, it is quite valid to write

```
if(no)
```

rather than the longer, but more explicit,

```
if (no != 0)
```

We can take the definition of the term *expression* one stage further and include assignment. Hence an `if` statement such as

```
no2 = 2;
if(no1 = 12-no2)
    cout << "TRUE\n";
```

not only assigns the value 10 to *no1*, but also evaluates this as **true** and the `cout` statement is executed.

Since C++ uses the strategy of reducing every expression to a single value, where the expression given is a Boolean expression (such as *no1 < 0*) the compiler reduces this to

1 if the Boolean expression is **true**
and 0 if the Boolean expression is **false**.

This then leads to the possibility of having an assignment statement containing a Boolean expression. For example, in the statement

```
days_in_feb = 28 + (year % 4 == 0);
```

C++ will first evaluate the Boolean expression (`year % 4 ==0`) which, assuming *year* has the value 1996 will be **true** and hence give a result of 1. At this point the assignment statement is equivalent to

```
days_in_feb = 28 + 1;
```

For other years which are not divisible by four, the statement would reduce to

```
days_in_feb = 28 + 0;
```

since `year % 4 == 0 would be` **false** and hence evaluate to zero.

TASK 3.2

Identify which of the following `if` statements are invalid. Where the statement is valid, indicate the final value of any variables which are modified and the overall value of the expression.

Assume the following definitions

```
int     no1 = 6, no2 = 2, no3 = 4;
char    letter = 'N';
```

```
1. if (no1 == 4)
2. if (letter > 'N')
3. if (7/6)
4. if (no1 == no2 + no3)
5. if (no1 = no2 + no3)
6. if (no1 = 'A')
7. if ('A')
```

It's worth pointing out at this stage that one of the most common mistakes that a beginner is likely to make when writing a Boolean expression, is to use the assignment operator (=) when attempting to test for equality (==). As you can see from TASK 3.2, both are valid so no compilation error will occur. BE CAREFUL!

TASK 3.3

What output is produced by the following code?

```
void main( )
{
    int no1=6,no2=2,ans1,ans2;
    ans1 = no1 - no2;
    ans2 = no1 + no2;
    if (ans1 == ans2)
        cout << "TRUE 1\n";
    if (ans1 = ans2/ans1)
        cout << "TRUE 2\n";
    if (ans2 < ans1*4)
        cout << "TRUE 3\n";
}
```

Compound Relations - AND and OR Operators

Simple conditions or expressions, such as those used in the examples above, can be combined using the AND and OR operators to form compound relational tests.

A token is a group of one or more characters that the compiler treats as a single component of the program. Reserved words, variable names, constants and operators are all examples of tokens.

In C++, AND is represented by the **token** `&&` while OR is represented by `||`. Where the AND construct is used to link expressions, then all conditions must be **true** (i.e. non-zero) for the overall result to be **true** (i.e. 1). When OR is used, at least one of the conditions must be **true** for the result to be **true**. It is also possible to construct complex expressions involving several AND and OR operators. Where this is done it may be necessary to insert additional parentheses to adjust the priority of the operators or simply to clarify the meaning of the condition. TABLE-3.4 gives several examples of Structured English statements and the C++ equivalent.

C++ evaluates compound expressions such as the final example in TABLE-3.4 using the following rules:

1. Reduce individual (simple) expressions to an `int` value.

2. Evaluate `&&` operators (left to right if more than one).

3. Evaluate `||` operators (left to right if more than one).

TABLE-3.4

Compound Expressions

Structured English	C++ Code
IF *no1* = 6 AND *no2* < 0 THEN	`if(no1==6 && no2<0)`
IF *sex* = 'M' OR *sex* = 'F' THEN	`if(sex=='M' || sex=='F')`
IF letter not uppercase THEN	`if(letter<'A' || letter>'Z')`
IF *temp* in the range 15 to 20 THEN	`if(temp>=15 && temp<=20)`
IF female AND older than 59 OR male AND older than 64 THEN	`if((sex=='F'&& age>59)|| (sex=='M'&& age>64))`

If we assume *no1* = 5 and *no2* = *10* in the statement

```
if (no3 = 0 && no1 > 0 || no2 == 10)
```

then the final value of the compound expression is determined by first evaluating each simple expression:

`no3 = 0` (**false**, hence evaluates to 0)
`no1 > 0` (**true**, hence 1)
`no2 == 10` (**true**, hence 1)

This results in the expression being reduced to:

```
if (0 && 1 || 1)
```

Since the AND operator has a higher priority than OR, the result of the expression 0&&1 is determined first:

`0 && 1` (**false**, hence 0)

which simplifies the original statement to

```
if (0 || 1)
```

which is evaluated to give the final result

```
if (1)
```

If we add parentheses to the original expression, giving

```
if (no3 = 0 && ( no1 > 0 || no2 == 10))
```

then, after the individual expressions are reduced to numeric values leaving

```
if (0 && (1 || 1))
```

the value of the inner parentheses is calculated:

```
(1||1)
```
(**true**, hence 1)

leaving

```
if(0 && 1)
```

which finally reduces to

```
if(0)
```

Nested parentheses are allowed in expressions. Where used, the inner-most brackets are evaluated first. Parentheses of equal depth are evaluated left to right.

TASK 3.4

Write the C++ equivalent for the following expressions:
(Assume any variables are already defined)

1. `IF weight > 16 THEN`
2. `IF code is not 17850 THEN`
3. `IF mark between 75 and 85 THEN`
4. `IF option = 'C' AND key = masterkey THEN`
5. `IF (command ='D' OR command ='A') AND quantity>100 THEN`

The NOT Operator

As well as using AND and OR to link simple expressions, we may negate the meaning of an expression by use of the NOT operator. In C++, NOT is implemented using the character exclamation mark (**!**).

The general structure is:

```
if ( ! (expression) )
```

The inner brackets are required because the NOT operator (!) has a higher priority than &&, ||, relational operators and assignment statements and hence would normally be evaluated first. TABLE-3.5 gives several examples of expressions involving NOT.

TABLE-3.5

Expressions using the NOT Operator

Structured English	Expression (using NOT)	Expression (without NOT)
IF *no* not equal to 10 THEN	`if(!(no == 10))`	`if(no != 10)`
IF *no1* not equal 10 AND *no2* not equal 6 THEN	`if(!(no1==10 || no2 == 6))`	`if(no1 != 10 && no2 != 6)`
IF *weight* not greater than 16 THEN	`if(!(weight > 16))`	`if(weight <= 16)`

TASK 3.5

Indicate which of the following expressions are invalid. Where an expression is valid, state its final value.

Assume the definition `int no = 4;`

1. `if (!(no==6))`
2. `if (!(no=6))`
3. `if (!(5+7))`
4. `if (!!(no < 5))`

Operator Precedence

We can see from the previous examples that, like arithmetic operators, relational operators (<, >, ==, etc.) and Boolean operators (&&, || and !) have an order of priority when evaluating expressions. TABLE-3.6 gives the priority of all operators we have encountered so far. This precedence list includes not only the arithmetic operators, but also conditional and assignment operators, since they can be used together. Highest precedence is at the top of the table.

TABLE-3.6

Operator Precedence

Items on the same line of the table have equal priority.

Where items of equal priority exist these are normally evaluated from left to right within the expression. However, those marked with an asterisk are processed from right to left.

Operator Precedence		
Operator	**Description**	
( )	Parentheses	
! -	Logical NOT, unary minus	*
++ --	Increment and decrement	*
* / %	Arithmetic multiply,divide,modulus	
+ -	Addition, subtraction	
< > >= <=	Inequality relational operators	
== !=	Equality relational operators	
&&	Logical AND	
||	Logical OR	
= += -= *= /= %=	Assignment	*

This operator precedence allows us to make sense of expressions such as

```
if (no1 = 6 == 3)
```

which, at first glance, may seem to be in error. However, if we follow the order of precedence then we begin by evaluating

```
6 == 3
```

which is **false** (i.e. zero), and giving the reduced expression

```
no1 = 0
```

This assigns the value zero to *no1* and, since the final result is zero, the expression is evaluated as **false**.

TASK 3.6

Which of the following pieces of code are invalid?

For valid code give the result of the expression and the final value of any variables involved.

Assume initial values of

```
ans = 3
no1 = 6
```

1. `ans = no1`
2. `ans = no1 == 5`
3. `ans == no1 = 5`
4. `ans = !no1`
5. `ans = !no1 ==0`
6. `ans = !(no1 ==6)`
7. `ans = 6 && no1 == 8`
8. `ans = !(no1 == 2)`
9. `ans = !no1 == 2`
10. `no1 = 3 == no1 + 1`

Compound Statements

Where there are several statements following the expression, then they must be enclosed in braces. The general form is shown below.

```
if (expression)
{
    statement;
    statement;
       .
    statement;
}
```

For example, the Structured English statement

```
IF ozs >= 16 THEN
    Add 1 to lbs
    Subtract 16 from ozs
ENDIF
```

is coded as

```
if(ozs >= 16)
{
    lbs++;
    ozs-=16;
}
```

The position of the braces and the use of indentation should be consistent throughout your program. Although the layout is of no concern to the compiler, we humans, who have to correct programs, sometimes weeks after they have been written, will find them much easier to decipher if a clear, neat style is used.

The rule is simple: indent any code within an `if` statement (or any of the other control structures we have yet to cover).

You may come across other styles of layout but this one makes finding missing braces (a common error) easy. Whatever style you decide on, be consistent!

if else

Like Structured English, C++ allows the `if` statement to be extended to include an `else` option which will be executed only if the condition specified is **false**.

Structured English uses the format

```
IF condition THEN
    statement
        .
    statement
ELSE
    statement
        .
    statement
ENDIF
```

C++ uses

```
if (expression)
    statement;
else
    statement;
```

where there is only one statement in the `else` option. However, where there is more than one statement in any section of the `if` statement, they must be enclosed in braces:

```
if (condition)
{
    statement;
        .
    statement;
}
else
{
    statement;
        .
    statement;
}
```

For example, the Structured English statement

```
IF no < 0 THEN
    Display "Negative"
    Add no to sumofnegativenumbers
ELSE
    Display "Positive"
    Add no to sumofpositivenumbers
ENDIF
```

translates in C++ to

```
if (no < 0)
{
    cout << "Negative\n";
    sumofnegativenumbers += no;
{
else
{
    cout << "Positive\n";
    sumofpositivenumbers += no;
}
```

The general form of the `if` statement is shown in FIG-3.1.

FIG-3.1

The `if` Statement

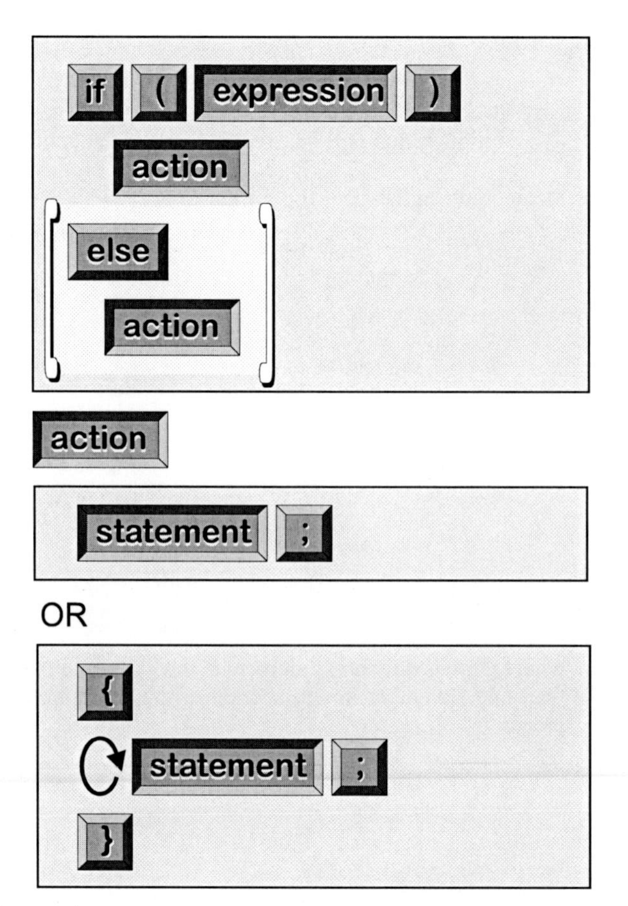

Nested `if` Statements

When dealing with more complex problems, it is sometimes necessary to place one `if` statement inside another. This is termed **nested `if`** statements. For example, we might divide males into those of working age and those of retirement age with the logic:

```
IF sex = 'M' THEN
    IF age >= 65 THEN
        Display "Retired male"
    ELSE
        Display "Working male"
    ENDIF
ENDIF
```

which in C++ is coded as:

```
if (sex == 'M')
    if (age >= 65)
        cout << "Retired male\n";
    else
        cout << "Working male\n";
```

Unfortunately, there is potential ambiguity in this structure since the `else` option could belong to the first `if` structure (`if (sex == 'M')`) rather than the second, as suggested by the indentation used. This uncertainty is avoided by applying the rule that an `else` is always assigned to the most recent `if` structure which does not already have a matching `else`.

Where the `else` statement is required to match with the first `if` rather than the second as in the logic:

```
IF sex = 'M' THEN
    IF age >= 65 THEN
        Display "Retired male"
    ENDIF
ELSE
    Display "Female"
ENDIF
```

then this can be achieved by separating the second `if` statement from the `else` using braces:

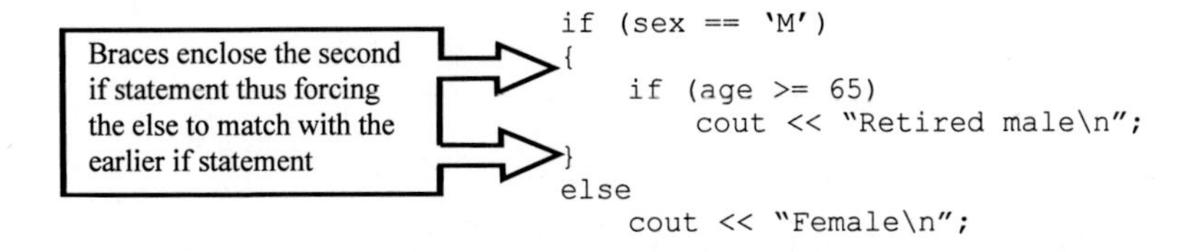

Braces enclose the second if statement thus forcing the else to match with the earlier if statement


```
if (sex == 'M')
{
    if (age >= 65)
        cout << "Retired male\n";
}
else
    cout << "Female\n";
```

> **TASK 3.7**
>
> Modify and extend the above `if` statement to print one of the four following messages:
>
> *Retired male*
> *Working male*
> *Retired female* (Females retiral age = 60)
> *Working female*

The `else if` Option

Although a simple `if..else` structure is ideal for choosing between two alternative actions, the nested `if` statements necessary to implement a wider range of choices can produce code which is less than easy to follow. For example, if a program requires to read in a transaction code and display one of the following messages

Code	**Message**
1	CASH
2	CREDIT
3	RETURNED
other	INVALID CODE

then this requires the logic·

```
IF code = 1 THEN
    Display "CASH"
ELSE
    IF code = 2 THEN
        Display "CREDIT"
    ELSE
        IF code = 3 THEN
            Display "RETURNED"
        ELSE
            Display "INVALID CODE"
        ENDIF
    ENDIF
ENDIF
```

which, if programmed using the conventional layout, produces

```
if(code == 1)
    cout << "CASH\n";
else
    if(code ==2)
        cout << "CREDIT\n";
```

```
    else
        if(code == 3)
            cout << "RETURN\n";
        else
            cout << "INVALID CODE\n";
```

Without affecting the logic of the code, the above layout can be improved by placing each `else` and subsequent `if` expression on the same line:

```
if(code == 1)
    cout << "CASH\n";
else if(code ==2)
    cout << "CREDIT\n";
else if(code ==3)
    cout << "RETURN\n";
else
    cout << "INVALID CODE\n";
```

The effect of executing such code is to test each expression in turn until one is found to be **true**. The instruction associated with that `if` statement is then executed. If no expression is **true** then the final `else` option is executed.

Where more than one statement is required after any of the options then, as usual, braces must be employed giving the general form for this structure:

```
if(expression)
{
    statement;
        .
    statement;
}
else if(expression)
{
    statement;
        .
    statement;
}
        .
        .
else
{
    statement;
        .
    statement;
}
```

PROGRAMMING EXERCISE 3.1

1. Read in a number and print NEGATIVE if the value is less than zero or POSITIVE otherwise.

```
    OUTLINE LOGIC:
        Read in number
        IF number is less than zero THEN
            Display "Negative"
        ELSE
            Display "Positive"
        ENDIF
```

Continued on next page

PROGRAMMING EXERCISE 3.1 (continued)

2. Read in two real numbers (*rno1, rno2*). If the second value is not zero calculate and display the value of *rno1/rno2*.

```
OUTLINE LOGIC:
    Read in values for rno1 and rno2
    IF rno2 isn't zero THEN
        Calculate result as rno1/rno2
        Display result
    ENDIF
```

3. Read in a letter and print VOWEL or CONSONANT as appropriate.

```
OUTLINE LOGIC:
    Read in value for letter
    IF letter is 'A', 'E', 'I', 'O' or 'U' THEN
        Display "VOWEL"
    ELSE
        Display "CONSONANT"
    ENDIF
```

4. Read in two numbers and display the smaller of the two. If both values are equal then display "EQUAL".

```
OUTLINE LOGIC:
    Read no1 and no2
    IF no1 < no2 THEN
        Display value of no1
    ELSE
        IF no2 < no1 THEN
            Display value of no2
        ELSE
            Display "EQUAL"
        ENDIF
    ENDIF
```

5. Modify Zeller's congruence program from the previous chapter to display the day of the week in text form.

```
OUTLINE LOGIC:
    Read date
    Determine day of week code for date
    IF
        code = 0:
            Display "Sunday"
        code = 1:
            Display "Monday"
        code = 2:
            Display "Tuesday"
        code = 3:
            Display "Wednesday"
        code = 4:
            Display "Thursday"
        code = 5:
            Display "Friday"
        code = 6:
            Display "Saturday"
    ENDIF
```

Continued on next page

PROGRAMMING EXERCISE 3.1(continued)

6. Gauss developed a formula for calculating the date on which Easter Sunday falls. The formula is:

   k = [year/100]
   a = year modulo 19
   b = year modulo 4
   c = year modulo 7
   q = [k/4]
   p = [(13+8k)/25]
   m = (15p+k+q)modulo 30
   d = (19a+m)modulo 30
   n = (4+k-q)modulo 7
   e = (2b+4c+6d+n)modulo 7

if d+e <=9	day = 22+d+e and month = 3
if d = 29 and e = 6	day = 19 month = 4
if d = 28 and e = 6 and a >10	day = 18 month = 4
all other cases	day = d+e-9 month = 4

   [x] = largest integer not greater than x.

   Write a program to read in a year and output the date on which Easter Sunday falls in that year.

```
OUTLINE LOGIC:
        Read year
        Calculate k as integer part of year/100
        Calculate a as year modulo 19
        Calculate b as year modulo 4
        Calculate c as year modulo 7
        Calculate q as integer part of k/4
        Calculate p as integer part of (13 + 8k)/25
        Calculate m as (15p + k+q) modulo 30
        Calculate d as (19a + m) modulo 30
        Calculate n as (4 + k-q) modulo 7
        Calculate e as (2b + 4c + 6d + n) modulo 7
        IF d+e <= 9 THEN
            Calculate day as 22+d+e
            Set month to 3
        ELSE
            IF d=29 AND e=6 THEN
                Set day to 19
                Set month to 4
            ELSE
                IF d=28 AND e=6 AND a > 10 THEN
                    Set day to 18
                    Set month to 4
                ELSE
                    Calculate day as d + e-9
                    Set month to 4
                ENDIF
            ENDIF
        ENDIF
        Display day and month
```

The Conditional Assignment Operator

In most languages, if we wish to assign one of two values to a variable then a selection construct would be used. For example, we might assign the smaller of two values to a third variable with the code:

```
if (no1 < no2)
    small = no1;
else
    small = no2;
```

This is quite allowable in C++ but a briefer style is available using the **conditional assignment operator**. This allows us to replace the above logic with the single statement:

```
small = (no1 < no2)? no1 : no2;
```

small is assigned the value following the question mark (i.e. the contents of *no1*) if the condition (`no1 < no2`) is **true** and assigned the value following the colon (*no2*) if the condition is **false**.

The general form of this statement is shown in FIG-3.2.

FIG-3.2

The Conditional Assignment Operator

where *variable* is assigned the value following the question mark if *expression* is **true**
variable is assigned the value following the colon if *expression* is **false.**
value is a variable, constant or expression.

TABLE-3.7 gives examples of the conditional assignment operator in use.

TABLE-3.7

The Conditional Assignment Operator

Structured English	C++

IF transactioncode = 'P' THEN
    Subtract amount from balance
ELSE
    Add amount to balance
ENDIF
	balance = (transactioncode == 'P')?
	    balance - amount:
	    balance + amount;

IF no < 0 THEN
    no = -no
ENDIF
	no = (no < 0)? -no : no;

TASK 3.8

Using the conditional assignment operator, produce the equivalent of:

```
if (no < 0)
    c = -c;
else
    c++;
```

Multi-way Selection

Multi-way selection means choosing one option from many. Although we have already dealt with this situation using nested `if` statements and the `else if` structure, there is an alternative approach which often results in clearer code. This is the `switch` statement. Earlier we looked at a program to read in a transaction code and display one of the following messages:

Code	Message
1	CASH
2	CREDIT
3	RETURNED
other	INVALID CODE

This could be coded in Structured English as:

```
IF
    code = 1:  Display "CASH"
    code = 2:  Display "CREDIT"
    code = 3:  Display "RETURNED"
    ELSE
               Display "INVALID CODE"
ENDIF
```

C++'s `switch` statement has a similar effect. One attempt at translating the Structured English to a `switch` statement might be:

```
switch (code)
{
    case 1  : cout << "CASH\n";
    case 2  : cout << "CREDIT\n";
    case 3  : cout << "RETURNED\n";
    default : cout << "INVALID CODE\n";
}
```

During execution, *code* (known as the **switch variable**) is evaluated and control jumps to the `case` statement whose value matches that of *code*. Where *code* does not match any of the `case` values, then control jumps to the `default` option.

This control structure may seem quite straight-forward but the `switch` statement has an unexpected characteristic: once the appropriate `case` option has been identified, and its associated instruction executed, the instructions in succeeding `case` statements are also executed. In other words, if, in the above example, *code* has the value 2, control jumps to `case 2:` and the word "CREDIT" is displayed, then execution continues through `case 3:` and `default:` resulting in the strings "RETURNED" and "INVALID CONTROL" also being displayed.

This is unlike multiway branch statements implemented in other languages where only one option is executed and all other options are skipped.

> **TASK 3.9**
>
> What output would be produced by the `switch` structure given above if a value of 3 was entered?

In most circumstances we would not want the subsequent statements specified in later `case` options to be executed. These can be bypassed by using another command: `break`.

When the break command is executed, control jumps immediately to the end of the switch statement.

We can now write the correct version of our code as:

```
switch (code)
{
    case 1  :   cout << "CASH\n";
                break;
    case 2  :   cout << "CREDIT\n";
                break;
    case 3  :   cout << "RETURNED\n";
                break;
    default :   cout << "INVALID CODE\n";
}
```

Note that there is no need to include a break after the default: option since it is the last one in the list.

Using this updated version, only one of the case options will be executed.

The default section of the switch statement is optional and may be omitted. Where there is no default option, and the value of the switch variable does not match any of those given in the cases which follow, then the whole switch structure is bypassed.

LISTING-3.1 allows the computer to be used as a simple calculator using the switch structure to choose the correct operation to be performed.

LISTING-3.1

Using switch

```
#include <iostream.h>

void main( )
{
  float    rno1, rno2, answer;
  char     option;

  // *** Get expression to be evaluated ***
  cout << "Enter expression (value operator value)\n";
  cin >> rno1 >> option >> rno2;

  // *** Execute appropriate choice ***
  int option_ok = 1;
  switch(option)
  {
      case '+'  :   answer = rno1+rno2 ;
                    break;
      case '-'  :   answer = rno1 - rno2;
                    break;
      case '/'  :   answer = rno1 / rno2;
                    break;
      case '*'  :   answer = rno1 * rno2;
                    break;
      default   :   cout << "\nUnknown operator\n";
                    option_ok = 0;
  }
  // *** If a valid operator used, display result ***
  if (option_ok)
      cout <<'\n' << rno1 << option << rno2 << '='
           << answer << endl;
}
```

There are some potential problems with this program. The case study at the end of this chapter gives a more robust version.

You can see from LISTING-3.1 that the switch structure can be implemented using character values as well as integers; real and string values are not allowed.

It is also possible to have two or more case options relating to the same section of code. For example, LISTING-3.1 expects the asterisk ('*') to be entered when using the multiply option but non-programmers are much more likely to enter an 'x'. Therefore, an improvement to the program would be to allow for both options. Since we already know that the `switch` statement falls through each `case` option where there is no `break` statement included, we need simply write

```
case '*'   :  ;
case 'x'   :  answer = rno1 * rno2;
              break;
```

at the appropriate point in our structure. However, C++ permits a certain freedom in this situation allowing the semi-colon in the empty `case` option (`case '*':;`) to be omitted giving simply:

```
case '*'   :  // *** No semi-colon required ***
case 'x'   :  answer = rno1 * rno2;
              break;
```

Unfortunately, there is no neat way of supplying a continuous range of values to a `case` option. For example, if we wished to grade an exam mark as *fail*, *pass* or *distinction* corresponding to scores in the ranges 0 - 45, 46 - 80, 81 - 100 this would not be easily coded using the `switch` construct and we would have to revert to the `else if` format.

The general format of the `switch` statement is shown in FIG-3.3.

FIG-3.3

The `switch` Statement

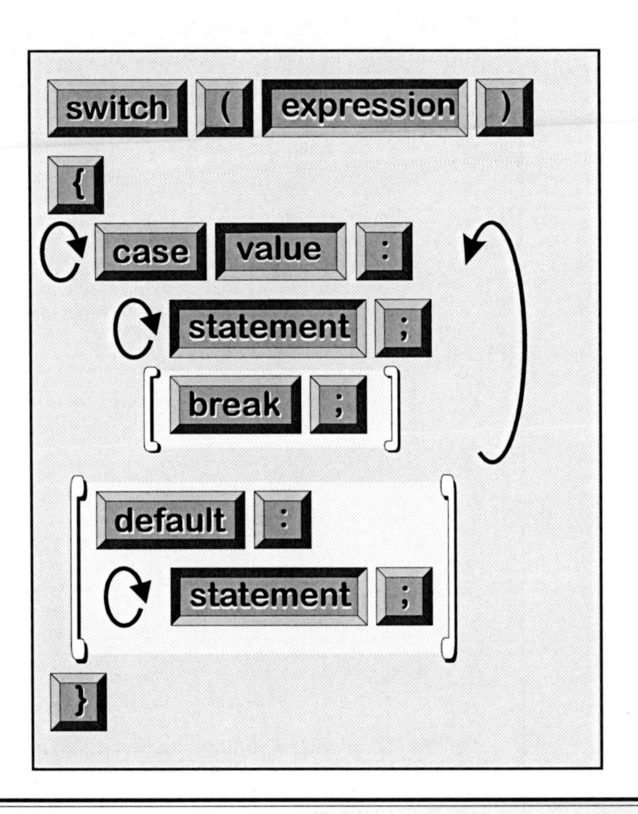

TASK 3.10

Using a `switch` statement, write C++ coding which reads in a positive decimal integer value and a character representing the number base in which the integer is to be displayed. ('O' for Octal, 'H' for Hexadecimal and 'D' for Decimal). Both upper and lower case letters should be acceptable. You need not validate the input. Display the entered numeric value in the base requested.

Summary

- **Boolean expressions** are given the value 1 if **true** and the value 0 if **false**.
- **Variables, constants and expressions** may used anywhere a **true/false** result is required. A numeric value of 0 is considered to be equivalent to **false**; any other value is equivalent to **true**.
- Since **Boolean expressions** return numeric values, such expressions **can be part of an arithmetic expression**.
  (e.g. `YC = year - (month <=3);`)
- **Expressions can be linked by && (AND) or || (OR).**
  (e.g. `no1 < 4 && no2 > 6`)
- **A logic value can be reversed using ! (NOT).**
  (e.g. `!(age > 18)`)
- **Nested `if` structures** can be used where a choice between more than two options has to be made.
- The **conditional operator** allows one of two values to be assigned to a variable depending on a given condition.
  (e.g. `YC = (month <= 3) ? year - 1 : year;`)
- **The `switch` statement** can also be used to choose from more than one alternative.
- **The `switch` statement will begin execution at the first `case` option found to be true.**

  Normally, all subsequent case options will also be executed.
- **Use of the `break` statement** will cause control to jump to the end of the `switch` structure.
- **Where none of the options in the `switch` statement are appropriate, the `default` option is executed.**

  Where there is no `default` statement, the whole `switch` structure is bypassed.
- **Values in the `case` options may be integer or character constants**; not real or string.
- **Several `case` options can be specified together.**
  (e.g.
  ```
  case 'a':
  case 'b':
  case 'c': cout << "A,B, or C\n";
  ```
)
- **`case`** cannot specify a range of values.
  (e.g. `case 0..45:` is not valid)
- **When `if` statements are nested,** `else` statements match with the last `if` section which is not already linked to an `else` statement.

  This may be overridden using parentheses.

Operator Priority

Items on the same line of the table have equal priority.

Where items of equal priority exist these are normally evaluated from left to right within the expression. However, those marked with an asterisk are processed from right to left.

Operator Precedence	
Operator	**Description**
( )	Parentheses
! -	Logical NOT, unary minus *
++ --	Increment and decrement *
* / %	Arithmetic multiply,divide,modulus
+ -	Addition,subtraction
< > >= <=	Inequality relational operators
== !=	Equality relational operators
&&	Logical AND
||	Logical OR
= += -= *= /= %=	Assignment *

Statement Formats:

Items enclosed in square brackets are optional and may be omitted.

```
    if
            if(expression)
                action
        [   else
                action              ]

    Conditional Operator
            variable = (expression)?value1:value2


    switch
            switch(expression)
            {
                case value1:
        [       case valuex: ...    ]
                    action
                    break;
        [       case value2:
                    action
                    break;
                      .                     ]
        [       default:
                    action
            } ]

where
    action
            statement;
    or
            {
                statement;
                      .
                statement;
            }
```

ITERATION

C++ has three distinct iterative structures. However, the C++ structures differ slightly in format and operation from those of Structured English and care should be taken when translating your iteration logic to C++.

The `while` Structure

The `while` structure is probably the easiest to understand, since it is identical in operation to the **while** of Structured English. This is an **entry controlled loop**; that is, the condition to be tested is at the start of the loop. If the condition is **true** the loop body is executed; if not, then the loop body is bypassed. For example, we might define the logic determining the number of times one integer divides into another as:

```
Get values for dividend and divisor
Set count to zero
WHILE dividend >= 0 DO
    Add 1 to count
    Subtract divisor from dividend
ENDWHILE
Subtract 1 from count
```

which can be coded in C++ as:

```
cin >> dividend >> divisor;
count = 0;
while (dividend >= 0)
{
    count++;
    dividend -= divisor;
}
count—;
```

Like the `if` statement, a `while` structure requires that, where there is more than one statement in the loop body, those statements are enclosed in braces. The structure of the statement is shown in FIG-3.4.

FIG-3.4

The `while` Statement

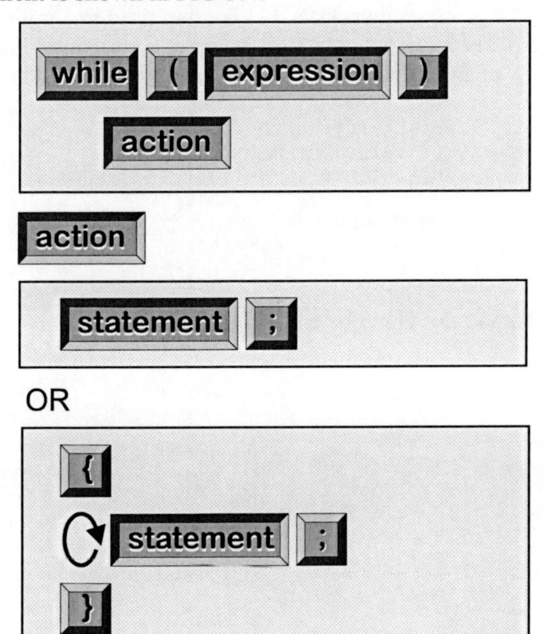

TABLE-3.8 gives several examples of Structured English *while* statements and the equivalent C++ code.

TABLE-3.8

`while` Structures

Structured English	C++

Get month
WHILE month outside range 1 - 12 DO
    Display "Invalid month"
    Get month
ENDWHILE
	cin >> month;
	while (month < 1 || month > 12)
	{
	    cout << "Invalid month\n";
	    cin >> month;
	}

Get value
WHILE value not zero DO
    Add value to total
    Get value
ENDWHILE
	cin >> value;
	while (value != 0)
	{
	    total += value;
	    cin >> value;
	}

TASK 3.11

Write the C++ equivalent of the following Structured English:

```
Get previousvalue
Get currentvalue
WHILE previousvalue not equal to currentvalue DO
    Set previousvalue equal to currentvalue
    Get currentvalue
ENDWHILE
```

Using the Comma Operator

See Chapter 2 for details of the comma operator.

The comma operator (`,`) is often used in conjunction with the `while` statement to create briefer code. For example, a Structured English solution to validate the input of a numeric value for a variable *month* would be:

```
Prompt for month
Get value for month
WHILE month is outside the range 1 to 12 DO
    Display error message
    Prompt for month
    Get value for month
ENDWHILE
```

and this could be coded as:

```
cout << "Enter month : ";
cin >> month;
while (month <1 || month > 12)
{
    cout << "Month must be in range 1 to 12\n";
    cout << "Enter month : ";
    cin >> month;
}
```

but, by using the comma operator, the code becomes

```
while(cout << "Enter month : ", cin >> month,
                                    (month < 1 || month > 12))
    cout << "Month must be in the range 1 to 12\n";
```

However, don't be tempted to overuse this technique since it does tend to lead to hard-to-read code.

The `do..while` Structure

The `do..while` statement is as close as C++ comes to supplying a **REPEAT .. UNTIL** structure. However, the two statements differ in more than syntax, since, although both have the condition at the end of the control structure, **REPEAT .. UNTIL** exits its loop body when the given condition is **true** whereas `do .. while` exits when its condition is **false**. In other words, the `do .. while` structure is more like a `while` statement with the condition moved to the end of the loop body. This means that the translation of a **REPEAT .. UNTIL** loop in Structured English to a `do..while` loop in C++ involves inverting the condition for the C++ version. For example, the logic

```
REPEAT
    Get value
    Add value to total
UNTIL value is zero
```

is coded as:

```
do
{
    cin >> value;
    total += value;
}
while (!(value == 0));
```

Note the negation of the original Structured English expression

Note that it would be quite possible to have coded the expression in the above `while` statement as `value != 0` rather than `!(value == 0)`. However, the latter technique of simply placing a NOT operator in front of the original Structured English condition is less prone to error, especially when the condition is a complex one.

For example, if a REPEAT loop contained the condition

```
month < 1 OR month > 12
```

this could be coded in a `while` structure as

```
!(month < 1 || month > 12)
```

rather than the equally correct

```
month >= 1 && month <= 12
```

which involves more changes from the original and hence is more likely to introduce an error in translation.

The `do..while` requires additional braces when there is more than one statement in the loop body. The general form of the statement is shown in FIG-3.5.

FIG-3.5

The `do..while` Statement

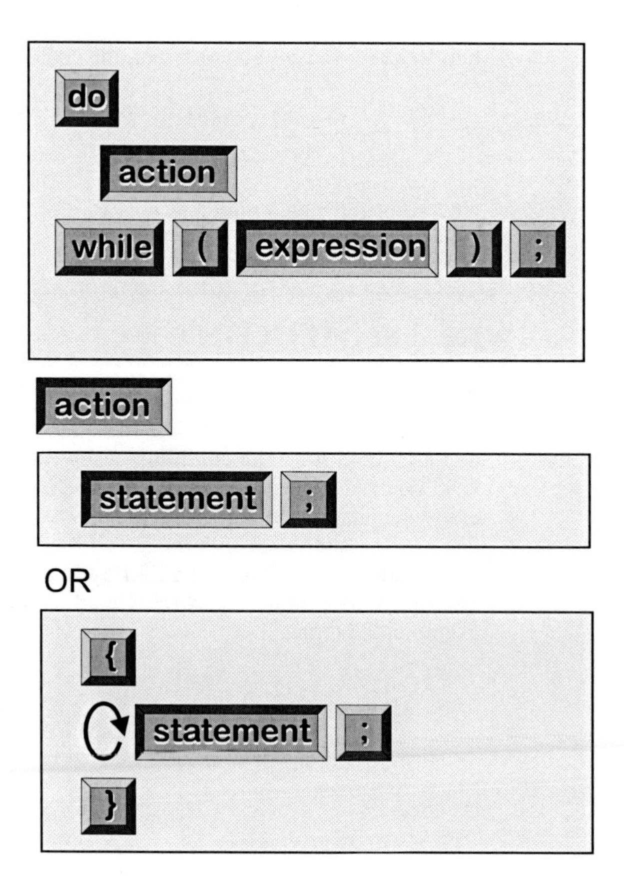

TABLE-3.9 gives some examples of Structured English **REPEAT .. UNTIL** loops and the equivalent C++ `do..while` structures.

TABLE-3.9

`do..while` Structures

Structured English	C++

Set target to 401
REPEAT
    Get score
    Subtract score from target
UNTIL target <= 0
	target = 401;
	do
	{
	    cin >> score;
	    target -= score;
	}
	while (!(target <= 0));

Set total to zero
Set count to zero
REPEAT
    Get number
    Add number to total
    Add 1 to count
UNTIL count = 10 OR number = 0
	total = 0;
	count = 0;
	do
	{
	    cin >> number;
	    total += number;
	}
	while (!(++count == 10||number ==0));

The `for` Structure

Like Structured English, C++ contains a `for` structure. In Structured English, this control structure can perform a sequence of tasks a fixed number of times using logic such as:

```
FOR each student DO
    Get student's mark
    Add mark to total
ENFOR
```

which, should there be 10 students, would carry out the statements

```
Get student's mark
Add mark to total
```

10 times.

When we want to perform this type of loop in C++, we usually need to define a **loop counter variable** which the `for` loop increments each time the loop body is executed. For example, the 10 students would have their marks totalled by the code:

count is the loop counter variable

```
int total=0,count,mark;

for(count = 1; count <= 10; count++)
{
    cin >> mark;
    total += mark;
}
```

The parentheses following the word `for` contains three main components. The first of these, `count = 1`, is known as the **initialisation statement** and is executed before the loop body is entered. The second, `count <= 10`, is the condition to be tested at the start of each iteration - only if the condition is **true** will the loop body be executed. The third and final part, `count++`, is executed at the end of the loop body before returning to the beginning of the loop and testing the condition.

The same logic can be implemented in a `while` loop as:

```
count = 1;              // part 1 before loop body
while (count <= 10)     // part 2 condition tested at start
{                       // of loop
    cin >> mark;
    total += mark;
    count++;            // part 3 executed at the end of the
}                       // loop body
```

Like the other iteration structures, parentheses are required where there is more than one statement in the `for` loop body.

TASK 3.12

What output will be produced from the code below :

```
for(no = 0; no < 5; no++)
    cout << no << '\n';
```

The format of the `for` statement is shown in FIG-3.6.

FIG-3.6

The `for` Statement

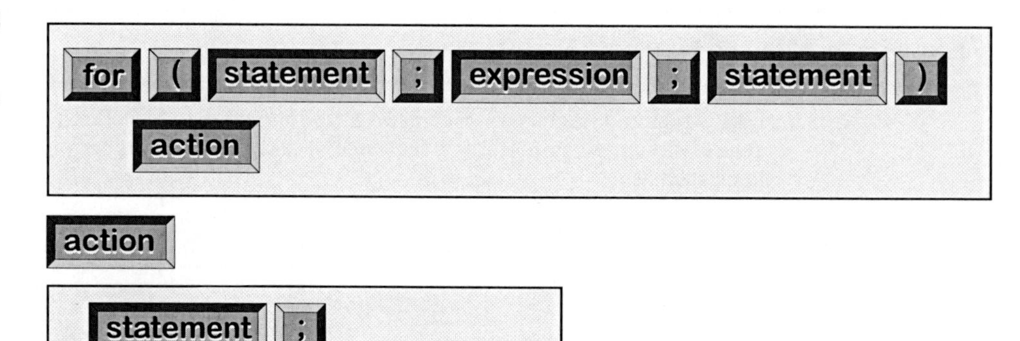

action

statement ;

OR

Using `for` to Implement Other Iterative Structures

In most programming languages, the condition which must hold when iterating a counting loop is never explicitly stated. For example, in the Pascal statement

```
FOR count := 1 TO 10 DO
```

the implied loop entry condition which must hold to continue iteration is *count <=10*. As we have seen, C++ requires such conditions to be stated explicitly. Hence the equivalent C++ statement would be:

```
for(count = 1; count <= 10; count++)
```

This apparently clumsy format is, in fact, very powerful. Since there is no restriction on exactly what condition is specified, it need have nothing to do with the loop counter. For example, if we needed to count the number of values in a list of numbers which terminates with a zero, our Structured English solution might be:

```
Set count to zero
Get number
WHILE number not zero DO
    Add 1 to count
    Get number
ENDWHILE
```

C++ can code this as:

The C++ statements are executed in a slightly different order from the Structured English but give the same result.

```
cin >> number;
for(count = 0; number != 0; count++)
    cin >> number;
```

We can take this variation on the standard `for` loop a stage further and create a C++ `for` loop which has no loop counter. The following code totals a list of values, stopping when the total exceeds 99.

```
for(total = 0; total < 100; total += no)
    cin >> no;
```

The equivalent Structured English is:

```
Set total to zero
WHILE total < 100 DO
    Get no
    Add no to total
ENDWHILE
```

Omitting Parts of the `for` Statement

It is possible to omit one or more parts of the `for` statement. For example, we may remove the initialisation part as in the example below:

```
const int terminator = -1;
int no;

//*** List each value entered ***
cout << "Enter number : ";
cin >> no;
for(; no != terminator; cout << no)
{
    cout << "Enter number : ";
    cin >> no;
}
```

Note that, although the initialisation statement has been omitted, the semi-colon must remain.

It is also valid to omit the post loop body statement. For example:

```
cout << "Enter number : ";
cin >> no;
for(total = no; no != 0;)
{
    cout << "Enter number : ";
    cin >> no;
    total += no;
}
```

It is even possible to omit the loop condition but, of course, this would normally result in an infinite loop which is unlikely to be what you are after.

```
for( ; ; )
    cout << "Looping forever\n";
```

Using The Comma Operator

It is possible to include additional statements in any component of the `for` loop by separating these by a comma. For example, we can initialise both a count and total before entering the loop body by beginning the `for` statement with:

```
for(i = 1, total = 0;
```

These same variables can be adjusted at the end of the loop body with

```
;i++, total += no)
```

The complete structure for summing 10 numbers would be:

```
for(i = 1, total = 0; i <= 10; i++, total += no)
{
    cout << "Enter number : ";
    cin >> no;
}
```

This approach can be useful for initialising several variables at the start of the loop or modifying several variables at the end of the loop.

Although useful, the technique should be used sparingly since it does nothing to aid readability.

Defining Variables in `for` Loops

Since C++ allows variables to be defined at any point in a program, it is the common practice of many C++ programmers to define the loop counter inside the `for` loop structure. For example:

```
for(int i = 1; i <= 10; i++)
```

Of course, this can be extended to apply to any other variables used exclusively in or after the loop body.

```
for(int i = 1, total = 0; i <= 10; i++, total += no)
```

This example also shows the double purpose of the comma symbol. Initially, it is used as a separator in a variable definition

```
int i = 1, total = 0;
```

while in the final part of the statement it is used as an operator in its own right:

```
i++, total += no
```

You will find many of the symbols used in C++ have differing functions depending on the context in which they are used.

TABLE-3.10 gives some examples of the `for` structure.

TABLE-3.10

`for` Structures

Structured English	C++

Set total to zero
FOR no := 1 TO 10 DO
    Add no to total
ENDFOR
	total = 0;
	for(no = 1; no <= 10; no++)
	    total += no;

Set total to zero
Get no of students
FOR each student DO
    Get student's mark
    Display student's mark
    Add student's mark to total
ENDFOR
Calculate average as
    total/no of students
	total = 0;
	cin >> noofstudents;
	for(i=1;i<=noofstudents;i++)
	{
	    cin >> mark;
	    cout << mark;
	    total += mark;
	}
	average = total/noofstudents;

Jump Statements

Statements which transfer the flow of control to some other part of a program are classified as **jump statements**. There are four such statements: `break`, `continue`, `goto` and `return`. The `return` statement will be dealt with later, in Chapter 5.

The `break` Statement

The `break` statement, which we have already encountered in the `switch` structure, can be used in any of the loop structures to allow early termination of the loop. For example, where we require to read in a maximum of 10 numbers, but with the possibility of terminating sooner if a zero is entered, we can use the code:

```
for(i = 0; i < 10; i++)
{
    cout << "Enter value " << i << " : ";
    cin >> no;
    if (no == 0)
        break;  //*** for loop terminated by this statement
    total += no;
}
cout << "total was " << total << " after " << i << " numbers\n";
```

Included in the code is the conditional statement

```
if(no == 0)
    break;
```

which, when its expression `(no == 0)` is **true**, will cause control to jump to the `cout` statement following the `for` loop body, hence terminating the execution of the loop (see FIG-3.7).

FIG-3.7

The `break` Statement

```
for(i=0; i<10;i++)
{
      cout << "Enter value "<<i<<" : ";
      cin >> no;
      if(no==0)
          break;
      total +=no;
}
cout<<"Total was "<<total<<" after "<<i
      <<" numbers\n";
```

Control moves to the end of the control structure

In general, the use of `break` in the manner described above is not considered good technique and should be avoided by rewriting the code.

The `continue` Statement

There is another statement which can be included in any loop structure. When executed, the `continue` statement causes the remaining statements in the loop to be skipped and transfers control back to the start of the loop.

When used with `for` loops, although the loop body is skipped, the incremental statement will be executed before returning to the beginning of the loop body.

The following code accepts 10 numbers, summing those which are positive.

```
total = 0;
for(i = 1; i <= 10; i++)
{
    cout << "Enter number ";
    cin >> no;
    if (no <= 0)
        continue;
    total += no;
}
cout << "Total of positive values entered is " << total;
```

Where `no <= 0` is **true** the remainder of the loop body, `total += no`, will be bypassed but the incremental statement, `i++`, will be executed before returning to the beginning of the loop. Hence the `for` structure will terminate after 10 iterations irrespective of how often the `continue` statement is executed (see FIG-3.8).

FIG-3.8

The `continue` Statement

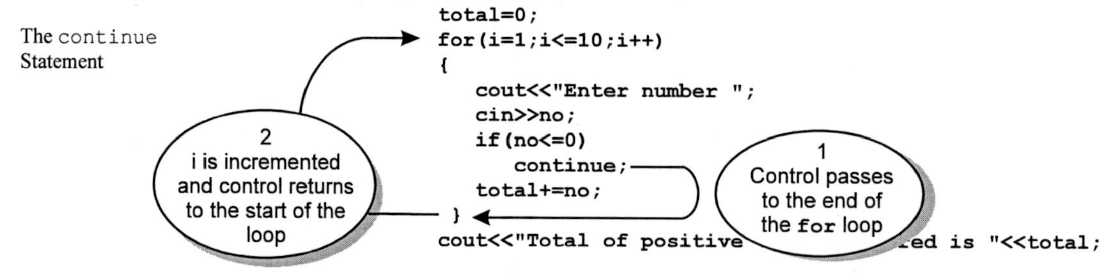

total=0;
for(i=1;i<=10;i++)
{
cout<<"Enter number ";
cin>>no;
if(no<=0)
continue;
total+=no;
}
cout<<"Total of positive
ed is "<<total;
2
i is incremented and control returns to the start of the loop
1
Control passes to the end of the for loop

> **TASK 3.13**
>
> Write a section of C++ code which makes use of the `continue` statement to accept and sum exactly 10 positive integers.

Like `break`, `continue` should be avoided since it makes a program difficult to follow and debug.

The `goto` Statement

The `goto` statement transfers control to a specified line of code. The destination line is identified by preceding it by a label. A label is any valid name followed by a colon.

```
total = 0;
for(i = 0; i < 10; i++)
{
    cin >> no;
    if(no == 0 && i == 1)  // goto finish if first number is
        goto finish;       // zero
    total += no;
}
average = total / i;
cout << "Average is " << average << '\n';
finish:                    // label for goto statement
cout << "Program terminated\n";
```

C++ will not allow a `goto` statement to jump past any variable definitions. For example, the following extract is invalid:

```
goto next;
    .
int total = 0; //cannot bypass definitions
    .
next:
```

It is also possible to jump to a label given earlier in the program code but since this creates a looping situation it would be more appropriate to use one of the iterative statements (`while, do` or `for`).

Unlike `break` and `continue,` which can only be used inside control structures, the `goto` statement can be used anywhere in a program. Nevertheless, most guides to good programming technique would suggest its use should be avoided.

Nested Loops

A common requirement is to produce nested loops, that is situations where one loop control structure appears within another. For example, if we want to read in and average six exam marks, each of which needs to be in the range 0 to 100, we could describe this logic as:

```
1.  Set total to zero
2.  FOR each exam DO
3.      Get valid mark
4.      Add mark to total
5.  ENDFOR
6.  Calculate average as total/6
7.  Display average
```

This appears to have only a single loop structure beginning at statement 2 and ending at statement 5. However, if we add detail to statement 3, this gives us

```
3.  Get valid mark
    3.1 Read mark
    3.2 WHILE mark is invalid DO
    3.3     Display"Mark must be between zero and 100"
    3.4     Read mark
    3.5 ENDWHILE
```

which, if placed in the original solution, results in

```
1.  Set total to zero
2.  FOR each exam DO
3.1     Read mark
3.2     WHILE mark is invalid DO
3.3         Display"Mark must be between zero and 100"
3.4         Read mark
3.5     ENDWHILE
4.      Add mark to total
5.  ENDFOR
6.  Calculate average as total/6
7.  Display average
```

giving a nested loops structure, where a WHILE loop appears inside a FOR loop.

Nested FOR Loops

Perhaps the most troublesome situation is where FOR loops are nested. The following example demonstrates the characteristics of such a structure. Consider the first two digits of a car's odometer. They begin set to 00. As the car moves, the least-significant digit (*units*) increments while the most significant digit (*tens*) remains unchanged (see FIG-3.9). But when the *units* value reaches 9, the *tens* value increments and the *units* is reset to zero(see FIG-3.10).

FIG-3.9

Incrementing the Inner Loop Counter

FIG-3.10

Incrementing the Outer Loop Counter

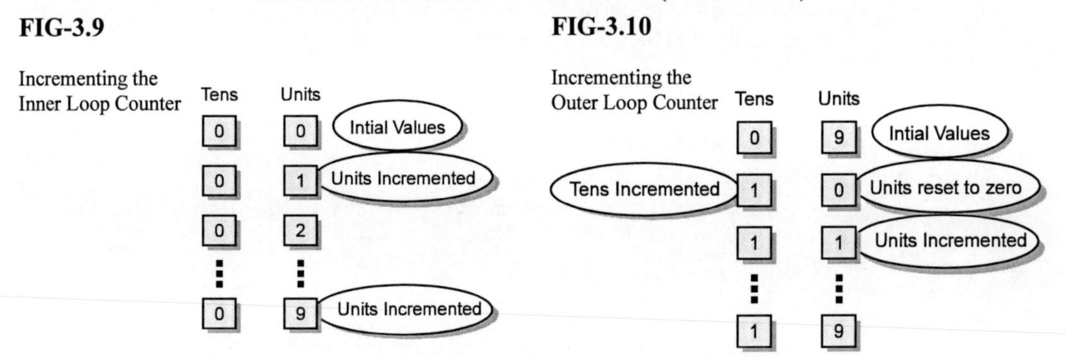

This process continues, with the *tens* value being incremented for every ten increments of the units.

This situation is matched exactly by the code below:

```
int units,tens;

for( tens=0;tens<=9;tens++)
    for(units=0;units<=9;units++)
        cout<<tens<<' '<<units<<'\n';
```

The *tens* loop is known as the **outer loop**, while the *units* loop is known as the **inner loop**.

A few points to note about nested `for` loops:

1. The inner loop increments fastest.
2. Only when the inner loop is complete does the outer loop variable increment.
3. The inner loop variable is reset to its starting value each time the outer loop counter is incremented.

A common mistake, when implementing nested loops, is to use the same loop counter variable name in both `for` structures:

```
for(count = 1 .....
{
        .
        .
    for(count = 1 ......
```

This makes it impossible to maintain two independent counts for both the inner and outer for loops - leading to disastrous results.

TASK 3.14

What would be the output of the following code?

```
for(no1 = -2;no1 <= 1;no1++)
    for(no2 = 0;no2 <= 6;no2+=3)
        cout << no1 << ' ' << no2 << '\n';
```

Translating from Structured English

The nested iterative structures seen in the Structured English of Chapter 1 can be produced by simple translation. Where 10 students each sit six exams with a maximum possible mark of 100 for each exam, we can calculate each student's average mark using the following logic:

```
FOR each student DO
    Set total to zero
    FOR each exam DO
        Get mark
        WHILE mark is invalid DO
            Display "Mark must be in the range 0 to 100"
            Get mark
        ENDWHILE
        Add mark to total
    ENDFOR
    Calculate average as total / 6 (rounded)
    Display student number and average
ENDFOR
```

The corresponding code is

```
int student, exam,mark, total, average;

for(student = 1; student <= 10; student++)
{
    total = 0;
    for(exam = 1; exam <= 6; exam++)
    {
        cout << "Enter mark for exam " << exam << ' ';
        cin >> mark;
        while (mark < 0 || mark > 100)
        {
            cout << "Mark must be in the range 0 to 100\n";
            cin >> mark;
        }
        total += mark;
    }
    average = total / 6.0 + 0.5;
    cout << "The average for student " << student
          << " was " << average << '\n';
}
```

`continue` and `break` in Nested Structures

Where `continue` or `break` is used in an inner control structure, as in

```
for(j = 1; j <= 3; j++)
{
    total = 0;
    for(i = 1; i <= 10; i++)
    {
        cout << "Enter number ";
        cin >> no;
        if(no <= 0)
            continue;
        total += no;
    }
    cout << "Total of positive values entered is " << total;
}
```

control jumps to the end of the control structure in which it is placed. In the case of a `for` loop structure, any post-loop body instruction is performed as normal. If the exit condition for the loop is not met, control returns to the beginning of the loop and iteration goes on as normal. Hence, in the above example, only the statement `total += no` is skipped and iteration of the *j* `for` loop is not affected.

TASK 3.15

What results would be produced from the code

```
int total = 0;
for(m = 1; m <= 3; m++)
    for(n = 1; n <= 5; n++)
    {
        cout << "Enter number : ";
        cin >> no;
        if(!no)
            break;
        total += no;
    }
cout << total;
```

if the values entered are 6,0,3,1,0,0,7,8,0,5,0?

PROGRAMMING EXERCISE 3.2

1. Write a program to display all numbers between 1 and 20 which are not divisible by 4 or 5.
   HINT: a number (x) is exactly divisible by some other number (y) when x divided by y gives no remainder.

```
OUTLINE LOGIC:
    FOR no := 1 TO 20 DO
        IF no is not divisible by 4 or 5 THEN
            Display no
        ENDIF
    ENDFOR
```

2. Write a program to read in two values (*column* and *line*) and place the character 'x' at the specified column and row on the screen. Check that *column* is between 1 and 80, the *line* between 1 and 24.

```
OUTLINE LOGIC:
    Get column
    WHILE column outside range 1 to 80 DO
        Display error message
        Get column
    ENDWHILE
    Get line
    WHILE line outside the range 1 to 24 DO
        Display error message
        Get line
    ENDWHILE
    Clear screen (move cursor to top left of screen)
    FOR line-1 times DO
        Move down one line
    ENDFOR
    Set width of display to column
    Display 'x'
```

3. One method of testing if a value is divisible by 37 is to split the value into groups of 3 digits which are then added. If the resulting sum is divisible by 37 then so is the original.
   e.g. 143412 = 143 + 412 = 555.
   Program this test and print an appropriate message.

```
OUTLINE LOGIC:
    Set sum to zero
    Get no
    WHILE no is not zero DO
        Extract the three least significant digits of no
        Add this extracted value to sum
        Remove the three least significant digits from no
    ENDWHILE
    IF sum is exactly divisible by 37 THEN
        Display "Value divisible by 37"
    ELSE
        Display "Value not divisible by 37"
    ENDIF
```

Continued on next page

PROGRAMMING EXERCISE 3.2 (continued)

4. The number of ways that *r* objects can be chosen from *n* objects is given by the formula

$$^{n}C_{r} = n!/((n-r)!*r!)$$

Write a program to read *r* and *n* (validate that $r < n$) and print the result.
NOTE: *r!* is pronounced *r* factorial and is *r * (r-1) * (r-2) *...... *1*

```
OUTLINE LOGIC:
    Get value for n
    Get value for r
    WHILE r>= n DO
        Display error message
        Get value for n
        Get value for r
    ENDWHILE
    Set factorialn to 1
    FOR I := 2 TO n DO
        Multiply factorialn by I
    ENDFOR
    Set factorialr to 1
    FOR I := 2 TO r DO
        Multiply factorialr by I
    ENDFOR
    Set factorialn_r to 1
    FOR I := 2 TO n-r DO
        Multiply factorialn_r by I
    ENDFOR
    Calculate nCr as Factorialn /(Factorialn_r*factorialr
    Display nCr
```

5. In ice skating, a number of judges (*N*) award marks. The highest and lowest of these are ignored and the others averaged to give a result. Write a program to input *N*, followed by *N* marks, and display the average score. (Scores range from 0.0 to 6.0 in increments of 0.1.)

```
OUTLINE LOGIC:
    Get first score
    Set highest_score to score
    Set lowest_score to score
    Set total to score
    Get value for N
    FOR N-1 times DO
        Get score
        Add score to total
        IF score is greater than highest_score THEN
            Set highest_score to score
        ELSE
            IF score is less than lowest_score THEN
                Set lowest_score to score
            ENDIF
        ENDIF
    ENDFOR
    Subtract highest_score and lowest_score from total
    Calculate average as total/(N-2)
    Display average
```

Continued on next page

PROGRAMMING EXERCISE 3.2 (continued)

6. If X_i is an approximation of the cube root of N then a closer approximation is:

$$X_{i+1} = (N/X_i^2 + 2X_i)/3$$

Write a program to calculate the cube root to 5 decimal places.

```
OUTLINE LOGIC:
    Get a value for N
    Set newx to N/3
    REPEAT
        Set oldx to newx
        Calculate newx as (N/(oldx*oldx)+2*oldx)/3
    UNTIL N-newx*newx*newx < 0.000005 AND
            newx*newx*newx - N < 0.000005
    Display newx
```

7. Making use of the date program written earlier, write a program which allows any date to be entered and the calendar for the month involved displayed in the form:

```
      Sun   Mon   Tue   Wed   Thu   Fri   Sat
                                  1     2     3
        4     5     6     7     8     9    10
       11    12    13    14    15    16    17
       18    19    20    21    22    23    24
       25    26    27    28    29    30
OUTLINE LOGIC:
    Get date
    Calculate day of week on which first day of month fell
    Display table heading
    Position cursor in correct column
    Display 1
    Display other day numbers on row 1
    Display numbers in subsequent rows
```

Summary

■ Iteration Structures

```
while
        while(expression)
            action

do..while
        do
            action
        while(expression);

for
        for(statement1; expression; statement2)
            action

action
        statement;
or
        {
            statement;
                .
            statement;
        }
```

- **In the `while` structure,** *expression* is evaluated before each iteration of the loop body.

- **The `while` loop body** may be iterated a minimum of zero times.

- **The `while` loop terminates** when *expression* is **false** (zero).

- **On termination of the `while` loop**, execution jumps to the statement following the `while` structure.

- **In the `do..while` structure,** *expression* is evaluated after each iteration of the loop body.

- **The `do..while` body** may be iterated a minimum of once.

- **The `do` loop terminates** when *expression* is **false**.

- **On termination of the `do` loop**, execution jumps to the statement following the `do..while` structure.

- **In the `for` structure,** *expression* is evaluated before each iteration of the loop body.

- **The `for` loop body** may be iterated a minimum of zero times.

- **The `for` loop terminates** when *expression* is **false**.

- **On termination of the `for` loop**, execution jumps to the statement following the `for` structure.

- **The `for` structure,**

```
for(statement1; expression; statement2)
    action;
```

  is exactly equivalent to

```
statement1;
while(expression)
{
    action
    statement2;
}
```

- **In the `for` structure,** *statement1*, *expression* and *statement2* may be omitted but the semi-colons must be retained.

- **Omitting *expression*** will result in an infinite loop.

- **In the `for` structure,** *expression* need not refer to a loop counter variable.

- **The comma operator** may be employed in all of the loop structures.

```
e.g.    while(cout<<"Enter no : ",cin>>no,no!=0)
            count+=no;

        for(i=1,sum=0;i<=10;i++,sum+no,cin>>no);
```

- **Using `break` in an iterative structure** transfers control to the first statement following the loop.

- **Using `continue` in an iterative structure** transfers control to the end of the action defined in the loop body. However, the loop itself is not exited.

- **Where loops are nested,** `break` and `continue` affect only the loop body in which they are used. That is, if they are defined in the inner loop control will be transferred to the end of that inner loop's body (`continue`); or to the first statement following the inner loop (`break`).

- **`goto` transfers control to the specified label** at some other point in the program.

- **`goto` can transfer control** either to an earlier or later point in the program code.

- **Use of `break`, `continue` or `goto` (especially `goto`) should be avoided** where possible since they can result in hard-to-follow code and violate guidelines of structured programming.

TESTING CONTROL STRUCTURES

In an ideal world we would check our programs by entering every possible value and combination of values as test data. However, this is not practical even for simple programs since the time and effort required is prohibitive. Instead, a compromise is required.

One strategy used to test a piece of code is to create test data based on the structure of that code, the aim being to pick relevant test values, each of which checks differing parts of the code. This technique is called **white box** or **glass box** testing - so called, because we need to look at the internal structure of the program in order to create appropriate test values.

A minimum requirement of white box testing is that every statement in the code is executed by the test data. However, as we will see, this is a relatively poor strategy which can be improved on.

Testing Sequences

To test a sequence of statements such as

```
cout << "Enter a number : ";
cin >> no1 >> no2;
 result = no1 * no2;
cout << no1 << " * " << no2 << " = " << result << '\n';
```

we need only one set of test values (e.g. 12 and 2). This will result in all statements being executed.

Testing Selection

Simple `if` Statements

The simplest selection statement is an `if` statement without an `else` option. For example:

```
int no;

cin >> no;
if(no < 0)
    cout << "This is a negative value\n";
```

Although we can ensure that all parts of this statement are executed by using any value for *no* which results in the expression `(no < 0)` evaluating to **true**, it is also important to test the structure where the expression evaluates to **false**. Why is this?

Consider the code

```
int no1,no2,ans;

cin >> no1 >> no2;
if(no2 != 0)
    ans = no1 / no2;
cout << ans << '\n';
```

If we test this code by entering the values 6 and 2, the result will be 3 and all the statements will have been executed.

However, if we use the values 6 and 0, *ans* will not be assigned a value and the resulting output will be unpredictable.

Obviously, we want to detect such problems while testing the code. It is therefore important that even simple `if` statements are tested with two sets of data: one which evaluates the expression as **true**; the other giving a **false** result.

`if .. else` Structures

Where an `else` is used, the need to test for both **true** and **false** situations is more obvious since this is the only way to execute all the instructions in the control structure. Hence, we might test the code

```
if(no < 0)
    cout << "Negative\n";
else
    cout<<"Positive or zero\n";
```

with the values *no* = -8 and *no* = 3.

Other Boolean Expressions

In C++, Boolean expressions turn up in other commands such as the conditional assignment statement:

```
discount = (total < 20)?0.05 : 0.10;
```

or even in an arithmetic statement

```
days_in_month = 28 + (year%4 == 0);
```

Statements such as these need to be treated like `if` statements and hence should be tested with values which give both **true** and **false** results for the expression involved.

Nested `if` Statements

Since the path taken through an `if` statement is dependent on the truth of the statement's expression, where two `if` statements are nested, there are three possible paths. For example, in the code

```
if(sex == 'M')
    if(age >= 65)
        cout << "Retired\n";
    else
        cout << "Working\n";
else
    cout << "Female";
```

we can identify the possible truth combinations for the expressions (`sex == 'M'`) and (`age >= 65`) (see TABLE-3.11).

TABLE-3.11

Possible Combinations for Two Boolean Expressions

Expression	
(sex=='M')	(age>=65)
TRUE	TRUE
TRUE	FALSE
FALSE	TRUE
FALSE	FALSE

The last two combinations (**false**,**true** and **false**,**false**) execute the same section of code:

```
else
    cout << "Female\n";
```

and hence we need only three combinations of data values to test the above code.

TASK 3.16

For the following code

```
if(sex == 'M')
   if(age >= 65)
       cout << "Male retired\n";
   else
       cout << "Male working\n";
else
   if(age >= 60)
       cout << "Female retired\n";
   else
       cout << "Female working\n";
```

1. List all the expressions to be tested.

2. List all **true/false** combinations for the expressions involved?

3. Which of these **true/false** combinations can actually be tested?

Complex Boolean Expressions

Where a Boolean expression is complex (i.e. contains linking AND or OR operators), as in

```
if(sex == 'M' && age >= 65)
    cout << "Male retired\n";
```

it is important to create test data which gives all possible combinations of **true** and **false** from the individual component of the expression. Hence, for the expression `(sex=='M' && age >= 65)`, test values resulting in each of the four possibilities shown in TABLE-3.11 is required.

Why is it important to perform all possible combinations? Consider the situation where we had mistakenly written the above code as:

```
if(sex == 'M' || age >= 65)
    cout << "Male retired\n";
```

The test data *sex='M', age=66* (**true**,**true**) and *sex='F', age=23* (**false**,**false**) would test both **true** and **false** options of the `if` statement without showing up any problems. However, by including the other combinations, for example, with the test data *sex='M', age=45* (**true**,**false**) and *sex='F', age=70* (**false**,**true**), the error in the code will be detected.

`switch` Statements

Since a `switch` statement is equivalent to a series of mutually exclusive `if` statements (assuming a `break` command ends each option), testing requires values corresponding to each of the `case` options as well as the `default` option. For example, given the code

```
switch(day)
{
    case 0: cout << "Sunday\n";
            break;
    case 1: cout << "Monday\n";
            break;
    case 2: cout << "Tuesday\n";
            break;
    case 3: cout << "Wednesday\n";
            break;
    case 4: cout << "Thursday\n";
            break;
    case 5: cout << "Friday\n";
            break;
    case 6: cout << "Saturday\n";
            break;
    default:cout << "Invalid value for day\n";
}
```

then the test values required for *day* will be 0,1,2,3,4,5,6 and some invalid value, say, -1.

As with the simple `if` statement, where we need to test both **true** and **false** option, even when no `else` section exists, so we need to include a test value for the `default` option in a `switch` statement even when there is no explicit code for that option.

Where two or more `case` options execute the same code, each `case` value should be tested separately. Hence the section of code

```
    case 'a':
    case 'e':
    case 'i':
    case 'o':
    case 'u':   cout << "Vowel\n";
                break;
```

would require that the values 'a','e','i','o','u' are all used as part of the test data.

Testing Iteration

Infinite Loops

Iteration instructs the machine to carry out a sequence of instructions repeatedly. In order to stop this looping, the program must contain some loop-terminating condition. For example, in the code

```
cin >> no;
while(no > 10)
    no--;
```

iteration of the single statement, `no–`, terminates when *no* is less than or equal to 10. No matter what value we enter, iteration will eventually halt. On the other hand, the code

```
cin >> no;
while(no != 10)
    no--;
```

may never exit if we give *no* a starting value of less than 10.

This situation is known as an **infinite loop**. If you are unlucky, you may have to reboot your computer to get out of this situation once your program has begun executing.

Infinite looping can occur in any of the three loop structures in C++.

We can minimise the chances of an infinite loop by checking that the loop body has an affect on the loop's exit-condition, which will eventually lead to loop termination.

Testing `for` Loops

Where a `for` loop is coded for a fixed number of iterations, such as in the code

```
total = 0;
for(int c = 1; c <= 5; c++)
{
     cout << "Enter number : ";
     cin >> no;
    total += no;
}
cout << "Average is " << (total / 5) << '\n';
cout << "Last number entered was " << no << '\n';
```

we have no influence over the number of times the loop will be executed and hence, only the five values required to be input need be supplied as test data.

However, it is important that we check that such loops do actually execute the expected number of times since the exit condition could easily be coded wrongly. For example, writing

```
for(int c = 1; c < 5; c++) //*** Equal sign omitted ***
```

will result in the loop iterating four, rather than five times.

Loops which iterate either one too few, or one too many times are so common that these errors are often tested for explicitly.

However, if the exit condition involves a variable as in

```
total = 0;
cout << "How many values are to be entered : ";
cin >> m;
for(int c = 1; c <= m; c++)
{
    cout << "Enter number : ";
    cin >> no;
    total += no;
 }
cout << "Average is " << (total / m) << '\n';
cout << "Last number entered was " << no << '\n';
```

we can influence the number of times the `for` loop is executed. In this situation, test data should be produced to execute the loop structure, zero, one and multiple times. For the example above, that would mean values of 0,1 and, perhaps, 4 for the variable *m*.

A run-time error is one which occurs while the program is executing and results in the program terminating early.

Not only do such checks ensure that the loop does not execute too many or too few times, but also highlights certain errors which only appear when a loop is executed a specific number of times. For example, the code above will result in a run-time error when $m = 0$ and hence the loop iterates zero times. This is because the expression (*total/m*) will give a division-by-zero fault.

TASK 3.17

1. Identify the error in the following code:

```
int total, m;
cin >> m;
for(int c = 1; c <= m; c++)
{
    total = 0;
    cout << "Enter number : ";
    cin >> no;
    total += no;
}
if(m > 0)
{
    cout << "Average is " << (total / m) << '\n';
    cout << "Last number entered was " << no << '\n';
}
```

2. In which case(s) will the above error be detected?
   a) During zero iterations test
   b) During one iteration test
   c) During multiple iteration test

Testing `while` and `do..while` Loops

The `while` loop contains an entry-condition at the beginning of the loop body and, as such, is fundamentally the same structure as a `for` loop. The two structures should therefore be tested in the same fashion with test data to perform zero, one and multiple iterations.

On the other hand, the `do..while` loop has the entry-condition placed at the end of the loop structure. This means that it is normally impossible to test for zero iterations but one and multiple iterations should still be tested.

Testing Complete Programs

Most programs will consist of a combination of control structures. To test the whole program, each control structure must be identified and test data constructed.

The following design describes a program which is intended to read in 10 values in the range 1 to 100 and count how many of the values entered are divisible by exactly 3 or 4.

Program Logic:

```
Set total to zero
FOR 10 times DO
    Read valid number
    IF number is divisible by 3 or 4 THEN
        Add 1 to total
    ENDIF
ENDFOR
IF any values were divisible by 3 or 4 THEN
    Display total
ELSE
    Display "No values are divisible by 3 or 4"
ENDIF
```

Program Code :

LISTING-3.2

White Box Testing of a Program

```
#include<iostream.h>
void main()
{
    int total = 0, number;


    for(int count = 1; count <= 10; count++)
    {
        //*** Read valid number ***
        cout << "Enter number : ";
        cin >> number;
        //*** While value entered is invalid re-enter it ***
        while(number < 0 || number > 100)
        {
            cout << "Invalid entry. Re-enter : ";
            cin >> number;
        }
        //*** If number divisible by 3 or 4 add 1 to total ***
        if(number % 3 == 0 || number % 4 == 0)
            total++;
    }
    //*** Display the total numbers divisible by 3 or 4 ***
    if(total > 0)
        cout << "Number of values divisible by 3 or 4 :"
             << total << '\n';
    else
        cout << "No values are divisible by 3 or 4\n";
}
```

Identifying the Test Requirements

> **TASK 3.18**
>
> Identify all selection and iteration control structures in LISTING-3.2.

We have two iterative and two selection structures in LISTING-3.2 to be tested.

Of these, the `for` structure is fixed to 10 iterations, hence zero and one iteration tests are not possible.

The `while` structure contains multiple conditions and therefore, as well as being tested for zero, one, and multiple iterations, should also be tested for all possible combinations of **true** and **false** within the Boolean expression itself. Note that the combination **true**, **true** is not possible since *number* cannot be both less than zero and greater than 100 at the same time.

There are also two selection structures, both `if`'s.

The first of these also has a complex Boolean expression and this can be tested for all four possibilities.

The second `if` statement is a simple one and needs only **true** and **false** tests.

These test requirements are summarised in TABLE-3.12.

TABLE-3.12

White Box Test Requirements

Structure to be tested	Purpose of test
`for(int count = 1;count<=10;count++)`	Test multiple iterations
`while(number<0||number>100)`	Zero iterations One iteration Multiple iterations true, false false, true false, false
`if(number%3==0||number%4==0)`	false, false false, true true, false true, true
`if(total>0)`	true false

Choosing the Test Data

One data value may test several parts of the code. For example, if we assign the value 21 to *number* then the `while` loop,

```
while(number < 0 || number > 100)
{
     cout << "Invalid entry. Re-enter : ";
     cin >> number;
}
```

will be iterated zero times. Not only does this value perform the zero iterations test, but, since the Boolean expressions

```
    number < 0
and number > 100
```

are both **false** when *number* is 21, this also tests the **false**, **false** combination for the expression `(number<0||number>100)`.

Once the `while` loop has been passed, the `if` statement

```
if(number%3 == 0 || number%4 == 0)
     total++;
```

will be executed. With *number* equal to 21, the first condition, `number % 3 == 0` is **true** while, the second is **false**. Hence another of our test requirements is performed.

Since all of this code is within the `for` loop which is to be executed 10 times, other values must be chosen for *number* during subsequent iterations.

TASK 3.19

Write down a value for *number* which:

a) gives a **true/false** result for `while(number<0||number>100)`
b) gives a **false/false** result for `if(number%3==0||number%4==0)`

We need to continue this process of choosing values until all the required tests will be performed by the data. Each test value, the tests they are designed to perform and the expected results should then be listed in test documentation (see TABLE-3.13).

TABLE-3.13

White Box Test Data

Run	Test Data	Reason for Test	Expected Result	Actual Result
1	number =			
	21	while iterated zero times		
		while false,false		
		if(number%3... true,false	total = 1	
	-6, 5	while iterated once	-6 rejected with error	
		while true,false	message	
		if(number%3... false,false	total unchanged	
	101,-3,8	while iterated more than once	101 and -3 rejected	
		while false,true		
		if(number%3... false,true	total= 2	
	12	if(number%3... true,true	total= 3	
	100		total= 4	
	0		total unchanged	
	1		total unchanged	
	13		total unchanged	
	31		total unchanged	
	17		total unchanged	
		for loop iterated 10 times		
		if(total>0) true	Displays	
			Number of values divisible	
			by 3 or 4 : 4	
2	number =			
	1			
	2			
	5			
	7			
	10			
	11			
	13			
	14			
	17			
	19	if(total>0) false	Displays	
			No values are divisible	
			by 3 or 4.	

There are a few points to note from TABLE-3.13 :

The RUN column refers to the program execution run number. This program will have to be run twice to test both options of the final `if` statement:

```
if(total > 0)
    cout<<"Number of values divisible by 3 or 4 :"<<total<<'\n';
else
    cout<<"No values are divisible by 3 or 4\n";
```

The TEST DATA column gives the values to be used when running the program. In this case, only one variable, *number*, needs to be supplied with a value. Where several variables are to be given values, the name of the variable to which a test value is to be assigned must be clearly stated in this column. Where a single variable is given more than one value on a single line (e.g. 101,-3,8), all but the last of these represent values which will be rejected by the input validation code.

The REASON FOR TEST column states the control structure and condition being tested by that specific test value. Where test data exercises a program condition already tested by an earlier piece of data, it need not be restated as a reason for test.

The EXPECTED RESULTS column states the expected reaction of the program to the data. This may specify the value to be taken by other variables or the output to be produced.

The ACTUAL RESULTS column is completed as the program is run. Hopefully, we may simply add an "as expected" message in this column with a reference to any printout produced during the test. But if the program should produce unexpected results, then this column should contain those results and reference made to other documentation detailing the error and the changes made to the program in attempting to correct that error.

If errors are detected during any test run, then all ealier test runs should be redone after corrections have been made. After all, the corrections may have introduced new errors. Where corrections have introduced new control structures or Boolean expressions, additional test data will have to be added.

PROGRAMMING EXERCISE 3.3

Type in the program in LISTING-3.2 and run it using the test data given in TABLE-3.13.

Debugging

Testing attempts to highlight errors in a program. When errors are discovered, their causes must be determined by examining the code and then changing the faults detected. This is known as **debugging**.

Borland supply several debugging aids to help track down errors in your code. Of these, the simplest and most useful are:

- Single step execution
- Watch facilities
- Breakpoints

Single Step Execution

The debugging features may be activated by different keys in your version of C++. Check your manual for details.

Single stepping allows us to execute a program one line at a time. The program code appears on the screen and the next line to be executed is highlighted. A line of the program is executed each time the F8 key is pressed.

```
#include<iostream.h>
void main()
{
    int total = 0, number;


    for(int count=1;count<=10;count++)
    {
        //***Read valid number ***
        cout<<"Enter number : ";
        cin>>number;
            .
```

Highlight bar showing next line to be executed

This allows us to see which lines of code are being executed and hence allows us to detect when an unexpected route is taken through the program. We may, for example, detect an `if` statement being treated as **true** when we were expecting it to be **false**.

Once the cause of an error has been detected, we can halt execution of the program without running it to completion by choosing the PROGRAM RESET or TERMINATE PROGRAM option.

The Watch Facility

Watches allow us to observe the value of any number of variables as the program executes. Hence we may see the value of *total* as our program counts the number of values divisible by 3 or 4.

The watch feature is switched on using the WATCH option in the DEBUG menu. This may be achieved using *Ctrl F7* or *Ctrl F5* depending on which version of C++ you are using. The debugger prompts you for the name of the variable whose value is to be displayed.

Once chosen, the variable's value will be displayed as you single step your way through the program. Any changes in the variable's value will be indicated instantly in the Watch window.

Any number of variables may be displayed.

Breakpoints

Single stepping through a large program or one containing loop structures can sometimes be awkward and tedious. It may be that the part of the code we wish to step through is several hundreds of lines into the program. To avoid this time-consuming approach, we may set a breakpoint at any line in our program. Having set a breakpoint, we start execution of our program in the normal way However, when the machine attempts to execute the line containing the breakpoint, we are returned to single-step mode at that point in the code.

To set a breakpoint, move the cursor to the line at which the break is required and press *Ctrl F8* or choose the SET BREAKPOINT option in the DEBUG menu.

Breakpoints may be made conditional. That is, they will only operate if a specified condition is **true** at the time the line containing the breakpoint is executed, otherwise the program continues normal execution.

When no longer required, breakpoints must be removed. This is done by returning the cursor to the line containing the breakpoint and again choosing the TOGGLE BREAKPOINT option in the DEBUG menu.

PROGRAMMING EXERCISE 3.4

By placing a watch on *total*, and single-stepping through your program, find and correct the error in the program given in LISTING-3.2.

Does the correction require changes to the test data? If so suggest additional test values, if no additional data is required state why.

Testing in this Book

As you can see, testing even a small piece of code is quite lengthy - and there are more testing techniques to cover yet! This means that, because of a lack of space, test data is generally missing or inadequate throughout this book.

Summary

- **White box testing** is designed to test the control structures in a program.
- **All sections of code** should be executed at least once.
- **All simple conditions** should be tested for both **true** and **false** outcomes.
- **All complex Boolean expressions** should be tested for every possible **true** and **false** combination of the component expressions.
- **All** `if` **statements** should be tested for both **true** and **false** outcomes.
- **Conditional assignment** and other assignments containing Boolean expressions should be tested for both **true** and **false** situations.
- **All** `switch` **statements** should be tested for every specified case option and the `default` option.
- **Iterative structures** should be checked for possible infinite looping before testing begins.
- **All** `for` **statements** should, where possible, be tested for zero, one and multiple iterations.
- **All** `while` loops should be tested for zero, one and multiple iterations.
- **All** `do .. while` **loops** should be tested for one and multiple iterations.
- **The test requirements for the code under test** should be identified and test data created to meet these tests.
- **A single test data value** may check several code situations.
- **The results of test runs** should be documented.
- **Where errors are discovered and corrected**, the changes made to the program code should be documented and all tests redone.

LIFETIME, SCOPE, AND VISIBILITY

Lifetime

A block is the sequence of instructions enclosed between an opening brace and the corresponding closing brace.

A variable is first allocated space in the computer's memory at the moment its definition statement is encountered during program execution. This variable continues to exist until the block in which it was defined is exited, at which point, the memory space is deallocated (the variable is **destroyed**). The time during which a variable exists is known as the **lifetime** of the variable and the variable is said to be **local** to that block. Hence, in the code shown in LISTING-3.3 the variable *no2* exists only between the lines indicated.

LISTING-3.3

Variable Lifetime

```
#include <conio.h>
#include <iostream.h>

void main()
{
   int no1;

   clrscr();
   cout << "Enter a value : ";
   cin >> no1;
   if (no1 > 0 )
   {
         int no2;

         no2 = no1*3
         cout << "no2 is " << no2
   }

   cout << "no1 is " << no1 << '
}
```

no2 created here

no2 destroyed here

PROGRAMMING EXERCISE 3.5

Enter the above program and run it.
Next, add a final line

```
cout<<no2<<'\n';
```

to the code and attempt to recompile the program.

As you can see from your results, attempting to reference a variable outside its block results in a compilation error.

A variable can be recreated if it is defined in a block of code which is re-entered. This can occur in an iterative structure. For example, in LISTING-3.4 the variable *no2* is recreated on each iteration of the `for` loop.

LISTING-3.4

Recreated Variables

```
#include <conio.h>
#include <iostream.h>

void main()
{
   int no1;
```

Continued on next page

LISTING-3.4
(continued)

Recreated Variables

```
    clrscr();
    for (int i=0;i<10;i++)
    {
        cout << "Enter a value ";
        cin >> no1;
        if (no1 > 0 )
        {
            int no2;
            no2 = no1*3;

            cout << "no2 is " << no2 << '\n';
        }
    }
    cout << "no1 is " << no1 << '\n';
}
```

no2 is recreated each time this statement is executed

> **PROGRAMMING EXERCISE 3.6**
>
> Use the debug features to watch *no2* and single-step through the program in LISTING 3.4.

Global Variables

It is also possible to declare a variable outside any block:

no1 defined outside the program block.

```
int no1;

void main()
{
    .
    .
}
```

Such variables are said to be **global** (or **external**) **variables** and are created at the start of program execution and exist until the program terminates.

Automatic Variables

Most variables are created and destroyed automatically during execution; these are known as **automatic variables**. In fact, we may explicitly declare a variable as automatic by preceding the definition with the term `auto`. For example:

```
auto int no1,no2;
```

However, since this is the default option, the term is rarely used.

Static Variables

A variable can also be defined as **static**:

```
static int no1,no2;
```

A **static variable** is created as soon as execution of the program begins, no matter where in the program that variable is defined, and exists until the program terminates.

A static variable has the same lifetime as a global variable.

PROGRAMMING EXERCISE 3.7

Enter the following program

```
#include <conio.h>
#include <iostream.h>

void main()
{
   for(int i = 1;i < 3;i++)
   {
        for(int j = 1;j < 4;j++)
        {
             int sum = 0;
             sum += j;
             cout << "In j loop\n";
             cout << sum << '\n';
        }
        cout << "In i loop block\n";
   }
}
```

1. Run the program and note the values displayed.

2. Change the line

```
int sum = 0;
```

to

```
static int sum=0;
```

and re-run the program, noting the values displayed.

3. After the line

```
cout << "In i loop block\n";
```

add

```
cout << sum << '\n';
```

and recompile the program.

The results from the above task highlight two characteristics of static variables:

- The area of code in which the variable can be accessed is, as with automatic variables, restricted to the block in which it is defined.
- The value of a static variable is retained when the block in which it is defined is exited.

Register Variables

A final possibility when declaring variables, is to request a **register variable** using a statement such as:

```
register int count;
```

While other variables are allocated space in the computer's main memory, register variables may be allocated one of the registers within the processor itself. Since a processor's registers can be accessed much more quickly than main memory, using register variables can result in faster execution of a program.

There are a limited number of registers in any processor, therefore only a very few variables can be allocated such space. The programmer should make requests for a variable to be assigned a register with care: likely candidates are loop counters or variables involved in time-critical processes.

C++ imposes its own restrictions on what variables may be defined as register variables:

- Variables must be of an integer type (`char`, `int`, `unsigned`, etc.).
- Variables must be local.

In addition, declaring a register variable is only a request to use a processor's register; the compiler may decide not to allocate a register if none are available or where it decides its use would be inappropriate.

Scope

The section of a program in which a variable may be accessed is known as the **scope** of the variable. In the case of automatic and global variables the scope and lifetime are identical. However, for static variables these differ, resulting in a lifetime that extends throughout the program, and a scope which is limited to the block in which the variable is defined.

TASK 3.20

Identify the scope and lifetime of the variables in the following code.

```
#include <conio.h>
#include <iostream.h>


void main()
{
   int no;

   clrscr();
   for(int i = 1; i <= 6; i++)
   {
       cout << "Enter number : ";
       cin >> no;
       if(no < 0)
       {
           static int x;
           x = -no;
           cout << x << '\n';
       }
       else
           cout << no;
   }
   getch();
}
```

Visibility

It is quite allowable to have two variables with the same name as long as they are defined in different blocks. If the second variable is defined within the scope of the first, then the first cannot normally be accessed while the second remains in scope. The first variable is not **visible** in this part of the code.

For example, in LISTING-3.5 there are two variables called *sum*. The first of these, defined in the line

```
int readings,sum=0;
```

is in scope throughout the whole program, but is not visible inside the `do` loop after the second *sum* variable is defined. Hence, whereas the line

```
cout<<"Total number of readings so far "<<sum<<'\n';
```

references to the first sum variable, the line

```
cout<<"Running total for this batch is "<<sum<<'\n';
```

is a reference to the second.

LISTING-3.5

Visibility

First *sum* variable visible in this area

First *sum* variable not visible in this area

First *sum* variable visible in this area

```
#include <conio.h>
#include <iostream.h>

void main()
{
    int readings,sum=0;    //*** First variable called sum
    char reply;

    do
    {
        cout << "Enter number of readings in batch ";
        cin >> readings;
        sum+=readings;
        cout<<"Total number of readings so far "<<sum<<'\n';
        int sum=0;              //*** Second variable called sum
        for(int i=1;i<=readings;i++)
        {
            int value;
            cout << "Enter value of reading "<<i<<' ';
            cin>>value;
            sum+=value;
            cout<<"Running total for this batch is "<<sum<<'\n';
        }
        cout<<"Any more batches? (Y/N) ";
        cin>>reply;
    }
    while (reply!='N');
}
```

The Scope Resolution Operator (: :)

When a global variable has the same name as a local variable, as in

```
int no;
void main()
{
    int no;
```

any reference to *no* in `main()` will give access to the local variable. However, the global one can be accessed by prefixing the variable name by the symbol :: (known as the **scope resolution operator**). Hence

```
::no = 12;
```

gives access to the global variable.

Of course, it is bad practice to allocate the same name to different variables in any circumstances but this may happen when several programmers are working on a project at the same time.

Summary

- **Local variables** have a lifetime extending from the point at which they are defined to the end of the block in which they are defined.
- **Global** (or **external**) **variables** have a lifetime from start to end of the program.
- **Automatic variables** are created and destroyed automatically during program execution.
- **Static variables** are created at the start of program execution irrespective of where they are defined within the program. The word `static` must be used when defining such variables.
- **The lifetime** of a variable defines the section of a program for which memory space is allocated to that variable.

  For automatic variables, this will be from the statement in which it is defined to the end of that block.

  For static this will be from start of execution until program termination.
- **A variable may be reincarnated** if the block in which it is defined is re-entered.
- **The scope** of a variable defines the area of code in which it may, theoretically, be accessed. This is from definition point to the end of the definition block.
- **Visibility** defines the area of code in which a variable may be accessed. This is usually identical to scope unless two (or more) variables of the same name are in scope, in which case only the most-recently defined variable is visible.
- **Register variables** may be allocated a register within the processor rather than an area in main memory.
- **Register variables must be an integer type and local.**
- **A register variable is allocated a processor register** at the discretion of the compiler.
- **Processor registers** can be accessed more quickly than main memory locations.
- The **scope resolution operator** (::) allows access to global variables which are otherwise hidden by local variables of the same name.

CASE STUDY

The Problem

A program is required to allow the computer to be used as a simple calculator. The user should be able to enter simple expressions such as 10.1 * 10 and see the result displayed in the form *10.1*10=101.0* .

Clarification

The program need only solve expressions with a single arithmetic operator. Any of the following may be used:

+	Addition
-	Subtraction
*	Multiplication
/	Division

Any other character entered as the operator should result in an error message being displayed.

Attempting division by zero should also result in an error message being displayed.

The program should continue to accept expressions until specifically terminated.

The Algorithm

We begin with an overview of the solution:

```
1   Get expression
2   WHILE not terminating expression DO
3       Attempt to process expression
4       IF valid expression THEN
5           Display result
6       ENDIF
7       Get expression
8   ENDWHILE
```

These can then be expanded to give sufficient detail to produce the program code:

```
1   Get expression
    1.1 Clear screen
    1.2 Display prompt
    1.3 Get expression (value1 operator value2)

3   Attempt to process expression
    3.1 IF
    3.2     operator is +:
    3.3         Calculate result as value1 + value2
    3.4     operator is -:
    3.5         Calculate result as value1 - value2
    3.6     operator is *:
    3.7         Calculate result as value1 * value2
    3.8     operator is /:
    3.9         IF value2 isn't zero THEN
    3.10            Calculate result as value1 / value2
    3.11        ELSE
    3.12            Display "Divide by zero error"
    3.13        ENDIF
```

```
    3.14    ELSE
    3.15        Display "Invalid operator"
    3.16 ENDIF

7   Get expression
    7.1 Display prompt
    7.2 Get expression (value1 operator value2)
```

This gives us a final version of the logic from which to produce code:

```
1.1 Clear screen
1.2 Display prompt
1.3 Get expression (value1 operator value2)
2   WHILE not terminating expression DO
3.1     IF
3.2         operator is +:
3.3             Calculate result as value1 + value2
3.4         operator is -:
3.5             Calculate result as value1 - value2
3.6         operator is *:
3.7             Calculate result as value1 * value2
3.8         operator is /:
3.9             IF value2 isn't zero THEN
3.10                Calculate result as value1 / value2
3.11            ELSE
3.12                Display "Divide by zero error"
3.13            ENDIF
3.14        ELSE
3.15            Display "Invalid operator"
3.16    ENDIF
4       IF valid expression THEN
5           Display result
6       ENDIF
7.1     Display prompt
7.2     Get expression (value1 operator value2)
8   ENDWHILE
```

The Program

LISTING 3.6

The Calculator Program

```
// *********************************************************
// * PROGRAM      : Calculator                             *
// * AUTHOR       : Patricia Stamp                         *
// * DATE         : 7/10/94                                *
// * VERSION      : 0.1                                    *
// * DESCRIPTION  : Calculates the results of single       *
// *                operator expressions                   *
// * HARDWARE     : PC Compatible                          *
// * SOURCE       : Turbo C++ v4.0                         *
// *********************************************************

#include <iostream.h>
#include <conio.h>

void main()
{
   float value1,value2;  // *** Values used in expression
   char op;              // *** Expression operator
   float result;         // *** Result of expression
   int valid;            // *** Indicates validity of expression
                         //   0 - invalid
                         //   1 - valid
```

Continued on next page

LISTING 3.6
(continued)

The Calculator Program

The terminating value (-9999) must be agreed and documented.

Note that the program code differs from the design in that 'x' is accepted as an alternative to '*'. This is only acceptable if agreed with the customer and fully documented.

```
    // *** Get expression ***
    clrscr();
    cout << "OPERATIONS AVAILABLE\n";
    cout << "\n\n+\tAddition\n";
    cout << "-\tSubtraction\n";
    cout << "*\tMultiplication\n";
    cout << "/\tDivision\n";
    cout << " Set first value to -9999 to terminate program\n\n";
    cout << "Enter expression (value operator value): ";
    cin >> value1 >> op >> value2;

    // *** While not terminating value process expression ***
    while (value1 != -9999)
    {
         // *** Assume operation valid ***
         valid = 1;
         // *** Perform appropriate arithmetic calculation ***
         switch (op)
         {
              case '+':
                   result = value1 + value2;
                   break;
              case '-':
                   result = value1 - value2;
                   break;
              case '*':
              case 'x':
                   result = value1 * value2;
                   break;
              case '/':
                   // *** If the second value is zero division not ***
                   // *** allowed and operation is invalid         ***
                   if (!value2)
                   {
                        cout << "Division by zero not allowed\n";
                        valid = 0;
                   }
                   else
                        result = value1/value2;
                   break;
              default:
                   // *** Error message if operator invalid ***
                   cout << "Invalid operator\n";
                   valid = 0;
         }
         // *** If valid input then display result ***
         if(valid)
              cout<<value1 << op << value2 << "=" << result;

         // *** Enter next expression ***
         cout << "\n\nEnter expression : ";
         cin  >> value1 >> op >> value2;
    }
}
```

Testing

By examining the program code we can identify several control structures:

```
while (value1 != -9999)
case '+':
case '-':
case '*':
case 'x':
case '/':
if(!value2)
default:
if(valid)
```

To test the program we'll need to:

Execute the `while` loop zero, one and multiple times
Execute each `case` option and the `default` option in the `switch` statement
Execute each `if` statement for both **true** and **false** situations.

The test data is shown in TABLE-3.14.

TABLE 3.14

Test Data

Run	Test Data	Reason for Test	Expected Result	Actual Result
1	value1 = -9999 op = '+' value2 = 0	while iterated zero times	Program terminates	
2	value1 = 6 op = '+' value2 = 3 value1 = -9999 op = '*' value2 = 0	while iterated one time case '+': if(valid), true	6+3 = 9 Program terminates	

3	value1 = 7
	op = '-'
	value2 = 12
	value1 = 9
	op = '/'
	value2 = 2
	value1 = 7
	op = '/'
	value2 = 0
	value1 = 8
	op = '*'
	value2 = 2
	value1 = 3
	op = 'x'
	value2 = -6
	value1 = 8
	op = '?'
	value2 = 1
	value1 = -9999
		while iterated more than once
		case '-':
		
		case '/':
		if(!value2), false
		
		if(!value2), true
		if(valid), false
		case '*':
		
		case 'x':
		
		default:
		if(valid), false
			7-12 = -5
			
			9/2 = 4.5
			
			Displays
			Division by zero not allowed
			
			8*2 = 16
			
			3*-6 = -18
			
			Displays
			Invalid operator	

PROGRAMMING EXERCISE 3.8

Enter and run the LISTING 3.6 using the above test data.

Problems

When using values containing fractions, the results may be slightly out because of the inaccuracy that is unavoidable when storing real numbers in binary.

Also, the method of terminating the program is somewhat clumsy, but is not easily avoided at this stage.

INVESTIGATION

1. What effect does placing a semi-colon at the end of the first line of an `if`, `while` or `for` loop have on the execution of code?

2. When the instruction

```
no1 =  (no2 < 0) ? a++ : b++;
```

is executed, are both *a* and *b* incremented or only the one used in assigning a value to *no1*?

3. What effect does placing an Boolean expression in a case option have on a program. For example:

```
switch()
{
    case no < 0:  .....
```

4. Can the scope opertor (::) be used to access a variable contained in a higher level block. For example:

```
{
    int no1
        .
    {
        int no1;
            .
        ::no1 = ....    //Is this allowed? If so, does it
                        // reference the outer no1?
```

5. Can a `for` loop use character constants as start and finish values? For example:

```
for(char c = 'A';c <= 'Z'; c++)
```

6. If nested `if` statements exist within a loop structure, will a `break` statement in the inner-most `if` jump control to the end of the outer `if` or the end of the loop structure? For example:

```
for(int c = 1 ; c<=10;c++)
{
    if (c >= 4 && c <= 8)
    {
        cout << c << '\n';
        if(c == 6)
            break;
    }                   // Control jumps to here
}                       // or here
```

SELF-ASSESSMENT REVIEW

1. What numeric values are considered to be:
   a) **false**
   b) **true**

   when an expression is evaluated?

2. What is the final value of the following expression?
```
(no=5||a==no&&no<0)
```

3. What value is output by the following statement?
```
if(0.5)
    cout<<"TRUE\n";
else
    cout<<"FALSE\n";
```

4. What is the output from
```
if(no1=0,no2=3,no1==no2,no1++)
    cout << no1;
else
    cout << no2;
```

5. Write the Structure English equivalent of
```
while(cout<<"Enter no : ",cin>>no,no<0)
    cout<<"Invalid. Please re-enter.\n"
```

6. What is the effect of the following code?
```
loop:
    cout << "hello\n";
    goto loop;
```

THE HENLEY COLLEGE LIBRARY

Solutions

TASK 3.1

```
2. let1 = let2
```

An assignment statement

TASK 3.2

All statements are valid

TASK 3.3

True 2

TASK 3.4

```
1. if(weight > 16)
2. if(code != 17850)
3. if(mark >= 75 && mark <= 85)
4. if(option == 'C' && key == masterkey)
5. if((command == 'D' || command == 'A') &&
   quantity > 100)
```

TASK 3.5

1. 1
2. 0
3. 0
4. 1

TASK 3.6

1. ans = 6
2. ans = 0
3. Invalid
4. ans = 0
5. ans = 1
6. ans = 0
7. ans = 0
8. ans = 1
9. ans = 0
10. no1 = 0

TASK 3.7

```
if(sex=='M')
    if(age >=65)
        cout << "Retired male\n";
    else
        cout <<"Working male\n";
else
    if(age(>=60)
        cout << "Retired female\n";
    else
        cout << "Working female\n";
```

PROGRAMMING EXERCISE 3.1

```
1.
#include <iostream.h>
#include <conio.h>
void main()
{
    int no;

    cout << "Enter number : ";
    cin >> no;
    if (no<0)
        cout << "Negative\n";
    else
        cout << "Positive\n";
}
```

```
2.
#include <iostream.h>
#include <conio.h>

void main()
{
    float rno1, rno2;
    float result;

    clrscr();
    cout<<"Enter two numbers : ";
    cin >> rno1>>rno2;
    if (rno2)
    {
        result = rno1/rno2;
        cout<<rno1<<'/'<<rno2<<"="<<result<<endl;
    }
}
```

```
3.
#include <iostream.h>
#include <conio.h>

void main()
{
    char letter;

    clrscr();
    cout<<"Enter a character : ";
    cin >> letter;
    if (letter == 'A'||letter=='E'
    ||letter=='I'||letter=='O'||letter=='U')
        cout << "Vowel\n";
    else
        cout << "Consonant\n";
}
```

```
4.
#include <iostream.h>
#include <conio.h>

void main()
{
    int no1,no2;

    clrscr();
    cout<<"Enter two numbers : ";
    cin >> no1 >> no2;
    if (no1 < no2)
        cout << no1;
    else
        if (no2 < no1)
            cout << no2;
        else
            cout << "Equal\n";
}
```

```
5.
#include <iostream.h>
#include <conio.h>

void main()
{
    int day,month,year;
    int M,CY,C,Y,temp,d;

    //*** Clear screen ***
    clrscr();
    //*** Get date ***
    cout<<"Enter date (dd mm yyyy) : ";
    cin>>day>>month>>year;
    //***Determine modified version of date ***
    M = (month+9)%12+1;
    CY = year-M/11;
    C  = CY/100;
    Y  = CY%100;
    temp = 2.6*M-0.2;
    d = ((temp+day+Y+Y/4+C/4-2*C)%7+7)%7;
    //*** Display result ***
    cout<<day<<'/'<<month<<'/'<<year<<" is a ";
    if(d == 0)
        cout << "Sunday\n";
    else if(d == 1)
        cout << "Monday\n";
    else if(d == 2)
        cout << "Tuesday\n";
    else if(d == 3)
        cout << "Wednesday\n";
```

Continued on next page

PROGRAMMING EXERCISE 3.1 (continued)

```
        else if(d == 4)
            cout << "Thursday\n";
        else id(d == 5)
            cout << "Friday\n";
        else if(d == 6)
            cout << "Saturday\n";
        }
}

6.
#include <iostream.h>
#include <conio.h>

void main()
{
    int day,month,year;
    int k,a,b,c,q,p,m,d,n,e;

    clrscr();
    cout << "Enter year : ";
    cin >> year;
    k = year/100;
    a = year % 19;
    b = year % 4;
    c = year % 7;
    q = k/4;
    p = (13+8*k)/25;
    m = (15*p+k+q)%30;
    d = (19*a+m)%30;
    n = (4+k-q)%7;
    e = (2*b+4*c+6*d+n)%7;
    if ((d+e) <= 9)
    {
        day = 22+d+e;
        month = 3;
    }
    else if (d==29 && e==6)
    {
        day = 19;
        month = 4;
    }
    else if (d==28 && e==6 && a > 10)
    {
        day = 18;
        month = 4;
    }
    else
    {
        day = d+e-9;
        month = 4;
    }
    cout << "Easter Sunday falls on "
         <<day<<'/'<<month<<'/'<<year;
}
```

TASK 3.8

```
c = (no <0)? -c : c+1;
```

TASK 3.9

RETURNED
INVALID CODE

TASK 3.10

```
#include <iostream.h>
#include <conio.h>

void main()
{
    int no;
    char base;

    cout << "Enter number and base (nnnb) : ";
    cin >> no >> base;
    switch(base)
    {
        case 'o':
        case 'O':
            cout << oct<<no<< " in octal\n"<<dec;
            break;
        case 'h':
        case 'H':
            cout << hex<<no<<" in hexadecimal\n"
                 <<dec;
            break;
        case 'd':
        case 'D':
            cout <<no<<"in decimal\n";
            break;
        default:
            cout << "Invalid letter;
    }
}
```

TASK 3.11

```
cout << "Enter first value : ";
cin >> previousvalue;
cout << "Enter next value : ";
cin >> currentvalue;
while (previousvalue != currentvalue)
{
    previousvalue = currentvalue;
    cout << "Enter next value : ";
    cin >> currentvalue;
}
```

TASK 3.12

0
1
2
3
4

TASK 3.13

```
int count = 0,sum=0,no;
.
.
for(;count<10;)
{
    cout << "Enter number : ";
    cin >> no;
    if (no < 0)
        continue;
    sum+=no;
    count++;
}
```

TASK 3.14

-2,0
-2,3
-2,6
-1,0
-1,3
-1,6
0,0
0,3
0,6
1,0
1,3
1,6

TASK 3.15

10

PROGRAMMING EXERCISE 3.2

1.
```
#include <iostream.h>
#include <conio.h>

void main()
{
    clrscr();
    cout << "The following numbers between 1 "
        "and 20 are not divisible by 4 or 5\n\n\n";
    for(int no = 1;no<=20;no++)
        if(no%4!=0&&no%5!=0)
            cout << no<<'\n';
}
```

2.
```
#include <iostream.h>
#include <conio.h>
#include <iomanip.h>

void main()
{
    int column,row;

    clrscr();
    while(cout << "Enter column : ",
    cin >> column,(column<1||column>80))
        cout << "Invalid column. Must be between"
            " 1 and 80. Please re-enter.\n";
    while(cout << "Enter row : ",
     cin >> row,(row<1||row>25))
        cout << "Invalid row. Must be between"
            " 1 and 25. Please re-enter.\n";
    clrscr();
    for(int i = 1;i<row;i++)
        cout << '\n';
    cout << setw(column)<<'x';
}
```

3.
```
#include <iostream.h>
#include <conio.h>

void main()
{
    long int sum=0,no;

    clrscr();
    cout << "Enter number : ";
    cin >> no;
    while(no)
    {
        sum+=no%1000;
        no/=1000;
    }
    if (sum % 37 == 0)
        cout << "Value divisible by 37\n";
    else
        cout << "Value not divisible by 37\n";
}
```

4.
```
#include <iostream.h>
#include <conio.h>

void main()
{
    int n,r;
    double factorialn=1,factorialr=1,factorialnr=1;
    double NoOfWays;

    clrscr();
    while (
            cout << "Enter number of objects : ",
            cin >> n,
            cout << "Enter number of objects to be "
                "chosen : ",
            cin >> r,
            r>n
        )
        cout << "Number chosen cannot be greater"
            " than number of objects\n";
    for(int i = 2;i<=n;factorialn*=i,i++);
    for(i=2;i<=r;factorialr*=i,i++);
    for(i=2;i<=(n-r);factorialnr*=i,i++);
    NoOfWays = factorialn/(factorialnr*factorialr);
    cout<< r<<" objects can be chosen from "<<n
        <<" objects in "<<NoOfWays<<" ways\n";
}
```

5.
```
#include <iostream.h>
#include <conio.h>
#include <iomanip.h>

void main()
{
    float score,highest,lowest,total,average;
    int judges,count;

    clrscr();
    cout << "Enter number of judges : ";
    cin >> judges;
    cout << "Enter score : ";
    cin >> score;
    highest = score;
    lowest = score;
    total = score;
    for(count = 2; count <= judges; count++)
    {
        cout << "Enter next score : ";
        cin >> score;
        total+=score;
        if (score < lowest)
            lowest = score;
        else if (score > highest)
            highest = score;
    }
    average  = (total-highest-lowest)/(judges-2);
    cout << "Overall score : "
    <<setprecision(2)<<average<<'\n';
}
```

6.
```
#include <iostream.h>
#include <conio.h

void main()
{
    double N,oldx,newx;

    clrscr();
    cout << "Enter value : ";
    cin >> N;
    newx = N/3;
    do
    {
        oldx = newx;
        newx = (N/(oldx*oldx)+2*oldx)/3;
    }
    while (N-newx*newx*newx >0.000005 ||
    newx*newx*newx-N > 0.000005);
    cout << "The cube root of " << N << " is "
        << newx << endl;
}
```

7.
```
#include <iostream.h>
#include <conio.h>
#include <iomanip.h>

void main()
{
    int day,month,year,M,CY,C,Y,temp,d,i,daysinmonth;
    char ch1,ch2;
    // *** Clear screen ***
    clrscr();
    // *** Get date ***
    cout << "Please enter a date in the form"
        " dd/mm/yyyy : ";
    cin >>day>>ch1>>month>>ch2>>year;
    //*** Change to first day of month ***
    day = 1;
    // *** Determine modified version of date ***
    M = (month+9) % 12 + 1;
    CY = year - M/11;
    C = CY/100;
    Y = CY%100;
    // *** Determine day of week ***
    temp = 2.6*M-0.2;
    d = ((temp + day + Y + Y/4 + C/4 - 2*C)%7+7)%7;
    // *** Calc  days in month ***
    if ( month==1||month==3||month==5||month==7||
      month==8||month==10||month==12)
        daysinmonth = 31;
    else if (month==2)
        daysinmonth = 28+(year%4==0);
        // *** Accurate between 1901 and 2099
    else
        daysinmonth = 30;
    // *** Print calendar ***
    cout <<"   Sun "<<" Mon "<<" Tue "<<" Wed "
        <<" Thu "<<" Fri "<<" Sat\n";
    // *** Print calendar ***
    // * Display day one at correct position *
```

```
        cout << setw(5+5*d)<<day++;
        // * Display remainder of first line *
        for(i=1;i< 7-d;i++)
            cout << setw(5)<<day++;
        cout<<'\n';
        // * Display other lines *
        for(i=1;day<=daysinmonth;i++,day++)
        {
            cout<<setw(5)<<day;
            if(i%7==0)
                cout<<'\n';
        }
    }
```

TASK 3.16

1.
The expressions used in the code are:
sex == 'M'
age >= 65
age >= 60

2.
Since there are three expressions in the code, the possible combinations are:

sex == 'M'	age >= 65	age >= 60
false	false	false
false	false	true
false	true	false
false	true	true
true	false	false
true	false	true
true	true	false
true	true	true

giving a total of 8 possibilities.

3.
Not all combinations are possible. For example, age >= 65 cannot be true when age >= 60 is false. This leaves us with the following combination:

sex == 'M'	age >= 65	age >= 60
false	false	false
false	false	true
false	true	true
true	false	false
true	false	true
true	true	true

These 6 combinations test all paths in the code.

TASK 3.17

1. *total* is zeroised within the `for` loop.

2. c). *total* will be reset to zero before each input.

TASK 3.18

```
for(int count=1;count<=10;count++)
while(number<0||number>100)
if(number%3==0||number%4==0)
if(total>0)
```

TASK 3.19

a) Any value less than zero. e.g. -5
b) Any positive value under 101 which is not divisible by 3 or 4. e.g. 7

PROGRAMMING EXERCISE 3.4

To ensure that zero is not considered to be a value which is divisible by 3 or 4 we need to change the first if statement to

```
if((number%3==0||number%4==0)&&number != 0)
```

Test data changes are required. With three expressions there are nine possible combinations. Some of these cannot occur. For example, **false/false/false** would mean that *number* gives a remainder when divided by 3 or 4 and is zero which is a contradiction.

Possible combinations	Possible value
false/false/true	1
false/true/true	4
true/false/true	3
true/true/false	0
true/true/true	12

TASK 3.20

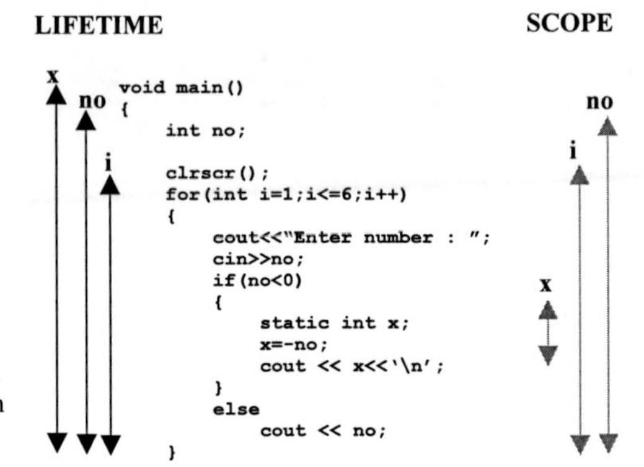
LIFETIME
SCOPE
x
no
i
no
i
x
void main()
{
int no;
clrscr();
for(int i=1;i<=6;i++)
{
cout<<"Enter number : ";
cin>>no;
if(no<0)
{
static int x;
x=-no;
cout << x<<'\n';
}
else
cout << no;
}
}

CHAPTER 4

Functions

This chapter covers the following topics:

- Calling Functions
- Default Parameters
- Function Declaration
- Function Definition
- Function Overloading
- Function Parameters
- Inline Functions
- Returning Values from a Function
- Standard Functions
- Structure Diagrams
- Test Drivers
- User Defined Functions

STANDARD FUNCTIONS

What are Functions?

Functions in Mathematics

Anyone with a basic knowledge of mathematics will have come across functions. For example, a typical statement in trigonometry might be:

$$x = \cos(75)$$

This equation uses the function *cos* which calculates the cosine of an angle. The angle, in this case 75°, is known as the **argument** of the function. Mathematical functions act on the argument to produce a **result**. In the example above, the function *cos* produces the cosine of 75° which happens to be 0.25882.

We may interpret the equation

$$x = \cos(75)$$

as short-hand for

x is equal to the cosine of 75°.

Functions in C++

In this text C++ functions are identified by including parentheses after the function name. This makes it easy to differentiate variable names from function names.

In C++, a function is a separate piece of code which performs some specific action. Every function has an identifying name and zero or more arguments. Not all functions need return a result.

C++ contains a function called `cos()` for calculating the cosine of an angle (given in radians rather than degrees). The program in LISTING-4.1 reads in an angle in radians and displays the cosine of that angle.

LISTING-4.1

Using a Function

```
#include <iostream.h>
#include <math.h>
#include <conio.h>



void main()
{
   double angle, answer;

   // *** Get angle ***
   clrscr();
   cout << "\nEnter angle in radians : ";
   cin >> angle;

   // *** Call function and assign value returned to answer ***
   answer = cos(angle);

   // *** Display results ***
   cout << "\nAngle of " << angle << " radians has cosine of "
        << answer << endl;
}
```

An Explanation of the Code

`#include <math.h>` — Before any function can be used the header file containing the information about that function must be included in the program. The header file *math.h* contains these details for the function `cos()`.

`answer = cos(angle);` — Calls the function `cos()` and supplies it with the value, *angle*. The result returned by the function is assigned to the variable *answer*.

Using Functions

Declaring Functions

Header files contain the **function prototypes** of routines such as `cos()`. A function prototype gives the name of a function, the types of any arguments to be supplied to the function and the type of value returned by the function. The function prototype for `cos()` is shown in FIG-4.1.

FIG-4.1

Function prototype for *cos()*

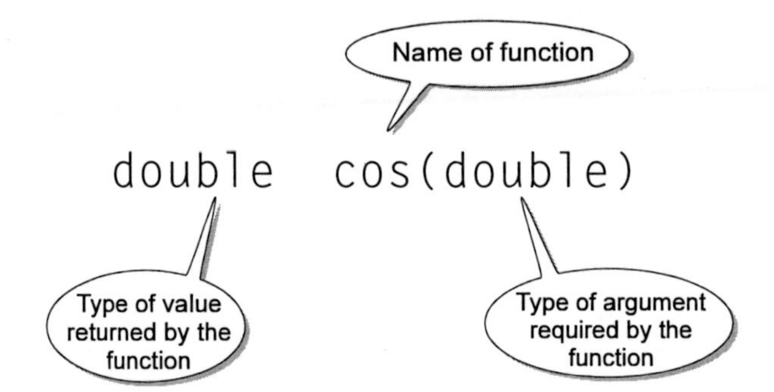

Many header files are supplied with C++, each containing prototypes for related functions. For example, unsurprisingly, *math.h* (used in LISTING-4.1) contains the prototypes for the mathematical functions.

By including the function prototype in a program, we are declaring the syntax of the function and allowing the compiler to check the validity of any subsequent function calls in our program code.

If the header file were to be omitted from the program, the compiler would fail to recognise the call to function `cos()` in the program and an error message would be issued.

Calling Functions

The argument of a function, as well as being a constant, can be a variable or an expression. This allows expressions such as

```
cos(no);
```

and

```
cos(no*3-0.6);
```

Where the argument is not a constant, C++ will evaluate the variable or expression involved and use the resulting value as the argument passed to the function.

The value returned by a function can be assigned to any variable allowing statements such as:

These statements assume the appropriate variables have been declared.

```
y = cos(x);
```
and
```
ans = cos(0.5);
```

A function call may be placed anywhere in a program that it would be appropriate to place a constant of the type returned by that function. Therefore, it is quite acceptable to write

```
cout << cos(1.6);
```

since a `double` constant at that point (e.g. `cout << -0.029`) would be valid.

This means statements such as

```
if (cos(angle) < 0.4) ...
```
and
```
y = (angle < 1.57)?cos(angle):-cos(angle);
```

are legal instructions.

C++ makes calling a function even easier. As with assignment statements, it will, before calling the function, perform automatic type conversion on any arguments which are not of the type required by the function . Hence we may write a statement such as

```
cout<<cos(1);
```

and the integer argument will automatically be converted to a `double` before being used as the argument in the call to `cos()`.

Similarly, return values will be converted to match the type of the receiving variable.

Arguments and Return Values

We have already used other functions in previous chapters. In fact, LISTING-4.1 contains a call to another function - `clrscr()`.

This function differs from `cos()` in that it has no arguments. Where a function has no arguments, the parentheses are nevertheless retained. This allows the compiler to differentiate between function calls and variable names. Also, `clrscr()` does not return any value, since its purpose is to clear the screen rather than perform some calculation.

To indicate that a function returns no value, the term `void` is used in the prototype. Where there are no arguments, again the term `void` may be used or alternatively the parentheses may simply be left empty. Hence, the prototype for `clrscr()` can be written as:

```
void clrscr(void)
```
or
```
void clrscr()
```

When a function returns no value it may be called as a separate instruction rather than as part of some other command. The contrast can be seen in LISTING-4.1 in the lines:

```
clrscr();   // Calls a function which does not return a value
```
and
```
answer = cos(angle); // Calls a function which returns a value
```

The call to `clrscr()` is on a line by itself while the call to `cos()` (which returns a value) is performed as part of an assignment statement.

Some functions have several arguments. One of these is `pow()` whose prototype is

```
double pow(double,double)
```

In order to explain the purpose of a function such as `pow()`, it is often useful to give names to the function arguments in the prototype. Hence we may write the prototype of `pow()` as

```
double pow(double x,double y)
```

and then use these names in the function's description:

The purpose of the function `pow()` *is to return the value* x^y.

While some functions can accept any value, others take a restricted range of values. For example, the function `cos()` will calculate the cosine of any `double` value, whereas `pow()`, whose arguments are also defined as type `double`, will fail if the values of *x* and *y* are both zero or where *y* is a value containing a fraction and *x* is negative (e.g. $-6.1^{3.5}$). Hence, in describing a function we must specify the conditions which the arguments must meet for that function to perform correctly. In the case of `pow()` this condition would be

x and y are not both zero AND if x is negative, y is a whole number

This is known as the **pre-condition** of the function. Where the function can accept any value (as with `cos()`), the pre-condition is simply written as **none.**

The following sections describe some of the routines available in Borland's TURBO C++ compiler. Each entry gives the prototype of the function and the header file in which the prototype is located. This is followed by the pre-condition placed on the arguments of the function, a description of the purpose of the function, and an example of it in use.

Mathematical Functions

The following are some of the mathematical functions available. For a full list consult your Borland C++ Library manual.

Prototype : `int abs(int x)` **Header** : stdlib.h
Pre-condition: None

Description : Returns the absolute value of *x*.

Example :

```
cout << abs(-6);            // Displays 6

difference = abs(x-y);      // Absolute difference
                            // between x and y
```

Prototype : `double acos(double x)` **Header** : math.h
Pre-condition: -1 <= x <= 1

Description : Returns the angle (in radians) for which x is the cosine. The value returned will be in the range 0 to π.

Example : `y = acos(cosine);`

Prototype : `double asin(double x)` **Header** : math.h
Pre-condition: -1 <= x <=1

Description : Returns the angle (in radians) for which x is the sine. Returns a value in the range -π/2 and π/2.

Example : `ans = asin(0.9);`

Prototype : `double atan(double x)` **Header** : math.h
Pre-condition: None

Description : Returns the angle (in radians) for which x is the tangent. Returns a value in the range -π/2 to π/2.

Example : `cout <<atan(1.2);`

Prototype : `double atan2(double x, double y)` **Header** : math.h
Pre-condition: y <> 0

Description : Returns the angle (in radians) for which x/y is the tangent. Returns a value in the range -π to π.

Example : `ans = atan2(3.1/2.5);`

Prototype : `double cos(double x)` **Header** : math.h
Pre-condition: None

Description : Returns the cosine of angle x (given in radians). Returns a value in the range -1 to 1.

Example : `cout << cos(0.73);`

Prototype : `double exp(double x)` **Header** : math.h
Pre-condition: None

Description : Returns e^x.

Example : `cout << exp(-0.68);`

Prototype : `double floor(double x)` **Header** : math.h
Pre-condition: None

Description : Returns the largest whole number not greater than *x*.

Example :

```
ans = floor(12.9);     // returns 12
ans = floor(-12.9);    // returns -13
```

Prototype : `double log(double x)` **Header** : math.h
Pre-condition: $x > 0$

Description : Returns the natural log of *x*.

Example :

```
result = log(rno);
```

Prototype : `double log10(double x)` **Header** : math.h
Pre-condition: $x > 0$

Description : Returns $\log_{10} x$

Example :

```
cout << log10(1.5);
```

Prototype : `double pow(double x, double y)` **Header** : math.h
Pre-condition: *x* and *y* must not both be zero AND if *x* is negative, *y* is an integer.

Description : Returns x^y

Example :

```
result = pow(1.2,0.6);
```

Prototype : `double pow10(double x)` **Header** : math.h
Pre-condition: None

Description : Returns 10^x.

Example :

```
cout << pow10(3.5);
```

Prototype : `int random(int x)` **Header** : stdlib.h
Pre-condition: None

Description : Returns a random number between zero and *x*-1 which is generated by the computer.

This function is normally used only after a call to the function `randomize()` which seeds the algorithm used by `random()` to generate values.

Example :

```
diethrow = random(6)+1;
```

Prototype : `void randomize(void)` **Header** : stdlib.h
Pre-condition: None

Description : Initialises the random number generator. This command should be used before calling the `random()` function, otherwise the program using `random()` will generate the same sequence of values each time the program is executed.

Example :

```
randomize(); // Initialise random number
             // generator before using
             // random()
dart = random(20)+1;
```

Prototype : `double sin(double x);` **Header** : math.h
Pre-condition: None

Description : Returns the sine of angle *x* (given in radians).

Example :

```
cout <<sin(0.11);
```

Prototype : `double sqrt(double x)` **Header** : math.h
Pre-condition: $x >= 0$

Description : Returns the square root of *x*.

Example :

```
cout << sqrt(no);

hypotenuse = sqrt(side1*side1 + side2*side2);
```

Prototype : `double tan(double x)` **Header** : math.h
Pre-condition: None

Description : Returns the tangent of angle *x* (given in radians).

Example :

```
tangent = tan(angle);
```

Using Maths Functions

The following programs illustrate the use of mathematical functions:

LISTING-4.2 lists the sine, cosine and tangent of all angles between 0° and 90°.

Program Logic:

```
Display headings
FOR angle := 0 TO 90 DO
    Convert angle to radians
    Display the sine, cosine and tangent of the angle
ENDFOR
```

Program Code:

LISTING-4.2

Angle Table

```
#include <iostream.h>
#include <conio.h>
#include <iomanip.h>
#include <math.h>

void main()
{
  double radians;

  // *** Display column headings ***
  clrscr();
  cout << "Angle (degrees)" << "    Sine   " << "  Cosine   "
       << " Tangent\n";

  // *** FOR each 5 degrees DO ***
  for (int angle=0;angle<=90;angle+=5)
  {
      // ** Convert to radians **
      radians = angle*3.1415/180;
      // ** Display sine, cosine and tangent of angle **
      cout     << setw(5) << angle<<setw(7) << " "
               << setw(10) << setprecision(2) << sin(radians)
               << setw(10) << setprecision(2) << cos(radians)
               << setw(10) << setprecision(2) << tan(radians)
               << '\n';
  }
}
```

The second program (LISTING-4.3) generates a number between 1 and 200 using `random()`, and allows the user up to seven guesses to determine the value of the number generated.

Program Logic:

```
Generate number
Issue prompt
FOR up to 7 guesses DO
    Get guess
    IF guess is correct THEN
        Display winning message
        terminate FOR loop
    ELSE
        IF guess is too low THEN
            Display "TOO LOW"
        ELSE
            Display "TOO HIGH"
        ENDIF
    ENDIF
ENDFOR
IF the number wasn't guessed THEN
    Display failure message and value of number
ENDIF
```

Program Code:

LISTING-4.3

Guessing Random Number

```
#include <iostream.h>
#include <conio.h>
#include <iomanip.h>
#include <stdlib.h>
```

Continued on next page

LISTING-4.3
(continued)

Guessing Random Number

```
void main()
{
   int guess,number;

   // *** Generate number ***
   randomize();
   number = random(200)+1;
   // *** Issue prompt ***
   clrscr();
   cout << "GUESS NUMBER between 1 and 200\n\n";
   // *** For up to seven times DO ***
   for(int made = 1;made <= 7;made++)
   {
        // ** Get guess **
        cout << "Enter your guess : ";
        cin >> guess;
        // ** If guess is correct issue message and quit **
        if (guess == number)
        {
             cout << "Correct after " << made << " guesses.\n";
             break;
        }
        // ** If guess wrong issue TOO HIGH or TOO LOW message **
        if (guess < number)
             cout << "Too low\n";
        else
             cout << "Too high\n";
   }
   // *** If all guesses wrong give message and original value ***
   if (guess != number)
        cout << "You failed to guess the number.
                  Number was " << number << '\n';
}
```

PROGRAMMING EXERCISE 4.1

1. Write the code necessary to display the square root of all integer values between 1 and 20 inclusive.

2. Write a program to generate and display six numbers between 1 and 49.

Console Input/Output

Streams are dealt with in detail in a later chapter.

The C++ language treats all I/O as data coming from or going to a **stream**. Although the details of this concept are covered in a later chapter, it is appropriate to define a few relevant terms at this point.

Normally input is taken from a stream known as **stdin** (short for *standard in*). By default, this stream is linked to the keyboard. Hence any attempt to read from **stdin** allows data to be entered at the keyboard.

Output is sent to a stream called **stdout** (*standard out*) which is linked to the screen.

The standard I/O operations such as those involving `cin` and `cout` use these streams when reading and writing data. However, Borland have added several more I/O functions which read directly from the keyboard and write directly to the screen.

Why are such additional routines necessary? I/O performed using the standard C++ calls is relatively slow whereas the Borland functions are very fast. Also, the range of operations available using the Borland routines is much greater. The down side is that the Borland functions will not be recognised if you are trying to create your program with some other manufacturer's C++ compiler.

The standard C++ I/O operations are declared in the header file **stdio.h**, while the Borland routine prototypes are in **conio.h**.

Standard I/O Functions

Prototype : `int getchar()` **Header** : stdio.h
Pre-condition: None

Description : Reads a single character from the **stdin** stream and displays (echoes) it on the screen. The code of the character pressed is returned as an unsigned integer.
If the character read is the end-of-file character the value returned is the named constant EOF (this has the value -1). The RETURN key must be pressed before the character is read when input is from the keyboard .

Example : `ch = getchar();`

Prototype : `int putchar(int ch)` **Header** : stdio.h
Pre-condition: None

Description : Outputs a single character to the **stdout** stream.
If successful, `putchar()` returns the value of *ch* otherwise it returns the value EOF.

Example : `putchar(ch);`

It may seem surprising, in the above descriptions, to talk in terms of end-of-file and failure to output a character, but such events may occur when the **stdin** and **stdout** streams are not directed to the keyboard and screen. How this is done is described in a later chapter.

Where this redirection of **stdin** is likely to be used, it may be necessary to write any code involving calls to `getchar()` in terms of detecting the end-of-file character. This character can be simulated at the keyboard by entering **Ctrl-Z**.

Strings and related functions are dealt with in a later chapter. However, this is such a useful function that it is included here to be used when displaying string constants.

Prototype : `int puts(string-constant)` **Header** : stdio.h
Pre-condition: None

Description : Outputs a string to the **stdout**. It returns the numeric value of the last character of the string. Like `putch()`, *\n* moves the cursor vertically down but does not return it to the beginning of the line.

Example : `puts("Hello");`

Two other functions found in **stdio.h** are `scanf()` and `printf()`. These two routines were the mainstay of keyboard and screen I/O in C but are little used in C++ (having been replaced by `cin` and `cout`). The parameters for both routines can be long and somewhat tortuous with many formatting options, hence they are omitted from this text. However, if you should require them, the compiler's help facilities and language manuals give a full explanation.

Borland's Console I/O Functions

These routines are designed specifically to read from the keyboard and write to the screen. As such, they are more specific than the functions in *stdio.h*, execute faster and offer many more features.

One of the functions available is `getch()`, which reads a single character from the keyboard.

This function differs from `getchar()` in two major respects:

- There is no need to press the ENTER key to indicate the end of input.
- The character read is not displayed on the screen.

The following code uses `getch()` to accept a capital 'N' before continuing:

```
cout << "Press N to continue";
do
    ch = getch();
while (ch != 'N');
```

If, rather than require input of a capital 'N', any key was acceptable, we can reduce the code to:

```
cout << "Press any key to continue";
getch();
```

Notice in this second example, that the value returned by `getch()` is not assigned to any variable. This is quite acceptable in C++ and can be used with any function call where the returned value is of no interest.

Both `cin` and `getch()` halt program execution while awaiting input. In some situations this is not desirable. For example, when controlling the movement of a character in an interactive game, we expect the character to continue moving if no key has been pressed and to react instantly when a key is hit.

This situation can be handled by the `kbhit()` function which determines if any key has been pressed. Where a game contained the logic:

```
IF a key has been pressed THEN
    Determine which key has been pressed
    Carry out the appropriate command
ENDIF
```

this can be coded in C++ as:

```
if(kbhit())
{
    ch = getch(); // *** Read which key has been pressed  ***
    //*** Code to carry out appropriate action  goes here ***
}
```

When a key is pressed on the computer keyboard its code is transferred to an area of the computer's memory known as the **keyboard buffer**. The `kbhit()` function returns zero if there are no values in the keyboard buffer, otherwise it returns a non-zero value.

The keyboard buffer is only a few bytes long. If several keys are pressed while the machine is busy, the codes for these keys are placed in the buffer. This may lead to the buffer becoming full. Pressing other keys at this point will produce the familiar bleep to warn you that these latest keystrokes have not been stored.

The `getch()` function reads and removes the first byte from the keyboard buffer and will only cause the program to halt, awaiting input, if the keyboard buffer is empty. See FIG-4.2.

FIG-4.2

The Keyboard Buffer

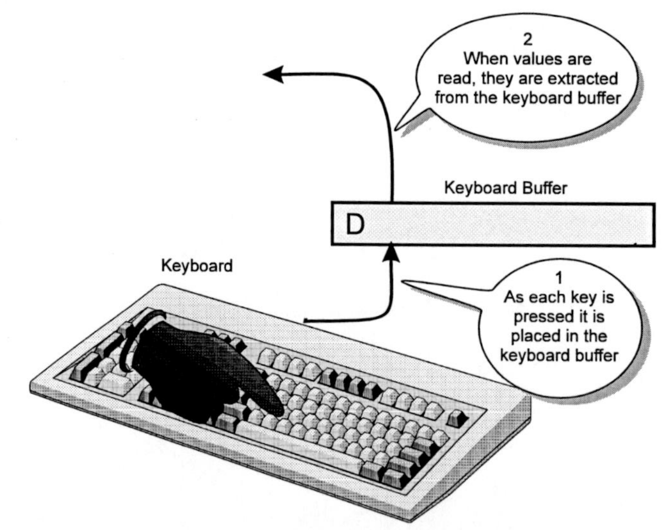

Some of the most commonly used I/O routines are given below.

Prototype : `int getch(void)` **Header** : conio.h
Pre-condition: None

Description : Reads a single character from the keyboard buffer and returns the code for that character as an integer value. The character is not displayed on the screen.

Example :

```
cout << "Do you want to continue (N/Y)? ";
do
    ch = getch();
while (ch!='Y'&&ch!='N');
```

Prototype : `int getche(void)` **Header** : conio.h
Pre-condition: None

Description : Reads a single character from the keyboard buffer and displays (echoes) it on the screen. The integer code of the character pressed is returned by the routine.

Example :

```
ch = getche();
```

Prototype : `int kbhit(void)` **Header** : conio.h
Pre-condition: None

Description : Checks to see if the keyboard buffer is occupied. Returns zero if the buffer is empty otherwise returns a non-zero value.

Example :

```
if (kbhit())
    ch = getch();
```

Prototype : `int putch(int ch)` **Header** : conio.h
Pre-condition: None

Description : Outputs the character whose code is *ch* to the screen. If output is successfully achieved then `putch()` returns the value of the character displayed, (i.e. the same value as *ch*) otherwise EOF (a named constant defined in *conio.h*) is returned.

Note that if the newline character (*n*) is displayed, it does not take the cursor back to the beginning of the next line; rather, the cursor is moved vertically down one line.

Example :

```
putch('X');     // Displays X

putch('A');
putch('\n');
putch('B');     // Displays    A
                                B
```

NOTE: This function will not operate when a program runs in Win16 mode.

Prototype : `int cputs(string-constant)` **Header** : conio.h
Pre-condition: None

Description : Outputs a string to the screen. It returns the numeric value of the last character of the string.
Like `putch()`, *n* moves the cursor vertically down but does not return it to the beginning of the line. To move to the start of a new line use the code "\n\r".

Example :

```
cputs("Hello");            // Displays Hello

cputs("Code\n\rTitle");    // Displays Code
                                       Title
```

Using Console I/O

The following program (LISTING-4.4) demonstrates how to filter key presses to a specified range. The code accepts up to 10 upper case alphabetic characters from the keyboard.

Program Logic:

```
Set count to zero
Read character from keyboard
WHILE character not ENTER DO
    IF character is an upper case letter AND count < 10 THEN
        Display character
        Add 1 to count
    ENDIF
    Read character from keyboard
ENDWHILE
```

Program Code:

LISTING-4.4

Filtering Keyboard Input

```
#include <conio.h>
#include <iostream.h>

void main()
{
    int count=0; // Counts the number of accepted characters
    int ch;          // Character entered at keyboard

    //***Read a key ***
    //*** WHILE it's not RETURN DO ***
    while((ch = getch()) != 13)
    {
        //*** IF ch is an upper case letter and count < 10 THEN ***
        if (ch >= 'A' && ch <= 'Z' && count < 10)
        {
            //*** Display character and add 1 to count ***
            putch(ch);
            count++;
        }
    }
}
```

Note the use of the code

```
while((ch=getch())!= 13)
```

in LISTING-4.4. This reads a character into *ch* and then tests the contents of *ch* to check for the RETURN character. The assignment part of the expression needs to be enclosed in parentheses since this has a lower priority than the test for inequality.

How the program reacts to the right cursor key depends on the target mode used by the program.

PROGRAMMING EXERCISE 4.2

Enter and run the program above.

When entering the 10 characters, press
- a) Combinations of numeric and punctuation keys
- b) Upper and lower case letters
- c) The backspace key
- d) The right cursor key.

Extended Code Keys

Notice that the right cursor key had the effect of adding a capital 'M' (this applies to DOS mode only) to the display (assuming you pressed it before 10 valid characters were entered). Why did this happen?

The description given here only applies when working in a DOS environment.

Under Windows certain key strokes, such as cursor keys, are captured by the Windows operating system and not passed to the application program.

We already know that all characters are stored using an 8-bit code. A quick look at these codes in Appendix A reveals that keys such as the function keys (labelled F1 to F12), the cursor keys and Page Up etc. are not shown. And yet, the computer must recognise these keys when they are pressed.

In the case of the special keys mentioned above, two 8-bit codes are generated by a single key press. These are known as the **extended code keys**. The first byte always contains the value zero; the second, some other value. For example, pressing the right cursor arrow generates the code 0,77. Both these bytes are stored in the keyboard buffer.

The function `getch()` reads only a single byte from the keyboard buffer. This has the potential to lead to some confusion when extended code keys are pressed. In the case of the program in LISTING-4.4, pressing the right cursor key places the values 0 and 77 in the keyboard buffer. The first call to `getch()` reads the value zero from the buffer. This value is not accepted as a valid character and ignored. On the next call, `getch()` returns 77 which is interpreted as a capital 'M'.

If we want to simply ignore all extended code keys by removing them from the keyboard buffer, we can use the logic

```
Read a byte from the keyboard buffer
WHILE byte has the value zero DO
    Read next byte from buffer//  This is the second byte
                                  of the key
    Read next byte from buffer//  First byte of next key press.
                                  This may also be from an
                                  extended code key
ENDWHILE
```

The function keys (F1 to F12) also generate different values if pressed, while the Alt, Ctrl or Shift keys are being held. A complete set of the values held in the second byte of extended code key is shown in TABLE-4.1.

TABLE-4.1

Extended Code Keys

Key	Normal	With Shift	With Ctrl	With Alt
F1	59	84	94	104
F2	60	85	95	105
F3	61	86	96	106
F4	62	87	97	107
F5	63	88	98	108
F6	64	89	99	109
F7	65	90	100	110
F8	66	91	101	111
F9	67	92	102	112
F10	68	93	103	113
F11	133	135	137	139
F12	134	136	138	140
Home	71			
Cursor Up	72			
Page Up	73			
Cursor Left	75			
Cursor Right	77			
End	79			
Cursor Down	80			
Page Dn	81			
Ins	82			
Del	83			

Backspacing

A second problem with LISTING-4.4 is that the backspace key can't be used to erase any characters entered by mistake.

To erase a character from the screen, we need to move the cursor one place to the left, erase the offending character by printing a space and then move the cursor back one more time. This can all be done using the single statement:

```
cout << "\b \b";
```

This statement should be executed when the backspace character has been pressed and there's something on the screen to delete. In addition, the count of how many characters are currently being displayed will have to be decremented.

PROGRAMMING EXERCISE 4.3

Re-program LISTING-4.4 to eliminate the extended code keys problem and to allow for backspacing.

```
OUTLINE LOGIC:
      Set count to zero
      Read a valid character code
      WHILE character not ENTER DO
          IF
              character is an upper case letter AND count < 10:
                  Display character
                  Add 1 to count
              character is BACKSPACE AND count > 0:
                  Remove last character from screen
                  Subtract 1 from count
          ENDIF
          Read a valid character code
      ENDWHILE
```

Screen Control (DOS Mode Only)

This section (to page 183) applies to DOS mode only and is not relevant to Windows based programs.

We have already used `cout` to produce screen displays, but the appearance of the display can be enhanced by using some of the many screen control functions available. For example, we can do such things as change text and background colours; specify exactly where on the screen we wish output to appear and restrict output to specified areas of the screen.

The Output Screen

Normally, the screen display consists of 25 lines each of 80 columns. Text can be placed anywhere on the screen by specifying the column and line at which output is to start; this position is called the **coordinates** of the character. Hence position (1,1) is the top left corner of the screen and (80,25) the bottom right (see FIG-4.3). Where sufficient output text is produced to occupy every line of the screen, scrolling will occur when subsequent lines are displayed.

FIG-4.3

Text Output Screen

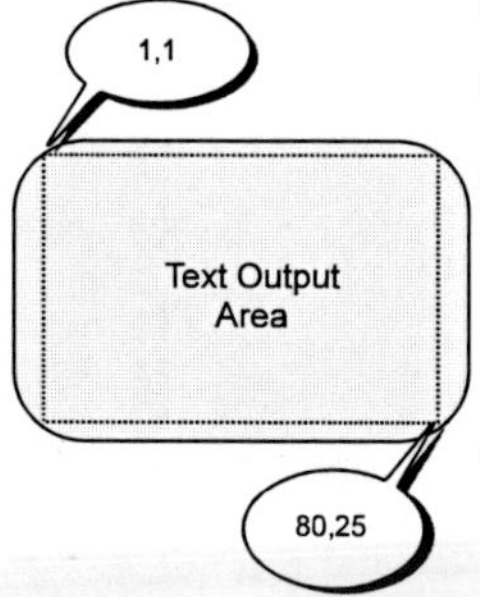

If a VGA video card or better is being used, the screen can be changed to a 50 lines by 80 columns display mode using the function call:

```
textmode(C4350);
```

To return to a 25 line, 80 column display use:

```
textmode(C80);
```

All other examples shown here assume a 25 lines by 80 columns display mode is being used.

The Text Window

The area of the screen in which output can occur is known as the **current text window**. Although the default text window is the whole screen, it is possible to

FIG-4.4

Text Window

41,1

Text Window

80,25

modify the current text window using the `window()` function. For example, we can force all output to the right-hand side of the screen by the command:

```
window(41,1,80,25);
```

This command specifies the screen coordinates of the top left and bottom right corners of the new text window (see FIG-4.4). Subsequent output will occur only in this area with automatic scrolling where necessary.

Screen and Text Window Coordinates

When a text window smaller than the whole screen is active, coordinates are usually specified relative to the top left corner of the current text window which is considered to have coordinates (1,1). Coordinates given from the top left of the whole screen are termed **screen coordinates**; those relative to the current text window are known as **window coordinates** (see FIG-4.5).

FIG-4.5

Screen & Text Window Coordinates

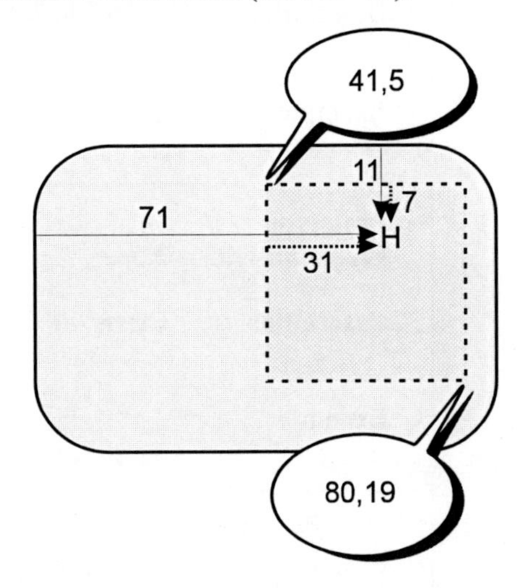

> **TASK 4.1**
>
> 1. Write the `window()` call necessary to set up the text window in the bottom right quarter (20 columns, 6 lines) of the screen.
>
> 2. The letter 'X' is placed at screen coordinates (75,21). What are the window coordinates of this character, assuming the window setup given in the first part of this question.

Screen Control

The function `clrscr()` will clear the current text window (not the whole screen) and move the cursor to the top left corner of that window. Any subsequent output would normally begin at this position but it is possible to move the cursor to any position in the current text window using `gotoxy()`. This function takes two arguments, which specify the column and line to which the cursor is to be moved. Text window coordinates are used. For example:

```
gotoxy(12,3);
cout << "Hello\n";
```

Places the 'H' of "Hello" at column 12, line 3 of the current text window.

The most commonly used screen output routines are described below.

Prototype : `void clreol(void)` **Header** : conio.h
Pre-condition: None

Description : Clears the screen from the current cursor position to the end of the current line in the text window. The cursor does not move.

Example :
```
gotoxy(65,12);
clreol();
```

Prototype : `void clrscr(void)` **Header** : conio.h
Pre-condition: None

Description : Clears the text window and moves the cursor to the top left corner of the text window.

Example :
```
clrscr();
```

Prototype : `void delline(void)` **Header** : conio.h
Pre-condition: None

Description : Clears the line containing the cursor and moves up any subsequent lines within the current text window.

Example :
```
gotoxy(1,8);
delline(); //** Deletes 8th line of text window
```

Prototype : `void gotoxy(int x, int y)` **Header** : conio.h
Pre-condition: (x,y) must lie within the current text window

Description : Moves the cursor to column *x*, line *y* within the text window. *x* and *y* must be given in text window coordinates.

Example :
```
gotoxy(10,3); // ** Moves cursor to Column 10,
              //    Line 3 of current window
```

Prototype : `void highvideo(void)` **Header** : conio.h
Pre-condition: None

Description : Characters output subsequently are highlighted (brighter). Only a restricted number of output functions produce this effect. For example, output produced by `cout` will not be affected. See output functions later for details.

Example :
```
highvideo();
cputs("Hello\n");
```

Prototype : `void insline(void)` **Header** : conio.h
Pre-condition: None

Description : Inserts a blank line at the cursor position in the current text window. Subsequent lines are moved down. The bottom line will be lost.

Example :

```
gotoxy(1,8);
insline(); //** Inserts blank line at line 8
           //** of the text window
```

Prototype : `void normvideo(void)` **Header** : conio.h
Pre-condition: None

Description : Displays subsequent characters in normal intensity.

Example :

```
highvideo();
cputs("Bright\n");
normvideo();
cputs("Normal\n");
```

Prototype : `void _setcursortype(int c_type)` **Header** : conio.h
Pre-condition: None

Description : Changes the shape of the text cursor. The constants associated with this command are:

_NOCURSOR	No cursor
_NORMALCURSOR	Normal underscore cursor
_SOLIDCURSOR	Solid block cursor

Example :

```
_setcursortype(_SOLIDCURSOR);
```

Prototype : `void textmode(int mode)` **Header** : conio.h
Pre-condition: None

Description : Sets the screen display into a specified text display mode The following constants can be used:

LASTMODE	Previous text mode
BW40	Black & white; 40 columns
C40	Colour; 40 columns
BW80	Black & white; 80 columns
C80	Colour; 80 columns
C4350	Colour; 50 lines VGA ; 43 lines EGA

Example :

```
textmode(C4350);     //** 43 lines if using EGA
                     //** 50 lines if using VGA

textmode(LASTMODE); //** Returns screen to previous
                    //** mode
```

Prototype : `int wherex(void)` **Header** : conio.h
Pre-condition: None

Description : Returns the *x* coordinate (i.e. column) of the cursor in the current text window coordinates.

Example :
```
cout << wherex();
```

Prototype : `int wherey(void)` **Header** : conio.h
Pre-condition: None

Description : Returns the *y* coordinate (i.e. line) of the cursor in current text window coordinates.

Example :
```
gotoxy(wherex(),wherey()+1);
             // ** Moves cursor down one line
```

Header : conio.h
Prototype : `void window(int x1, int y1, int x2, int y2)`
Pre-condition: Must be a valid set of positions.

Description : Defines the current text window. The values given are in screen coordinates. The upper left corner having coordinates (*x1,y1*); the lower right corner (*x2,y2*). Clears the text window created and moves the cursor to the top left corner of the window.

Example :
```
window(20,5,40,15);
```

Header : conio.h
Prototype :
```
int movetext(int x1, int y1, int x2, int y2,
         int nx1, int ny1)
```
Precondition : (*x1,y1*), (*x2,y2*) and (*nx1, ny1*) must be valid screen coordinates.

Description : Copies the contents of the rectangular screen area defined by (*x1, y1*) and (*x2,y2*). The copy is placed with its upper left corner at position (*nx1, ny1*). The source area of the screen remains unchanged. Positions are given in absolute screen coordinates. The old and new positions may overlap. Returns a non-zero value if successful.

Example :
```
//*** Display characters (1,1) to (10,6)***
for(line=1;line<=6;line++)
{
    for(row=1;row<10;row++)
    putch(line*10+row+54);
    cputs("\n\r");
}
//*** Copy to (20,12) ***
movetext(1,1,10,6,20,12);
```

Using Screen Control

The following programs illustrate the use of some of the above functions. LISTING-4.5 shows output within a text window.

Program Logic:

```
Fill the whole screen with the character 'X'
Create a window in the left half of the screen
Fill window with the character 'A'
Add more output to window (shows text scrolling)
Clear window
Create a new window at the bottom left of screen
Fill window with the character 'B'
Restore window to full screen
Clear window
```

Program Code:

LISTING-4.5

Using Text Windows

```
#include <conio.h>
#include <iostream.h>


void main()
{
   int count;

   // *** Fill screen with X's ***
   for(count = 1;count<2000;count++)
        cout << 'X';
   getch();

   // *** Create window in right half of screen ***
   window(41,1,80,25);

   // *** Fill with A's ***
   for(count = 1;count < 1000;count++)
        cputs("A");

   // *** Add more text to make window scroll ***
   cputs("A");
   for(count = 1;count < 200;count++)
        cputs(".");
   getch();

   // *** Clear window ***
   clrscr();
   getch();

   // *** Create window in bottom left of screen ***
   window(1,12,40,25);

   // *** Fill with B's ***
   for(count = 1;count < 560;count++)
        cputs("B");
   getch();

   // *** Make whole screen the text window and clear ***
   window(1,1,80,25);
   clrscr();
   getch();
}
```

The following program (LISTING-4.6) uses `wherex()` and `wherey()` in association with `getch()` to allow a character to be moved about the screen. The cursor is switched off during the program.

Program Logic:

```
Switch off cursor
Clear the screen
Display character in middle of screen
Read key
WHILE key not ENTER DO
    IF
        key = 'U':
            IF character not at top of screen THEN
                Move character vertically up
            ENDIF
        key = 'D':
            IF character not at bottom of screen THEN
                Move character vertically down
            ENDIF
        key = 'L':
            IF character not at left edge of screen THEN
                Move character one place to the left
            ENDIF
        key = 'R':
            IF character not at right edge of screen THEN
                Move character one place to the right
            ENDIF
    ENDIF
    Read key
ENDWHILE
```

Program Code:

LISTING-4.6

Controlling Movement

```
#include <conio.h>
#include <iostream.h>

void main()
{
  const char shape = 65;
  int ch;

  // *** Hide cursor and clear screen ***
  _setcursortype(_NOCURSOR);
  clrscr();

  // *** Place character in the middle of the screen ***
  gotoxy(40,13);
  putch(shape);

  // *** While key pressed is not ENTER DO ***
  while (ch=getch(),ch!=13)
  {
      //*** Move up, down, left or right as appropriate ***
      switch (ch)
      {
          case 'U':                               //UP
                  if (wherey() > 1)
                  {
                      cputs("\b \b");
                      gotoxy(wherex(),wherey()-1);
                      putch(shape);
                  }
                  break;
          case 'D':                               //DOWN
                  if (wherey() < 25)
                  {
                      cputs("\b \b");
                      gotoxy(wherex(),wherey()+1);
                      putch(shape);
                  }
                  break;
```

Continued on next page

LISTING-4.6
(continued)

Controlling Movement

```
            case 'L':                              //LEFT
                if (wherex() > 1)
                {
                    cputs("\b \b");
                    gotoxy(wherex()-1,wherey());
                    putch(shape);
                }
                break;
            case 'R':                              //RIGHT
                if (wherex() < 80)
                {
                    cputs("\b \b");
                    gotoxy(wherex()+1,wherey());
                    putch(shape);
                }
        }
    }
}
```

Screen Colours

The information displayed on the screen is also stored in an area of the computer's memory known as the **video RAM**. Whenever output is directed to the screen the data to be output is first copied into the video RAM. The contents of the video RAM is then transformed into a video signal, which is sent to the monitor resulting in the screen display. If any changes are made to the video RAM, then a corresponding change will take place on the screen.

Each character output to the screen is represented in video RAM by two bytes. One byte contains the ASCII code for the character itself, while the second byte contains the colours used when displaying that character. There are two colours defined: the the colour of the character itself and the colour of the background. In addition, this second byte can be used to make the character flash on and off. Details of how a single character is stored are shown in FIG-4.6.

FIG-4.6

Video RAM Storage

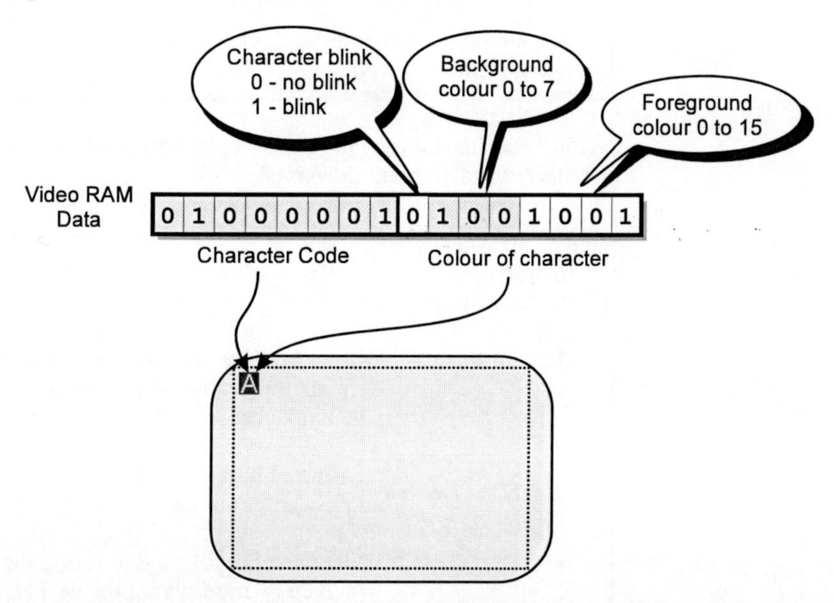

The colour of both text and background output can be defined from a set of limited colours. The background colour can be one of 8 colours (since only three bits are allocated to this value) while the text can be one of 16 different colours (four bits allocated). The final bit is set to 1 to make the character blink on and off. The colours available and their numeric values are given in TABLE-4.2.

TABLE-4.2

Colour Constants

Symbolic Name	Numeric Value	
BLACK	0	↑ Background limited to colours 0 to 7
BLUE	1	
GREEN	2	
CYAN	3	
RED	4	
MAGENTA	5	
BROWN	6	
LIGHTGRAY	7	↓
DARKGRAY	8	
LIGHTBLUE	9	
LIGHTGREEN	10	
LIGHTCYAN	11	
LIGHTRED	12	
LIGHTMAGENTA	13	
YELLOW	14	
WHITE	15	

The constants defined in TABLE-4.2 can be used with the `textcolor()`, `textbackground()` and `textattr()` functions, to set up the colours you require.

Any text can be made to blink on and off by adding 128 to its colour value. This is usually achieved using the named constant, BLINK, which is assigned the value 128. (see `textcolor()` function on the next page).

TASK 4.2

1. Give the four digit hexadecimal number required in the two bytes of video RAM to display a light red capital 'A' on a blue background. ('A' has the ASCII code 41_{16}).

2. What colours are being displayed when the colour byte of a character contains the value AE_{16}?

NOTE: the functions given below only operate when used in conjunction with output routines declared in *conio.h*.

Prototype : `void textattr(int colours)` **Header** : conio.h

Pre-condition: None

Description : Allows both the text and background colours to be defined. Subsequent output will use the colours specified. The blink attribute bit may also be set. The value specified in the call to this function is transferred to the attribute byte of each character subsequently output. To set the background colour correctly the basic colour value must be shifted four bits to the left; this can be achieved by multiplying the background colour by 16.

Example :

```
textattr(GREEN*16+WHITE); // White text on a
cputs("HELLO");           // green background
```

Prototype :	`void textbackground(int colour)` **Header** : conio.h	
Pre-condition:	colours 0 to 7 only	
Description :	Sets background colour for subsequent output.	
Example :	`textbackground(BROWN);` `clrscr();              // Clears screen to brown`	

Prototype :	`void textcolor(int colour)` **Header** : conio.h
Pre-condition:	Colour 0 to 15 (+ 128 if character blinking is required)
Description :	Subsequent text output will be shown in the colour specified by *colour*.
Example :	`textcolor(BLINK + RED);` `cputs("WARNING");      // Flashing red output`

The following program (LISTING-4.7) outputs the first 15 characters of the alphabet using different colours for each.

Program Logic:

```
Clear screen
FOR 15 times DO
    Change background colour
    Change text colour
    Display character
ENDFOR
```

Program Code:

LISTING-4.7

Text Colours

```
#include <conio.h>
#include <iostream.h>


void main()
{
  int backgroundcolour, textcolour;
  int count;

  // *** Clear screen ***
  clrscr();

  // *** Display text in various colours ***
  for (count = 0; count < 16;count++)
  {

      //*** Set the foreground and background colours ***
      backgroundcolour = count % 8; // background 0 to 7 only
      textcolour = 15 - count;        // Use other colour for text
      textattr(backgroundcolour * 16 + textcolour);

      //*** Output character ***
      putch(count + 65);
  }
  getch();
}
```

Classification Functions

Many functions are available for determining a character's classification. For example, we may use the function `isalnum()` to determine if the contents of a character variable are alphanumeric.

Such functions can be useful when checking the format of data entered at the keyboard.

A list of the most widely used functions is given below.

Prototype : `int isalnum(int ch)` **Header** : ctype.h
Pre-condition: None

Description : Returns non-zero if *ch* is the ASCII code of a letter (A..Z or a..z) or a number (0..9), otherwise zero is returned.

Example :

```
while(!isalnum(letter = getch()))
    cout << "Not alphanumeric\n";
```

Prototype : `int isalpha(int ch)` **Header** : ctype.h
Pre-condition: None

Description : Returns non-zero if *ch* is the ASCII code of a letter (upper or lower case), otherwise zero is returned.

Example :

```
if(isalpha(letter))
    cout << "Alphabetic\n";
```

Prototype : `int isascii(int ch)` **Header** : ctype.h
Pre-condition: None

Description : Returns non-zero if *ch* has a value in the range 0 to 127, otherwise zero is returned.

Example :

```
if(!isascii(received))
    cout << "Invalid transmission\n";
```

Prototype : `int isdigit(int ch)` **Header** : ctype.h
Pre-condition: None

Description : Returns a non-zero value if *ch* contains the ASCII code for a numeric digit, otherwise zero is returned.

Example :

```
ch = getch();
if (isdigit(ch))
    cout << "Numeric\n";
else
    cout << "Non-numeric\n";
```

Prototype : `int iscntrl(int ch)` **Header** : ctype.h
Pre-condition: None

Description : Returns non-zero if *ch* is a control character (codes 0..31) or a delete character (code 127), otherwise returns zero.

NOTE: Your keyboard DELETE key does NOT generate the code 127. However, you may enter the code when using `getch()` by holding down the ALT key and pressing the digits 1, 2, 7 on the numeric keypad.

Example :

```
if (iscntrl(key))         // if control character
    if (key ==127)        // if delete
        cputs("\X8");     //   delete character
    else                  // else
        putch(7);         //    beep
```

Prototype : `int isgraph(int ch)` **Header** : ctype.h
Pre-condition: None

Description : Returns non-zero if *ch* is a visible, printable character (i.e. all ASCII codes between 33 and 126), otherwise zero is returned.

Example :

```
c1 = getch();
if (isgraph(ch))
    putch(ch);
```

Prototype : `int islower(int ch)` **Header** : ctype.h
Pre-condition: None

Description : Returns a non-zero value if *ch* is a lower case letter (i.e. a .. z), otherwise zero is returned.

Example :

```
while(islower(ch=getch()))
    cout << "Must be upper case. Re-enter.\n";
```

Prototype : `int isprint(int ch)` **Header** : ctype.h
Pre-condition: None

Description : Returns non-zero if *ch* is a printable character (i.e. all ASCII codes between 32 and 126), otherwise zero is returned.

NOTE: This is similar to `isgraph()` except here, the space character returns a non-zero value.

Example :

```
if(isprint(letter))
    cout << "Non-space printable character\n";
```

Prototype : `int ispunct(int ch)` **Header** : ctype.h
Pre-condition: None

Description : Returns zero for any printing character which is not a letter, number or space. All other values return zero.

The function name is somewhat misleading since characters such as $ and £ will return non-zero values.

Example :

```
if(ispunct(letter))
    cout << "Punctuation mark\n";
```

Prototype : `int isspace( int ch)` **Header** : ctype.h
Pre-condition: None

Description : Returns non-zero if *ch* is a tab, return, newline, vertical tab form feed, or space character (i.e. codes 9..14 or 32), otherwise zero is returned.

Example :

```
if (isspace(letter))
    cout << "White space character\n";
```

Prototype : `int isupper(int ch)` **Header** : ctype.h
Pre-condition: None

Description : Returns a non-zero value if *ch* is an upper case letter, otherwise zero is returned.

Example :

```
if (isupper(ch))
    cout << "Upper case letter\n";
```

Prototype : `int isxdigit(int ch)` **Header** : ctype.h
Pre-condition: None

Description : Returns a non-zero value if *ch* is a hexadecimal character (i.e. 0..9, 'A'..'F' or 'a'..'f'), otherwise zero is returned.

Example :

```
while(!isxdigit(c1=getch()))
    cout <<  "Must be hexadecimal digit\n";
```

As well as testing the classification of characters, some functions are available to convert values from one classification to another.

Prototype : `int toascii(int ch)` **Header** : ctype.h
Pre-condition: None

Description : Returns an ASCII code between 0 and 127 derived by clearing all but the least-significant 7 bits of *ch*.

Example :

```
simasc = toascii(parascii);
                // converts parity coded
                // byte to one without
                // parity coding.
```

Prototype : `int tolower(int ch)` **Header** : ctype.h
Pre-condition: None

Description : If *ch* is a upper case letter (A..Z), the value returned is the code of the lower case equivalent, otherwise the returned value is identical to that of the argument.

Example :

```
if (tolower(letter)=='f')
    cout << "Female\n";
```

Prototype : `int toupper(int ch)` **Header** : ctype.h
Pre-condition: None

Description : If *ch* is a lower case letter (a..z), the value returned is the code of the upper case equivalent, otherwise the returned value is identical to that of the argument.

Example :

```
while(ch=getch(),toupper(ch)!='Y'&&
 toupper(ch)!='N')
    cout <<"Must be Y or N\n";
```

Miscellaneous Functions (DOS Mode Only)

These final functions don't fall into any of the previous categories. They allow such things as halting the program for a specified time (`delay()` and `sleep()`) and creating sounds (`sound()` and `nosound()`).

Prototype : `void delay(unsigned time)` **Header** : dos.h
Pre-condition: None

Description : Delays processing for *time* milliseconds

Example :

```
cout<<"Stopping for 2 seconds\n";
delay(2000);
```

Prototype :	`void sleep(unsigned time)`	**Header** : dos.h
Pre-condition:	None	
Description :	Delays processing for *time* seconds	
Example :	`cout<<"Stopping for 2 seconds\n";` `sleep(2);`	

Prototype :	`void sound(unsigned Hz)`	**Header** : dos.h
Pre-condition:	None	
Description :	Produces a sound at *Hz* Hertz. The sound will continue until the function `nosound()` is executed.	

Example :	`sound(500);`
	`delay(300);`
	`nosound();`	

Prototype :	`void nosound(void)`	**Header** : dos.h
Pre-condition:	None	
Description :	Switch off sound. If no sound is currently being produced this routine has no effect.	

Example :	`cout<<"Enter frequency in hertz : ";`
	`cin>>hertz;`
	`cout<<"Enter duration in tenth of a second : ";`
	`cin>>tenths;`
	`sound(hertz);`
	`delay(tenths*100);`
	`nosound();`	

The following program (LISTING-4.8) plays a sequence of noises, first in ascending, then in descending frequency.

LISTING-4.8

Making Noise

```
#include<dos.h>

void main()
{
   int note = 440,count;
// *** Rising frequency ***
   for(count = 0;count <= 7;count++)
   {
        sound(note+count*55);
        delay(300);
        nosound();
   }
// *** Falling frequency ***
   for(count = 7;count >= 0;count--)
   {
        sound(note+count*55);
        delay(300);
        nosound();
   }
}
```

These are just a few of the functions available in C++. Some of the others will be covered in later chapters.

Summary

Function Name	Return Type	Input Type	Header File	Description
MATHS				
abs	int	int x	stdlib.h	Returns absolute value of *x*.
acos	double	double x	math.h	Returns arc-cosine of *x*.
asin	double	double x	math.h	Returns arcsine of *x*.
atan	double	double x	math.h	Returns arctan of *x*($\pi/2$ to $\pi/2$).
atan2	double	double x double y	math.h	Returns arctan of *x* ($-\pi$ to π).
cos	double	double x	math.h	Returns cosine of *x*(-1 to 1).
exp	double	double x	math.h	Returns e^{x}.
floor	double	double x	math.h	Returns the largest whole number not greater than *x*.
log	double	double x	math.h	Returns ln x.
log10	double	double x	math.h	Returns log *x*.
pow	double	double x double y	math.h	Returns x^{y}.
pow10	double	double x double y	math.h	Returns 10^{x}.
random	int	int x	stdlib.h	Returns a random number between 0 and *x*-1. Use **randomize()** first.
randomize	void	void	stdlib.h	Provides a starting value for the random number generator.
sin	double	double x	math.h	Returns sine of *x*.
sqrt	double	double x	math.h	Returns square root of of *x*.
tan	double	double x	math.h	Returns tangent of *x*.
STANDARD I/O				
getchar	int	void	stdio.h	Returns the next character from stdin as an **int** value (**EOF** if end-of-file encountered).
putchar	int	int c	stdio.h	Sends the value *c* to *stdout*. returns the value of *c* if successful.
puts	int	string s	stdio.h	Sends s to *stdout*.
CONSOLE I/O				
getch	int	void	conio.h	Reads a single byte from the keyboard buffer. Waits for input if the buffer is empty.
getche	int	void	conio.h	As **getch()** but echoes character to screen.
kbhit	int	void	conio.h	Returns zero if the keyboard buffer is empty else returns a non-zero value.
putch	int	int c	conio.h	Outputs *c* to the screen. If successful returns the value of *c* otherwise returns **EOF**.
cputs	int	string s	conio.h	Outputs *s* to the screen. Returns the numeric value of the last character in *s*.
SCREEN CONTROL				
clreol	void	void	conio.h	Clears screen from cursor to end of current line. Cursor unmoved.
clrscr	void	void	conio.h	Clears text window and places cursor at top left.
delline	void	void	conio.h	Deletes current line. Subsequent lines move up.
gotoxy	void	int x int y	conio.h	Moves the cursor to (*x*,*y*).
highvideo	void	void	conio.h	Succeeding output brighter.

Function Name	Return Type	Input Type	Header File	Description
SCREEN CONTROL				
insline	void	void	conio.h	Inserts line at current cursor position.
normalvideo	void	void	conio.h	Subsequent output at normal brightness.
_setcursortype	void	int	conio.h	Changes shape of cursor Uses **_NOCURSOR** **_NORMALCURSOR** **_SOLIDCURSOR**
textmode	void	int x	conio.h	Sets the screen display to mode *x*. Uses **LASTMODE** **BW40** **C40** **BW80** **C80** **C4350**
wherex	int	void	conio.h	Returns the *x* ordinate of cursor.
wherey	int	void	conio.h	Returns the *y* ordinate of cursor.
window	void	int x1 int y1 int x2 int y2	conio.h	Defines the current text window using absolute screen coordinates.
movetext	int	int x1 int y1 int x2 int y2 int nx1 int ny1	conio.h	Copies the text within the rectangle(*x1,y1*) (*x2,y2*) to (*nx1,ny1*). Uses absolute screen coordinates.
SCREEN COLOURS				
textattr	void	int c	conio.h	Sets the text and background colours. The 4 least significant bits of *c* define text colour. The next 3 bits define background colour. Final bit defines blink mode.
textbackground	void	int c	conio.h	Sets the background colour to *c*. Can use **BLACK** **BLUE** **GREEN** **CYAN** **RED** **MAGENTA** **BROWN** **LIGHTGRAY**
textcolor	void	int c	conio.h	Sets the text colour to *c*. Can use **BLACK** **BLUE** **GREEN** **CYAN** **RED** **MAGENTA** **BROWN** **LIGHTGRAY** **DARKGRAY** **LIGHTBLUE** **LIGHTGREEN** **LIGHTCYAN** **LIGHTRED** **LIGHTMAGENTA** **YELLOW** **WHITE** **BLINK**

Function Name	Return Type	Input Type	Header File	Description
CLASSIFICATION				
isalnum	int	int c	ctype.h	Returns non-zero if *c* is alphanumeric.
isalpha	int	int c	ctype.h	Returns non-zero if *c* is alphabetic.
isacii	int	int c	ctype.h	Returns non-zero if *c* is valued 0 to 127.
iscntrl	int	int c	ctype.h	Returns non-zero if *c* is valued 0 to 31 or 127.
isdigit	int	int c	ctype.h	Returns non-zero if *c* is numeric.
isgraph	int	int c	ctype.h	Returns non-zero if *c* is valued 33 to 126.
islower	int	int c	ctype.h	Returns non-zero if *c* is valued 'a' to 'z'.
isprint	int	int c	ctype.h	Returns non-zero if *c* is valued 32 to 126.
ispunct	int	int c	ctype.h	Returns non-zero if *c* is not a letter, number or space.
isspace	int	int c	ctype.h	Returns non-zero if *c* is whitespace character.
isupper	int	int c	ctype.h	Returns non-zero if *c* is valued 'A' to 'Z'.
isxdigit	int	int c	ctype.h	Returns non-zero if *c* is a hexadecimal character.
RE-CLASSIFICATION				
toascii	int	int c	ctype.h	Returns the least significant bits of *c*. All other bits in returned value are zero.
tolower	int	int c	ctype.h	If *c* is an upper case letter then the lower case equivalent is returned, otherwise *c* is returned.
toupper	int	int c	ctype.h	If *c* is a lower case letter then the upper case equivalent is returned, otherwise *c* is returned.
MISCELLANEOUS				
delay	void	unsigned t	dos.h	Halts the program for *t* msecs.
sleep	void	unsigned s	dos.h	Halts the program for *s* secs.
sound	void	unsigned h	dos.h	Produces sound at *h* hertz.
nosound	void	void	dos.h	Switches off sound produced by **sound()**.

USER-DEFINED FUNCTIONS

Introduction

As well as using the standard library functions supplied with C++, we can also create functions of our own.

By creating a function for each of the main tasks to be performed by a program, we construct a set of building blocks which can then be linked to produce the complete software system.

This modular approach has many benefits. It allows each function to be created and tested in isolation before being linked to others to form the final program. This tends to lead to shorter development time and more robust software.

The General Format of a Function

Since `main()` itself is a function, we are already familiar with the general layout of a function definition as shown in FIG-4.7.

FIG-4.7

The Format of a Function Definition

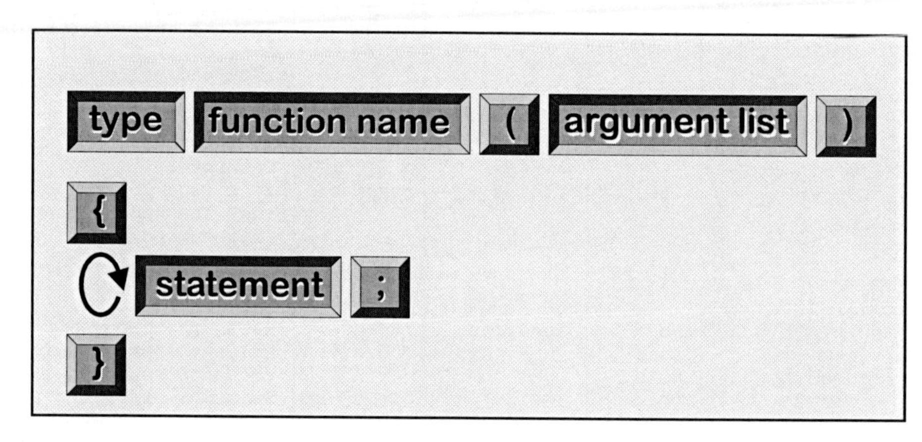

KEY to FIG-4.7

type Specifies the type of value returned by the function. Typical values are `int`, `char`, `float`, etc. Where no value is returned the term `void` is used.

function name Specifies the name of the function.

argument list Defines the type of values passed to the function. Each argument must be named since the instructions which follow will reference to these parameters.
Where there are no arguments, the term `void` may be used or the parentheses simply left empty.

statement A statement may be either a variable definition or an instruction to be carried out when the function is executed. Where a function does return a value, the function should contain the statement `return` followed by the actual value to be returned by the function.

The following example of a user-defined function displays a line of asterisks.

```
void line()
{
    cout <<"*****************************\n";
}
```

This is known as the **function definition**.

Function Prototypes

When using a standard function, we are required to include the appropriate header file containing the function prototype. This allows the compiler to check the validity of the function call, ensuring the name and number of parameters are correct.

User-defined function names are shown in itialics.

Since there is no header file for our own functions, we need to add a prototype to the program. For *line()* this prototype would be

```
void line();
```

or

```
void line(void);
```

This is also known as the **function declaration**.

Calling a Function

With the function coded and the function declaration included in the program, we are now free to call that function. This is achieved in the same manner as calling standard functions. Hence our call to *line()* would be:

```
line();
```

A Complete Program

LISTING-4.9 below uses `line()` to create the output

LISTING-4.9

User-Defined Function

```
#include <iostream.h>

// *** Function Declaration ***
void line();

void main()
{
  // *** Call function        ***
  line();
  cout << "              Hello\n";
  // *** Call function again ***
  line();
}

// *** Function definition ***
void line()
{
  cout << "******************************\n";
}
```

PROGRAMMING EXERCISE 4.4
Enter and run the program in LISTING-4.9.

How the Program Executes

Every program instruction is stored in the computer's memory. Although these instructions are in machine code, they are equivalent to the original C++ statements. Hence, we may consider, for the purpose of this explanation, that the program is held as a sequence of C++ instructions.

We can identify two main sections of code in LISTING-4.9 : the code for `main()` and that for *line()* (see FIG-4.8).

FIG-4.8

Code Held in Memory

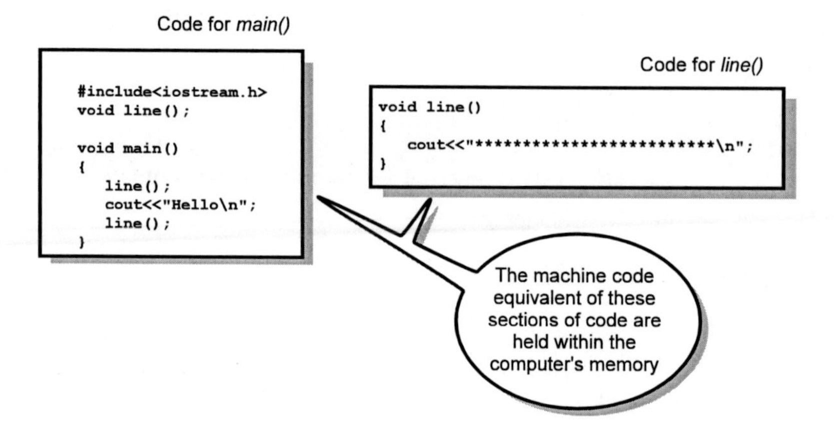

As always, execution begins in `main()`. However, the first statement in `main()` is a call to *line()* the code of which is then executed. When this is complete, the control returns to the statement in `main()` following the original function call and continues execution of `main()`. The stages involved in the execution of LISTING-4.9 are shown in FIG-4.9.

FIG-4.9

Executing a Function

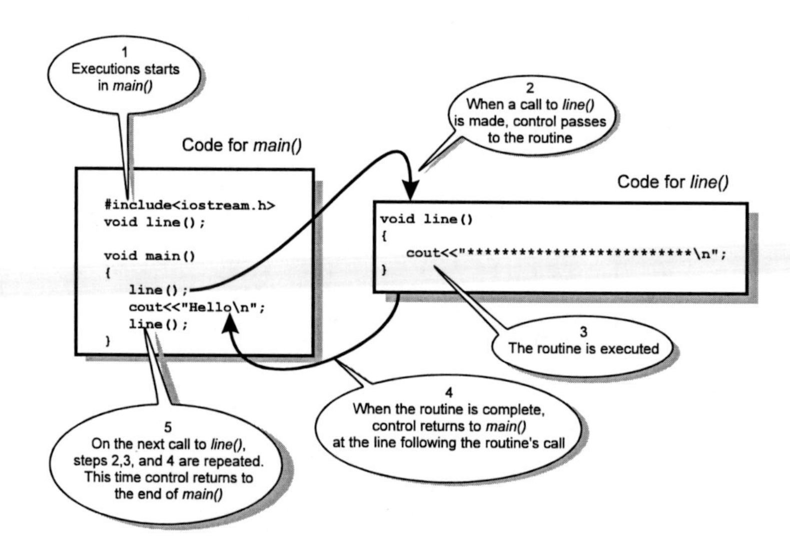

Key to FIG-4.9

1. Execution starts at the beginning of `main()`.
2. When a call to *line()* is encountered control jumps to the routine.
3. The *line()* is executed.
4. Control returns to the statement in `main()` following the function call (`cout`). Execution of `main()` continues until the next call to *line()* is encountered.
5. Control jumps to *line()*.
   line() is executed.
   Control returns to `main()`.
   Execution of `main()` terminates.

PROGRAMMING EXERCISE 4.5

Type in LISTING-4.9 and use the single step trace facilities of the debugger to watch the execution of the program.

PROGRAMMING EXERCISE 4.6

Write a function, *Box()*, which draws a 10 by 10 square of asterisks.

Passing Parameters

A Single Parameter

The *line()* function is not very useful as it stands since the length of the line is predetermined. A better routine would allow us to pass the required length as a parameter. Assuming a parameter, *length*, the new version of *line()* has the logic

```
FOR length TIMES DO
    Display a single asterisk (keeping cursor on the same line)
ENDFOR
Move cursor to start of next line
```

which is coded as:

```
void line(int length)
{
    int c;

    //*** Output a single asterisk the required number
    //*** of times
    for(c = 1;c <= length;c++)
        cout << '*';

    //*** Output a final newline character ***
    cout << '\n';
}
```

This routine has a prototype:

```
void line (int);
```

The new version of *line()* uses a `for` loop to display a single '*' *length* times. This requires the routine to declare a variable (*c*) to be used as the loop counter. Since *c* is declared inside *line()* it is known as a **local variable** and is allocated space in the computer's memory only while *line()* is executing. This is also true for *length*, which, although a parameter of the routine, is also created as a local variable in *line()*.

When our new version of *line()* is called, a value must be supplied in the parentheses. For example:

```
line(15);
```

This argument supplied is also known as the **actual parameter** of the function. When the function is called, the value of the actual parameter is copied into the formal parameter variable before execution of the function begins. In the example above, this means that the value 15 is copied to *length* (see FIG-4.10).

FIG-4.10

Passing Parameters

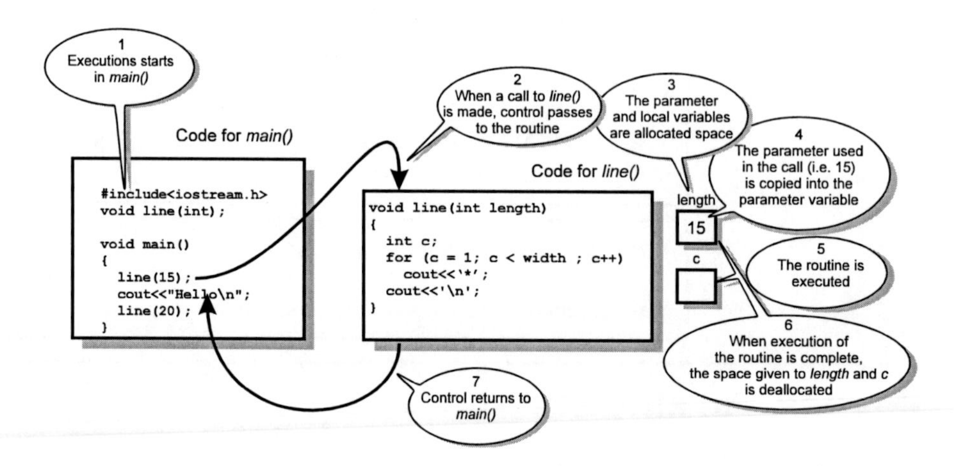

The actual parameter may be a variable or expression as well as a constant. For example:

```
int no = 12;
line(no);       // *** Variable parameter ***
line(no*2);     // *** Expression parameter ***
```

> **PROGRAMMING EXERCISE 4.7**
>
> Modify your *Box()* function to allow the size of the square to be defined as a parameter.

Multiple Parameters

The function *line()* would be even more flexible if we could specify which character is to be used to create the line. This is achieved by making the character to be used in constructing the line another parameter of the function:

```
void line(int length, char shape)
{
    int c;

    for(c = 1; c <= length; c++)
        cout << shape;
    cout << '\n';
}
```

The new function prototype is

```
void line(int,char);
```

and a typical call might be:

```
line(30,'=');
```

When calling a function, it is your responsibility as the programmer to ensure that the actual parameters (30 and '=' in the call to *line()* above) are given in the correct order - integer followed by character. Failure to do so can lead to some unexpected results. We might be tempted to assume that a call such as `line('=',40);` would be trapped at compile time but, since C++ performs automatic type conversions, the compiler will let the call pass.

PROGRAMMING EXERCISE 4.8

Update the program from PROGRAMMING EXERCISE 4.5 to include the latest version of *line()*.

Delete the first call to *line()* and replace the second with the statement:

```
line('=',40);
```

Explain the results obtained.

Default Parameters

Sometimes one or more of the actual parameters passed to a function will be the same value each time the function is called. For example, it may be that although we can specify any character when calling `line()`, in the majority of cases, the underscore (_) is used. In this situation, it is possible to define a default value for that parameter. This is given in the function prototype:

```
void line(int,char = '_');
```

The function definition remains unchanged. When the function is called, the second actual parameter may be omitted

```
line(12);
```

in which case the *shape* parameter is assumed to be the underscore.

When some other character is required to construct the line, the second parameter is specified in the call:

```
line(12,'+');
```

If helpful, the *length* parameter could also be given a default value:

```
line(int = 10, char = '_');
```

which allows both actual parameters to be omitted in the function call:

```
line()
```

Such a call would result in a line of 10 underscores. With this version of the prototype, all of the following calls are valid:

```
line();         // *** Produces __________   (10 underscores)
line(6);        // *** Produces ______       (6 underscores)
line(3,'=');    // *** Produces ===          (3 equal signs)
```

Limitations

There are some rules that must be observed when using default parameter values:

- When a function parameter is given a default value, all the parameters to its right must also be given default values.

```
void line(int = 10, char);
```

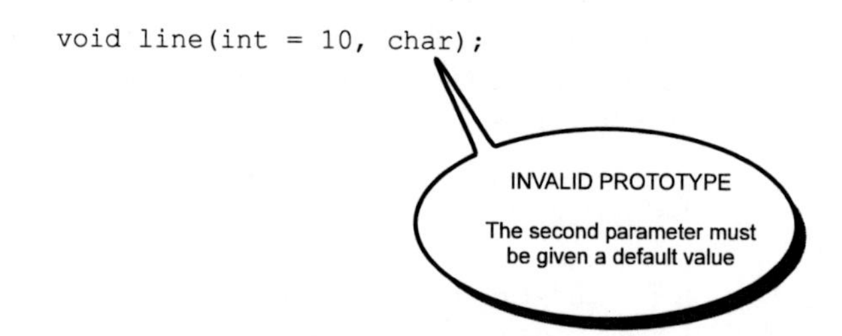

INVALID PROTOTYPE
The second parameter must be given a default value

- When a defaulted parameter is given an actual value in the function call then all the parameters to the left must also be given actual values (even if these are the same as the default value).

```
void line(int=10,char='_'); // *** Prototype ***

   line(10,'=');
```

NOTE

A value must be given to the first parameter when the second parameter's default is overridden

TASK 4.3

Identify the errors in the following code.

```
#include <iostream.h>
#include <conio.h>
#include <stdlib.h>

void stars(int = 100, char = '*');

void main()
{
    clrscr();
    stars(20);
    stars('x');
    stars();
    getch();
}

void stars(int no=100, char star='*')
{
    for(int i = 1;i <= no;i++)
    {
        gotoxy(random(80)+1,random(24)+1);
        cout << star;
    }
}
```

Returning Values from a Function

Returning a Single Value

Most functions return a value and to do this in C++ the function name must be preceded by the return type. For example, a routine which returns the smaller of two values would be coded as:

```
int smaller(int no1, int no2)
{
    if (no1 < no2)
        return no1;
    else
        return no2;
}
```

The `return` statement forces the function to terminate execution of the routine and return the value specified.

It is possible to call the function without referencing the value returned:

```
smaller(n1,n2);
```

Called in this way, the returned value is lost. Although this can be what is wanted on some occasions, it is more likely that we will wish the returned value to be displayed, assigned to a variable, or used in some expression. Typical calls are:

```
cout << smaller(n1,n2);         // *** Result displayed
charges = smaller(n1,n2)*5;     // *** Result used in expression
if (smaller(n1,n2) < 0)         // *** Result used in Boolean exp
    cout <<"Smaller value is negative \n";
line(smaller(n1,n2),'*');       // *** Result used as parameter in
                                //         other function
```

TASK 4.4

In the final example above, the result of *smaller()* is used as an argument in a call to *line()*. Use this technique, write down a single instruction involving calls to *smaller()* which returns the smallest of four values.

PROGRAMMING EXERCISE 4.9

Write a function which accepts a single character argument and returns the succeeding character (as defined in the extended character set given in APPENDIX A).

Returning Several Values

Some functions require to return more than a single value. For example, if an imperial weight is stored over two variables, one containing the pounds value, the other the ounces, and a routine is required which takes two such weights and returns their sum, then the function will have to return two values.

Our first attempt at the prototype of such a function might be

```
void addweights(int lbs1, int oz1, int lbs2, int oz2,
                        int anslbs, int ansoz)
```

with the returned values added to the parameter list.

This isn't quite enough, as the compiler is going to have to differentiate between values entering the function and those returning from it. To do this, an ampersand (&) is added to the types of the returning values.

```
void addweights(int lbs1, int oz1, int lbs2, int oz2,
                    int& anslbs, int& ansoz)
```

In fact, this does more than separate input parameters (*lbs1, oz1, lbs2, oz2*) from output ones (*anslbs, ansoz*), it also changes the way in which the parameters are treated during execution of the function.

Parameters without the ampersand are known as **pass by value** parameters. This means that the values of the actual parameters are copied into the formal parameters (space for which is created when the function is called - as previously described in FIG-4.10).

Parameters with ampersands are **call by reference** parameters. The precise mechanism of how such parameters operate is given in the next chapter, but for the moment we may think of formal reference parameters as being replaced throughout the function by the actual parameters at call time. For example, the `addweights()` routine declared above could be coded as:

```
void addweights(int lbs1, int oz1, int lbs2, int oz2,
                int& anslbs, int& ansoz)
{
    ansoz = (oz1 + oz2) % 16;
    anslbs = lbs1 + lbs2 + (oz1 + oz2) / 16;
}
```

and if it were to be called in the statement

```
addweights(8,12,6,9,lb,oz);
```

the routine would execute as if it contained the code

```
    oz = (oz1 + oz2) % 16;
    lb = lbs1 + lbs2 + (oz1 + oz2) / 16;
```

A full program using this function is given in LISTING-4.10.

LISTING-4.10

Returning Several Values from a Function

```
#include <conio.h>
#include <iostream.h>

void addweights(int,int,int,int,int&,int&);

void main()
{
  int p1, o1, p2, o2, pounds, ounces;

  // *** Get both weights ***
  clrscr();
  cout << "Enter first weight :";
  cin >> p1 >> o1;
  cout << "Enter second weight :";
  cin >> p2 >> o2;

  // *** Call function to add weights ***
  addweights(p1,o1,p2,o2,pounds,ounces);
```

Continued on next page

LISTING-4.10
(continued)

Returning Several Values from a Function

```
    // *** Display results returned ***
    cout << pounds<<" lbs "<<ounces<<" ozs\n";
    getch();
}

void addweights(int lbs1,int oz1, int lbs2, int oz2,
                              int& anslbs, int& ansoz)
{
    ansoz = (oz1 + oz2)%16;
    anslbs = lbs1 + lbs2 + (oz1+oz2)/16;
}
```

Even when only a single value is returned, it may be useful to use a call by reference parameter. For example, should we require a routine which subtracts 10 from a number, we could code this as:

```
int sub10(int no)
{
    return (no-10);
}
```

If we were then to use this function to subtract 10 from a variable, say *value*, then the call statement would be:

```
value = sub10(value);
```

However, by rewriting the function with a call by reference parameter

```
void sub10(int& no)
{
    no -= 10;
}
```

the call can be simplified to

```
sub10(value);
```

A final reason for using call by reference is to eliminate local copies of the actual parameters within the routine. We'll meet examples of this in the next chapter.

Inline Functions

The Problem with Normal Functions

The mechanism used to execute a function is designed to minimise the memory requirements of a program. However, the price paid for this is slower execution. The reduction in speed is caused by the necessity of saving the return address, creating space for local variables, and copying actual parameter values to formal ones before beginning execution of the function, as well as having to de-allocate local variable space and retrieve the return address when the routine is terminated.

Although this penalty is only a small percentage of the time taken to execute the function itself and hence is acceptable in most cases, for short, simple functions the time spent in these activities may become a more significant percentage. An alternative solution, in this case, is to create an **inline** function.

When a routine is declared as an inline function, each call to the function is substituted by the actual code of the function. Hence, if our original version of the function *line()* was defined as an inline function

The key word `inline` is required at the start of the routine.

```
inline void line()// *** Definition of inline function
{
    cout << "*******************\n";
}
```

and `main()` contained the code

```
void main()
{
    line();
    cout << "      Hello\n";
    line();
}
```

then `main()` would be expanded to

```
void main()
{
    cout << "*******************\n";
    cout << "      Hello\n";
    cout << "*******************\n";
}
```

before execution begins.

If the inline function has parameters, then the actual parameters replace the formal parameters in the text. For example, if *line()* was now coded as

```
inline void line(int length)
{
    int count;
    for(count = 1;count <= length;count++)
        cout << '*';
    cout << '\n';
}
```

and `main()`

```
void main()
{
    line(15);
    cout << "      Hello\n";
    line(20);
}
```

the expansion of `main()` would be

```
void main()
{
    {
        int count;
        for(count = 1;count <= 15;count++)
            cout << '*';
        cout << '\n';
    }
    cout << "      Hello\n";
    {
        int count;
        for(count = 1;count <= 20;count++)
            cout << '*';
        cout << '\n';
    }
}
```

Using an inline function results in faster execution, but at the price of greater memory requirements if the function is called frequently in a program.

Defining Inline Functions

The definition of an inline function must appear in a program before any call is made to that function otherwise the compiler ignores the inline request and treats the routine as a normal function. This means that there is normally no need for a function prototype.

By placing the reserved word `inline` at the beginning of a function's definition, we are issuing a request to the compiler to treat that routine as an inline one. Note the word 'request'. The compiler may decide not to make the function an inline one if the code involved is too large or complex. What it considers too large or complex is not defined in the documentation of most compilers.

Function Overloading

Occasionally, we require several functions all of which perform similar tasks but have different parameters. For example, we might need one function to find the smallest of three integer values, while another is required to find the smallest of four values. Possible declarations for these functions could be:

```
int smallest1(int, int, int);
int smallest2(int,int,int,int);
```

Perhaps yet another routine is required to find which of three letters, irrespective of case, is nearest the start of the alphabet. This could be declared as:

```
char smallestletter(char,char,char);
```

Anyone wishing to use these routines needs a good memory! It would be considerably easier if we could give each routine the same name since they all perform similar operations. C++ allows us to do just that. Hence the three routines above can be declared as:

```
int smallest(int,int,int);
int smallest(int,int,int,int);
char smallest(char,char,char);
```

Declaring several identically named functions is called **function overloading**.

The compiler doesn't have a problem with this since it can identify each routine from the number and type of parameters supplied when the routine is called. The program in LISTING-4.11 shows the three routines declared above in use.

LISTING-4.11

Function Overloading

```
#include <conio.h>
#include <iostream.h>
#include <ctype.h>



int  smallest (int, int, int);
int  smallest (int, int, int, int);
char smallest (char, char, char);
```

Continued on next page

LISTING-4.11
(continued)

Function Overloading

```
void main()
{
  int n1,n2,n3,n4;
  char c1, c2, c3;

  clrscr();

  // *** Smallest of three integers ***
  cout << "Enter three numbers : ";
  cin >> n1>>n2>>n3;
  cout << "The smallest number is "<<smallest(n1,n2,n3)<<'\n';

  // *** Smallest of four numbers ***
  cout << "Enter four numbers : ";
  cin >> n1>>n2>>n3>>n4;
  cout << "The smallest number is "<<smallest(n1,n2,n3,n4)<<'\n';

  // *** Smallest of three letters ***
  cout << "Enter three letters : ";
  cin >> c1>>c2>>c3;
  cout << "The smallest char is "<<smallest(c1,c2,c3)<<'\n';

  getch();
}

int smallest(int no1, int no2, int no3)
{
  int temp;
  if (no1 < no2)
       temp = no1;
  else
       temp = no2;
  if(no3 < temp)
       return no3;
  else
       return temp;
}

int smallest(int no1, int no2, int no3, int no4)
{
  int temp1,temp2;

  if (no1 < no2)
       temp1 = no1;
  else
       temp1 = no2;
  if (no3 < no4)
       temp2 = no3;
  else
       temp2 = no4;
  if(temp1<temp2)
       return temp1;
  else
       return temp2;
}

char smallest(char p1, char p2, char p3)
{
  char temp;

  if(toupper(p1) < toupper(p2))
       temp = p1;
  else
       temp = p2;
  if(toupper(p3)<toupper(temp))
       return p3;
  else
       return temp;
}
```

PROGRAMMING EXERCISE 4.10

Enter and run the program in LISTING-4.11.

When using function overloading, some versions of C++ treat `char`, `unsigned char` and `signed char` as three distinct types. This means we can use the declarations

```
int convert(char);
int convert(unsigned char);
```

and

```
int convert(signed char);
```

without the compiler raising any objections.

A function name can only be overloaded if the type of parameters or the number of parameters differ between each definition. It is not sufficient to vary only the return type. Hence, attempting to declare two functions with prototypes

```
int increment(int);
```

and

```
long int increment(int);
```

throws up a compilation error, since these differ only in the type of value returned.

PROGRAMMING EXERCISE 4.11

Write a program containing an overloaded function, `print()`. One version of the routine displays a specified integer value at the current cursor position, while a second version prints an integer value at a specified screen position.

Some words of caution when using overloaded functions: what might at first appear to be a good idea can sometimes lead to time-consuming problems if not handled with care.

Overloading should only be used where routines perform identical operations on either different data types or on different quantities of data. As such, our *smallest()* functions in LISTING-4.11 are acceptable as overloaded functions whereas *print()* defined in PROGRAMMING EXERCISE 4.11 is a more doubtful candidate for overloading.

Overloading and Default Parameters

Making use of both function overloading and default parameters values can lead to ambiguity. For example, if we attempt to declare two functions named *line()* as

```
void line(void);
```

and

```
void line(int = 20, char = '*');
```

then the call

```
line();
```

is ambiguous, since it could be taken as a call to either version of the function. Because of this, the compiler will not allow both definitions of the function to be used, flagging an error at compile time.

Type Casting

C++ attempts to match the actual parameter types to the types of the formal parameters when a function is called. When the actual and formal parameter types match exactly then there's no problem.

PROGRAMMING EXERCISE 4.12

Enter and run the following program to determine which version of `convert()` is called.

```
#include <conio.h>
#include <iostream.h>

void convert(char);
void convert(unsigned char);
void convert(signed char);

void main()
{
  clrscr();
  convert('A');
  getch();
}

void convert(char c)
{
  cout << "char convert executed\n";
}

void convert(unsigned char c)
{
  cout << "unsigned char convert executed\n";
}

void convert(signed char c)
{
  cout << "signed char convert executed\n";
}
```

However, if the formal and actual parameters differ in type, then, although conversion is normally performed automatically during execution, where a function has been overloaded the compiler may signal an ambiguous function call. For example, if we have three functions whose prototypes are

```
void convert(char);
void convert(unsigned char);
```

and

```
void convert(signed char);
```

the compiler will issue an error message when presented with the instruction

```
convert(65);
```

since the actual parameter, 65, does not match any formal parameter types and hence there is no way to know which of the three functions should be called.

To resolve this ambiguity, and to force a call to the desired version of a routine we can specify the type to which the actual parameter is to be converted. For example we can ensure the *convert(char)* version of the routine is called by using the instruction:

```
convert(char(65));
```

This technique is known as **typecasting** or **coercion** and can be used at any point in a program to force a value to be converted to a specific type. For example, `float(12)`, `long(8)` and `(signed char)65` result in `float`, `long int` and `signed char` values respectively.

The formats of a typecast are given in FIG-4.11.

FIG-4.11

Typecasting

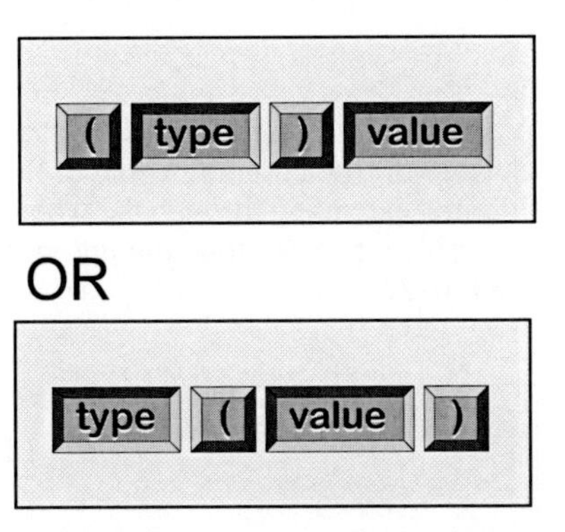

The first syntax in FIG-4.11 is inherited from C and should be used when the type requires two words as in `(unsigned char) 65`; the second comes from C++ and is the preferred method since it uses the same structure as a function call.

Various circumstances in which typecasting can be useful are shown in TABLE-4.3.

TABLE-4.3

Using Typecasting

Circumstances	Example
To force a real result when dividing two integers	`6/float(4)`
To ensure intermediate results produced in evaluating an expression are stored to sufficient accuracy	`30000 * long(120)`
To force the required type when calling overloaded functions	`convert(char(65))`
To change the type of value returned by a function	`int(sqrt(x)) % 5`
To force `cout` to use the required interpretation of the data	`int no = 65;` `cout<<char(no);`

TASK 4.5

Write typecasts for the following:

1. `'A'` to `int`
2. `-9` to `signed char`
3. the variable *x* to `float`
4. the expression (`8%5+3`) to `double`
5. `-125` to `unsigned int`

Functions and Lifetime, Scope, and Visibility

Lifetime

Variables defined in a function are local to that function and cannot be accessed outside the function. A variable defined immediately after the first brace has a lifetime extending through the whole function, while any variables declared within inner blocks of the function are local only to that block. An example is shown in FIG-4.12.

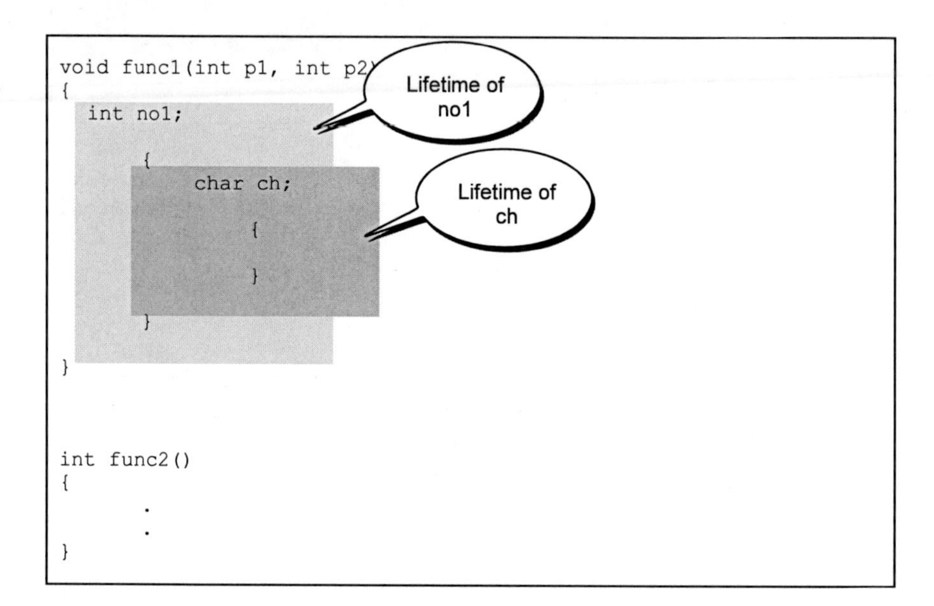

FIG-4.12

Variable Lifetime in a Function

The parameters to a function are also treated as local variables defined at the beginning of the function, hence their lifetime extends throughout the function.

Scope

Variables local to a function can be defined as `static`. However, the variable is created as soon as execution of the program begins, but is only in scope within their definition block.

Parameters variables are in scope throughout the execution of the function.

TASK 4.6

Identify the scope and lifetime of the variables in the following code:

```
#include <conio.h>
#include <iostream.h>

void CountSevens(int);
void main()
{
  int no;

  clrscr();
  for(int i = 1;i <= 6;i++)
  {
      cout << "Enter number : ";
      cin >> no;
      CountSevens(no);
  }
  getch();
}

void CountSevens(int x)
{
  int static count=0;

  if(x == 7)
      count++;
  cout << "Count of sevens so far " << count << '\n';
}
```

Global Variables

Any global variables (those defined outside all program blocks) may be accessed from anywhere in a program. For example, in the code skeleton below

```
void funct1(int);
int funct2(int,int);

int sum;

void main()
{


}

void funct1(int n)
{

}

int funct2(int x, int y)
{

}
```

the variable *sum* is global and is in scope within `main()`, *funct1()* and *funct2()*.

As a general rule, global variables are dangerous since any accidental changes to them in one part of the code can have repercussions throughout the program.

PROGRAMMING EXERCISE 4.13

Write functions to perform each of the tasks detailed below:

1. Draw a rectangle using the extended code graphic characters (see APPENDIX A). Parameters should be the coordinates of the top-left corner, rectangle width and height.

```
OUTLINE LOGIC:
    Move cursor to top left corner
    Display top left corner symbol (char 218)
    Display (width-2) horizontal line characters (196)
    Display top right corner symbol (191)
    FOR height-2 times DO
        Move cursor to correct position under left corner
        Display vertical line symbol (179)
        Move cursor horizontally under right corner
        Display vertical line symbol  (179)
    ENDFOR
    Move to bottom left corner position
    Display bottom left corner symbol (192)
    Display (width-2) horizontal line symbols (196)
    Display bottom right corner symbol (217)
```

2. Return the second largest of four numbers.

```
OUTLINE LOGIC:
    IF n1> n2 THEN
        largest := n1
        second := n2
    ELSE
        largest := n2
        second := n1
    ENDIF
    IF n3 > largest THEN
        second := largest
        largest := n3
    ELSE
        IF n3 > second
            second := n3
        ENDIF
    ENDIF
    IF n4 > largest THEN
        second := largest
        largest := n4
    ELSE
        IF n4 > second
            second := n4
        ENDIF
    ENDIF
    return second
```

Continued on next page

PROGRAMMING EXERCISE 4.13 (continued)

3. Identify a character parameter as a vowel, consonant or non-alphabetic character (return 1, 2 or 3 respectively).

```
OUTLINE LOGIC:
    IF ch is alphabetic THEN
        IF ch is a vowel THEN
            return 1
        ELSE
            return 2
        ENDIF
    ELSE
        return 3
    ENDIF
```

4. Return the value 1 if a specified year is a leap year, otherwise return zero. Implement this as an `inline` function.

```
OUTLINE LOGIC:
    IF (year exactly divisible by 4 but not 100)
        OR(year exactly divisible by 400) THEN
        return 1
    ELSE
        return zero
    ENDIF
```

5. Return the number of days in a specified month. Ignore the possibility of leap years.

```
OUTLINE LOGIC:
    IF month is 4,6,9 or 11 THEN
        return 30
    ELSE
        IF month = 2 THEN
            return 28
        ELSE
            return 31
        ENDIF
    ENDIF
```

6. Reads a single key from keyboard and returns the integer value of that key. Where the key pressed is one which generates an extended code (e.g. cursor right) then the routine is to return the value of the second byte as a negative value. Hence, if 'M' (ASCII 77) is pressed, the routine returns 77 and cursor right key (which generates 0, 77) returns the value -77.

Make use of the functions you have already produced in the previous questions in this exercise.

Name the routine *ReadKey()*.

```
OUTLINE LOGIC:
    Read byte from keyboard buffer
    IF byte is zero THEN
        Read byte from keyboard buffer
        Make byte negative
    ENDIF
    Return byte
```

PROGRAMMING EXERCISE 4.13 (continued)

7. Read a date entered in the form day/month/year. If the date as a whole is invalid, it is to be re-entered. Accept all entries from the same area of the screen. The date should be returned in three integer variables.

```
OUTLINE LOGIC:
    REPEAT
        Set invalid to FALSE
        Read day,month,year
        IF month outside the range 1 to 12 THEN
            Set invalid to TRUE
        ENDIF
        IF year before 1600 THEN
            Set invalid to TRUE
        ENDIF
        Calculate  days in month
        IF month is February AND its a leap year THEN
            Add 1 to days in month
        ENDIF
        IF day outside range 1 to days in month THEN
            Set invalid to TRUE
        ENDIF
    UNTIL NOT invalid
```

Name this routine *DateToJulian*

8. Accept a date (as three parameters) and return the number of days since 1/1/4713BC.
   The formula for this is

```
    Y=year+(month-2.85)/12
    days=[[[[367.0* Y]-[Y]-0.75*[Y]+day]-0.75*2.0]+1721115.0]
```

   where
   [x] is the largest integer smaller than or equal to *x*.

Name this routine *JulianToDate*

9. Accept the number of days since 1/1/4713BC and return the corresponding date.
   The formula for this is

```
    temp1 = (days - 1721119.0)+2.0
    year = [(temp1 - 0.2)/365.25]
    temp2 = temp1 - [365.25*year]
    M = [(temp2-0.5)/30.6]
    day = temp2 - 30.6 * M + 0.5
    IF M > 9 THEN
        month = M - 9
        year = year+1
    ELSE
        month = M+3
    ENDIF
```

10. Write two overloaded inline functions which convert imperial distances to metric.
    The first function accepts a `double` value representing a distance in miles and returns the equivalent distance in kilometres.
    The second function accepts two `int` values representing a distance in miles and yards and returns the equivalent distance in kilometres.
    (1 mile = 1.6 kilometres; 1 mile = 1760 yards)

11. Reads in an integer value and returns another integer whose digits are the reverse of the accepted value (e.g. 145 will return 541).

Summary

- **User-defined functions** require both a function declaration (also called function prototype) and function definition.

- A **function declaration** has the format:

```
return-type function-name (parameter type list);
```

- A **function definition** has the format:

```
return-type function-name (named parameter list)
{
    action
}
```

- A **function call** transfers control to the function code. When the function terminates, control returns to the next statement in the calling routine.

- **When a function is called**, any input parameters are created as local variables in the routine.

- **The actual parameter values** are transferred to the formal parameters before the function is executed.

- Parameters can be assigned **default values** in the function declaration.

- **All parameters to the right** of a defaulted parameter must also be defaulted.

- **If a function's default value is over-ridden**, all actual parameters to the left of this value must be specified.

- **Function overloading** allows two or more functions to share the same name so long as the parameter list for each is different.

- **Using default parameters and function overloading** may give rise to ambiguity. This will be flagged by the compiler.

- **The term `void` is used** where no value is returned by a function.

- **Where variables in the parameter list are to be modified** within the function body, an ampersand (&) is included after the parameter type in both the function declaration and definition.

- **Each call to an `inline` function** is substituted by the actual function code (at the compiler's discretion) during the pre-processing stage.

- The **definition of an `inline` function** must appear in a program before any call to that function otherwise the function cannot be made inline by the compiler.

- Since an **inline** function's definition must appear before any call to that function, normally a **function prototype is not required**.

- **Typecasting** can be used to force a value to be stored as a different type.

- **Global variables** are in scope in every function defined after that variable.

CASE STUDY

The Problem

A program is required to perform a variety of tasks involving dates. The operations required are:

1. To calculate the number of days between two dates.
2. To calculate the resulting date when adding a number of days to a specified date.
3. To calculate the resulting date when subtracting a number of days from a specified date.
4. To determine the day of the week on which a specified date falls.

Clarification

The program should display the options available in the form of a menu. Invalid entries should be flagged with appropriate error messages.

The Algorithm

A basic description of logic required is given by:

```
1.  REPEAT
2.      Display Menu
3.      Get option
4.      Process option
5.  UNTIL QUIT option chosen
```

Rather than continue to stepwise refine the algorithm, an alternative approach is to identify statements which may be converted to functions in the final program and treat these as separate problems to be tackled independently. In the above logic, steps 2, 3 and 4 seem likely candidates.

The details of each routine are given in what is known as a Mini-Specification (or Mini-Spec). For example, the Mini-Spec for a menu function would be:

NAME	:	DisplayMenu
PARAMETERS		
IN	:	None
OUT	:	None
IN/OUT	:	None
PRECONDITION	:	None
DESCRIPTION	:	User options are displayed on screen
OUTLINE LOGIC	:	

```
Display "1  -  Days between dates"
Display "2  -  Add days to date"
Display "3  -  Subtract days from date"
Display "4  -  Day of week"
Display "5  -  QUIT"
Display "Enter option (1 to 5)"
```

As you can see, a Mini-Spec bears some resemblance to the description of a standard function. However, there are some differences: rather than supplying a prototype, separate lines are used to define the routine's name, parameters and return type.

IN parameters are equivalent to those passed on a *read only* or *pass by value* basis in a function. For example, a routine which calculated a employee's wage based on the number of hours worked would require the hours worked to be passed as an IN parameter.

An OUT parameter indicates a value returned by the routine. For example, in the wage calculating routine the employee's wage would be an OUT parameter.

When the routine described in the Mini-Spec is finally coded in C++, where there is a single OUT parameter, this can be the value returned by the routine; where there is more than one value, these would become *call by reference* parameters. Hence, the routine to calculate an employee's wage which takes the hours worked and returns the gross wage would have a C++ prototype of:

```
float CalculateWage(float hrswrked);
```

A similar routine which returned the gross pay and deductions would have the prototype:

```
void CalculateWage(float hrswrked, float& gspay, float& ded);
```

IN/OUT parameters are those where the actual parameter's value is examined and changed by the function. For example, if a routine subtracts a withdrawal from the balance in a bank account, then *balance* would be an IN/OUT parameter. Again, this would be a *call by reference* parameter in the function.

The OUTLINE LOGIC gives details, in a Structured English, of the steps required to program the routine.

The routine required to get the user's option has the Mini-Spec:

NAME	:	GetOption
PARAMETERS		
IN	:	None
OUT	:	option : INTEGER
IN/OUT	:	None
PRECONDITION	:	None
DESCRIPTION	:	*option* set to value entered at keyboard. *option* should be in range 1 to 5. Values outside this range should result in an error message with the user being allowed to re-enter a value for *option.*
OUTLINE LOGIC	:	

```
Display "Enter option"
Get option
WHILE option outside range 1 to 5 DO
    Display "Invalid option. Must be in
            the range 1 to 5"
    Display "Please re-enter option "
    Get option
ENDWHILE
```

```
NAME             :  ProcessOption
PARAMETERS
    IN           :  option : INTEGER
    OUT          :  None
    IN/OUT       :  None
PRE-CONDITION    :  1<=option<=5

DESCRIPTION      :  option specified is executed.

OUTLINE LOGIC    :
                    IF
                        option = 1:
                            Get first date
                            Get second date
                            Change first date to Julian days
                            Change second date to Julian days
                            Display the absolute difference
                            between the first and second
                            Julian days
                        option = 2 :
                            Get date
                            Get days
                            Convert date to Julian days
                            Add days to Julian days
                            Convert Julian days to date
                            Display new date
                        option = 3 :
                            Get date
                            Get days
                            Convert date to Julian days
                            Subtract days to Julian days
                            Convert Julian days to date
                            Display new date
                        option = 4 :
                            Get date
                            Convert to day of week
                            Display day of week
                    ENDIF
```

The outline logic for *ProcessOption()* highlights some complex tasks:

```
Get first date
Get second date
Convert first date to Julian days
Convert second date to Julian days
Convert Julian days to date
Convert to day of week code
Display day of week text
```

Some of these tasks, such as `Get first date` and `Get second date` are basically the same task with different parameters. Recognising this, we can reduce our list of tasks to:

```
Get date
Convert date to Julian days
Convert Julian days to date
```

```
Convert date to day of week code
Display name of day corresponding to day of week code
```

Now each of these can be defined as functions in their own right:

NAME	:	GetDate
PARAMETERS		
IN	:	None
OUT	:	day, month, year : INTEGER
IN/OUT	:	None
PRE-CONDITION	:	None
DESCRIPTION	:	Valid values for *day, month* and *year* accepted from keyboard.
OUTLINE LOGIC	:	

```
REPEAT
    Set invalid to FALSE
    Clear area of screen used
    Read day,month,year
    IF month outside the range 1 to 12
    THEN
        Set invalid to TRUE
    ENDIF
    IF year before 1600 THEN
        Set invalid to TRUE
    ENDIF
    Calculate days in month
    IF month is February AND
     year is a leap year THEN
        Add 1 to days in month
    ENDIF
    IF day outside range 1 to
     days in month THEN
        Set invalid to TRUE
    ENDIF
UNTIL NOT invalid
```

NAME	:	DateToJulian
PARAMETERS		
IN	:	day,month,year : INTEGER
OUT	:	noofdays : INTEGER
IN/OUT	:	None
PRE-CONDITION	:	*day, month* and *year* form a valid date
DESCRIPTION	:	Sets *noofdays* to the number of days since 1/1/4713BC to *day/month/year* inclusive.
OUTLINE LOGIC	:	

```
Y = year+(month-2.85)/12
noofdays = [ [ [367.0* Y]-[Y]-0.75*[Y]
+day]-0.75*2.0]+1721115.0
```

NAME	:	JulianToDate
PARAMETERS		
IN	:	noofdays : INTEGER
OUT	:	day, month, year : INTEGER
IN/OUT	:	None
PRE-CONDITION	:	noofdays >=0
DESCRIPTION	:	Returns the date (*day/month/year*) which is *noofdays* since 1/1/4713BC
OUTLINE LOGIC	:	

```
temp1 := (noofdays - 1721119.0)+2.0
temp2 := temp1 - [365.25*temp1]
M := [(temp2-0.5)/30.6]
day := temp2 - 30.6 * M + 0.5
year := [(temp1 - 0.2)/365.25]
IF M > 9 THEN
    month := M - 9
    year := year+1
ELSE
    month := M+3
ENDIF
```

NAME	:	DateToDayofWeek
PARAMETERS		
IN	:	day, month, year : INTEGER
OUT	:	dow : INTEGER
IN/OUT	:	None
PRE-CONDITION	:	*day, month* and *year* form a valid date
DESCRIPTION	:	Returns the code for the day of the week on which the date *day/month/year* fell. (0 - "Sunday" .. 6 - "Saturday").
OUTLINE LOGIC	:	

```
M   := (month+9) modulo 12+1
CY  := year-[M/11]
C   := [CY/100]
Y   := CY modulo 100
temp:= 2.6*M-0.2
dow := (temp+day+Y+[Y/4]+[C/4]-2*C)
          modulo 7
```

```
NAME              :  DisplayDayOfWeek
PARAMETERS
    IN            :  dow : INTEGER
    OUT           :  None
    IN/OUT        :  None
PRE-CONDITION     :  0<=dow<=6

DESCRIPTION       :  Displays name of day corresponding to dow.
                     (e.g. displays "Sunday" if dow = 0;
                         "Saturday" if dow = 6)

OUTLINE LOGIC     :
                     IF
                         dow = 0:
                             Display "Sunday"
                         dow = 1:
                             Display "Monday"
                         dow = 2:
                             Display "Tuesday"
                         dow = 3:
                             Display "Wednesday"
                         dow = 4:
                             Display "Thursday"
                         dow = 5:
                             Display "Friday"
                         dow = 6:
                             Display "Saturday"
                     ENDIF
```

The detailed logic of *GetDate()* introduces the possibility for yet more routines: one to determine if a year is a leap year and another to return the number of days in a specified month. This generates two additional Mini-Specs:

```
NAME              :  IsLeapYear
PARAMETERS
    IN            :  year : INTEGER
    OUT           :  result : INTEGER
    IN/OUT        :  None
PRE-CONDITION     :  1600<year

DESCRIPTION       :  Returns a 1 if year is a leap year, otherwise
                     returns zero.

OUTLINE LOGIC     :
                     IF (year divisible by 4 but not 100)
                     OR(year  divisible by 400) THEN
                         return 1
                     ELSE
                         return zero
                     ENDIF
```

```
NAME              :  DaysinMonth
PARAMETERS
    IN            :  month : INTEGER
    OUT           :  days : INTEGER
    IN/OUT        :  None
PRE-CONDITION     :  1<=month<=12
DESCRIPTION       :  Returns the number of days in the month
                     specified. No account is taken of leap years.
OUTLINE LOGIC     :
                     IF month is 4,6,9 or 11 THEN
                         return 30
                     ELSE
                         IF month = 2 THEN
                             return 28
                         ELSE
                             return 31
                         ENDIF
                     ENDIF
```

Since `main()` itself is also a function, it should be described in a mini-specification:

```
NAME              :  main
PARAMETERS
    IN            :  None
    OUT           :  None
    IN/OUT        :  None
PRE-CONDITION     :  None
DESCRIPTION       :  Offers a selection of date processing operations.
                     Option 1 -  the number of days between two
                                 dates.
                     Option 2 - Add a number of days to a given date.
                     Option 3 - Subtract days from a given date.
                     Option 4 - Display the day of the week on
                                which a date fell.
OUTLINE LOGIC     :
                     REPEAT
                         Display menu
                         Get option
                         Perform option chosen
                     UNTIL quit option chosen
```

Structure Diagrams

FIG-4.13

Representing a Routine in a Structure Diagram

Process Option

With so many routines used in the program, we are in danger of losing sight of the overall structure of the program. One graphical method of representing this overview is with a **Structure Diagram.**

A Structure Diagram shows the relationship between the routines of the system. That is, it shows calling/called relationship between routines and the values that are passed between these routines.

Each routine is represented by a labelled rectangle (see FIG-4.13).

Where one routine is called by another, this is shown by linking the corresponding rectangles (see FIG-4.14).

In the diagram, the **called routine** is placed beneath the **calling routine**.

Where data passes between the routines, this is shown using the symbol ↗○ and the name of the data items being transferred. The direction of the arrow indicates the direction in which the information is passed (see FIG-4.15).

If an item of data is updated by a routine (i.e. it's an IN/OUT parameter) it is shown as passing both into and out of the called routine (see FIG-4.16).

FIG-4.14

Calling and Called Routines

FIG-4.15

Returning Values from the Called Routine

FIG-4.16

Representing an IN/OUT Parameter

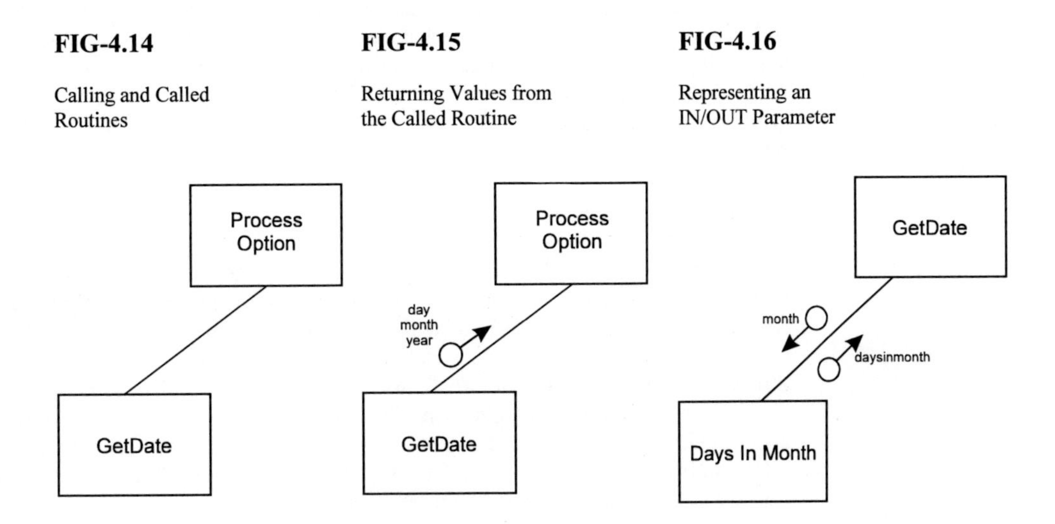

Using these basic principles, we can construct the Structure Diagram for our program (FIG-4.17).

FIG-4.17

The Case Study's Structure Diagram

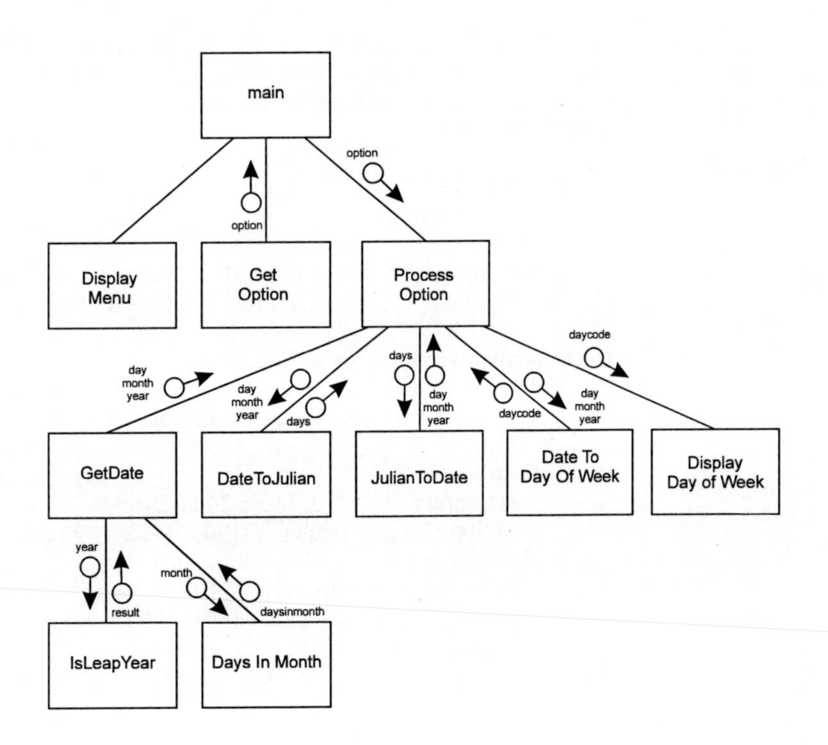

There are several details that do not show up on the Structure Diagram:

- The order in which routines are called
- How often a routine is called
- The actual parameters used in the routine call

Testing the Routines

We've already seen in the previous chapter that test data can be created by examining the actual code of a program. This is called white box testing. By separating a program into several routines we can apply this technique to each routine. As long as routines are kept small and uncomplicated then the amount of white box test data required for each should be held at a level which can be easily handled.

Black Box Testing

One problem with white box testing is that it only tests those control structures actually present in the code. If we've mistakenly omitted code from a program then tests which should be carried out will not be generated by this approach.

Another way to test code is to create test data based on the actions that the program or routine is supposed to perform. For example, if we know a routine called *IsLeapYear()* is meant to return **true** when the year given as an argument is a leap year and **false** when it is not, then we might use the values 1992 and 1995 to check that we get the expected results under both circumstances.

We have created test data without reference to the code of the routine. In fact, the test data could be generated as soon as a complete description of the purpose of the routine is given, long before any code is ever written. This approach is known as **black box testing**.

The aims of black box testing is to identify the general group of responses that may occur in a routine, and from this to define the set of input values which should lead to each response. In the case of *IsLeapYear()*, the responses are **true** or **false** and the input sets are:

1. Leap years
2. Non-Leap years

These input sets are known as **equivalence classes** since members of a given set or class should elicit the same response from the program.

Occasionally, we may want to divide an equivalence class into sub-classes simply because we feel this might result in more rigorous testing. Hence we might decide to identify the equivalence classes for *IsLeapYear()* as

1. Leap years
   a) Century years (i.e. 1600, 2000, 2400 etc.)
   b) Non-Century years (i.e. 1904, 1952, 1996 etc.)
2. Non-Leap years
   a) Century years (i.e. 1900, 2100,2200 etc.)
   b) Non-Century years (i.e. 1901, 1973, 2001 etc.)

Again, we would use a single value from each class to test the routine.

THE HENLEY COLLEGE LIBRARY

TASK 4.7

Identify the responses for *DaysInMonth()* which returns the number of days in a specified month. The routine accepts an integer value in the range 1 to 12 and takes no account of leap years.

Notice that invalid input also forms a valid equivalence class since the routine has a different response to such data.

Boundary Values

Some equivalence classes are linear in nature. For example, one sub-class of rejected values in *DaysInMonth()* is that containing integer values of 13 or more.

Experience has shown that with such classes the values on the boundary between one equivalence class and the next, when used as test data, often highlight problems in a piece of software. Hence, these **boundary values** should be used, along with some other value from each class, as test data.

Creating Black Box Test Data

To summarise: creating black box test data involves six steps:

- Identify the differing responses of the routine to be tested.
- Identify the equivalence classes for parameters or input data.
- Sub-divide the main classes where thought to be useful.
- Choose a value from each class as test data.
- Where the values of a class are linear, add all boundary values to the test data.
- Identify the expected response for each test value.

Testing *DaysInMonth()*

Responses:
Pre-condition not met
28
30
31
Equivalence classes:
1. Invalid month
   a) Less than 1
   b) Greater than 12
2. 2 (February)
3. 4,6,9,11 (April, June, September, November)
4. 1,3,5,7,8,10,12 (January, March, May, July, August, October, December)

Test Data is shown in TABLE-4.4.

TABLE-4.4

Black Box Test Data

Class	Test Data	Expected Result
1 a)	-7	Not executed
1 a) Boundary	0	Not executed
1 b)	20	Not executed
1 b) Boundary	13	Not executed
2	2	28
3	6	30
4	5	31

Black box testing is not an alternative to white box testing. Rather, they complement each other and increase the likeliehood of discovering errors in our code. For example, once we code *DaysInMonth()* we'll end up with the following control structures:

```
if (month<1||month>12)
if (month==4||month==6||month==9||month==11)
if (month == 2)
```

and these will determine the white box test data required.

As we create white box test values, we can incorporate, where possible, the values already chosen for the black box technique. The white box test data is shown in TABLE-4.5 with values extracted from the black box test data marked with an asterisk.

TABLE-4.5

White Box Test Data for *DaysInMonth()*

Run	Test Value	Reason for Test	Expected Result	Actual Result
1	month = -7*	if(month<1|| t,f	return 0	
2	month = 13*	if(month<1|| f,t	return 0	
3	month = 4	if(month<1|| f,f if(month==4||t,f,f,f	return 30	
4	month = 6*	if(month==4||f,t,f,f	return 30	
5	month = 9	if(month==4||f,f,t,f	return 30	
6	month = 11	if(month==4||f,f,f,t	return 30	
7	month = 2*	if(month==4||f,f,f,f if(month==2) t	return 28	
8	month = 5*	if(month==2) f	return 31	

In addition to this, the test data table has to be extended to include any test values not yet incorporated from the black box test values. In the case of *DaysInMonth()*, this would require two more test runs using the values 0 and 20. These would appear on the final test data table as the test data values for runs 9 and 10.

A Test Driver

Like the components in a piece of equipment, the functions that go to make up the whole program should be tested separately. This is achieved by isolating the routine to be tested from the rest of the program and writing a small `main()` program to call up the routine and display any results it produces.

This program is known as a **test driver**. Each routine should have its own test driver.

The results produced by a test driver should be compared with the expected results and, where there are differences, these should be documented and corrections made to the routine being tested.

Normally, testing begins at the lowest level of routine. LISTING-4.12 shows the program required to test *DaysinMonth()*.

LISTING-4.12

Test Driver for *DaysInMonth()*

```
#include <iostream.h>
#include <conio.h>

int DaysinMonth(int);

// *** Driver for DaysinMonth() ***
void main()
{
  int month;

  do
  {
       clrscr();
       //*** Read test value ***
       cout<<"Enter month (1 to 12) : ";
       cin >> month;
       //*** Call routine to be tested and display result ***
       cout<<"Days in month "<<month<<"= "<<DaysinMonth(month)
            <<'\n';
       getch();
  }
  //*** Stop when -99 entered ***
  while(month != -99);
}

// *** Code for DaysinMonth ***
int DaysinMonth(int month)
{
  //*** IF precondition not met THEN return 0 ***
  if(month<1||month>12)
       return 0;
  //*** IF April,June,September or November THEN return 30 ***
  if (month==4||month==6||month==9||month==11)
       return 30;
  //*** IF February THEN return 28 ***
  else if (month == 2)
       return 28;
  //*** Otherwise return 31 ***
  else
       return 31;
}
```

The test data and drivers required by the other routines are omitted for the sake of brevity. The listing of the complete program is given in LISTING-4.13.

LISTING-4.13

Date Program

```
#include <conio.h>
#include <iomanip.h>
#include <iostream.h>
#include <math.h>


//*** Program constant ***
const int QUIT = 5;

//*** Function prototypes ***
long DateToJulian(int,int,int);
void JulianToDate(long,int&,int&,int&);
void DisplayMenu();
void GetOption(int&);
void ProcessOption  (int);
void GetDate(int&,int&,int&);
int DateToDayofWeek(int,int,int);
int DaysinMonth(int);
void DisplayDayofWeek(int);
```

Continued on next page

LISTING-4.13
(continued)

Date Program

```
//*** Inline Leap year routine ***
inline int IsLeapYear(int year)
{
  return((year%4==0&&year%100!=0)||(year%400==0));
}



void main()
{
  int option;

  do
  {
      clrscr();
      DisplayMenu();
      GetOption(option);
      ProcessOption(option);
  }
  while (option != QUIT);
}



//*** Display the menu options ***
void DisplayMenu()
{
  cout<<setw(37)<<' '<<"MENU\n\n\n";
  cout<<"1  -  Days between dates\n";
  cout<<"2  -  Add days to date\n";
  cout<<"3  -  Subtract days from date\n";
  cout<<"4  -  Day of week\n";
  cout<<"5  -  QUIT\n\n";
  cout<<"Enter option (1 to 5) :";
}


//***     Get  menu option      ***
void GetOption(int& opt)
{
  while(cin>>opt,(opt<1||opt>QUIT))
      cout<<"Invalid option\nMust be in range 1 to "<<QUIT<<'\n';
}


//***     Execute Option        ***
void ProcessOption(int opt)
{
  int d1,d2,m1,m2,y1,y2,days;
  double temp;

  switch (opt)
  {
      case 1:  // *** DIFFERENCE BETWEEN TWO DATES ***
               // *** Get dates ***
               GetDate(d1,m1,y1);
               GetDate(d2,m2,y2);
               // *** Display Difference ***
               cout<<"There are "<<abs(DateToJulian(d1,m1,y1)-
                        DateToJulian(d2,m2,y2))
                    <<" days between "<<d1<<'/'<<m1<<'/'<<y1
                    <<" and "<<d2<<'/'<<m2<<'/'<<y2<<'\n';
               // *** Press any key to continue ***
               getch();
               break;
```

Continued on next page

LISTING-4.13
(continued)

Date Program

```
        case 2: // *** ADD DAYS TO DATE ***
                // *** Get date and days ***
                GetDate(d1,m1,y1);
                cout<<"Enter number of days : ";
                cin>>days;
                // *** Convert to Julian date and add days ***
                temp=DateToJulian(d1,m1,y1)+days;
                // *** Convert result to date ***
                JulianToDate(temp,d2,m2,y2);
                // *** Display result ***
                cout<<d1<<'/'<<m1<<'/'<<y1<<"+"<<days<<" days is "
                <<d2<<'/'<<m2<<'/'<<y2<<'\n';
                // *** Press any key to continue ***
                getch();
                break;

        case 3: // *** SUBTRACT DAYS FROM DATE ***
                // *** Get date and days ***
                GetDate(d1,m1,y1);
                cout<<"Enter number of days : ";
                cin>>days;
                // *** Convert to Julian and subtract days ***
                temp=DateToJulian(d1,m1,y1)-days;
                // *** Convert result to date ***
                JulianToDate(temp,d2,m2,y2);
                // *** Display date ***
                cout<<d1<<'/'<<m1<<'/'<<y1<<"-"<<days<<" days is "
                    <<d2<<'/'<<m2<<'/'<<y2<<'\n';
                // *** Press any key to continue ***
                getch();
                break;

        case 4: // *** DETERMINE DATE'S DAY OF WEEK ***
                // *** Get date ***
                GetDate(d1,m1,y1);
                // *** Convert to numeric day of week ***
                int dow=DateToDayofWeek(d1,m1,y1);
                // *** Display result ***
                cout<<d1<<'/'<<m1<<'/'<<y1<<" fell on a ";
                DisplayDayofWeek(dow);
                // *** Press any key to continue ***
                getch();
  }
}

void GetDate(int& day, int& month, int& year)
{
  char ch1,ch2;
  int invalid;
  int posx,posy;

  posx=wherex();
  posy=wherey();
  do
  {
      invalid = 0;
      gotoxy(posx,posy);
      cout<<"Enter date: "<<"          \b\b\b\b\b\b\b\b\b\b";
      cin>>day>>ch1>>month>>ch2>>year;
      if (month<1||month>12)
          invalid = 1;
      if(year < 1600)
          invalid = 1;
      if(day>DaysinMonth(month)+(IsLeapYear(year)&&month==2))
          invalid = 1;
  }
  while(invalid);
}
```

Continued on next page

LISTING-4.13
(continued)

Date Program

```
//*** Convert date to days ***
long DateToJulian(int day,int month,int year)
{
   double temp;

   temp = year+(month-2.85)/12;
   return(floor(floor(367.0*temp)-floor(temp)-0.75*floor(temp)+day)
                                          -0.75*2.0)+1721115.0;
}

//*** Convert days to date ***
void JulianToDate(long no, int& day, int& month, int& year)
{
   double t1,t2,y1,m1;

   t1=(no-1721119.0)+2.0;
   y1=floor((t1-0.2)/365.25);
   t2=t1-floor(365.25*y1);
   m1=floor((t2-0.5)/30.6);
   day = (t2-30.6*m1+0.5);
   year = (y1+(m1>9));
   month = (m1+3-((m1>9)*12));
}

//*** Give day of week date fell on ***
int DateToDayofWeek(int d,int m,int y)
{
   int M,CY,C,Y,temp;

   M = (m+9)%12+1;
   CY = y-M/11;
   C    = CY/100;
   Y    = CY%100;
   temp = 2.6*M-0.2;
   return(((temp+d+Y+Y/4+C/4-2*C)%7+7)%7);
}

//*** Display day's name ***
void DisplayDayofWeek(int daycode)
{
   switch (daycode)
   {
        case 0:  cout<<"Sunday\n";
                 break;
        case 1:  cout<<"Monday\n";
                 break;
        case 2:  cout<<"Tuesday\n";
                 break;
        case 3:  cout<<"Wednesday\n";
                 break;
        case 4:  cout<<"Thursday\n";
                 break;
        case 5:  cout<<"Friday\n";
                 break;
        case 6:  cout<<"Saturday\n";
   }
}

//*** Calculate the days in a given month ***
int DaysinMonth(int month)
{
   if(month==4||month==6||month==9||month==11)
        return 30;
   else if(month==2)
        return 28;
   else
        return 31;
}
```

INVESTIGATION

1. What happens to a library function, such as *sqrt()* and *pow()*, when an invalid parameter is passed to it?

2. What assumptions does the compiler make if a user-defined function is declared and defined without a return type? (e.g. `myfunction(int);`)

3. What happens where a user-defined function which is declared as returning a value (say `int`) is coded without returning any value?

4. The parameters passed to a function may be *call by reference* parameters. Can the return value from a function be *call by reference*? If so, what type of result is returned by the routine?

5. If a function returns two values, can the same variable name for both parameters be used when calling the routine?

   e.g. Is it possible with a routine declared as

   ```
   void myfunct(int&, int&);
   ```

   to call the routine with the statement

   ```
   myfunct(x,x);
   ```

SELF-ASSESSMENT REVIEW

1. What function should be called prior to executing random()?

2. What term is used to specify the return type in a function which returns no value?

3. What is the purpose of a function prototype?

4. What is function overloading?

5. What is wrong with the following prototype?

```
int myfunct(int, int= 6, float, char);
```

6. In what way does an inline function differ from other user-defined functions?

7. How does C++ handle a parameter to a function when the parameter is not of the same type as specified in the function's prototype?

8. A function has the prototype

```
void myfunct(int, float=2.1, char='A');
```

   What is wrong with the following function call?

```
myfunct(7,'C');
```

9. What does the term int& signify in the following prototype?

```
void myfunct(int, int&);
```

10. What is the purpose of a call by reference parameter?

11. What is typecasting?

12. State three reasons for using explicit typecasting.

13. Which of the following prototypes are valid function overloads?

    a)
```
int myfunct(int);
void myfunct(int);
```

    b)
```
myfunct();
myfunct(char='A');
```

    c)
```
void myfunct(signed char);
void myfunction(unsigned char);
```

14. State the characteristics of a program which are tested by white box testing?

15. What tests would normally be applied to a `while` structure using white box testing?

16. What is an equivalence class?

17. Identify the structures to be examined under white box testing in the following code:

```
    x=wherex();
    y=wherey();
    do
    {
        invalid=0;
        gotoxy(x,y);
        cout<<"          \b\b\b\b\b\b\b\b\b\b";
        cin>>day>>c1>>month>>c2>>year;
        if(month<1||month>12)
            invalid=1;
        if(year<1600)
            invalid=1;
        maxdays=DaysInMonth(month)+
            (month==2&&IsLeapYear(year));
        if(day<1||day>maxdays)
            invalid=1;
    }
    while(invalid);
}
```

Solutions

PROGRAMMING EXERCISE 4.1

```
1.
#include<iostream.h>
#include<math.h>
#include<conio.h>
#include<iomanip.h>

void main()
{
    int no;

    cout<<"Number\tSquare\tSquare Root\n";
    for(no=1;no<=20;no++)
        cout<<setw(3)<<no<<'\t'<<setw(4)
        <<no*no<<'\t'<<sqrt(no)<<'\n';
    getch();
}

2.
#include<iostream.h>
#include<stdlib.h>
#include<conio.h>

void main()
{
    int no;

    randomize();
    for(no=1;no<=6;no++)
        cout<<random(49)+1<<"  ";
    cout<<'\n';
    getch();
}
```

PROGRAMMING EXERCISE 4.3

```
#include<conio.h>
#include<iostream.h>

void main()
{
    int count=0;
    int ch;

    ch=getch();
    while(!ch)
    {
        ch=getch();
        ch=getch();
    }

    while(ch!=13)
    {
        if(ch>='A'&&ch<='Z'&&count<10)
        {
            putch(ch);
            count++;
        }
        else if(ch==8&& count>0)
        {
            cout<<"\b \b";
            count-;
        }
        ch=getch();
        while(!ch)
        {
            ch=getch();
            ch=getch();
        }
    }
}
```

TASK 4.1

1. window(61,19,80,25)

2. 15,3

TASK 4.2

1. 0X4114

2. Flashing Yellow on a Green background.

PROGRAMMING EXERCISE 4.6

```
#include<conio.h>
#include<iostream.h>

void Box();

void main()
{
    Box();
    getch();
}
void Box()
{
    int no;
    int atx, aty;

    atx=wherex();
    aty=wherey();
    cout<<"**********";
    for(no=1;no<=8;no++)
    {
        gotoxy(atx,aty+no);
        cout<<'*';
        gotoxy(atx+9,aty+no);
        cout<<'*';
    }
    gotoxy(atx,aty+9);
    cout<<"**********\n";
}
```

PROGRAMMING EXERCISE 4.7

```
#include<conio.h>
#include<iostream.h>

void Box(int);

void main()
{
    int length;

    cout<<"Enter required size : ";
    cin>>length;
    Box(length);
    getch();
}
void Box(int size)
{
    int no;
    int atx, aty;

    atx=wherex();
    aty=wherey();
    for(no=1;no<=size;no++)
        cout<<'*';
    cout<<'\n';
    for(no=1;no<=size-2;no++)
    {
        gotoxy(atx,aty+no);
        cout<<'*';
        gotoxy(atx+size-1,aty+no);
        cout<<'*';
    }
    gotoxy(atx,aty+size-1);
    for(no=1;no<=size;no++)
        cout<<'*';
    cout<<'\n';
}
```

PROGRAMMING EXERCISE 4.8

The equal sign ('=') has an ASCII code of 61 and 40 is the ASCII code for '('. Automatic type casting results in a line of 61 '('s.

TASK 4.3

`stars('x');` should be `stars(100,'x');`
If the second default parameter is given a value, the first one must also be explicitly specified.

`void stars(int no=100,char star='*');` should be
`void stars(int no, char star);`
The default values should not be specified in the function definition. Additionally, the identifier '*star*' is not a good choice of name since it is so similar to the function name.

`random()` should not normally be used without a preceding call to `randomize()`.

TASK 4.4

```
smaller(smaller(a,b),smaller(c,d))
```

PROGRAMMING EXERCISE 4.9

```
#include<conio.h>
#include<iostream.h>

char Next(char);

void main()
{
    char letter;

    cout<<"Enter character: ";
    cin>>letter;
    cout<<letter<<" next is "<<Next(letter);
    getch();
}

char Next(char letter)
{
    return letter+1;
}
```

PROGRAMMING EXERCISE 4.11

```
#include<conio.h>
#include<iostream.h>

void print(int);
void print(int,int,int);

void main()
{
    int no;

    cout<<"Enter number: ";
    cin>>no;
    print(no);
    print(15,8,no);
    getch();
}

void print(int n)
{
    cout<<n;
}

void print(int x, int y, int n)
{
    gotoxy(x,y);
    cout<<n;
}
```

TASK 4.5

```
1.  int('A');

2.  (signed char)-9

3.  float(x)

4.  double(8%5+3)

5.  -125 cannot be stored in an unsigned int.
```

TASK 4.6

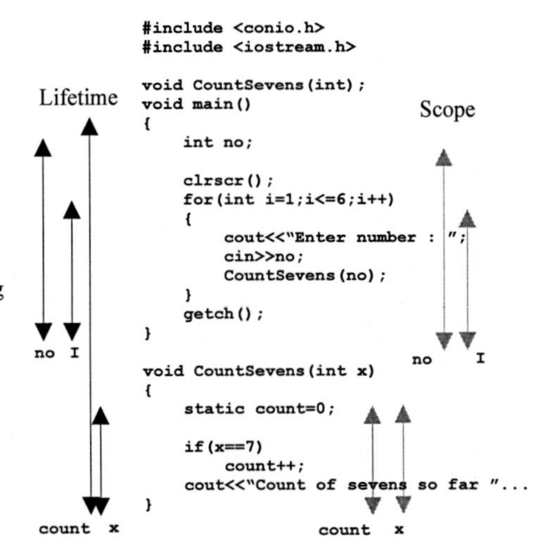

Lifetime
Scope
#include <conio.h>
#include <iostream.h>
void CountSevens(int);
void main()
{
int no;
clrscr();
for(int i=1;i<=6;i++)
{
cout<<"Enter number : ";
cin>>no;
CountSevens(no);
}
getch();
}
no I
no I
void CountSevens(int x)
{
static count=0;
if(x==7)
count++;
cout<<"Count of sevens so far "...
}
count x
count x

PROGRAMMING EXERCISE 4.13

```
1.
#include <iostream.h>
#include <conio.h>

void Rectangle(int,int,int,int);

void main()
{
    int x,y,length,height;

    clrscr();
    cout<< "Enter position of top left corner : ";
    cin>>x>>y;
    cout<< "Enter length and height : ";
    cin>>length>>height;
    Rectangle(x,y,length,height);
    getch();
}

void Rectangle(int x, int y, int length, int
height)
{
    int i;
    gotoxy(x,y);
    cout<<char(218);
    for(i= 1;i<=length-2;i++)
        cout<<char(196);
    cout<<char(191);

    for(i=1;i<=height-2;i++)
    {
        gotoxy(x,y+i);
        cout<<char(179);
        gotoxy(x+length-1,y+i);
        cout<<char(179);
    }
    gotoxy(x,y+height-1);
    cout<<char(192);
    for(i= 1;i<=length-2;i++)
        cout<<char(196);
    cout<<char(217);
}

2.
#include<iostream.h>
#include <conio.h>

int SecLargest(int,int,int,int);

void main()
{
    int no1, no2, no3, no4;

    clrscr();
    cout<<"Enter four numbers : ";
    cin>>no1>>no2>>no3>>no4;
    cout<<"Second largest value is "
        <<SecLargest(no1,no2,no3,no4)<<'\n';
    getch();
}
```

Continued on next page

```
int SecLargest(int n1, int n2, int n3, int n4)
{
    int largest,second;

    if(n1>n2)
    {
        largest=n1;
        second=n2;
    }
    else
    {
        largest=n2;
        second=n1;
    }
    if(n3>largest)
    {
        second=largest;
        largest=n3;
    }
    else if(n3>second)
        second=n3;
    if(n4>largest)
    {
        second=largest;
        largest=n4;
    }
    else if(n4>second)
        second=n4;
    return second;
}
```

3.

```
#include <iostream.h>
#include <conio.h>
#include <ctype.h>

int Classify(char);

void main()
{
    char ch;

    cout<<"Enter character : ";
    cin>>ch;
    switch(Classify(ch))
    {
        case 1: cout<<"Vowel\n";
                break;
        case 2: cout<<"Consonant\n";
                break;
        case 3: cout<<"Non-alphabetic\n";
    }
    getch();
}

int Classify(char ch)
{
    if(isalpha(ch))
        if(toupper(ch)=='A'||toupper(ch)=='E'
        ||toupper(ch)=='I'||toupper(ch)=='O'
        ||toupper(ch)=='U')
            return 1;
        else
            return 2;
    else
        return 3;
}
```

4.

```
#include <iostream.h>
#include <conio.h>

inline int IsLeapYear(int y)
{
    if((y%4==0&&y%100!=0)||y%400==0)
        return 1;
    else
        return 0;
}

void main()
{
    int year;

    clrscr();
    cout<<"Enter year : ";
    cin>>year;
    if(IsLeapYear(year))
        cout<<"Leap year\n";
    else
        cout<<"Non-leap year\n";
    getch();
}
```

5.

```
#include <iostream.h>
#include <conio.h>

int DaysInMonth(int);

void main()
{
    int month;

    clrscr();
    cout<<"Enter month : ";
    cin>>month;
    cout<<"Month "<<month<<" has "
        <<DaysInMonth(month)<<" days\n";
    getch();
}

int DaysInMonth(int m)
{
    if(m==4||m==6||m==9||m==11)
        return 30;
    else if(m==2)
        return 28;
    else
        return 31;
}
```

6.

```
#include<conio.h>
#include<iostream.h>

int ReadKey();

void main()
{
    cout<<ReadKey()<<endl;
    getch();
}

int ReadKey()
{
    int ch;

    ch=getch();
    if(ch==0)
    {
        ch=-getch();
    }
    return ch;
}
```

7.

```
#include <iostream.h>
#include <conio.h>

inline int IsLeapYear(int y)
{
    if((y%4==0&&y%100!=0)||y%400==0)
        return 1;
    else
        return 0;
}

void GetDate(int&, int&, int&);
int DaysInMonth(int);

void main()
{
    int day,month,year;
    clrscr();
    cout << "Enter date : ";
    GetDate(day,month,year);
    cout<<day<<'/'<<month<<'/'<<year<<'\n';
    getch();
}

void GetDate(int& day, int& month, int& year)
{
    char c1,c2;
    int invalid;
    int x,y;
    int maxdays;

    x=wherex();
    y=wherey();
    do
    {
        invalid=0;
        gotoxy(x,y);
        cout<<"          \b\b\b\b\b\b\b\b\b\b";
        cin>>day>>c1>>month>>c2>>year;
        if(month<1||month>12)
            invalid=1;
```

Continued on next page

```
        if(year<1600)
            invalid=1;
        maxdays=DaysInMonth(month)+
                (month==2&&IsLeapYear(year));
        if(day<1||day>maxdays)
            invalid=1;
    }
    while(invalid);
}

int DaysInMonth(int m)
{
    if(m==4||m==6||m==9||m==11)
        return 30;
    else if(m==2)
        return 28;
    else
        return 31;
}
```

8.

```
#include <iostream.h>
#include <conio.h>
#include <math.h>
long DateToJulian(int,int,int);
inline int IsLeapYear(int y)
{
    if((y%4==0&&y%100!=0)||y%400==0)
        return 1;
    else
        return 0;
};
void GetDate(int&, int&, int&);
int DaysInMonth(int);

void main()
{
    int day,month,year;

    clrscr();
    GetDate(day,month,year);
    cout<<DateToJulian(day,month,year)
        <<" days  between 1/1/4713BC and "
        <<day<<'/'<<month<<'/'<<year<<'\n';
    getch();
}

long DateToJulian(int day,int month,int year)
{
    double temp;
    temp = year+(month-2.85)/12;
    return(floor(floor(367.0*temp)-floor(temp)
        -0.75*floor(temp)+day)
        -0.75*2.0)+1721115.0;
}

void GetDate(int& day, int& month, int& year)
{
    char c1,c2;
    int invalid;
    int x,y;
    int maxdays;

    x=wherex();
    y=wherey();
    do
    {
        invalid=0;
        gotoxy(x,y);
        cout<<"          \b\b\b\b\b\b\b\b\b\b";
        cin>>day>>c1>>month>>c2>>year;
        if(month<1||month>12)
            invalid=1;
        if(year<1600)
            invalid=1;
        maxdays=DaysInMonth(month)+
            (month==2&&IsLeapYear(year));
        if(day<1||day>maxdays)
            invalid=1;
    }
    while(invalid);
}

int DaysInMonth(int m)
{
    if(m==4||m==6||m==9||m==11)
        return 30;
    else if(m==2)
        return 28;
    else
        return 31;
}
```

9.

```
#include <iostream.h>
#include <conio.h>
#include <math.h>

void JulianToDate(long no, int& day, int& month,
int& year);

void main()
{
    long days;
    int day,month,year;

    clrscr();
    cout<<"Enter number of days : ";
    cin>>days;
    JulianToDate(days,day,month,year);
    cout<<day<<'/'<<month<<'/'<<year<<" is "
        <<days<<" days since 1/1/4713BC\n";
    getch();
}
void JulianToDate(long no, int& day, int& month,
int& year)
{
    double t1,t2,y1,m1;

    t1=(no-1721119.0)+2.0;
    y1=floor((t1-0.2)/365.25);
    t2=t1-floor(365.25*y1);
    m1=floor((t2-0.5)/30.6);
    day = (t2-30.6*m1+0.5);
    year = (y1+(m1>9));
    month = (m1+3-((m1>9)*12));
}
```

10.

```
#include <iostream.h>
#include <conio.h>

inline float ToKilometres(int m)
{
    return (m*1.6);
}

inline float ToKilometres(int m, int y)
{
    return (m*1.6+y/1760*1.6);
}


void main()
{
    int miles,yards;
    int option;

    clrscr();
    cout<<"1 - Miles to kilometres\n";
    cout<<"2 - Miles and yards to kilometres\n";
    cout<<"\n    Enter option (1,2) : ";
    cin>>option;
    if(option==1)
    {
        cout<<"Enter miles : ";
        cin>>miles;
        cout<<miles<<" miles is "
            <<ToKilometres(miles)<<" kilometres\n";
    }
    else
    {
        cout<< "Enter miles : ";
        cin>>miles;
        cout<< "Enter yards : ";
        cin>>yards;
        cout<<miles<<" miles "<<yards<<" yards is "
            <<ToKilometres(miles,yards)
            <<" kilometres\n";
    }
    getch();
}
```

11.

```
#include <iostream.h>
#include <conio.h>

long Reverse(long);

void main()
{
    long no;

    clrscr();
    cout<<" Enter number : ";
    cin>>no;
```

Continued on next page

```
    cout<<no<<" reverses digits to "
        <<Reverse(no)<<'\n';
    getch();
}

long Reverse(long no)
{
    long temp=0;

    while(no)
    {
        temp = temp*10+no%10;
        no/=10;
    }
    return temp;
}
```

TASK 4.7

1. Invalid month
    a) Less than 1
    b) Greater than 12
2. Months returning 28
3. Months returning 30
4. Months returning 31

Chapter 5

Data Structures

This chapter covers the following topics:

Bit Fields

Bit Manipulation Operators

Double Indirection

Dynamic Space Allocation

Enumerated Types

One-Dimensional Arrays

Pointer Variables

String Functions

Strings

Structure Definitions

Type Definition

Union

POINTERS

Introduction

FIG-5.1
Allocating Memory

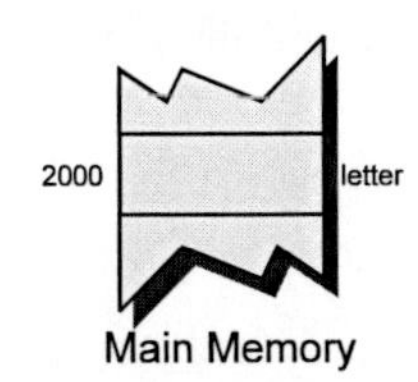

When we define a variable, it is allocated one or more bytes in the computer's memory. This, in effect, associates each variable with an unique address within that memory. Hence, the definition

```
char letter;
```

might allocate the memory location at address 2000 to the variable *letter* (see FIG-5.1).

FIG-5.2
Allocating More Memory

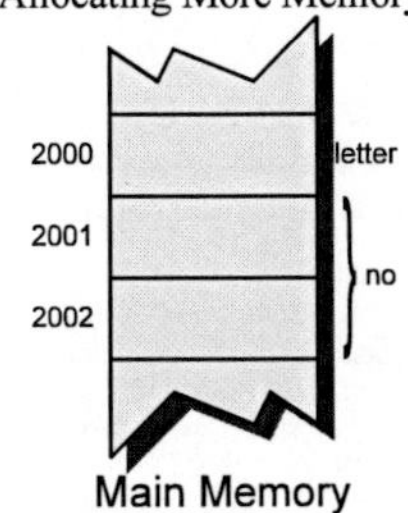

Where a variable is allocated two or more bytes, the variable is identified by the address of the first byte allocated to it. For example, if the definition

```
char letter;
short no;
```

results in the space allocation shown in FIG-5.2, then the variable *no* is associated with the address 2001.

The *Address Of* Operator, &

The address allocated to a variable can be determined using the **address of** operator, **&**. For example, while we can display the contents of *no* with the statement

```
cout<<no;
```

we can display the address of the first byte allocated to *no* using the statement

```
cout<<&no;
```

Assuming the addresses in FIG-5.2, the above statement would result in the value 2001 being displayed. However, in practice, there is no way of knowing in advance the exact memory locations allocated by the compiler to a variable.

Pointer Variables

What is a Pointer?

As well as variables to hold numeric and character values, C++ allows us to create variables designed to hold memory addresses. These are known as **pointer variables**. This is because a pointer variable contains an integer value representing the address of some location in memory and, hence, they can be thought of as pointing to (or **referencing**) some memory location.

Since addresses are simply integer values (e.g. 2001), you may be tempted to assume that normal integer variables could be used to hold this information, but pointer variables have their own unique set of operations and are treated differently from other variable types by the compiler.

Defining Pointers

Like any other variable, a pointer must be defined. A variable is identified as a pointer by being preceded by an asterisk in the definition statement (e.g. `*ptr`). A pointer definition also specifies a type. For example:

```
short *sptr;
```

The type (`short`, in the above example) identifies the type of value expected at the location pointed to by the variable. Hence we may read the above definition as

sptr is a pointer to a `short` *value.*

or

sptr will contain an address of `short` *value*

> **TASK 5.1**
>
> Write the definition necessary to create variables *iptr1* and *iptr2* which are pointers to `int` values and *fptr* which references a `float` value.

Using Pointers

Allocating a Value to a Pointer

FIG-5.3
Allocating Pointer Space

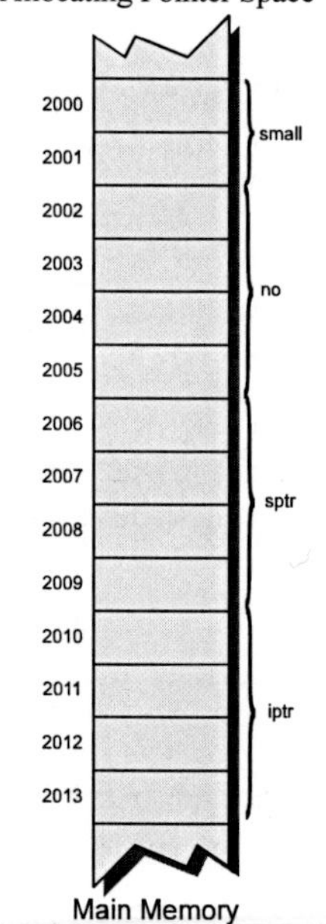

If we assume a program begins with the definitions

```
short   small;  //simple short variable
long    no;     //simple long variable
short   *sptr;  //pointer to a short value
long    *iptr;  //pointer to an long value
```

then the memory allocated by the compiler might be as shown in FIG-5.3, with each pointer being allocated 4 bytes.

For clarity we may simplify this diagram to show only each variable and its start address (FIG-5.4).

> **TASK 5.2**
>
> Draw a simplified memory allocation diagram for the following declaration:
>
> ```
> float   rno1,*rptr;
> long    lno,*lptr;
> ```
>
> Assume space is allocated in sequential order, beginning at location 3010.

FIG-5.4
Simplified Variable Allocation

2000 small
2002 no
2006 sptr
2010 iptr
Main Memory

While program assignments such as

```
small = 12;
no = 65;
```

result in values being stored in the simple variables *small* and *no*, the pointer variables can be allocated the addresses of *small* and *no* using the statements:

```
sptr = &small;
iptr = &no;
```

FIG-5.5
Allocating Addresses

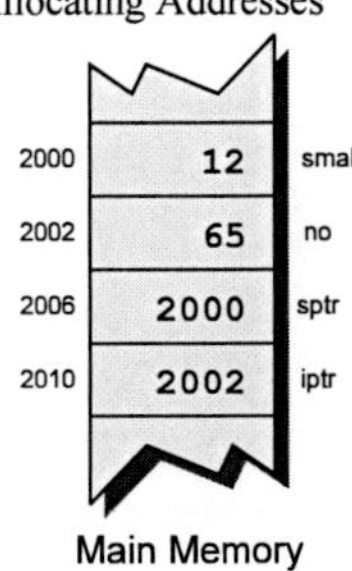

The results of these four statements are shown in FIG-5.5.

Note that we must allocate the address of a `short` value to the `short` pointer and an `int` value to the `int` pointer, otherwise unexpected results will occur.

Since, in practice, we are unlikely to know the actual addresses involved when variables are allocated memory space, we can show that *sptr* references *small* and *iptr* points to *no* using the more abstract style shown in FIG-5.6.

FIG-5.6

Referencing: Generalised

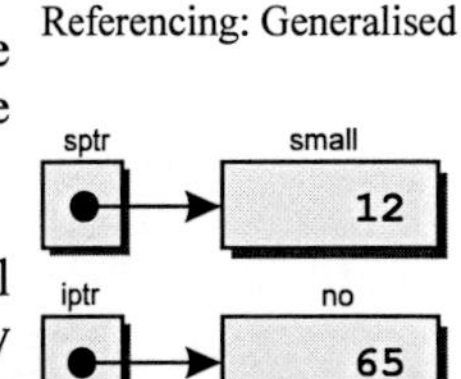

Dereferencing a Pointer

Once a pointer contains a valid address, it can be used to access the data at that address. This is known as **dereferencing** the pointer.

To access the contents of the referenced address, we use the pointer name preceded by an asterisk. Hence, the statement

```
cout << *sptr;
```

Using the line **`cout << sptr;`** would display the address held in *sptr*.

will display the contents held at the address pointed to by *sptr* (i.e. 12).

In this context, the asterisk is known as the **indirection operator**.

Dereferencing can be used in any situation where a normal variable name might be used. This allows statements such as:

```
no = 65;
```

to be replaced by

```
*iptr = 65;
```

TABLE-5.1 gives several examples showing normal variable statements and the dereferenced equivalents.

TABLE-5.1

Pointer Equivalents

Standard Commands	Pointer Equivalent
`no++;`	`*iptr++;`
`cin>>small ;`	`cin>>*sptr;`
`if(small== 14)`	`if(*sptr==14)`
`cout<<10-no;`	`cout<<10-*iptr;`
`for(no=0;no<5;no++)`	`for(*iptr=0;*iptr<5;*iptr++)`

There are situations in which dereferencing can confuse the compiler. For example, if the expression

`12/no;` is replaced by `12/*iptr;`

the compiler will take the /* as the start of a comment and your program will suddenly produce a glut of new errors. This is overcome by enclosing the pointer dereference in parentheses or placing a space between the two characters:

`12/(*iptr);` or `12/ *iptr;`

Alternatively, a statement such as

`cout <<5*no;` if replaced by `cout<<5**iptr;`

may confuse a programmer rather than the compiler. Again, this can be clarified by using parentheses or additional spacing:

`cout << 5*(*iptr);` or `cout << 5 * *iptr;`

HINT: Add 3 pointer variables and use these to hold the addresses of *no1, no2* and *ans*.

PROGRAMMING EXERCISE 5.1

Using only pointer notation, produce a program equivalent to:

```
#include <iostream.h>
#include <conio.h>
void main()
{
   int no1,no2,ans;

   clrscr();
   cout<<"Enter two numbers : ";
   cin>>no1>>no2;
   if (no1<no2)
       ans = no1;
   else
       ans = no2;
   cout<<"Smaller value is "<<ans<<'\n';
}
```

Initialising Pointers

To indicate that a pointer variable does not contain an address we can assign it the value **NULL**. For example:

```
int *iptr=NULL;
```

The graphical representation of an empty pointer is shown in FIG-5.7.

FIG-5.7

Null Pointer Symbol

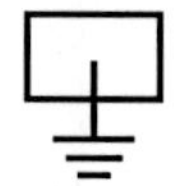

The term NULL is defined in several header files such as *stdlib.h.* One of these header files must be included in your program if you are using NULL. NULL sets all the bits of the pointer variable to zero. Hence, the same effect can be achieved by the statement

```
int *iptr=0;
```

or by any other constant, such as '\0', which has a zero value.

It is also possible to initialise a pointer to the address of a previously defined variable.

```
int n1=5;       // Normal variable
int *iptr=&n1; // iptr references n1
```

Two or more pointer variables may reference the same address. Hence, assuming the definitions

```
int no, *iptr1, *iptr2;
```

both pointers can reference *no* by using the statements

```
iptr1 = &no;
iptr2 = &no;
```

or

```
iptr1 = &no;
iptr2 = iptr1;
```

FIG-5.8
Referencing the same Address

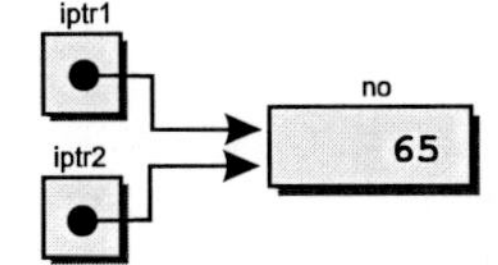

This last method copies the contents of one pointer variable (*iptr1*) to another (*i*ptr2), with the result that both then contain the same address (see FIG-5.8).

> **TASK 5.3**
>
> Write the `if` statement necessary to check if two integer pointers, *iptra* and *iptrb*, reference:
>
> 1. the same address
> 2. the same value

Pointers and Constants

Pointers to Constants

If your program contains constant definitions such as

```
const float pi=3.1415;
const float e=2.7183;
```

then an attempt to create a pointer to one of these values with a statement such as

```
float *fptr = &pi;
```

will not compile, since *fptr* is a pointer to a `float` value whereas *pi* is a `const float` value.

The correct definition is

```
const float *fptr=&pi;
```

which states that *fptr* is a pointer to a `const float`, in this case, *pi*.

Since *fptr* points to a constant, the referenced value cannot be changed. Hence, a statement such as

```
*fptr = 3.1516;
```

would be flagged as an error.

However, the content of the pointer itself is NOT a constant, which allows *fptr* to reference other `const float` values. For example,

```
fptr = &e;
```

is valid.

Constant Pointers

If necessary, the address held by a pointer can be fixed by defining the pointer itself to be a constant. For example,

```
int no1, no2;
int const *iptr = &no1;
```

fixes the address held by *iptr* to be that of *no1*.

And while we may change the contents of the referenced address with statements such as

```
*iptr =12;
```

it is not possible to change the contents of *iptr* itself with commands such as

```
iptr = &no2;
```

which would be flagged as an error by the compiler.

Constant Pointers to Constants

A final option is to create a constant pointer to a constant value where neither the address held by the pointer nor the referenced value may be changed. For example,

```
const float pi = 3.1416;
const float const *fptr = &pi;
```

Note, that the definition of *fptr* above is a combination of formats from the earlier definitions.

> **TASK 5.4**
>
> Write definitions for the following:
>
> 1. A pointer, *icptr*, to `const int MAX=10;`
> 2. A constant pointer, *fptr*, to `float x;`
> 3. A constant pointer, *cfptr*, to `const float tax=0.25;`

Pointers and Functions

Pointers as Function Parameters

In C, *call by reference* parameters, are not available. This means that the only way to modify the value of a parameter to a function, is to use pointer notation.

For example, while C++ allows us to write a function, *times2()*, which doubles the value of the specified parameter (LISTING-5.1), C achieves the same result using a pointer as the parameter (LISTING-5.2).

LISTING-5.1

Reference Parameter

```
#include <conio.h>
#include <iostream.h>

void times2(int&);

void main()
{
   int number=3;

   clrscr();
   times2(number);
   cout << number << '\n';
   getch();
}

// *** Doubles value of specified parameter ***
void times2(int &no)
{
   no *= 2;
}
```

LISTING-5.2

Pointer Parameter

```
#include <conio.h>
#include <iostream.h>

void times2(int *);

void main()
{
   int number=3;

   clrscr();
   times2(&number);
   cout << number << '\n';
   getch();
}

void times2(int *no)
{
   *no *= 2;
}
```

Specifies an **int** pointer as the parameter type

Gives the address of the actual parameter

Dereference pointer to change value

There are three differences in the two versions of the routine:

- The function parameter is specified as a *call by reference* parameter in LISTING-5.1 and as an `int` pointer in LISTING-5.2.

- The function call specifies the actual parameter name in LISTING-5.1 and the address of the actual parameter in LISTING-5.2.

- The body of the function uses a normal assignment statement in LISTING-5.1 and pointer dereferencing in LISTING-5.2.

A final point to note is that where a pointer parameter is required, the address of a variable or constant of the same type may be used instead. Hence the code

```
int number = 3;

times2(&number);
```

is equivalent to

```
int number=3;
int *iptr;
    .
iptr = &number;
    .
times2(iptr);
```

Both methods of defining functions can be used in C++, but since the *call by reference* results in more easily understood code, this is the method of preference. However, there are circumstances in which pointer parameters need to be used (these are discussed later in this chapter).

The truth is, that C++ implements *call by reference* by using pointers - it just hides the details from the programmer!

Returning an Address

Chapter 4 contained a function which returned the smallest of three values. Should we require a similar function which returned, not the smallest value, but the address of the variable containing the smallest value, then the function would have the prototype:

```
int *smallest(int&,int&,int&);
```

In order to return the address of the variable containing the smallest value, the addresses of the three variables involved must be passed to the routine.

Although we might have created pointer variables as in

```
int n1=3,n2=6,n3=2;
int *p1=&n1,*p2=&n2,*p3=&n3;
int *s;
```

and called the function using

```
s=smallest(p1,p2,p3);
cout << s;
```

since *call by reference* is implemented using pointers, we can omit the pointer variables and simplify the code to

```
int n1=3,n2=6,n3=2;
int *s;

s=smallest(n1,n2,n3);
cout << s;
```

Even the pointer *s* may be omitted to give a final version of

```
int n1=3,n2=6,n3=2;

 cout << smallest(n1,n2,n3);
```

The full program is shown in LISTING-5.3.

LISTING-5.3

Returning an Address

```
#include <conio.h>
#include <iostream.h>

int*smallest(int&,int&,int&);

void main()
{
   int n1=3,n2=6,n3=2;
   clrscr();
   // *** Display the address of each variable              ***
   cout << &n1 << ' ' << &n2 << ' ' << &n3 << '\n';
   // *** Display the address of the variable containing the ***
   // ***smallest value                                      ***
   cout << smallest(n1,n2,n3) << '\n';
   getch();
}


// *** Function to return address of variable containing the***
// *** smallest value                                        ***
int* smallest(int& no1,int& no2,int& no3)
{
   int temp;

   if(no1 < no2 && no1 < no3)
        return &no1;
   else if(no2 < no1 && no2 < no3)
        return &no2;
   else
        return &no3;
}
```

Pointers to Functions

Just as a variable name is associated with the address of the first memory location allocated to it, so a function name is associated with the start address of its first instruction. Because of this, we are at liberty to create a pointer to a function.

Whereas a variable pointer must specify the type of value it will reference, a function pointer must list the type of value returned by the function it is to point to, as well as the number and type of values in the function parameter list. For example, if the pointer variable, *fnptr*, is to be used to reference the function *line()* whose prototype is

```
void line(int,char);
```

then the function pointer's definition would be

```
void (*fnptr)(int,char);
```

If we require several function pointers to functions with identical return types and parameter lists, these are listed within the first set of parentheses:

```
void(*fnptr1,*fnptr2)(int,char);
```

The general format for declaring function pointers is given in FIG-5.9.

FIG-5.9
Defining Function Pointers

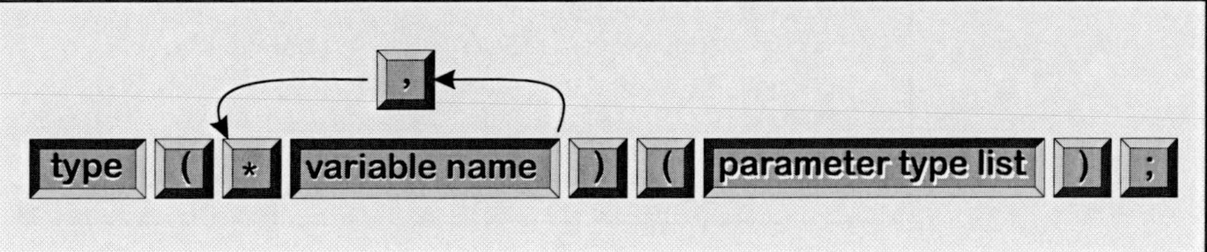

where

type is the type of value returned by the function.

variable name is the name given to the pointer. Several variable names can be specified, each separated from the next by a comma.

parameter list is the list of parameter types required by the function. Each item in the list is separated from the next by a comma. Only the parentheses are shown if there are no parameters.

Since the address of a function is associated with that function's name, the function pointer name must be enclosed in parentheses, otherwise the compiler assumes a function called which returns a pointer value. For example,

```
int *fnptr(char,char);
```

would be taken as a function called *fnptr* which returns an `int` pointer.

PROGRAMMING EXERCISE 5.2

Type in and execute the following program which displays the address of the function *line()*.

```
#include <iostream.h>
#include <conio.h>
void line();

  void main()
{
  clrscr();
  cout << "Address of line() : " << line << '\n';
  getch();
}
void line()
{
  cout << "*************************\n";
}
```

To assign the address of the function *line()* to *fnptr* we use the statement:

```
fnptr = line;  //*** Note, the function parentheses are omitted
```

PROGRAMMING EXERCISE 5.3

Modify the program given in PROGRAMMING EXERCISE 5.2 to read:

```
void main()
{
  void(*fnptr)();

  fnptr = line;       //*** Reference function
  clrscr();
  cout << "Address of line() : " << line << '\n';
  cout << "Address in pointer :" << fnptr << '\n';
  getch();
}
```

Execute the program and check that both addresses displayed are the same.

Once the pointer references the function, rather than use the conventional statement

```
line();
```

to call the function, we can achieve the same effect by replacing the function name by that of the pointer:

```
fnptr();
```

Once *fnptr* references *line()*, we may think of *fnptr* as being an alternative name for the function.
Hence both terms (*line* and *fnptr*) can be used interchangeably.

PROGRAMMING EXERCISE 5.4

Modify `main()` from PROGRAMMING EXERCISE 5.3 to call the *line()* function using both methods described above.

The next programming example shows a single function pointer being used to call one of two functions. The program logic is as follows:

```
Assign values to three variables
Get users option to find largest or smallest
Assign function pointer to largest or smallest function
Call function referenced by pointer
Display result
```

The corresponding code is given in LISTING-5.4.

LISTING-5.4

Function Pointer

```
#include <iostream.h>
#include <conio.h>

int smallest(int,int,int);
int largest(int,int,int);


void main()
{
   int (*fptr)(int,int,int);   // *** Function pointer ***
   int n1=8,n2=10,n3=5;
   int option;
   //*** Select option ***
   clrscr();
   cout << "Enter option:\n\t1 - Highest\n\t2 - Lowest\n";
   cin >> option;
   //*** Reference selected function ***
   if(option == 1)
       fptr = largest;           // *** Assign function pointer
   else
       fptr = smallest;          // *** Assign function pointer
   //*** Call selected function ***
   cout << fptr(n1,n2,n3);
   getch();
}


int smallest(int no1, int no2, int no3)
{
   int temp;

   if(no1 < no2)
       temp = no1;
   else
       temp = no2;
   if(no3 < temp)
       temp = no3;
   return temp;
}
```

Continued on next page

LISTING-5.4
(continued)

Function Pointer

```
int largest(int no1, int no2, int no3)
{
   int temp;

   if(no1 > no2)
       temp = no1;
   else
       temp = no2;
   if(no3 > temp)
       temp = no3;
   return temp;
}
```

An Explanation of the Code

`int (*fptr)(int,int,int);` Defines a pointer, *fptr*, to a function returning an `int` value which requires three `int` parameters.

```
if(option==1)
    fptr = largest;
else
    fptr = smallest;
```

Assigns the address of *largest()* or *smallest()* to *fptr* (depending on option chosen).

`cout << fptr(n1,n2,n3);` Calls the function referenced by *fptr*. *n1*, *n2* and *n3* are the parameters to the function and the value returned is displayed.

This method of using function pointers has done nothing to increase the efficiency or clarity of the program.

TASK 5.5

Write function pointer definitions for each of the following functions (use variable names *fnptr1* and *fnptr2*):

1. `float f1(float);`
2. `int f2();`
3. `void f3();`
4. Two pointers to `int f4(int,float);`

A function pointer can only be assigned the address of a function which exactly matches the return type and parameters specified in the pointer definition. For example, if a program contains three functions: largest(), *big()* and *smallest()* whose prototypes are

```
int smallest(int,int,int);
int big(int,int);
```

and

```
int largest(int,int,int);
```

fptr may reference either *smallest()* or *largest()* but not *big()*, since it takes only two `int` parameters.

Dynamic Allocation

new

Since pointer dereferencing can be used to replace a variable name in a program, the final stage in this process is to eliminate the need to define the normal variable in the first place. This is done by allocating the space referenced by a pointer using the `new` command. Assuming the definition

```
int *iptr;
```

we can reserve space in which to store an integer value and at the same time make *iptr* hold the address of that memory space with the single command

```
iptr = new int;
```

The effects of this command are shown in FIG-5.10.

FIG-5.10

Dynamic Allocation

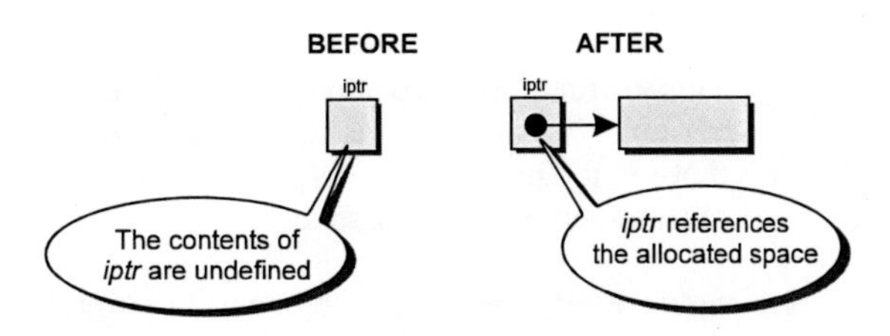

This technique is known as **dynamic space allocation**.

Since the allocated space has no name of its own, its contents can only be accessed by dereferencing *iptr*.

The program in LISTING-5.5 shows this technique in practice.

LISTING 5.5

Using Dynamic Allocation

```
#include <iostream.h>
#include <conio.h>

void main()
{
  int *iptr;

  clrscr();
  iptr = new int;          //*** Allocate space
  *iptr = 12;              //*** Store value in space
  cout << *iptr<<'\n';     //*** Display value in space
  getch();
}
```

Since we can only access the dynamically allocated data area via the pointer, it is important that the content of the pointer variable is not changed. For example, if, after allocating space using *iptr*, we execute the command

```
iptr = NULL;
```

the connection between pointer and allocated space will be lost (see FIG-5.11) - and there is no way to get it back!

FIG 5.11

Losing a Pointer Link to Dynamically Allocated Variables

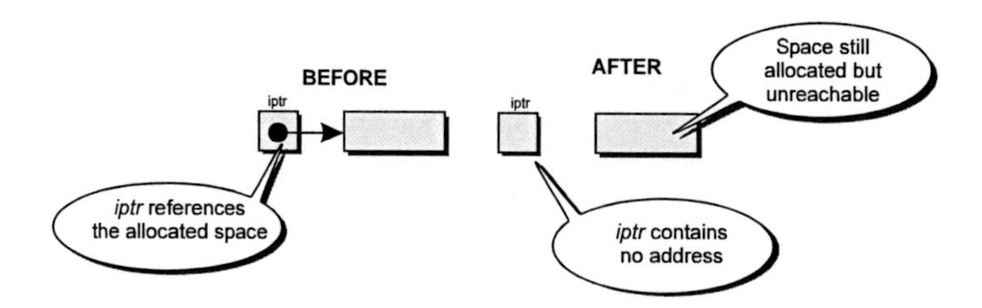

delete

The space assigned to normal variables is deallocated at the end of their lifetime (see Chapter 3), but dynamically allocated space remains allocated until it is deallocated with the `delete` command. To delete the space referenced by *iptr* use

```
delete iptr;
```

This instruction deallocates the space but does not modify the contents of the pointer variable. It is important to deallocate space when it is no longer required, otherwise there is a danger, when large amounts of memory are dynamically allocated, of running out of memory space.

Since attempting to dereference the pointer after the space it points to has been deallocated, can have disastrous results, it is good policy to follow the `delete` statement by a command to reset the pointer involved to NULL:

```
delete iptr;    //*** Deallocate space ***
iptr = NULL;    //*** Reset pointer    ***
```

Dynamic allocation of space is a very powerful tool, allowing a program to allocate and deallocate data space as and when required. We will see more of this later.

void Pointers

Sometimes it is useful not to declare the type of value that the pointer is to reference. This can be done by defining a `void` pointer with a statement such as:

```
void *ptr;
```

Such a pointer can then be used to point to a variable of any type:

```
int no1;
float discount;

void *ptr;          //*** void pointer

ptr = &no1;         //*** ptr points to an int variable
ptr = &discount;    //*** ptr points to a float variable
```

We can also use a `void` pointer when allocating space:

```
ptr = new int;
```

However, the compiler cannot deal with dereferencing a `void` pointer, since there is no way of knowing how to interpret the binary pattern at the referenced address.

When accessing the contents of the referenced address, it is necessary to cast the `void` pointer to the appropriate type (see FIG-5.12):

FIG-5.12

Casting a void Pointer

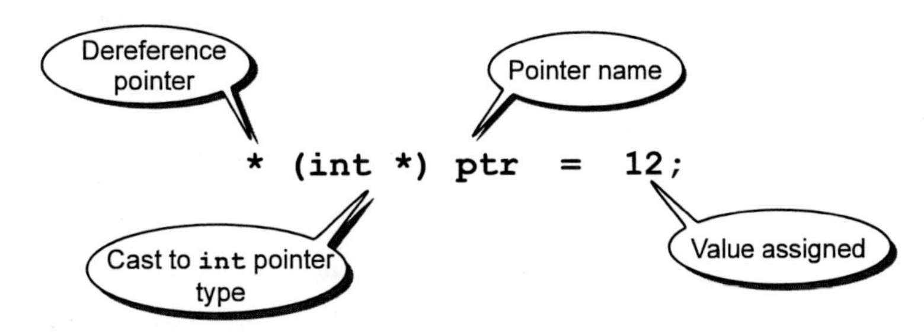

This format must be used each time the pointer is to be dereferenced.

An example of this technique is given in LISTING-5.6.

LISTING-5.6

Casting a void Pointer

```
#include <iostream.h>
#include <conio.h>


void main()
{
   void    *ptr;
   int     no;
   float   real;

   ptr = &no;            //*** Points to an int
   no = 9;
   *(int*)ptr = 12;
   cout << *(int*)ptr << endl;
   ptr = &real;          //*** Points to float
   getch();
}
```

PROGRAMMING EXERCISE 5.5

Modify the program in LISTING-5.6 to:

1. Reference the variable *real*; assign it the value 3.14, and display its value.
2. Dynamically allocate space for a `long int` value which is to be read from the keyboard and displayed.

PROGRAMMING EXERCISE 5.6

Write programs to perform the following tasks:

1. Display the address and contents of two `long int` variables, *v1* and *v2* (which should have previously been assigned values).
2. Create a pointer to an `int` variable, *no*, and, using that pointer, read in and display the value of *no*.

Continued on next page

PROGRAMMING EXERCISE 5.6 (continued)

3. Create a function called **Sub2** which subtracts 2 from the `int` variable specified in the parameter list. Use a pointer variable rather than a *call by reference* parameter. The function does not return a value.

4. Create a function as described below

NAME	:	RetAddr
PARAMETERS		
IN	:	no : INTEGER
		ano1, ano2: INTEGER address
OUT	:	rno : INTEGER address
PRE-CONDITION	:	no = 1 OR no = 2
DESCRIPTION	:	Returns the address of *ano1* if *no* = 1, otherwise returns the address of *ano2*.

5. Write two functions. Function 1 returns an integer constructed from reversing the digits of an input parameter. Function 2 returns the sum of the digits of an input parameter.
   Using a function pointer, call each of these routines.

6. Using dynamic allocation, read in two values and display their sum and difference.

Allocating Blocks of Memory

It is often necessary to allocate space for more than one value when using dynamic memory allocation. For example, when operating in DOS mode, it is possible to copy an area of the screen's video RAM to another area of memory using the function `gettext()`. This function copies a rectangular area of the screen to an area of memory specified by a pointer. You may recall that every character on the screen occupies 2 bytes of video RAM (1 byte containing the ASCII character code while the other contains display colour information). It follows that were we to copy the first 2 lines of the screen we would require 320 bytes (two lines of 80 characters at 2 bytes per character). To achieve this, first we need a `void` pointer

```
void *scrptr;
```

which then needs to allocate and reference the 320 bytes of space required to hold a copy of the video RAM area. This is done using an extended form of the `new` command which allows the number of memory storage units allocated to be specified. Hence, to reserve the 320 bytes we need to write

```
scrptr = new char[320];
```

which allocates space for 320 `char` values. Alternatively, knowing that an `int` variable occupies 2 bytes, we could have written

```
scrptr = new int[160];    // Allocates space for 160 int values
```

TASK 5.6

Write the `new` command necessary to allocate 320 bytes of memory using

a) `float`
b) `double`

as the basic unit.

To delete the block of memory the `delete` operator needs to be called using the format:

```
delete [] scrptr;
```

The brackets indicate to the compiler that a block of memory, rather than a single storage unit, needs to be deallocated. In fact, Borland C++ allows the brackets to be omitted but this is not standard C++ and is probably best avoided.

The function `gettext()`, which copies an area of screen memory, requires five parameters:

the coordinates of the rectangular area of the screen to be saved
and *a pointer to the allocated memory space* into which the image is to be copied

The memory space must be allocated before calling `gettext()`.

The saved area can be restored to the screen using `puttext()` which requires the same five parameters. The saved data need not be restored to the same area of the screen from which it originated.

Both routines are defined more formally below.

Use in DOS mode only.

Prototype :	`int gettext(int x1, int y1, int x2, int y2, void *ptr)`	**Header** : conio.h
Precondition :	(*x1*,*y1*) and (*x2*,*y2*) must be valid screen coordinates AND *ptr* must have previously been allocated sufficient space.	
Description :	Copies the contents of the video RAM for the area of screen defined to the memory referenced by *ptr*. Screen coordinates (not text window coordinates) must be used. If successful the function returns 1, otherwise it returns zero.	
Example :	See text below.	

Use in DOS mode only.

Prototype :	`int puttext(int x1, int y1, int x2, int y2, void *ptr)`	**Header** : conio.h
Precondition :	(*x1*,*y1*) and (*x2*,*y2*) must be valid screen coordinates AND the memory referenced by *ptr* must already contain a copy of the screen image to be displayed.	
Description :	Copies the contents of the area referenced by *ptr* to the rectangular area of the screen specified by (*x1*,*y1*), (*x2*,*y2*). Returns 1 if successful, otherwise returns zero.	
Example :	See text below.	

The program in LISTING-5.7 uses these functions to restore an area of the screen after it has been overwritten with new output.

Program Logic:

```
Determine the area of the screen to be saved
Allocate sufficient space for copy of screen area
Copy screen area to allocated space
Perform any other operations required
Restore saved area to screen
Deallocate space
```

Program Code:

LISTING-5.7

Copying Screen Areas

Use in DOS mode only.

```
#include <iostream.h>
#include <conio.h>

void main()
{

   void *scrptr;
   int i;

   //*** Fill screen with Xs ***
   for(i=1;i<2000;i++)
        cout<<X;

   //*** Save top left section of screen ***
   scrptr = new char [100];        //*** Allocate space
   gettext(1,1,10,5,scrptr);       //*** Copy screen image
   gotoxy(20,12);
   cout<<"   Top left saved - Press any key to continue   ";
   getch();
   gotoxy(20,12);
   cout<<"XXXXXXXXXXXXXXXXXXXXXXXXXXXXXXXXXXXXXXXXXXXXXXX";

   //*** Overwrite that area of screen ***
   window(1,1,10,6);
   for(i=1;i<=50;i++)
        putch(.);
   window(1,1,80,25);
   gotoxy(20,12);
   cout<<"   Top left overwritten. Press any key   ";
   gotoxy(20,12);
   getch();
   cout<<"XXXXXXXXXXXXXXXXXXXXXXXXXXXXXXXXXXXXXXX";

   //*** Restore original contents ***
   puttext(1,1,10,5,scrptr);
   getch();

   //*** Delete allocated space ***
   delete [] scrptr;
}
```

PROGRAMMING EXERCISE 5. 7

Write a modified version of the program in LISTING-5.7 which accepts the coordinates of the screen area to be saved; saves the specified part of the screen; clears the area and then restores the original image.

Double Indirection

If we can have pointers to any of the basic data types, what about pointers to pointers? Well, this is allowed too, and gives rise to the sort of situation shown graphically in FIG 5.13. A pointer to a pointer is sometimes referred to as an **indirect pointer**. Since the data is two steps away from such a pointer, we need to use the indirection operator twice to access the data; this is known as **double indirection**.

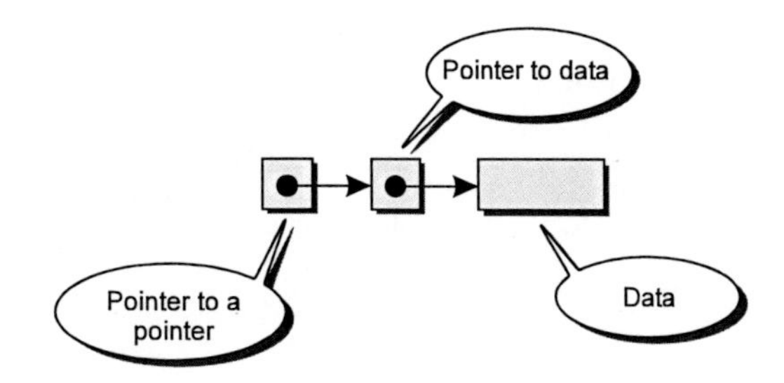

FIG-5.13

An Indirect Pointer

Defining an Indirect Pointer

When we define a normal pointer, we specify the type of value to be referenced; the name to be given to the pointer variable, and the fact that it is a pointer. Hence, a statement such as that in FIG-5.14

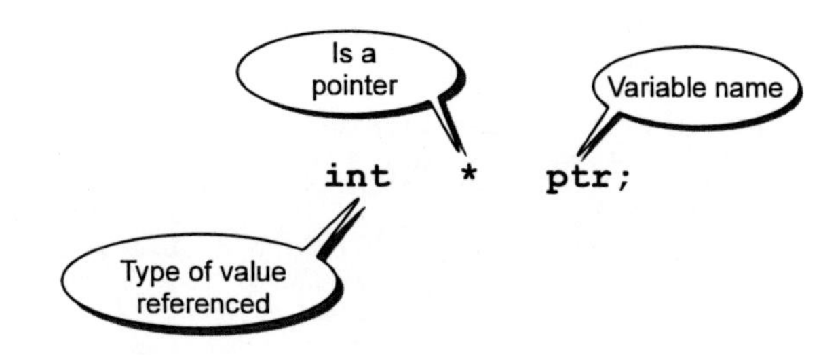

FIG-5.14

Defining a Pointer

creates a pointer, *ptr*, to an `int` value.

The same basic rules apply when creating a pointer to a pointer (see FIG-5.15).

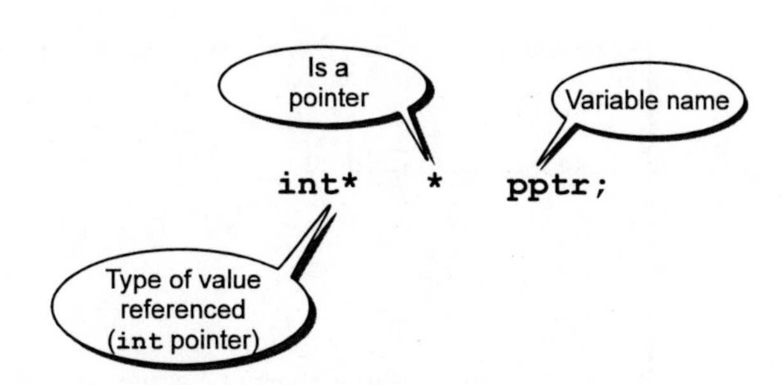

FIG-5.15

Defining an Indirect Pointer

Usually, this is written without spaces between the asterisks, giving the less clear result:

```
int **pptr;
```

Where several such variables are required, the double asterisks must be included for each:

```
int **pptr1, **pptr2, **pptr3;
```

Using an Indirect Pointer

The program in LISTING-5.8 gives an example of double indirection in operation.

Program Logic:

```
Set pointers to reference data
Access data using double indirection
Display results using double indirection
```

Program Code:

LISTING-5.8

Using Indirect Pointers

```
#include <iostream.h>
#include <conio.h>

void main()
{
   int no;                          //*** int variable
   int *ptr;                        //*** Pointer to int
   int **pptr;                      //*** Indirect pointer to int

   //*** Set variables ***
   ptr = &no;                       //*** Holds address of no
   pptr = &ptr;                     //*** Holds address of ptr
   //*** Access data using double indirection ***
   clrscr();
   cout<<"Enter value : ";
   cin>>**pptr;                     //*** Accesses no
   //*** Display data using double indirection ***
   cout<<"Value entered was "<<**pptr<<endl;
   cout<<"Value in no is : "<<no<<endl;    //*** Prove no affected

   getch();
}
```

The above program shows the mechanisms required to manipulate indirect pointers, but is hardly of any practical use. However, there are situations in which double indirection is required.

TASK 5.7

Assuming the definitions

```
int no;
int *ptr=&no;
int **pptr = &ptr;
```

show how the variable *no* can be assigned the value 8 using

a) *no*
b) *ptr*
c) *pptr*

Indirect Pointers and Function Parameters

The program given earlier in LISTING-5.3 returns the address of a data value. The prototype for this function was:

```
int* smallest(int&,  int&, int&);
```

If we wanted to return that address in one of the parameters of the function, then we need to declare a *call by reference* pointer as a parameter of the function:

```
void smallest(int&, int&, int&, int*&);
```

Call by reference pointer

Now, we already know that normal *call by reference* parameters (such as `int&`) are implemented within the function body using pointers, hence it should come as no surprise that *call by reference* pointer parameters are implemented using indirect pointers.

In C++, the use of indirect pointers in this situation is hidden from the programmer. This can be seen in the example below (see LISTING 5.9) which uses *smallest()* as declared above to return the address of the smallest value passed to the function.

LISTING-5.9

Indirect Pointers and Functions

```
#include <iostream.h>
#include <conio.h>

void smallest(int&, int&, int&, int*&);

void main()
{
   int no1,no2,no3;              //***Three values
   int *ptr;                     //***Pointer to int

   //*** Get three values ***
   clrscr();
   cout<<"Enter three values : ";
   cin>>no1>>no2>>no3;
   //*** Call smallest, result in ptr ***
   smallest(no1,no2,no3,ptr);
   //*** Display results ***
   cout<<"Address of variables are : "<<&no1<<' '<<&no2<<' '
       <<&no3<<endl;
   cout<<"Address of variable with smallest value is :  "
       <<ptr<<endl;

   getch();
}

//*** Definition of smallest() ***
void smallest(int& n1, int& n2, int& n3, int*& p)
{
   if(n1<n2&&n1<n3)
       p=&n1;
   else if(n2<n3&&n2<n1)
       p=&n2;
   else
       p=&n3;
}
```

The C Approach

C++ can generally be thought of as an extension to C, so the old techniques for handling indirect pointers still exists within the new language. In the case of *call by reference* pointers, C requires that we use the indirect pointer format in the function prototype. This would require the prototype for *smallest()* to be:

```
void smallest(int*, int*, int*, int**);
```

The routine's code must also change to use pointer notation (see LISTING-5.10)

LISTING-5.10

Using Indirect Pointer Notation

```
#include <iostream.h>
#include <conio.h>

void smaller(int*, int*, int*, int**);      //***Pointers and
                                            //***indirect pointer

void main()
{
   int no1,no2,no3;
   int *ptr;

   cout<<"Enter three values : ";
   cin>>no1>>no2>>no3;
   smaller(&no1,&no2,&no3,&ptr);            //*** Give addresses
   cout<<"Address of variables are : "<<&no1<<' '<<&no2<<' '
       <<&no3<<endl;
   cout<<"Address of variable with smallest value is : "
       <<ptr<<endl;
   getch();
}

void smaller(int* n1, int* n2, int* n3, int** p)
{
   //*** Requires pointer notation ***
   if(*n1<*n2&&*n1<*n3)
       *p=n1;
   else if(*n2<*n3&&*n2<*n1)
       *p=n2;
   else
       *p=n3;
}
```

PROGRAMMING EXERCISE 5.8

As well as using an `int` pointer variable (`int * ptr`) in LISTING-5.10, an indirect pointer (`int **pptr`) may be used.
Modify the program in LISTING-5.10 so that *pptr* is used as the actual parameter to *smaller()*.
HINT : You need to retain *ptr* as an `int` pointer.

Summary

- The **address of** operator (`&`) can be used to access the start address of a simple variable.
- A **pointer variable** contains an address.
- **A pointer to data is defined** using the format

  `type * variable [, * variable]`

- The **indirection operator** (*) can be used to access the data at the address held in a pointer variable.
- The term **NULL** may be used to assign a value to a pointer variable, which is taken to mean that the pointer references no valid address.
- **A function's name is treated as a pointer constant** containing the start address of that function.

- **A pointer to a function is defined** using the format

```
return type ( * variable)(funct parameter list)
```

- **Using the asterisk as part of the return type** in a function indicates that a pointer (i.e. address) to a value of that type is returned by the function.

- **Using an asterisk with a parameter to a function** in the function header indicates that the actual parameter should be a pointer or address.

- **`new`** is used to dynamically allocate memory space for a variable. The pointer specified is made to reference that space.

- **`delete`** deallocates the space referenced by a pointer. The contents of the pointer remains unchanged.

- **A pointer should be assigned the value NULL** after being used in a **`delete`** command.

- A **`void` pointer** can reference any type of value or a function.

- **`void`** pointers must normally be **typecast** before they are dereferenced.

- **A block of memory can be allocated** by extending the format of the `new` operator to include the number of storage units required:

```
pointer_name = new type [ units ]
```

- **Deallocating a block of memory** requires the delete operator to include brackets:

```
delete [ ] pointer_name
```

- **The function `gettext()`** copies an area of screen memory to another area of memory.

- **The function** `puttext()` places the contents of a memory block on the screen.

- **An indirect pointer** is a pointer to a pointer.

- **Indirect pointers are defined** using the format

```
type ** variable [, **variable]
```

- **Indirect pointers are used** when pointer parameters to a function need to be modified by the function.

DEFINING TYPES

Although C++ limits the number of types available, the programmer is allowed to define alternative identifiers for existing types. This is achieved in a `typedef` statement. For example, we may write

```
typedef  int mytype;
```

and then define variables using this new name:

```
mytype no1,no2;
```

This is identical in effect to the statement

```
int no1, no2;
```

but, nevertheless, this may be a useful device to simplify terms in both variable definitions and function headings.

Hence, instead of writing

```
float *fptr1, *fptr2;
```

we can declare a type

```
typedef float* FloatPtrType;
```

and use this to define pointer variables:

```
FloatPtrType fptr1, fptr2;
```

Note from the example that there is no need to add an asterisk before each variable as in the standard declaration.

Function pointer types can be similarly defined:

```
typedef int(*FunctPtrType)(int,int,int);

FunctPtrType fnptr1, fnptr2;
```

The `typedef` statement does not create new types, rather they allow alternative names to be used in place of the standard definition format. As a consequence, these alternative names cannot be used to differentiate between types when overloading a function. For example, the following is an invalid attempt at overloading a function:

```
typedef int MyType;

void MyFunction(int);
void MyFunction(MyType);
```

Invalid since *MyType* is equivalent to *int*

TASK 5.8

Write `typedef` statements to define the following types:

1. A `char` pointer
2. A function which returns an `int` pointer and requires a `long` parameter.

ARRAYS

Problems with Simple Variables

All the variables we have encountered up to this point are known as **simple variables**. A simple variable is capable of holding only a single value. For example,

```
int no;
```

defines a simple variable *no*, which can store a single integer value.

However, there are certain problems which cannot easily be solved using this type of variable. For example, if we need to read in five numbers and then display them, the relevant code might be:

```
int no1,no2,no3,no4,no5;
cout << "Enter 5 numbers ";
cin >> no1 >> no2 >> no3 >> no4 >> no5;
cout<<no1<<' '<<no2<<' '<<no3<<' '<< no4<<' '<<no5<<endl;
```

Although somewhat inelegant, this approach might be acceptable when only five values are used, but would prove more unwieldy if 50 or 100 values were involved.

TASK 5.9

Consider possible approaches to tackling the following problems:

1. Read in 20 integer values in the range 1 to 5 and print out how often each value occurred. (e.g. 1 occurred 4 times; 2 occurred 7 times etc.)

2. Read in 15 integer values. Next, read in another value and then display a message saying whether the last value is repeated anywhere in the original 15 values (display FOUND or NOT FOUND as appropriate).

Hopefully, you can see from attempting TASK 5.9 that any solution to these problems is going to be long and cumbersome if simple variables are used.

One Dimensional Arrays

What is an Array ?

An array is a collection of elements. Each of these elements can hold a single data value. That is, an element in an array performs the same role as a simple variable.

All elements of an array are of the same type (i.e. `int`, `float`, `char`, etc.).

Like other variables, an array must be given a name; individual cells in the array are identified by a number: the first cell being 0, the second 1, etc.

Visually, we can conceive of an array as shown in FIG-5.16.

FIG-5.16

Array Characteristics

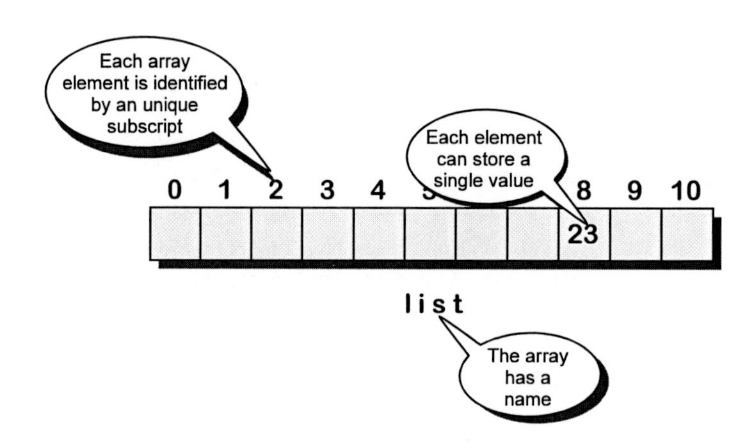

We can summarise the characteristics of an array as:

- It has an identifying name.
- It has a number of elements. The exact number being stated when the array is defined.
- It has a defined type, which specifies the type of values which may be held within the elements of the array.

Each element in an array has :

- An unique integer value identifying its position in the array (starting at zero).
- A value assigned to it which may be changed (as with simple variables).

Defining Arrays

When an array is defined, all the characteristics given above must be specified. For example

```
int list[11];
```

defines an array called *list* containing eleven elements, each of which can store an `int` value. The elements are numbered 0 to 10.

TASK 5.10

Write array definitions for the following data items.

1. An array called *results* which stores exam marks for 15 students.

2. An array called *weights* which stores 10 weights in kilograms.

Initialising Arrays

The contents of the elements of an array are initially undefined, but it is possible to initialise them as part of the definition. Hence we may set every element of an array *counts* to zero with the definition:

```
int counts[5]={0,0,0,0,0};
```

If there are too many values in the initialising list, then extra ones are ignored; if there are too few values in the list, the additional elements of the array are initialised to zero. Hence

```
int values[4]= {3,1};
```

assigns the values:

```
values[0]=3, values[1]=1, values[2]=0, values[3]=0
```

Knowing this, we could initialise the elements of *counts* to zero by simply writing

```
int counts[5]={};
```

Leaving thc parentheses empty is not allowed by all versions of the compiler; some insist that at least one zero is specified.

But this approach hardly leads to clear, self-documenting, program code!

When initialising an array it is acceptable to omit the number of elements in the array and allow the compiler to deduce this from the number of values given in the definition. Hence

```
float nos[] = {12.8, 6.9, -23.098}
```

will create a three element array (*nos[0]* to *nos[2]*).

TASK 5.11

Initialise an array, *bias*, containing 8 elements to contain the values 6, 2, 2, 5, 1, 3, 3, 2.

Accessing Arrays

A program cannot deal with an array as a single entity, but must access the individual elements of the array by specifying:

- The array name
- The number of the element to be accessed.

Hence, having made the declaration

```
int list[7];
```

we can assign the value 6 to the third element of the array, using the assignment statement :

```
list[2] = 6;
```

The value in the barckets after the array name is known as the array **subscript**.

In fact, we may use an array element in any statement where we might use a simple variable of the same type. Examples of valid statements are shown in FIG-5.17.

FIG-5.17

Using an Array

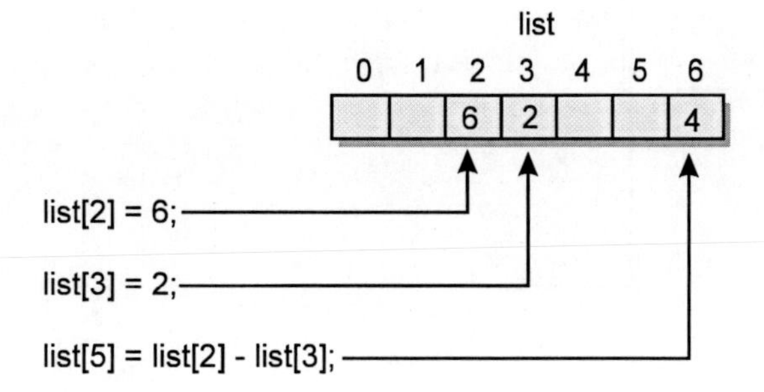
list
0 1 2 3 4 5 6
6
2
4
list[2] = 6;
list[3] = 2;
list[5] = list[2] - list[3];

C++ makes no attempt to check that the subscript given is a valid one. If the array subscript used is too large, as in

```
int nos[10];
nos[12] = 45;   //***Invalid subscript
```

then unpredictable things will happen as the program attempts to access areas of the computer's memory not allocated to the array.

If this were all that could be achieved when using arrays, their usefulness would be limited. However, the power of arrays lies in the fact that the subscript may be specified not only as an integer constant, but also as an integer variable or expression. This allows statements such as

```
p = 3;
list[p] = 12;
```

To execute the second assignment statement above, the machine will determine the value of the array subscript variable (3), and use that when determining which element of the array is to be accessed. This means that the two statements above are equivalent to

```
list[3] = 12;
```

Various examples are shown in FIG-5.18 below.

FIG-5.18

Variable Subscripts

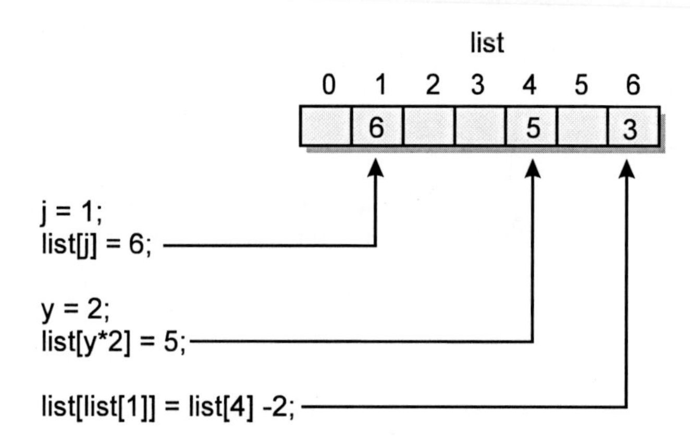
list
0 1 2 3 4 5 6
6
5
3
j = 1;
list[j] = 6;
y = 2;
list[y*2] = 5;
list[list[1]] = list[4] -2;

TASK 5.12

Assuming the definitions:

```
int list[]={-4,3,9,2,0,12};
int J;
```

State the contents of the array *list* after each of the following statements:

```
list[2] = 7;
J = list[1];
list[J] = -2;
list[J++] = 3;
list[++J] = 5;
for (J = 0;J <= 5;J++)
    list[J] = J*2;
```

Using Arrays

To get some experience of using arrays to solve real problems, we'll return to the task of reading in five numbers and then displaying them, the details of which are described below.

Program Logic:

```
FOR 5 times DO
    Read value into next element of array
ENDFOR
FOR 5 times DO
    Display the value in the next element of the array
ENDFOR
```

Program Code:

LISTING-5.11

Accessing Elements of an Array

```
#include <iostream.h>
#include <conio.h>

void main()
{
   const int size = 5;    //*** Used to set the size of the array
   int nos[size];
   int p;

   clrscr();

   // *** Read numbers into array ***
   for(p = 0;p < size;p++)
   {
        cout << "Enter number : ";
        cin >> nos[p];
   }

   // *** Display numbers ***
   for(p = 0;p < size;p++)
        cout << nos[p] << '\n';
}
```

Should we require to process 20 numbers, the only modification necessary is to change the first line to:

```
const int size = 20;
```

Looking back at TASK 5.9, we can produce an equally elegant solution for each of the other problems using arrays:

Problem : Read in 20 integer values in the range 1 to 5 and display how often each value occurs.

Rather than store the 20 numbers in the array, we need to store the counts in an array:

Program Logic:

```
Set all counts to zero
FOR 20 times DO
    Read valid number(1 to 5)
    Add 1 to the appropriate count
ENDFOR
Display counts
```

Program Code:

LISTING-5.12

Counting with Arrays

```
#include <iostream.h>
#include <conio.h>

void main()
{
   const int size = 20;
   int counts[6] ={0,0,0,0,0,0}; //*** Element zero not used
   int no,c;

   //*** Read in twenty numbers ***
   clrscr();
   for(c = 1;c <= size;c++)
   {
        cout << "Enter number : ";
        cin >> no;
        //*** Check number in range 1 to 5 ***
        while (no < 1 || no > 5)
        {
             cout << "Invalid value. Must be 1 to 5. Re-enter : ";
             cin >> no;
        }
        //*** Add 1 to the appropriate count ***
        counts[no] ++;
   }
   //*** Display results ***
   for(c = 1;c <= 5;c++)
        cout << "There are " << counts[c] << ' ' << c << "\'s\n";
   getch();
}
```

Problem: Read in 15 values followed by a final number. Search the first 15 values for one which is equal in value to the final number entered.

Program Logic:

```
Read all 15 values into an array
Get the value to be searched for
Starting at the first value in the array
WHILE value being examined does not match the value being
searched for AND not all values in the array have yet been
examined DO
    Move on to the next value in the array
ENDWHILE
IF a match was found THEN
    Display "Found"
ELSE
    Display "Not found"
ENDIF
```

Program Code:

LISTING-5.13

Searching an Array

```
#include<iostream.h>
#include<conio.h>

void main()
{
   const int size=15;
   int list[size];          //*** List of values to be searched
   int no;                  //*** Number to be searched for
   int count;               //*** Loop counter
```

Continued on next page

LISTING-5.13
(continued)

Searching an Array

```
    //*** Read in 15 values ***
    clrscr();
    for(count = 0;count < size;count++)
    {
        cout << "Enter number : ";
        cin >> list[count];
    }
    //*** Read value to be searched for ***
    cout << "Enter search value : ";
    cin >> no;
    //*** Search until match found or all numbers examined ***
    count = -1;
    while(list[++count] != no && count < size-1);
    //*** Display result ***
    if(list[count] == no)
        cout << "FOUND\n" << count << '\n';
    else
        cout << "NOT FOUND\n";

    getch();
}
```

PROGRAMMING EXERCISE 5.9

Write programs to perform the following tasks:

1. Enter six numbers; display the numbers in the same order as they were entered; display the numbers in the reverse order (i.e. last number entered displayed first).

```
OUTLINE LOGIC:
    Read numbers into an array
    Display contents of array starting at element zero
    Display contents of array starting at element five
```

2. Enter ten values and display only those in the odd numbered elements (i.e. elements 1,3,5,7,9).

```
OUTLINE LOGIC:
    Read numbers into array
    FOR position := 1 TO 9 DO
        IF position is an odd number THEN
            Display the element with that subscript
        ENDIF
    ENDFOR
```

3. Read in 10 characters and display how many E's are in the sequence. Both upper and lower case E's should be counted.

```
OUTLINE LOGIC:
    Set count to zero
    Read in 10 characters
    FOR each character DO
        IF upper case version of character is 'E' THEN
            Add 1 to count
        ENDIF
    ENDFOR
    Display count
```

Continued on next page

PROGRAMMING EXERCISE 5.9 (continued)

4. Read in 10 numbers in the range 1 to 50 and display how many fell into each of the categories 1..10, 11..20, 21..30, 31..40, 41..50.

```
OUTLINE LOGIC:
    Set all five counts to zero
    FOR 10 times DO
        Read in a valid number
        Determine which category the number falls into
        Add 1 to the appropriate count
    ENDFOR
    Display each count
```

5. Read in 10 numbers and display the smallest number in the list.

```
OUTLINE LOGIC:
    Read in 10 numbers
    Set smallest equal to the first number
    FOR each remaining number DO
        IF its smaller than smallest THEN
            Set smallest equal to that number
        ENDIF
    ENDFOR
    Display smallest
```

Arrays as Function Parameters

Since we can pass every other sort of value to a function, it should come as no surprise that were allowed to pass arrays to or from functions.

To pass an array to a function we begin by specifying in the function prototype that an array is to be used. For example, if we want to create a function *smallest()* which takes an array of numbers and returns the smallest value in that array, then the function prototype might be:

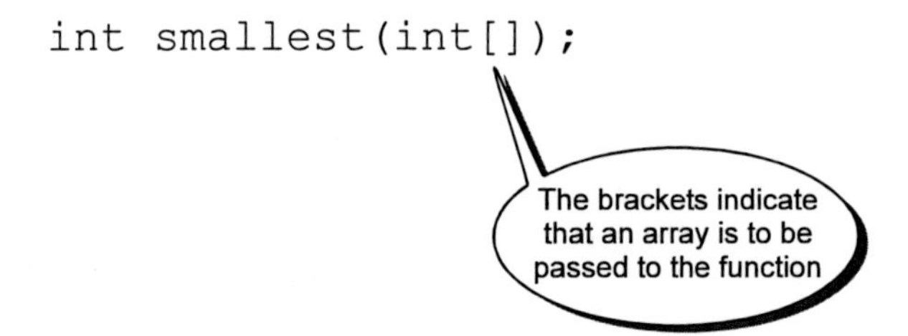
int smallest(int[]);
The brackets indicate that an array is to be passed to the function

Notice that the size of the array is not given within the array brackets in the prototype. This is to our advantage, because it means that we are allowed to pass any size of array to the function. However, the usual price for this flexibility is the need to add a second parameter to the prototype, which is used to specify how many elements there actually are at call time. This gives a new prototype of:

```
int smallest(int[],int);
```

The function definition includes parameter names in the usual manner:

```
int smallest(int list[],int size)
```

To call this function, the actual parameters include the array name and the number of elements in the array:

```
int nos[12];              //*** Defined in main()
        .
cout << smallest(nos,12); //*** Call function
```

A complete program defining and using this function is shown in LISTING-5.14.

LISTING-5.14

Passing an Array to a Function

```
#include <iostream.h>
#include <conio.h>

int smallest(int[],int);

void main()
{
    const int size = 10;
    int nos[size];
    //*** Read in values ***
    clrscr();
    for(int i = 0;i < size;i++)
    {
        cout << "Enter number " << (i+1) << " : ";
        cin >> nos[i];
    }
    //*** Display lowest value by calling smallest() ***
    cout << "Smallest value entered was "<< smallest(nos,size)
        << '\n';
    getch();
}


int smallest(int list[],int sz)
{
    int answer;

    answer = list[0];
    for(int i = 1;i < sz;i++)
        if(list[i] < answer)
            answer = list[i];
    return answer;
}
```

Updating a function parameter normally involves using the **address of** operator (`&`) in the prototype. For example, a function which adds 2 to an integer value would have the prototype:

```
void Add2(int&);
```

We might expect the same style in a function to update an array (perhaps `void Add2(int[]&,int)`). In fact, where the array passed to the function is to have its contents changed, this is not made explicit in the prototype which remains:

```
void Add2(int[],int);
```

The full program to update an array using such a function is given in LISTING-5.15.

LISTING-5.15

Updating an Array within a Function

```
#include <iostream.h>
#include <conio.h>
void Add2(int[],int);

void main()
{
    const int size = 10;
    int nos[size];
    int i;
```

Continued on next page

LISTING-5.15
(continued)

Updating an Array within a Function

```
    //*** Read in values ***
    clrscr();
    for(i = 0;i < size;i++)
    {
        cout << "Enter number " << (i+1) << " : ";
        cin >> nos[i];
    }

    //*** Add two to each value ***
    Add2(nos,size);

    //*** Display updated list ***
    for(i = 0;i < size;i++)
        cout << nos[i] << '\n';

    getch();
}

void Add2(int list[],int sz)
{
    for(int i = 0;i < sz;i++)
        list[i] += 2;
}
```

Arrays and Pointers

Why are arrays treated differently from simple variables? The truth is that an array name is, in fact, a pointer constant to the first address in the array. When we define an array in a statement such as

```
int list[10]
```

two things happen:

1. Space for each element of the array is reserved in memory.

2. A `int const` pointer to the first address in the reserved space is set up. This pointer derives its name from that of the array.

The effect of the definition is shown graphically in FIG-5.19.

FIG-5.19

The Array Name as a Pointer

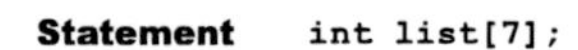
Statement int list[7];

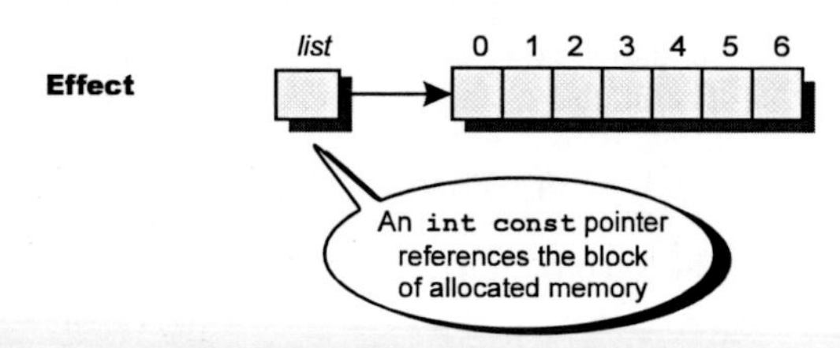
list
0 1 2 3 4 5 6
Effect
An int const pointer references the block of allocated memory

The pointer to the array is a constant and cannot be modified, although the contents of the array space it references can.

When we declare an array in the parameter list of a function we are, effectively, stating that a pointer constant parameter is to be used. Like any pointer passed to a function, it can then be used to update the area which it references.

The next programming exercise shows that an array name and a pointer variable are interchangeable.

PROGRAMMING EXERCISE 5.10

1. Enter and run the program in LISTING-5.15.
2. Add a pointer variable in `main()`
```
int *ptr;
```
3. Immediately preceding the call to *Add2()*, insert the line
```
ptr = nos; //*** ptr references the same address as nos
```
4. Change the call to *Add2()* to read
```
Add2(ptr,size);
```
5. Run the program again.
6. Remove the above changes from your program.
7. Change the prototype to
```
Add2(int*,int);
```
8. Change the first line of the function definition to
```
void Add2(int *list,int sz)
```
9. Run the program again.

All of this raises another problem for good software design: passing an array to a function gives that function the ability to change the contents of the array whether we want that ability or not! To inhibit this ability we can use the term `const` in the function prototype and definition. For example, the function *smallest()* (LISTING-5.14) can have its array parameter changed to a read-only mode by modifying the prototype to

```
void smallest(const int[], int);
```

and the first line of the definition to

```
void smallest (const int list[], int sz)
```

This approach should be used whenever an array is passed as an IN parameter to a function.

From everything that's gone before, pointers and arrays are obviously closely linked. We can create an array and a variable pointer to that array, with statements such as:

```
int list[]={2,4,6,8}; //*** Set up an array
int *aptr = list;     //*** Set pointer to the array
```

To display the first value in the array we can write:

`cout << list[0];` or `cout << *aptr;`

Although displaying the contents of the next element is simple using array notation (`cout<<list[1];`), to do the same using the pointer, we need to make the pointer reference element 1 rather than element zero.

An `int` is assumed to occupy 2 bytes in this text.

Remembering that a pointer variable simply contains an integer value which represents some address in memory, and since the next element of an `int` array will be two locations further along, maybe we can get at the next element by the statement

```
aptr += 2; //*** Add 2 to the address held in aptr?
```

If this were the technique we had to employ, we would also have to know how many memory locations a single value occupied. Since the storage requirements of each data type is not defined as part of the language, this can vary between compilers and might require us to modify our code whenever moving to a new compiler.

Luckily, pointers are smarter than this. When a pointer is incremented using a statement such as

```
aptr++;
```

its contents are incremented not by one, but by the number of memory locations allocated to the type referenced by the pointer. Hence incrementing a `char` pointer adds 1 to its contents while incrementing a `long` pointer adds 4. The effect of incrementing *aptr* is shown in FIG- 5.20.

FIG-5.20

Incrementing an Array Pointer

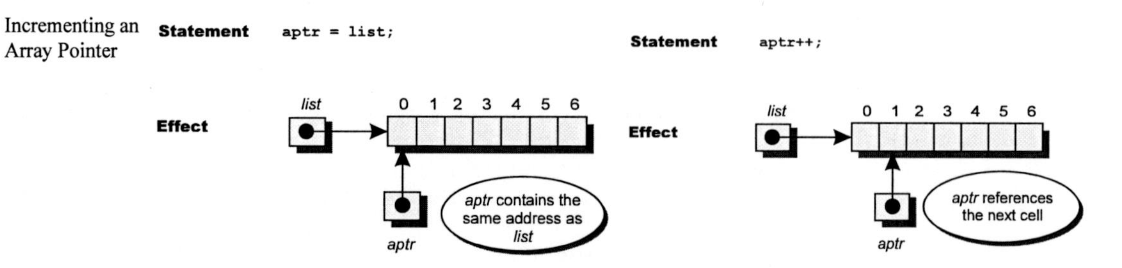

We can practice this technique by displaying the contents of an array using a pointer variable. The conventional method of displaying the contents of an array such as

```
int list[]={2,4,6,8};
```

would be

```
for(int i = 0; i < 4; i++)
    cout << list[i] << '\n';
```

Using a pointer this can be coded as:

```
int list[]={2,4,6,8};
int *aptr = list;

 for(int i = 0; i < 4; i++)
    cout << *aptr++ << '\n';
```

Now, if we think back to the last run in PROGRAMMING EXERCISE 5.5 which contained code equivalent to

```
for(int i = 0; i < 4; i++)
    cout << aptr[i] << '\n';
```

we see yet another way to access elements of an array via a pointer. That is, we can specify an address offset within the square brackets. This means that the terms

This assumes *aptr* currently contains the start addrress of list.

`aptr += 2` and `aptr[2];`

both allow element three of the array to be accessed, but the first approach modifies the contents of *aptr*; the second does not.

To access the contents of the array element we may write

`*aptr` or `aptr[2]`

Note that when a subscript is used with the pointer, there is no dereference operator This shouldn't really surprise us when we remember that the array name itself is a pointer constant. The value in brackets acts as an offset from the specified base address held in the pointer.

TASK 5.13

Assuming the definitions

```
int list[]={1,2,5,3,7,4};
int *aptr;
```

Explain the action of each of the following statements

1. `aptr = list;`
2. `aptr += 2;`
3. `cout << aptr[3];`
4. `aptr--;`
5. `aptr[2] = *aptr+*aptr++;`

Pointer Arithmetic

The next program (see LISTING-5.16) uses two pointers to indicate the addresses of the first two occurrences of the value 7 in an array.

Program Logic:

```
Read values into array
Set first pointer to start of array
WHILE referenced value not 7 AND not beyond end of array DO
    Increment pointer
ENDWHILE
Set second pointer to same address as first
REPEAT
    Increment pointer
 UNTIL pointer references the value 7
    OR pointer beyond the end of the array
IF both pointers within the array THEN
    Display addresses
ELSE
    Display Two 7s not found
ENDIF
```

Program Code:

LISTING-5.16

Referencing Array Elements using Pointers

```
#include<iostream.h>
#include<conio.h>

void main()
{
  int list[]={3,7,3,5,7,1,3};
  int *aptr1=list,*aptr2=NULL;

  //*** Search for first 7 ***
  while(*aptr1!=7&&aptr1<=list+6)
      aptr1++;
  aptr2 = aptr1;
  //*** search for second 7 ***
  do
      aptr2++;
  while(*aptr2 != 7 && aptr2 <= list+6);
  //*** If 7s found display details ***
  if(aptr1 <= list+6 && aptr2 <= list+6)
      cout << "Array starts at " << list << "\nFirst 7 at "
           << aptr1 << "\nSecond 7 at " << aptr2 << '\n';
  else
      cout << "Two 7s not found\n";
  getch();
}
```

A possible result for this program is shown in FIG-5.21.

FIG-5.21

Referencing Array Elements using Pointers

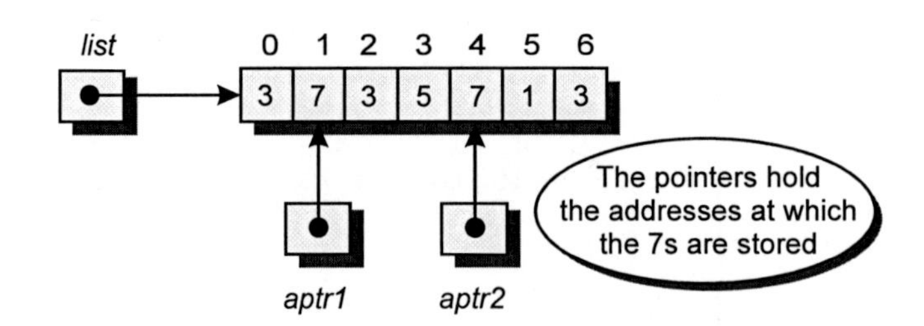

Should we require instead to display the number of elements between the first and second occurrence of the value 7, then we can use the expression:

```
aptr2 - aptr1
```

If we were to examine the contents of these two pointers they might contain values such as $27680FE6_{16}$ and $2768FE0_{16}$. This would suggest that the subtraction would give the result 6. In fact, we get an answer of 3. This is pointer intelligence at work: the program takes into account that we are dealing with two `int` pointers and, since an `int` value occupies two memory locations, the actual result of the subtraction is derived using the formula

$$\frac{\text{aptr2 - aptr1}}{\text{size of the data type}}$$

PROGRAMMING EXERCISE 5.11

1. Enter the program above (LISTING-5.16) and run it.
2. Change the display to show the number of array elements between the first and second occurrence of the value 7.

The `Address of` Operator and Arrays

The **address of operator** (`&`) can be used to retrieve the address of individual array elements. Hence, if we define *list* as

```
int list[7];
```

the address of `list[3]` is accessed using the term

```
&list[3];
```

Since the array name is a pointer constant to the start address of the array, the terms

`list` and `&list[0]`

are equivalent.

We can also use this approach to set a pointer variable to reference a specific element of an array:

```
int list[7];
int *aptr = &list[2];  //aptr contains the address of list[2]
```

PROGRAMMING EXERCISE 5.12

1. Write a function which takes two `int` arrays and returns 1 if the contents of the arrays are identical in value and order. If the contents are different, zero is returned.
2. Write a function which accepts an `int` array and returns the address of the first location containing a negative value. If no location returns a negative value, return NULL.
3. Using only pointer notation, read in and display the contents of a five element `int` array.

Dynamic Allocation of Arrays

We saw earlier, in the description of the function `puttext()`, that it is possible, using a pointer, to allocate large blocks of space. This technique can also be used to create normal data space. Hence, armed with the definition

```
int *ptr;
```

we can allocate space for 10 `int` values using the statement

```
ptr = new int[10];
```

and can then access this space using either normal pointer notation

```
for(int count=0;count<10;count++,ptr++)
    cin>>*ptr;
```

or, if we do not want to move the pointer, by using subscript notation:

```
for(int count=0;count<10;count++)
    cin>>ptr[count];
```

When no longer required, the space can be deallocated using

```
delete [] ptr;
```

Using the symbols [ ] in the `delete` command informs the program that a block of memory is to be deallocated. It is not necessary to specify the size of this block since the program itself contains this information.

PROGRAMMING EXERCISE 5.13

Write a program which performs the following logic:

```
Get the number of exam marks to be entered
Allocate space for the exam marks
Read in the exam marks
Calculate the average mark
Write all marks below average
Deallocate the space for the exam marks
```

Multi-dimensional Arrays

The Need for More Dimensions

If a student sits six exams, then an array containing 6 elements could be used to store this information:

```
int marks[6];
```

However, if there are eight students, we would need eight such arrays in order to contain all the data. The definition for this is

```
int marks[8][6];
```

FIG-5.22

A 2D Array

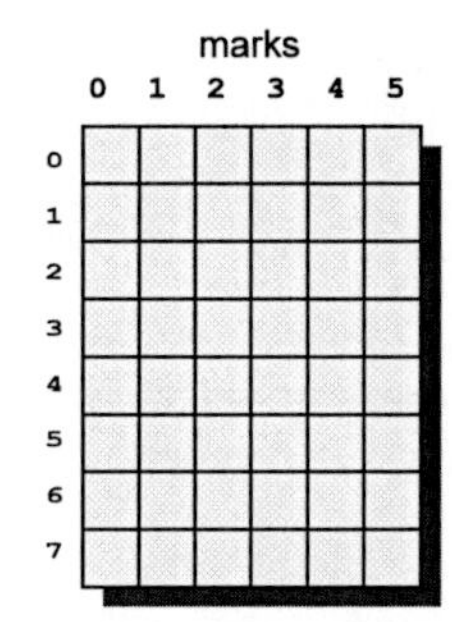

Literally, this defines 8 copies of a six element array.

The resulting data structure is a **two-dimensional array** (see FIG-5.22).

There are many situations which call for two-dimensional arrays. For example, a chess board is easily represented by an 8 by 8 array, while a class timetable could be held as a 7 by 5 array, representing seven subjects taught over five days.

These two-dimensional structures are often referred to as **matrices**.

To define a two-dimensional array, use the format

```
type identifier[value1][value2];
```

where

`type`	defines the type of value to be held in the elements of the array.
`identifier`	specifies the name of the array.
`value1`	specifies the number of rows in the array.
`value2`	specifies the number of columns.

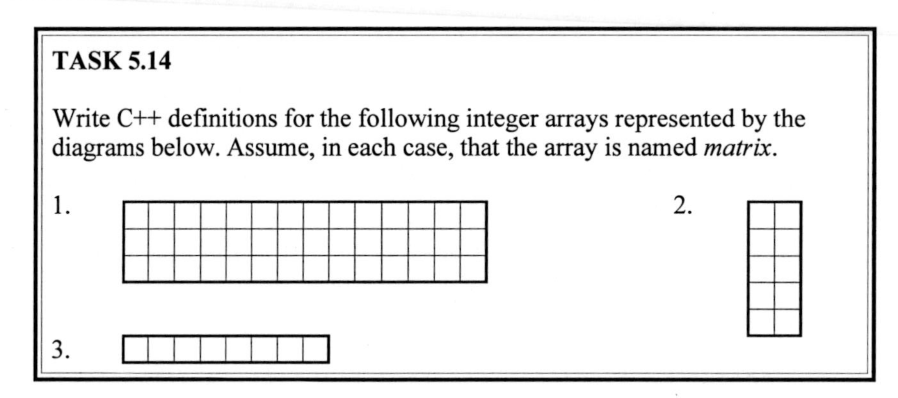

TASK 5.14

Write C++ definitions for the following integer arrays represented by the diagrams below. Assume, in each case, that the array is named *matrix*.

1.

2.

3.

Accessing the Array

To access an individual element in the array, we must give the array name and the row and column numbers (see FIG-5.23).

FIG-5.23

Accessing Elements in a 2D Array

```
int marks[8][6];
```

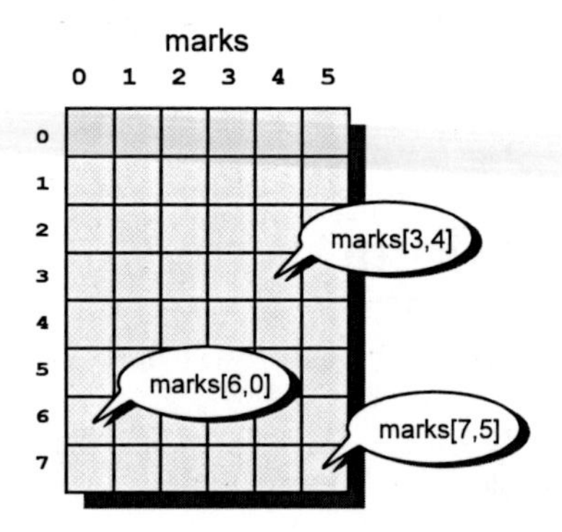

To read in the six marks for each of the eight students we employ the following logic:

```
FOR each student DO
    FOR each mark DO
        Read mark into appropriate element of marks
    ENDFOR
ENDFOR
```

A more program-like logic would be

```
FOR student := 0 TO 7 DO
    FOR exam := 0 TO 5 DO
        Read valid mark into marks[student][exam]
    ENDFOR
ENDFOR
```

the C++ code for this being

```
for(int student=0;student<=7;student++)
{
    cout << "Processing student " << (student+1) << '\n';
    for(exam = 0;exam <= 5;exam++)
    {
        cout << "Enter mark " << (exam+1) << " : ";
        cin >> marks[student][exam];
    }
}
```

Initialising

To initialise the array, as well as the normal set of braces enclosing the set of values, we bracket the values for each row in its own set of braces, separating each set of row values by a comma. For example,

```
int matrix[4][2]={{8,4},{1,1},{2,0},{5,5}};
```

PROGRAMMING EXERCISE 5.14

With an array, `int matrix[4][4]`, use nested `for` loops to set up the array in the following ways:

1	2	3	4
5	6	7	8
9	10	11	12
13	14	15	16

1	5	9	13
2	6	10	14
3	7	11	15
4	8	12	16

16	15	14	13
12	11	10	9
8	7	6	5
4	3	2	1

How the Array is Stored

Although we show the two-dimensional array as a matrix, computer memory is linear. That is, memory is equivalent to a one-dimensional array. To allocate space for a two-dimensional data structure in a one-dimensional memory, some mapping function is required. FIG-5.24 shows how this is done.

FIG-5.24 Mapping 2D Arrays to Memory

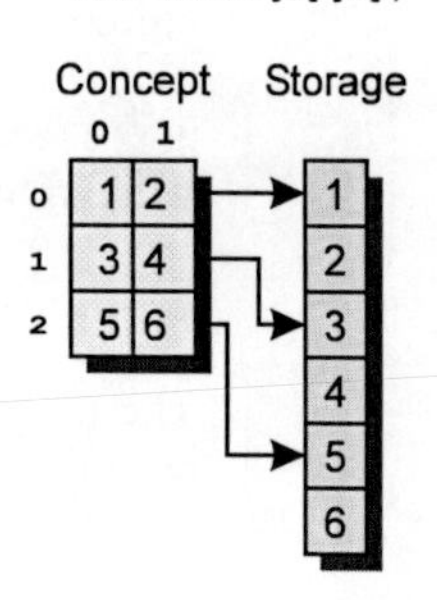

Pointers and Two-Dimensional Arrays

Whereas with one-dimensional arrays the array name is a pointer to the first element in the array, a two-dimensional array's name acts as a pointer constant to an array of pointers. This array contains pointers to the first value in each row of the original array. Hence, a definition such as

```
int matrix[3][2];
```

has the effect shown in FIG-5.25.

FIG-5.25

Pointers to 2D Arrays

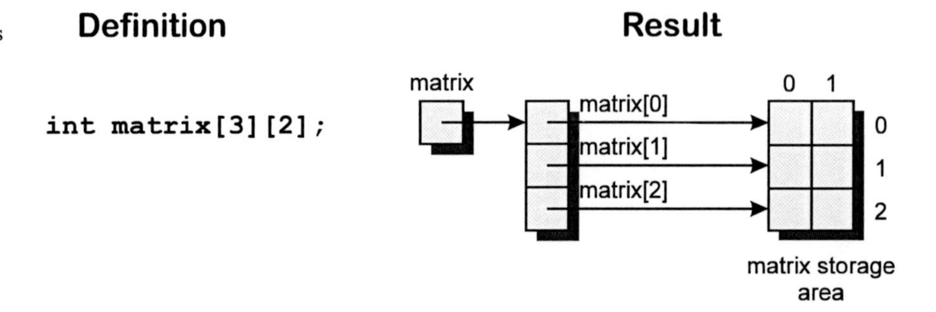

To create a pointer variable capable of referencing a two-dimensional array, we need to define a variable able to reference the same area as the pointer *matrix*. This requires a pointer definition of the form

```
int (*a2ptr)[2]= matrix;
```

which states that *a2ptr* is a pointer to an array with two columns. The pointer can then be used to reference any two column array, irrespective of the number of rows in that array.

To access the elements of the array using the pointer we may employ statements such as:

```
a2ptr[2][1]
```

From FIG-5.25 above, we can see that *matrix[0]* (and now *a2ptr[0]*) is a pointer to the first value in row 1. The following statements are therefore equivalent:

```
matrix[0][0]
*matrix[0]
a2ptr[0][0]
*a2ptr[0]
```

Two Dimensional Arrays As Parameters

Although two-dimensional arrays can be passed to a function, the number of columns in the array must be specified in the function parameter list. The number of rows, on the other hand, may be omitted. For example, a function which accepted a `float` array with 8 columns and the number of rows of that array as parameters, while returning a `float`, would have a prototype

```
float functname(float[][8],int);
```

The program in LISTING-5.17 demonstrates this type of parameter passing by returning the smallest value in a two-dimensional array.

LISTING-5.17

2D Arrays as Parameters

```
#include<iostream.h>
#include<conio.h>

int smallest(int[][3],int);


void main()
{
   int nos2[4][3]={{8,4,9},{7,7,7},{9,1,6},{8,3,9}};

   clrscr();
   cout << "Smallest value is " << smallest(nos2,4) << '\n';
   getch();



int smallest(int s[][3],int size)
{
   //*** Assume first element is smallest ***
   int small = s[0][0];
   //*** FOR each element DO ***
   for(int row = 0;row < size;row++)
        for(int col = 0;col < 3;col++)
             //*** IF current element is smallest so far save it ***
             if(s[row][col] < small)
                  small = s[row][col];
   return small;
}
```

Higher Dimensions

There are situations in which even two-dimensional arrays are inadequate. For example, if we want to store the minimum and maximum temperatures every hour for a 365 day period, then we need an array which is 365 x 24 x 2.

Such arrays can be defined by extending the existing definition format. Hence, we can define an array to hold temperatures as:

```
float temp[365][24][2];
```

Where initialisation is required for higher dimensional arrays, more braces are required. For example:

```
int arr[3][2][4] =
     {
          {
               {1,3,2,3},{1,1,1,1}
          },
          {
               {1,8,9,7},{6,5,4,3}
          },
          {
               {0,0,0,0},{6,6,6,6}
          }
     };
```

We can extend our definitions to an almost unlimited number of dimensions; although it is unusual to require more than three.

When passing these higher dimensional arrays to functions, all but the first value must be specified in the functions declaration and definition:

```
int smallest(int[][24][2],int);
```

Summary

■ **An array is** a sequence of elements. Each element can hold a single value. Each value in an array is of the same type.

■ **Single dimension array declaration**:

```
type name[number of elements]

e.g. int list[10];
```

■ **Elements in an array are numbered** from 0 to *number of elements* -1.

■ **Each element is identified** by the array name followed by a subscript enclosed in square brackets.

■ **Arrays can be initialised at definition time** using the format:

```
type name[value]={v1,v2,v3.....}
```

■ **Surplus values are ignored** when initialising arrays.

■ **Surplus elements are zero filled** when initialising arrays.

■ **The array subscript can be given as a constant, variable or expression.**

```
e.g.    list[4];        //*** Constant
        list[no];       //*** Variable
        list[no+2];     //*** Expression
```

■ **When passing an array to a function**, the prototype must contain a type followed by square brackets.

```
int myfunc( int[] .....
```

■ **Normally the contents of an array can be changed from within a function.**

■ **Use** `const` **with the function parameter to prevent changes to the array** within the function.

```
int myfunct(const int[] ....
```

■ **An array name is a pointer constant** to the first element in the array.

```
int myarray[10];
```

`myarray` is the same as `&myarray[0]`

■ **Incrementing a pointer** adjusts its value by the number of memory locations required by its referenced type.

```
int     no;
float   rno;
int     *iptr=&no;
float   *fptr=&rno;

iptr++ // Adds 2 to the value in iptr
       // (int occupies 2 bytes)
fptr++ // Adds 4 to fptr
       // (float occupies 4 bytes)
```

- **Subtracting two pointers** of the same type gives a result equal to the numeric difference between the pointers, divided by the number of memory locations allocated to the data type referenced by the pointers.

- **Array elements can be accessed** using incrementing pointers or offset pointers:

```
int list[10];
int* ptr=list;

//*** Access using pointer offset
for(int c=0;c<10;c++)
     cin>>ptr[c];

//*** Access using pointer incrementing
for(int c=0;c<10;c++,ptr++)
    cin>>*ptr;
```

- **The name of a two-dimensional array is a pointer constant** to an array of pointers. This array contains a pointer for every row in the original array. Each pointer references the first value in that row.

- **Multi-dimensional arrays** are defined using the format

```
type name[dim1][dim2]....
```

- **When passing a multi-dimensional array to a function**, all but the first dimension must be explicitly specified in the function prototype.

- To create pointers to multi-dimensional arrays use the form

```
type (*name)[dim2][dim3]....
```

STRING VARIABLES

Defining String Variables

We have already encountered string constants such as *"Hello world\n"*. But what about string variables? That is, variables capable of holding more than one character.

A string is a sequence of characters. As such, a string can be stored in an array of type `char`. Hence, if we require a variable in which a surname can be stored we may make the definition

```
char surname[12];
```

Initialising Strings

When initialising an `int` array, each element must be specified separately:

```
int nos[5]={3,1,8,4,9};
```

Just to make life a little easier, C++ allows some relaxation of its rules when handling strings, so rather than write

Strings need to be terminated with the NULL character (\0)

```
char surname[12]={'S','t','a','m','p','\0'};
```

which, although valid, is rather awkward to type,we can enter

```
char surname[12]="Stamp";
```

Note that this method does not require the terminating NULL character to be explicitly specified, since the compiler inserts it automatically.

Using Strings

Basic String I/O

This relaxation of the rules when handling strings extends to I/O commands. Hence, we may write

```
cin>>surname;
```

and

```
cout<<surname<<endl;
```

when inputting and displaying strings.

Storage

Where the string is defined to be larger than the data it is allocated, the contents of the elements after the terminating NULL character are undefined. For example, the code

```
char surname[12]="Smith";
```

results in the data storage shown in FIG-5.26.

FIG-5.26

Storing a String

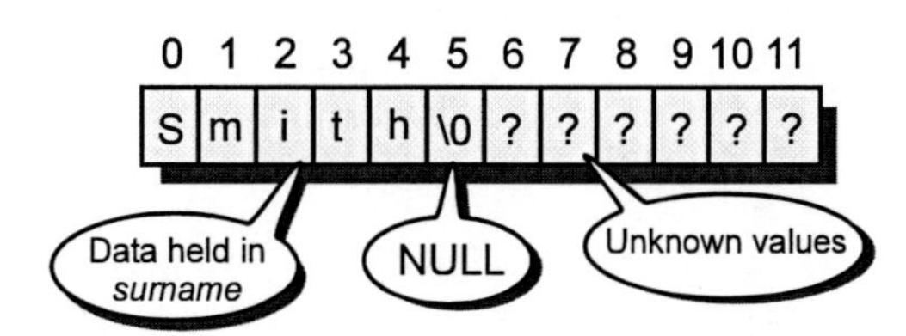

Because of the terminating character, *surname* can only store eleven data characters.

If we attempt to store a string which has more characters than the array being used, this results in the data overflowing into memory locations not allocated to that variable (see FIG-5.27).

FIG-5.27

Storage Overflow

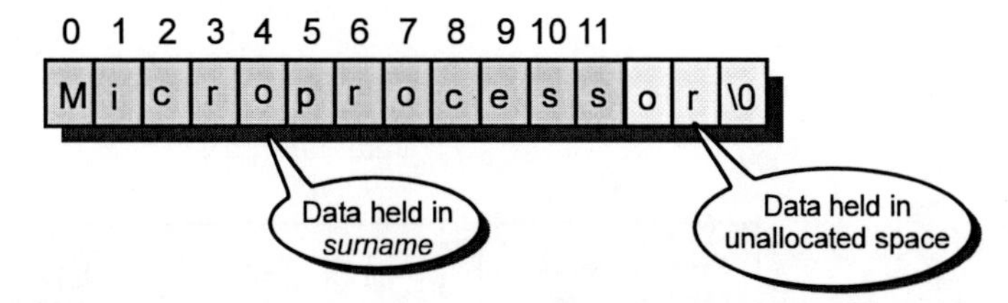

The short program below (LISTING-5.18) is used to illustrate the results of entering a string which is too long for the array to which it is allocated. If the data is only a few characters too large, the contents of *extra* will be affected; where the data is even longer the computer may hang or reboot.

LISTING-5.18

The Effects of Assigning too Large a Value to a String

```
#include <iostream.h>
#include <conio.h>

void main()
{
  char surname[12];
  char extra='X';

  clrscr();
  cout << "Enter surname : ";
  cin >> surname;
  cout << surname << ' ' << extra << '\n';
  getch();
}
```

PROGRAMMING EXERCISE 5.15

Enter the program above and enter the name as:

1. ABCD
2. ABCDEFGHIJKLMNPQR

As with other arrays, a string variable name is treated as a `char` pointer constant containing the start address of the string. In addition, string constants such as "*Hello world\n*" are also treated as address constants, when used in a program. Knowing this gives an insight into why a statement such as

```
surname = "Smith";
```

is invalid as an assignment operation. Whereas most other programming languages interpret the above instruction as a command to copy the string constant value *"Smith"* into the space allocated to a variable, *surname*, C++ looks on this as an attempt to copy the address of the string constant *"Smith"* to a `char` pointer constant and therefore generates an error condition.

To achieve the required effect, we must use a function, `strcpy()`, which copies the contents of one string to a string variable:

```
strcpy(surname,"Smith");
```

Entering Strings at the Keyboard

If we are using `cin` to enter a value for a string variable, there is another surprise waiting: `cin` interprets any whitespace character (space, tab, newline, return) as the terminating symbol of the string. This means that should we attempt to enter a value such as *"John Smith"* at the keyboard, the receiving string variable will only store the value *"John"*(see FIG-5.28).

FIG-5.28

String Entry Using `cin`

Code	Data entered at keyboard	Data Stored
`char name[20];` `cin << name;`	John Smith	John\0 (name)

`gets()` needs `#include <stdio.h>`

To overcome this problem, C++ offers other string handling functions such as `gets()`, which accepts a string terminating with the RETURN character. Hence, if we use the statement

```
gets(name);
```

to read in the name "*John Smith*", then the complete text will be transferred to the variable.

String Functions

Since string variables and constants are handled as addresses by the computer, many of the operations which we can perform on numeric variables cannot be treated in an identical fashion when dealing with strings. For example, the statements in TABLE-5.2 are either invalid or perform unexpectedly.

TABLE 5.2

Invalid String Operations

C++ Statement	Expected Meaning	Actual Meaning
`name = "FRED"`	Assign the value "FRED" to *name*	Attempt to copy the address of "FRED" to *name*.
`if(str1==str2)`	Compare the contents of *str1* and *str2*	Compare the addresses of *str1* and *str2*

Instead, these, and many other operations are performed using string functions. Many of these are listed below.

Most of the following functions are prototyped in the **string.h** header file.

Prototype : `char* strcat(char *s1, const char *s2)`
Pre-condition: *s1* is large enough to hold its original contents, plus the contents of *s2*.

Description : Appends *s2* to the end of *s1*.

Example :

```
char s1[40]="Hello ";
char s2[]="again";

strcat(s1,s2);          //s1 = "Hello again"
strcat(s1,",Sam\n");    //s1 = "Hello again,Sam"
```

Prototype : `char* strchr(const char *s, int c)`
Pre-condition: None

Description : Searches *s* for the first occurrence of the character *c*. The terminating NULL character is part of the area searched.
Returns a pointer to the character if found, otherwise NULL is returned.

Example :

```
char *cptr;
char text[30];

cin>>text;
cptr = strchr(text,'e');
if(cptr)
    cout<<"\'e\' occurs at position "
    <<cptr-text+1<<" in the text "<<text<<'\n';
```

Prototype : `char *strcpy(char *s1, const char *s2)`
Pre-condition: *s1* must have sufficient space to store *s2*.

Description : Copies the contents of *s2* to *s1*. The previous contents of *s1* are erased.

Example : `strcpy(surname,"Smith");   // surname = "Smith"`

size_t is defined in a `typedef` statement. It is equivalent to a `long int.`

Prototype : `size_t strlen(const char *s)`
Pre-condition: None

Description : Returns the number of characters in *s*. The NULL character is not included in the count.

Example : `cout<<strlen("Hello\n"); // displays 5`

Prototype : `int strcmp(const char* s1, const char *s2);`
Pre-condition: None

Description : Compares the strings *s1* and *s2*, one character at a time, beginning with the left most character.
There are three possible results:
1. *s1* is the same as *s2*
2. *s1* is less than *s2*
3. *s1* is greater than *s2*

s1 is less than *s2* if, at the first differing character, that character in *s1* has a smaller ASCII code value than that in *s2* or where the characters in *s1* match those in *s2* but there are still remaining characters in *s2*.
The value returned by this function is:
0 if $s1 = s2$
<0 if $s1 < s2$
>0 if $s1 > s2$
The comparison is case-sensitive.

Example :
```
cout<<strcmp("HE","he");//displays a neg. value

if (!strcmp(s1,s2))
    cout<<"Equal\n";
```

Prototype : `int stricmp(const char *s1, const char *s2)`
Pre-condition: None

Description : As `strcmp()` but is not case sensitive.

Example :
```
cout << stricmp("HE","he"); // displays zero
```

Prototype : `char *strlwr(char *s)`
Pre-condition: None

Description : Converts all upper case characters in *s* to lower case.
s is modified by this operation.
Returns a pointer to *s*.

Example :
```
cout << strlwr("Hello"); // displays hello
```

Prototype : `char *strncat(char*s1,const char*s2,size_t len)`
Pre-condition: *s1* must have sufficient space to hold *len* more characters.

Description : Appends at most *len* characters from *s2* to the end of *s1*.
If *s2* has less than *len* characters, then only those characters in *s2* are appended to *s1*.
Returns a pointer to *s1*.

Example :
```
char words[30]="De";

strncat(words,"capital",3); // words="Decap"
```

Prototype : `int strncmp(const char*s1, const char*s2, size_t len)`

Pre-condition: None

Description : Compares the first *len* characters of *s1* and *s2*.
The value returned by this function is:
0 if *s1* = *s2*
<0 if *s1* < *s2*
>0 if *s1* > *s2*
The comparison is case-sensitive.

Example :

```
if(!strncmp("Hello","Help",3))
    cout<<"First three characters equal\n";
```

Prototype : `char*strncpy(char*s1, const char*s2,size_t len)`

Pre-condition: *s1* has sufficient space for the number of characters copied.

Description : Copies the first *len* characters from *s2* to *s1*.
If s2 does not contain at least *len* characters, all of *s2* is copied to *s1*. The previous contents of *s1* is lost.
Returns a pointer to *s1*.

Example :

```
char text1[20],text2[]="Particle";

strncpy(text1,text2,4); // text1 = "Part"
```

Prototype : `char *strnset(char *s, int ch, size_t len)`

Pre-condition: *s* should contain some valid string value before this routine is called.

Description : Copies the character *ch* into the first *len* positions of *s*.
However if `strlen(s)` < *len*, then only `strlen(s)` characters are set to *ch*.

Returns a pointer to *s*.

Example :

```
char test[20]="Start value";

strnset(test,*,4); // test = "****t value"

strnset(test,-,50); // test= "————-"
```

Prototype : `char *strupr(char *s)`

Pre-condition: None

Description : Converts the contents of *s* to upper case.

Example :

```
cout<<strupr("Hello"); // Outputs HELLO

strupr(name);      //Upcases the contents
                   //of name
```

Prototype : `char *strpbrk(const char *s1, const char *s2)`
Pre-condition: None

Description : Returns a pointer to the first occurrence in *s1* of any character in *s2*.
If there is no match, NULL is returned.

Example :

```
char sent[]="Mary had a little lamb.";
char find[]=",.? ";
char *foundat;


foundat = strpbrk(sent,find);
if(foundat)
    cout << "First word is " << (foundat-sent)
    << " characters long\n";
```

Prototype : `char *strrchr(const char *s, int ch)`
Pre-condition: None

Description : Returns a pointer to the last position in *s* at which the character *ch* occurs.
If *ch* does not appear in *s*, NULL is returned.

Example :

```
char sent[]="Mary had a little lamb.";
char *foundat;


foundat = strrchr(sent,'e');
if(foundat)
    cout << "The last \'e\' is at position
    << (foundat-sent+1) << '\n';
```

Prototype : `char *strstr(const char *s1 const char *s2)`
Pre-condition: None

Description : Returns a pointer to the start of the first occurrence of the sub-string *s2* in *s1*.
If *s2* does not occur within *s1*, NULL is returned.

Example :

```
char sent[]="Mary had a little lamb.";
char find[]="ad";
char *foundat;


foundat = strstr(sent,find);
if(foundat)
    cout << foundat;
```

Prototyped in *stdlib.h*

Prototype : `double strtod(const char *s, char **stopptr)`
Pre-condition: None

Description : Converts *s* to the equivalent `double` value. If *s* does not contain a valid sequence of characters for conversion to a numeric value, *stopptr* holds the address of the first character in *s* which is invalid. If the conversion is successful, *stopptr* is set to NULL.
Note, when using this function, the parameter ***stopptr* is given as the address of a `char` pointer (see details of **indirect pointers** earlier in this chapter).

Example :

```
char entry[20], *check;
double value;

do
{
    gets(entry);
    value = strtod(entry,&check);
}
while (check);
```

Prototype : `char *strtok(char *s1 const char *s2)`
Pre-condition: None

Description : This function treats *s1* as a series of **tokens**. A token is defined as the sequence of characters terminated by any one of the characters specified in *s2*.
Calling the function returns the address of the first token in *s1*.
In addition, the terminating character of the token in *s1* is changed to a NULL character.
If subsequent calls to `strtok()` use NULL as the first argument, the effect is to work through the original string from token to token. The example below uses this technique.
If there are no more tokens in *s1*, NULL is returned.

Example :

```
char sent[]="Mary had a little lamb";
char term[]=".,?! ";
char *cptr;

//*** Display each word in sentence ***
//*** Displays each word of sent on a
//*** separate line
cptr=strtok(sent,term);
while(cptr)
{
    cout << cptr << '\n';
    cptr = strtok(NULL,term);
}
```

Prototyped in *stdlib.h*

Prototype : `long strtol(const char*s,char**stopptr, int radix)`

Pre-condition: None

Description : Converts *s* to a `long int` value. *s* may be in decimal, octal or hexadecimal value.
If *s* does not contain a valid sequence of characters for conversion to a numeric value, *stopptr* holds the address of the first character in *s* which is invalid.
If the conversion is successful, *stopptr* is set to NULL.
The parameter ***stopptr* is given as the address of a `char` pointer.
radix specifies which number base the string represents.

Example :

```
char entry[20], *check;
long value;

do
{
    gets(entry);
    value = strtol(entry,&check);
}
while (check);
```

The following functions are in the header file **stdio.h**.

Prototype : `char *gets(char *s)`
Pre-condition: None

Description : Accepts a string of characters from the input device.
Input is terminated by the **newline** character (generated by pressing the **return** key when entering data at the keyboard).
The stored string has a terminating NULL character added automatically.
The start address of *s* is returned if the input is successful, otherwise the function returns NULL.

Example :

```
char name[20];
gets(name);
```

Prototype : `int puts(char *s)`
Pre-condition: None

Description : Copies *s* to the output device. The cursor moves to the start of the next line after output.
Returns a non-negative value if successful, otherwise returns EOF.

Example :

```
puts("Hello world");
```

Accessing Individual Characters in a String

Although an array of type `char` is often treated as a single string entity, it is also possible to access the individual characters in such a string. For example, if we make the definition

```
char words[]="Mary had a little lamb";
```

then we can access the third character in this string using the term

```
words[2];
```

The following function (LISTING-5.19) returns a count of how often a specified character occurs in a string by comparing each character in the string with the required one.

LISTING-5.19

Counting a Specified Character

```
int countletter(const char s[], char ch)
{
  for(int total = 0,p = 0; p < strlen(s);p++)
      if(s[p] == ch)
          total++;
  return total;
}
```

Arrays of Strings

If we need to retain several linked strings, this can be achieved by declaring an array of strings. Such an array is, in effect, a two-dimensional `char` array, where each row contains one string. This can be declared with a statement such as:

```
char names[5][25];
```

To access one of these strings, the array name and first subscript only are supplied:

Recall that these are pointers to individual rows in a two-dimensional array.

```
strcpy(names[0],"Liz Heron");
gets(names[1]);
```

Initialising an Array of Strings

If an array of strings is to be initialised during definition, the second dimension must be specified but the first may be omitted:

```
char names[][25]={"Spock","Scotty","Bones","Jean Luc","Data"};
```

or

```
char names[5][25]={"Spock","Scotty","Bones","Jean Luc","Data"};
```

Pointers and Strings

Where a program uses a single string, the string variable name is a pointer constant to the strings data. However, as you can see from the previous section, when we are dealing with an array of strings, the array name followed by the row subscript is also treated as a pointer constant to the string held in that row. Hence, assuming the definition

```
char names[5][25];
```

`names[0]` is a pointer to the first string in this array. This means that the terms `names[0]` and `&names[0][0]` are equivalent.

If we create a pointer variable,

```
char *cptr;
```

this can be made to point to any string or part of a string. Hence

```
cptr = names[0];       //points to first string
cptr = names[2];       //points to third string
cptr = &names[0][3];   //points to the third character in the
                       // first string
```

Since we can only create `char` pointers rather than string ones, how does the compiler tell if we wish to access a single character in a string or the whole string?

The potential problem is solved by the differing ways in which strings and characters are handled: strings always supply an address while characters supply the actual value.

In practice, this means that, assuming the code

```
name[] = "James Dean";
char *cptr = name;
```

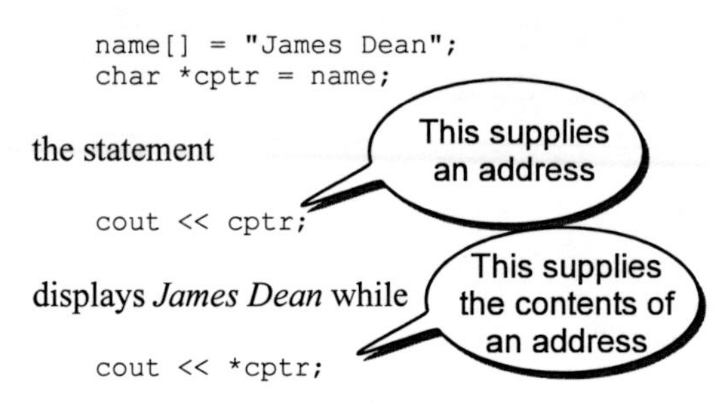

the statement

```
cout << cptr;
```

displays *James Dean* while

```
cout << *cptr;
```

displays the single letter *J*.

Passing Strings to Functions

Passing a single string to a function is treated in exactly the same manner as passing any other array. Hence, the prototypes

```
void myfunct(char[]);
```
and
```
void myfunct(char *);
```

both declare a `char` pointer parameter.

Where the string is not to be changed by the function, the term `const` should be included. This can be done using either:

```
void myfunct(const char[]);
```
or
```
void myfunct(const char *);
```

as the prototype.

When passing an array of strings, only the first subscript may be omitted:

```
void myfunct (char[][25]);
```

This example allows any number of strings, each of a maximum 24 characters, to be passed.

Converting Numbers to Strings

A few functions exist which convert numeric values to null-terminated strings. The space required to store the resulting strings (and the terminating null) must already be allocated before calling any of these routines. The functions, listed below, are all declared in **stdlib.h**.

Prototype : `char *fcvt(double v, int dp, int *pd, int *sign)`
Pre-condition: None

Description : Converts *v* to a null-terminated string. The string contains *dp* digits after the decimal point.
The decimal point is not stored in the string itself; *pd* returns the position of the decimal point relative to the start of the string. Where the value returned is negative this indicates that the decimal point is to the left of the returned string.
If *v* is positive, *sign* is zero, otherwise *sign* is non-zero.

Example :

```
char result[10];
int decpnt, sign;
result = fcvt(12.6761,2,&decpnt,&sign)
```

result = "1268"
decpnt = 2
sign = 0

```
result = fcvt(-0.00000198,8,&decpnt,&sign);
```

result = "198"
decpnt = -5
sign = 1

Prototype : `char *itoa(int v, char *str, int base)`
Pre-condition: None

Description : Converts *v* to a null-terminated string stored in *str*. *base* is the number base used when converting the number. This must lie between 2 to 36. If *v* is negative and *base* is 10 the first character in *str* will be '-'.

Example :

```
char result[10];
itoa(123,result,10);
```

result = "123"

```
itoa(255,result,16);
```

result = "FF"

Prototype : `char *ecvt(double v,int totd,int *pd,int *sign)`
Pre-condition: None
Description : Converts *v* to a null-terminated string. The string contains *totd* digits.
The decimal point is not stored in the string itself; *pd* returns the position of the decimal point relative to the start of the string. Where the value returned is negative this indicates that the decimal point is to the left of the returned string.
If *v* is positive, *sign* is zero, otherwise *sign* is non-zero.

Example :

```
char result[10];
int decpnt, sign;
result = ecvt(12.6761,2,&decpnt,&sign)
```

result = "13"
decpnt = 2
sign = 0

```
result=ecvt(0.00000198,8,&decpnt,&sign);
```

result = "19800000"
decpnt = -5
sign = 1

Prototype : `char *ltoa(long v, char *str, int base)`
Pre-condition: None

Description : Converts *v* to a null-terminated string stored in *str*. *base* is the number base used when converting the number. This must lie between 2 to 36. If *v* is negative and *base* is 10 the first character in *str* will be '-'.

Example :

```
char result[10];
ltoa(-123L,result,10); //result = "-123"

ltoa(255L,result,8);    //result = "377"
```

Prototype : `char *ultoa(unsigned long v,char *str,int base)`
Pre-condition: None

Description : Converts *v* to a null-terminated string stored in *str*. *base* is the number base used when converting the number. This must lie between 2 to 36.

Example :

```
char result[10];
unsigned long no = 12345678
ultoa(no,result,10);        //result = "12345678"

ultoa(255UL,result,16);     //result = "FF"
```

THE HENLEY COLLEGE LIBRARY

PROGRAMMING EXERCISE 5.16

Write programs to achieve the following tasks:

1. Create a function which returns how often each letter occurs in a string.

```
OUTLINE LOGIC:
   FOR each character in string DO
       IF character is a letter THEN
           Add 1 to appropriate count
       ENDIF
   ENDFOR
   return set of counts
```

2. Create a function which reverses the contents of a string.

```
OUTLINE LOGIC:
   set first to zero
   set last to length of string-1
   WHILE first<last DO
       Swap characters at positions first and last
       Increment first
       Decrement last
   ENDWHILE
```

3. Capitalise the first character in every word of a sentence.

```
OUTLINE LOGIC:
   Capitalise first letter
   FOR every other character in the string DO
       IF the preceding character is a space THEN
            Capitalise letter
       ENDIF
   ENDFOR
```

4. Create a function which accepts a string (*s*) such as “xka..ej” and returns a string (*result*) in which the additional characters implied by the symbols “..” have been inserted. In the string shown here, the returned value would be “xka**bcd**ej”. The “..” notation may occur several times within the original string. You may assume the resulting string is less than 256 characters.

```
OUTLINE LOGIC:
   Empty result
   Copy first char from s to result
   FOR all but the last 2 characters DO
       IF the next two char of s are “..” THEN
           FOR letter = char before “..” TO char after “..” DO
               Copy letter into result
           ENDFOR
           Skip past “..” chars
       ELSE
           Copy char from s to result
       ENDIF
   ENDFOR
   Copy any remaining chars from s to result
   Add NULL character to result
```

Continued on next page

PROGRAMMING EXERCISE 5.16 (continued)

5. Create a function *GetData()*, which returns a string entered from the keyboard. The string should be constructed from characters from a specified set, and by no more than a specified number of characters in length. The specified character set should be given in abbreviated form and expanded using the function created in 4 above.

```
OUTLINE LOGIC:
    Set count to zero
    Expand abbreviated character set
    Set result to an empty string
    Read a valid character
    WHILE character not ENTER DO
        IF
            character is in specified set AND count<maximum :
                Display character
                Add 1 to count
                Add character to result
            character is BACKSPACE AND count > 0 :
                Remove last character from screen
                Remove last character from result
                Subtract 1 from count
        ENDIF
        Read a valid character code
    ENDWHILE
    return result
```

Summary

- A **string constant** is zero or more characters enclosed in double quotes.
- **String values are terminated** by the **NULL** character ('\0').
- A **string variable** is an array of type `char`.
- **String variables may overflow their storage space**, since there is no range checking when dealing with arrays. This can lead to unpredictable results.
- **String input terminates when a whitespace character is encountered** where `cin` is used.
- **Normally, `gets()` should be used to input a string value.**
- **Use a subscript to access individual characters** in a string.

  e.g. *name*[2] to access the third character in *name*.
- **A two-dimensional array of** `char` can be used to hold an array of strings.
- When using an array of strings, **the array name followed by one subscript specifies the address of a string. The array name followed by two subscripts, specifies a character within a string.**

  e.g. *list[4]* - accesses the fifth string in *list*.
  list[4][0] - accesses the first character of the fifth string.

Function Name	Return Type	Input Types	Header File	Description
gets	char*	char* s	stdio.h	Accepts a value for *s* from the input device. Returns the address of *s*.
puts	int	char* s		Displays *s* on the output device.
strcat	char*	char* s1 const char* s2	string.h	Appends *s2* to *s1*.
strchr	char*	const char* s int ch	string.h	Returns address of first occurrence of *ch* in *s* else NULL.
strcmp	int	const char* s1 const char* s2	string.h	Compares *s1* and *s2*. Returns <0 if *s1*<*s2* 0 if *s1*=*s2* >0 if *s1*>*s2*
stricmp	int	const char* s1 const char* s2	string.h	As strcmp() but not case sensitive.
strcpy	char*	char* s1 const char* s2	string.h	Copies *s2* into *s1*.
strlen	size_t	const char* s	string.h	Returns the number of characters in *s*.
strlwr	char*	char* s	string.h	Converts all lower case characters in *s* to upper. Returns a pointer to *s*.
strncat	char*	char* s1 const char* s2 size_t len	string.h	Appends at most *len* characters from *s2* to *s1*. Returns a pointer to *s1*.
strncmp	int	const char* s1 const char* s2 size_t len	string.h	Compares the first *len* characters in *s1* and *s2*. Returns <0 if *s1*<*s2* 0 if *s1*=*s2* >0 if *s1*>*s2*
strncpy	char*	char* s1 const char* s2 size_t len	string.h	Copies the first *len* characters of *s2* into *s1*. Returns a pointer to *s1*.
strnset	char*	char* s int ch size_t len	string.h	Copies ch into the first *len* characters of *s*. Returns a pointer to *s*.
strpbrk	char*	const char* s1 const char* s2	string.h	Returns a pointer to the first occurrence in *s1* of any character in *s2*.
strrchr	char*	const char* s int ch	string.h	Returns a pointer to the last position in *s* at which *ch* occurs.
strstr	char*	const char* s1 const char* s2	string.h	Returns a pointer to the first occurrence of *s2* in in *s1*.
strtod	double	const char* s char **stopptr	string.h	Converts *s* to a double. Returns the address of first character which cannot be converted, in *stopptr* else NULL.
strtok	char*	char* s1 const char* s2	string.h	Identifies the tokens in *s1*. Any character from *s2* is taken as a token terminator.
strtol	long	const char* s char **stopptr int radix	string.h	Converts *s* to a long. *radix* defines the radix used in *s*. Returns the address of first character which cannot be converted else NULL.
strupr	char*	char* s		Converts all characters in *s* to uppercase.
fcvt ecvt	char*	double v int dp int *pd int *sign	stdlib.h	Converts *v* to a string held to *dp* decimal places (total digits for *ecvt()*) *pd* indicates position of decimal point. *sign* zero for positive values else non-zero.
itoa ltoa	char*	int/long/ unsigned long v char* str int base	stdlib.h	Converts *v* to a string,in *str*. *base* is the number base.

ENUMERATED TYPES

Introduction

There are some situations in which neither numbers nor strings are really appropriate ways of representing data. For example, if we want to model a set of traffic lights which use the repeating sequence: RED, RED-AMBER, GREEN, AMBER, although we might use strings

```
char lights[][10]={"RED","RED-AMBER","GREEN","AMBER"}
char state[10] = lights[0];
```

moving from one traffic light state to another is rather clumsy:

```
strcpy(state,lights[1]);
```

On the other hand, using a numeric value

```
int state = 0;
```

hides the descriptive value of the lights.

Using Enumerated Types

Declaring an Enumerated Type

An alternative is to create an **enumerated type**. By declaring an enumerated type we are permitted to declare a specific set of values which may be assigned to any variables defined as this type. Hence, we may first declare *lights* as an enumerated type with the statement:

NOTE: The values listed are not strings and must not be enclosed in quotes.

```
enum lights {RED,RED_AMBER,GREEN,AMBER};
```

As well as defining the possible values which any variable of this type may be given, an order is also imposed on these values (AMBER is after GREEN, RED_AMBER is before GREEN). The listed values are known as the **members** of the enumerated type.

Normally, the declaration will appear above `main()` thus allowing us to define variables of this type anywhere in our program.

Defining and Using EnumeratedVariables

Once we create a variable of this type, for example,

```
lights trafficlights;
```

we can then set it to any of the defined values:

```
trafficlights = RED;
```

Increment and decrement operators can be used to change the variable's contents to an adjacent value in the list:

```
trafficlights = RED;
trafficlights++;   //*** now equal to RED_AMBER***
```

```
trafficlights = AMBER;
trafficlights--;          //*** now equal to GREEN
```

In reality, enumerated types are implemented using contiguous integer values, the first member being assigned the value zero.

It is possible to override the integer values associated with the listed members by specifying the associated integer in the `enum` statement:

```
enum lights{RED=1,RED_AMBER,GREEN=5,AMBER}
```

Those members not given an explicit value are automatically given ascending values from the left (e.g. RED = 1, RED_AMBER=2, GREEN=5, AMBER=6}

The downside of using enumerated types is that their value can neither be entered from the keyboard nor displayed on the screen. This leaves their usefulness limited to variables used exclusively for internal representational purposes.

The program in LISTING-5.20 shows an enumerate type in use. The program accepts the number of hours worked on the days Monday to Friday and then displays the data entered.

Note that the program uses an enumerated type variable as a subscript to an array.

LISTING-5.20

Using Enumerated Types

```
#include <iostream.h>
#include<conio.h>
#include<iomanip.h>


void main()
{
   //*** Declare enumerated type ***
   enum Days {Mon,Tues,Wed,Thurs,Fri};
   //*** Define string equivalents ***
   char dow[5][10]=
        {"Monday","Tuesday","Wednesday","Thursday","Friday"};

   Days today;
   float workload[5];

   //*** Enter values hours worked each day ***
   for(today = Mon;today <= Fri;today++)
   {
        cout << "Enter hours worked on "<<dow[today]<<" : ";
        cin >> workload[today];
   }
   //*** Display data entered ***
   clrscr();
   cout << setw(35) << "Workload for Week\n\n\n";
   for(today = Mon;today <= Fri;today++)
        cout << setw(10) << dow[today] << ' ' << workload[today]
        << endl;

   getch();
}
```

There are a couple of points worth looking at in LISTING-5.20:

The array *dow* is used to contain the actual text corresponding to the values of the enumerated type. This technique overcomes the problem of not being able to display the value of an enumerated variable.

We might have been tempted to define the `float` array using the statement

```
float workload[Fri];
```

which has the benefit of emphasising the strategy used in the program, but this does not have the desired effect since the value *Fri* is represented internally as the integer value 4 and will result in an array with four, rather than five elements. Hence the correct definition would be

```
float workload[Fri+1];
```

TASK 5.15

Write the declaration of an enumerated type for the months of the year. Each month should be assigned the numeric value equivalent to the number of days which have passed from the beginning of the year to the end of that month; hence, *Jan* = 31 and *Dec* = 365.

COMPOSITE STRUCTURES

Introduction

An array is only useful when the data items to be stored are all of the same type. Where the collection of data items is of differing types, another data structure is required. This is known as a **record**. A record is a collection of individual data items or **members** or **fields**. Each data item may be of any type.

Defining a Record Structure

If we wanted to retain the identity code, sex and score of a student who had taken part in an aptitude test, then we might declare this collection of information using the following Structured English :

```
TYPE
    IQType =
        RECORD
            idcode  : INTEGER
            sex     : CHAR
            score   : INTEGER
        ENDRECORD
```

This acts as a blueprint for any subsequent variables defined as this type. For example:

```
st1,st2 :   IQType
```

In contrast, C++ uses the keyword `struct` to declare a record's format:

```
struct IQType
{
    int     idcode;
    char    sex;
    int     score;
}
```

The identifier *IQType* is known as the **structure tag** and is then used when defining variables of that structure:

```
IQType st1,st2;
```

The resulting allocation of memory space is shown in FIG-5.29.

FIG-5.29

Record Structures

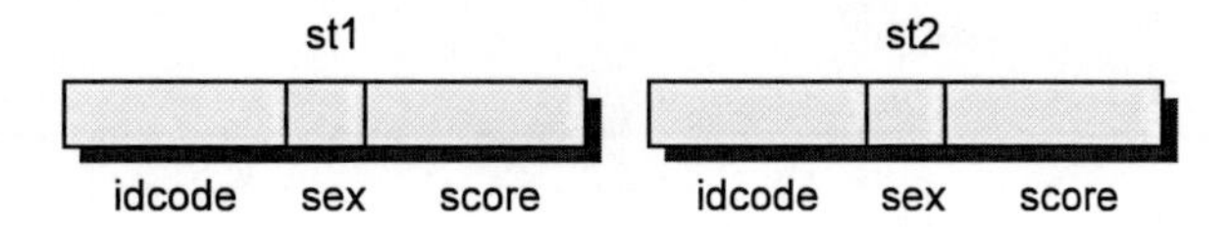

An alternative approach is to define the variables at the end of the structure declaration; in which case the structure tag may be omitted:

```
struct
{
    int     idcode;
    char    sex;
    int     score;
} st1, st2;
```

A final possibility is to define the structure in a `typedef` statement:

```
typedef struct
{
    int     idcode;
    char    sex;
    int     score;
} IQType;
```

Note that the type name comes at the end of the structure definition and no structure tag is required.

Variables are then defined with statements such as:

```
IQType st1, st2;
```

The first of these three methods is the most widely used since the other offer no advantages.

TASK 5.16

Using the first approach given above, write the definition of a structure, *details,* containing *age* (in years), *height* (in metres) and *weight* (in kilos). Define three variables, *w1*, *w2* and *w3* of this structure.

Record structures are often used even when the data they contain are of the same type - a situation in which we might normally think of using arrays. For example, time information might be held in a record structure defined as

```
struct Time
{
    int hrs, mins, secs;
}
```

since this allows us to give a name to each component in the data; something that isn't possible when using an array.

Initialising a Structure Variable

Structure variables are initialised in much the same way as an array, with the values for each field enclosed in braces. For instance, we can set the *idcode, sex* and *score* fields of a variable *st1* to 123,'M' and 115 respectively with the definition

```
IQType st1={123,'M',115};
```

The values must be given in the same order as the fields to which they are to be assigned.

Structure Members

Accessing Structure Members

A field within a structure variable can be accessed using the member selector operator (.).

Hence, assuming the definition

```
IQType st1,st2;
```

we can access the *score* field in *st1* using the term

```
st1.score
```

This term can be employed at any point in the program where it would be legal to use an `int` variable. For example:

```
st1.score = 120;
cout << st1.score;
cin >> st1.score;
if (st1.score >100)
        ....
```

The following program (LISTING-5.21) makes use of record variables in determining the average aptitude score for two students.

Program Logic:

```
Read details of first student
Read details of second student
Calculate average score
Display average score
```

Program Code:

LISTING-5.21

Using structs

```
#include<iostream.h>
#include<conio.h>

struct IQType
{
  int idcode;
  char sex;
  int score;
};

void main()
{
  IQType st1,st2;         //Holds details of students

  //*** Get student details ***
  clrscr();
  cout<<"Enter id of first student : ";
  cin>>st1.idcode;
  cout<<"Enter sex : ";
  cin>>st1.sex;
  cout<<"Enter score : ";
  cin>>st1.score;
  cout<<"Enter id of second student : ";
  cin>>st2.idcode;
  cout<<"Enter sex : ";
  cin>>st2.sex;
  cout<<"Enter score : ";
  cin>>st2.score;
  //*** Calculate average ***
  float average = (st1.score+st2.score)/2.0;
  //*** Display average score ***
  cout<<"Average score = "<<average<<endl;

  getch();
}
```

PROGRAMMING EXERCISE 5.17

Write a program to determine the height of the tallest of three people. The following information is held on each person: *age, height* and *weight.*

Field Types

Record structure fields may be arrays, other structures or pointers as well as user-defined types. For example, if we want to hold the score achieved by a student in each of six exams we could declare the structure:

```
//*** Declare structure ***
struct StudentDetails
 {
    int     idcode;
    char    sex;
    int     score[6]; //An array with a struct
};
```

Defining and initialising a variable is achieved by statements such as:

```
//*** Define variable and initialise variable ***
StudentDetails student1 = { 123, 'M',{47,52,91,68,73,78}};
```

To access the third score we use a combination of member selection (using .) and array element access ([2]) :

```
//*** Access field in struct ****
student1.score[2]
```

> **TASK 5.17**
>
> Write code to sum the six marks of variable *student1* defined above.

To add the student's name to our structure we include a string field:

```
//*** Declare struct using string variable***
struct StudentDetails
{
    int     idcode;
    char    name[30];
    char    sex;
    int     score[6];
};
```

An alternative is to simply include a `char` pointer within the record structure:

```
//*** Declare struct using string pointer ***
struct StudentDetails
{
    int     idcode;
    char    *name;
    char    sex;
    int     score[6];
};
```

This approach can be useful when we have an array of *StudentDetails,* where allocating 30 character spaces for each name, many of which will require significantly less characters, would be wasteful of memory space.

Using this setup, the programming requirements for reading in a name would be:

```
Read name into a temp string variable
Allocate dynamic space for the name referenced by the pointer
 within the students record.
Copy name into allocated space
```

The relevant code is given overleaf:

```
//*** Declare record structure ***
struct StudentDetails
{
    int     idcode;
    char    *name;
    char    sex;
    int     score[6];
};

//*** Define variables ***
StudentDetails st;      //Student's record
char temp[30];          //Temporary storage for name

//*** Read name into temp variable ***
gets(temp);
//*** Allocate space for name ***
st.name=new char[strlen(temp)+1]; //extra byte for NULL char
//*** Copy name into allocated space ***
strcpy(st.name,temp);
```

The effect of this is shown in FIG-5.30.

FIG-5.30

Using Pointer in a struct

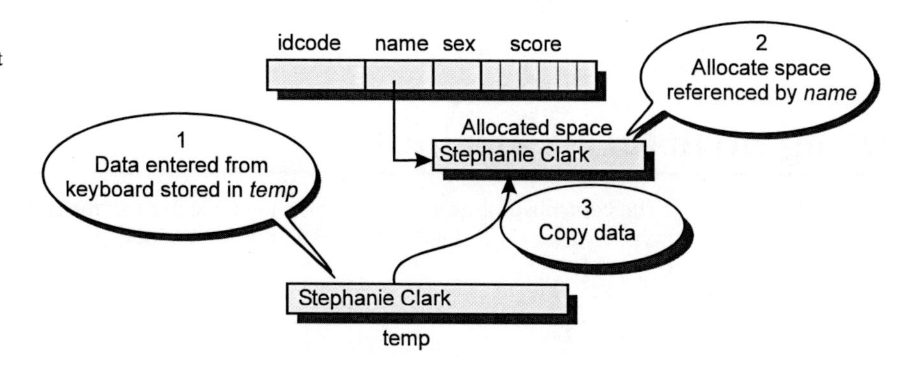

Disk files are discussed in the next chapter.

A disadvantage of this method occurs when the contents of such structures are saved to a disk file. Using a pointer for *name* will mean that only the contents of the pointer will be saved. That is, only the address of where the actual name is stored is saved rather than the name itself. This address will be meaningless when the contents of the record are subsequently read from disk at a later date and, hence, the actual data will be lost.

Where a record does contain a pointer member, the de-reference operator, when used, should be placed before the record variable name. Hence, to access the *name* field in the structure referenced by *st* we use

```
*st.name
```

Nested Record Structures

A common requirement is to store a date. Although this might be held using a simple string variable, because we often require to access the day, month and year components of a date separately, it is more appropriate to use a record structure such as

```
struct DateType
{
    char    day;
    char    month;
    int     year;
};
```

Where a date is required as part of a larger record, then the result is a **nested structure**. For example, to add the date of birth to our student record the new declaration would be

```
struct StudentDetails
{
    int         idcode;
    char        name[30];
    DateType    dob;
    char        sex;
    int         score[6];
};
```

Assuming the definition

```
StudentDetails st1;
```

we can access the *dob* fields components using the terms

```
st1.dob.day
st1.dob.month
```
and
```
st1.dob.year
```

Using Structure Variables

The contents of a structure variable may be copied to another variable of the same type by a single assignment statement. For example:

```
StudentDetails st1=
        {1234,"Liz Heron",{26,10,1961},'F'{67,78,95,89,99,100}}
,st2;

//*** Copy the complete contents of st1 to st2 ***
st2 = st1;
```

If only specified fields are to be copied then the fields must be copied separately:

```
//*** Copy date of birth and name ***
st2.dob=st1.dob;
strcpy(st2.name,st1.name);
```

Structures and Pointers

Making a pointer of the appropriate type reference a record structure, is achieved using the same methods as that for simple variables such as `int` and `float` values

```
//*** Define pointer and record variables ***
StudentDetails *rptr,st1;

//*** Copy the address of st1 to the pointer ***
rptr = &st1
```

and accessing the record's fields requires the pointer to be de-referenced:

```
(*rptr).name
```

Note that the de-reference operation must be enclosed in parentheses since the member selector operator (.) has a higher priority than the de-reference operator (*).

However, since this format looks rather awkward, the language provides an alternative operator to achieve the same effect. The **structure pointer operator** (->) consists of two keyboard characters: a *minus* sign and a *greater than* symbol with no spaces between. Using this symbol, we can access the structure's fields using expressions such as:

```
rptr->sex
```

Rather than reference an existing record, we can create the record space dynamically. This is done using the expression

```
rptr = new StudentDetails;
```

with field access as before

```
rptr->sex;
```

Function Parameters and Structures

Passing a structure to or from a function involves the same techniques used to pass simple types such as `int` and `float` values.. For *call by value*, simply specify the structure tag in the prototype at the appropriate position. For example, to pass a StudentDetails record to a function the relevant code would be

```
int HighestMark(StudentDetails);


int HighestMark(StudentDetails st)
{
    .
    .
}
```

A *call by reference* structure parameter requires the **address of** operator:

```
int Update(StudentDetails&);

int Update(StudentDetails& st)
{
    .
    .
}
```

Arrays of Records

If we need to retain the details of several students then one possibility is to define an array of records. This is done with the definition

```
StudentDetails studentlist[7];
```

To access a specific student's record the array name and element number must be specified. For example:

```
studentlist[4]
```

To access a field within that record we need the structure member operator and the field name:

`studentlist[4].dob.day` (see FIG-5.31)

FIG-5.31

Arrays of Records

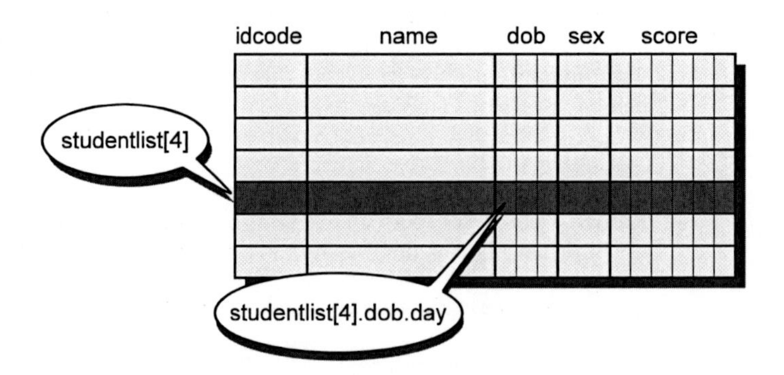

> **PROGRAMMING EXERCISE 5.18**
>
> Write a program using a record structure which reads in the *account number*, *name*, *address* and *balance* of a bank customer. The name should be sub-divided into *surname*, *first name* and *initials*; the address should be divided into *first line*, *second line*, *third line*, *town*, *district* and *post code*. The balance entered should be increased by 5% after which all details should be displayed on the screen.

Summary

- **A record is a collection of fields.**
- C++ uses the term `struct` to declare a record structure.
- The fields within a `struct` are often referred to as **members** of the `struct`.
- **The commonest format** when defining a `struct` is

```
struct structure_tag
{
   type field1;
   type field2;
     .
   type lastfield;
 };
```

- **Use the structure_tag when defining variables**

```
structure_tag variable1, variable2...
```

- **To initialise the fields** of a `struct` variable use the form

```
structure_tag variable = {value1, value2...}
```

- **To access a `struct` field:**

```
simple member           variable_name.field_name
array element           variable_name.array_name[subscript]
de-referenced pointer   *variable_name.field_name
```

- **To access the field of a pointer referenced `struct`:**

```
        (*pointer).field_name
or      pointer->field_name
```

- **To make a pointer reference a `struct`** variable:

```
struct_name *pointer;
pointer = &struct_variable;
```

- **To dynamically allocate a** `struct` **data item**:

```
struct_name *pointer;
pointer = new struct_name;
```

- **When passing a *call by value*** `struct` **to a function** use the structure tag in the function declaration and definition.

```
myfunct(struct_tag)
```

- **When passing a *call by reference*** `struct` **to a function** use the structure tag followed by the *address of* operator in the function declaration and definition.

```
myfunct2(struct_tag&)
```

- **When using an array of** `struct`, a field may be accessed using the format

```
array_name[subscript].field_name
```

- **To copy one `struct`** variable to another of the same type, use the normal assignment command:

```
struct_var1 = struct_var2;
```

BITS

Bit Fields

All the data items we have encountered so far occupy a given number of bytes. However, it is possible to define data components which occupy as little as a single bit. This may be desirable to minimise the storage requirements of information. For example, if we need to record the sex of a student, we could define an appropriate variable using the statement

```
char sex;
```

But this variable requires a byte (8 bits) of storage whereas we could store the same information in a single bit simply by setting that bit to 1 for *male* or 0 for *female*.

Although this may not be a significant saving where the sex of a single person is involved, when thousands of occurrences of such data are to be stored the savings can be considerable.

Another possible situation in which a small group of bits needs to be defined is in performing low level operations such as interrogating the state of pins on an INPUT/OUTPUT port. Here, each pin can be represented by a single bit.

Although C++ does not allow separate bit-sized variables, you can define structures which contain bit-sized fields. These fields must be declared as `int` or `unsigned int` types but, unlike normal fields, the syntax is extended to allow the number of bits the field is to occupy to be stated. The format for declaring such fields are:

```
type field_name : number of bits (max of 16 bits)
```

For example, you may recall that, in DOS mode, a single character on the screen is held in two bytes of video RAM: one byte containing the ASCII code for the character while the other contains details of the colours used in displaying the character (see FIG-5.32).

FIG-5.32

Screen Character Structure

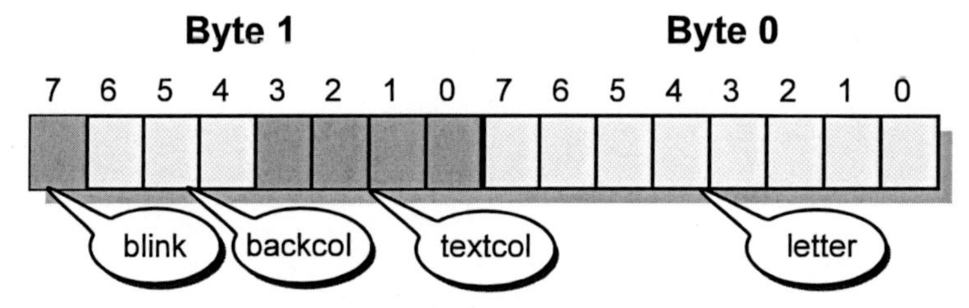

This structure may be defined as

```
struct VideoChar
{
    char letter;
    unsigned textcol   : 4;
    unsigned backcol   : 3;
    unsigned blink     : 1;
};
```

We can then define variables of this type in the usual fashion:

```
VideoChar c;
```

and access fields with statements such as:

Colour constants such as YELLOW are defined in conio.h.
Note, only uppercase symbolic names will be recognised.

```
c.letter = 'A';
c.textcol = YELLOW;
c.backcol = BLUE;
```

The program in LISTING-5.22 uses the above structure to place a single character directly on the screen. Video RAM addresses begin at $B8000000_{16}$ if a VGA display is being used.

Program Logic:

```
Set up data to be written to screen in data structure
Set pointer to address of first byte in video RAM
Clear screen
Copy data to area referenced by pointer
```

Program Code:

LISTING-5.22

Accessing the Video RAM using Bit Fields

NOTE: This program will only operate correctly if your machine is 100% IBM PC compatible.

This line casts the hexadecimal value B8000000 to a *VideoChar* pointer type hence allowing it to be assigned to the pointer variable, *scrptr*.

```
#include <conio.h>

struct VideoChar
{
  char letter;
  unsigned textcol:4;
  unsigned backcol:3;
  unsigned blink:1;
};

void main()
{
   VideoChar c={'A',YELLOW,BLUE,0};    //Data for screen

   //*** Set pointer to start of video RAM ***
   VideoChar *scrptr=(VideoChar*)0XB8000000L;//Cast address to
   //*** Clear screen ***                            correct type
   clrscr();
   //*** Copy data to area referenced by pointer ***
   *scrptr=c;
   getch();
}
```

TASK 5.18

Every screen character occupies two bytes and screen memory is allocated on a line by line basis. Hence, the second character on the first line is allocated memory locations $B8000002/3_{16}$
What addresses are allocated to:
1. the last character on line 1
2. the last character on line 25.

Aligning Bits to a Location Boundary

Where the structure contains fields which do not fit in a single location, the data items may straddle memory locations. For example, the definition

```
struct MOREBITS
{
    unsigned first    :12;
    unsigned second   :5;
    unsigned third    :4;
};
```

whose storage requirements are shown in FIG-5.33, contains fields which cross byte boundaries. This can result in a deterioration of program efficiency as the machine generates the code necessary to access data which does not start on a location boundary.

FIG-5.33

Bit Fields Straddling Byte Boundaries

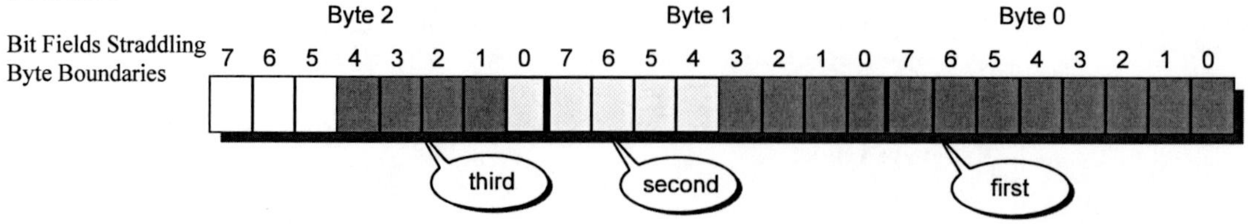

To ease this problem, we can force bit fields to start on a location boundary by adding unnamed fields within our structure:

```
struct MOREBITS
{
    unsigned first    :12;
    unsigned          : 4;
    unsigned second   : 5;
    unsigned          : 3;
    unsigned third    : 4;
};
```

You can even get the compiler to do the hard work of calculating how many unnamed bits to insert by specifying 0 bits in the declaration:

```
struct MOREBITS
{
    unsigned first    :12;
    unsigned          : 0;
    unsigned second   : 5;
    unsigned          : 0;
    unsigned third    : 4;
};
```

Of course, although this will result in faster access, it means a larger storage requirement for the structure and cannot be used where the positioning of the bits is critical as in *VideoChar*.

Bit-Manipulation Operators

In addition to defining bit fields, it is possible to manipulate the bits of other simple data types.

Bit Complement Operator (~)

This unary operator inverts the bits of a value, giving a result in which the 1's of the original value are replaced by zeros and the original zeros by 1's. A typical piece of code might be:

```
char no1 = 0XB2;
char no2 = 0X7;
char ans;
ans = ~no1;
```

ans will then contain the value 0X4D (see FIG-5.34).

FIG-5.34

Bit Complement

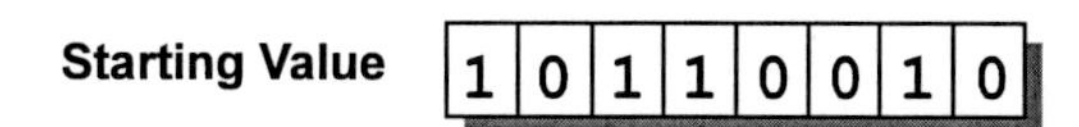

Operation : ~

Result 0 1 0 0 1 1 0 1

> **TASK 5.19**
>
> What is the result of the expressions
> 1. ~0X7C09
> 2. ~196
>
> Give your results in both hexadecimal and binary.

Shift Left Operator (<<)

This allows us to move a value a specified number of bits to the left. For example:

```
no1 = 0XB2;
ans = no1 << 3;
```

The result of this example is shown in FIG-5.35.

FIG-5.35

Shift Left

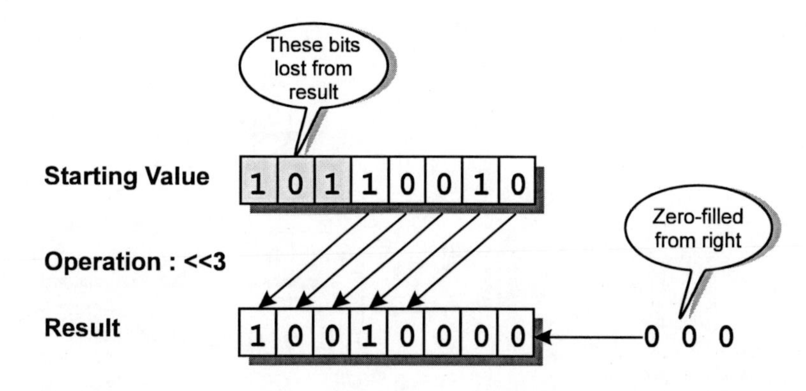

Note that the left hand bits of the original value are lost, while the right-hand bits are zero-filled.

The shift left operator can be used as an efficient way of multiplying a value by any power of two. Hence to multiply a value by 8 (2^3), we simply move it 3 places to the left.

It can also be used to determine the value of a specific bit. For example, if we want to find out if the third bit (counting from the right) of an `int` value contains a 1, we can simply shift the value 5 places to the left and test if the result is less than zero (remembering that a 1 in the left-most bit of a signed integer will result in the contents being interpreted as a negative value).

PROGRAMMING EXERCISE 5.19

Write a function which displays the contents of an `int` value in binary.

```
OUTLINE LOGIC:
   FOR each bit DO
      IF value negative THEN
         Display '1'
      ELSE
         Display 0
      ENDIF
      Shift value one place to left
   ENDFOR
```

Shift Right Operator (>>)

This operator, rather obviously, moves a value a specified number of places to the right. This is a good way to perform integer division by any power of two. Hence, to divide the contents of *no1* by 16 (2^4) we need merely write

```
ans = no1 >> 4;
```

The effects of this operation are shown in FIG-5.36.

FIG-5.36

Shift Right

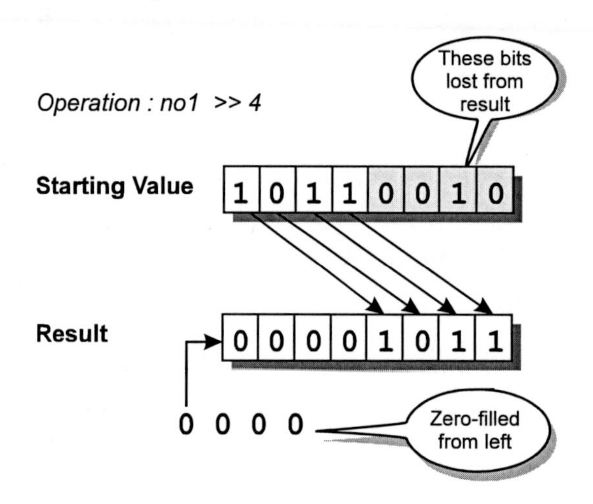

Bit-wise AND (&)

This AND's the bits of two values. A bit in the result is 1 if the corresponding operand bits are both 1, otherwise the result bit is zero. A typical statement might be

```
ans = no1 & 0X04;
```

The second value specified in this, and the remaining operations, is often referred to as a **mask**, since it can be used as a mask or filter out parts of a value. For example, suppose we want to know if bit 3 of a `char` variable contains a 1. One way to do this is to copy only bit 3 of the variable into a second variable and if this result is zero then the original bit 3 was also zero. To stop the other bits of the original value being copied across to the result we use the bit-AND operator with a mask value of 0X04 (see FIG-5.37).

FIG-5.37

Bit AND

Operation : no1 & 0X04

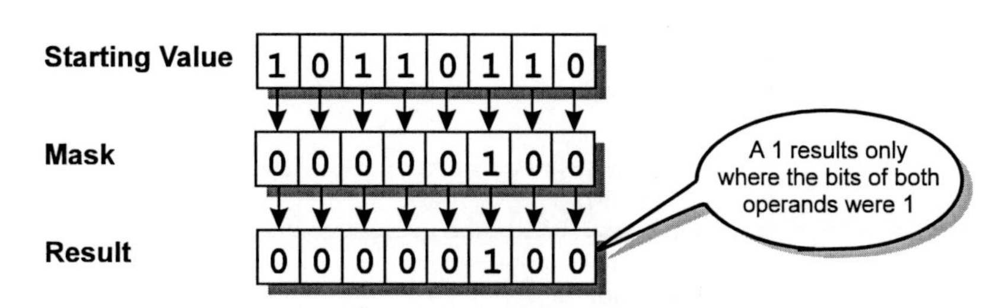

Bit-wise OR (|)

This operator OR's the bits of two values, giving a result of 1 where either or both of the corresponding operand bits are 1, otherwise giving a zero. Typically,

```
ans = no1 | 0X0F;
```

The result of the above example is shown in FIG-5.38.

FIG-5.38

Bit OR

Operation : no1 | 0X0F

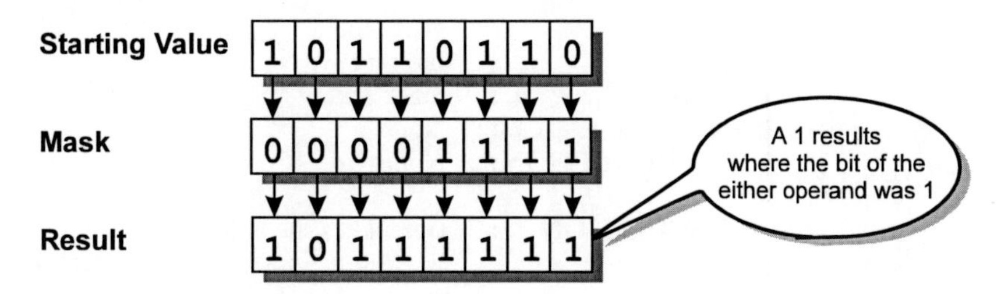

Bit-wise Exclusive OR (^)

A given bit in the result is set to 1 if the corresponding bits in the two operands are of differing values (0, 1 or 1,0); a result of zero is given where both bits are the same (0,0 or 1,1). A typical statement might be

```
ans = no1 ^ no2;
```

An example is shown in FIG-5.39.

FIG-5.39

Exclusive OR

Operation : no1 ^ 0X0F

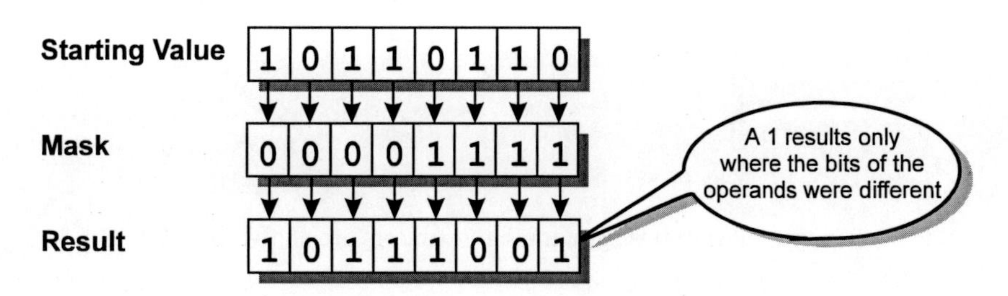

TASK 5.20

1. Write down the result of the operation
   01011101
   01110000 XOR

2. Using the result of 1 above, XOR it with the same value as before (01110000).

The result from the above Task highlights an important feature of the exclusive OR operation: performing XOR twice produces the original value.

This can be very useful when dealing with screen output. For example, we can change the background colour of an area on the screen without affecting the character or foreground colour by using an exclusive OR mask on the required area of the video RAM and then change it back to the original colour by performing the same XOR operation.

PROGRAMMING EXERCISE 5.20

Write a function which conforms to the following Mini-Spec:

NAME	:	CreateMask
PARAMETERS		
IN	:	start : int req : int
OUT	:	mask : int
IN/OUT	:	None
PRE-CONDITION	:	None
DESCRIPTION	:	Calculates the value of *mask* required such that when *start* is XORed with *mask* the result is *req*.
OUTLINE LOGIC	:	`mask = start XOR req`

Bit Assignment Operators

Just as we can write

```
sum += no;
```

rather than

```
sum = sum + no;
```

we may also code statements such as

```
no1 = no1<<5;
```

as

```
no1<<=5;
```

All bitwise assignment operators are shown in TABLE-5.3.

TABLE 5.3

Bitwise Assignment Operators

<table>
<tr><th>Operator</th><th>Description</th><th>Example</th><th>Equivalent</th></tr>
<tr><td><<=</td><td>Shift left assignment</td><td>no1<<=2</td><td>no1 = no1<<2</td></tr>
<tr><td>>>=</td><td>Shift right assignment</td><td>no1>>=3</td><td>no1 = no1>>3</td></tr>
<tr><td>&=</td><td>Bit AND assignment</td><td>no1 &= 0X0F</td><td>no1 = no1&0X0F</td></tr>
<tr><td>|=</td><td>Bit OR assignment</td><td>no1 |= no2</td><td>no1 = no1 | no2</td></tr>
<tr><td>^=</td><td>Bit Exclusive OR assignment</td><td>no1^=0X07</td><td>no1 = no1 ^ 0X07</td></tr>
</table>

Summary

- **A bit field can only be declared within a** `struct`.
- **Bit fields must be of type** `int` **or** `unsigned int`.
- The number of bits to be allocated must be specified when declaring a bit field (max. 16).
- **The format for declaring a bit field is**

```
type field_name : no. of bits
```

- **Unnamed bit fields can be included** to ensure byte alignment within memory.
- **The compiler will automatically allocate the number of bits** required to reach the next byte boundary if the number of bits is given as zero.
- **Bit operators can be applied to integer values.**
- **The bit operators available are**

<table>
<tr><th>Operator</th><th>Description</th><th>Example</th></tr>
<tr><td>~</td><td>Bit Complement</td><td><code>ans = ~no1</code></td></tr>
<tr><td><<</td><td>Shift Left</td><td><code>ans = no1<<5</code></td></tr>
<tr><td>>></td><td>Shift Right</td><td><code>ans = no1>>3</code></td></tr>
<tr><td>&</td><td>Bit-wise AND</td><td><code>ans = no1&no2</code></td></tr>
<tr><td>|</td><td>Bit-wise OR</td><td><code>ans = no1 | no2</code></td></tr>
<tr><td>^</td><td>Bit-wise Exclusive OR</td><td><code>ans = no1 ^ no2</code></td></tr>
<tr><td><<=</td><td>Shift left assignment</td><td><code>no1<<=2</code></td></tr>
<tr><td>>>=</td><td>Shift right assignment</td><td><code>no1>>=3</code></td></tr>
<tr><td>&=</td><td>Bit AND assignment</td><td><code>no1 &= 0X0F</code></td></tr>
<tr><td>|=</td><td>Bit OR assignment</td><td><code>no1 |= no2</code></td></tr>
<tr><td>^=</td><td>Bit Exclusive OR assignment</td><td><code>no1^=0X07</code></td></tr>
</table>

UNION

A union is a derived data type constructed from two or more members. However, where a union differs from a `struct` is that each member of a union shares the same memory space. For example, the declaration

```
union same
{
    int     no;
    char    ch[2];
};
```

and subsequent definition:

```
same v;
```

results in 2 bytes being reserved for the variable. These two bytes can be treated as a single integer value if we use the term

```
v.no
```

or as two separate character elements in an array using the terms

`v.ch[0]` and `v.ch[1]`

The setup is shown in FIG-5.40.

FIG-5.40

A union Structure

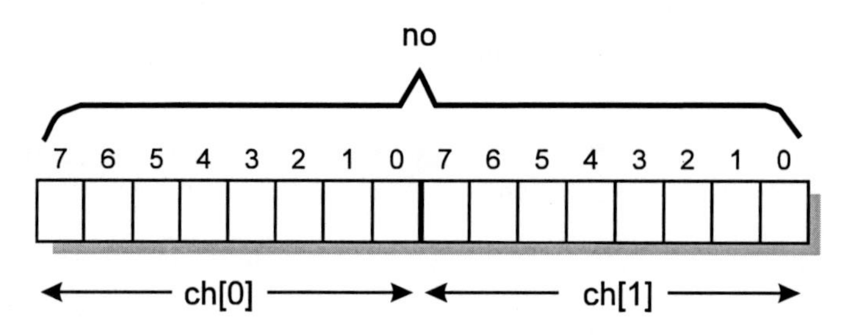

If we store the characters 'A' and 'B' in *v.ch[0]* and *v.ch[1]* respectively the two allocated bytes now contain the binary pattern

```
01000001  01000010
```

using the output statement

```
cout<<v.ch[0]<<v.ch[1];
```

will result in the letters 'A' and 'B' being displayed. However, if we employ the term

```
cout<<v.no;
```

the same two memory locations will be treated as a single `int` value and 16706 will be displayed (this being the decimal value of the binary pattern held over the two bytes).

DOS mode only.

A practical example of union in use is given in the following program (see LISTING-5.23) which changes the background colour of the top left character of the screen without changing any other characteristics at that position. To do this we need to XOR the background colour details in the video RAM. FIG-5.41 shows the operation required to change the background from BLUE to RED.

FIG-5.41

Changing the Background Colour

DOS mode only.

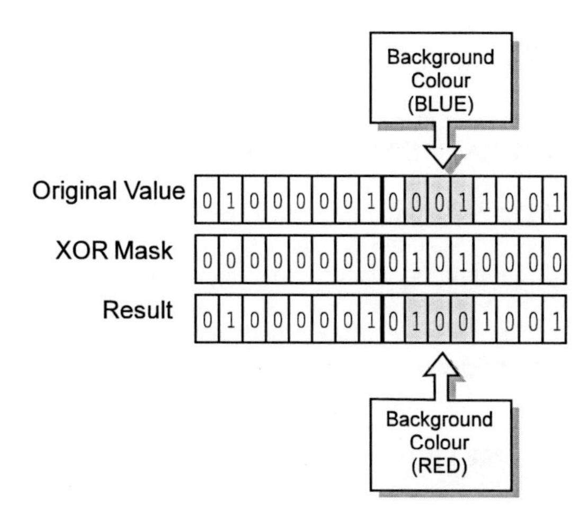

The program uses the following strategy:

Program Logic:

```
Get the required new background colour
Determine the value of the mask
XOR the necessary video RAM and the mask
```

Program Code:

LISTING-5.23

Using union

The terms XOR and EOR are often used to identify the Exclusive OR operation.

DOS mode only.

```
#include <conio.h>

//*** Define the video character structure ***
struct VideoChar
{
  char letter;
  unsigned textcol:4;
  unsigned backcol:3;
  unsigned blink:1;
};

//*** Allow alternate interpretation of a video character ***
union VideoLoc
{
  VideoChar vidch;
  unsigned  vidint;
};


void main()
{
  VideoChar c={'A',YELLOW,BLUE,0};        //**Video Char details
  VideoLoc mask={{'\0',0,0X5,0}};         //**Mask
  VideoLoc *scrptr=(VideoLoc*)0XB8000000L;//**Pointer to start
                                          //of video RAM
  //*** Place character on screen ***
  clrscr();
  scrptr->vidch=c;
  getch();

  //*** XOR screen RAM with mask ***
  scrptr->vidint ^= mask.vidint;
  getch();
}
```

Why do we need a union in the program above? The main task of the program is to XOR the video RAM location with the mask. Unfortunately, C++ will not allow us to use the XOR operator on a *VideoChar* value; it is therefore necessary to redefine the structure as a single `int` value which can then be used when performing the XOR operation.

PROGRAMMING EXERCISE 5.21

DOS mode only.

1. Modify the program in LISTING-5.23 to accept the screen position and new background colour. Use the function *CreateMask()* written in the last Programming Exercise to assign a value to the mask.

DOS mode only.

2. Write a routine, *ChangeBackground(),* which conforms to the following Mini-Spec:

NAME : ChangeBackground
PARAMETERS
IN : x1,y1,x2,y2 : int
mask: int
OUT : None
IN/OUT : None
PRE-CONDITION: (*x1,y1*) and (*x2,y2*) are valid screen co-ordinates

DESCRIPTION : Changes the background colour of the rectangular are of the screen defined by the co-ordinates (*x1,y1*) and (*x2,y2*) to that resulting from XORing the current background with *mask*.

OUTLINE LOGIC:

```
FOR line := y1 TO y2 DO
    Calculate video RAM address of (x1,line)
    FOR col := x1 TO x2 DO
        XOR screen with mask
        Increment address
    ENDFOR
ENDFOR
```

Calculate the address of the video RAM with an auxiliary function, *CalcVideoAddr(),* which uses the formula:

```
address = (VideoLoc*)(0XB8000000+(line-1)*160+(col-1)*2)
```

NOTE: The above approach will not work if your machine is not 100% IBM PC compatible. An alternative algorithm which is not machine-dependent is:

```
Copy area of screen to be changed
XOR every second byte screen copy with mask
Restore copy to screen
```

3. Using the functions above, write a program to allow a user defined area of the screen to be changed to a specified background colour. On a key press the background colour should be returned to its original value.

We are not restricted to two descriptions of a memory space, nor do the alternatives need to occupy exactly the same number of bytes. For example, in the declaration

```
union alt3
{
    int no;
    char ch[2];
    float x;
}
```

Sufficient space will be allocated for a `float` value, but only the first two bytes of this space will be shared with the `char` array and `int` fields.

CASE STUDY

The Problem

A program is required which reads in up to 20 students' details. The details can be listed at the user's request and may be sorted if required. The details held for each student are:

- an unique identity code,
- name,
- sex,
- scores for exactly six exams.

Clarification

The user is to be presented with a menu of options. These options will be:

1. Enter a student's details
2. Sort the student list
3. Display the student list
4. Quit

Where the sort option is chosen, the user can select to sort on either the student's identity code or surname.

The Algorithm

A basic logic used is

```
1.  REPEAT
2.      Display menu
3.      Get option
4.      Process option
5.  UNTIL QUIT option chosen
```

The process option step can be further detailed to

```
4.  Process option
    4.1     IF
    4.2         option is Enter Student details:
    4.3             Get student details
    4.4             Add student details to list
    4.5         option is sort:
    4.6             Display sort options
    4.7             Get sort option
    4.8             Sort on option chosen
    4.9         option is display:
    4.10            Display the details of every student
    4.11        option is QUIT:
    4.12            Clear data from list
    4.13    ENDIF
```

This represents a sufficiently detailed solution to allow us to begin a more detailed design of our system.

The Data Structure

The information for one student can be held in a structure declared in C++ as

```
struct StudentDetails
{
    int     idcode;
    char    name[31];
    char    sex;
    int     scores[6];
};
```

In order to accommodate the information of 20 students, we require an array of such records:

```
StudentDetails data[20];
```

However, we also need to keep track of how many students details have been entered, and for this a count must be maintained. Since this count has such a close relation to the array, it would be good policy to reflect this relationship by grouping the two values together:

```
struct ListType
{
    StudentDetails data[20];  //**All students' details
    int            count;     //**Number of students in list
};
```

A Final Adjustment

Rather than reserve space for all 20 records, some of which may never by used, a more memory efficient approach would be to allocate space for each student's details as and when the need arises. To achieve this we need to define the array, *data*, as a series of pointers:

```
struct ListType
{
    StudentDetails *data[20];
    int             count;
};
```

The Mini-Specifications

By examining the outline logic for the system we can identify most of the routines needed. These are given below in the form of Mini-Specs.

NAME	:	GetOption
PARAMETERS		
IN	:	None
OUT	:	option : INTEGER
IN/OUT	:	None
PRE-CONDITION	:	None
DESCRIPTION	:	Accepts users menu option from keyboard.
OUTLINE LOGIC	:	Display "Enter option : " Read option

```
NAME                 :  ProcessOption
PARAMETERS
     IN              :  option : INTEGER
     OUT             :  None
     IN/OUT          :  None
PRE-CONDITION        :  None

DESCRIPTION          :  Performs the action requested by user.
                        Option 1 allows new data to be entered for
                            one student.
                        Option 2 sorts the list.
                        Option 3 lists the details of every student.
                        Option 4 quits the system.
OUTLINE LOGIC        :  IF
                            option = 1:
                                Get student details
                                Add details to list
                            option = 2:
                                Display sort menu
                                Get user option
                                Sort list according to option
                            option = 3:
                                Display details of every student
                            option = 4:
                                Clear data from list
                         ENDIF
```

```
NAME                 :  DisplayMenu
PARAMETERS
     IN              :  None
     OUT             :  None
     IN/OUT          :  None
PRE-CONDITION        :  None

DESCRIPTION          :  Displays the main options available.
OUTLINE LOGIC        :  Clear the screen
                        Display "   Menu"
                        Display "1 - Enter students details"
                        Display "2 - Sort student list"
                        Display "3 - List every student"
                        Display "4 - QUIT"
```

```
NAME                 :  DisplaySortMenu
PARAMETERS
     IN              :  None
     OUT             :  None
     IN/OUT          :  None
PRE-CONDITION        :  None

DESCRIPTION          :  Displays the list of options available for sort.
OUTLINE LOGIC        :  Display "1 - Sort on idcode"
                        Display "2 - Sort on surname"
```

```
NAME             :  GetStudentDetails
PARAMETERS
    IN           :  None
    OUT          :  stdtls : StudentDetails
    IN/OUT       :  None
PRE-CONDITION    :  None

DESCRIPTION      :  Accepts a single student's details from the
                    keyboard into stdtls.
OUTLINE LOGIC    :  Get the student's idcode
                    Get student's name
                    Get student's sex
                    Get student's score for all 6 exams
```

```
NAME             :  AddToList
PARAMETERS
    IN           :  stdtls : StudentDetails
    OUT          :  ind :INTEGER
    IN/OUT       :  stlist : ListType
PRE-CONDITION    :  None

DESCRIPTION      :  Adds stdtls to the end of the list stlist if space is
                    available. Sets ind to 1 if the stdtls was added
                    to stlist else sets ind to zero.
OUTLINE LOGIC    :  IF stlist not full THEN
                        Allocate space using the first free
                        pointer element in stlist.data
                        Copy stdtls to the space allocated
                        Increment stlist.count
                        Set ind to 1
                    ELSE
                        Set ind to 0
                    ENDIF
```

```
NAME             :  Sort
PARAMETERS
    IN           :  None
                    comp    : pointer to compare function
    OUT          :  None
    IN/OUT       :  stlist  : ListType
PRE-CONDITION    :  None

DESCRIPTION      :  Sorts the data in stlist according to the compare
                    function being used.
OUTLINE LOGIC    :  FOR pass := 1 TO st.count-1 DO
                        FOR p := 1 TO st.count-pass DO
                            IF st.data[p] and st.data[p+1]
                                in wrong order
                            THEN
                                swap them
                            ENDIF
                        ENDFOR
                    ENDFOR
```

NAME	:	DisplayList
PARAMETERS		
IN	:	stlist : ListType
OUT	:	None
IN/OUT	:	None
PRE-CONDITION	:	None
DESCRIPTION	:	Lists the details of each entry in *stlist*.

OUTLINE LOGIC :

```
Display headings
FOR each entry in stlist DO
    Display its details
ENDFOR
```

NAME	:	DeleteDetails
PARAMETERS		
IN	:	None
OUT	:	None
IN/OUT	:	stlist:ListType
PRE-CONDITION	:	None
DESCRIPTION	:	Deletes all of the space allocated for the records referenced by the elements of *stlst.data*.

OUTLINE LOGIC :

```
FOR each element of stlist.data DO
    deallocate the referenced space
    Reset the pointer to NULL
ENDFOR
```

NAME	:	main
PARAMETERS		
IN	:	None
OUT	:	None
IN/OUT	:	None
PRE-CONDITION	:	None
DESCRIPTION	:	Allows student's details to be entered, sorted and listed. The user specifies which option is required. The sort may be on the identity number or surname.

OUTLINE LOGIC :

```
REPEAT
    Display menu
    Get option
    Process option
UNTIL QUIT option chosen
```

TASK 5.21

Draw a structure diagram for this system showing the calling relationship between the functions defined above.

Program Listing

LISTING-5.24

Student List

```
//******************************************
//* PROGRAM      : Student Details List     *
//* AUTHOR       : Patricia Stamp           *
//* DATE         : 24/3/1995                *
//* VERSION      : 0.4                      *
//* DESCRIPTION  : Allows up to 20 students'*
//*              details to be entered and*
//*              stored. Records can be   *
//*              sorted on idcode or      *
//*              surname.                 *
//* HARDWARE     : PC Compatible            *
//* SOURCE       : BorlandC++ V4.0          *
//******************************************

#include<iostream.h>
#include<conio.h>
#include<stdio.h>
#include<iomanip.h>
#include<string.h>

//*** Main menu quit value ***
const int QUIT = 4;
//*** Student record structure ***
struct StudentDetails
{
   int  idcode;
   char name[31];
   char sex;
   int  score[6];
};
//*** Students list structure ***
struct ListType
{
   StudentDetails *data[20];
   int count;
};
//*** Define Function pointer type name ***
typedef int(*CompFPointer)(StudentDetails,StudentDetails) ;
//*** Function Prototypes ***
int  AddToList(ListType&,StudentDetails);
int  CompareId(StudentDetails,StudentDetails);
int  CompareSurname(StudentDetails,StudentDetails);
void DeleteDetails(ListType&);
void DisplayList(ListType);
void DisplayMenu();
void DisplaySortMenu();
void GetStudentDetails(StudentDetails&);
int  GetOption();
void ProcessOption(int);
void Sort(ListType&,CompFPointer);


void main()
{
   char option;

   clrscr();
   do
   {
        DisplayMenu();
        option=GetOption();
        ProcessOption(option);
   }
   while(option!=QUIT);
}
```

Continued on next page

LISTING-5.24
(continued)

Student List

```
//*** Add new record to List ***
int AddToList(ListType& stlst,StudentDetails sd)
{
   //*** If list isn't full then add new record ***
   if(stlst.count<20)
   {
        stlst.data[stlst.count]=new StudentDetails;
        *stlst.data[stlst.count++]=sd;
        //** Return the number of records held ***
        return stlst.count;
   }
   else
        //*** Return zero to indicate that list is full ***
        return 0;
}

//*** Compare student id ***
int CompareId(StudentDetails st1,StudentDetails st2)
{
   //***  return 1 if first larger else return 2 ***
   if(st1.idcode>st2.idcode)
        return 1;
   else
        return 2;
}


//***Compare surnames ***
int CompareSurname(StudentDetails st1,StudentDetails st2)
{
   //*** return 1 if first larger else return 2 ***
   if(strcmp(strrchr(st1.name,' ' ),strrchr(st2.name,' ' ))>0)
        return 1;
   else
        return 2;
}


//*** Delete dynamic space ***
void DeleteDetails(ListType& st)
{
   //*** Delete area referenced by each pointer ***
   for(int j=0;j<st.count;j++)
   {
        delete st.data[j];
        st.data[j]=NULL;
   }
}

//*** Display list of student details ***
void DisplayList(ListType stlst)
{
   //*** Display headings ***
   cout<<"\t\t\tSTUDENT DETAILS LIST\n\n";
   cout<<" ID\t\tNAME\t\t    SEX\t\t    SCORES\n";

   //***FOR each record in list DO ***
   for(int j=0; j<stlst.count;j++)
   {
        //**Display its details **
        cout<<setw(5)<<stlst.data[j]->idcode<<' '
             <<stlst.data[j]->name;
        cout<<setw(30-strlen(stlst.data[j]->name))
             <<stlst.data[j]->sex;
        for(int exam=0;exam<=5;exam++)
             cout<<setw(5)<<stlst.data[j]->score[exam];
        cout<<'\n';
   }
}
```

Continued on next page

LISTING-5.24
(continued)

Student List

```
//*** Display main menu ***
void DisplayMenu()
{
  clrscr();
  cout<<"\n\t\tMENU\n";
  cout<<"1 - Enter student\'s details\n";
  cout<<"2 - Sort student list\n";
  cout<<"3 - List every student\n";
  cout<<"\n4 - QUIT\n";
}


  //*** Display options for sort key ***
void DisplaySortMenu()
{
  cout<<"\n\n\t\tSORT \n";
  cout<<" 1 - On Student\'s Id\n";
  cout<<" 2 - On Student\'s surname\n";
}



//*** Get a student's details ***
void GetStudentDetails(StudentDetails& sd)
{
  clrscr();
  //*** Get student's id ***
  cout<<"Enter student\'s id    : ";
  cin>>sd.idcode;
  //*** Get student's name ***
  cout<<"Enter student\'s name  : ";
  gets(sd.name);
  //*** Get student's sex ***
  cout<<"Enter student\'s sex : ";
  cin>>sd.sex;
  //*** Get marks for six tests ***
  cout<<"Enter student's marks\n";
  for(int j=0;j<6;j++)
  {
      cout<< "Score for test "<<(j+1)<<" : ";
      cin>>sd.score[j];
      while (sd.score[j]<0||sd.score[j]>100)
      {
          cout<<"Score must be between 0 and 100 : ";
          cin>>sd.score[j];
      }
  }
}


//*** Get user's option ***
int GetOption()
{
  int op;

  cout<<"\nEnter option : ";
  cin>>op;
  return op;
}
```

Continued on next page

LISTING-5.24
(continued)

Student List

```
//*** Execute user's option ***
void ProcessOption(int op)
{
  static ListType studentlist;   //Contains all students' details
  StudentDetails sd;             //Details of an individual
  CompFPointer CFPtr;            //Pointer to comparison function
  int ops;

  //***Execute option chosen ***
  switch(op)
  {
      case 1:
          //*** Add a new student to list ***
          GetStudentDetails(sd);
          AddToList(studentlist,sd);
          break;
      case 2:
          //*** Sort list ***
          //** Get sort key **
          DisplaySortMenu();
          ops=GetOption();
          //** Set function pointer to correct Compare function
          if(ops==1)
              CFPtr=CompareId;
          else
              CFPtr=CompareSurname;
          //** Perform sort **
          Sort(studentlist,CFPtr);
          break;
      case 3:
          //*** Display contents of list ***
          clrscr();
          DisplayList(studentlist);
          cout<<"Press any key to continue\n";
          getch();
          break;
      case 4:
          //*** Delete allocated space ***
          DeleteDetails(studentlist);
  }
}

//*** Sort Student Records ***
void Sort(ListType& stlst,CompFPointer cfptr)
{
   StudentDetails *temp;

  //*** Sort Pointers ***
  for(int times=1;times<=stlst.count-1;times++)
      for(int comp=0;comp<=stlst.count-2;comp++)
          //** If wrong order swap position of pointers **
          if(cfptr(*stlst.data[comp],*stlst.data[comp+1])==1)
          {
              temp = stlst.data[comp];
              stlst.data[comp]=stlst.data[comp+1];
              stlst.data[comp+1]=temp;
          }
}
```

PROGRAMMING EXERCISE 5.22

1. Modify the above program to ensure that non-numeric and out-of-range values entered for the *option*, *mark* and *student id* are correctly handled.

2. Add new *Compare()* functions which can be used to sort the list in:
   a) Descending *idcode* order.
   b) Descending *average score* order

INVESTIGATION

1. Can a dynamically assigned data area be given an initialising value? For example:
```
int *ptr;
ptr = new int = 7;
```

2. Is it possible to use an indirect pointer to reference a two dimensional array? For example:
```
int matrix[3][5];
int **pptr;
pptr = matrix;
```

3. Is it possible to dynamically allocate a two dimensional array? For example:
```
int **pptr;
pptr = new int [10][5];
```

4. When using an enumerated variable such as
```
lights = {RED, RED_AMBER,GREEN,AMBER};
state = AMBER;
```
is it possible to:
   a) perform assignments involving arithmetic expressions such as
   ```
   state = RED+RED_AMBER;
   ```
   b) assign a value outside the specified range
   ```
   state = AMBER;
   state++;
   ```
   c) use enumerated values in a `switch` statement:
   ```
   switch(state)
   {
       case RED:
             .
   ```

5. We cannot copy one string variable to another using a statement such as
```
str1 = str2;
```
However, such a statement is possible when using two `struct` variables. If a single string field is enclosed in a `struct` definition as in
```
struct test
{
    char str[30];
};
```
is it possible to copy such strings from one variable to another? For example, are the following statements valid:
```
test s1, s2={"Copy this"};
s1 = s2;
```

6. Since a function name is an address, what happens when an attempt is made to de-reference it?

SELF-ASSESSMENT REVIEW

1. What type of value does a pointer variable hold?
2. How many bytes does a pointer variable occupy?
3. What numeric value does NULL assign to a pointer?
4. What formula does the machine use when calculating the difference between two pointer variables?
5. What is the shortest (least typing) way to initialise all the elements of an array to zero?
6. How is a string value terminated?
7. Why is it usually inappropriate to use `cin` when reading a string value from the keyboard?
8. What will the effect be on your program of overflowing the storage area of a string.
9. What is the normal method used for copying the contents of one string variable to another?
10. List two ways of defining a `struct` variable.
11. What does the term XOR mean?
12. If a value is XORed with a mask, and the result is XORed with the same mask, what final value is obtained?
13. What effect on the numeric value on an `int` will shifting it two bits to the left have?
14. How can we ensure that a bit field starts on a byte boundary?
15. How does a `union` variable differ from that of a `struct`?

Solutions

TASK 5.1

```
int *iptr1, *iptr2;
float *fptr;
```

TASK 5.2

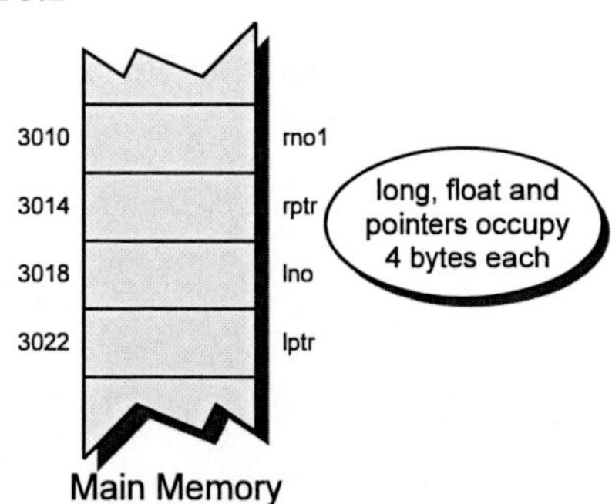

PROGRAMMING EXERCISE 5.1

```
#include <iostream.h>
#include <conio.h>

void main()
{
    int no1,no2,ans;
    int *no1ptr=&no1, *no2ptr=&no2, *ansptr=&ans;

    clrscr();
    cout<<"Enter two numbers ";
    cin>>*no1ptr>>*no2ptr;
    if(*no1ptr<*no2ptr)
        *ansptr=*no1ptr;
    else
        *ansptr = *no2ptr;
    cout<<"Smallest value is "<<*ansptr<<'\n';
}
```

TASK 5.3

```
1.  if(iptra == iptrb)
2.  if(*iptra == *iptrb)
```

TASK 5.4

```
1. const int *icptr = &MAX;
2. float const *fptr = &x;
3. const float const *cfptr = &tax;
```

TASK 5.5

```
1.  float (*fnptr1)(float);
2.  int (*fnptr1)();
3.  void (*fnptr1)();
4.  int(*fnptr1, *fnptr2)(int,float);
```

PROGRAMMING EXERCISE 5.5

```
1.
*(float*)ptr = 3.14;
cout<<*(float*)ptr<<endl;

2.
ptr = new long;
cin>>*(long*)ptr;
cout<<*(long*)ptr<<endl;
```

PROGRAMMING EXERCISE 5.6

```
1.
#include <iostream.h>
#include <conio.h>
void main()
{
    long int v1=65,v2=66;
    clrscr();
    cout<<"Address of v1 : "<<&v1
        <<" value : "<<v1;
    cout<<"\nAddress of v2 : "<<&v2
        <<" value : "<<v2;
    getch();
}

2.
#include <iostream.h>
#include <conio.h>
void main()
{
    int no;
    int *iptr=&no;
    clrscr();
    cout<< "Enter number : ";
    cin>>*iptr;
    cout<< "Value entered was : "<<*iptr<<'\n';
    getch();
}

3.
#include <iostream.h>
#include <conio.h>
void Sub2(int*);
void main()
{
    int no;
    clrscr();
    cout<< "Enter number : ";
    cin>>no;
    Sub2(&no);
    cout<< "New value : "<<no<<'\n';
    getch();
}

void Sub2(int *v)
{
    *v-=2;
}

4.
#include <iostream.h>
#include <conio.h>
int* RetAddr(int&, int&);
void main()
{
    int no1,no2;
    clrscr();
    cout<<"Address no1 = "<<&no1;
    cout<<"\n Address no2 = "<<&no2;
    cout<<"\n Smaller value at : "
        <<RetAddr(no1,no2);
    getch();
}

int *RetAddr(int& ano1, int& ano2)
{
    if(ano1<ano2)
        return &ano1;
    else
        return &ano2;
}

5.
#include <iostream.h>
#include <conio.h>
int Reverse(int);
int Sum(int);
void main()
{
    int no1;
    int (*fnptr)(int);
    clrscr();
    cout<< "Enter value : ";
    cin>>no1;
    fnptr=Reverse;
    cout<<"Reverse value is "<<fnptr(no1)<<'\n';
    fnptr=Sum;
    cout<<"Sum of digits is "<<fnptr(no1)<<'\n';
    getch();
}
```

Continued on next page

```
int Reverse(int v)
{
    int ans=0;

    while(v)
    {
        ans = ans*10+v%10;
        v/=10;
    }
    return ans;
}

int Sum(int v)
{
    int ans=0;

    while(v)
    {
        ans+=v%10;
        v/=10;
    }
    return ans;
}
```

```
6.
#include <iostream.h>
#include <conio.h>


void main()
{
    int *iptr1,*iptr2;

    clrscr();
    iptr1 = new int;
    iptr2 = new int;
    cout<<"Enter two values : ";
    cin>>*iptr1>>*iptr2;
    cout<<"Sum "<<(*iptr1+*iptr2)
        <<"Difference "<<(*iptr1-*iptr2)<<'\n';
    getch();
}
```

TASK 5.6

```
a) scrptr = new float[80];
b) scrptr = new double[40];
```

PROGRAMMING EXERCISE 5.7

```
#include <iostream.h>
#include <conio.h>

void main()
{

    void *scrptr;
    int i;
    int x1,y1,x2,y2;

    //*** Get area of screen to be saved ***
    clrscr();
    cout<<"Enter cordinates of area to be saved : ";
    cin>>x1>>y1>>x2>>y2;

    //*** Fill screen with X's ***
    for(i=1;i<2000;i++)
        cout<<'X';

    //*** Save selected area of screen ***
    //**Calculate and allocate space required**
    int space = (x2-x1+1)*(y2-y1+1)*2;
    scrptr = new char [space];
    gettext(x1,y1,x2,y2,scrptr);
    gotoxy(20,12);
    cout<<" Area saved-Press any key to continue ";
    getch();
    gotoxy(20,12);
    cout<<"XXXXXXXXXXXXXXXXXXXXXXXXXXXXXXXXXXXXXXX"
        <<"XXXXXXXXXXXX";
    //*** Overwrite that area of screen ***
    window(x1,y1,x2,y2);
    for(i=1;i<space/2;i++)
        putch('.');
    window(1,1,80,25);
    gotoxy(20,12);
    cout<<" Area overwritten. Press any key ";
    gotoxy(20,12);
    getch();
    cout<<"XXXXXXXXXXXXXXXXXXXXXXXXXXXXXXXXXXXXXXX"
        <<"XXXXXX";
    //*** Restore original contents ***
    puttext(x1,y1,x2,y2,scrptr);
    getch();
    //*** Delete allocated space ***
    delete [] scrptr;
}
```

TASK 5.7

```
a)  no = 8;
b)  *ptr = 8;
c)  **ptr = 8;
```

PROGRAMMING EXERCISE 5.8

```
#include <iostream.h>
#include <conio.h>
void smaller(int*, int*, int*, int**);

void main()
{
    int no1,no2,no3;
    int *ptr;
    int **pptr=&ptr;    //Define indirect pointer

    cout<<"Enter three values : ";
    cin>>no1>>no2>>no3;
    smaller(&no1,&no2,&no3,pptr);
    //*** Give addresses
    cout<<"Address of variables are : "<<&no1<<' '
        <<&no2<<' '<<&no3<<endl;
    cout<<"Address of smallest value is : "
        <<*pptr<<endl;
    getch();
}

void smaller(int* n1, int* n2, int* n3, int** p)
{
    if(*n1<*n2&&*n1<*n3)
        *p=n1;
    else if(*n2<*n3&&*n2<*n1)
        *p=n2;
    else
        *p=n3;
}
```

TASK 5.8

```
1.  typedef char *CptrType
2.  typedef int*(*FPtrType(long);
```

TASK 5.9

```
1.  Set all counts to zero
    FOR 20 times DO
        Read a number
        IF
            number = 1:
                Add 1 to first count
            number = 2:
                Add 1 to second count

                    etc


2.  Read 15 values into variables n1, n2, n3 etc
    Read in search value
    IF
        search value = n1:
            Display Found
        search value = 2:
            Display Found

                etc
    ELSE
        Display Not found
    ENDIF
```

TASK 5.10

```
1.  int result[15];
2.  float weights[10];
```

TASK 5.11

```
int bias[]={6,2,2,5,1,3,3,2};
```

TASK 5.12

Statement	Array contents
`int list[]={-4,3,9,2,0,12}`	-4,3,9,2,0,12
`list[2] = 7;`	-4,3,7,2,0,12
`list[J]=-2`	-4,3,7,-2,0,12
`list[J++]=3`	-4,3,7,3,0,12
`list[++J]=5`	-4,3,7,3,0,5
`for(J=0;J<=5;J++) list[J] = J*2;`	0,2,4,6,8,10

PROGRAMMING EXERCISE 5.9

```
1.
#include <conio.h>
#include <iostream.h>

void main()
{
    int list[6];

    //*** Read in numbers ***
    for(int i=0;i<=5;i++)
    {
        cout<<"Enter number "<<(i+1)<<" : ";
        cin>>list[i];
    }
    //*** Display numbers in same order ***
    cout << "Numbers entered were : ";
    for(i=0;i<=5;i++)
    {
        cout<<list[i]<< ;
    }
    //*** Display in reverse order ***
    cout << "\nIN reverse order     : ";
    for(i=5;i>=0;i)
    {
        cout<<list[i]<<' ';
    }
    getch();
}
```

```
2.
#include <conio.h>
#include <iostream.h>

void main()
{
    int list[10];

    //*** Read in numbers ***
    for(int i=0;i<=9;i++)
    {
        cout<<"Enter number "<<(i+1)<<" : ";
        cin>>list[i];
    }
    //*** Display numbers in odd locations ***
    cout<<"Numbers at odd subscript locs were : ";
    for(i=1;i<=9;i++)
    {
        if(i%2==1)
            cout<<list[i]<<' ';
    }

    getch();
}
```

```
3.
#include <conio.h>
#include <iostream.h>

void main()
{
    char list[10];

    //*** Read in characters ***
    cout<<"Enter 10 characters : ";
    for(int i=0;i<=9;i++)
        cin>>list[i];
    //*** Count number of E's ***
    int count = 0;
    for(i=0;i<=9;i++)
    {
        if(toupper(list[i])=='E')
            count++;
    }
    //*** Display count ***
    cout<<"There are "<<count<<" E\'s\n";

    getch();
}
```

```
4.
#include <conio.h>
#include <iostream.h>
void main()
{
    int counts[5]={0,0,0,0,0};
    int no;
    int place;

    for(int i=0;i<=9;i++)
    {
        //*** Read a number ***
        cout<<"Enter number : ";
        cin>>no;

        //*** Calculate which count to
        //      be incremented ***
        place = (no-1)/10;

        //*** Increment count ***
        counts[place]++;
    }

    //*** Display counts ***
    for(i=0;i<=4;i++)
        cout<<"Numbers in the range "
            <<(i*10+1)<<'-'<<((i+1)*10)
            <<" : "<<counts[i]<<'\n';

    getch();
}
```

```
5.
#include <conio.h>
#include <iostream.h>

void main()
{
    int list[10];

    //*** Read in 10 numbers ***
    for(int i=0;i<=9;i++)
    {
        cout<<"Enter number : ";
        cin>>list[i];
    }
    //*** Set smallest equal to list[0] ***
    int smallest = list[0];

    //*** Check rest of list for smaller value ***
    for(i=1;i<=9;i++)
        if(list[i]<smallest)
            smallest = list[i];

    //*** Display smallest ***
    cout<<"Smallest number is : "<<smallest<<'\n';
    getch();
}
```

TASK 5.13

1. aptr references *list[0]*
2. aptr is incremented to reference *list[2]*
3. Outputs the value located at *aptr + 3* i.e. *list[5]*
4. Decrements aptr to reference list[1]
5. *list[3]=list[1]+list[1]* and aptr is increment to reference *list[2]*

PROGRAMMING EXERCISE 5.11

Change the final if statement to

```
if(aptr1<=list+6 && aptr2<= list+6)
    cout<<"There are "<<aptr2-aptr1
        <<" elements between both 7s\n";
else
    cout<<"Two 7s not found\n";
```

PROGRAMMING EXERCISE 5.12

```
1.
#include <conio.h>
#include <iostream.h>

int AreEqual(int[],int[],int);

void main()
{
    int list[6],list2[6];

    clrscr();
    //*** Read values into arrays ***
    for(int i = 0;i<6;i++)
    {
        cout<<"Enter value "<<(i+1)
            <<" for first array: ";
        cin>>list[i];
    }
    for(i = 0;i<6;i++)
    {
        cout<<"Enter value "<<(i+1)
            <<" for second array: ";
        cin>>list2[i];
    }
    //*** Display appropriate message ***
    if(AreEqual(list,list2,6))
        cout<<"Arrays are equal\n";
    else
        cout<<"Arrays not equal\n";

    getch();
}


int AreEqual(int l1[], int l2[], int size)
 {
    //*** Assume arrays are equal ***
    int equal=1;
    //*** If any elements are different
    //      then not equal ***
    for(int i=0;i<size&&equal==1;i++)
        if(l1[i]!=l2[i])
            equal=0;
    return equal;
}


2.
#include <conio.h>
#include <iostream.h>
int *FirstNeg(int[],int);

void main()
{
    int list[6];

    clrscr();
    //*** Read values into arrays ***
    for(int i = 0;i<6;i++)
    {
        cout<<"Enter value "<<(i+1)<<" : ";
        cin>>list[i];
    }

    //*** Display address of array and      ***
    //*** element containing negative value ***
    cout<<"Array starts at "<<list
        <<"\nFirst negative value at : "
        <<FirstNeg(list,6)<<'\n';
    getch();
}


int *FirstNeg(int list[], int size)
{
    int *result=NULL;
    //*** If any elements are different ***
    //*** then not equal                ***
    for(int i=0;i<size&&result==NULL;i++)
        if(list[i]<0)
            result=&list[i];
    return result;
}


3.
#include <conio.h>
#include <iostream.h>

void main()
{
    int list[5], *aptr=list;

    clrscr();
    //*** Read values into arrays ***
    for(int i = 0;i<5;i++)
    {
        cout<<"Enter value "<<(i+1)<<" : ";
        cin>>aptr[i];
    }
    //*** Display contents of array ***
    cout<<"\nValues are : ";
    for(i=0;i<5;i++)
    {
        cout<<aptr[i]<<' ';
    }

    getch();
}
```

PROGRAMMING EXERCISE 5.13

```
#include<iostream.h>
#include <conio.h>

void main()
{
    int noofmarks;
    int *marks;

    //*** Get no. of marks ***
    clrscr();
    cout<<"Enter number of exams : ";
    cin>>noofmarks;
    //*** Allocate space for marks ***
    marks = new int[noofmarks];
    //*** Read in marks ***
    for(int c=0;c<noofmarks;c++)
    {
        cout<<"Enter mark "<<(c+1)<<" : ";
        cin>>marks[c];
    }
    //*** Calculate average ***
    int total = 0;
    for(c=0;c<noofmarks;c++)
        total+=marks[c];
    float average = total/float(noofmarks);
    //*** Display all marks below average ***
    cout<<"\n\nMarks are below average:\n";
    for(c=0;c<noofmarks;c++)
        if(marks[c]<average)
            cout<<marks[c]<<endl;
    //*** Deallocate space ***
    delete [] marks;

    getch();
}
```

TASK 5.14

```
1.  int matrix[3][14];
2.  int matrix[5][2];
3.  int matrix[8]; // One dimensional
```

PROGRAMMING EXERCISE 5.14

```
1.
#include <iostream.h>
#include <conio.h>
#include<iomanip.h>

void main()
{
    int matrix[4][4];
    //*** Assign values ***
    for(int row=0;row<4;row++)
        for(int col=0;col<4;col++)
            matrix[row][col]=row*4+col+1;

    //*** Display values ***
    for(row=0;row<4;row++)
    {
        for(int col=0;col<4;col++)
            cout<<setw(4)<<matrix[row][col];
        cout<<'\n';
    }
}
```

Continued on next page

```
2.
#include <iostream.h>
#include <conio.h>
#include<iomanip.h>

void main()
{
    int matrix[4][4];
    //*** Assign values ***
    for(int col=0;col<4;col++)
        for(int row=0;row<4;row++)
            matrix[row][col]=col*4+row+1;

    //*** Display values ***
    for(int row=0;row<4;row++)
    {
        for(col=0;col<4;col++)
            cout<<setw(4)<<matrix[row][col];
        cout<<'\n';
    }
    getch();
}
```

```
3.
#include <iostream.h>
#include <conio.h>
#include<iomanip.h>

void main()
{
    int matrix[4][4];

    //*** Assign values ***
    for(int row=0;row<4;row++)
        for(int col=0;col<4;col++)
            matrix[row][col]=16-(row*4+col);

    //*** Display values ***
    for(row=0;row<4;row++)
    {
        for(int col=0;col<4;col++)
            cout<<setw(4)<<matrix[row][col];
        cout<<'\n';
    }
    getch();
}
```

PROGRAMMING EXERCISE 5.16

```
1.
#include <iostream.h>
#include <conio.h>
#include <ctype.h>
#include <string.h>
#include <stdio.h>

void LetterCount(const char *, int[26]);

void main()
{
    int totals[26]={0}; //Set all totals to zero
    char sentence[80];

    clrscr();
    cout<<"Enter string : ";
    gets(sentence);
    LetterCount(sentence,totals);
    for(int i=0;i<26;i++)
    {
        cout<<"The letter "<<char(i+65)<<" occurs "
            <<totals[i]<<" times\n";
        if(i==20)
        {
            cout<<"PRESS ANY KEY TO CONTINUE\n";
            getch();
        }
    }
    getch();
}

void LetterCount(const char * s, int counts[26])
{
    for(int c = 0;c<26;c++)
        counts[c]=0;
    for(c=0;c<strlen(s);c++)
        if (isalpha(s[c]))
            counts[toupper(s[c])-65]++;
}
```

```
2.
#include <iostream.h>
#include <conio.h>
#include <ctype.h>
#include <string.h>
#include <stdio.h>
void Reverse(char *);

void main()
{
    char sentence[80];
    clrscr();
    cout<<Enter string : ;
    gets(sentence);
    Reverse(sentence);
    cout<<sentence<<'\n';
    getch();
}


void Reverse(char *s)
{
    char temp;
    int first = 0;
    int last = strlen(s)-1;

    while(first<last)
    {
        temp = s[first];
        s[first]=s[last];
        s[last]=temp;
        first++;
        last—;
    }
}
```

```
3.
#include <iostream.h>
#include<conio.h>
#include<string.h>
#include<ctype.h>
#include<stdio.h>

void Capitalise(char*);

void main()
{
    char sentence[80];

    clrscr();
    cout<<"Enter string to be capitalised : ";
    gets(sentence);
    Capitalise(sentence);
    cout<<"Capitalised version : "<<sentence<<endl;

    getch();
}

void Capitalise(char *s)
{
    //*** Return if string empty ***
    if (strlen(s)==0)
        return;
    int c=0;    //Position in string
    //*** Capitalise first character ***
    s[c]=toupper(s[c]);
    c++;
    //*** WHILE not end of string ***
    while(s[c])
    {
        //** IF start of word, capitalise **
        if (isalpha(s[c])&& isspace(s[c-1]))
            s[c]=toupper(s[c]);
        c++;
    }
}
```

```
4.
#include<conio.h>
#include<iostream.h>
#include<string.h>

void ExpandString(char*);

void main()
{
    char text[256];

    //** Read in text ***
    clrscr();
    cout<<"Enter text to be expanded : ";
    cin>>text;
    //*** Expand text ***
    ExpandString(text);
    //*** Display result ***
    cout<<"The expanded version is : "<<text<<endl;

    getch();
}
```

Continued on next page

```
void ExpandString(char* s)
{
    char temp[256]=""; //Empty temporary storage
    //***Copy the first character accross ***
    temp[0]=s[0];
    //*** For all but the last 2 chars DO ***
    for(int c=1,p=1;c<=int(strlen(s))-3;c++)
    {
        //**If two periods ***
        if(s[c]=='.'&&s[c+1]=='.')
        {
            //* Insert range of chars implied *
            for(char ch=s[c-1]+1;ch<=s[c+2];ch++)
                temp[p++]= ch;
            //* Move past this part of the text *
            c+=2;
        }
        else
            //**If not two dots, copy char **
            temp[p++]=s[c];
    }
    //***Copy any remaining characters ***
    while(s[c])
        temp[p++]=s[c++];
    //*** Insert final NULL character ***
    temp[p]='\0';
    strcpy(s,temp);
}
```

NOTE: it is necessary to cast *strlen(s)* as an *int* (it returns a *size_t*, which is actually an *unsigned int*) otherwise we will not get a negative value from the expression *strlen(s)-3* when dealing with small strings.

```
5.
#include<conio.h>
#include<iostream.h>
#include<string.h>

void ExpandString(char*);
void GetData(char*, int, char*);

void main()
{
    char text[256];

    //** Read in text ***
    clrscr();
    cout<<"Enter text : ";
    GetData("a..zA..Z 0..9",10,text);
    getch();
}

void GetData(char* allowed,int max,char* result)
{
    const int ENTER=13;
    const int BACKSPACE = 8;

    char ch;                 // char from keyboard
    int count=0;             // chars entered
    char expandedset[256];   // allowable chars

    //*** Expand set of allowed characters ***
    strcpy(expandedset,allowed);
    ExpandString(expandedset);
    //*** Start with empty result ***
    strcpy(result,"");
    //*** Read a character ***
    ch=getch();
    //*** WHILE return key not pressed DO ***
    while(ch!=ENTER)
    {
        //*** If allowed char & result not full ***
        if(strchr(expandedset,ch)&&count<max)
        {
            //**Display char and add to result ***
            cout<<ch;
            count++;
            result[count-1]=ch;
            result[count]=0;
        }
        //*** ELSE if delete & result not empty ***
        else if(ch==BACKSPACE&&count>0)
        {
            //** Remove last char **
            cout<<"\b \b";
            count-;
            result[count]=0;
        }
        //*** Read another character ***
        ch=getch();
    }
    cout<<endl;
}
```

```
void ExpandString(char* s)
{
    char temp[256]=""; //Empty temporary storage
    //***Copy the first character accross ***
    temp[0]=s[0];
    //*** For all but the last 2 chars DO ***
    for(int c=1,p=1;c<=int(strlen(s))-3;c++)
    {
        //**If two dots ***
        if(s[c]=='.'&&s[c+1]=='.')
        {
            //* Insert range of chars implied *
            for(char ch=s[c-1]+1;ch<=s[c+2];ch++)
                temp[p++]= ch;
            //* Move past this part of the text *
            c+=2;
        }
        else
            //**If not two dots, copy char ***
            temp[p++]=s[c];
    }
    //***Copy any remaining characters ***
    while(s[c])
        temp[p++]=s[c++];
    //*** Insert final NULL character ***
    temp[p]='\0';
    strcpy(s,temp);
}
```

TASK 5.15

```
enum months
{Jan=31,Feb=59,Mar=90,Apr=120,May=151,Jun=181,
Jul=212,Aug=243,Sep=273,Oct=304,Nov=334,Dec=365}
```

TASK 5.16

```
struct Details
{
    int age;
    float height;
    float weight;
}
```

PROGRAMMING EXERCISE 5.17

```
#include <iostream.h>
#include<conio.h>

void main()
{
     struct Details
     {
        int age;
        float height;
        float weight;
     };

    Details w1,w2,w3;

    //*** Get details ***
    cout<<Enter details of first person  : ;
    cin>>w1.age>>w1.height>>w1.weight;
    cout<<Enter details of second person : ;
    cin>>w2.age>>w2.height>>w2.weight;
    cout<<Enter details of third person  : ;
    cin>>w3.age>>w3.height>>w3.weight;
    //*** Determine tallest ***
    float tallest = w1.height;
    if(w2.height>tallest)
        tallest=w2.height;
    if(w3.height>tallest)
        tallest=w3.height
    //*** Display result ***
    cout<<"The tallest has a height of "
        <<tallest<<" metres\n";

     getch();
}
```

TASK 5.17

```
for(int i=0,sum=0;i<6;i++)
     sum+=student1.score[i];
```

PROGRAMMING EXERCISE 5.18

```
#include <iostream.h>
#include <conio.h>
#include <iomanip.h>
#include <stdio.h>

void main()
{
    struct Name
    {
        char surname[20];
        char forename[20];
        char initials[8];
    };

    struct Address
     {
        char firstline[30];
        char secondline[30];
        char thirdline[30];
        char town[18];
        char district[18];
        char postcode[10];
    };

    struct Account
    {
        int accno;
        Name name;
        Address address;
        float balance;
    };

    Account customer;

    //*** Get details ***
    clrscr();
    cout<<"Enter customers name : ";
    cin  >>customer.name.forename
         >>customer.name.initials
         >>customer.name.surname;
    cout<<"Enter address : \n";
    gets(customer.address.firstline);
    gets(customer.address.secondline);
    gets(customer.address.thirdline);
    gets(customer.address.town);
    gets(customer.address.district);
    gets(customer.address.postcode);
    cout<<"Enter balance : ";
    cin>>customer.balance;

    //*** Add interest ***
    customer.balance*=1.05;

    //*** Display details ***
    clrscr();
    cout<<setw(45)<<"CUSTOMER DETAILS\n";
    cout<<"Name :    "<<customer.name.surname
        <<, <<customer.name.forename
        << <<customer.name.initials<<'\n';
    cout<<"Address: "
    <<customer.address.firstline<<'\n'
    <<"          "<<customer.address.secondline<<'\n'
    <<"          "<<customer.address.thirdline<<'\n'
    <<"          "<<customer.address.town<<'\n'
    <<"          "<<customer.address.district<<'\n'
    <<"          "<<customer.address.postcode<<'\n';
    cout<<"Balance: "<<customer.balance<<'\n';
    getch();
}
```

TASK 5.18

1. line 1   col 80 = 0XB800009E
2. line 25 col 80 = 0XB800081E

TASK 5.19

1. 83F6   1000 0011 1111 0110
2. FF3A   1111 1111 0011 1010

PROGRAMMING EXERCISE 5.19

```
#include<iostream.h>
#include <conio.h>

void Binary(int);

void main()
{
    int no;

    clrscr();
    cout<<"Enter number to be converted : ";
    cin>>no;
    Binary(no);

    getch();
}

void Binary(int no)
{
    for(int c=1; c<=sizeof(int)*8;c++)
    {
        if (no<0)
            cout<<1;
        else
            cout<<0;
        no<<=1;
    }
}
```

NOTE: *sizeof(int)*8* is used to determine how many bits are in an int. Being system-independent this should operate correctly with any compiler.

TASK 5.20

0101 1101	
0111 0000	XOR
0010 1101	=
0111 0000	XOR
0101 1101	=

NOTE: By performing XOR twice we arrive back at the original value.

PROGRAMMING EXERCISE 5.20

```
#include<conio.h>
#include<iostream.h>

int inline CreateMask(int curback,int reqdcol)
{
    return curback ^ reqdcol;
}


void main()
{
    int start=BLUE, reqd=RED;
    int mask;
    mask = CreateMask(start,reqd);
    cout<<"Mask value is : "<<hex<<mask<<endl;

    getch();
}
```

PROGRAMMING EXERCISE 5.21

```
1.

#include <conio.h>
#include<iostream.h>

//*** Define the video character structure ***
struct VideoChar
{
    char letter;
    unsigned textcol:4;
    unsigned backcol:3;
    unsigned blink:1;
};
```

Continued on next page

```
//*** Allow alt. interpretation of video char ***
union VideoLoc
{
    VideoChar vidch;
    unsigned  vidint;
};


int inline CreateMask(int curback,int reqdcol)
{
    return curback ^ reqdcol;
}

int GetBackColour(int,int);


void main()
{
    VideoChar c={'A',YELLOW,BLUE,0};
    int backmask;
    VideoLoc mask = {{'\0',0,0,0}};
    VideoLoc *scrptr;
    int line, col;
    int colour;         //New background

    //*** Clear screen ***
    textbackground(BLACK);
    clrscr();

    //*** Get position and colour ***
    cout<<"Enter screen position for display : ";
    cin>>col>>line;
    cout<<"Enter the new background (0 to 7) ";
    cin>>colour;

    //*** Calculate mask ***
    mask.vidch.backcol = CreateMask(BLUE,colour);

    //*** Set pointer to screen area and output ***
    scrptr= (VideoLoc*)(0XB8000000L+
            ((line-1)*160+col-1)*2);
    scrptr->vidch=c;

    //*** Change background colour ***
    getch();
    (*scrptr).vidint=scrptr->vidint^mask.vidint;

    getch();
}
```

```
2 & 3
#include <conio.h>
#include <iostream.h>

//*** Structure for a video character ***
struct VideoChar
{
    char letter;
    unsigned textcol:4;
    unsigned backcol:3;
    unsigned blink:1;
};

//*** Redefinition of video character ***
union VideoLoc
{
    VideoChar vidch;
    unsigned  vidint;
};


inline int CreateMask(int curback,int reqdcol)
{
    return curback ^ reqdcol;
}

inline VideoLoc* CalcVideoAddr(int col,int line)
{
    return (VideoLoc*)(0XB8000000L+
            (line-1)*160+(col-1)*2);
}

int GetBackColour(int,int);
void ChangeBackground(int,int,int,int,int);

void main()
{
    int backmask;
    int x1,y1,x2,y2;
    int newback;

    //*** Clear screen ***
    textbackground(BLACK);
    clrscr();

    //*** Get screen coordinates ***
    cout<<"Enter area of screen to be changed : ";
    cin>>x1>>y1>>x2>>y2;

    //*** Get new background ***
    cout<<"Enter new background colour : ";
    cin>> newback;

    //*** Fill screen with X's ***
    clrscr();
    for(int i=0;i<=1800;i++)
        cout<<'X';

    //*** Calculate mask ***
    cout<<"Back : "<<GetBackColour(1,1);
    backmask =
        CreateMask(GetBackColour(1,1),newback);

    //*** Change background of specified area ***
    ChangeBackground(x1,y1,x2,y2,backmask);

    //*** Change back to original colour ***
    getch();
    ChangeBackground(x1,y1,x2,y2,backmask);

    getch();
}

int GetBackColour(int col, int line)
{
    VideoLoc *address;
    VideoLoc mask = {{'\0',0,7,0}};

    address = (VideoLoc*)(0XB8000000L+
              (line-1)*160+(col-1)*2);
    return (address->vidint & mask.vidint)>>12;
}

void ChangeBackground
    (int x1, int y1, int x2, int y2, int mask)
{
    int line,col;
    VideoLoc *address;
    VideoLoc screenmask = {{'\0',0,mask,0}};

    for(line=y1;line<=y2;line++)
    {
        address = CalcVideoAddr(x1,line);
        for(col=x1;col<=x2;col++)
        {
            address->vidint ^=screenmask.vidint;
            address++;
        }
    }
}
```

PROGRAMMING EXERCISE 5.22

1.
We can use the *GetData()* routine to get more control over data entry. However, additional checks are required for the *sex* and *score* fields.

GetData:

```
void GetData(const char *s,int max,char *result)
{
    const int ENTER=13;
    const int BACKSPACE = 8;
    char ch;
    int count=0;

    strcpy(result,"");
        ch=getch();
    while(ch!=ENTER)
    {
        if(strchr(s,ch)&&count<max)
        {
            cout<<ch;
            count++;
            result[count-1]=ch;
            result[count]=0;
        }
        else if(ch==BACKSPACE&&count>0)
        {
            cout<<\b \b;
            count;
            result[count]=0;
        }
        ch=getch();
    }
     cout<<\n;
}
```

Continued on next page

PROGRAMMING EXERCISE 5.22 (cont.)

The new version of *GetStudentDetails()* is

```
void GetStudentDetails(StudentDetails& sd)
{
    char temp[10];  //Holds numeric values as
                    //string before conversion
    char *error;
    clrscr();

    //*** Get student id ***
    long result;
    do
    {
        cout<<"Enter student id : ";
        GetData("0..9",5,temp);
        result=strtol(temp,&error,10);
    }
    while(result<=0||result>32767);
    sd.idcode=result;

    //*** Get name ***
    cout<<"Enter student name : ";
    GetData("A..Za..z .-",29,sd.name);

    //*** Get sex ***
    cout<<"Enter student's sex : ";
    //** Make sure a M or F entered
    //   (could press ENTER first) **
    do
    {
        //** Clear string **
        temp[0]=0;
        GetData("MF",1,temp);
    }
    while (temp[0]!='M'&&temp[0]!='F');
    //***Copy character to sex ***
    sd.sex=temp[0];

    //*** Get marks ***
    cout<<"Enter student's marks : \n";
    for(int j=0;j<6;j++)
    {
        //** Make sure marks in range 0 to 100 **
        do
        {
            cout<<"Enter score for test "<<(j+1)
                <<" : ";
            temp[0]=0;
            GetData("0..9",3,temp);
            sd.score[j]=strtol(temp,&error,10);
        }
        while (sd.score[j]<0||sd.score[j]>100);
    }
}
```

2.
The new routines are defined below.

```
int CompareIdDescending(StudentDetails st1,
StudentDetails st2)
{
    if(st1.idcode<st2.idcode)
        return 1;
    else
        return 2;
}


int CompareAverage( StudentDetails st1,
StudentDetails st2)
{
    int total1=0,total2=0;

    for(int i=0;i<6;i++)
    {
         total1 += st1.score[i];
        total2 += st2.score[i];
    }
    if(total1 < total2)
         return 1;
    else
        return 2;
}
```

In addition, these need to be incorporated in the Sort menu and in the code assigning the function pointer.

TASK 5.21

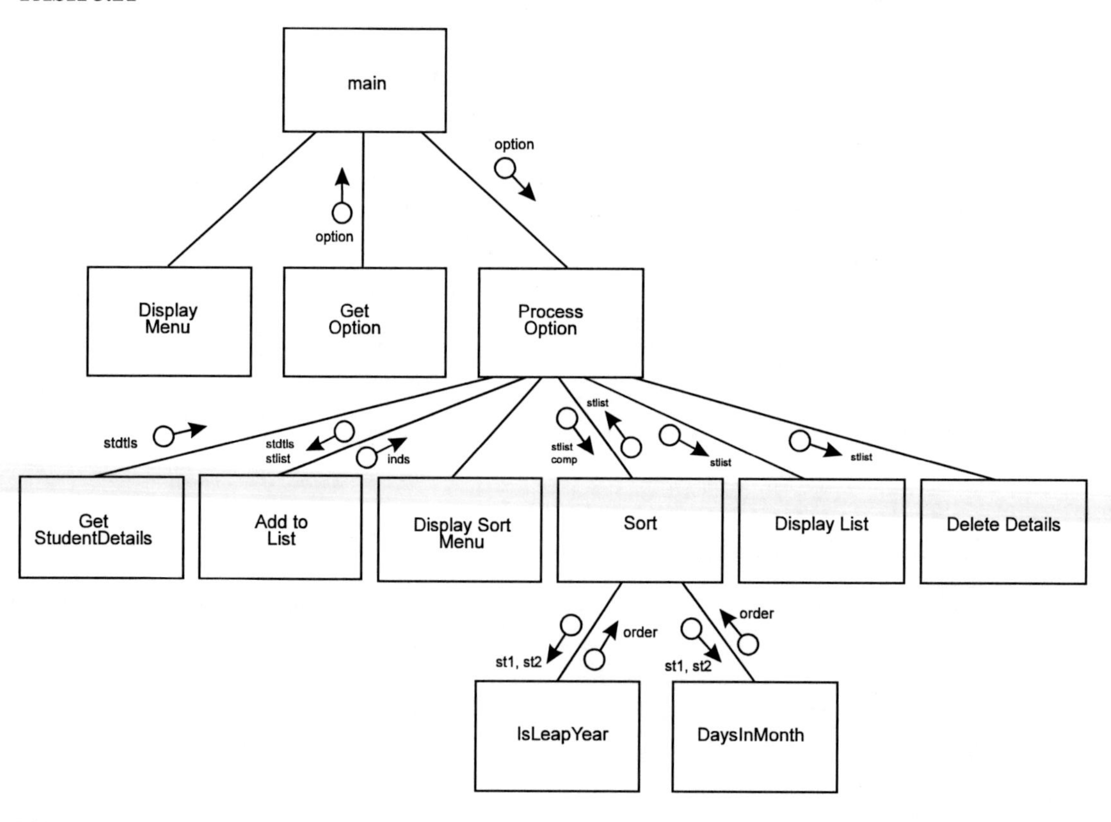

CHAPTER 6
File Handling

This chapter covers the following topics:

Binary File Format

Block I/O

Calling DOS Commands

Deleting Records

Formatted I/O

Housekeeping Functions

Random Access

Reading from Files

Streams

Text File Format

Updating Records

Writing to Files

FILE HANDLING

Introduction

Data held exclusively within the variables of a program is going to be lost when that program is terminated. Hence, it is normal to store important data which is likely to be required at a later date in a more permanent form. This means using disk files in which information can be held indefinitely.

C++'s ancestor, C, defines a complete set of functions for handling files. And, since C++ is a superset of C, these functions are also available in the new language.

We need to begin by looking at the way in which C++ (and C) views the transfer of information to and from peripheral devices. The philosophy of the language is to make this transfer of information independent from the physical devices which may be linked to your computer. This is achieved by doing all input/output (I/O) via a **stream**.

We can consider a stream as a store of sequential characters. To use a stream, we must, normally, link it to a physical device. The devices themselves are called **files**. In C++, there is no basic difference between linking a stream to a disk file or some other peripheral such as a printer - all are considered to be files (see FIG-6.1).

FIG-6.1

Streams are linked to Devices

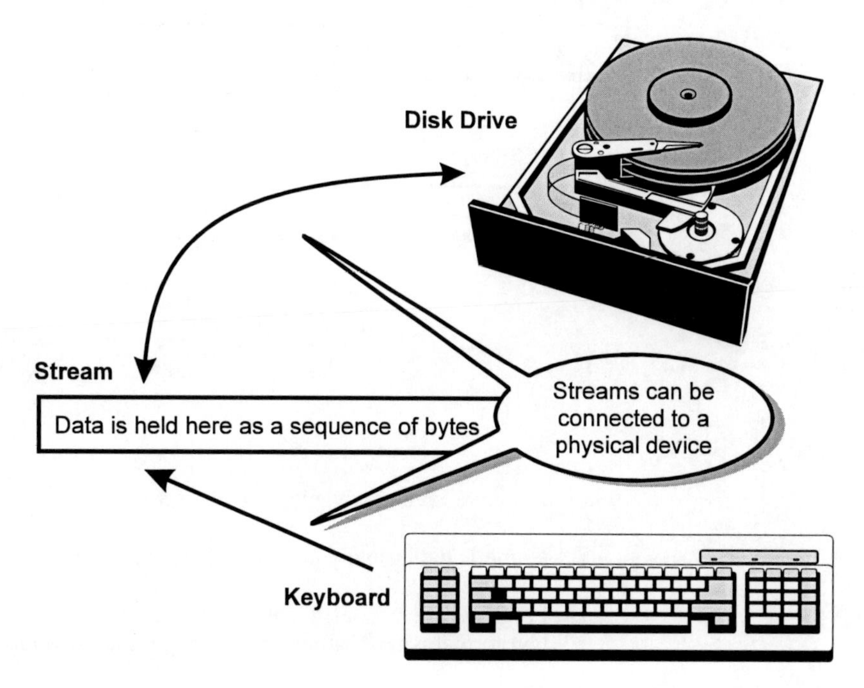

`cin` is an example of a stream and is normally linked to `stdin` (the keyboard). This link is created automatically in the case of `cin`, but normally we need to define such links explicitly within our program.

The majority of the examples that follow involve streams which are linked to disk files.

Disk Files Background

File Formats

Before using a disk file, we'll start by examining how information is stored in such a file. C++ allows us two methods of storage:

Text
and Binary

The main difference between these two formats is a simple one: a text file holds all its information as ASCII characters, while binary files hold numeric values in the same binary format as the variables from which the data comes. The difference in storage methods for three variables, *name, sex* and *age*, which contain the values

"Fred Bloggs" 'M' 23

is shown in FIG-6.2.

FIG-6.2

Text and Binary Storage Formats

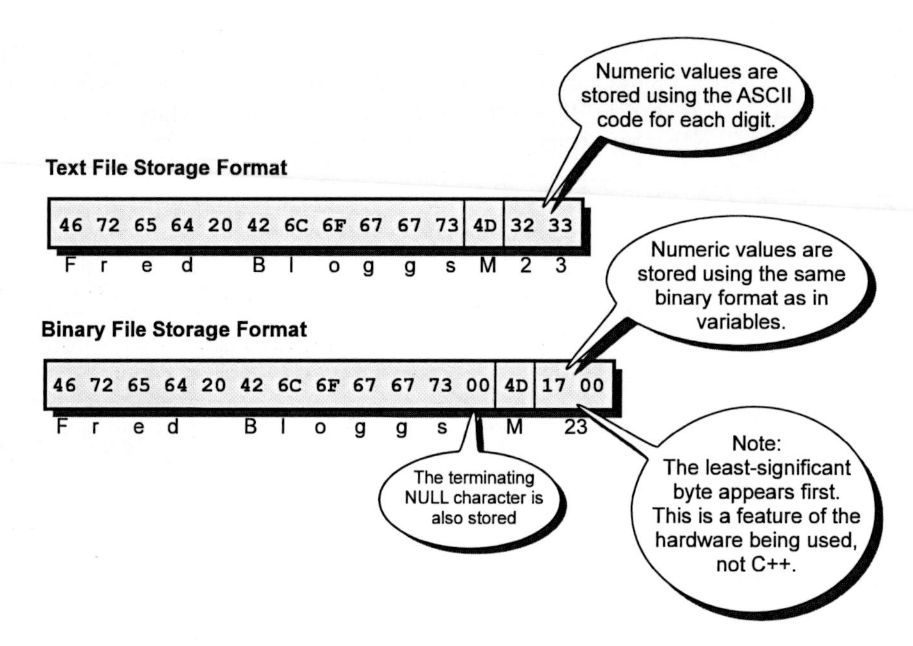

Binary files have several advantages over text files:

- Numeric data usually occupies less bytes in binary mode.
- Programs are more efficient since there is no requirement to convert to/from text format when reading and writing numeric values.
- Binary files can be accessed randomly.

Using Files

To use a disk file, we need to apply the following logic:

```
Define a stream pointer variable
Associate variable with a DOS file name
Open the file in the required mode
Read/Write records to the file
Close the file
```

The Stream Pointer

Once linked the terms *file* and *stream* tend to be used interchangeably.

A **stream pointer** is used to reference a stream. The data areas set up by a stream include the file name and status as well as a buffer area to store information transferred to/from the stream.

Stream pointers are defined as type `FILE` which is, itself, defined in *stdio.h*. Any program using streams will contain a definition such as:

```
FILE *fptr;
```

Opening a File

Having defined a stream pointer, it needs to be initialised by supplying three additional pieces of information about the file to which it is to be linked:

1. The DOS name of the file to be opened.
2. The file's format (Text or binary).
3. The I/O mode to be used.

The actual file name is usually a string specifying the drive, path and filename (e.g. "C:\\MYDIR\\MYDATA.DAT"). However, the file name may also be a peripheral device such as a printer (name: "prn") or keyboard and screen (name: "CON")

This link between the file and stream is performed using the function `fopen()` which is defined below:

***fopen()* is prototyped in stdio.h**

Prototype : `FILE* fopen(const char *fname, const char *mode)`

Pre-condition: None

Description : Opens the file specified by *fname* and returns a reference to the stream associated with the file.
The *mode* parameter specifies the file format and I/O mode to be used.
Basic values for *mode* are:

mode	Meaning
"r"	Open for reading only. The file must exist.
"w"	Open for writing. If the file does not exist, it is created. If it does exist, its contents are erased.
"a"	Open for writing. If the file does not exist, it is created If it does exist, new data is added after existing data.
"r+"	Opens a file for updating. The file must exist. The current contents can be read and modified.
"w+"	Open a file for updating. If the file does not exist, it is created. If it does exist, its contents are erased.
"a+"	Open a file for updating. If the file does not exist, it is created. If it does exist, new data is added after existing data.

Add "t" (for "text") or "b" ("binary") to the end of the *mode* string to specify the file format being used. (e.g. "wb"-open binary file for writing)

Closing a File

When a program has finished with a file, that file must be closed. This is done using the `fclose()` function which is defined as:

Prototype :	`int fclose(FILE *stream)`	**Header** : stdio.h
Pre-condition:	*stream* must have been used in a previous *fopen()* call.	
Description :	Closes the stream referenced by *stream*. The buffer area associated with the stream is flushed (if the stream is opened for output, this will result in any data remaining in the buffer being written to the associated file) and deallocated. Returns zero if the stream is closed successfully, otherwise EOF (-1) is returned.	

Writing to a File

Text Files

Only strings and characters can be written to a text file; any numeric values (`int`, `float`, etc.) must first be converted to a string before being output to the file.

To write a string to a text file we use the `fputs()` function. For example:

```
fputs("Fred Bloggs", testfile);
```

outputs the text "*Fred Bloggs*" to the stream referenced by *testfile*.
Characters are output using `fputc()`. For example:

```
fputc('M',testfile);
```

The two routines are defined formally below.

***fputs()* is prototyped in stdio.h**

Prototype :	`int fputs(const char* str,FILE *stream)`
Pre-condition:	*stream* must have been opened for writing.
Description :	Outputs the string *str* to *stream*. The terminating NULL character of *str* is not written to the stream. The function returns EOF if an error occurs, otherwise a non-zero value is returned.

***fputc()* is prototyped in stdio.h**

Prototype :	`int fputc(int ch,FILE *stream)`
Pre-condition:	*stream* must have been opened for writing.
Description :	Outputs the character *ch* to *stream*. Returns the character written if successful, otherwise EOF is returned

The program in LISTING-6.1 writes the three values shown earlier ("Fred Bloggs", 'M' and 23) to a text file.

LISTING-6.1

Writing to a Text File

```
#include<iostream.h>
#include<stdio.h>
#include<stdlib.h>

void main()
{
   FILE *testfile;
   char temp[10];
   //*** Open a text file for writing ***
   testfile=fopen("C:\\TEST.DAT","wt");
   //*** Output string to file ***
   fputs("Fred Bloggs",testfile);
   //*** Output character to file ***
   fputc('M',testfile);
   //*** Output int value by first converting it to a string ***
   itoa(23,temp,10);
   fputs(temp,testfile);
   //*** Close file ***
   fclose(testfile);
}
```

PROGRAMMING EXERCISE 6.1

Enter and run the above program.

The DOS command, EDIT, allows the contents of a text file to be displayed and edited. Examine the contents of the file you've just created by typing:

   EDIT C:\TEST.DAT

Once you've checked that the file contains the expected data, exit the EDIT program by choosing

   FILE|EXIT

FILE|EXIT is shorthand for selecting EXIT from within the FILE menu.

A more technical examination of the file is possible using the DOS DEBUG program. This will display the contents of the file in both hexadecimal and character formats. To use DEBUG type

   DEBUG C:\TEST.DAT

The DEBUG prompt is the hyphen. When this appears type

   D

D tells DEBUG to display the contents of a block of memory.

to display the contents of the file. A typical display from DEBUG is shown below.

```
C:\>DEBUG TEST.DAT
-d
1878:0100  46 72 65 64 20 42 6C 6F-67 67 73 4D 32 33 0D 0A   Fred BloggsM23..
1878:0110  00 6A 00 6A 00 57 E8 39-F8 89 46 FE 34 00 67 18   .j.j.W.9..F.4.g.
1878:0120  8B F7 8B 1E B4 52 C1 E6-02 8B 40 02 89 46 F8 50   .....R....@..F.P
1878:0130  FF 76 0A FF 76 08 FF 76-06 FF 76 04 E8 07 F9 89   .v..v..v..v.....
1878:0140  46 FE 0B C0 74 20 8B F7-C1 E6 02 8B 1E B4 52 FF   F...t ........R.
1878:0150  70 02 E8 AD F8 8B F7 C1-E6 02 8B 1E B4 52 FF 70   p.............R.p
1878:0160  02 E8 9E F8 EB 68 8B 76-0C 8B DF 8B 44 0A 8B CF   .....h.v....D...
1878:0170  C1 E3 02 C4 3E 50 56 26-29 01 8B 46 F6 8B FB C4   ....>PV&)..F....
-
```


DEBUG displays a block of main memory into which TEST.DAT has been loaded. Since the file's contents is much smaller than the block displayed, much of what appears in the display is of no interest to us.

Use Q to quit DEBUG.

If we look at the contents of the file we've created, we'll see that the data is held as a continuous sequence of characters:

```
Fred BloggsM23
```

Holding information in this way can make reading the data back later rather difficult since there is no way to tell where one piece of information ends and another begins.

One way round this is to write a newline character after each piece of data. LISTING-6.2 contains a modified version of the previous program, which separates the three data items using this approach.

LISTING-6.2

Adding newline Characters in the Text File

```
#include<iostream.h>
#include<stdio.h>
#include<stdlib.h>

//*** Adds a newline character after each data item ***
void main()
{
   FILE *testfile;
   char temp[10];
   //*** Open a text file for writing ***
   testfile=fopen("C:\\TEST.DAT","wt");
   //*** Output string to file ***
   fputs("Fred Bloggs",testfile);
   fputc('\n',testfile);
   //*** Output character to file ***
   fputc('M',testfile);
   fputc('\n',testfile);
   //*** Output integer value by first converting to a string ***
   itoa(23,temp,10);
   fputs(temp,testfile);
   fputc('\n',testfile);
   //*** Close file ***
   fclose(testfile);
}
```

PROGRAMMING EXERCISE 6.2

Run the program in LISTING-6.2 and use EDIT and DEBUG to examine the contents of the TEST.DAT. Identify the bytes written to the file after each three strings.

Notice that the newline character ($0A_{16}$) specified in LISTING-6.2 is written to the file as two characters: a RETURN ($0D_{16}$) and NEWLINE ($0A_{16}$).

PROGRAMMING EXERCISE 6.3

Write a program which accepts one student's details from the keyboard and saves this information to disk file.
The student's information is defined as

```
struct StudentDetails
{
    int idcode;
    char name[30];
    char sex;
    int score[6];
};
```

The file should be named "STUDENT.DAT".

Reading a Text File

Reading One Character at a Time

One way to access the data in a text file is to read through it one character at a time. The function required to do this is `fgetc()` which, unlike the familiar `getc()` function, requires a stream pointer argument. When reading from the file, we need to detect when the end of the data is reached. `fgetc()` reports this situation by returning EOF when an attempt is made to read past the last character in the file. The function `fgetc()` is defined as:

Prototype :	`int fgetc(FILE *stream)`	**Header**: stdio.h
Pre-condition:	*stream* must have been opened for reading.	
Description :	Returns the next character from the input stream. If successful, the value of the character is returned, otherwise EOF (-1) is returned.	

The program in LISTING-6.3 reads TEST.DAT one character at a time.

Program Logic:

```
Open text file for reading
IF file cannot be found THEN
    Display error message
    Terminate program
ENDIF
Read a character from the file
WHILE character is not EOF marker DO
    Display character
    Read a character from the file
ENDWHILE
Close file
```

Program Code:

LISTING-6.3

Reading a Text File One Character at a Time

Note the requirement of checking that the file has been successfully opened.

```
#include<iostream.h>
#include<stdio.h>
#include<stdlib.h>
#include<conio.h>
void main()
{
  FILE *testfile;
  char temp;

  //*** Open text file for reading ***
  testfile=fopen("C:\\TEST.DAT","rt");
  //*** If file not found, error message ***
  if(!testfile)
  {
      cout<<"Error opening file\n";
      exit(1);
  }
  //*** Read and display a character until EOF encountered ***
  while((temp=fgetc(testfile))!=EOF)
      cout<<temp;
 //*** Close file ***
  fclose(testfile);
  getch();
}
```

How is the program able to detect the end of the file? First, the program detects the file's length by reading this information from the disk's file directory where every file's length is specified, then, by keeping a count of how many characters have been read from the file, the program is able to detect when the end of the file has been reached. When the program attempts to read past the end of the file, a value of -1 (EOF) is returned by the `fgetc()` function. Note that no special character is stored in the file itself to indicate the end of file.

> **PROGRAMMING EXERCISE 6.4**
>
> 1. Write a program to display the contents of your STUDENT.DAT file.
>
> 2. Display the contents of STUDENT.DAT as a sequence of hexadecimal values.
>   (HINT: use `cout<<hex<<int(ch)<<' ';`)
>
>   Notice that the character sequence RETURN NEWLINE is read as a single NEWLINE character.
>
> 3. Modify your previous program to count the number of characters read from STUDENT.DAT. Compare this with the number of characters reported in the file using DIR STUDENT.DAT.

The End-Of-File Marker

When reading a file, the operating system detects the end-of-file condition by comparing the number of bytes read with the length of the file (taking into account how RETURN/NEWLINE combinations are handled) but the end-of-file condition will also be reported if any byte read from the file has the value $1A_{16}$.

The use of $1A_{16}$ as an end-of-file marker is a hangover from the days of the CP/M operating system (an ancestor of MSDOS) which used this technique.

> **PROGRAMMING EXERCISE 6.5**
>
> 1. Use DEBUG to place the value $1A_{16}$ at the eleventh character position in STUDENT.DAT. To do this:
>
>   Enter DOS mode
>   Type:
>   DEBUG C:\STUDENT.DAT
>   Type:
>   d
>   E xxxx:010A 1A
>   W
>   Type:
>   Q
>
> 2. Run your program to report the length of the file.

Replace xxxx with the address given on the left-hand side of the first line of the display.

Reading a String at a Time

An alternative way to read a text file is to read one string at a time (a string is every character up to the next NEWLINE character). To do this we need to reserve enough space for the largest possible string, and use the function `fgets()` to read the string from the file. This function is described overleaf.

fgets() is prototyped in stdio.h

Prototype :	`char*fgets(char* buff,int maxch,FILE*stream)`
Pre-condition:	*fname* must be a text file open for reading.
Description :	Places up to *maxch*-1 characters from *stream* into *buff*. If a NEWLINE character is encountered, the transfer will stop at that point. The NEWLINE character, if encountered, will be added to the end of the string. A terminating NULL character is appended to the returned value. If succesful, `fgets` returns the string referenced by *buff*. If end-of-file or an error is detected, it returns NUL.

The program in LISTING-6.4 uses this approach to read TEST.DAT.

LISTING-6.4

Read a Text File One Line at a Time

```
#include<iostream.h>
#include<stdio.h>
#include<stdlib.h>
#include<conio.h>


void main()
{
  FILE *testfile;
  char temp[201];

  clrscr();
  //*** Open file ***
  testfile=fopen("C:\\TEST.DAT","rt");
  if(!testfile)
  {
       cout<<"Error opening file\n";
       exit(1);
  }
  //*** Read and display contents of file ***
  while(fgets(temp,200,testfile)!=NULL)
       cout<<temp;
  //*** Close file ***
  fclose(testfile);
  getch();
}
```

PROGRAMMING EXERCISE 6.6

Write a program to read back, a string at a time, the information contained in STUDENT.DAT.

TASK 6.1

Often, the NEWLINE character held in the strings read from a file will be unwanted. Detail how these characters may be removed from such a string.

Appending to a File

If we continue to use the file writing programs given earlier, any existing data will be erased on the next occasion we execute our program. However, it is likely that we will often want to add the new data to that already in the file and to do this we must open the file for writing using the append option ("at").

The program in LISTING-6.5 adds new information to TEST.DAT.

LISTING-6.5

Appending Data to a File

```
#include<iostream.h>
#include<stdio.h>
#include<stdlib.h>

void main()
{
  FILE *testfile;
  char temp[10];

  //*** Open a text file for writing ***
  testfile=fopen("C:\\TEST.DAT","at");
  //*** Output string to file ***
  fputs("Shabnam Latif",testfile);
  fputc('\n',testfile);
  //*** Output character to file ***
  fputc('F',testfile);
  fputc('\n',testfile);
  //*** Output integer value by first converting to a string ***
  itoa(20,temp,10);
  fputs(temp,testfile);
  fputc('\n',testfile);
  //*** Close file ***
  fclose(testfile);
}
```

PROGRAMMING EXERCISE 6.7

Write a program to allow additional student records to be added to STUDENT.DAT.

The program should allow any number of records to be added, stopping when the student's id is entered as -1.

Formatted I/O

Formatted Output

An alternative way of outputting to a text file is to use the function `fprintf()` which not only allows us to write several items of data to a file in a single instruction, but also allows us to specify the exact format of that output.

For example, if we want to output *name*, *sex*, *age* and *weight* values to TEST.DAT we can use the command

```
fprintf(testfile,"%s%c%d%f",name,sex,age,weight);
```

The string following the stream name is known as the **format string** and determines how the value, given after the format string, are to be output. The format string is constructed using **format specifiers**.

The format specifier *%s* signifies a string output; *%c*, a character; *%d*, a decimal integer and *%f*, a real value. *name,age, sex* and *weight* are the values to be used in each case.

If we want a NEWLINE character between each data item we add these to the format string:

```
fprintf(testfile,"%s\n%c\n%d\n%f\n",name,sex,age,weight);
```

Any non-formatting characters in the format string will become part of the data output to the stream.

The function `fprintf()` is defined formally below:

***fprintf()* is prototyped in stdio.h**

Prototype : `int fprintf(FILE *stream, const char* form [,arg,...])`

Pre-condition: *stream* must be open for writing. The number of *args* must equal the number of format specifiers in *form*.

Description : Accepts a list of arguments (*arg*,...) and applies the format specifiers in *form* when outputting these values to *stream*. If successful, the number of bytes output is returned, otherwise EOF is returned.
Format specifiers have the format
%[flags][width][precision]type

type:

This is the minimum option required by a format specifier. The following options are available:

type char	arg type	Output Format
d	Integer	Signed decimal int
i	Integer	Signed decimal int
o	Integer	Unsigned octal int
u	Integer	Unsigned dec int
x	Integer	Unsigned hex int (uses a,b,c,d,e,f)
X	Integer	Unsigned hex int (uses A,B,C,D,E,F)
f	Real	Signed fixed-point
e	Real	Signed scientific (uses e)
E	Real	Signed scientific (uses E)
c	Character	Character
s	String	String

flags:

Controls output justification, signs, decimal places, hexadecimal and octal prefixes

flag	Effect
-	Left-justify output within field. Defaults to right-justified.
+	Adds + to positive numeric values; - to negative numeric values.
space	Adds a space to positive numeric values; - to negative ones.
#	arg converted to an "alternative form". This symbol is used in conjunction with the type character described above:

Effect of # on	Effect
0	Zero prefixed to non-zero values
x	0x prefixed to value
X	0X prefixed to value
e,E,f	Decimal point included in output even when no digits follow (normally, there would be no decimal point).

Continued on next page

width:
This integer value sets the minimum number of characters produced when outputting. Where this is larger than the value itself, the other positions are space-filled; where width is too small, it is ignored and number of characters required to output the value is used.

precision:
This is normally included to specify the number of decimal places required when outputting real values. Values will be rounded. The value is always preceded by a decimal point.
A value of .0 will mean no decimal places are given

Example : `fprintf(tfile,"%s%8.2f",name,weight);`

The next program (LISTING-6.6) demonstrates the use of this function.

LISTING-6.6

Formatted Text Output

```
#include<iostream.h>
#include<stdio.h>
#include<stdlib.h>


void main()
{
  FILE *testfile;
  char temp[10];
  //*** Open a text file for writing ***
  testfile=fopen("C:\\TEST.DAT","wt");
  //*** Output string to file ***
  fprintf(testfile,"%s\n%c\n%d\n%f\n","Shabnam",'F',20,43.5);
  //*** Close file ***
  fclose(testfile);
}
```

This has several advantages over the previous methods:

- All output can be achieved by a single statement
- Numeric values are automatically converted to strings.
- The exact format of the stored values can be specified.

Generally, field size will be omitted so as to ensure that the data is held in the minimum number of bytes possible and hence save disk space.

Formatted Input

There is a corresponding function `fscanf()` for reading information from a formatted text file. To read data, this function must be supplied with a format string which indicates how to interpret the data read from the file (as a string, character, integer etc.) and the address of the variables in which the information read is to be placed. Hence, we might use the statement

```
fscanf(testfile,"%s %c %d %f",name,&sex,&age,&weight);
```

to read the details of an individual from TEST.DAT.

This seems a lot easier than reading individual strings and characters from the file. Also conversion between string and numeric formats will be handled automatically.

However, there's one big drawback: like `cin`, `fscanf()` assumes that a space character signifies the end of a string. This means that where the data in TEST.DAT begins with *"Fred Bloggs"* only *Fred* will be read into *name* and subsequent variables (*sex*, *age* and *weight*) will contain meaningless values.

This failing means that `fscanf()` is of limited use when handling strings, but where the data held in the text file is numeric then this is an ideal way to read its contents.

The formal definition for `fscanf()` is given below:

Prototype : `int fscanf(FILE *stream, const char *form [,address...])`

Pre-condition: *stream* must be opened for reading. There must be a format identifier for each address.

Description : Reads from stream and places the data at the addresses specified. The characters read from the stream are interpreted using the information in the format string. The number of values transferred is returned. If the end of the data is reached an EOF(-1) value is returned. Generally, a format specifier will have the format

`% type`

type specifies the type of data expected from the stream and the type of variable receiving the data.
The type options are:

type	Expected input	Receiving variable
d	Decimal integer	int
D	Decimal integer	long
o	Octal integer	int
O	Octal integer	long
x	Hexadecimal integer	int
X	Hexadecimal integer	long
u	Unsigned decimal	int
U	Unsigned decimal	long
c	Character	char
s	String	char array

The code in LISTING-6.7 uses `fscanf()`, to read the file created by LISTING-6.6.

LISTING-6.7

Reading a Formatted File

```
#include<iostream.h>
#include<stdio.h>
#include<stdlib.h>
#include<conio.h>
void main()
{
  FILE *testfile;
  char name[30];
  char sex;
  int  age;
  float weight;

  clrscr();
```

Continued on next page

LISTING-6.7
(continued)

Reading a Formatted File

NOTE: Variable addresses must be used

```
    //*** Open file ***
    testfile=fopen("C:\\TEST.DAT","rt");
    if(!testfile)
    {
        cout<<"Error opening file\n";
        exit(1);
    }
    //*** Read and display contents of file ***
    fscanf(testfile,"%s %c %d %f",name,&sex,&age,&weight);
    cout<<name<<' '<<sex<<' '<<age<<' '<<weight<<endl;
    //*** Close file ***
    fclose(testfile);

    getch();
}
```

Binary Files

As already stated, one of the main differences between binary and text files is that binary files store numeric values (`int`, `float`, etc.) in the same format as used within main memory while text files store all data in character format. As well as this, NEWLINE characters are written to binary files as a single $0A_{16}$ byte and where a file contains the combination $0D_{16}$ $0A_{16}$ this is read as two separate bytes. Finally, no value in a binary file is recognised as an end-of-file marker; hence, $1A_{16}$ is simply taken as another byte of data in the file.

We have to tell the program that a binary file is being used by employing a 'b' in place of 't' in the `fopen()` call. Hence, we would use "wb" to open a binary file for writing.

Normally, it is wise only to open in binary format files which have been created as binary files. However, this rule is not imposed on us by the language itself and the program in LISTING-6.8 reads through the contents of the text file TEST.DAT, displaying and counting the number of characters in the file.

LISTING-6.8

Reading a Text File in Binary Mode

```
#include<iostream.h>
#include<stdio.h>
#include<stdlib.h>
#include<conio.h>
void main()
{
    FILE *testfile;
    char temp;

    clrscr();
    //*** Open binary file for reading ***
    testfile=fopen("C:\\TEST.DAT","rb");
    //*** If file not found, error message ***
    if(!testfile)
    {
        cout<<"Error opening file\n";
        exit(1);
    }
    //*** Read a character until EOF encountered ***
    int count=0;
    while((temp=fgetc(testfile))!=EOF)
    {
        cout<<hex<<int(temp)<<' ';
        count++;
    }
```

Continued on next page

LISTING-6.8
(continued)

Reading a Text File in

```
   //*** Close file ***
   fclose(testfile);
   //*** Display the number of characters read ***
   cout<<"\n\nThere were "<<dec<<count
       <<" characters in the file\n";

   getch();
}
```

PROGRAMMING EXERCISE 6.8

1. Enter and run the above program using your STUDENT.DAT file, noting the result.

2. Change the file open mode to "rt" and re-run the program noting the result.

   Explain the difference between the two results.

Reading and Writing Records

So far, writing and reading your *StudentDetails* record has involved dealing with each field separately. Since this approach seems a little long-winded, a more desirable method would be to read and write a whole record in one go. When using binary files we can do this by using **block I/O**.

Block I/O uses the function `fwrite()` to write information to a file and `fread()` to retrieve that information. These functions read/write data in **blocks**. The size of a block, and the number of blocks to be transferred need to be specified. For example, if a program contains the definition

```
StudentDetails list[10];
```

and creates a file with the code

```
FILE *stfile;
stfile=fopen("C:\\STUDENT.DAT","wb");
```

we can write the contents of all ten elements of *list* to a binary file with the statement,

```
fwrite(list,sizeof(StudentDetails),10,stfile);
```

In the above statement

`list`	is the start address of the data to be written to the file.
`sizeof(StudentDetails)`	is the number of bytes in a single block.
`10`	is the number of blocks to be written.
`stfile`	is the address of the stream to which the data is to be written.

When the file is open for reading, the statement

```
fread(list,sizeof(StudentDetails),1,stfile);
```

will read a single block (one record) from *stfile* and place the data in *list[0]*.

These two functions are defined as:

fwrite() **is prototyped in stdio.h**

Prototype : `size_t fwrite(const void *dptr, size_t bksz, size_t nblks, FILE *stream)`

Pre-condition: *stream* should be open for writing in binary

Description : Writes *nblks* blocks of *bksz* bytes, starting at location *dptr*, to *stream*.
Returns the number of blocks transferred to *stream*. Normally, this will be *nblks*; if there are problems, the returned value will be less than *nblks*.

fread() **is prototyped in stdio.h**

Prototype : `size_t fread(void *dptr, size_t bksz, size_t nblks, FILE *stream)`

Pre-condition: *stream* must be a binary file open for reading.

Description : Reads *nblks* blocks of each of *bksz* bytes from *stream* and stores the information in the area referenced by dptr. If successful, the value of *nblks* is returned to indicate the number of blocks successfully read from the file, otherwise a value less than *nblks* is returned.

The programs in LISTING-6.9 and LISTING-6.10 show how records are transferred to and from files using this approach.

Program Logic for LISTING-6.9:

```
Open binary file for writing
Read a record from the keyboard
WHILE name field is not empty DO
    Write record to file
    Read a record from the keyboard
ENDWHILE
Close file
```

Program Code:

LISTING-6.9

Writing Blocks to a Binary File

```
#include<iostream.h>
#include<stdio.h>
#include<stdlib.h>
#include<conio.h>
#include<string.h>

//*** Record structure declaration ***
struct Details
{
  char name[30];
  char sex;
  int age;
};

//*** Prototype for reading a record from keyboard function ***
void ReadDetails(Details&);

void main()
{
  FILE *testfile;
  Details det;
```

Continued on next page

LISTING-6.9 (continued)

Writing Blocks to a Binary File

```
   //*** Open binary file for writing ***
   testfile=fopen("C:\\TEST.DAT","wb");
   //*** If file not found, error message ***
   if(!testfile)
   {
       cout<<"Error opening file\n";
       exit(1);
   }
   //*** Read a record's details from the keyboard ***
   ReadDetails(det);
   //*** WHILE not terminate message DO ***
   while(strcmp(det.name,""))
   {
       //*** Write data to file ***
       fwrite(&det,sizeof(det),1,testfile);
       //*** Read more details from the keyboard ***
       ReadDetails(det);
   }
   //*** Close file ***
   fclose(testfile);
}

//*** Read record from Keyboard function ***
void ReadDetails(Details& p)
{
   //*** Get data from keyboard ***
   clrscr();
   cout<<"Enter name : ";
   gets(p.name);
   if(!strcmp(p.name,""))
       return;
   cout<<"Enter sex : ";
   cin>>p.sex;
   cout<<"Enter age : ";
   cin>>p.age;
}
```

Program Logic for LISTING-6.10:

```
Open binary file for reading
Read a record from the file
WHILE the end of file has not been read DO
    Display record
    Read a record from the file
ENDWHILE
Close file
```

Program Code:

LISTING-6.10

Reading Blocks from a Binary File

```
#include<iostream.h>
#include<stdio.h>
#include<stdlib.h>
#include<conio.h>
//*** Record structure declaration ***
struct Details
{
   char name[30];
   char sex;
   int age;
};
void main()
{
   FILE *testfile;
   Details p;
```

Continued on next page

LISTING-6.10
(continued)

Reading Blocks from a Binary File

```
    //*** Open binary file for reading ***
    testfile=fopen("C:\\TEST.DAT","rb");
    //*** If file not found, error message ***
    if(!testfile)
    {
        cout<<"Error opening file\n";
        exit(1);
    }
    clrscr();
    cout<<"THE FILE CONTAINS THE FOLLOWING DATA\n\n";
    //*** Read data from file ***
    while(fread(&p,sizeof(p),1,testfile)==1)
    {
        //*** Display data read ***
        cout<<p.name<<' '<<p.sex<<' '<<p.age<<endl;
        getch();
    }
    cout<<"End of file reached\n";
    //*** Close file ***
    fclose(testfile);

    getch();
}
```

PROGRAMMING EXERCISE 6.9

Produce both reading and writing programs for your *StudentDetails* structure. Your program should add checks for handling possible error conditions when reading or writing to the file.

The third parameter of `fwrite()` and `fread()` can be useful when an array of data is to be written or read.

For example, if a program contains the definition

```
Details list[15];
```

we could save the contents of the first five elements of list using the statement

```
fwrite(list,sizeof(list[0]),5,testfile);
```

Of course, to save the whole array we can write either

```
    fwrite(list,sizeof(Details),15,testfile);
or  fwrite(list,sizeof(list),1,testfile);
```

Random Access

When we write information to a file, each new record is placed immediately after the last; when we subsequently read information from that file, the records are read one by one in the same order in which they were written. However, there are occasions when we want to go directly to a record without accessing the preceding ones (in much the same way as we might want to go to track 5 on a CD without playing the first four).

In binary files, where the data is stored as a sequence of fixed size records we achieve this random access by using the `fseek()` function.

All files maintain their own file pointer. This is a hidden variable which references the next byte to be accessed in that file. When a file is first opened, its file pointer points to the first byte in that file. Reading or writing to the file moves the pointer through the file in much the same way as the screen cursor moves along the screen as we type.

Just as the function `gotoxy()` allows us to move the screen cursor to some desired position, so `fseek()` allows us to place the file pointer at any position within the file's data. The definition of `fseek()` is given below.

***fseek()* is prototyped in stdio.h**

Prototype : `int fseek(FILE *stream, long offset, int post)`
Pre-condition: *stream* must be open.

Description : Moves the file pointer of *stream* by *offset* bytes from position *post*.
post must be 0. 1, or 2 or the equivalent named constant:

Symbolic Name	Value	Starting position
SEEK_SET	0	Start of file
SEEK_CUR	1	Current position
SEEK_END	2	End of file

Returns 0 if successful, otherwise non-zero.

The program in LISTING-6.11 demonstrates the use of random file access.

Program Logic:

```
Open binary file for reading
Read position of required record
WHILE not terminate program DO
    Seek record
    Read record
    IF record read THEN
        Display its details
    ELSE
        Display error message
    ENDIF
    Read record
ENDWHILE
Close file
```

Program Code:

LISTING-6.11

Random Access Files

```
#include<iostream.h>
#include<stdio.h>
#include<stdlib.h>
#include<conio.h>
struct Details
{
  char name[30];
  char sex;
  int age;
};
void main()
{
  FILE *testfile;
  Details p;
  //*** Open binary file for reading ***
  testfile=fopen("C:\\TEST.DAT","rb");
```

Continued on next page

LISTING-6.11
(continued)

Random Access Files

```
    //*** If file not found, error message ***
    if(!testfile)
    {
        cout<<"Error opening file\n";
        exit(1);
    }

    //*** Read record position ***
    clrscr();
    cout<<"Enter record required : ";
    int post;
    cin>>post;
    //*** WHILE not terminate option DO ***
    while(post!=-1)
    {
        //*** Seek required record ***
        fseek(testfile,sizeof(p)*(post-1),0);
        //*** IF record read from file THEN***
        if (fread(&p,sizeof(p),1,testfile)==1)
        {
            //*** Display data read ***
            cout<<p.name<<' '<<p.sex<<' '<<p.age<<endl;
            getch();
        }
        else
        //*** ELSE display error message ***
        {
            cout<<"Invalid record number. Press any key\n";
            getch();
        }
        //*** Read record position ***
        cout<<"Enter record required : ";
        cin>>post;
    }
    cout<<"Program terminated\n";
    //*** Close file ***
    fclose(testfile);
    getch();
}
```

The current value of the file pointer can be found using another function, `ftell()`, which returns the number of bytes the file pointer has moved from the start of the file. The routine is defined as:

Prototype : `long ftell(FILE * stream)` **Header**: stdio.h
Pre-condition: *stream* must be an opened file.

Description : Returns the value of *stream*'s file pointer.
If the file pointer is at the beginning of the file, zero is returned.
If the operation fails, -1 is returned.

Example :

```
testfile = fopen("C:\\TEST.DAT","rb");
//*** Move to end of file ***
fseek(testfile,0,2);
//*** Calculate records in file ***
noofrecs = ftell(testfile)/sizeof(Details);
//*** Display results ***
cout<<"There are "<<noofrecs<<"in the file\n";
//*** Move pointer back to start of file ***
fseek(testfile,0,0);
```

Updating Files

The contents of most files will need to be changed periodically. There are only three basic operations required when files are updated:

- Adding new records
- Modifying existing records
- Deleting records

We've already seen how records are added to a file using the append operation.

Modifying a Record

To change the contents of a record we must first read the record from the file into some variable; next we need to modify the required field(s), and, finally, the record must be written back to the file.

It's important that the updated record is exactly the same as the original version since it needs to be placed back in the same "slot" in the file. Generally, this won't be a problem when dealing with binary files because each field is of a fixed size. However, this is not true of text files where numeric values will occupy a varying number of bytes based on the number of digits in any numeric values written to the file.

The program in LISTING-6.12 allows the user to change the name in a specified record in TEST.DAT.

Program Logic:

```
Open file for updating
Calculate and display the number of records in the file
Get the number of the record to be changed
WHILE number not -1 DO
    Seek record
    IF found THEN
        Display record
        Get new name
        Move file pointer back to the record just read
        Write updated record to file
    ELSE
        Display error message
    ENDIF
    Get the number of the record to be changed
ENDWHILE
Close file
```

Program Logic:

LISTING-6.12

Modifying Records

```
#include<iostream.h>
#include<stdio.h>
#include<stdlib.h>
#include<conio.h>
struct Details
{
  char name[30];
  char sex;
  int age;
};
```

Continued on next page

LISTING-6.12
(continued)

Modifying Records

```
void main()
{
   FILE *testfile;
   Details p;

   //*** Open binary file for updating ***
   testfile=fopen("C:\\TEST.DAT","r+b");
   //*** If file not found, error message ***
   if(!testfile)
   {
        cout<<"Error opening file\n";
        exit(1);
   }
   clrscr();
   //*** Calculate how many records are in the file ***
   fseek(testfile,0,2);
   int noofrecs=ftell(testfile)/sizeof(p);
   cout<<"The file contains "<<noofrecs<<" records\n";
   fseek(testfile,0,0);
   //*** Read record position ***
   cout<<"Enter record required (-1 to stop): ";
   int post;
   cin>>post;
   //***WHILE not terminate option DO
   while(post!=-1)
   {
        //*** Seek required record ***
        fseek(testfile,sizeof(p)*(post-1),0);
        //*** IF record read from file THEN ***
        if (fread(&p,sizeof(p),1,testfile)==1)
        {
             //*** Display data read ***
             cout<<p.name<<' '<<p.sex<<' '<<p.age<<endl;
             //*** Get replacement name ***
             cout<<"Enter the new name : ";
             gets(p.name);
             //*** Move file pointer to record just read ***
             fseek(testfile,(post-1)*sizeof(p),0);
             //*** Rewrite the record to the file ***
             fwrite(&p,sizeof(p),1,testfile);
        }
        else
        //*** ELSE display error message ***
        {
             cout<<"Invalid record number. Press any key\n";
             getch();
        }
        //*** Read record position ***
        cout<<"Enter record required (-1 to stop): ";
        cin>>post;
   }
   cout<<"Program terminated\n";
   //*** Close file ***
   fclose(testfile);
   getch();
}
```

PROGRAMMING EXERCISE 6.10

Write a menu driven program for your *StudentDetails* file which allows you to add new records, display a specific record, display all records, modify a record.
Your program should make use of routines already written. These include: *DisplayMenu(); GetOption(); GetData()* and *ExpandString()*.

Deleting a Record

The usual way to delete a record from a file is to make a new copy of the file in which the record to be deleted has been omitted. Such a program would use the logic:

```
Open old file for reading
Open new file for writing
Read a record from the original file
WHILE not at end of original file DO
    IF record read is not to be deleted THEN
        Write the record to the new file
    ENDIF
ENDWHILE
Close both files
Delete old file
Rename new file to that given to the original file
```

The program in LISTING-6.13 deletes the third record from TEST.DAT.

LISTING-6.13

Deleting Records

```
#include<conio.h>
#include<iostream.h>
#include<stdio.h>

struct Details
{
   char name[30];
   char sex;
   int age;
};


void main()
{
   FILE *infile, *outfile;
   Details sd;

   //*** Open files ***
   infile=fopen("C:\\TEST.DAT","rb");
   outfile=fopen("C:\\TEMP.DAT","wb");
   //*** Set count to zero ***
   int count = 1;
   while(fread(&sd,sizeof(sd),1,infile)==1)
   {
        //*** If it's not third record, copy it to new file ***
        if(count!=3)
             fwrite(&sd,sizeof(sd),1,outfile);
        //** Add 1 to count **
        count++;
   }
   //*** Close files ***
   fclose(infile);
   fclose(outfile);
   //*** Delete old file ***
   system("DEL C:\\TEST.DAT");
   //*** Rename new file ***
   system("REN C:\\TEMP.DAT TEST.DAT");
}
```

The above program introduces a new function: `system()`. This routine is used to execute any DOS command or other program. The command to be executed and any parameters it requires are given as a string argument to the function. This string should include path information where required.

A formal definition for `system()` is given overleaf.

Prototype :	`int system(const char *command)` **Header** :stdlib.h
Pre-condition:	None
Description :	Executes the DOS command, batch,.EXE, or .COM file specified by *command*. Returns 0 if execution is successfully started, and -1 is returned when an error occurs. The program to be executed must be in the current directory or in one of the directories listed in PATH otherwise the path information must be included in the command.

PROGRAMMING EXERCISE 6.11

Write a program, based on LISTING-6.13 above, which will delete a record in STUDENT.DAT by specifying its *id* value.

This approach to deleting records in a file can be rather time consuming if the file is a large one and records are removed frequently. An alternative approach is to simply mark records for deletion without actually removing them.

However, this still requires us to develop a program which can be used periodically to physically remove the records marked for deletion from the file.

The program in LISTING-6.14 allows records to be marked for deletion.

Program Logic:

```
Open file for updating
Get position in file of record to be deleted
WHILE position not -1 DO
    Find required record
    Change id field to DELETED indicator
    Get position in file of record to be deleted
ENDWHILE
    Close file
```

Program Code:

LISTING-6.14

Marking Deleted Records

```
#include<conio.h>
#include<iostream.h>
#include<stdio.h>
#include<string.h>
#include<stdlib.h>
struct Details
{
  char name[30];
  char sex;
  int age;
};

void main()
{
  const char DELETED[] = "-1";
  const int QUIT = -1;
  FILE *stfile;
  Details sd;
```

Continued on next page

LISTING-6.14 (continued)

Marking Deleted Records

```
    //*** Open files ***
    if((stfile=fopen("C:\\TEST.DAT","r+b"))==NULL)
    {
        cout<<"Error opening file\n";
        exit(1);
    }
    //*** Get the position of record to be marked for deletion ***
    cout<<"Enter record position (-1 to stop): ";
    int post;
    cin>>post;
    //*** WHILE not -1 DO ***
    while(post!=QUIT)
    {
        //*** Find required record ***
        fseek(stfile,(post-1)*sizeof(sd),SEEK_SET);
        //*** IF found THEN ***
        if(fread(&sd,sizeof(sd),1,stfile)==1)
        {
            //*** Mark for deletion ***
            strcpy(sd.name,DELETED);
            //*** Rewrite to file ***
            fseek(stfile,(post-1)*sizeof(sd),SEEK_SET);
            fwrite(&sd,sizeof(sd),1,stfile);
        }
        else
        //*** ELSE display error message ***
        {
            cout<<"Record not found\n";
            getch();
        }
        //*** Get position of next record ***
        cout<<"Enter record position : ";
        cin>>post;
    }
    //*** Close files ***
    fclose(stfile);
}
```

PROGRAMMING EXERCISE 6.12

Create a program, based on the one above, which will mark records in your student file for deletion.
Check that your program is operating correctly by examining the contents of the student file after the program has been run.

We now need a second program which copies those records not marked for deletion into another file.

The Structure English description of such a program is

```
Open original file for reading
Open new file for writing
Read a record from original file
WHILE not EOF DO
    IF record not marked for deletion THEN
        Write record to new file
    ENDIF
    Read a record from original file
ENDWHILE
Close both files
Delete the original file
Make a copy of the new file under the original name
Delete the new file
```

PROGRAMMING EXERCISE 6.13

Write a program based on the Structured English given above. Include the ability for the user to specify the name of the source file being copied.

Using Command Line Arguments

Specifying a File Name from DOS

Many DOS commands allow the user to specify a file name on the same line as the command. For example,

```
EDIT A:myfile.dat
```

This ability to pass these command-line arguments to a program can also be implemented in C++. To do this we need to make use of the, up-to-now, empty parentheses of `main()`. If we start the definition of `main()` with

```
void main(int argc, char *argv[ ])
```

which states that two arguments will be passed to `main()`: the second is an array of strings and the first the number of strings in that array.

The program in LISTING-6.15 can be called in this way and displays the values of *argc* and *argv[]*.

Program Logic:

```
Display the argument count
Display each argument
```

Program Code:

LISTING-6.15

Accessing Command Line Arguments

```
#include<iostream.h>
#include<conio.h>

void main(int argc, char *argv[])
{
  clrscr();
  cout<<"Argument count : "<<argc<<endl;
  for(int c=0; c<argc;c++)
      cout<<argv[c]<<endl;
  getch();
}
```

If we compile the above program, creating an .EXE file, for example, MYPROG.EXE, then running the program from DOS with the command

```
C:\MYDIR\MYPROG arg1 arg2 arg3 arg4
```

will produce the output

```
5
C:\MYDIR\MYPROG.EXE
arg1
arg2
arg3
arg4
```

Notice that we do not supply a value for *argc*, which, in fact, is created automatically by the system. Also, the first argument string is the full path/file name for the executed program.

During program testing, when it may be more convenient to run your program from the Integrated Development Environment, you can set up the arguments to be passed to your program by choosing the RUN|Arguments option from the menu bar. This will open an edit window where the arguments required can be entered.

We can use this technique of passing arguments in our file copy program to allow the user to specify the source file name. The program is given in LISTING-6.16.

Program Logic:

```
Check file name supplied from operating system
IF no name given THEN
    Get filename
ENDIF
Open original file for reading
Open new file for writing
Read a record from original file
WHILE not EOF DO
    IF record not marked for deletion THEN
        Write record to new file
    ENDIF
    Read a record from original file
ENDWHILE
Close both files
Delete the original file
Copy the new file using the old file name
Delete the new file
```

Notice that the RENAME option is not used when the records have been transferred to the new file. This is because the command line file names may include path information which is invalid when specifying the new name in RENAME.

Program Code:

LISTING-6.16

Using Command Line Arguments

```
#include<iostream.h>
#include<conio.h>
#include<string.h>
#include<stdio.h>
#include<stdlib.h>
struct Details
{
  char name[30];
  char sex;
  int age;
};
const char DELETED[] = "-1";
const int QUIT = -1;

void main(int argc, char *argv[])
{
  Details sd;
  char filename[25];
  if (argc==1)
  {
      cout<<"Enter the name of the file to be copied : ";
      cin>>filename;
  }
  else
      strcpy(filename,argv[1]);
  FILE *sourcefile, *destfile;
```

Continued on next page

LISTING-6.16
(continued)

Using Command Line Arguments

```
    if((sourcefile=fopen(filename,"rb"))==NULL)
    {
        cout<<"Source file not found\n";
        exit(1);
    }
    destfile=fopen("c:\\TEMP.DAT","wb");
    while(fread(&sd,sizeof(sd),1,sourcefile)==1)
        if(strcmp(sd.name,DELETED)!=0)
            fwrite(&sd,sizeof(sd),1,destfile);
    //*** Close files ***
    fclose(sourcefile);
    fclose(destfile);
    //*** Delete old file ***
    char command[30]="DEL ";
    strcat(command,filename);
    system(command);
    //*** Copy temp file ***
    strcpy(command,"COPY C:\\TEMP.DAT ");
    strcat(command,filename);
    system(command);
    //*** Delete temp file ***
    strcpy(command,"DEL C:\\TEMP.DAT");
    system(command);
}
```

Using the Printer

The printer is simply another file, which, when linked to a stream, can be used as an output file. The symbolic file name for the printer is “prn”.

The program in LISTING-6.17 copies the contents of TEST.DAT to the printer.

Program Logic:

```
Open TEST.DAT for reading
Open PRN for writing
Read a record from TEST.DAT
WHILE not EOF DO
    Copy record to printer
    Read a record from TEST.DAT
ENDWHILE
Close both files
```

The actual program is a little more complicated than the outline logic would suggest because, if we are to make sense of the printed output, we must treat the printer as a text file.

Program Code:

LISTING-6.17

Outputting to the Printer

```
#include<iostream.h>
#include<stdio.h>
#include<stdlib.h>
#include<conio.h>
#include<string.h>

struct Details
{
    char name[30];
    char sex;
    int age;
};
```

Continued on next page

LISTING-6.17
(continued)

Using the Printer

```
void main()
{
   FILE *testfile, *printer;
   Details p;
   //*** Open binary file for reading ***
   testfile=fopen(“C:\\TEST.DAT”,"rb");
   //*** If file not found, error message ***
   if(!testfile)
   {
       cout<<“Error opening file\n”;
       exit(1); }
   printer=fopen(“prn”,"wt");
   //*** If no printer, error message ***
   if(!printer)
   {
       cout<<“Error opening printer\n”;
       exit(1);
   }
   clrscr();
   fprintf(printer,"THE FILE CONTAINS THE FOLLOWING DATA\n\n");
   //*** WHILE reading a record does no detect EOF DO ***
   while(fread(&p,sizeof(p),1,testfile)==1)
       //*** Write to printer ***
       fprintf(printer,"%s  %c  %d\n",p.name,p.sex,p.age);
   cout<<“End of file reached\n”;
   fprintf(printer,"\XC");
   //*** Close file ***
   fclose(testfile);
   fclose(printer);
}
```

Summary

- **A stream** can be thought of as a sequence of bytes.
- **Streams are used to handle all I/O.**
- **Streams are linked to files** using `fopen()`.
- **A file's data** can be held in text or binary format.
- **Text files**

  Store all data in ASCII format
  Store a NEWLINE character ($0A_{16}$) as RETURN/NEWLINE ($0D_{16}$ $0A_{16}$)
  Treat the value $1A_{16}$ as an end-of-file marker
  Read the RETURN/NEWLINE combination as a single NEWLINE character

- **Binary Files**

  Store numeric values using the same format as the corresponding variables
  Store newline characters in a single byte ($0A_{16}$)
  Read the RETURN/NEWLINE combination as two separate bytes
  Does not treat $1A_{16}$ as an end-of-file marker

- **Files can be opened for:**

  Reading
  Writing
  Updating

- **Text files can be written**

    One character at a time
    One string at a time
    Using formatted output

- **Data items should be written to a text file with separation characters** (normally the newline character).

- **Binary files are written in blocks.**

- **Binary files will generally require less storage space** than the equivalent text file.

- **The contents of a file** can be examined using the DEBUG command from MSDOS.

- **Records can only be modified** within a file if the new data occupies the same number of bytes as the original data.

- **Deleting records** requires the contents of the file to be copied to a new file.

- **It is more efficient to mark records for deletion** and physically delete using a separate program.

- **New records** must be added at the end of the current data.

- **Records in a binary file** can be accessed randomly using `fseek()`.

- **Move to the start of a file** using

```
fseek(stream,0,0);
```

- **Move to the end of a file** using

```
fseek(stream,0,2);
```

- **Move to a specified record position** in a file using the code

```
fseek(stream,(rec_post-1)*sizeof(rec_type),0);
```

- **The number of records (blocks) in a file** can be determined using the code

```
fseek(stream,0,2);     //Move pointer to end of file
no_of_recs = ftell(stream)/sizeof(rectype);
```

- Values can be passed to a program **from the DOS prompt by specifying parameters in `main()`.**

- **DOS commands,** batch files and executable programs can be run from within your program using `system()`.

- **Output to the printer** can be achieved by opening a file named "prn".

- The file functions available are listed on the next page:

Function Name	Return Type	Input Type	Header File	Description
fopen	FILE*	char * fname char *mode	stdio.h	Opens the file specified by fname and returns a reference to stream associated with the file. mode specifies the mode in which the file is opened. "r" Open for reading. Must exist. "w" Open for writing. Created or overwritten. "a" Open for writing. Created or appends new data. "r+" Open for updating. Must exist. "w+" Open for updating. Created or emptied. "a+" Open for updating. Created or appended. Add "t" to mode to open in text mode. Add "b" to mode to open in binary mode.
fclose	int	FILE* stream	stdio.h	Closes stream. Flushes data in buffer.
Text Files				
fputc	int	int ch FILE* stream	stdio.h	Outputs *ch* to *stream*. Returns *ch* if OK, else EOF.
fputs	int	char* str FILE* stream	stdio.h	Outputs *str* to *stream*.. NULL not written to file. Returns non-zero if OK, else EOF.
fgetc	int	FILE* stream	stdio.h	Returns the next character from *stream* if OK , else EOF.
fgets	char*	char* buff int maxch FILE* stream	stdio.h	Reads next max*ch*-1 characters from *stream* into *buff.* Reads less if NEWLINE encountered. NULL added to *buff.* Returns a pointer to *buff.*
fprintf	int	FILE* stream char* format args	stdio.h	Outputs a set of values given in *args* to *stream* using the format given in format. Returns number of bytes output if OK, else EOF. Format specifiers have the format. %[flags][width][precision]type ***type:*** This is the minimum option required by a format specifier. The following options are available: **type char** / **arg type** / **Output Format** d Integer signed decimal int i Integer signed decimal int o Integer Unsigned octal int u Integer Unsigned dec int x Integer Unsigned hex int (uses a,b,c,d,e,f) X Integer Unsigned hex int (uses A,B,C,D,E,F) f Real Signed fixed-point e Real Signed scientific (uses e) E Real Signed scientific (uses E) c Character Character s String String ***flags:*** Controls output justification, signs, decimal places, hexadecimal and octal prefixes flag Effect - Left-justify output within field. Defaults to right-justified. + Adds + to positive numeric values; - to negative numeric values. space Adds a space to positive numeric values; - to negative ones. # arg converted to an "alternative form". This symbol is used in conjunction with the type character described above: **Effect of # on** / **Effect** 0 Zero prefixed to non-zero values x 0x prefixed to value X 0X prefixed to value e,E,f Decimal point included in output even when no digits follow (normally, there would be no decimal point).
fscanf	int	FILE* stream char *format args	stdio.h	Reads values from stream and places those values in the addresses given by *args*. The characters read from stream are interpreted using the information in format.

Function Name	Return Type	Input Type	Header	Description
Binary Files				
fwrite	size_t	void *ptr size_t bksz size_t n FILE *stream	stdio.h	Writes *n* blocks of *bksz* characters held at ptr to *stream* Returns the number of blocks transferred to *stream.*
fread	size_t	void *ptr size_t bksz size_t n FILE *stream	stdio.h	Reads *n* blocks of *bksz* bytes from *stream* and places the data at *ptr.*
fseek	int	FILE *stream long offset int post	stdio.h	Moves the *stream*'s file pointer *offset* bytes from position *post.*
ftell	long	FILE *stream	stdio.h	Returns the value of the file pointer for *stream* as the number of bytes from the start of the file. Returns zero if at the start of the file; returns -1 if the routine fails.
system	int	char *command	stdlib.h	Executes a DOS command, batch file or .EXE or .COM file as specified in *command.*

CASE STUDY

The Problem

When we need to examine the contents of a text file it's easy enough to load it into a text editor. Looking at a binary file is a different problem since all its numeric values will appear as random ASCII characters when displayed in an editor.

Normally, we need to write specific programs to display the contents of binary files, with a different program for each record format. However, a more useful program would allow us to enter the format of the record and use this to interpret and display the contents of the file.

Clarification

We require a program which will display the contents of any binary file by allowing us to specify that file's record structure which is then used when displaying the contents of the file.

We will assume a maximum record size of 80 characters and no more than 20 fields in each record.

The Algorithm

Although the implementation of this program uses some unusual code, the logic behind it is quite simple and is given in the algorithm below:

```
Set up a general record variable
Get the filename
Display possible field types
Get type of first field
WHILE not end of fields DO
    IF field is a string THEN
        Get length of string
    ENDIF
    Record field's type and size
    Get type of next field
ENDWHILE
Calculate size of record in bytes
FOR each field in record DO
    Set pointer to start of field position in general record
ENDFOR
Open file for reading
Read data into record variable
WHILE not EOF DO
    FOR each field pointer DO
        Cast pointer to field type
        Display contents of field
    ENDFOR
    Read data into record variable
ENDWHILE
Close files
```

The program is given in LISTING-6.18

LISTING-6.18

Generic Binary File Reader

```
#include<iostream.h>
#include<stdio.h>
#include<conio.h>
#include<string.h>
#include<stdlib.h>

//*** Function prototypes ***
int DisplayMenu(char*);
int GetOption(int);

void main()
{
   int typesize[4]={1,2,1,4}; //Size of string/int/char/float
   char filename[20];          //Name of file to be read
   char record[80];            //Storage space for one record
   int fieldinfo[10][2];       //Type and size of up to 10 fields
   void *fieldptr[10];         //Pointers to the starting location
                               //of each field
   int size;                   //Actual size of a single record
   FILE * stream;              //Stream pointer

   //*** Get the filename ***
   clrscr();
   cout<<"Enter the name of the file to be opened : ";
   gets(filename);
   //*** Display possible field types ***
   int noofops = DisplayMenu("1  - String\n2  - int\n3  - char\n4
- float\n5  - QUIT\n");
   //*** Get user's choice ***
   int option= GetOption(noofops);
   //*** WHILE not end of fields DO ***
   for(int fields = 0; option!=noofops;fields++)
   {
       //*** Record field type and size ***
       fieldinfo[fields][0]=option;
       fieldinfo[fields][1]=typesize[option-1];
       //*** IF its a string THEN ***
       if(option==1)
       {
           //*** Get its length ***
           cout<<"Enter length of string field : ";
           cin>>size;
           fieldinfo[fields][1]=size;
       }
       //*** Get next field type ***
       option= GetOption(noofops);
   }
   //*** Calculate record size ***
   int recsize=0;
   for(int c = 0 ;c<fields;c++)
       recsize+=fieldinfo[c][1];
   cout<<"Record size = "<<recsize<<endl;
   //*** Set pointers for each field ***
   int offset=0;
   for(c=0;c<fields;c++)
   {
       fieldptr[c] = &record[offset];
       offset+=fieldinfo[c][1];
   };
   //*** Open file ***
   if((stream=fopen(filename,"rb"))==NULL)
   {
       cout<<"File not found\n";
       exit(1);
   }
```

Continued on next page

LISTING-6.18
(continued)

Generic Binary File

```
    //*** Read a record ***
    while(fread(record,recsize,1,stream)==1)
    {
        //*** Interpret and display record's data ***
        for(c=0;c<fields;c++)
        {
            switch(fieldinfo[c][0])
            {
                case 1:  //*** Display string ***
                    cout<<(char*)fieldptr[c]<<' ';
                    break;
                case 2:  //*** Display int ***
                    cout<<*(int*)fieldptr[c]<<' ';
                    break;
                case 3:  //*** Display char ***
                    cout<<*(char*)fieldptr[c]<<' ';
                    break;
                case 4:  //*** Display float ***
                    cout<<*(float*)fieldptr[c]<<' ';
                    break;
            }
        }
        cout<<endl;
    }
    //*** Close file ***
    fclose(filename);
}


int DisplayMenu(char * m)
{
    cout<<m;
    int count=0;
    for(int c=0;c<=strlen(m);c++)
        if(m[c]=='\n')
            count++;
    return count;
}

int GetOption(int max)
{
    char opstr[3];

    cout<<"Enter option : ";
    gets(opstr);
    int op=atoi(opstr);
    while(op<1||op>max)
    {
        cout<<"\a?:";
        gets(opstr);
        op=atoi(opstr);
    }
    return op;
}
```

INVESTIGATION

1. What happens if we attempt to read from the A: drive and there is no disk in the drive?

2. What happens when a program attempts to write to a floppy disk which is write protected?

3. What happens when an attempt is made to read past the end of a file's data area?

4. How does a program react when a formatted read statement does not match the structure of the data in the file being read?

5. Can data written to a file using `fputs()` and `fputch()` be read using `fscanf()`?

6. What are the consequences of opening a file in "r+t" mode when the file name specified is "con"?

SELF-ASSESSMENT

1. What is a stream?

2. How is a stream linked to a file?

3. List the differences between text and binary file formats.

4. If an `int` variable holds the value 1234, how many bytes will this value occupy in
    a) A binary file?
    b) A text file?

5. If a file is opened in “r+b” mode, what does this signify?

6. Why may the length of a file, as given in a DIR listing, differ from the count of characters read from the same file when opened in “rt” mode?

7. What is the problem with using `fscanf()` to read a string value from a text file?

8. Why can random access not normally be used when dealing with text files?

9. a) What is the intended purpose of the following statement:

    ```
    fseek(myfile,-sizeof(myrec),1);
    ```

    b) In what way must the statement be modified in order to function correctly?

Solutions

PROGRAMMING EXERCISE 6.3

```
#include<iostream.h>
#include<conio.h>
#include<stdio.h>
#include<stdlib.h>

struct StudentDetails
{
    int idcode;
    char name[30];
    char sex;
    int score[6];
};

void main()
{
    FILE *stfile;   //Student file
    char temp[10]; //stores any number as a string
    StudentDetails sd;  //Student's details

    //*** Get the student's details ***
    clrscr();
    cout<<"Enter student's id   : ";
    cin>>sd.idcode;
    cout<<"Enter student's name : ";
    gets(sd.name);
    cout<<"Enter student's sex  : ";
    cin>>sd.sex;
    for(int c=0;c<6;c++)
    {
        cout<< "Enter score "<<(c+1)<<"  : ";
        cin>>sd.score[c];
    }
    //*** Write details to file ***
    //** Open file **
    stfile = fopen("C:\\STUDENT.DAT","wt");
    //** Change id to string **
    itoa(sd.idcode,temp,10);
    //** Write id to file **
    fputs(temp,stfile);
    fputc('\n',stfile);
    //**Write name **
    fputs(sd.name,stfile);
    fputc('\n',stfile);
    //**Write sex **
    fputc(sd.sex,stfile);
    fputc('\n',stfile);
    //**Write scores **
    for(c=0;c<6;c++)
    {
        //* Convert score to string *
        itoa(sd.score[c],temp,10);
        //* Write score *
        fputs(temp,stfile);
        fputc('\n',stfile);
    }
    //*** Close file ***
    fclose(stfile);
}
```

PROGRAMMING EXERCISE 6.4

1.

```
#include<iostream.h>
#include<conio.h>
#include<stdio.h>
#include<stdlib.h>

void main()
{
    FILE *stfile;   //Student file
    char ch;        //Holds byte read from file

    //** Open file **
    if((stfile = fopen("C:\\STUDENT.DAT","rt"))
                    ==NULL)
    {
        cout<<"Error opening file\n";
        exit(1);
    }
    //*** Read & display char until EOF ***
    while((ch=fgetc(stfile))!=EOF)
        cout<<ch;
    //*** Close the file ***
    fclose(stfile);
}
```

2.

```
#include<iostream.h>
#include<conio.h>
#include<stdio.h>
#include<stdlib.h>

void main()
{
    FILE *stfile;   //Student file
    char ch;        //Holds byte read from file

    //** Open file **
    if((stfile = fopen("C:\\STUDENT.DAT","rt"))
                    ==NULL)
    {
        cout<<"Error opening file\n";
        exit(1);
    }
    //*** Read & display a char until EOF ***
    while((temp=fgetc(stfile))!=EOF)
        cout<<hex<<int(ch)<<' ';
    //*** Close the file ***
    fclose(stfile);
}
```

3.

```
#include<iostream.h>
#include<conio.h>
#include<stdio.h>
#include<stdlib.h>

void main()
{
    FILE *stfile;   //Student file
    char ch;        //Holds byte read from file
    int count=0;    //Holds the file byte count

    //** Open file **
    if((stfile = fopen("C:\\STUDENT.DAT","rt"))
                    ==NULL)
    {
        cout<<"Error opening file\n";
        exit(1);
    }
    //*** Read & display a char until EOF ***
    while((ch=fgetc(stfile))!=EOF)
    {
        count++;
        cout<<hex<<int(ch)<<' ';
    }
    //*** Close the file ***
    fclose(stfile);
    //*** Display count ***
    cout<<"\n\nThe file contains "<<count
        <<" characters\n";
    getch();
}
```

PROGRAMMING EXERCISE 6.6

```
#include<iostream.h>
#include<conio.h>
#include<stdio.h>
#include<stdlib.h>

void main()
{
    FILE *stfile;   //Student file
    char temp[30];  //Holds string read from file

    //** Open file **
    if((stfile = fopen("C:\\STUDENT.DAT","rt"))
                    ==NULL)
    {
        cout<<"Error opening file\n";
        exit(1);
    }
    //*** Read & display the contents of file ***
    while((fgets(temp,200,stfile))!=NULL)
        cout<<temp;
    //*** Close the file ***
    fclose(stfile);
    getch();
}
```

TASK 6.1

The NEWLINE character at the end of the string can be removed by changing it to a NULL character with the statement

```
string[strlen(string)]='\0';
```

PROGRAMMING EXERCISE 6.7

```
#include<iostream.h>
#include<conio.h>
#include<stdio.h>
#include<stdlib.h>

struct StudentDetails
{
    int idcode;
    char name[30];
    char sex;
    int score[6];
};

void main()
{
    FILE *stfile;   //Student file
    char temp[10]; //stores number as a string
    StudentDetails sd;  //Student's details

    //*** Get the student's details ***
    clrscr();
    cout<<"Enter student's id   : ";
    cin>>sd.idcode;
    cout<<"Enter student's name : ";
    gets(sd.name);
    cout<<"Enter student's sex  : ";
    cin>>sd.sex;
    for(int c=0;c<6;c++)
    {
        cout<< "Enter score "<<(c+1)<<"  : ";
        cin>>sd.score[c];
    }
    //*** Write details to file ***
    //** Open file **
    stfile = fopen("C:\\STUDENT.DAT","at");
    //** Change id to string **
    itoa(sd.idcode,temp,10);
    //** Write id to file **
    fputs(temp,stfile);
    fputc('\n',stfile);
    //**Write name **
    fputs(sd.name,stfile);
    fputc('\n',stfile);
    //**Write sex **
    fputc(sd.sex,stfile);
    fputc('\n',stfile);
    //**Write scores **
    for(c=0;c<6;c++)
    {
        //* Convert score to string *
        itoa(sd.score[c],temp,10);
        //* Write score *
        fputs(temp,stfile);
        fputc('\n',stfile);
    }
    //*** Close file ***
    fclose(stfile);
}
```

PROGRAMMING EXERCISE 6.9

```
#include<iostream.h>
#include<conio.h>
#include<stdio.h>
#include<stdlib.h>

struct StudentDetails
{
    int idcode;
    char name[30];
    char sex;
    int score[6];
};

void ReadDetails(StudentDetails&);

void main()
{
    FILE *stfile;   //Student file
    StudentDetails sd;  //Student's details

    //*** Open the file ***
    if(!(stfile = fopen("C:\\STUDENT.DAT","rb")))
    {
        cout<<"Error opening file\n";
        exit(1);
    }
    //*** Get students' details from file***
    clrscr();
    //*** WHILE read does not detect EOF DO ***
    while(fread(&sd,sizeof(sd),1,stfile)==1)
    {
        //*** Display record ***
        cout<<sd.idcode<<' '<<sd.name<<' '<<sd.sex
            <<' ';
        for(int c=0;c<6;c++)
            cout<<sd.score[c]<<' ';
        cout<<endl;
    }
    //*** Close file ***
    fclose(stfile);
    getch();
}

//*** Get the student's details ***
void ReadDetails(StudentDetails& sd)
{
    cout<<"Enter student's id   : ";
    cin>>sd.idcode;
    if(sd.idcode==-1)
        return;
    cout<<"Enter student's name : ";
    gets(sd.name);
    cout<<"Enter student's sex  : ";
    cin>>sd.sex;
    for(int c=0;c<6;c++)
    {
        cout<< "Enter score "<<(c+1)<<"  : ";
        cin>>sd.score[c];
    }
}
```

PROGRAMMING EXERCISE 6.10

```
#include<iostream.h>
#include<conio.h>
#include<stdio.h>
#include<stdlib.h>
#include<string.h>
#include<ctype.h>

//*** Record structure declaration ***
struct StudentDetails
{
    int idcode;
    char name[30];
    char sex;
    int score[6];
};
//*** Named constants ***
const int QUIT=5;

//*** Function prototypes ***
void ReadDetails(StudentDetails&);
int DisplayMenu(char*);
int GetOption(int);
void GetData(char*, int, char*);
void ExpandString(char*);
void ExecuteOption(int, FILE*);
void ChangeField(FILE*,int,int,char*);
void DisplayRec(FILE*,int);
long RecsInFile(FILE*);

void main()
{
    FILE *stfile;   //Student file

    //*** Open the file ***
    if(!(stfile = fopen("C:\\STUDENT.DAT","r+b")))
    {
        cout<<"Error opening file\n";
        exit(1);
    }
    int option;
    //*** Display menu, execute option ***
    do
    {
        clrscr();
        int noofops=DisplayMenu("1 - Add a record\n"
        "2 - Modify a record\n3 - Display a record\n"
        "4 - Display the file\n5 - QUIT\n");
        option = GetOption(noofops);
        ExecuteOption(option,stfile);
    }
    while(option!=QUIT);
```

Continued on next page

```
    //*** Close file ***
    fclose(stfile);
    getch();
}

//*** Get the student's details ***
void ReadDetails(StudentDetails& sd)
{
    char temp[40];

    //*** Get id ***
    cout<<"Enter student's id   : ";
    GetData("0..9",4,temp);
    sd.idcode=atoi(temp);
    if(sd.idcode==-1)
        return;
    //*** Get name ***
    cout<<"Enter student's name : ";
    GetData("A..Za..z -'.",29,sd.name);
    //*** Get sex ***
    cout<<"Enter student's sex  : ";
    GetData("MFmf",1,temp);
    sd.sex=toupper(temp[0]);
    //*** Get scores ***
    for(int c=0;c<6;c++)
    {
        cout<< "Enter score "<<(c+1)<<"  : ";
        GetData("0..9",3,temp);
        sd.score[c]=atoi(temp);
    }
}

//*** Display and count menu options ***
int DisplayMenu(char * m)
{
    cout<<m;
    int count=0;
    for(int c=0;c<=strlen(m);c++)
        if(m[c]=='\n')
            count++;
    return count;
}

//*** Get user menu option ***
int GetOption(int max)
{
    char opstr[3];
    cout<<"Enter option : ";
    gets(opstr);
    int op=atoi(opstr);
    while(op<1||op>max)
    {
        cout<<"\a?:";
        gets(opstr);
        op=atoi(opstr);
    }
    return op;
}

//*** Get Data value from keyboard ***
void GetData(char* allowed, int max, char*
result)
{
    const int ENTER=13;
    const int BACKSPACE = 8;

    char ch;          // char read from keyboard
    int count=0;      // how many valid chars entered
    char expandedset[256]; // full set of
                           //allowable characters

    //*** Expand set of allowed characters ***
    strcpy(expandedset,allowed);
    ExpandString(expandedset);
    //*** Start with empty result ***
    strcpy(result,"");
    //*** Read a character ***
    ch=getch();
    //*** WHILE return key not pressed DO ***
    while(ch!=ENTER)
    {
        //*** If allowed char & result not full ***
        if(strchr(expandedset,ch)&&count<max)
        {
            //**Display char and add to result ***
            cout<<ch;
            count++;
            result[count-1]=ch;
            result[count]=0;
        }
        //*** ELSE if delete & result not empty ***
        else if(ch==BACKSPACE&&count>0)
        {
            //** Remove last char from screen & result **
            cout<<"\b \b";
            count--;
            result[count]=0;
        }
        //*** Read another character ***
        ch=getch();
    }
    cout<<endl;
}

//*** Expand compressed string ***
void ExpandString(char* s)
{
    char temp[256]="";  //Empty temporary storage

    //***Copy the first character accross ***
    temp[0]=s[0];
    //*** For all but last two chars DO ***
    for(int c=1,p=1;c<=int(strlen(s))-3;c++)
    {
        //**If two periods ***
        if(s[c]=='.'&&s[c+1]=='.')
        {
            //* Insert range of character assumed *
            for(char ch=s[c-1]+1;ch<=s[c+2];ch++)
                temp[p++]= ch;
            //* Move past this part of the text *
            c+=2;
        }
        else
            //**If not two periods, copy char ***
            temp[p++]=s[c];
    }
    //***Copy any remaining characters ***
    for(int k=c;k<=strlen(s)-1;k++,c++)
        temp[p++]=s[c];
    //*** Insert final NULL character ***
    temp[p]='\0';
    strcpy(s,temp);
}

//*** Execute user option ***
void ExecuteOption(int opt, FILE *stfile)
{
    const int
fieldsizes[8]={29,1,3,3,3,3,3,3};//Size of
fields in record
    char fieldchars[8][13]={"A..Za..z .-",
    "MFmf","0..9","0..9","0..9",
    "0..9","0..9","0..9"};
              //Character sets for fields
    StudentDetails sd;  //student record
    int nooffields;     //No. of ops in sub-menu
    int key;            //Record position
    int c;              //Loop counter
    long noofrecs;      //No. of recs in file
    int fieldchanged;   //No. of field to change
    char newvalue[30];  //New value for field
    char temp[30];      //User input - temp storage

    switch(opt)
    {
        case 1: //*** New record ***
            //*** Get record data ***
            ReadDetails(sd);
            //*** Move to end of file ***
            fseek(stfile,0,2);
            //*** Write new rec to file ***
            fwrite(&sd,sizeof(sd),1,stfile);
            break;
        case 2: //*** Modify a record ***
            //*** Display no. of recs in file ***
            clrscr();
            noofrecs=RecsInFile(stfile);
            cout<<"The file contains "<<noofrecs
                <<" records\n";
            //*** Get post of rec to be changed ***
            cout<<"Enter position of record"
                  " to be modified : ";
            GetData("0..9",4,temp);
            key = atoi(temp);
            //*** IF position valid THEN ***
            if(key>=1&&key<=noofrecs)
            {
                //*** Get field to be changed ***
                nooffields = DisplayMenu(
                "1 - Name\n2 - sex\n3 - Score 1\n"
                "4 - Score 2\n5 - Score 3\n"
                "6 - Score 4\n7 - Score 5\n"
                "8 - Score 6\n9 - Return to main"
                "menu\n");
                fieldchanged=GetOption(nooffields);
                //*** IF valid field THEN ***
                if (fieldchanged != 9)
                {
                    //*** Enter new value ***
                    cout<<"Enter new value : ";
                    GetData(fieldchars[fieldchanged-1],
                    fieldsizes[fieldchanged-1],newvalue);
                    //*** Change record's field ***
                    ChangeField(stfile,key,fieldchanged,
                    newvalue);
```

```
            }
        }
        break;
    case 3: //*** Display specific record ***
        //*** Display no. of recs in file ***
        noofrecs = RecsInFile(stfile);
        cout<<"The file contains "
            <<noofrecs<<" records\n";
        //*** Get post of rec to display ***
        cout<<"Enter position of record"
                " to be displayed : ";
        GetData("0..9",4,temp);
        key = atoi(temp);
        //*** IF valid position THEN ***
        if(key>=1&&key<=noofrecs)
        {
            //*** Display record ***
            DisplayRec(stfile,key);
            getch();
        }
        break;
    case 4:     //*** Display whole file ***
        //*** Go to start of file ***
        fseek(stfile,0,2);
        //*** Determine no. of recs in file ***
        noofrecs = ftell(stfile)/sizeof(sd);
        //*** Display each rec ***
        for(c=1;c<=noofrecs;c++)
            DisplayRec(stfile,c);
        getch();
        break;
    case 5: //*** Terminate program ***
        cout<<"PROGRAM TERMINATED\n";
        break;
    }
}

//*** Change contents of a record's field ***
void ChangeField(FILE *stfile,int key,
                        int field, char *nv)
{
    StudentDetails sd;

    //*** Read record from file ***
    fseek(stfile,(key-1)*sizeof(sd),0);
    fread(&sd,sizeof(sd),1,stfile);
    //*** Modify field ***
    switch(field)
    {
        case 1: //*** Modify name ***
            strcpy(sd.name,nv);
            break;
        case 2:     //*** Modify sex ***
            sd.sex=nv[0];
            break;
        default: //*** Modify score ***
            sd.score[field-3]=atoi(nv);
    }
    //*** Rewrite record ***
    fseek(stfile,-long(sizeof(sd)),1);
    fwrite(&sd,sizeof(sd),1,stfile);
};

//*** Display a record ***
void DisplayRec(FILE *stfile, int key)
{
    StudentDetails sd;

    //*** read record from file ***
    fseek(stfile,(key-1)*sizeof(sd),0);
    fread(&sd,sizeof(sd),1,stfile);
    //*** Display record ***
    cout<<sd.id<<' '<<sd.name<<' '<<sd.sex<<' ';
    for(int c=0;c<6;c++)
        cout<<sd.score[c]<<' ';
    cout<<endl;
}

//*** Calculate no. of recs in file ***
long RecsInFile(FILE* st)
{
    long current;
    long ans;

    //*** Save current file pointer position ***
    current = ftell(st);
    //*** Move to end of file ***
    fseek(st,0,2);
    //*** Calculate no. of recs ***
    ans=ftell(st)/sizeof(StudentDetails);
    //*** Reset file pointer to original position ***
    fseek(st,current,0);
    return ans;
}
```

PROGRAMMING EXERCISE 6.11

```
#include<conio.h>
#include<iostream.h>
#include<stdio.h>
#include<stdlib.h>

struct StudentDetails
{
    int id;
    char name[30];
    char sex;
    int score[6];
};
void main()
{
    FILE *infile, *outfile;
    StudentDetails sd;
    //*** Open files ***
    if((infile=fopen("C:\\STUDENT.DAT","rb"))
                ==NULL)
    {
        cout<<"File not found\n";
        getch();
        exit(1);
    }
    outfile=fopen("C:\\TEMP.DAT","wb");
    //*** Get id of record to be deleted ***
    int recid;
    cout<<"Enter id of record to be deleted : ";
    cin>>recid;
    //***Transfer all recs but one matching id ***
    while(fread(&sd,sizeof(sd),1,infile)==1)
    {
        //*** If not a match, copy to new file ***
        if(sd.id!=recid)
            fwrite(&sd,sizeof(sd),1,outfile);
    }
    //*** Close files ***
    fclose(infile);
    fclose(outfile);
    //*** Delete files ***
    system("DEL C:\\STUDENT.DAT");
    //*** Rename new file ***
    system("REN C:\\TEMP.DAT STUDENT.DAT");
}
```

PROGRAMMING EXERCISE 6.12

```
#include<conio.h>
#include<iostream.h>
#include<stdio.h>
#include<string.h>
#include<stdlib.h>

struct StudentDetails
{
    int id;
    char name[30];
    char sex;
    int score[6];
};

void main()
{
    const int DELETED = -1;
    const int QUIT = -1;
    FILE *stfile;
    StudentDetails sd;

    //*** Open files ***
    if((stfile=fopen("C:\\STUDENT.DAT","r+b"))==NULL)
    {
        cout<<"Error opening file\n";
        exit(1);
    }
    //*** Get post of rec to be deleted ***
    cout<<"Enter position of record to be deleted"
          " (-1 to stop): ";
    int post;
    cin>>post;
    //*** WHILE not -1 DO ***
    while(post!=QUIT)
    {
        //*** Find required record ***
        fseek(stfile,(post-1)*sizeof(sd),SEEK_SET);
        //*** IF found THEN ***
        if(fread(&sd,sizeof(sd),1,stfile)==1)
        {
            //*** Mark for deletion ***
            sd.id =DELETED;
            //*** Rewrite to file ***
            fseek(stfile,(post-1)*sizeof(sd)
                                ,SEEK_SET);
            fwrite(&sd,sizeof(sd),1,stfile);
```

```
        }
        else
        //*** ELSE display error message ***
        {
            cout<<"Record not found\n";
            getch();
        }
        //*** Get position of next record ***
        cout<<"Enter record position : ";
        cin>>post;
    }
    //*** Close files ***
    fclose(stfile);
}
```

PROGRAMMING EXERCISE 6.13

```
#include<conio.h>
#include<iostream.h>
#include<stdio.h>
#include<string.h>
#include<stdlib.h>

struct StudentDetails
{
    int id;
    char name[30];
    char sex;
    int score[6];
};

void main()
{
    FILE *sourcefile, *destfile;
    StudentDetails sd;

    //*** Open files ***
    if((sourcefile=fopen("C:\\STUDENT.DAT","rb"))==NULL)
    {
        cout<<"Error opening source file\n";
        exit(1);
    }
    if((destfile=fopen("C:\\TEMP.DAT","wb"))==NULL)
    {
        cout<<"Error opening destination file\n";
        exit(1);
    }
    //*** WHILE not end of source file DO ***
    while(fread(&sd,sizeof(sd),1,sourcefile)==1)
        //*** IF not deleted rec THEN ***
        if(sd.id!=-1)
            //*** Copy to new file ***
            fwrite(&sd,sizeof(sd),1,destfile);
    //*** Close files ***
    fclose(sourcefile);
    fclose(destfile);
    //*** Delete original file ***
    system("DEL C:\\STUDENT.DAT");
    //*** Rename new file ***
    system("REN C:\\TEMP.DAT STUDENT.DAT");
}
```

Chapter 7
Tables

This chapter covers the following topics:

- Abstract Data Types
- Bubble Sort
- Comparing Search Efficiency
- Comparing Sort Efficiency
- Direct Access Tables
- Hash Tables
- Insertion Sorts
- Linear Searching Techniques
- Non-Linear Searching Techniques
- Selection Sorts
- Simple Tables
- Table Efficiency

ABSTRACT DATA TYPES

Introduction

Concrete Data Types

This range of values assumes a 16 bit int.

Most languages have built-in data types. For example, C++ has `int`, `float` and `char` types. The data type of a variable determines what type and range of values may be held in that variable. Hence, we know that in Borland C++ V 4.5 an `int` variable may hold any value between -32,768 and +32,767. In addition, a variable's type also determines what operations can be performed on the variable. In the case of `int` variables, we can perform operations such as addition, subtraction, multiplication, and integer division as well as comparisons using <, >, ==, etc.

From this informal description we can produce a definition for data types:

A data type defines not only the type and range of values which may be held in a variable of that type, but also the set of operations which may be performed on it.

The data types available within a programming language are known as **concrete data types**.

Abstract Data Types

During the design of most software systems the need for new data types, which are not part of the final programming language, will be highlighted. For example, we might identify the need to record imperial weights in pounds and ounces. Such weights will have to be assigned a value, converted to kilogrammes, or the component parts of the weight *(pounds* and *ounces*) accessed.

One way to handle these requirements is to define a new data type containing *pounds* and *ounces* data components with *setWeight, ConvertToKilos, getPounds* and *getOunces* operations.

A vital part of the specifications of such a data structure is that no details of how the structure is to be implemented must be given. This abstraction ensures that the description can remain a simple one and also allows the programmer, who will later implement the new data type, complete freedom in the method chosen when coding the design requirements. Data structures defined in this way are known as **abstract data structures**.

Designing Abstract Data Types

In the initial stages of the design, we will want to describe the data components and operations of our new data type. The purpose of an abstract data type is to describe the data type without specifying any details of how the data components and operations should be implemented in the target programming language.

The general format for describing an abstract data type is:

```
ADT new_data_type_name IS
    DATA
        description of the data components
    OPERATIONS
        description of each operation
END ADT
```

Data

This area contains a description of the data values held and, where necessary, the range of value which may be assigned.

Operations

Each operation is described separately in mini-spec format containing the headings

```
NAME
PARAMETERS
    IN
    OUT
    IN/OUT
PRE-CONDITION
POST-CONDITION
```

The POST-CONDITION describes the state of the data type after the operation is complete. We might think of this as a description of what happens when the operation is performed.

A Weight ADT

Let's assume a software system under design identifies the need to record imperial weights given in pounds and ounces. Four operations on this data are also required. These operations will allow a value to be assigned to the weight, convert the weight to kilograms, return the pounds part of the weight, and return the ounces part of the weight.

From this informal description we can now write the specification for a *Weight* abstract data type:

```
ADT Weight IS
    DATA
        A weight is stored in terms of pounds and ounces, where pounds can
        be any non-negative integer value and ounces has an integer value
        between 0 and 15 inclusive.
    OPERATIONS
        NAME                :   SetWeight
        PARAMETERS
            IN              :   lbs : integer
                                oz : integer
            OUT             :   w : Weight
            IN/OUT          :   None
        PRE-CONDITION       :   lbs >= 0 AND  0 <= oz <= 15
        POST-CONDITION      :   w is set to lbs pounds, oz ounces

        NAME                :   ConvertToMetric
        PARAMETERS
            IN              :   w : Weight
            OUT             :   result : real
            IN/OUT          :   None
        PRE-CONDITION       :   None
        POST-CONDITION      :   result is assign the kilogramme equivalent of
                                imperial weight w
```

```
NAME                :   GetPounds
PARAMETERS
    IN              :   w : Weight
    OUT             :   result : integer
    IN/OUT          :   None
PRE-CONDITION       :   None
POST-CONDITION      :   result = w.pounds

NAME                :   GetOunces
PARAMETERS
    IN              :   w : Weight
    OUT             :   result : integer
    IN/OUT          :   None
PRE-CONDITION       :   None
POST-CONDITION      :   result = w.ounces

END ADT
```

Once such a data structure has been implemented in code, an application programmer could then declare variables of this type

```
Weight w1;
```

and make use of the associated operations:

```
SetWeight(12,10,w1)        //Sets w1 to 12 pounds 10 ounces
cout << ConvertToKilos(w1) // Displays the kilogramme equivalent
                           // of 12lbs 10 oz
cout << GetPounds(w1) << lbs "<< GetOunces(w1) << "oz\n");
                           //Displays 12lbs 10oz
```

TASK 7.1

Write an ADT definition for a *Distance* type which can record distances in yards, feet and inches (12 inches = 1 foot; 3 feet = 1 yard).
The operations required are:

SetDistance	-	which takes three integer values and assigns these to the yards, feet and inches of the distance.
ConvertToMetric	-	which converts the distance to metres.
GetYards	-	which returns the yards component of the distance.
GetFeet	-	which returns the feet component of the distance.
GetInches	-	which returns the inches component of the distance.

Implementation

Implementing Weight

When the designer has completed his work, the description of the new *Weight* data type will be passed to the programmer who has the task of implementing the type in a programming language.

The programmer should have complete freedom in the method of implementation chosen. He is likely to try and find an approach which will result in the shortest, clearest and fastest code with the minimum of storage space requirements. Usually, however, not all of these goals are attainable.

First we begin by defining the data components. These might reflect exactly the structure suggested by the design:

```
struct Weight
{
    int pounds;
    int ounces;
};
```

Next, the operations must be coded. Again, the programmer has complete freedom but must ensure that the name and parameters of the operations match those given in the abstract design.

Often this will be done by first adding Outline Logic to the mini-spec. So for example, the expanded mini-spec for *SetWeight* might be:

NAME	:	SetWeight
PARAMETERS		
IN	:	lbs : integer
		oz : integer
OUT	:	w : Weight
IN/OUT		: None
PRE-CONDITION	:	*lbs* >= 0 AND 0 <= *oz* <= 15
POST-CONDITION	:	*w* is set to *lbs* pounds, *oz* ounces
OUTLINE LOGIC	:	*w.pounds = lbs*
		w.ounces = oz

The next step is to implement each routine in the target programming language (in this case, C++).

The function name and parameters must match those given in the mini-spec, so the first line of code for the *SetWeight()* function would be:

```
void SetWeight (int lbs, int oz, Weight& w)
```

Since only a single value is returned by the function, the program might instead write the first line as:

```
Weight SetWeight (int lbs, int oz)
```

Next, any pre-condition defined for the routine should be checked:

```
void SetWeight (int lbs, int oz, Weight& w)
{
    if (lbs <0 || oz <0 || oz > 15)
        return;
```

Notice, since the `if` statement is written in such a way as to terminate the operation when the pre-condition is not met, the actual conditions checked are exactly the opposite of those given in the mini-spec.

Finally, the code necessary to meet the post-condition can be added:

```
void SetWeight ( int lbs, int oz, Weight& w)
{
    if (lbs <0 || oz <0 || oz > 15)
        return;
    w.pounds = lbs;
    w.ounces = oz;
}
```

Coding and testing of each operation continues until the complete data type has been implemented. Each routine should, where possible, be tested separately using the strategies we developed in earlier chapters. Unfortunately, space restrictions make that impractical here. However, the complete code for the new data type and a `main()` test driver is given in LISTING-7.1.

LISTING-7.1

Implementing an Abstract Data Type

```
#include<iostream.h>

//***********************************
//*** Weight Data Type Declarations ***
//***********************************
//*** Data ***
struct Weight
{
  int pounds;
  int ounces;
};

//***Operations ***
void SetWeight(int lbs, int oz, Weight& w)
{
  if(lbs < 0 || oz < 0 || oz > 15)
      return;
  w.pounds = lbs;
  w.ounces = oz;
}

double ConvertToMetric(Weight w)
{
  return (w.pounds * 16 + w.ounces)*0.0283495;
}

int GetPounds(Weight w)
{
  return w.pounds;
}

int GetOunces(Weight w)
{
  return w.ounces;
}


//***********************************
//***    Test Driver for Weight    ***
//***********************************
void main()
{
  //*** Create the Weight Variable ***
  Weight w1;

  //*** Initialise to Zero ***
  SetWeight(0,0,w1);

  //*** Read values for weight ***
  cout<<"Enter pounds: ";
  int lbs;
  cin>>lbs;
  cout<<"Enter ounces: ";
  int oz;
  cin>>oz;

  //*** Assign value to weight variable ***
  SetWeight(lbs, oz , w1);
  //*** Display the weight in pounds and ounces ***
  cout << "The weight entered was " << GetPounds(w1) <<
  " lbs "<< GetOunces(w1)<<" oz"<<endl;
  //*** Display the weight in kilos ***
  cout << "This is " << ConvertToMetric(w1)<<" kilos"<<endl;
```

1 inch = 0.0254 metres

> **PROGRAMMING EXERCISE 7.1**
>
> Code and test the operations for *Distance* data type as defined in TASK 7.1.

An Alternative Implementation

Of course, the programmer is free to implement an Abstract Data Type in any way. For example, an alternative approach to coding *Weight* type might be to begin with the data component declaration:

```
struct Weight
{
    float value;
};
```

With this method, the ounces component of a weight would be stored as a fraction of a pound. Hence, 5 lbs 4 oz would be held in *value* as 5.25.

Obviously, this will have an effect on how the operations of the data structure are to be coded. Some will be easier to implement. For example, *SetWeight()* can now be written as

```
void SetWeight(int lbs, int oz, Weight& w)
{
    if (lbs <0 || oz <0 || oz > 15)
        return;
    w.value = lbs + oz/16.0;
}
```

while *getPounds()* becomes:

```
int GetPounds(Weight w)
{
    return (int)w.value;
}
```

However, irrespective of the implementation, the parameters of the operations must remain the same. This means that any application programmer who has been using the previous version of the *Weight* data type will continue to use variables of this type in exactly the same way as before.

sex should be assigned either M or F

score values should lie in the range 0 to 100.

> **TASK 7.2**
>
> Create an ADT for an abstract data type named *StudentDetails*. The data components of this type are: *idcode* (integer), *name, sex, score* (6 integers). The operations are:
>
> | | | |
> |---|---|---|
> | *SetId* | - | Assigns a value to the *idcode* field. |
> | *SetName* | - | Assigns a value to the *name* field. |
> | *SetSex* | - | Assigns a value to the *sex* field. |
> | *SetScore* | - | Assigns a value to a specified *score* element. |
> | *GetId* | - | Returns the value of the *idcode* field. |
> | *GetName* | - | Returns the value of the *name* field. |
> | *GetSex* | - | Returns the value of the *sex* field . |
> | *GetScore* | - | Returns the value of a specified *score* element. |

> **PROGRAMMING EXERCISE 7.2**
>
> Implement and test the *StudentDetails* data type.

Summary

- **A Data Type** is defined by the set of values it may be assigned and the operations which can be performed on those values.

- **Concrete Data Types** are those data types built-in to a language.

- **Abstract Data Types** (ADT) are user-designed types without any details of how they are to be implemented.

- **The definition of an abstract data type** is given in the form:

```
ADT type_name IS
    Data
        Description of the data components
    Operations
        Description of each operation
END ADT
```

- **Each operation is defined** using a mini-spec.

- **Abstract Data Types** are implemented using concrete data types.

- **The programmer is free to use any implementation method** but aims for efficiency.

- **Operation names and parameters** must not be changed during the implementation stage.

SIMPLE TABLES

Introduction

It is often necessary to maintain a list of data within the computer's main memory. The advantage of this approach over reading records one at a time from a disk file is simply that of speed: accessing information held in memory is many hundreds of times faster than trying to get at the same data held on disk. Of course, disk storage is still required for long-term storage and where there is too much data to be held within main memory.

Where a collection of data exists, it is likely that the value in one or more of the record fields will be unique. Such a field can be used as the record's key. For example, in our student records disk file (see previous chapter), the value of the *idcode* field was unique for each student.

This data list is often known as a **table**.

Designing a Table

Tables, like most data collections, require three basic operations:

Insertion of new entries
Deletion of existing entries
Modification of existing entries

With these come some requirements for additional functions such as

Creating an empty table
Finding a specific entry in the table
Displaying the contents of the table

Using a table of *StudentDetails* entries, we'll create a formal definition of an abstract data type:

```
ADT StudentTable IS
    Data
        A list of StudentDetails values. The idcode field of StudentDetails is
        to be used as the key field and must be unique to each entry.

    Operations
        NAME                :   CreateTable
        PARAMETERS
            IN              :   None
            OUT             :   t : StudentTable
            IN/OUT          :   None
        PRE-CONDITION       :   None
        POST-CONDITION      :   t is empty.

        NAME                :   Add
        PARAMETERS
            IN              :   st : StudentDetails
            OUT             :   None
            IN/OUT          :   t : StudentTable
```

PRE-CONDITION	:	*st.idcode* does not match any in *t* AND *t* is not full.
POST-CONDITION	:	*st* is added to *t*.
NAME	:	Delete
PARAMETERS		
IN	:	key : INTEGER
OUT	:	None
IN/OUT	:	t : StudentTable
PRE-CONDITION	:	*key* matches an *idcode* in *t*.
POST-CONDITION	:	The entry whose *idcode* is equal to *key* is removed from *t*.
NAME	:	Display
PARAMETERS		
IN	:	t : StudentTable
OUT	:	None
IN/OUT	:	None
PRE-CONDITION	:	None
POST-CONDITION	:	The contents of *t* is displayed on the screen.
NAME	:	GiveRecord
PARAMETERS		
IN	:	key : INTEGER t : StudentTable
OUT	:	st : StudentDetails
IN/OUT	:	None
PRE-CONDITION	:	*key* must match an idcode value in *t*.
POST-CONDITION	:	*st* contains a copy of the entry in *t* whose *idcode* field has the value *key*.
NAME	:	UpdateRecord
PARAMETERS		
IN	:	st : StudentDetails
OUT	:	None
IN/OUT	:	t : StudentTable
PRE-CONDITION	:	The *idcode* in *st* should match an existing entry in *t*.
POST-CONDITION	:	The record *st* replaces the entry with the same *idcode* in *t*.
NAME	:	IsFull
PARAMETERS		
IN	:	t : StudentTable
OUT	:	result : INTEGER
IN/OUT	:	None
PRE-CONDITION	:	None
POST-CONDITION	:	If *t* is full, *result* is set to 1. If *t* is not full, *result* is set to zero.

END ADT

Implementing a Table

Data Components

One of the simplest ways of implementing a table is to hold the data in an array of records. Hence, we could declare a table structure for our student details as:

```
const int SIZE=20;

struct StudentDetails
{
    int idcode;
    char name[31];
    char sex;
    int score[6];
};


struct StudentTable
{
    int count;
    StudentDetails list[SIZE];
};
```

The number of elements required in the array *(list)* would be determined by the analysis of the system which should reveal the maximum number of entries required.

We need to maintain a count of how many entries are held in *list* at any time and this is the purpose of the *count* field.

Operations

Creating An Empty Table

The CreateTable has an Outline Logic of a single line

```
Set t.count to zero
```

There is no need to empty the contents of the array.

The code for the function is

```
void CreateTable(StudentTable& t)
{
    t.count = 0;
}
```

The effect of the routine is shown graphically in FIG-7.1 (see overleaf).

Adding a New Entry to the Table

Before looking at the logic behind this operation, we can see the effect of adding two new entries to our table in FIG-7.2.

Note the two effects of each operation:

The new entry is added at the first empty position in the table.
The count field is incremented after each record is inserted.

FIG-7.1

An Empty StudentTable Variable

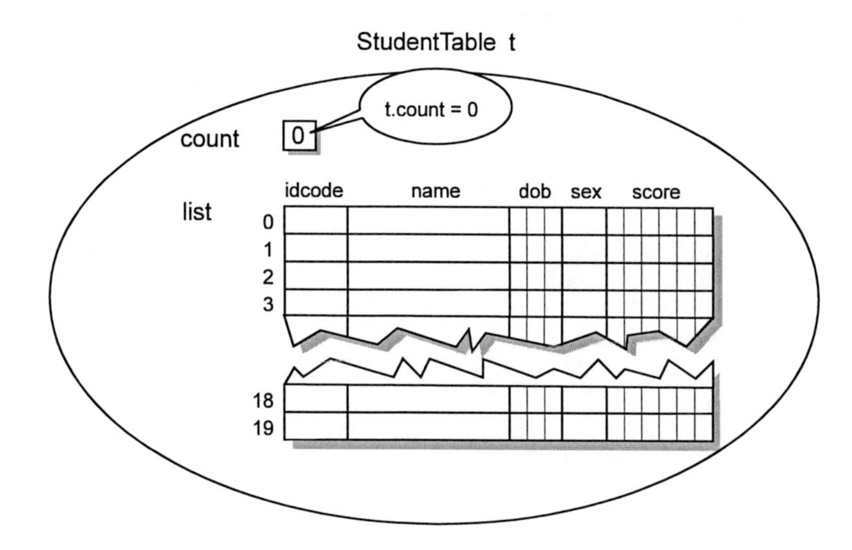

The lines of code necessary for each of the effects are:

```
t.list[t.count] = st;  //Places st in first empty position
t.count++;             //Adds 1 to t.count
```

FIG-7.2

Adding records to the Table

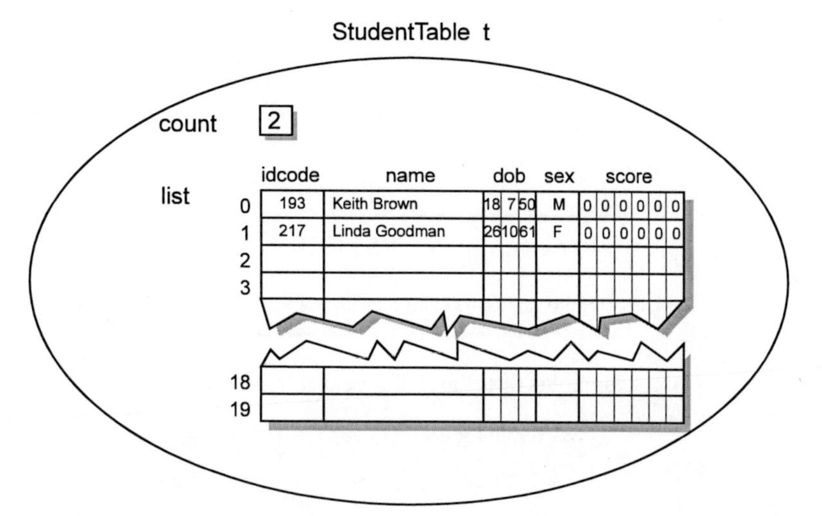

It's important that we don't try to insert a new record which contains the same *idcode* number as an existing record in the table so, when describing the *Add* operation, we need to include a pre-condition stating that a record with the same key must not already exist. Another condition we need to check for before attempting to insert a new record is that the table is not already full. Hence, before we can code the *Add()* routine, we'll need to produce the *IsFull()* function (as defined in the ADT). The coding for this simple routine is:

```
int IsFull(t:StudentTable)
{
    if(t.count==SIZE)
        return 1;
    else
        return 0;
}
```

It would also be useful to create an auxiliary function which detects if the new record's *idcode* matches an existing one. We'll call this new routine *IsAt* and design it to return the position in the table containing a match for a specified *idcode* value; if there is no match, it will return -1.

The description of the new function doesn't belong in the design of the ADT as it has only been created to aid the coding of other operations.

In order to determine if the key is already in the list we are going to have to search the list. Searching is such an important operation that we'll dedicate a section of this chapter to that task, but for the moment we'll use the simplest approach which can be described informally as:

```
Start at the beginning of the list
Compare the idcode value of each entry in the list until a match
is found or the last record in the list is reached.
IF a match was found THEN
    result is the position at which a match was found
ELSE
    result is -1
ENDIF
```

or more formally as

```
Set position to 0
WHILE t.list[position].idcode not equal req'd key
    AND position < count-1
DO
    Increment post
ENDWHILE
IF t.list[position].idcode=req'd key THEN
    result := position
ELSE
    result := -1
ENDIF
```

PROGRAMMING EXERCISE 7.3

Create an *IsAt()* function based on the description above.

Using this new function, we can return to the coding of the *Add()* function:

```
void Add(StudentDetails st, StudentTable& t)
{
    if(IsAt(st.idcode,t)==-1 || IsFull(t))
        return;
    t.list[t.count]=st;
    t.count++;
}
```

Any good application programmer using a *StudentTable* data structure in his program will write code in such a way as to check the success of the *Add()* function. After all, we can see from *Add()* that it will fail if the *idcode* field in the new record matches any already in the table.

The programmer using our *StudentTable* structure should write code such as:

```
if(IsAt(st.idcode,t)!=-1&&!IsFull(t))
    Add(st,t);
else
{
    cout<<"Key already exists.\nRecord not added\n"
        <<"Press any key to continue\n";
    getch();
}
```

But this is very inefficient code since *IsAt()* will be executed twice if the record is successfully added to the table: once before *Add()* is called, and again inside *Add()* itself. How can we avoid this? A simple way to get round this problem is to make the *Add()* function return some indicator of its success. Such a change needs to be reflected in a reworking of the ADT's definition of that operation. The new descriptor would be

NAME	:	Add
PARAMETERS		
IN	:	st:StudentDetails
OUT	:	success : INTEGER
IN/OUT	:	t : StudentTable
PRE-CONDITIONS	:	None
POST-CONDITIONS	:	If *t* is full or *st.idcode* matches an *idcode* in *t* *success* is set to zero and *t* is unchanged, otherwise *st* is added to *t* and *success* is set to 1.

Now we can create code to match the new definition:

```
int Add(StudentDetails st, StudentTable& t)
{
    if(IsAt(st.idcode,t)!=-1 || IsFull(t))
        return 0;
    t.list[t.count]=st;
    t.count++;
    return 1;
}
```

This allows the application programmer to write more succinct code such as:

```
if(!Add(st,t))
{
    cout<<"Key already exists.\nRecord not added\n"
        <<"Press any key to continue\n";
    getch();
}
```

Displaying the Contents of StudentTable

It would be useful if we could check that the operations we've created so far perform correctly. To do that, we need to be able to display the contents of the table, so the next operation to code is *Display*, the Outline Logic of which is:

```
IF t.count = 0 THEN
    Display "Table empty"
ELSE
    FOR post := 1 TO t.count DO
        Display t.list[post]
    ENDFOR
ENDIF
```

> **PROGRAMMING EXERCISE 7.4**
>
> Create a menu-driven program, to operate on a *StudentTable* structure, which contains all of the routines described so far.
>
> Check that the program operates correctly when attempting to:
> display an empty table
> add a record containing a duplicate *idcode* field
> add a record to a full table

Returning an Entry

Often the application programmer will want to retrieve a specific entry from the table. This may be in order to examine the contents of some of the fields or to display its contents.

> **TASK 7.3**
>
> Write an updated version of the mini-spec for *GiveRecord* which returns a *success* indicator.

> **PROGRAMMING EXERCISE 7.5**
>
> Add the *GiveRecord* function to your *StudentTable* program.

Deleting a Record

We may need to remove a record from the table because it has been entered in error or because the student has left the course.

Removing the last record in the list isn't really a problem: all we have to do is reduce the count by one (we don't even need to remove the record's data from the list). But when the record being erased is at some other position in the table, then there's a bit more involved. The stages required are shown in FIG-7.3.

FIG-7.3

Deleting an Entry from the Table

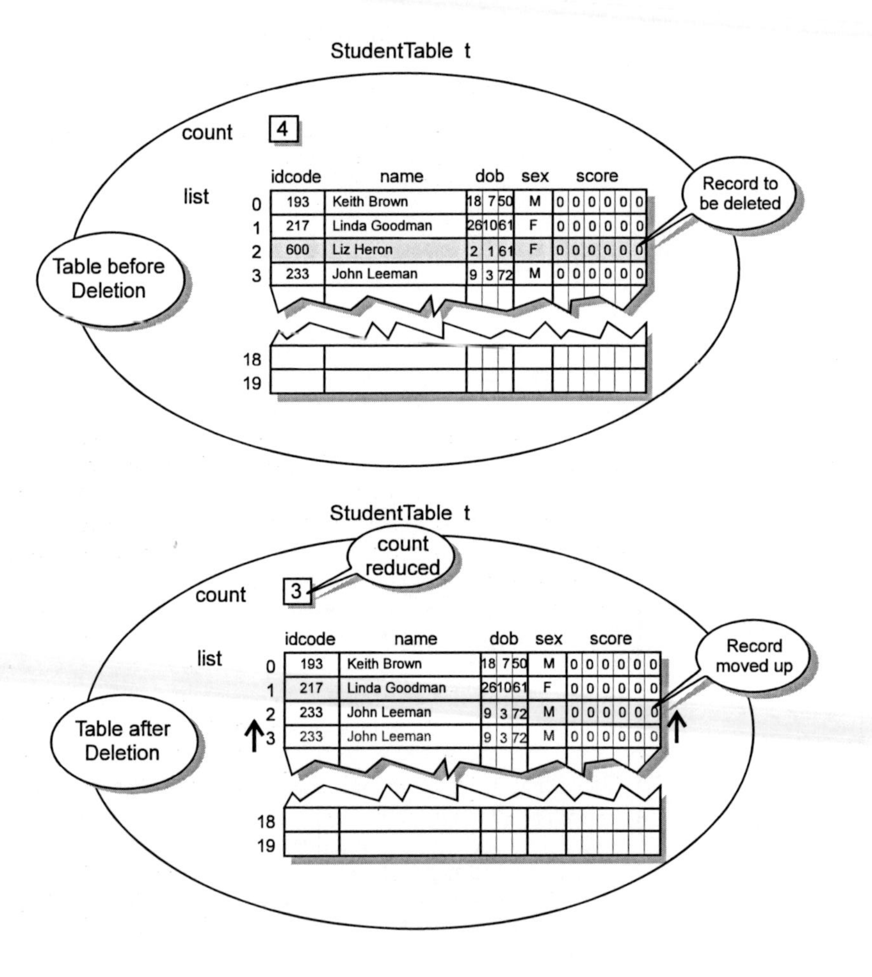

Like the *Add* operation, it will be worth going back to the original design and adding a success/fail indicator to the operation. The new mini-spec being:

NAME	:	Delete
PARAMETERS		
IN	:	key:INTEGER
OUT	:	success:INTEGER
IN/OUT	:	t : StudentTable
PRE-CONDITION	:	None
DESCRIPTION	:	If *key* matches any *idcode* in *t* then *success* is set to zero and *t* is unchanged, otherwise the entry whose *idcode* field is equal to *key* is removed from *t* and *success* is set to 1.

The Outline Logic for the routine is

```
Find position of record to be deleted
IF record not found THEN
    Set success to 0
ELSE
    Move all records below the one to be
    deleted up one position in the list
    Decrement the count
    Set success to 1
ENDIF
```

and the C++ code is

```
int Delete(int key, StudentTable& t)
{
    //*** If no match in table exit routine ***
    int post;
    if((post=IsAt(key,t))==-1)
        return 0;
    //*** Move all lower records up one position ***
    for(int c=post+1;c count;c++)
        t.list[c-1]=t.list[c];
    //*** Decrement count ***
    c.count-;
    //*** Success ***
    return 1;
}
```

Modifying a Record

There are many reasons which may cause us to change the contents of a record once it has been stored in the table. For example, we may start off with no scores recorded and later need to enter such information. The only restriction in allowing changes is that it is not good policy to allow the key field (in this case, the *idcode* field) to be changed; where this is necessary use the delete operation to remove the original record, and then insert a new record containing the required *idcode* value. That ensures that there is no possibility of ending up with two records with the same key in the table.

Changing the contents of any field in a single *StudentDetails* record is an operation properly defined within the *StudentDetails* ADT; for example, we have already defined *ChangeName* and *ChangeScore* operations. So, the only operation required to be defined for *StudentTable* is one which allows us to overwrite a record whose *idcode* matches one already in the table. This allows the application program to employ the following strategy to update a table entry:

```
Get the required record from the table (using GiveRecord)
Make changes to this copy (using ModifyName or ModifyScore)
Write the copy back to the table (using UpdateRecord)
```

As with other operations, we'll start by modifying the definition of *UpdateRecord* so that it returns a success/fail indicator:

NAME	:	UpdateRecord
PARAMETERS		
IN	:	st : StudentDetails
OUT	:	success : INTEGER
IN/OUT	:	t : StudentTable
PRE-CONDITION	:	None
POST-CONDITION	:	If the *idcode* of *st* matces an entry in *t*, then *st* replaces the entry with the same *idcode* in *t* and *success* is set to 1, otherwise *success* is set to zero.

The corresponding function is

```
int UpdateRecord(StudentDetails st, StudentTable& t)
{
    int position;  //Holds position at which match found

    //*** Determine position of match ***
    position=IsAt(st.idcode,t);
    //*** IF no match in table return fail indicator ***
    if(position==-1)
        return 0;
    else
    //*** ELSE update entry and return success indicator ***
    {
        t.list[position]=st;
        return 1;
    }
}
```

PROGRAMMING EXERCISE 7.6

Add the *UpdateRecord* operation to your table program.

Allow either the name or a score to be modified.

Other Operations on the Table

As well as changing the contents of the table, we may want to retrieve information held in the table or generate statistical data. For example, we might require an operation to return the number of students of a specified sex or the *idcode* value of all students with an average score of at least 50.

It may be that we cannot predict all the operations required by the application programmer. The solution to this problem is to include operations to return a specific record from the table. The application programmer can then interrogate the entry's data in any way necessary.

Now, we already have a *GiveRecord* operation, but that is not sufficient. For example, to determine the total number of females in the table using *GiveRecord*, the *idcode* value of each entry would have to be supplied in order to retrieve the data from the table and this is impractical. When every entry in the table needs to be examined, the best approach is to define another operation which returns a specific entry in the table. The difference between *GiveRecord* and this new routine (let's call it *GiveRecordAt*) is that the new routine takes the position in the table of the record required rather than its key.

The mini-spec for the new routine is:

NAME	:	GiveRecordAt
PARAMETERS		
IN	:	post : INTEGER t : StudentTable
OUT	:	st : StudentDetails success : INTEGER
IN/OUT	:	None
PRE-CONDITIONS	:	None
POST-CONDITIONS	:	If *post* lies between 1 and the number of entries *t* then *st* returns the entry at position post in *t* and *success* is set to 1, otherwise success is set to zero.

The code for this routine is simply:

```
int GiveRecordAt(int post, const StudentTable& t,
                                            StudentDetails& st)
{
    if(post<1||post>t.count)
        return 0;
    st = t.list[post-1];
    return 1;
}
```

PROGRAMMING EXERCISE 7.7

Create a final version of your *StudentTable* program containing all of the operations defined so far.

Add a *NoOfSex* operation which returns the number of students of a given sex. Check for an invalid sex parameter which should result in a sex count of -1.

Summary

- **A table is** a list of composite values.
- One or more fields in the composite value is used as **the key field.**
- **Key field values should be unique** to each table entry.
- **The basic operations** required of a table are:

  Adding a new entry
  Deleting an entry
  Modifying an entry

- **A table may be implemented** as a sequential array of records.
- **Adding an entry**. One option is to add a new entry at the end of the occupied area of the table.
- **Deleting an entry**. This will mean moving all entries 'below' the one being removed.
- **Modifying an entry**. This allows an entry within the table to be overwritten with a record containing the same key value.

- It can be useful to design these operations in such a way as to return a value which indicates the success or failure of the operation when called.

- The main table operations give rise to **additional operations** such as

  IsFull
  IsAt
  Display
  GiveRecord

SEARCHING

Introduction

In implementing the insert, delete and modify operations for a table, you should have noted that each requires the table to be searched for an appropriate entry in the list. This task is so common, that much time and effort has gone into developing efficient methods of searching and into ways of measuring the efficiency of these methods.

Implementation Efficiency and Searching

If a table contains thousands of items then the speed of any search operation can be a major influence on the way in which that table is implemented.

The main factors which are considered when determining the efficiency of a search technique are:

1. Average number of comparisons required to determine if the required value is in the list being searched.
2. The complexity of the routine required to code the search method.

Linear Searching Techniques

A linear search technique is one where each entry in the list is searched in turn, until the possibility of a match is determined.

There are several search techniques which fall into this class.

Serial Searching

In a serial search the list of values being searched are not held in key field order.

For example, let us assume we want to search a *StudentTable* structure containing the values shown in FIG-7.4.

FIG-7.4

The Table to be Searched

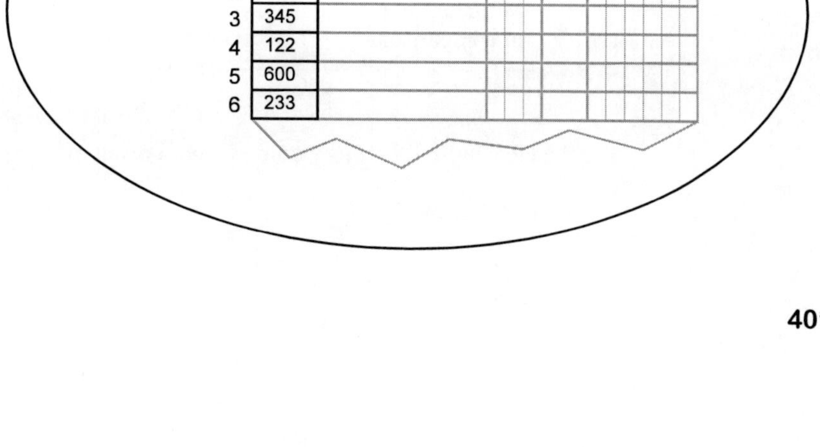

Only the *idcode* field is shown since it is the only part of the table involved in the search process.

StudentTable t

count 7

list

	idcode	name	dob	sex	score
0	588				
1	251				
2	701				
3	345				
4	122				
5	600				
6	233				

The search progresses by comparing the *idcode* field in each table entry in turn with the required key value. When a match is found the search terminates. We can formalise this algorithm as:

```
Starting at the beginning of the table
WHILE current entry's idcode not equal to req'd key
    AND not at end of table
DO
    Move to next entry in the table
ENDWHILE
IF the idcode of the current table entry = req'd key THEN
    found is TRUE
ELSE
    found is FALSE
ENDIF
```

FIG-7.5 shows the search path taken when searching the student table for an *id* value of 122.

FIG-7.5

Performing a Serial Search

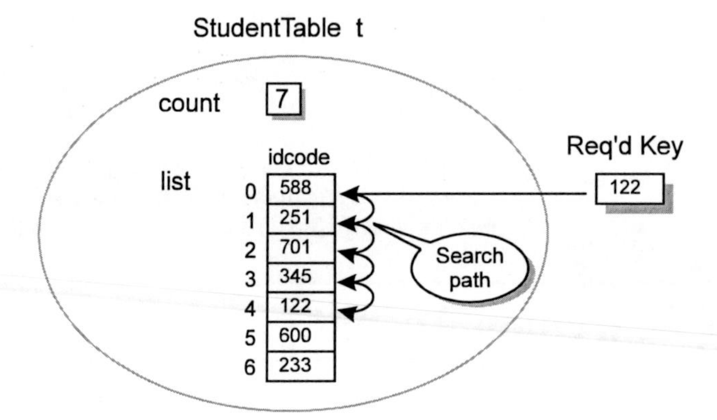

As has already been stated, one criteria used when judging the efficiency of a search method is the average number of comparisons required to find a match.

Using a serial search, the number of comparisons required before finding the matching entry equals the position of the required entry in the list,

so	122 requires	5 comparisons before being found
	701 requires	3 comparisons
	etc.	

Assuming that each entry in the list has an equal probability of being the one required, then the average number of comparisons is given by:

> *Total number of comparisons required to search for each entry in the list separately* divided by *the total number of entries in the list.*

Alternatively, since the number of comparisons increases linearly, the average number of comparisons =

$$\frac{\text{Minimum number of comparisons} + \text{Maximum number of comparisons}}{2}$$

For the table in FIG-7.5 this would give us a result of

$(1 + 7)/ 2 = 4$

TASK 7.4

What would be the average number of comparisons required if the list contained

a) 255 entries
b) N entries

What if the entry we were looking for was not in the table? For example, FIG-7.6 shows the search path for the *idcode* value 181.

FIG-7.6

Serial Searching - No match Found

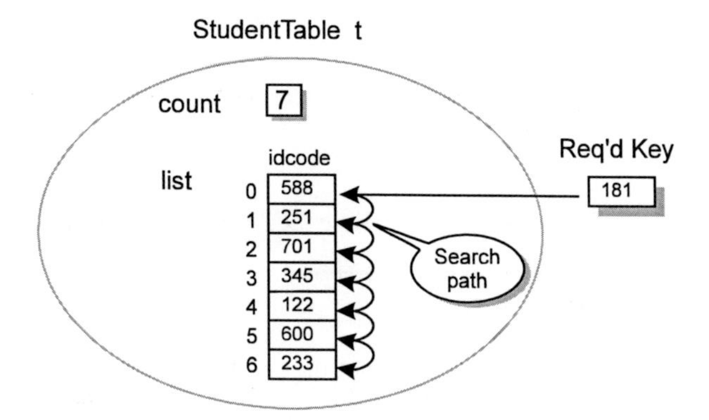

We can see from the diagram that the whole table must be searched before we can be sure that no match exists.

In the above example, that means 7 comparisons. For a table containing *N* entries then *N* comparisons would be required.

The Serial Search algorithm as used in *IsAt()* was coded as:

```
int IsAt(int key, const StudentTable& t)
{
    int position = 0;
    while(t.list[position].idcode != key && position<t.count-1)
        position++;
    if(t.list[position].idcode==key)
        return position;
    else
        return -1;
}
```

We have stated that the efficiency of the search depends on the average number of comparisons required, but another factor is the efficiency of the coded algorithm. The most critical part of the algorithm is the search loop

```
while(t.list[position].idcode != key && position<t.count-1)
    position++;
```

since all other parts of the routine are executed only once, while the coding within the loop may be executed many times (depending on the size of list to be searched and the position of the required value).

There are three components to the loop in *IsAt()*. These are:

```
t.list[position].idcode != key
position<t.count-1)
position++;
```

Each of these components will take some portion of time to execute. Let's assume the following timings:

If we assume that the execution times of the statements are:

Accessing an array element is a relatively slow process while incrementing is very fast.

`t.list[position].idcode != key`	3 time units
`position<t.count-1)`	2 time units
`position++`	1 time unit

In a table containing 10,000 entries (i.e. N = 10,000), the average search time to find a key match would be:

$$(10000 + 1)/2 * 6 = 30003 \text{ units of time}$$

And, where there is no match, the search time would be:

$$10000*6 = 60000 \text{ units of time}$$

If we can reduce this time then obviously the algorithm will be more efficient.

> **TASK 7.5**
>
> What is the purpose of the condition *position < g.count-1* in the algorithm?

We can only be rid of this condition from the code if we can be certain that a match for the required key will be found within the table. And the only way we can be certain of that is to add it ourselves!

Before starting the search, we can add the required key at the first empty position in the table (this assumes that at least one empty position exists in the table). FIG-7.7 shows the results of such a technique when searching for both matched and unmatched keys.

FIG-7.7

Adding the Search Key to the Table

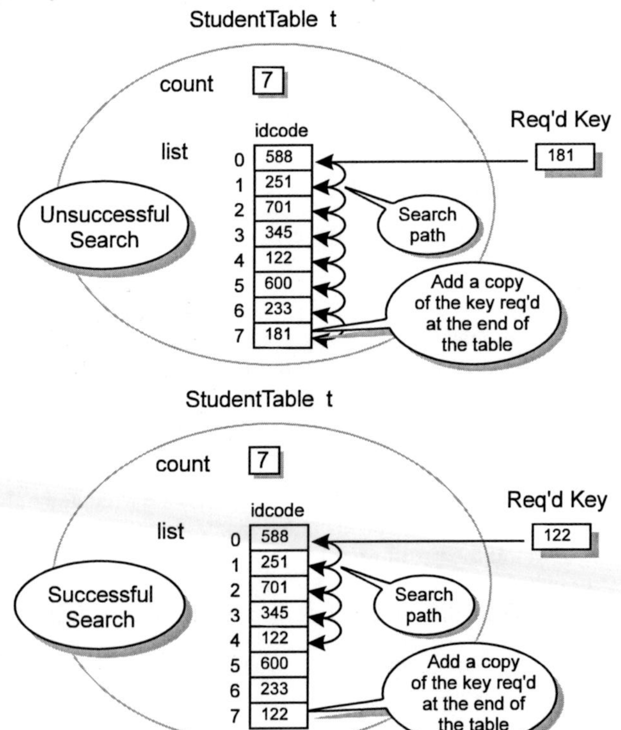

Notice that where a matching key already existed in the table, it is the first occurrence of the key that is found (not our inserted copy) but where the key did not originally exist in the table, the search stops at the matching value inserted at the end of the table. This gives us the strategy for the new algorithm:

NOTE: To ensure there will always be space for the extra entry in the table we should create the table with SIZE+1 elements in the array.

```
Add copy of req'd key to end of table
Starting at beginning of table
WHILE no match found DO
    move to next position in table
ENDWHILE
If match found at inserted key position THEN
    result is -1
ELSE
    result is position where match found
ENDIF
```

By eliminating *position* < *g.count-1* the execution time of the algorithm becomes:

Average search for match = (10000 + 1)/2 * 4 = 20002
Search for non-match = 10001 * 4 = 40004

PROGRAMMING EXERCISE 7.8
Code this new version of *IsAt()* and add it to your *StudentTable* program.

So is this more efficient? That depends: making a copy of the *idcode* value in the table will take time, and the table has to be made one element larger to ensure there is always one free space in which to place this copy. However, if the table is a large one, chances are we will have a faster search method using this new approach. However, for our small table, we'll ignore this approach from now on.

Sequential Searching

Can we improve the efficiency of the search by arranging the entries in order?

For example, FIG-7.8 shows the search path to find value 251 within a sorted table.

FIG-7.8

Sequential Searching

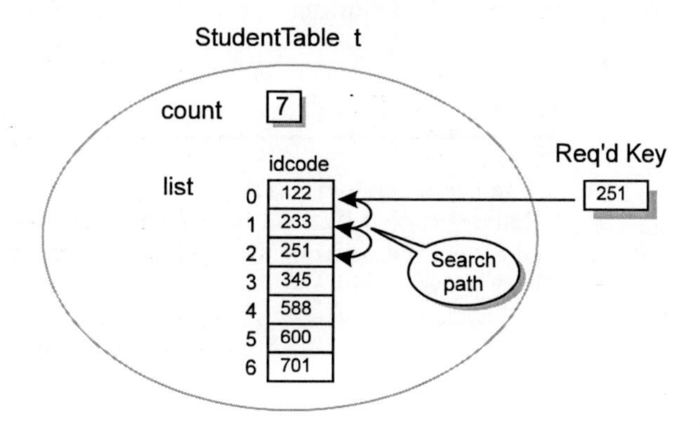

The number of comparisons required to find 251 was 3, whereas searching for 122 would have required 1 comparison and searching for 701 would have required 7 comparisons. In other words, the number of comparisons required is given by the position of the required entry in the list being searched (as it was with the serial search).

So the average number of comparisons to find a match is the same as that for the serial search - there has been no improvement in the figures by sorting the list to be searched.

Now let us look for a value which is not in the list, say 219 (see FIG-7.9).

FIG-7.9

Unsuccessful Search of a Sorted Table

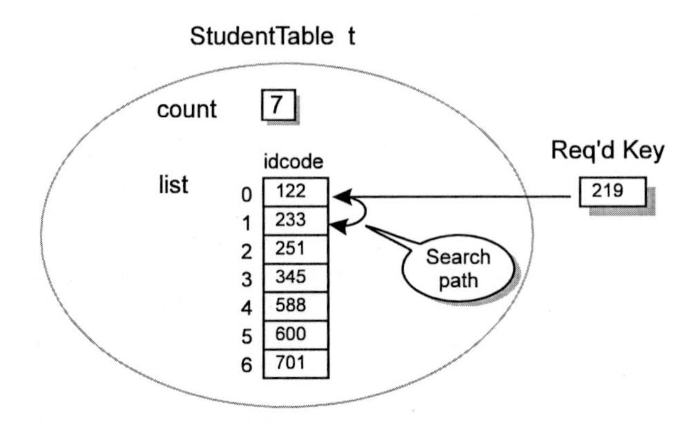

Notice that it is not necessary to search the whole list since, as soon as we reach an entry with an *idcode* value greater than the one we seek, there is no possibility of a match being found further along the list.

Three comparisons were required to establish that key 219 was not present. If 219 had been in the list it would have been in position 3. We can generalise this to produce the rule:

> *When a value is not present in a sorted list, the number of comparisons required to determine this fact is equal to the position in the list at which that value would have been placed.*

TASK 7.6

Using the table in FIG-7.9, how many comparisons would be required to determine if the following *idcode* values existed in the table:

a) 100
b) 599
c) 800

So the number of comparisons required equals the position in the list that the value would have occupied if it had been present. At best the number of comparisons required is one, and, at worst, is equal to the number of entries in the table (seven in FIG-7.9 above).

Hence the average number of comparisons required when searching for a value which is not in the list is :

$$
\begin{aligned}
&(\text{min comps} + \text{max comps}) / 2 \\
= \; &(1 + 7) / 2 \\
= \; &4
\end{aligned}
$$

For a list of N elements we get:

$$(1+N)/2$$

Using a sorted table, we can rewrite the logic for *IsAt()* as:

```
Starting at beginning of table
WHILE idcode of current entry < req'd key
    AND not at end of table
DO
    move to next position in table
ENDWHILE
If match found THEN
    result is position where match found
ELSE
    result is -1
ENDIF
```

Should we maintain a sorted table? First, we can see that only in the search for unmatched keys does a sorted list offer an improvement in our search efficiency. So, unless a large number of searches are for unmatched values, the improvement is of little significance. And, as usual, there is a price to be paid for maintaining a sorted table: we need to modify the *Add()* routine so that new records are added at the appropriate position in the table (we'll look at this in detail later).

Estimated Entry

The search methods described above are fairly obvious approaches. But how good are they? For example, confronted with a telephone directory (which is an ordered list), would we use a sequential search? If we did, it would take a very long time to find John Smith's phone number.

To find an entry in the phone book, we make an initial guess about where that entry should be and begin searching from there. If this initial guess starts us before the required name, we need to search forward through the book until we find a match OR until we pass the position where the entry should have been.

On the other hand, if we start beyond the required name, we need to search backwards through the book until we find a match OR until we pass where the name should be.

The main problem of such an algorithm is how to make the initial guess. That depends on several factors including:

- The type of values held in the list (numeric or alphabetic)
- The length of the list being searched

Let's assume that all the *idcode* values in our students' table lie in the range 100 to 999. If we also assume these values are allocated on an apparently random basis, then 1/9 of all keys should be in the 100-199 range, 1/9 in the 200-299 range etc.

For a table containing 20 elements we would expect the first 20/9 elements to contain idcode in the range 100 - 199; the next 20/9 elements to contain idcodes in the range 200 - 299, etc.

To translate a key into a position in the table we need to use formula:

[(key's most significant digit - 1)*20/9 +0.5]

[x] means the largest integer values less than or equal to

So if we were looking for a match for the value 820 we should start looking at position [(8-1) * 20/9+0.5] which is element 16 (see FIG-7.10).

The efficiency of this method depends to a great extent on the effectiveness of the initial starting position.

However, it can be seen from the example that this method seems much quicker than any previous technique.

FIG-7.10

The Estimated-Entry Search

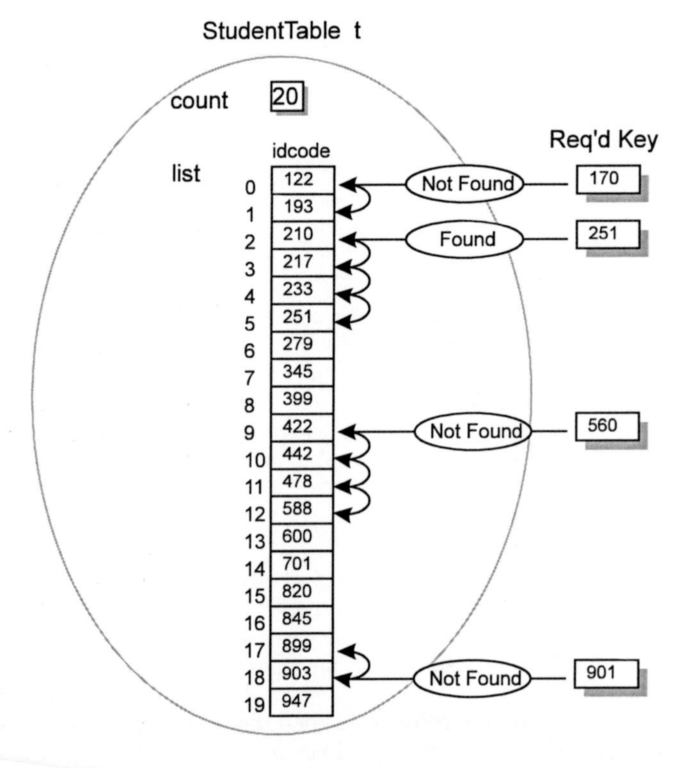

If the values in the list are changed in such a way as to give an unbalanced distribution, then the efficiency drops (see FIG-7.11).

FIG-7.11

Estimated-Entry with a Biased Key Range

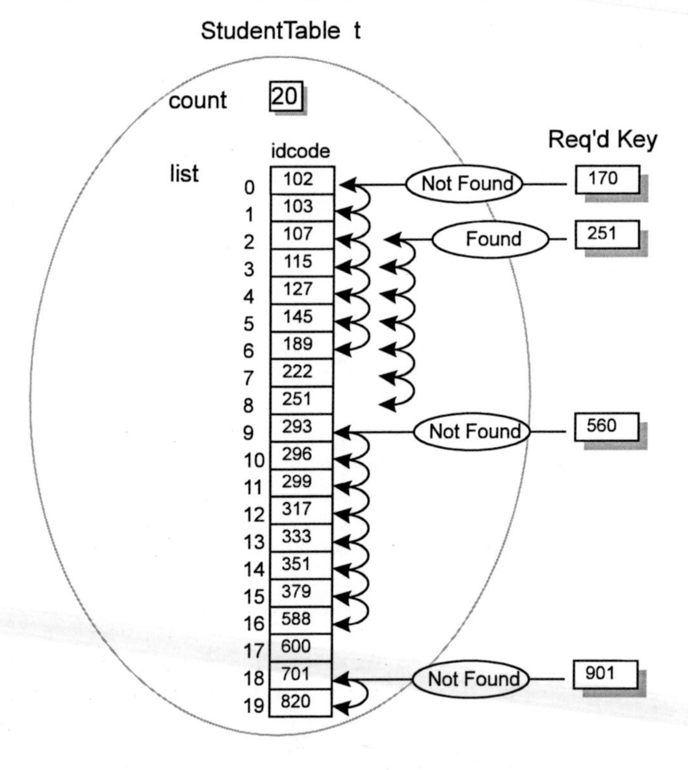

The number of comparisons required has increased because our entry point into the table, which was based on there being an average of 1/9*20 entries in each key range 0 - 099, 100 - 199 etc., gives a poor estimate of the required value's actual position.

Even if the algorithm appears to work well initially it may become less efficient as values are added and deleted from the table, hence changing the spread of values.

However, even for a relatively poor estimation algorithm, the estimated entry approach tends to give better figures for the average number of comparisons required than any of the previous methods.

Non-linear Searching

The Binary Search

The initial guess method seems to give the best search method so far. However, if we return to the every day searching situation of using a telephone directory it is obvious that, in practice, the method employed is none of those described previously.

If the guess at where in the book the entry we require is likely to be is a poor one, then we make other estimates based on each preceding estimate. So if we are looking for SMITH in the directory and the first page we open at (say page 340) contains McELROY then we know that SMITH is somewhere further on and make our next guess accordingly (between page 340 and the end of the directory). If that results in opening at TAYLOR (on page 612) then our next guess is made between the pages containing McELROY and TAYLOR (between pages 340 and 612) etc.

The next computer searching technique to be examined uses this "divide and conquer" strategy and is known as the **binary search**.

The search uses the following strategy:

```
Starting at the middle of the occupied area of the table
WHILE no match AND search area not empty DO
    IF entry's idcode is less than req'd key THEN
        Eliminate top half of table from search area
    ELSE
        Eliminate bottom half of table from search area
    ENDIF
    Examine the middle entry in the search area
ENDWHILE
IF search area is empty THEN
    found := -1
ELSE
    found := 0
ENDIF
```

FIG-7.12 shows the strategy in practice for a 15 entry table. The steps involved in searching for key 442 are:

1. Compare the middle entry (at position 7) with the required key.
2. Since the key at position 7 (345) is smaller than the required key, we can eliminate the top half of the table (positions 0 to 7) since they contain values smaller than the one required.
3. We are left with positions 8 to 14 in the search area. The middle of these is position 11 which is compared with the required key.
4. This time the key examined (478) is too large. This means that positions 11 to 14 can be eliminated as they contain idcode values which are too large.
5. Now only elements 8 to 10 remain in the search area. Element 9 is used in the next comparison.
6. Since it is too small, positions 8 and 9 are eliminated.
7. Only element 10 remains, and on this comparison a match is found.

FIG-7.12

The Binary Search

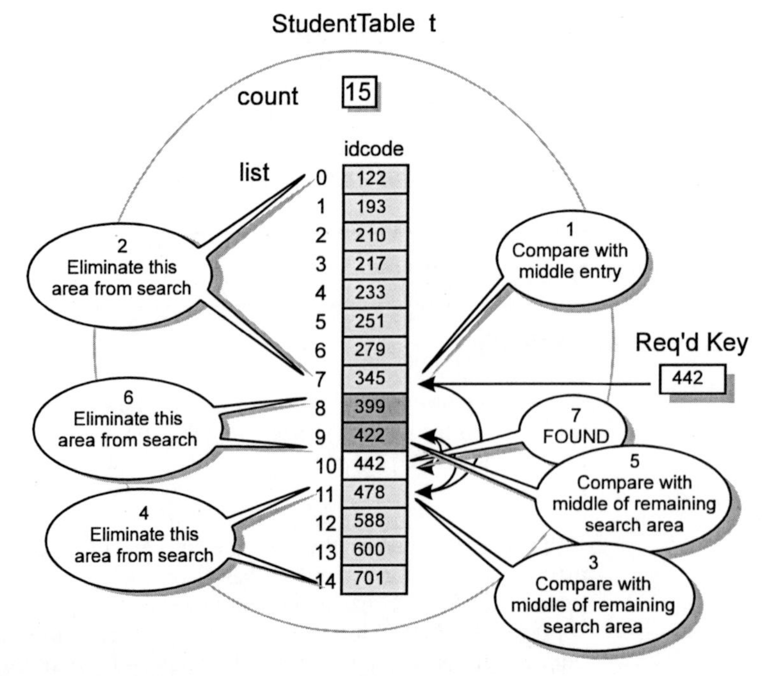

In this example we had to reduce the search area to a single element before a match was found, but if we had been searching for *idcode* 345 it would have been found after only one comparison, and 478 after two comparisons.

> **TASK 7.7**
>
> 1. List the number of comparisons required to reach each of the entries in the table using the binary search approach.
>
> 2. How many entries in the table can be found after:
>   a) 1 comparison?
>   b) 2 comparisons?
>   c) 3 comparisons?
>   d) 4 comparisons?
>
> 3. What is the average number of comparisons required to find an entry?

From the results of TASK 7.7 you can see that the maximum number of comparisons required to find an entry is 4. This seems to be the most effective search method so far. You can see from the example, that the worst search case occurs when we have to reduce the search area to a single entry. How many comparisons does this require?

If we begin with a table of N entries, after 1 comparison (assuming a match is not found) there will be N/2 entries remaining in the search area (since we will have halved the search area). After the next comparison, there will be N/4 entries remaining (again a halving of the search area).

> **TASK 7.8**
>
> How many entries remain after:
>   a) 3 comparisons?
>   b) 4 comparisons?

If we write the numbers 2,4,8,16 as powers of 2, we get

$$2 = 2^1$$
$$4 = 2^2$$
$$8 = 2^3$$
$$16 = 2^4$$

Using this notation in stating the size of the search area

No of comparisons	Size of search area
1	$N/2^1$
2	$N/2^2$
3	$N/2^3$
4	$N/2^4$

we can see that the size of the search area is related to the number of comparisons made. Hence we can generalise and say that after x comparisons, the size of the search area is $N/2^x$ elements.

Now, after some number of comparisons (say p) we must reach a stage where the search area has been reduced to one element (i.e. when $N/2^p = 1$). At that point (if not earlier) we will discover if a match exists or not. So the maximum number of comparisons required for a list of N elements is p when $N/2^p = 1$. This can be re-arranged to give:

$$p = \log_2 N$$

The maximum number of comparisons must obviously be an integer. Since the expression $\log_2 N$ will not always give an integer result, we need to modify this slightly to:

$$p = [\log_2 N+1]$$

TASK 7.9

Using the formula above, calculate the maximum number of comparisons for a table of size:

a) 15
b) 16
c) 1,000
d) 10,000

The maximum comparisons required to find a match is also the number of comparisons required to discover that a key is not in the table.

One way to calculate the average number of comparisons (rather than the maximum) has already been shown in TASK 7.7. Since such a calculation would be long and tedious for a list of any significant length, an approximation can be obtained using the formula

$$\text{Average comparisons} = (\log_2 N) - 1$$

where N is the number of entries in the table.

The accuracy of this approximation increases as N becomes large.

Implementing the Binary Search

Assuming we are willing to maintain a sorted table, the binary search approach seems to be the approach to use when coding our *IsAt()* function.

To indicate which part of the table remains in the search area, we need to maintain two indicator variables, *lowest* and *highest*. These hold the lowest and highest element numbers still in the search area. Hence, at the start of our search, in a table containing 15 entries, *lowest* would contain the value zero and *highest* 14. The middle of the search area can be found using the formula:

```
[(lowest+highest) /2]
```

> **TASK 7.10**
>
> List the values of *lowest* and *highest*, during the search shown in FIG-7.12.

The detailed logic and code for the new version of *IsAt()* is given below:

Outline Logic:

```
lowest := 0
highest := t.count
mid := (lowest+highest)/2
WHILE not a match AND search area not empty DO
    IF table's idcode < req'd key THEN
        lowest := mid+1
    ELSE
        highest := mid -1
    ENDIF
    mid := (lowest+highest)/2
ENDWHILE
IF search area not empty THEN
    post := mid
ELSE
    post = -1
ENDIF
```

Function Code:

```
int IsAt(int key, const StudentTable& t)
{
    int lowest=0, highest=t.count-1;
    int mid = (lowest+highest)/2;
    while(t.list[mid].idcode != key && lowest<=highest)
    {
        if(t.list[mid].idcode< key)
            lowest = mid + 1;
        else
            highest = mid - 1;
        mid = (lowest+highest)/2;
    }
    if(lowest<=highest)
        return mid;
    else
        return -1;
}
```

> **PROGRAMMING EXERCISE 7.9**
>
> Update your *StudentTable* program to include this version of *IsAt()*.
> (Ensure the table entries are sorted by adding them in the correct order.)

A Final Comparison

A comparison of the Sequential and Binary searches (see TABLE-7.1) shows that, using only this criteria, the Binary search is an obviously superior method.

TABLE 7.1

Comparison of Sequential and Binary Searching

Size of List	Average number of comparisons (seq)	(binary)
10	5.5	2.9
100	50.5	5.8
1000	500.5	9.0
10000	5000.5	12.4

However, the search loop of the Binary Search is more complex which implies that each comparison will require more time than with the earlier methods.

If the time taken for one iteration of the sequential search is t_s and the time for the Binary search t_b then the average time for a binary search must be less than that for the sequential search to make it worthwhile. That is

$$t_b(\log_2 N - 1) < t_s((N+1)/2)$$

In practice this point occurs long before the list reaches 100 elements.

Choosing An Implementation

The discussion on searching should highlight the sort of thing a designer has to take into consideration when choosing the method of implementation for a data structure.

If an array is to be used, should the values contained in that array be held in order (even if the application does not require it) since this will allow faster search methods to be employed (i.e. the binary search)?

The price that must be paid for maintaining an ordered list is the effort of inserting and deleting entries in such a list. These operations involve moving existing entries about within the array to create space for a new entry or to remove an entry. This movement will take a long time (in computer terms) and hence degrade the efficiency of the program.

Generally, the programmer may decide on a sorted array if the number of new entries and deletions are expected to be small (and hence minimise the amount of data movement involved) but if many such insertions and deletions are expected some other method will probably be chosen.

Summary

- **Search method efficiency** is determined by
  - The average number of comparisons required to find a given value.
  - The efficiency of the algorithm used to implement the method.

■ **Linear search methods** include

- Serial search
- Sequential Search
- Estimated entry Search

■ **The binary search is a non-linear method.**

DIRECT ACCESS TABLES

Introduction

As we've seen from the analysis of the techniques, both ordered and unordered tables give relatively poor performance when searched. Even the best method, Binary Search, suffers from the overhead having to maintain a sorted list.

When minimising search time is our top priority, one method of achieving this is to use a **direct access** table. A direct access table contains a position for every possible key value. For example if the *idcode* field in our *StudentTable* contained values between 0 and 999 the table would have 1000 elements (see FIG-7.13).

FIG-7.13

Creating a Direct Access Table

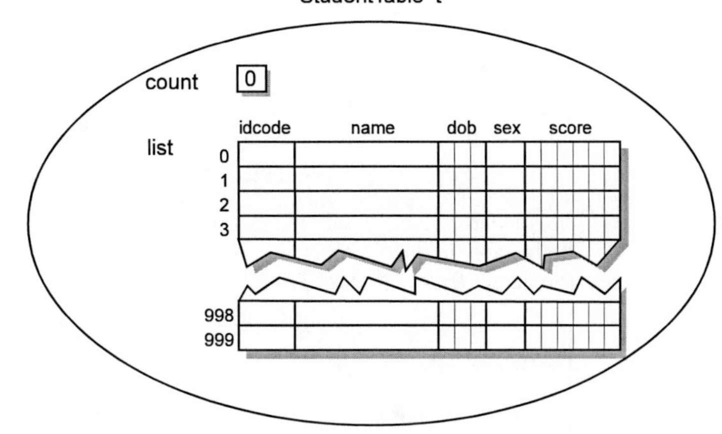

The code for this structure would be:

```
struct StudentTable
{
    int count;
    StudentDetails list[1000];
};
```

New entries to the table are inserted at the position in the table which corresponds to their key value. Hence, if adding records for students 1 3 and 998 then the table would be as shown in FIG-7.14.

FIG-7.14

Adding Records to a Direct Access Table

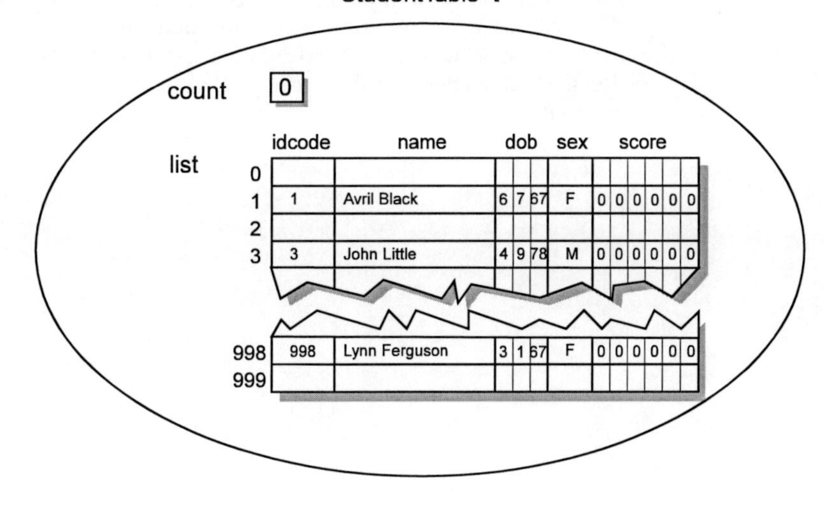

Notice that there is no requirement to store the actual *idcode* field, since the record's position in the table is the same as its *idcode* value. This would allow us to redefine the table's structure and omit the *idcode* field from the array's record structure.

Implementation

Since we need to differentiate between an occupied and unoccupied position in the table's array, the *CreateTable()* function will have to set each entry in the array to a value corresponding to "empty".

We might do this by setting the *name* field to blank with the code

```
void CreateTable(StudentTable& t)
{
    t.count = 0;
    for(int c=0;c<1000;c++)
        strcpy(t.list[c].name,"");
}
```

The code for *IsAt()* now becomes trivial. To find a record, we simply examine the position in the table corresponding to the student's *idcode*. If there's an entry , the routine returns the position in the table of the matching record; if not, -1 is returned.

This means we have reduced the number of comparisons required to find an entry in the table to one. In other words, we can access the required entry directly; hence the name: **Direct Access Table**.

TASK 7.11

1. Write the code for *IsAt()* function using the strategy described above.

2. Write the *Delete()* function for removing an entry in the table.

We have created the ultimate in fast access tables, and there are several advantages:

- The key field does not need to be saved
- Access to a record is immediate with no searching
- Inserting and deleting a record does not involve moving any of the remaining entries

So why isn't this the way all tables are implemented? Unfortunately, direct access tables have one overwhelming drawback: the size of the array. Our table requires 1000 entries, and if we don't have many students, only a few elements of the array will ever be occupied. For a six-digit numeric key, we'd need 1,000,000 entries and for a 30 character key field, such as name, we'd need more storage than any computer's memory is capable of holding.

THE HENLEY COLLEGE LIBRARY

HASH TABLES

Introduction

The hash table is a structure which attempts to gain the fast access characteristic of direct access tables without the corresponding large storage requirements. To achieve this, the hash table is created with an array which is approximately 50% larger than the number of records it is likely to hold and the key field of any new records is transformed (or hashed) to give the position in the table where the record should be stored.

For example, assume we need to store information on five students in a table containing 20 positions. One way of deciding where in the table each record should be placed is to store the record in the position corresponding to the last digit of the *idcode* number. So, if we assume the data for the five students is

```
1162    Keith Brown    M   61 21 32 11 21 19
7914    Linda Goodman  F   45 67 21 34 23 12
2635    James Allen    M   10 12 16 13 18 14
2937    Carol Wight    F   65 45 53 37 41 57
1329    Fiona Black    F   87 79 65 45 62 16
```

then the position of the records in the hash table would be as shown in FIG-7.15.

FIG-7.15

Manipulating a Record's Key to Generate an Insert Position

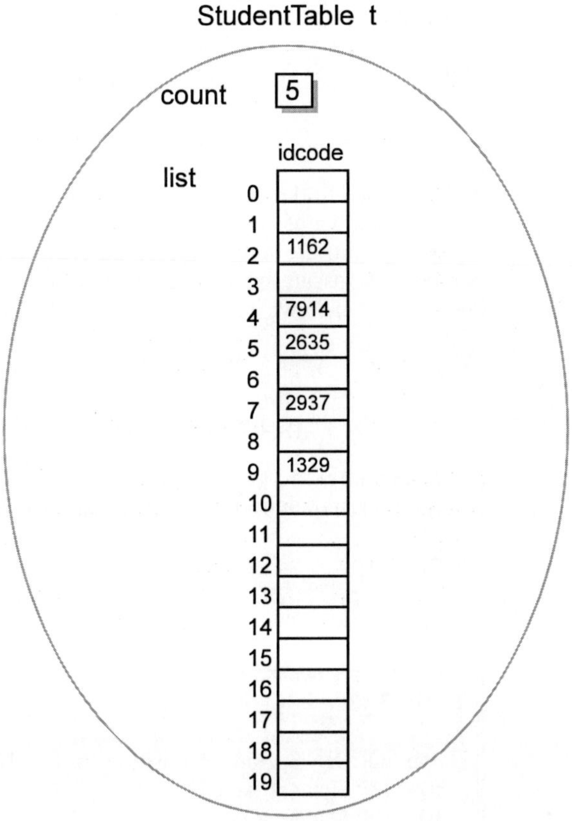

StudentTable t

count 5

list

	idcode
0	
1	
2	1162
3	
4	7914
5	2635
6	
7	2937
8	
9	1329
10	
11	
12	
13	
14	
15	
16	
17	
18	
19	

Unlike direct access tables, we have to store the key field since the position of the record is not identical to the key.

This isn't a very good method of deciding where to place the entries since only positions 0 to 9 will ever be occupied. It's important therefore that we choose a good hashing algorithm. Some of the more popular are described below.

Key Transformation Algorithms

The main criteria in choosing a method of key transformation is that the table entries should spread as evenly as possible throughout the table and not cluster in one area of the table. Secondly, the time taken to carry out the translation should be kept to a minimum.

Modular Division

In this technique, the key is divided by the number of elements in the table and the remainder is taken as the position. For example, assuming the use of a table with 17 elements (numbered 0 to 16) then an entry with key 615 would have its position calculated as:

key modulo table size
= 615 MOD 17
= 3

It can be shown (but we will not do so here!) that the best results are obtained when division is by a prime number. That is, the number of elements in the table should be a prime number.

Modular Division is one of the best general purpose hashing algorithms.

Folding

In this method the key is divided into separate segments, with each segment having the same number of digits as contained in the index of the last element of the table. These segments are added together to give a result in the range of the table length. For example, assuming a table size of 100 (0 to 99) and a 6 digit key, then for the key value 242586 we get

242586 = 24 + 25 + 86
= 135
= position 35 (the most-significant digit is ignored)

For a larger table, the key is split into larger sections. For example, assuming a table size of 1000 (0 to 999), the result for the same key (242586) is

242586 = 242 + 586
= 828
= position 828

TASK 7.12

Using FOLDING, find the position for key 102438 in a
a) 100 element table
b) 1000 element table

Mid-Square

Using this method, the key is squared and a group of digits from the middle of the result are used to specify the position. The size of the group is decided by the number of elements in the table. For example, assuming a table of 100 elements and a 4 digit key, then for the key 4573 we get the result

$$4573^2 = 20912329$$
$$= \text{position 12 (taken from the middle 2 digits)}$$

If the table contained 1000 elements then the address would have been 912 or 123 depending on which group of digits were chosen (it is obviously important to be consistent).

Hashing String Fields

So far the key fields to be hashed have been numeric ones. This isn't an unreasonable assumption since many computer systems do use numeric keys. However, this is not always the case. For example, a National Insurance number contains both letters and numbers, while a small table might even use a person's name as the key field. The simplest way to handle such fields is simply to convert part of the field to a numeric value which can then be hashed using one of the methods described above. For example, in a small table using a client's name as the key field, we might take the first 4 bits of the first letter and the first 4 bits of the last letter in the name to create a single 8 bit numeric value (giving values in the range 0 to 255) which can then be hashed to lie within the table size.

TASK 7.13

Write the code necessary to create such an 8-bit value from a string.
(HINT: you may find the remainder operator useful.)

Handling Collisions

FIG-7.16 shows where various records are stored using the hashing algorithm *idcode* modulo 17.

FIG-7.16

Using Modular Division Hashing

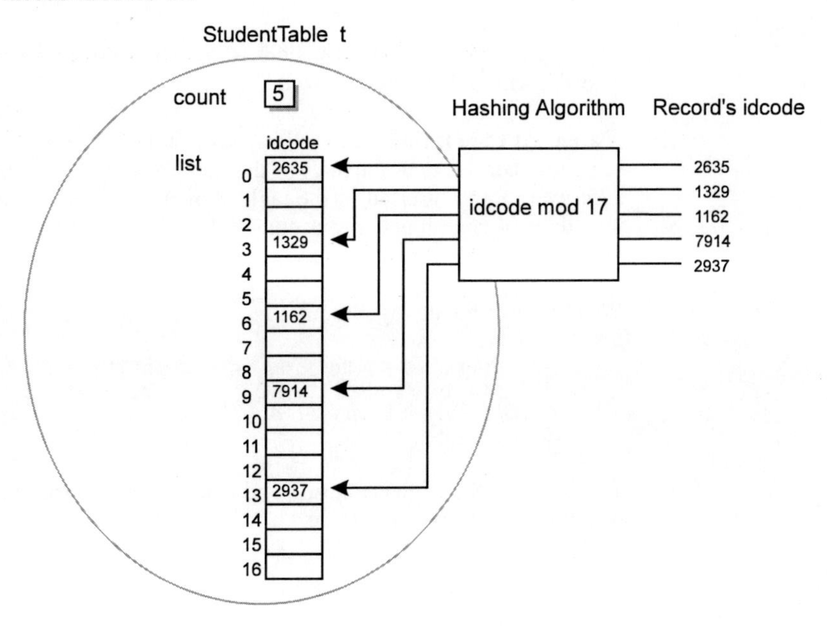

TASK 7.14

Using the same hashing algorithm, calculate the insertion points for the records whose *idcode* values are:

8838
6627
4895
1995

The last value in TASK 7.14 highlights the problem with hashing. What happens when two or more keys hash to the same position in the table?

When a new record hashes to an already occupied location, we have a collision. The simplest way to deal with this situation is to insert the new record in the first empty space available (see FIG-7.17).

FIG-7.17

Handling Collisions

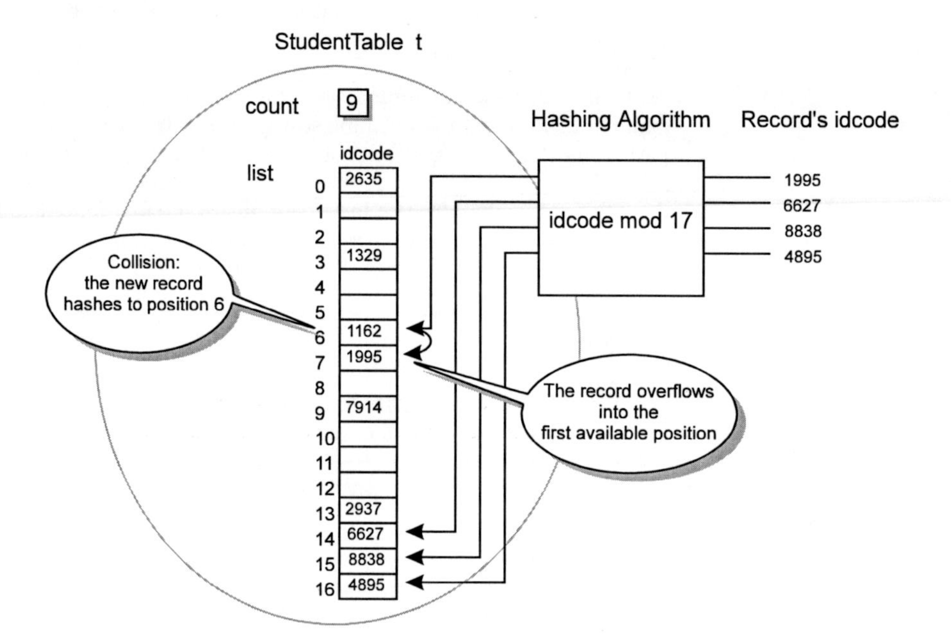

This approach to handling collisions is known as **linear probing** and the displaced record is said to have **overflowed.**

If a record cannot find an overflow position before the end of the list is reached searching continues at the start of the list. For example, if the record with idcode 1765 were to be inserted in the table shown in FIG-7.17, its initial hash position would be 14, and, this being occupied, locations 15, 16, 0 and 1 would be probed to find an empty table element.

We can describe the logic required to add an entry to the hash table as:

```
Hash record's key to find insert position
WHILE position occupied DO
    move to next position
ENDWHILE
```

This assumes the table is not full, and when the end of the table is reached, the next position is the start of the table.

Implementation

Our hash table will contain records of *StudentDetails* type. The *list* component of the table consists of 17 elements (too small to gain any practical advantage from hashing but large enough to demonstrate the theory of hash tables).

Defining the StudentTable

The only difference in the declaration of the table's structure from earlier versions is that, from what's been said already, it will be more efficient to make sure that the list component's size is a prime number: in this case 17. This gives us the declaration:

```
struct StudentDetails
{
    int idcode;
    char name[30];
    char sex;
    int score[6];
};

const int SIZE = 17;

struct StudentTable
{
    int count;
    StudentDetails list[SIZE];
};
```

Creating the Table

As in the direct access table, we need to mark every element in the list as empty, as well as setting the count field to zero. This time, we'll use the value 0 in the *idcode* field to indicate an empty position.

So, assuming the global definition

```
const int EMPTY = 0;
```

we can code this routine as:

```
CreateTable(StudentTable& t)
{
    t.count = 0;
    for(int c = 0;c < SIZE;c++)
        t.list[c].idcode = EMPTY;
};
```

Creating the Hash Function

Since transforming the record's key field will be such a common occurrence, this can be written as a function, which can be made more efficient by defining it as inline.

```
inline unsigned Hash(int key)
{
    return key % SIZE;
}
```

In other tables, with non-numeric keys, the hashing algorithm will obviously be adjusted appropriately.

Adding an Entry to the Table

To add a new student we need to make sure that the *idcode* value is not already in the table. If it isn't, then we need to calculate where in the table the new record needs to be placed.

As with our earlier table, we'll start by creating an *IsAt()* function. This needs to look through the table for a match. Finding a match is easy: we just hash the key and use the same strategy employed to insert the record in the first place. But how do we know a record isn't in the table? We could search the whole table, but that would negate many of the advantages of the hash table. Instead, we need only look at the section of the table in which the record should have been placed.

The mini-spec for the routine is similar to that for the standard table:

```
NAME            :  IsAt
PARAMETERS
    IN          :  key:INTEGER
                   t:StudentTable
    OUT         :  post:INTEGER
    IN/OUT      :  None
PRE-CONDITION   :  None.
POST-CONDITION  :  Returns in post, the position in t of the record whose
                   idcode value is key. Where no match exists, post is set to -1.
```

The Outline Logic for the routine is

```
Calculate starting position by hashing key
WHILE no match AND position not EMPTY
  AND complete table not searched
DO
    Move to next position in the table
ENDWHILE
IF id at stopping position is equal to key THEN
    Set post to stopping position
ELSE
    Set post to -1
ENDIF
```

From this we get the code

```
int IsAt(int key, const HashTable& t)
{
    int post = Hash(key);
    int start=post;
    while(t.list[post].idcode!=key&&t.list[post].idcode!=EMPTY)
    {
        post=(post+1)%SIZE;
        if(post==start)
            break;
    }
    if(t.list[post].idcode!=key)
        return NOTFOUND;
    else
        return post;
}
```

NOTFOUND is a named constant assigned the value -1

The function contains the line

```
post = (post+1) % SIZE ;
```

which is a shorter, if more obscure, way of writing

```
if (post<SIZE-1)
    post++;
else
    post=0;
```

We can then make use of *IsAt()* to make sure any *Add* operation does not allow two or more entries to contain the same *idcode* value.

The mini-spec for the *Add* operation is

NAME	:	Add
PARAMETERS		
IN	:	st:StudentDetails
OUT	:	success:INTEGER
IN/OUT	:	t: StudentTable
PRE-CONDITION	:	None
POST-CONDITION	:	If *t* is full or *st.idcode* matches an *idcode* in *t*, *success* is set to zero and *t* is unchanged, otherwise *st* is added to *t* and *success* is set to 1.

The Outline Logic is

```
IF table is full OR st.idcode matches an entry in t THEN
    success := 0
ELSE
    Calculate insert position by hashing st.idcode
    WHILE no match AND position occupied DO
        move to next position
    ENDWHILE
    Insert new record at position
    Increment count
    success:=1
ENDIF
```

The code for this is

```
int Add(StudentDetails st, StudentTable& t)
{
    //*** IF full, or already exists, return 0 ***
    if(IsFull(t)||IsAt(st.idcode,t)!=-1)
        return 0;
    //*** Find insert point ***
    int post = Hash(st.idcode);
    while(t.list[post].idcode!=EMPTY)
        post= (post+1)%SIZE ;
    //*** Insert record ***
    t.list[post]=st;
    t.count++;
    return 1;
}
```

Displaying the Table

Since much of the table will be empty, the display function must look at each position in the table displaying only the contents of occupied positions. This requires the logic:

```
Starting at the first position in the table
REPEAT
    IF the position is occupied THEN
        Display its contents
    ENDIF
UNTIL the end of the table is reached
```

Returning a Single Table Entry

Previously, we had two functions for returning a single record: *GiveRecord()* and *GiveRecordAt()*. However, the second of these, designed to return the entry at a specified position in the table is of little use in this situation where the position of an entry cannot be easily predicted. The mini-spec for *GiveRecord* is repeated below.

```
NAME                 :    GiveRecord
PARAMETERS
    IN               :    key : INTEGER
                          t : StudentTable
    OUT              :    st : StudentDetails
                          success: INTEGER
    IN/OUT           :    None
PRE-CONDITIONS       :    None
POST-CONDITIONS      :    If key does not match idcode of an entry in t,
                          success is set to 0, otherwise success is set
                          to 1 and st contains a copy of the entry in t
                          whose idcode field has the value key.
```

When using a hash table, the Outline Logic for *GiveRecord()* is

```
Calculate position by hashing key
WHILE no match AND t.list[position] is not EMPTY DO
    move to next position
ENDWHILE
IF t.list[position].idcode=key THEN
    reccopy = t.list[position]
    success=1
ELSE
    success=0
ENDIF
```

> **TASK 7.15**
>
> Based on the logic given above, produce the code for *GiveRecord()*.

Deleting a Table Entry

It's much easier to delete a record from a hash table than from serial and sequential tables. This is because there is no need to move any of the other entries in the table when deleting from a hash table. All we need to do is to find the required entry and place a marker in its key field.

The question is, what sort of marker? Perhaps we should simply mark it with an EMPTY value. At first sight, this might seem a reasonable choice, since, once deleted, the record's position will be free to take a new entry. But there's a major problem: if we mark a deleted record as EMPTY, the search procedure may fail (see FIG-7.18).

To avoid this problem, we need to use a distinct marker for deleted records. This way, the search algorithm won't stop too early.

FIG-7.18

Breaking the Search Path

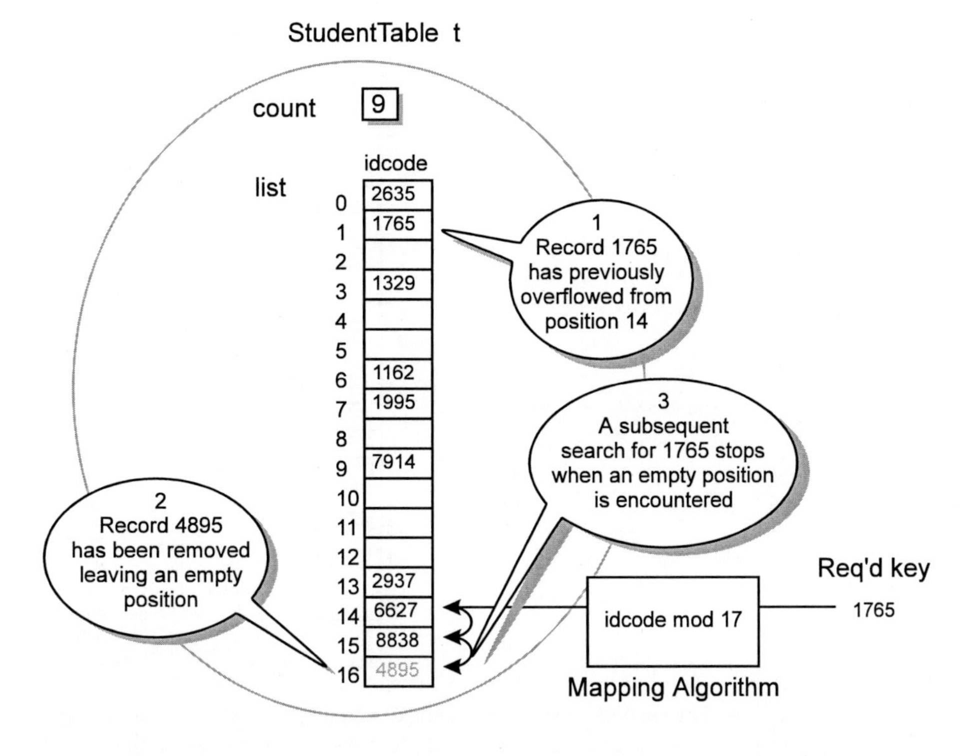

There's one final tweak to get the whole thing working: the *Add()* function needs to change from

```
while(t.list[post].idcode!=EMPTY)
```

to

```
while(t.list[post].idcode!=EMPTY&&t.list[post].idcode!=DELETED)
```

which allows us to insert new entries at deleted as well as empty positions in the table.

> **PROGRAMMING EXERCISE 7.10**
>
> Create a hash table implementation of *StudentTable*.

An Alternative Method of Dealing with Overflow

Problems With Linear Probing

For a hash table to be efficient it is important that we keep the number of comparisons required to find an entry to a minimum. If the required entry has not overflowed then the number of comparisons required during a search will be 1. However, if overflow has occurred this figure will increase. The actual figure depends on the length of the search path through the table.

Linear probing, the method of overflow that we dealt with above, has some problems in this area. You can see from FIG-7.19 that if several entries hash to the same position in a table, they follow the same route when searching for an empty position. This situation obviously leads to a reduction in the efficiency of the search and needs to be eliminated.

FIG-7.19

Overflowing in the Footsteps of Others

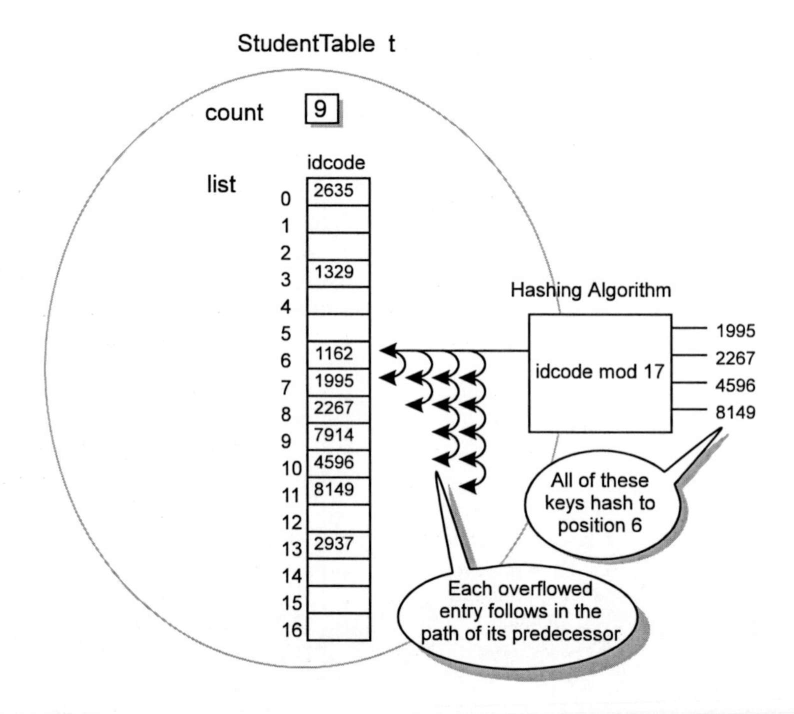

The second method of overflow we are going to examine attempts to eliminate this following in the footsteps of previous synonyms which linear probing suffers from.

Double Hashing

This technique is similar to linear probing but instead of probing the next element of the table when a collision occurs double hashing calculates a step size which is then used to calculate the next position to be probed. For example, if a new entry such as 8149 hashes to an occupied position 6 in our table then a step size is calculated. Assuming a step size of 11, the table would be probed for an empty (or deleted) element at positions 0 ((6+11)%17), 1 1, 5 , 16, etc. until an insert position is found (see FIG-7.20).

FIG-7.20

Using an Overflow Step Size

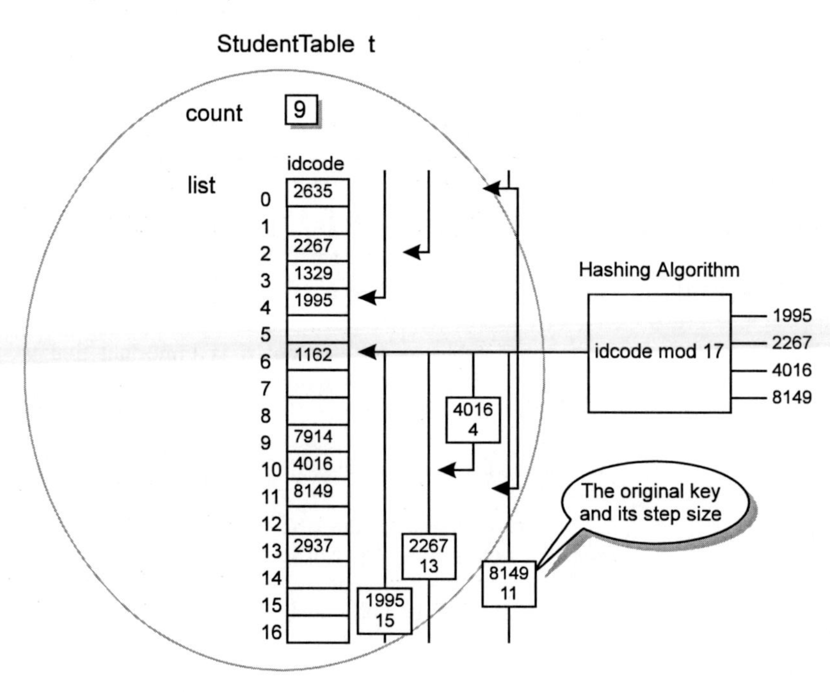

Calculating the step Size

To calculate the step size, the original key is transformed using a second (different) hashing algorithm.

To be effective, the second hashing algorithm must have the following characteristics:

1. It must not return a step size of zero.
   Obviously, with a step size of zero the search position would be unchanged from the original hash position.

2. It should not return a value which divides exactly into the length of the table.
   This would mean that not all elements of the table could be probed. (e.g. if a table had 8 elements and a new entry which mapped to position 6 overflowed using a step size of 2 then the elements which could be probed are 8,2,4,6,8,2... etc.). This problem is easily solved by making the number of positions in the table a prime number and the step size some lesser value.

3. It must return a different step size for keys which are synonyms under the first hashing algorithm. For example, keys 1995 and 4016 both map to position 6, under the second hash algorithm they should have differing step sizes say 15, and 4. This restriction is necessary otherwise overflowing entries will still follow each other's 'footsteps' in a search for insert position.

A good second transformation algorithm for a table containing N elements is:

(N-2) - (key MOD (N-2))

In our example N = 17, so the step size is calculated as:

15 - (key MOD 15)

Using this double hashing approach, the *Add* operation would be coded using the logic:

```
IF new entry's idcode matches an existing one OR table full THEN
    Set success to zero
ELSE
    Transform the key to get insert position
    IF position in table is not empty or deleted THEN
        Calculate step size by hashing new entry's key
        (using second hash algorithm)
        REPEAT
            Calculate next position as
                        (current position + step size)MOD SIZE
        UNTIL table position empty or deleted
    ENDIF
    Insert new entry
    Add 1 to count
    Set success to 1
ENDIF
```

PROGRAMMING EXERCISE 7.11

Modify your hash table program to use Double Hashing overflow.

Hash Table Efficiency

The hash table gives a very small average number of comparisons when searching. When the table is around 50% full, the average number of comparisons required is approximately 1.625. Also, this value does not vary with the size of the table but rather with the percentage occupied. Hence a table which has 200 elements and is 50% full will have the same average number of comparisons when searching as one which has 5000 elements and is 50% full. Double hashing gives a slight improvement in the average over linear probing. When the table is over 70% full the average climbs rapidly and the best solution is to rehash all the entries into a larger table.

Summary

- **A hash table** is designed to give fast access to entries without excessive storage requirements.
- **The key field of the record is hashed** using a mapping algorithm to determine the point of insertion within the table.
- **Modular division** is the commonest method of hashing.
- **Synonyms** are keys which hash to the same value.
- **A collision** occurs when a record attempts insertion at a position already occupied.
- **A record overflows** into some other position in the table when the required insert position is already occupied.
- **Linear probing** searches forward one position at a time for an insert point.
- **Double hashing** calculates a step size when choosing the next position to be examined as a possible insert position.
- **Double hash algorithm must**:

  Not give a zero step size
  Not give a step size which divides exactly into the table size
  Not produce the same step size for all synonyms

SORTING

Introduction

Sorting is the act of arranging a list of items into a specific order. Typical examples of sorted information include:

- The entries in a telephone directory have been sorted into alphabetic order of the subscriber's name.
- A football league table has been sorted according to the points gained by each team.
- The entries in a bank statement have been sorted in order of date of transaction.

Consider a set of records held by a bookseller, giving details of the items in stock. Such a record could have the following structure:

```
BookRec =
RECORD
    Isbn    : INTEGER
    Title   : STRING
    Author  : STRING
    InStock : INTEGER
ENDRECORD
```

If the books are to be arranged in order of the author's name then the field, *Author*, is said to be the record's **sort key**.

The sort key is defined as the set of characters within a record that is used to determine order during the sorting process. This is sometimes simply referred to as the key. A key can consist of:

Part of a field
A single field
or Several fields

Sort Order

Sorting may arrange the data in either ascending or descending order. Ascending order is, by far, the more commonly used of the two organisations.

TASK 7.16

Write down the order of the following records after sorting them in ascending order using the Author field as the sort key.

ISBN	TITLE	AUTHOR	QTY
330	Childhood's End	A.C.Clarke	8
708	Janissaries	J.Pournelle	6
586	Hiero's Journey	S.E.Lanier	3
090	2001	A.C.Clarke	7
911	A Martian Odyssey	S.G.Weinbaum	1
569	2010	A.C.Clarke	2
255	I,Robot	I.Asimov	4

Since there are three books by A.C.Clarke in the data given in TASK 7.16, any arrangement of these three records would conform to the definition of a sorted list.

To define a unique order for the above records, the sort key specified must incorporate one or more additional fields. For example, the sort key could be *Author* followed by *Isbn*. That is, the sort can be thought of as the action of sorting the books by *Author* then for records with the same author, the *Isbn* is used to determine their order. The term used is sorting on ***ISBN within Author***.

Using *Author/Isbn* would give the Clarke books an order of:

```
090 2001                A.C.Clarke 7
330 Childhood's End     A.C.Clarke 8
569 2010                A.C.Clarke 2
```

In this situation, *Author* is termed the **major key**; *Isbn* is the **minor key**.

In practice, the sorting algorithm concatenates the fields that make up the key into a single string that is then used as the sort key.

A key made up of non-contiguous fields is known as a **split-key**.

Why Sort?

Some of the main reasons for sorting data are:

- The order in which items are stored often has a profound effect on the speed and simplicity of the algorithms that manipulate them.

  Example
  The binary search requires data to be in key field order.

- So that the output can be presented in a useful and meaningful form.

  Example
  Sales figures could be sorted to show
  a) Sales by branch
  b) Sales by item
  c) Sales by date

- So that calculations that require data in a particular order can operate efficiently.

  Example
  Sales forecasting would require sales data to be in chronological order.

- To facilitate the retrieval of information.

  Example
  Telephone directories would be difficult to use if not sorted by name.

Types of Sorts

There are two main classes of sorts:

Internal sorts

Here the data to be sorted is held entirely within the main memory of the machine. Obviously, this can only be used if the amount of data is relatively small.

External sorts

The data to be sorted is held on backing store. A batch of records from the data is read into main memory from backing store. These records are then sorted using internal sorting techniques and then written to a new file on backing store. This process continues until all of the original data has been read in, sorted and written to various files on disk (or tape). These files are then merged to form a single sorted file. We'll be looking at this in more detail later.

We will examine internal sorts only in this chapter.

Generally, internal sorts are faster than external sorts since all records to be sorted are held in main memory, the access to which is much faster than backing store access. The data is normally held in an array of records.

Types of Internal Sorts

Internal sorts may be sub-divided into 3 groups:

Selection sorts

These scan an unsorted list repeatedly, selecting the record with the smallest key on each scan through the list. The record selected is then added to the sorted list.

Insertion sorts

Each record in the unsorted list is taken in turn, starting at the first, and inserted into the correct position in a sorted list.

Exchange sorts

The keys of two records are compared and if the records are out of order with respect to each other they exchange positions. This process is repeated until the whole list is sorted.

The Selection Sorts

Simple Selection

This is possibly the simplest of all sort algorithms, being little more complicated than just finding the minimum value in a list.

We begin with two lists (in this case, we'll continue to use tables). One of the lists contains the records to be sorted (let's call it *t1*); the other (*t2*) is empty. Now, *t1* is scanned from start to finish in search of the record containing the lowest key. Once identified, this record is copied to the first empty position in *t2*. To ensure that the same record is not picked on the next pass through *t1*, each record transferred to t2 is erased from the unsorted list. This is usually achieved by replacing the key field with a value greater than any possible for a valid key.

These three steps constitute one **pass** of the sort and are shown in FIG-7.21.

The steps are repeated until all records have been transferred.

FIG-7.21

Simple Selection Sort

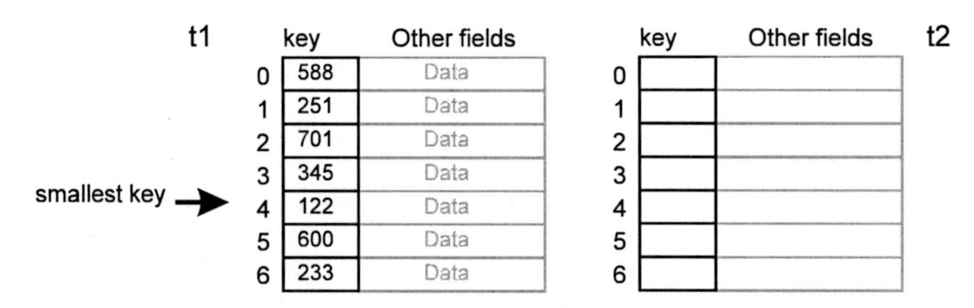

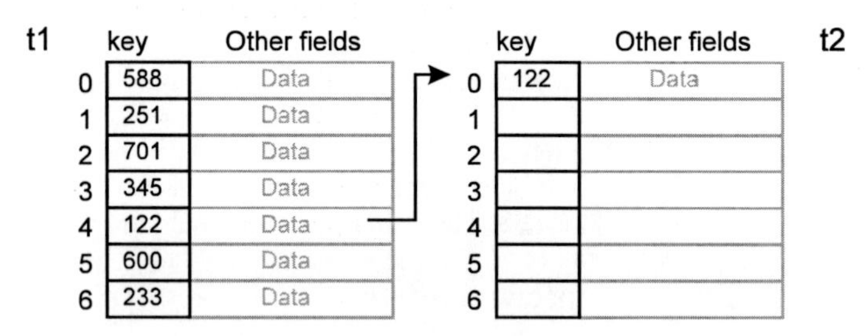

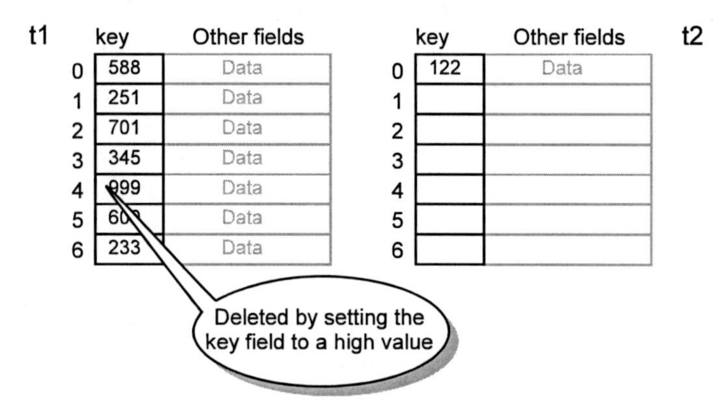

> **TASK 7.17**
>
> How many passes will be required before all 7 records shown in FIG-7.21 are transferred?

The number of passes required by a sort is one of the characteristics used to determine the efficiency of the sort.

The Simple Selection sort performed on a list of N entries can be described in Structured English as:

```
FOR N passes DO
    Find the smallest key in the unsorted list
    Copy the corresponding record to the first empty position
     in the sorted list
    Delete the record from the unsorted list
ENDFOR
```

PROGRAMMING EXERCISE 7.12

Using the table structure created in PROGRAMMING EXERCISE 7.9:

a) Create a function *SmallestAt()* which returns the position of the smallest *idcode* in a *StudentTable* variable.
b) Create a sort operation which will copy the contents of one table in sorted order to another.

(HINT: Use 32,767 when setting a record's *idcode* to a high value.)

We need to discover a few more facts before deciding the efficiency of this sort method.

TASK 7.18

1. To sort a list of *N* elements how many record storage elements are required?
2. How many comparisons are required to find the minimum key in the unsorted list during
    a) Pass 1
    b) Pass 2
    c) Pass *N*
3. What is the total number of comparisons carried out during the whole sorting process ?
4. How many record movements are there on each pass?
5. How many record movements does the sort require in total?

To summarise, when deciding on the efficiency of a sorting technique the following factors are taken into account:

- the storage requirements;
- the total number of comparisons involved;
- the total number of record movements required.

Selection With Exchange

The big problem with the Simple Selection sort that we looked at earlier was the space requirement: 2*N* record positions to sort *N* records. The obvious refinement is to reduce this to a single list of records so only *N* locations are required. In the Selection with Exchange sort, the minimum key in the list is found as before. However, this time the record involved is not moved to a different list but is swapped with the record at the top of the list. The process is shown in FIG-7.22.

This is the end of pass 1 and at this point we have the record with the smallest key in the first position (element 0) in the list. This means that only elements 2 and upwards have still to be sorted.

In the second pass we again search for the smallest key but only in the unsorted portion of the list (i.e. elements 1 to 6). When the smallest key in that array is found its record is exchanged with the record at the second position in the list. Now only elements 2 through 6 are unsorted. This continues until the search area is reduced to the last two records in the list. When the smallest of these two is found and repositioned then, as a consequence, the last record must be in the correct position also. FIG-7.23 shows the progression of the sort.

FIG-7.22

Selection with Exchange - The First Pass

Step 1: Find the smallest key in t1

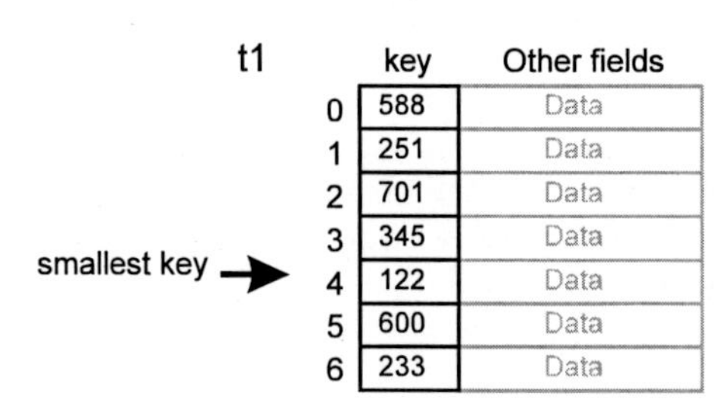

Step 2: Swap the first and smallest records

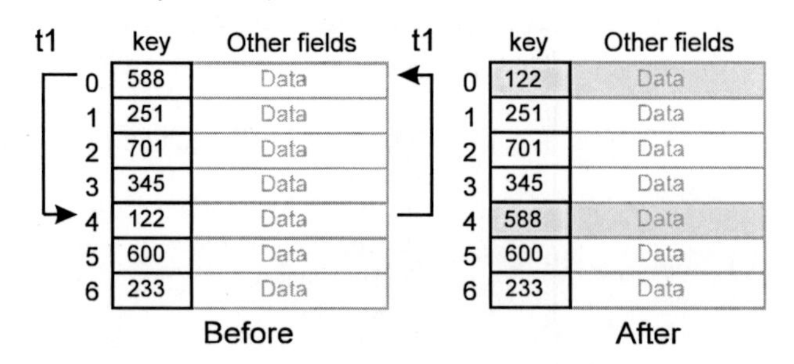

FIG-7.23

Selection with Exchange - Subsequent Passes

Pass 2:

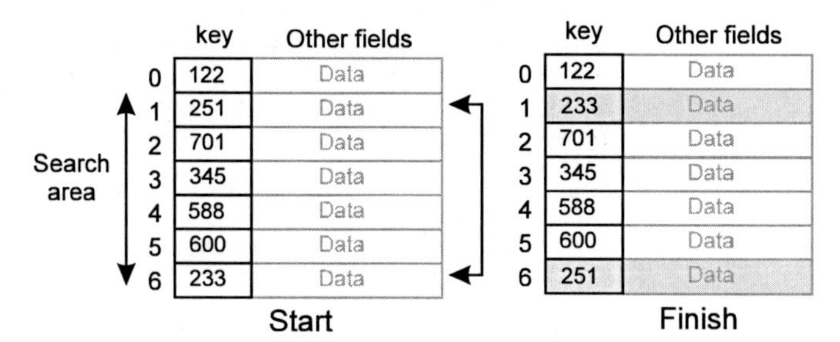

Pass 3:

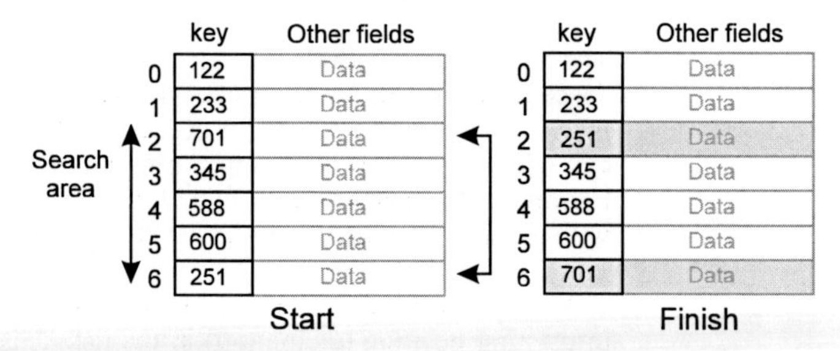

Pass 6:

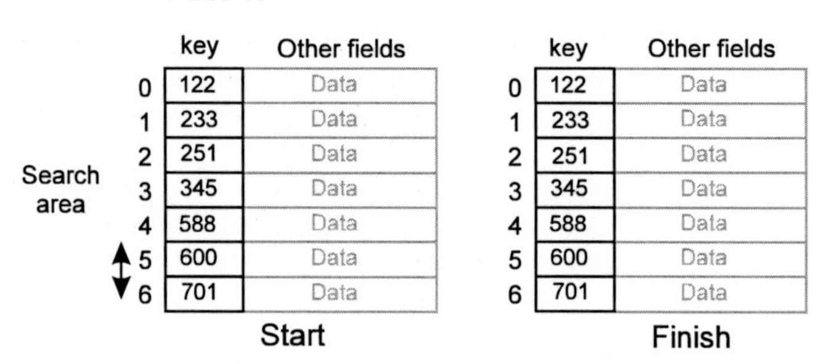

Since the last two elements sort on the final pass only 6 passes were required to sort the 7 element list in the example above. When a list containing *N* elements is sorted using this technique *N*-1 passes are required.

Note that the list contains a sorted area at the beginning of the list that grows larger by at least one record on each pass (2 on the last pass) and an unsorted area that correspondingly decreases on each pass. However, it is possible that, depending on the original ordering of the records, the sort may be completed in fewer passes. In the previous example, the sort was complete after only 3 passes.

The sort can be described in Structured English as:

```
FOR N-1 PASSES DO
    Find the smallest key in the unsorted part of the list
    Swap its record with the one at the top of the unsorted area
ENDFOR
```

TASK 7.19

1. How many comparisons are required to find the minimum key for a list of N elements on:
   a) Pass 1
   b) Pass 2
   c) Pass 3
   d) Pass *N*-1
2. What is the total number of comparisons required?
3. How many record movements are performed on each pass?
4. How many movements are performed in total?

PROGRAMMING EXERCISE 7.13

Change the sort operation written in PROGRAMMING EXERCISE 7.18 to use the Selection with Exchange sort method.

If we compare the statistics of the two Selection sorts we can see that while one has a smaller number of moves, the other has a smaller number of comparisons. These are the elements which are going to affect the execution time of the sort but which takes the longest to perform a comparision or a move?

The answer is - it depends. It depends on the length of the key and the length of the record. Keys will be compared a word at a time, so integer keys can be compared quickly, while a 15 digit character key will take longer. Also, record movement will depend on the length of the record - obviously a 50 character record can be moved more quickly than a 500 character record.

However, if a record is short (less than 100 characters) and the key is only a word or two long, then the time taken to perform a comparison can be taken as approximately equal to the time to move a record.

In that case, if we want to make a comparison of the likely execution time of two sort methods, then this can be achieved by adding the total number of moves and the total number of comparisons for each and comparing the figures.

The only time that the Simple Selection sort is the more efficient is when the records being moved are large, in which case the time taken to execute a move is much greater than the time required for a comparison. But since you'll need 2*N* locations the chances are you'll run out of space!

The Insertion Sorts

Simple Insertion

In the Simple Insertion sort, like the Simple Selection sort, two lists are used. One list contains the unsorted records, the other is initially empty. The records of the unsorted list are transferred one at a time, working from the start of the unsorted list to the second list. This second list is maintained in order at all times. This requirement usually involves moving records about within the second list. The first stages of the sort are shown in FIG-7.24.

FIG-7.24

The Simple Insertion Sort

Starting Condition: Copy the first record in t1 to t2

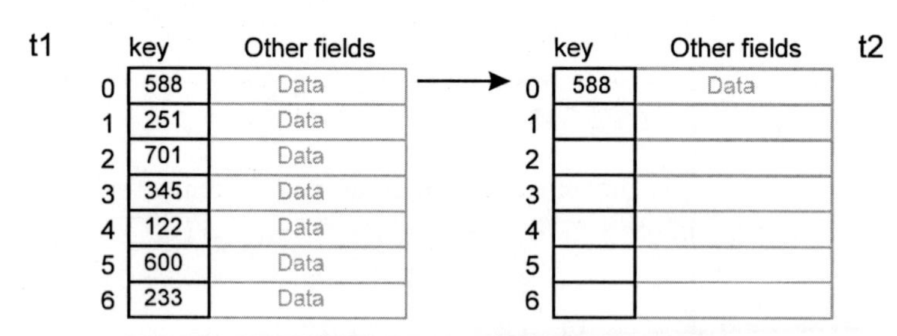

Step 1: Using the next record in t1, determine its insert point in t2

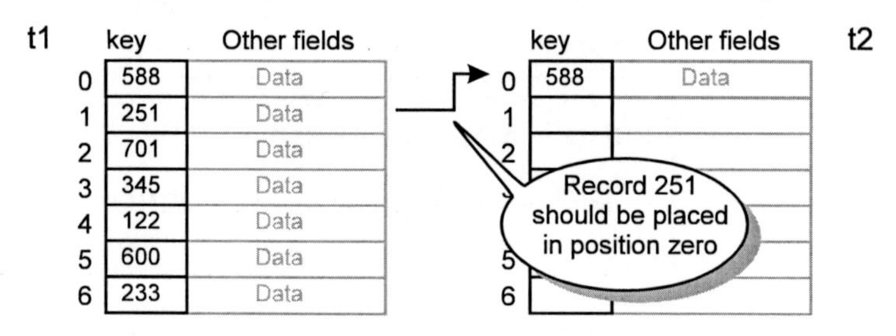

Step 2: Create a gap in t2 for the new record from t1

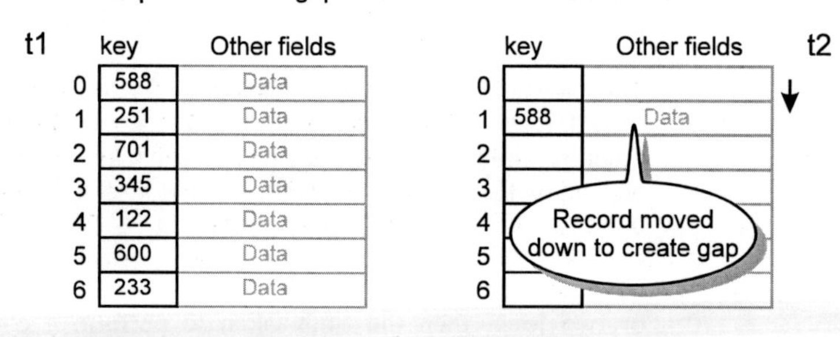

Step 3: Insert new record from t1

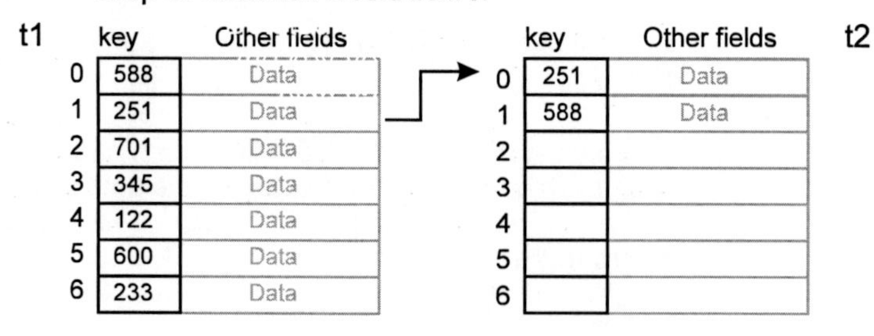

Steps 1 to 3 make up a single pass of the sort. Since the first record of t1 is simply copied across to t2, at the beginning of the sort, only 6 passes are required to sort the 7 records. Hence a list of *N* records requires *N-1* passes.

The sort Outline Logic is:

```
Move the first record to the sorted list
FOR N-1 passes DO
    Find the insert point in the sorted list for the next record
    Move the necessary records in the sorted list to make room
    for the new record
    Copy record from unsorted to sorted list
ENDFOR
```

The code for this is

```
void InsertionSort(const StudentTable& t1, StudentTable& t2)
{
    //*** Insert first record ***
    t2.list[0] = t1.list[0];
    t2.count = 1;
    //*** For each remaining record ***
    for(int pass=1; pass<t1.count;pass++)
    {
        //*** Find insert point ***
        int placeat = InsertAt(t1.list[pass].idcode,t2);
        //*** Move down lower records ***
        for(int post=t2.count-1;post>=placeat;post—)
        {
            t2.list[post+1]=t2.list[post];
        }
        //***Insert new record ***
        t2.list[placeat]=t1.list[pass];
        t2.count++;
    }
}
```

The auxiliary function, *InsertAt()*, is coded as:

```
int InsertAt(int id, const StudentTable& t)
{
    int post=0;
    while(t.list[post].idcode < id && post<t.count)
        post++;
    return post;
}
```

Although the example earlier shows the data to be sorted held in an array, the Insertion sort is often used when sorting an incomplete set of data. For example, if transactions are being entered at a keyboard at random intervals for an application which requires the transactions to be in sorted order at all times (perhaps for easy interrogation), then the Insertion sort is ideal since it does not require the complete set of data to be present before sorting is commenced. This is not true of other sorting methods.

PROGRAMMING EXERCISE 7.14

Modify your table program's *Add()* function to maintain a sorted table

As has been already stated, the number of comparisons and moves required by a sort gives an indication of its efficiency. However, these figures are not as easy to calculate for the Simple Insertion sort since they can vary. For example, FIG-7.25 shows the possible range of comparisons and moves involved when inserting a new entry in the sorted list.

FIG-7.25

Simple Insertion - The Range of Comparisons and Moves

Minimum Comparisons - Maximum Moves

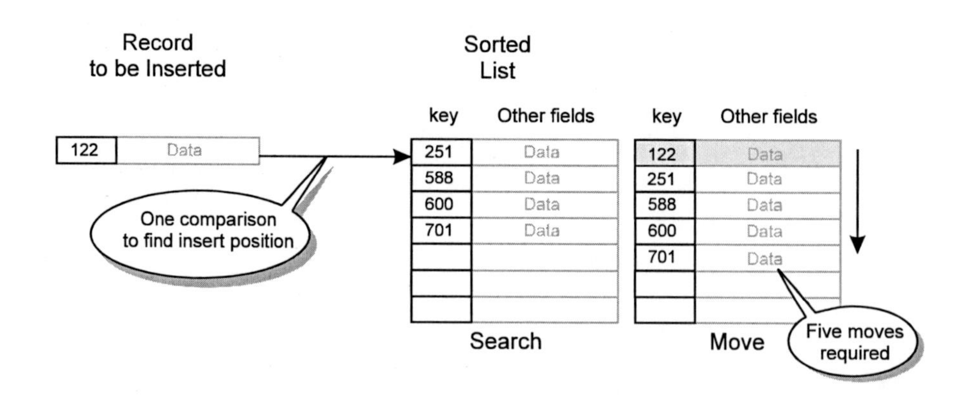

Maximum Comparisons - Minimum Moves

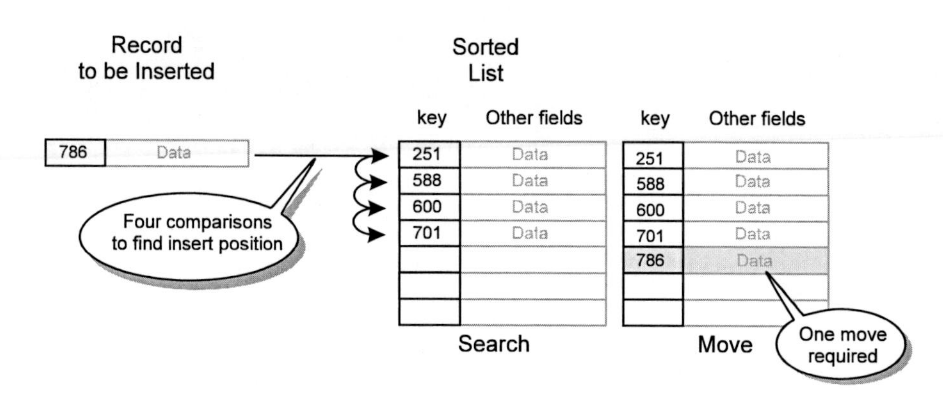

This requires us to talk in terms of the minimum and maximum moves and comparisons which can arise during each pass.

> **TASK 7.20**
>
> 1. Assuming a list contains *N* records, state the minimum and maximum moves and comparisons required during:
>   a) Pass 1
>   b) Pass 2
>   c) Pass 3
>   d) Pass *N*-1
> 2. What is the average number of moves and comparisons required to complete the sort?

It is in the nature of this sort that the better the original order of the list, the more comparisons (but less moves) there will be. Conversely, the worse the original order, the fewer comparisons and more moves. So the sort is slightly better at dealing with a source list which is already quite well ordered.

Finally, if we assume that a comparison and move take the same amount of time, then the moves and comparisons can be combined to give a figure of approximately:

$$N^2/2$$

Insertion With Exchange Sort

Just as we improved the simple selection sort by restricting the memory requirements to one list, so the Simple Insertion can be improved in the same way. When using only one list, we can think of it as consisting of sorted and unsorted areas.

At the beginning of the sort, the sorted area occupies only the first element of the list, but with each pass more and more of the list becomes sorted.

Initially the first entry in the list is considered to be in the sorted area. The keys of the first and second records are compared. If the records are in the wrong order they are exchanged. At this point the sorted area is two records in length.

Now the key of the third record is compared in turn with each of those in the sorted area (starting at record 2 and working backwards) until a key less than that of record 3 is encountered or the start of the list is reached. Record 3 is inserted at that point. The process continues until the whole list is sorted. FIG-7.26 shows the sort in action.

FIG-7.26

Selection with Exchange

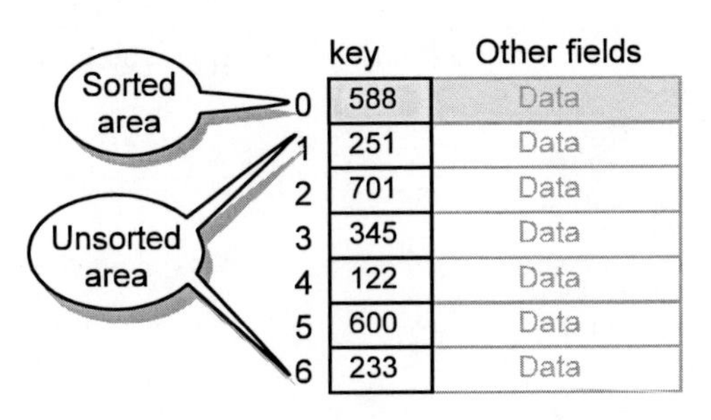

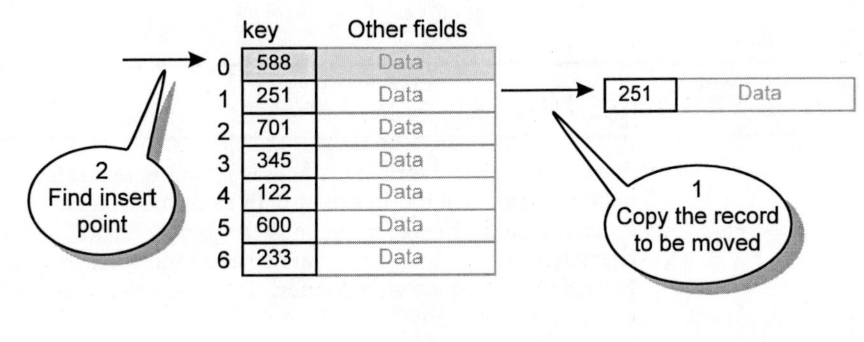

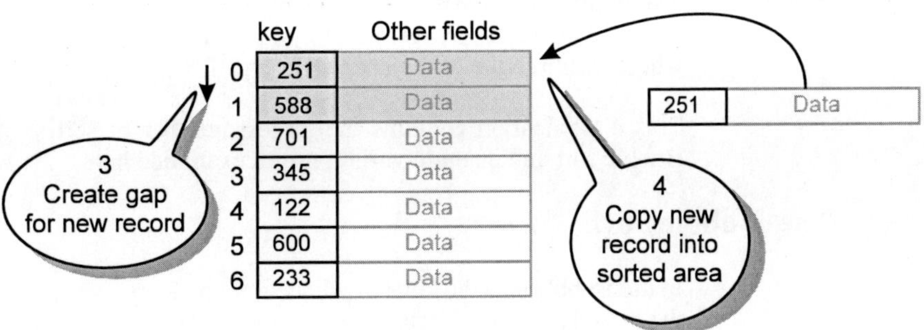

The logic of the Insertion with Exchange sort is:

```
FOR N-1 passes DO
    Make a copy of the record to be inserted
    Find the insert position in the unsorted area
    Create space for the new record in the sorted area
    Insert record at appropriate point
ENDFOR
```

For the *StudentTable* structure we can code this as:

```
void InsertionwithExchangeSort(StudentTable& t1)
{
    StudentDetails st; //Holds copy of record

    for(int pass=1; pass<t1.count;pass++)
    {
        //*** Copy record ***
        st=t1.list[pass];
        //*** Find insert point ***
        int placeat = InsertAt(st.idcode,t1,pass);
        //*** Move down lower records ***
        for(int post=pass-1;post>=placeat;post—)
            t1.list[post+1]=t1.list[post];
        //***Insert new record ***
        t1.list[placeat]=st;
    }
}
```

This makes use of a modified *InsertAt()* function which examines only a specified area of the table:

```
int InsertAt(int id, const StudentTable& t, int max)
{
    int post=0;
    while(t.list[post].idcode < id && post<max)
        post++;
    return post;
}
```

This method requires N(N-1)/4 comparisons and a maximum of $(N^2-4)/2$ moves; the average total moves being $(N^2-4)/4$.

The Exchange Sorts

The classification of sorting methods is seldom entirely clear-cut. Both the selection with exchange and the insertion with exchange can be viewed in some ways as exchange sorts. However, there is a group of sort methods whose dominant characteristic is the comparison of two items and, if they are not in order with respect to each other, an exchange is made.

This comparison and possible exchange is repeated as the list of records is scanned. The scan may work from top to bottom or vice versa. There are also some variations where the direction of the scan alternates from pass to pass.

This classification contains the largest number of sorting algorithms. Only the Bubble sort and its main variations are examined here.

The Bubble Sort

In the Bubble sort the keys of adjacent records are compared and where necessary the records exchange positions.
FIG-7.27 shows the first pass of a Bubble sort.

FIG-7.27

The Bubble Sort

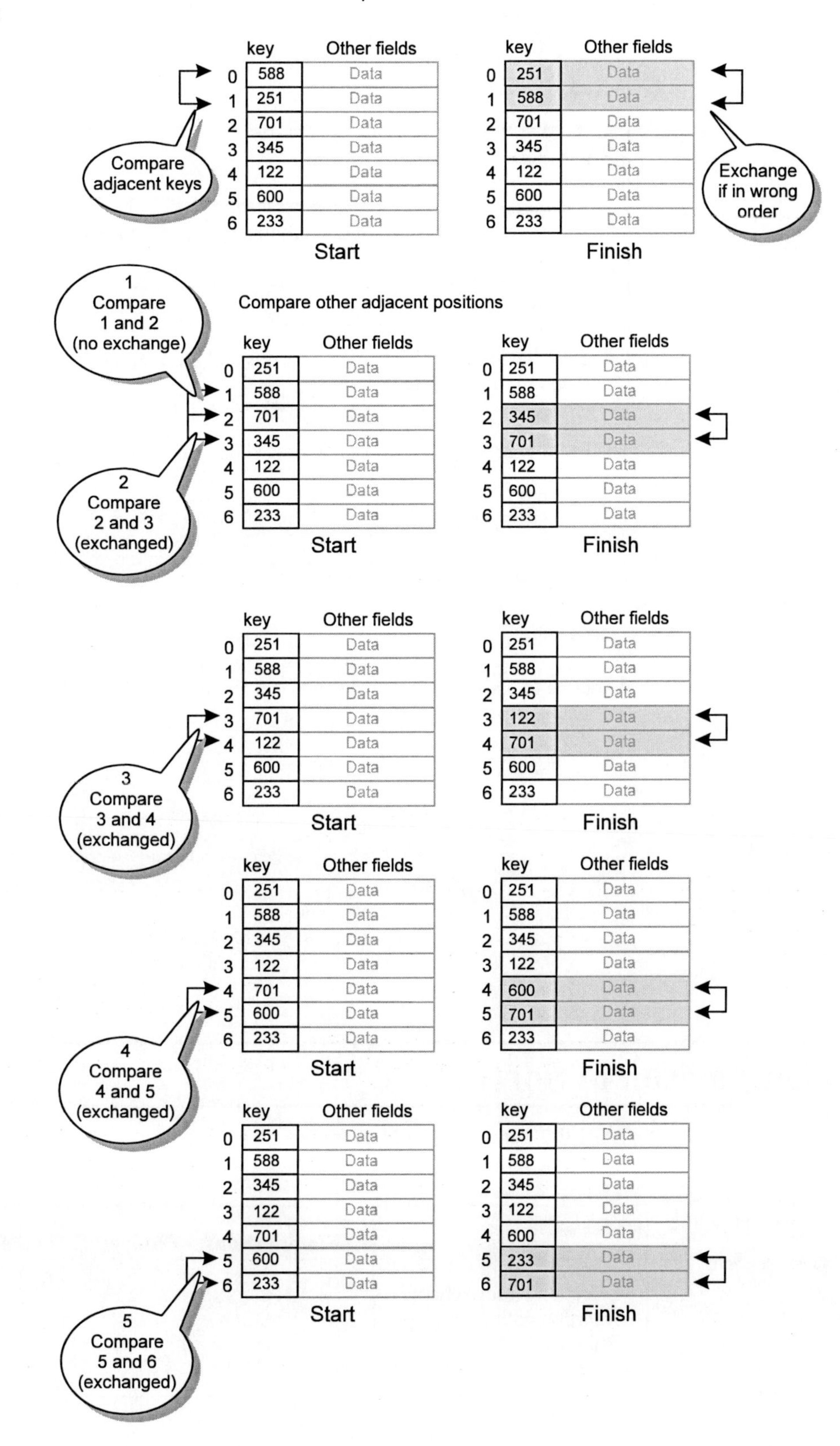

Note that by the end of the first pass, the record with the largest key has sunk to the bottom of the list. Again, we can think of the list containing a sorted area (this time at the bottom of the list) and an unsorted area. During the second pass we need only compare the records in the unsorted area (elements 0 to 5). When the second pass is complete, the record in the unsorted area with the largest key will have been moved to element 5 in the list, hence increasing the size of the sorted area by one.

TASK 7.21

1. Assuming a list of *N* records is to be sorted using the Bubble sort, state the number of comparisons and maximum moves required during:
   a) Pass 1
   b) Pass 2
   c) Pass 3
   d) Pass N-1
2. State the total number of comparisons and the average number of moves required to complete the sort.

The Bubble sort's algorithm can be described in Structured English as:

```
FOR N-1 passes DO
    Starting at the beginning of the list
    FOR number of records in the unsorted area of list -1 DO
        IF the next two records are out of order THEN
            Exchange them
        ENDIF
    ENDFOR
ENDFOR
```

A routine to perform the Bubble sort on a *StudentTable* variable is given below.

```
void BubbleSort(StudentTable& t1)
{
    StudentDetails st; //Holds copy of record

    for(int pass=1; pass<t1.count;pass++)
        for(int post = 0; post<t1.count-pass;post++)
            //*** IF wrong order, exchange records ***
            if(t1.list[post].idcode>t1.list[post+1].idcode)
            {
                st = t1.list[post+1];
                t1.list[post+1]=t1.list[post];
                t1.list[post]=st;
            }
}
```

Comparison of Sorts

TABLE-7.2 shows the average figures for sorting a list of 20 records using various sorting methods.

TABLE-7.2

Comparing Sorts

Sort	Comparisons	Moves	Total
Selection with Exchange	190	29	219
Insertion with Exchange	95	114	209
Bubble	190	285	475

The above table highlights how poor the Bubble sort is; the Insertion sort coming out best.

The Insertion sort's figures can be improved by using the Binary search during the scan of the sorted portion of the list.

Generally, sorts are compared on three standards:

1) Execution time.
   This is a function of the number of moves and comparisons which are affected by the order of the data.
2) Storage requirements.
3) The ease of implementation.

For short lists points 2) and 3) tend to be the most important but for longer lists and sorts which are to be executed often then factor 1) tends to be the most dominant.

Summary

- **Sorting involves** ordering data according to some data field(s).
- **Sorting may be required** for the presentation of data or the efficient processing of data.
- **Sorts may be classified** as either internal or external.
- **Internal sorts** hold all the data within the computer's memory.
- **External sorts** hold the data on back storage.
- **Internals sorts may be subdivided** into *Selection*, *Insertion* and *Exchange* sorts.
- **Selection sorting** involves finding the data with the lowest key and inserting it at the end of a list.
- **Insertion sorting** takes records in any order and adds them at the correct position in a sorted list.
- **Only Insertion sorts** may be used when not all the data is available at the start of the sort.
- **Exchange sorting** involves comparing two keys and swapping the position of the data if the keys are not in order.
- **Sort processes are compared** using the amount of storage space required, the number of comparisons, and the number of moves.

CASE STUDY

The Problem

Although a hash table gives very fast access to its data, any such structure is always limited in size to the amount of memory available.

An alternative is to create the hash table on disk where we are restricted only by the much larger capacity of the disk and get the bonus of having a permanent copy of our data.

Clarification

In this program we are simply going to create an alternative way of implementing *StudentTable*. All operations and their parameters must remain the same as before otherwise our original design will be compromised.

Implementing the Data Type

Data

We need to declare both a *StudentDetails* type and a *StudentTable* type, whereas the *StudentDetails* declaration is unchanged:

```
struct StudentDetails
{
    int idcode;
    char name[30];
    char sex;
    int score[6];
};
```

The declaration for *StudentTable* is simply a renaming of a FILE pointer type:

```
typedef FILE* StudentTable;
```

Operations

Although, as we will see, it is possible to write the existing operations of a *StudentTable* data type without violating the formal design definitions, it will be necessary to add two new operations: *OpenTable()* and *CloseTable()* which open and close the file used to hold the *StudentTable* structure.

These two operations are defined below:

```
NAME              :  OpenTable
PARAMETERS
    IN            :  filename:STRING
    OUT           :  t : StudentTable
    IN/OUT        :  None
PRE-CONDITION     :  None
POST-CONDITION    :  Opens a disk file named filename in which the
                     contents of t is stored.
```

NAME	:	CloseFile
PARAMETERS		
IN	:	t : StudentTable
OUT	:	None
IN/OUT	:	None
PRE-CONDITION	:	*t* has previously been opened
POST-CONDITION	:	Close the file holding the contents of t.

The main() program follows a simple menu driven logic:

```
Open table
REPEAT
    Display menu
    Get user option
    Execute option
UNTIL option is QUIT
Close table
```

Program Code

LISTING-7.2

Hashing to Disk

```
//***************************************************
//* PROGRAM     :   Disk Hash Table                 *
//* AUTHOR      :   Patricia Stamp                  *
//* DATE        :   30/5/1996                       *
//* VERSION     :   0.1                             *
//* DESCRIPTION :   Creates a disk-based hash table*
//* HARDWARE    :   PC Compatible                   *
//* SOURCE      :   Borland C++ v4.5                *
//***************************************************

#include<iostream.h>
#include<conio.h>
#include<string.h>
#include<ctype.h>
#include<stdio.h>
#include<stdlib.h>
#include<iomanip.h>

//*** Named constants ***
const int SIZE = 17;
const int EMPTY = 0;
const int DELETED = -1;
const int NOTFOUND = -1;

//*** Student record structure declaration ***
struct StudentDetails
{
  int idcode;
  char name[30];
  char sex;
  int score[6];
};

//*** Declare table type ***
typedef FILE* StudentTable;

//*************************************
//*** Table Operations Prototypes ***
//*************************************

//*** Main operations ***
void CreateTable(StudentTable&);
int Add(StudentDetails, StudentTable&);
```

Continued on next page

LISTING-7.2
(continued)

Hashing to Disk

```
void Display(const StudentTable&);
int Delete(int, StudentTable&);
//*** Auxiliary operations ***
int IsAt(int,const StudentTable&);
int Hash(int);
//*** New operations required for file handling ***
int OpenTable(char*,StudentTable&);
void CloseTable(StudentTable);

//************************************
//*** Other operation prototypes ***
//************************************
int DisplayMenu(char*);
int GetOption(int);
void ExecuteOption(int,StudentTable&);
void GetStudentDetails(StudentDetails&);



void main()
{
  StudentTable table;

  //***Open table ***
  if(OpenTable("C:\\MyDATA.dat",table)==0)
  {
      cout<<"Error!";
      exit(1);
  }
  int opt;
  int noofoptions;
  do
  {
      //*** Display menu ***
      clrscr();
      noofoptions=DisplayMenu("1-Create Table\n2-Add Student\n"
                  "3-Remove Student\n4-Display\n5-QUIT\n");
      //*** Get user option ***
      opt=GetOption(noofoptions);
      //*** Execute option ***
      ExecuteOption(opt,table);
  }
  while(opt!=noofoptions);
  //*** Close table ***
  CloseTable(table);
}


//**************************************
//*** Table Operations Definitions ***
//**************************************

//*** Create empty table ***
void CreateTable(StudentTable& t)
{
  StudentDetails st={EMPTY,"FRED",'M',{0,0,0,0,0,0}};
  //*** Move to start of file ***
  fseek(t,0,0);
  //*** Set every record's idcode file to EMPTY ***
  for(int c=1;c<=SIZE;c++)
      fwrite(&st,sizeof(st),1,t);
}

//*** Add new record to table ***
int Add(StudentDetails sd, StudentTable& t)
{
  if(IsAt(sd.idcode,t)!=-1)
      return 0;
```

Continued on next page

LISTING-7.2
(continued)

Hashing to Disk

```
    int post = Hash(sd.idcode);
    int start = post;
    StudentDetails st;
    //*** Seek the insert position ***
    fseek(t,post*sizeof(st),0);
    fread(&st,sizeof(st),1,t);
    while(st.idcode!=EMPTY&&st.idcode!=DELETED)
    {
        post++;
        if(post==start)
            return 0;
        fseek(t,post*sizeof(st),0);
        fread(&st,sizeof(st),1,t);
    }
    //*** Write new record to file ***
    fseek(t,post*sizeof(st),0);
    fwrite(&sd,sizeof(sd),1,t);
    return 1;
}

//*** Remove record from table ***
int Delete(int key, StudentTable& t)
{
    //*** Find entry ***
    int post = IsAt(key,t);
    //*** If not present, return ***
    if(post==NOTFOUND)
        return 0;
    //*** Delete by setting key field ***
    StudentDetails st;
    fseek(t,post*sizeof(st),0);
    fread(&st,sizeof(st),1,t);
    st.idcode = DELETED;
    fseek(t,post*sizeof(st),0);
    fwrite(&st,sizeof(st),1,t);
    return 1;
}

//*** Display contents of table ***
void Display(const StudentTable& t)
{
    StudentDetails st;
    fseek(t,0,0);
    while(fread(&st,sizeof(st),1,t)==1)
    {
        if(st.idcode != EMPTY&&st.idcode!=DELETED)
        {
            cout<<setw(6)<<st.idcode<<"  " <<st.name
                <<setw(20-strlen(st.name))<<' '<<setw(3)<<st.sex
                <<"   ";
            for(int d=0;d<6;d++)
                cout<<setw(4)<<st.score[d];
            cout<<endl;
        }
    }
}

//*** Open table's file ***
int OpenTable(char *filename, StudentTable& t)
{
    t=fopen(filename,"r+b");
    if(!t)
    {
        t=fopen(filename,"w+b");
        if(!t)
            return 0;
    }
    return 1;
}
```

Continued on next page

LISTING-7.2
(continued)

Hashing to Disk

```
//*** Close table's file ***
void CloseTable(StudentTable t)
{
  fclose(t);
}


//***************************************
///*** Auxiliary function Definitions ***
//***************************************

//*** Hash key to generate insert position ***
int Hash(int key)
{
  return key % SIZE;
}

//*** Find position of record in table ***
int IsAt(int key, const StudentTable& t)
{
  StudentDetails st;

  //*** Calculate insert position ***
  int post = Hash(key);
  int start = post;
  //*** Read record at that position ***
  fseek(t,post*sizeof(st),0);
  fread(&st,sizeof(st),1,t);
  //*** WHILE no match AND not empty DO ***
  while(st.idcode!=key&&st.idcode!=EMPTY)
  {
      post++;
      //*** IF searched all THEN exit loop ***
      if(post==start)
          break;
      //*** Read next record ***
      fseek(t,post*sizeof(st),0);
      fread(&st,sizeof(st),1,t);
  }
  //*** IF match found THEN return its position ***
  if(st.idcode!=key)
      return NOTFOUND;
  else
      //*** ELSE return -1 ***
      return post;
}

//**********************************
//*** Other function definitions ***
//**********************************

//*** Get student's details from keyboard ***
void GetStudentDetails(StudentDetails& sd)
{
  cout<<"Enter idcode : ";
  cin>>sd.idcode;
  cout<<"Enter name : ";
  gets(sd.name);
  cout<<"Enter sex (F or M) : ";
  cin>>sd.sex;
  cout<<"Enter test scores\n";
  for(int c=0;c<6;c++)
  {
      cout<<"for score "<<(c+1)<<" : ";
      cin>>sd.score[c];
  }
}
```

Continued on next page

LISTING-7.2
(continued)

Hashing to Disk

```
//*** Display menu ***
int DisplayMenu(char * m)
{
   cout<<m;
   int count=0;
   for(int c=0;c<=strlen(m);c++)
        if(m[c]=='\n')
             count++;
   return count;
}

//*** Get user option ***
int GetOption(int max)
{
   char opstr[3];
   cout<<"Enter option : ";
   gets(opstr);
   int op=atoi(opstr);
   while(op<1||op>max)
   {
        cout<<"\a?:";
        gets(opstr);
        op=atoi(opstr);
   }
   return op;
}

//*** Execute option ***
void ExecuteOption(int opt, StudentTable& t)
{
   switch(opt)
   {
        case 1:
             CreateTable(t);
             break;
        case 2:
             StudentDetails sd;
             GetStudentDetails(sd);
             Add(sd,t);
             break;
        case 3:
             cout<<"Enter idcode of record to be removed : ";
             int key;
             cin>>key;
             if(!Delete(key,t))
                  cout<<"Key not found\n";
             else
                  cout<<"Deleted\n";
             getch();
             break;
        case 4:
             clrscr();
             cout<<setw(45)<<"TABLE'S CONTENTS\n\n";
             cout<<" Idcode     Name";
             cout<<setw(13)<<' '<<"Sex            Scores\n";
             Display(t);
             getch();
             break;
        case 5:
             cout<<"TERMINATING PROGRAM\n";
             break;
   }
}
```

SELF-ASSESSMENT

1. What are the main parts of a data type?

2. Define the term **pre-condition**.

3. How is an operation's parameters affected by the method of implementation?

4. What is a table?

5. What are the main characteristics which should be considered when determining the efficiency of a search technique?

6. List three search methods.

7. What are the benefits of a direct access table?

8. Describe two methods of dealing with hash table collisions.

9. What are the two main types of sort?

10. What is the number of comparisons required when using a Simple Selection sort on a list of *N* records?

Solutions

TASK 7.1

ADT Distance is

DATA

A distance is stored in terms of yards, feet and inches. Where yards can be any non-negative integer value, feet has an integer value between 0 and 2, and inches has an integer value between 0 and 11.

OPERATIONS

NAME	:	SetDistance
PARAMETERS		
IN	:	nyards : INTEGER nfeet : INTEGER ninches : INTEGER
OUT	:	d : Distance
IN/OUT	:	None
PRE-CONDITION	:	*nyards*<=0 AND 0<=*nfeet*<=2 AND 0<=*ninches*<=11
POST-CONDITION	:	*d* is set to *nyards* yards, *nfeet* feet, *ninches* inches

NAME	:	ConvertToMetric
PARAMETERS		
IN	:	d : Distance
OUT	:	result : REAL
IN/OUT	:	None
PRE-CONDITION	:	None
POST-CONDITION	:	*result* is set to the kilometre equivalent of *d*

NAME	:	GetYards
PARAMETERS		
IN	:	d : Distance
OUT	:	result : INTEGER
IN/OUT	:	None
PRE-CONDITION	:	None
POST-CONDITION	:	*result* is set to *d.yards*

NAME	:	GetFeet
PARAMETERS		
IN	:	d : Distance
OUT	:	result : INTEGER
IN/OUT	:	None
PRE-CONDITION	:	None
POST-CONDITION	:	*result* is set to *d.feet*

NAME	:	GetInches
PARAMETERS		
IN	:	d : Distance
OUT	:	result : INTEGER
IN/OUT	:	None
PRE-CONDITION	:	None
POST-CONDITION	:	*result* is set to *d.inches*

END ADT

PROGRAMMING EXERCISE 7.1

```
#include<iostream.h>
//****************************************
//*** Distance Data Type Declarations ***
//****************************************
//*** Data ***
struct Distance
{
    int yards;
    int feet;
    int inches;
};

//***Operations ***
void SetDistance(int nyards, int nfeet, int
ninches, Distance& d)
{
    if(nyards < 0 || nfeet < 0 || nfeet > 2 ||
ninches < 0 || ninches > 11)
        return;
    d.yards = nyards;
    d.feet = nfeet;
    d.inches = ninches;
}

double ConvertToMetric(Distance d)
{
    return (d.yards*36+d.feet*12+d.inches)*0.0254;
}

int GetYards(Distance d)
{
    return d.yards;
}

int GetFeet(Distance d)
{
    return d.feet;
}

int GetInches(Distance d)
{
    return d.inches;
}

//****************************************
//***    Test Driver for Distance     ***
//****************************************

void main()
{
    //*** Create the Distance variable ***
    Distance d1;

    //*** Initialise to zero ***
    SetDistance(0,0,0,d1);

    //*** Read value for distance ***
    cout << "Enter yards : ";
    int y;
    cin >> y;
    cout << "Enter feet : ";
    int f;
    cin >> f;
    cout << "Enter inches : ";
    int i;
    cin >> i;
    //*** Assign value to distance variable ***
    SetDistance(y,f,i,d1);

    //*** Display distance in yds, ft, in ***
    cout<<GetYards(d1)<<" yds "<<GetFeet(d1)
        <<" ft "<<GetInches(d1)<<" in\n";

    //*** Display distance in metres ***
    cout<<ConvertToMetric(d1)<<" metres\n";
}
```

TASK 7.2

ADT StudentDetails is

DATA

A student's details are stored in terms of the student's idcode, name, sex and the scores achieved on six tests. The test scores should lie in the range 0 to 100.

OPERATIONS

NAME	:	SetId
PARAMETERS		
IN	:	newid : INTEGER
OUT	:	None
IN/OUT	:	st : StudentDetails
PRE-CONDITION	:	newid > 0
POST-CONDITION	:	*idcode* in *st* set to *newid*

```
NAME            : SetName
PARAMETERS
    IN          : newname: STRING
    OUT         : None
    IN/OUT      : st       : StudentDetails
PRE-CONDITION   : None
POST-CONDITION  : name part of st set to newname

NAME            : SetSex
PARAMETERS
    IN          : newsex  : CHAR
    OUT         : None
    IN/OUT      : st       : StudentDetails
PRE-CONDITION   : newsex = 'M' OR newsex = 'F'
POST-CONDITION  : sex part of st set to newsex

NAME            : SetScore
PARAMETERS
    IN          : newscore: INTEGER
                  scnum   : INTEGER
    OUT         : None
    IN/OUT      : st       : StudentDetails
PRE-CONDITION   : 0 <= newscore <= 100
                  AND 1<=scnum <=6
POST-CONDITION  : score[scnum] part of st set to
                  newscore

NAME            : GetId
PARAMETERS
    IN          : st       : StudentDetails
    OUT         : result
    IN/OUT      : None
PRE-CONDITION   : None
POST-CONDITION  : result set to idcode part of st

NAME            : GetName
PARAMETERS
    IN          : st       : StudentDetails
    OUT         : result
    IN/OUT      : None
PRE-CONDITION   : None
POST-CONDITION  : result set to name part of st

NAME            : GetSex
PARAMETERS
    IN          : st       : StudentDetails
    OUT         : result
    IN/OUT      : None
PRE-CONDITION   : None
POST-CONDITION  : result set to isex part of st

NAME            : GetScore
PARAMETERS
    IN          : st       : StudentDetails
                  scnum    : INTEGER
    OUT         : result
    IN/OUT      : None
PRE-CONDITION   : 1 <= scnum <= 6
POST-CONDITION  : result set to score[scnum]
                  part of st
END ADT
```

PROGRAMMING EXERCISE 7.2

```
#include<iostream.h>
#include<string.h>
#include<stdio.h>
//*****************************************
//*** Student Data Type Declarations  ***
//*****************************************
//*** Data ***
struct StudentDetails
{
    int idcode;
    char name[31];
    char sex;
    int scores[6];
};

//***Operations ***
void SetIdcode(int newid, StudentDetails& st)
{
    if(newid <= 0)
        return;
    st.idcode = newid;
}

void SetName(char newname[], StudentDetails& st)
{
    strcpy(st.name,newname);
}

void SetSex(char newsex, StudentDetails& st)
{
    if(newsex !='M' && newsex != 'F')
        return;
    st.sex = newsex;
}

void SetScore(int newscore, int scnum,
StudentDetails& st)
{
    if(newscore < 0 || newscore > 100 || scnum < 1
    || scnum > 6)
        return;
    st.scores[scnum-1] = newscore;
}

int GetIdcode(StudentDetails st)
{
    return st.idcode;
}

void GetName(StudentDetails st, char result[])
{
    strcpy(result,st.name);
}

char GetSex(StudentDetails st)
{
    return st.sex;
}

int GetScore(int scnum, StudentDetails st)
{
    if(scnum < 1 || scnum > 6)
        return -1;
    return st.scores[scnum-1];
}

//*****************************************
//***  Test Driver for StudentDetails ***
//*****************************************

void main()
{
    //*** Create the StudentDetails variable ***
    StudentDetails st;

    //*** Read value for idcode ***
    cout << "Enter idcode : ";
    int id;
    cin >> id;
    SetIdcode(id,st);
    //*** Read in and assign name ***
    cout << "Enter name : ";
    char name[31];
    gets(name);
    SetName(name,st);
    //*** Read in and set sex ***
    cout << "Enter sex : ";
    char sex;
    cin >> sex;
    SetSex(sex,st);
    //*** Read in and set all 6 scores ***
    int score;
    for(int c = 1; c <= 6; c++)
    {
        cout<<"Enter score "<<c<<" : ";
        cin>>score;
        SetScore(score,c,st);
    }
    //*** Display student's details ***
    cout<<"Idcode : "<<GetIdcode(st)<<endl;
    char ans[31];
    GetName(st,ans);
    cout<<"Name   : "<<ans<<endl;
    cout<<"Sex    : "<<GetSex(st)<<endl;
    for(c=1; c <= 6; c++)
        cout<<GetScore(c,st)<<"    ";
    cout<<endl;
}
```

PROGRAMMING EXERCISE 7.3

```
int IsAt(int key, const StudentTable& t)
{
    int position = 0;
    while(t.list[position].idcode != key
     && position<t.count-1)
        position++;
    if(t.list[position].idcode == key)
        return position;
    else
        return -1;
}
```

PROGRAMMING EXERCISE 7.4

```
#include<iostream.h>
#include<string.h>
#include<stdio.h>
#include<iomanip.h>
#include<conio.h>
#include<stdlib.h>
#include<ctype.h>


//***************************************
//***       StudentDetails Type      ***
//***************************************
//*** Data ***
struct StudentDetails
{
    int idcode;
    char name[31];
    char sex;
    int scores[6];
};

//***Operations ***
void SetIdcode(int newid, StudentDetails& st)
{
    if(newid <= 0)
        return;
    st.idcode = newid;
}

void SetName(char newname[], StudentDetails& st)
{
    strcpy(st.name,newname);
}

void SetSex(char newsex, StudentDetails& st)
{
    if(newsex !='M' && newsex != 'F')
        return;
    st.sex = newsex;
}

void SetScore(int newscore, int scnum,
StudentDetails& st)
{
    if(newscore < 0 || newscore > 100
    || scnum < 1 || scnum > 6)
        return;
    st.scores[scnum-1] = newscore;
}

int GetIdcode(StudentDetails st)
{
    return st.idcode;
}

void GetName(StudentDetails st, char result[])
{
    strcpy(result,st.name);
}

char GetSex(StudentDetails st)
{
    return st.sex;
}

int GetScore(int scnum, StudentDetails st)
{
    if(scnum < 1 || scnum > 6)
        return -1;
    return st.scores[scnum-1];
}

//*********************************************
//***         END StudentDetails Type       ***
//*********************************************

//*********************************************
//***           StudentTable Type           ***
//*********************************************
//*** Data ***
const SIZE =20;
struct StudentTable
{
    int count;
    StudentDetails list[SIZE];
};

//*** Operations ***
//*** Create empty table ***
void CreateTable(StudentTable& t)
{
    t.count=0;
}

//*** Find position of entry in table ***
int IsAt(int key, const StudentTable& t)
{
    int position = 0;
    while(t.list[position].idcode != key
    && position<t.count-1)
        position++;
        if(t.list[position].idcode==key)
            return position;
        else
            return -1;
}
//*** Add new record to table ***
int Add(StudentDetails st, StudentTable& t)
{
    if(IsAt(st.idcode,t)!=-1||t.count==SIZE)
        return 0;
    t.list[t.count]=st;
    t.count++;
        return 1;
}

//*** Display contents of table ***
void Display(const StudentTable& t)
{
    if (t.count==0)
        cout<<"Table is empty\n";
    else
    {
        cout<<setw(50)<<"STUDENT TABLE CONTENTS\n\n";
        for(int c=0;c<t.count;c++)
        {
            cout    <<setw(6)<<t.list[c].idcode
                    <<setw(20)<<t.list[c].name
                    <<setw(3)<<t.list[c].sex;
            for(int d=0;d<6;d++)
                cout<<setw(4)<<t.list[c].scores[d];
            cout<<endl;
        }
    }
}

//*********************************************
//***       END StudentTable Data Type     ***
//*********************************************


//*** Other Function Declarations ***
void GetData(char*,int,char*);
void ExpandString(char*);
void ReadStudentDetails(StudentDetails&);
int DisplayMenu(char*);
int GetOption(int);
void ExecuteOption(int,StudentTable&);

//*********************************************
//***         Test Driver for Table         ***
//*********************************************

void main()
{
    StudentTable table;
    int noofopts,op;
    CreateTable(table);
    do
    {
        noofopts =  DisplayMenu(
                "1 - Create Table\n"
                "2 - Add new student\n"
                "3 - Display Table\n4 - QUIT\n");
        op = GetOption(noofopts);
        ExecuteOption(op,table);
    }
    while(op!=noofopts);
}
```

```
//*********************************************
//***     Other routine definitions         ***
//*********************************************
void GetData(char *allowed, int max,char
*result)
{
    const int ENTER=13;
    const int BACKSPACE=8;
    char ch;
    int count=0;               //chars entered
    char expandedset[256];  //allowed chars

    //*** Expanded alowed char set ***
    strcpy(expandedset,allowed);
    ExpandString(expandedset);
    //***Start with empty result***
    strcpy(result,"");
    //*** Read a character ***
    ch=getch();
    //*** WHILE return key not pressed ***
    while(ch!=ENTER)
    {
        //*** If allowed char & result not full ***
        if(strchr(expandedset,ch)&&count<max)
        {
            //** Display char and add to result **
            cout<<ch;
            count++;
            result[count-1]=ch;
            result[count]=0;
        }
        //*** ELSE if delete&result not empty ***
        else if(ch==BACKSPACE&&count>0)
        {
            //** Remove last char **
            cout<<"\b \b";
            count--;
            result[count]=0;
        }
        //*** Read another character ***
        ch=getch();
    }
    cout<<endl;
}

void ExpandString(char *s)
{
    char temp[256]="";
    //Empty temp storage
    //*** Copy the first character across ***
    temp[0]=s[0];
    //*** For all but the last 2 chars DO ***
    for(int c=1,p=1;c<=int(strlen(s))-3;c++)
    {
        //** If two dots **
        if(s[c]=='.'&&s[c+1]=='.')
        {
            //* Insert range of chars implied *
            for(char ch=s[c-1]+1;ch<=s[c+2];ch++)
                temp[p++]=ch;
            //* Move past this part of the text *
            c+=2;
        }
        else
        //** Else copy char ***
        temp[p++]=s[c];
    }
    //*** Copy any remaining characters ***
    for(int k=c;k<=int(strlen(s))-1;k++,c++)
        temp[p++]=s[c];
    //*** Insert final NULL character ***
    temp[p]='\0';
    strcpy(s,temp);
}

void ReadStudentDetails(StudentDetails& st)
{
    char temp[31];  //Temp store for data entered
    //*** Get idcode ***
    //** Read up to 5 digits **
    cout<<"Enter id code : ";
    GetData("0..9 ",5,temp);
    //** Convert to numeric distance **
    st.idcode=atoi(temp);
    //*** Get name ***
    cout<<"Enter name : ";
    GetData("A..Za..z . -'",30,st.name);
    //*** Get sex ***    cout<<"Enter sex : ";
    cout<<"Enter sex : ";
    GetData("FMfm",1,temp);
    st.sex = toupper(temp[0]);
    //*** Get six scores ***
    for(int c=0;c<6;c++)
    {
        cout<<"Enter score "<<(c+1)<<" : ";
        GetData("0..9",3,temp);
        st.scores[c]=atoi(temp);
        while(st.scores[c]>100)
        {
            cout<<"\a?:";
            GetData("0..9",3,temp);
            st.scores[c]=atoi(temp);
        }
    }
}

int DisplayMenu(char * m)
{                       //char from keyboard
    cout<<m;
    int count=0;
    for(int c=0;c<=strlen(m);c++)
        if(m[c]=='\n')
            count++;
    return count;
}

int GetOption(int max)
{
    char opstr[3];
    cout<<"Enter option : ";
    gets(opstr);
    int op=atoi(opstr);
    while(op<1||op>max)
    {
        cout<<"\a?:";
        gets(opstr);
        op=atoi(opstr);
    }
    return op;
}

void ExecuteOption(int opt, StudentTable& t)
{
    switch(opt)
    {
        case 1:
            CreateTable(t);
            break;
        case 2:
            StudentDetails sd;
            ReadStudentDetails(sd);
            if(!Add(sd,t))
            {
                cout<<"Error could not be added\n";
                getch();
            }
            break;
        case 3:
            Display(t);
            getch();
            break;
        case 4:
            cout<<"TERMINATING PROGRAM\n";
            break;
    }
}
```

TASK 7.3

There's a slight complication here in as much as we are now required to return two values from the function.

This is no real problem for the ADT operations definition which is modified to:

NAME	:	GiveRecord
PARAMETERS		
IN	:	key : INTEGER t : StudentTable
OUT	:	success : INTEGER st : StudentDetails
IN/OUT	:	None
PRE-CONDITION	:	None
POST-CONDITION	:	If key matches an *idcode* in *t*, then *st* contains a copy of the entry in t whose *idcode* is *key* and *success* is set to 1. If *key* does not match an entry in *t*, *st* contains an *idcode* of -1 and *success* is set to zero.

PROGRAMMING EXERCISES 7.5 to 7.7

```
#include<iostream.h>
#include<conio.h>
#include<string.h>
#include<ctype.h>
#include<stdio.h>
#include<stdlib.h>
#include<iomanip.h>

//****************************************
//***       StudentDetails Type        ***
//****************************************
//*** Data ***
struct StudentDetails
{
    int idcode;
    char name[31];
    char sex;
    int scores[6];
};

//***Operations ***
void SetIdcode(int newid, StudentDetails& st)
{
    if(newid <= 0)
        return;
    st.idcode = newid;
}

void SetName(char newname[], StudentDetails& st)
{
    strcpy(st.name,newname);
}

void SetSex(char newsex, StudentDetails& st)
{
    if(newsex !='M' && newsex != 'F')
        return;
    st.sex = newsex;
}

void SetScore(int newscore, int scnum,
StudentDetails& st)
{
    if(newscore < 0 || newscore > 100
    || scnum < 1 || scnum > 6)
        return;
    st.scores[scnum-1] = newscore;
}

int GetIdcode(StudentDetails st)
{
    return st.idcode;
}

void GetName(StudentDetails st, char result[])
{
    strcpy(result,st.name);
}

char GetSex(StudentDetails st)
{
    return st.sex;
}

int GetScore(int scnum, StudentDetails st)
{
    if(scnum < 1 || scnum > 6)
        return -1;
    return st.scores[scnum-1];
}

//**********************************************
//***         END StudentDetails Type        ***
//**********************************************

//**********************************************
//***             StudentTable Type          ***
//**********************************************
//*** Data ***
const SIZE =20;
struct StudentTable
{
    int count;
    StudentDetails list[SIZE];
};

//*** Operations ***

//*** Create empty table ***
void CreateTable(StudentTable& t)
{
    t.count=0;
}

//*** Add new record to table ***
int Add(StudentDetails st, StudentTable& t)
{
    if(IsAt(st.idcode,t)!=-1||IsFull(t))
        return 0;
    t.list[t.count]=st;
    t.count++;
    return 1;
}

//*** Display contents of table ***
void Display(const StudentTable& t)
{
    if (t.count==0)
        cout<<"Table is empty\n";
    else
    {
        cout<<setw(50)<<"STUDENT TABLE CONTENTS\n\n";
        for(int c=0;c<t.count;c++)
        {
            cout    <<setw(6)<<t.list[c].idcode
                    <<setw(20)<<t.list[c].name
                    <<setw(3)<<t.list[c].sex;
            for(int d=0;d<6;d++)
                cout<<setw(4)<<t.list[c].scores[d];
            cout<<endl;
        }
    }
}

//*** Returns a specified entry in the table ***
int GetRecord(int key, const StudentTable& t,
                            StudentDetails& st)
{
    StudentDetails failed={0,"", ,{0,0,0,0,0,0}};
    int post;
    if((post=IsAt(key,t))!=-1)
    {
        st= t.list[post];
        return 1;
    }
    else
    {
        st = failed;
        return 0;
    }
}
int GiveRecordAt(int post, const StudentTable& t
                            ,StudentDetails& st)
{
    StudentDetails failed={0,"", ,{0,0,0,0,0,0}};
    if(post<1||post>t.count)
    {
        st=failed;
        return 0;
    }
    st= t.list[post-1];
    return 1;
}

//*** Delete a specified entry ***
int Delete(int key, StudentTable& t)
{
    int post;
    if((post=IsAt(key,t))==-1)
        return 0;
    for(int c=post+1;c<t.count;c++)
        t.list[c-1]=t.list[c];
    t.count;
    return 1;
}

int UpdateRecord(const StudentDetails& st,
                            StudentTable& t)
{
    int post;

    if((post=IsAt(st.idcode,t))==-1)
        return 0;
    else
    {
        t.list[post]=st;
        return 1;
    }
}

//*** Determine if table is full ***
int IsFull(const StudentTable& t)
{
    if(t.count==SIZE)
        return 1;
    else
        return 0;
};

//*** Determine number of given sex ***
int NoOfSex(char sex, const StudentTable& t)
{
    int count=0;
```

```
    char Sex = toupper(sex)

    if(Sex!=F&&Sex!=M)
        return -1;
    else
    {
        for(int c=0;c<t.count;c++)
            count+=(t.list[c].sex==Sex);
        return count;
    }
}

//*** Find position of entry in table ***
int IsAt(int key, const StudentTable& t)
{
    int position = 0;
    while(t.list[position].idcode != key
                        && position<t.count-1)
        position++;
    if(t.list[position].idcode==key)
        return position;
    else
        return -1;
}

//*******************************************
//***  END StudentTable Type Declaration  ***
//*******************************************

//*** Other Function Declarations ***
void GetData(char*,int,char*);
void ExpandString(char*);
void ReadStudentDetails(StudentDetails&);
int DisplayMenu(char*);
int GetOption(int);
void ExecuteOption(int,StudentTable&);


void main()
{
    StudentTable table;
    int noofopts,op;

    CreateTable(table);
    clrscr();
    do
    {
      clrscr();
      noofopts =    DisplayMenu(
        "1  - Create Table\n2  - Add new student\n"
        "3  - Modify name\n4  - Modify score\n"
        "5  - Delete Entry\n6  - Count sex\n"
        "7  - Display record at given position\n"
        "8  - Display table\n9  - QUIT\n");
      op = GetOption(noofopts);
      ExecuteOption(op,table);
    }
    while(op!=noofopts);
}

//**********************************************
//***        Other routine definitions        *
//**********************************************

void GetData(char *allowed, int max,
                              char *result)
{
    const int ENTER=13;
    const int BACKSPACE=8;

    char ch;                 //char from keyboard
    int count=0;             //chars entered
    char expandedset[256];   //allowed chars

    //*** Expanded alowed char set ***
    strcpy(expandedset,allowed);
    ExpandString(expandedset);
    //***Start with empty result***
    strcpy(result,"");
    //*** Read a character ***
    ch=getch();
    //*** WHILE return key not pressed ***
    while(ch!=ENTER)
    {
        //*** If allowed char & result not full ***
        if(strchr(expandedset,ch)&&count<max)
        {
            //** Display char and add to result **
            cout<<ch;
            count++;
            result[count-1]=ch;
            result[count]=0;
        }
        //*** ELSE if delete & result not em
        else if(ch==BACKSPACE&&count>0)
        {
            //** Remove last char **
            cout<<"\b \b";
            count;
            result[count]=0;
        }
        //*** Read another character ***
        ch=getch();
    }
    cout<<endl;
}

void ExpandString(char *s)
{
    char temp[256]=""; //Empty temp storage

    //*** Copy the first character across ***
    temp[0]=s[0];
    //*** For all but the last 2 chars DO ***
    for(int c=1,p=1;c<=int(strlen(s))-3;c++)
    {
        //** If two dots **
        if(s[c]==.&&s[c+1]==.)
        {
            //* Insert range of chars implied *
            for(char ch=s[c-1]+1;ch<=s[c+2];ch++)
                temp[p++]=ch;
            //* Move past this part of the text *
            c+=2;
        }
        else
            //** Else copy char ***
            temp[p++]=s[c];
    }
    //*** Copy any remaining characters ***
    for(int k=c;k<=int(strlen(s))-1;k++,c++)
        temp[p++]=s[c];
    //*** Insert final NULL character ***
    temp[p]=\0;
    strcpy(s,temp);
}

void ReadStudentDetails(StudentDetails& st)
{
    char temp[31];  //Temp store for data entered
    //*** Get idcode ***
    //** Read up to 5 digits **
    cout<<"Enter id code : ";
    GetData("0..9 ",5,temp);
    //** Convert to numeric distance **
    st.idcode=atoi(temp);
    //*** Get name ***
    cout<<"Enter name : ";
    GetData("A..Za..z . -'",30,st.name);
    //*** Get sex ***   cout<<"Enter sex : ";
    cout<<"Enter sex : ";
    GetData("FMfm",1,temp);
    st.sex = toupper(temp[0]);
    //*** Get six scores ***
    for(int c=0;c<6;c++)
    {
        cout<<"Enter score "<<(c+1)<<" : ";
        GetData("0..9",3,temp);
        st.scores[c]=atoi(temp);
        while(st.scores[c]>100)
        {
            cout<<"\a?:";
            GetData("0..9",3,temp);
            st.scores[c]=atoi(temp);
        }
    }
}

int DisplayMenu(char * m)
{
    cout<<m;
    int count=0;
    for(int c=0;c<=strlen(m);c++)
        if(m[c]==\n)
            count++;
    return count;
}

int GetOption(int max)
{
    char opstr[3];
    cout<<"Enter option : ";
    gets(opstr);
    int op=atoi(opstr);
    while(op<1||op>max)
    {
        cout<<"\a?:";
        gets(opstr);
        op=atoi(opstr);
    }
    return op;
}
                        pty ***
void ExecuteOption(int opt, StudentTable& t)
{
    int examno, exammark;
    char temp[30];
```

```
int id;
StudentDetails st;
int post;
char sex;
int total;

switch(opt)
{
    case 1: //*** Create Table ***
        CreateTable(t);
        break;
    case 2: //*** Add student ***
        StudentDetails sd;
        ReadStudentDetails(sd);
        if(!Add(sd,t))
        {
            cout<<"Error could not be added\n";
            getch();
        }
        break;
    case 3: //*** Change name ***
        cout<<"Enter idcode of record : ";
        GetData("0..9",4,temp);
        id = atoi(temp);
        if (!GetRecord(id,t,st))
        {
            cout<<"Record not found\n";
            getch();
        }
        else
        {
            cout<<"Enter new name : ";
            GetData("a..zA..Z .-",29,temp);
            SetName(temp,st);
            UpdateRecord(st,t);
        }
        break;
    case 4: //*** Change score ***
        cout<<"Enter idcode of record : ";
        GetData("0..9",4,temp);
        id = atoi(temp);
        if (!GetRecord(id,t,st))
        {
            cout<<"Record not found\n";
            getch();
        }
        else
        {
            cout<<"Enter exam number : ";
            GetData("1..6",1,temp);
            examno=atoi(temp);
            cout<<"Enter new mark : ";
            GetData("0..9",3,temp);
            exammark = atoi(temp);
            while (exammark>100)
            {
                cout<<"\a?:";
                GetData("0..9",3,temp);
                exammark = atoi(temp);
            }
            SetScore(examno,exammark,st);
            UpdateRecord(st,t);
        }
        break;
    case 5: // *** Delete a record ***
        cout<<"Enter id to be removed : ";
        GetData("0..9",5,temp);
        id=atoi(temp);
        if(Delete(id,t))
        {
            cout<<"Record deleted\n";
            getch();
        }
        else
        {
            cout<<"Record not found\n";
            getch();
        }
    case 6: //*** Number of given sex ***
        cout<<"Enter sex (M or F) : ";
        GetData("MFmf",1,temp);
        sex=toupper(temp[0]);
        total=NoOfSex(sex,t);
        if(sex==M)
            cout<<"There are "<<total
                <<" males\n";
        else
            cout<<"There are "<<total
                <<" females\n";
        break;
    case 7: //*** Display record at ***
        cout<<"Enter the records position : ";
        GetData("0..9",2,temp);
        post = atoi(temp);
        if(GiveRecordAt(post,t,st)==0)
        {
            cout<<"Invalid position\n";
            getch();
        }
        else
        {
            for(int c=0;c<t.count;c++)
            {
                cout<<setw(6)<<st.idcode
                    <<setw(20)<<st.name
                    <<setw(3)<<st.sex;
                for(int d=0;d<6;d++)
                    cout<<setw(4)<<st.scores[d];
                cout<<endl;
            }
            getch();
        }
        break;
    case 8:
        Display(t);
        getch();
        break;
    case 9:
        cout<<"TERMINATING PROGRAM\n";
        break;
    }
}
```

TASK 7.4

a) 128 i.e. (1+255)/2
b) (1+N)/2

TASK 7.5

This condition tests for the end of the entries being reached without finding a match.

PROGRAMMING EXERCISE 7.8

We need to start by modifying the declaration of *StudentTable* type to make sure there is always room for a copy of the search key by increasing the size of *list* by 1:

```
struct StudentTable
{
    int count;
    StudentDetails list[SIZE+1];
};


//*** Find position of entry in table ***
int IsAt(int key, StudentTable& t)
{
    int position = 0;

    //*** Copy reqd key to end of table ***
    t.list[t.count].idcode=key;
    //*** Find match for key ***
    while(t.list[position].idcode != key)
        position++;
    //*** IF found at inserted key position THEN ***
    if (position==t.count)
        //*** return not found ***
        return -1;
    else
        //*** ELSE return position of match ***
        return position;
}
```

Notice that the table is no longer passed as a `const` to *IsAt()*. This change is required since the table is modified by *IsAt()*.

Otherwise, the program is unchanged.

TASK 7.6

a) 1
b) 6
c) 7

TASK 7.7

1. The number of comparisons required to reach each key in the table is:

Key	Comparisons
122	4
1 93	3
210	4
217	2
233	4
251	3
279	4
345	1
399	4
422	3
442	4
478	2
588	4
600	3
701	4

2. a) 1
   b) 2
   c) 4
   d) 8

3. ((1*1)+(2*2)+(4*3)+(8*4))/15
   = 3.27

TASK 7.8

a) 1
b) None

TASK 7.9

a) 4
b) 5
c) 10
d) 14

TASK 7.10

	lowest	highest
Initially	0	15
After 1 comp	8	15
After 2	8	10
After 3	10	10

PROGRAMMING EXERCISE 7.9

The following changes are required from Programming Exercise 7.8:
The list size in the table declaration may be returned to its original length:

```
struct StudentTable
{
    int count;
    StudentDetails list[SIZE+1];
};
```

The new version of *IsAt()* is:

```
int IsAt(int key, const StudentTable& t)
{
    int lowest=0, highest=t.count-1;
    int mid = (lowest+highest)/2;
    while(t.list[mid].idcode != key &&
    lowest<=highest)
    {
        if(t.list[mid].idcode< key)
            lowest = mid + 1;
        else
            highest = mid - 1;
        mid = (lowest+highest)/2;
    }
    if(lowest<=highest)
        return mid;
    else
        return -1;
}
```

All other code remains unchanged.

TASK 7.11

1.

```
int IsAt(int key const StudentTable& t)
{
    if(t.list[key].idcode==key)
        return key;
    else
        return -1;
}
```

2.

```
int Delete(int key, StudentTable& t)
{
    if(t.list[key].idcode == idcode)
    {
        t.list[key].idcode=DELETED;
        return 1;
    }
    else
        return 0;
}
```

TASK 7.12

```
a)  10 + 24 + 38 = 72
b)  102 + 438 = 540
```

TASK 7.13

```
value = (key[0]&0X0F)<<4+
        key[strlen(key)-1]&0X0F
```

TASK 7.14

Key	Position
8838	15
6627	14
4895	16
1995	6

TASK 7.15

No change is required to this routine; only the function responsible for finding the table entry (*IsAt()*) requires modification.

The code for give *GiveRecord()* remains as:

```
//*** Returns a specified entry in the table
***
int GetRecord(int key, const StudentTable& t,
    StudentDetails& st)
{
    StudentDetails failed={0,"", ,{0,0,0,0,0,0}};
    int post;
    if((post=IsAt(key,t))!=-1)
    {
```

```
        st= t.list[post];
        return 1;
    }
    else
    {
        st = failed;
        return 0;
    }
}
```

PROGRAMMING EXERCISE 7.10

```
#include<iostream.h>
#include<conio.h>
#include<string.h>
#include<ctype.h>
#include<stdio.h>
#include<stdlib.h>
#include<iomanip.h>

//*********************************************
//***           StudentDetails Type        ***
//*********************************************
//*** StudentDetails code goes here
//*********************************************
//***         END StudentDetails Type      ***
//*********************************************

//*********************************************
//***           StudentTable Type          ***
//*********************************************
//*** Data ***
const SIZE = 17;
const int EMPTY = 0;
const int DELETED = -1;
const int NOTFOUND = -1;
struct StudentTable
{
    int count;
    StudentDetails list[SIZE];
};

//*** Operations ***
//*** Create empty table ***
void CreateTable(StudentTable& t)
{
    //*** Set count to zero ***
    t.count=0;
    //*** Set all key fields to empty ***
    for(int c=0;c<SIZE;c++)
        t.list[c].idcode=EMPTY;
}

//*** Add new record to table ***
int Add(StudentDetails st, StudentTable& t)
{
    //*** If the id exists OR table full return ***
    if(IsAt(st.idcode,t)!=NOTFOUND||IsFull(t))
        return 0;
    //*** Find insert position ***
    int post = Hash(st.idcode);
    while(t.list[post].idcode != EMPTY&&
                t.list[post].idcode != DELETED)
        post=(post+1)%SIZE;
    //*** Add new entry ***
    t.list[post]=st;
    t.count++;
    return 1;
}

//*** Display contents of table ***
void Display(const StudentTable& t)
{
    for(int c=0;c<SIZE;c++)
        if(t.list[c].idcode!=EMPTY&&
                    t.list[c].idcode!=DELETED)
        {
            cout<<setw(6)<<t.list[c].idcode
                <<setw(20)<<t.list[c].name
                <<setw(3)<<t.list[c].sex;
            for(int d=0;d<6;d++)
                cout<<setw(4)<<t.list[c].score[d];
            cout<<endl;
        }
}

//*** Returns a specified entry in table ***
int GetRecord(int key, const StudentTable& t,
                            StudentDetails& st)
{
    StudentDetails failed={0,"", ,{0,0,0,0,0,0}};
    int post;
    if((post=IsAt(key,t))!=-1)
    {
        st= t.list[post];
        return 1;
    }
    else
    {
        st = failed;
        return 0;
    }
}

//*** Delete a specified entry ***
int Delete(int key, StudentTable& t)
{
    //*** Find entry ***
    int post = IsAt(key,t);
    //*** If not present, return ***
    if(post==NOTFOUND)
        return 0;
    //*** Delete by setting key field ***
    t.list[post].idcode=EMPTY;
    t.count;
    return 1;
}

int UpdateRecord(const StudentDetails& st,
StudentTable& t)
{
    int post;

    if((post=IsAt(st.idcode,t))==-1)
        return 0;
    else
    {
        t.list[post]=st;
        return 1;
    }
}

//*** Determine if table is full ***
int IsFull(const StudentTable& t
{
    if(t.count==SIZE)
        return 1;
    else
        return 0;
};

//*** Determine number of given sex ***
int NoOfSex(char sex, const StudentTable& t)
{
    int count=0;
    char Sex = toupper(sex);
    if(Sex!=F&&Sex!=M)
        return -1;
    else
    {
        for(int c=0;c<SIZE;c++)
            if(t.list[c].idcode != EMPTY &&
                t.list[c].idcode != DELETED)
                count+=(t.list[c].sex==Sex);
        return count;
    }
}

//*** Find position of entry in table ***
int IsAt(int key, const StudentTable& t)
{
    int post = Hash(key);
    int start=post;
    while(t.list[post].idcode!=key&&
                t.list[post].idcode!=EMPTY)
    {
        post=(post+1)%SIZE;
        if(post==start)
            break;
    }
    if(t.list[post].idcode!=key)
        return NOTFOUND;
    else
        return post;
}

//*********************************************
//***         END StudentTable Type        ***
//*********************************************

//*** Other Function Declarations ***

void GetData(char*,int,char*);
void ExpandString(char*);
int DisplayMenu(char*);
int GetOption(int);
void ExecuteOption(int,StudentTable&);


void main()
{
    StudentTable table;
    int noofopts,op;
```

```
    CreateTable(table);
    clrscr();
    do
    {
      clrscr();
      noofopts =     DisplayMenu(
        "1  - Create Table\n2  - Add new student\n"
        "3  - Modify name\n4  - Modify score\n"
        "5  - Delete Entry\n6  - Count sex\n"
        "7  - Display table\n8  - QUIT\n");
      op = GetOption(noofopts);
      ExecuteOption(op,table);
    }
    while(op!=noofopts);
}

//**********************************************
//***         Other routine definitions         *
//**********************************************
//*** Definition of GetData goes here
//*** Definition of ExpandString goes here
//*** Definition of DisplayMenu goes here
//*** Definition of GetOption goes here

void ExecuteOption(int opt, StudentTable& t)
{
    int examno, exammark;
    char temp[30];
    int id;
    StudentDetails st;

char sex;
    int total;

    switch(opt)
    {
        case 1: //*** Create Table ***
            CreateTable(t);
            break;
        case 2: //*** Add student ***
            StudentDetails sd;
            Read(sd);
            if(!Add(sd,t))
            {
                cout<<"Error could not be added\n";
                getch();
            }
            break;
        case 3: //*** Change name ***
            cout<<"Enter idcode of record : ";
            GetData("0..9",4,temp);
            id = atoi(temp);
            if (!GetRecord(id,t,st))
            {
                cout<<"Record not found\n";
                getch();
            }
            else
            {
                cout<<"Enter new name : ";
                GetData("a..zA..Z .-",29,temp);
                ModifyName(temp,st);
                UpdateRecord(st,t);
            }
            break;
        case 4: //*** Change score ***
            cout<<"Enter idcode of record : ";
            GetData("0..9",4,temp);
            id = atoi(temp);
            if (!GetRecord(id,t,st))
            {
                cout<<"Record not found\n";
                getch();
            }
            else
            {
                cout<<"Enter exam number : ";
                GetData("1..6",1,temp);
                examno=atoi(temp);
                cout<<"Enter new mark : ";
                GetData("0..9",3,temp);
                exammark = atoi(temp);
                while (exammark>100)
                {
                    cout<<"\a?:";
                    GetData("0..9",3,temp);
                    exammark = atoi(temp);
                }
                ModifyScore(examno,exammark,st);
                UpdateRecord(st,t);
            }
            break;
        case 5: // *** Delete a record ***
            cout<<"Enter id of entry to be removed : ";
            GetData("0..9",5,temp);
            id=atoi(temp);
            if(Delete(id,t))
            {
                cout<<"Record deleted\n";
                getch();
            }
            else
            {
                cout<<"Record not found\n";
                getch();
            }
            break;
        case 6: //*** Number of given sex ***
            cout<<"Enter sex (M or F) : ";
            GetData("MFmf",1,temp);
            sex=toupper(temp[0]);
            total=NoOfSex(sex,t);
            if(sex==M)
                cout<<"There are "<<total
                    <<" males\n";
            else
                cout<<"There are "<<total
                    <<" females\n";
            getch();
            break;
        case 7:
            Display(t);
            getch();
            break;
        case 8:
            cout<<"TERMINATING PROGRAM\n";
            break;
    }
}
```

PROGRAMMING EXERCISE 7.11

Few changes are required to the previous program. These are:

1. The definition of a *StepSize()* function:

```
inline int StepSize(int key){return (SIZE-2)-key
% (SIZE-2);}
```

2. An update to the *Add()* function:

```
//*** Add new record to table ***
int Add(StudentDetails st, StudentTable& t)
{
    //*** If id exists OR table full return ***
    if(IsAt(st.idcode,t)!=NOTFOUND||IsFull(t))
      return 0;
    //*** Find insert position ***
    int post = Hash(st.idcode);
    if(t.list[post].idcode != EMPTY &&
           t.list[post].idcode != DELETED)
    {
        int step = StepSize(st.idcode);
        while(t.list[post].idcode != EMPTY &&t.
                  list[post].idcode != DELETED)
            post=(post+step)%SIZE;
    }
    //*** Add new entry ***
    t.list[post]=st;
    t.count++;
    return 1;
}
```

3. An update to *IsAt()* function:

```
//*** Find position of entry in table ***
int IsAt(int key, const StudentTable& t)
{
    int post = Hash(key);
    int start=post;
    if(t.list[post].idcode != key &&
                t.list[post].idcode != EMPTY)
    {
        int step = StepSize(key);
        while(t.list[post].idcode!=key &&
                t.list[post].idcode!=EMPTY)
        {
            post=(post+step)%SIZE;
            if(post==start)
                break;
        }
    }
    if(t.list[post].idcode!=key)
        return NOTFOUND;
    else
        return post;
}
```

TASK 7.16

The important thing here is not to be fooled into sorting on the surname. The computer will treat the name field as a simple string when organising the data.

The final result will give the records in the order

330
090
569
255
708
589
911

Since the first three records have the same author, these can be given in any order.

TASK 7.17

7 passes. One for each record transferred.

PROGRAMMING EXERCISE 7.12

a)

```
int SmallestAt(const StudentTable& t)
{
    int smallestid=t.list[0].idcode, post=0;
    for(int c=1;c<t.count;c++)
        if(t.list[c].idcode<smallestid)
        {
            smallestid = t.list[c].idcode;
            post = c;
        }
    return post;
}
```

b)

```
void SelectionSort(StudentTable& t1,
                   StudentTable& t2)
{
    for(int pass = 1;pass<=t1.count;pass++)
    {
        int post=SmallestAt(t1);
        t2.list[pass-1]=t1.list[post];
        t1.list[post].idcode=32767;
    }
    t2.count = t1.count;
}

void SelectionSort(StudentTable&,
StudentTable&);
```

TASK 7.18

1. 2N
2. a) N-1
   b) N-1
   c) N-1
3. N(N-1)   i.e. Passes * Comparisons per pass
4. 1
5. N

TASK 7.19

1. a) N-1
   b) N-2
   c) N-3
   d) 1   i.e. N - (N-1)
2. N(N-1)/2   i.e. Passes * Average comparisons per pass
3. 3
4. 3(N-1)

PROGRAMMING EXERCISE 7.13

Since we only want to search a restricted area of the table for the smallest key, we begin by rewriting *SmallestAt()* to specify the area of the table to be searched:

```
int SmallestAt(const StudentTable& t,int start)
{
    int smallestid=t.list[start].idcode,
        post=start;
    for(int c=start+1;c<t.count;c++)
        if(t.list[c].idcode<smallestid)
        {
            smallestid = t.list[c].idcode;
            post = c;
        }
    return post;
}
```

The new sort routine is coded as:

```
void SelectionWithExSort(StudentTable& t)
{
    for(int pass = 1 ; pass<t.count;pass++)
    {
        int post=SmallestAt(t,pass-1);
        StudentDetails st = t.list[pass-1];
        t.list[pass-1]=t.list[post];
        t.list[post]=st;
    }
}
```

PROGRAMMING EXERCISE 7.14

```
int Add(StudentDetails st, StudentTable& t)
{
    if(IsAt(st.idcode,t)!=-1)
        return 0;
    int placeat = InsertAt(st.idcode,t);
    //*** Move down lower records ***
    for(int post=t.count-1;post>=placeat;post)
        t.list[post+1]=t.list[post];
    //***Insert new record ***
    t.list[placeat]=st;
    t.count++;
    return 1;
}
```

TASK 7.20

1.

	Moves		Comparisons	
	Min	Max	Min	Max
a)	1	2	1	1
b)	1	3	1	2
c)	1	4	1	3
d)	1	N	1	N-1

2.

Min moves total	= N-1
Max moves total	= (N-1)(N+2)/2
Av. moves	= $(N^2+3N-4)/4$
Min comparisons total	= N-1
Max comparisons total	= N(N-1)/2
Av. comparisons	= $(N^2+N-2)/4$

TASK 7.21

1. a) Comparisons: N-1 Max moves : 3(N-1)
   b) Comparisons: N-2 Max moves : 3(N-2)
   c) Comaprisons: N-3 Max moves : 3(N-3)
   d) Comparisons: 1 Max moves : 3

2. Total comparisons : N(N-1)/2
   Total av. moves : 3N(N-1)/4

CHAPTER 8

Dynamic Linear Types

This chapter covers the following topics:

Creating Library Files

Creating a Linked List

Designing a Node

Doubly Linked Lists

Problems with Fixed Size Storage

Queues

Stacks

Using Library Files

LINKED LISTS

The Problem with Arrays

We have already seen that it is possible to define a pointer to any data type. For example, we might create a pointer to an `int` value using the definition

```
int *iptr;
```

One of the advantages of using pointers is that we are free to create and destroy data as and when required using the `new` and `destroy` commands.

Of course, with only one pointer, we can only reference a single item of data. What if we want to reference several data items using pointers?

One way to tackle this is to create an array of pointers (see the Case Study in the previous chapter). This approach is acceptable if we know in advance the maximum number of data items to be created, since we need to specify the size of the array (see FIG-8.1).

FIG-8.1

An Array of Pointers

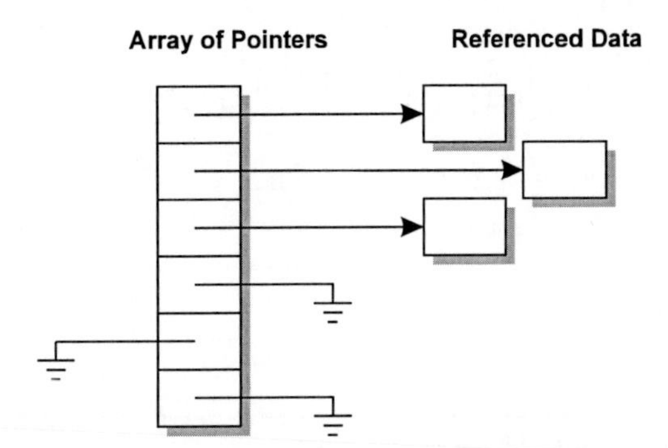

But when the number of items involved cannot be predicted this technique is of little use. What we need is some way of increasing the number of pointers available as our storage requirements grow. This is the purpose of a **linked list**.

Creating a Linked List

Adding a pointer field to a Structure

A standard structure might be declared as

```
struct Data
{
    // data fields declared here
};
```

The idea behind a linked list is to combine the pointer and the data in a single structure. Hence, the new structure would be:

Node is the usual term for a component of a linked list.

```
struct Node
{
    Data    value;
    Node    *next;
};
```

Manipulating a Linked List

How does this help us create a collection of data unlimited in size? The easiest way to see how this approach solves our problem is to follow a specific example. Let's assume that our declarations are

```
struct Data
{
    int     no;
};

struct Node
{
    Data    value;
    Node    *next;
};
```

and that our program has defined a pointer to this structure:

```
Node *start;
```

We can create space and store a value using the instructions

```
start = new Node;
start->value.no = 12;
start->next = NULL;
```

This situation is shown in FIG-8.2.

FIG-8.2

Pointer to a Node

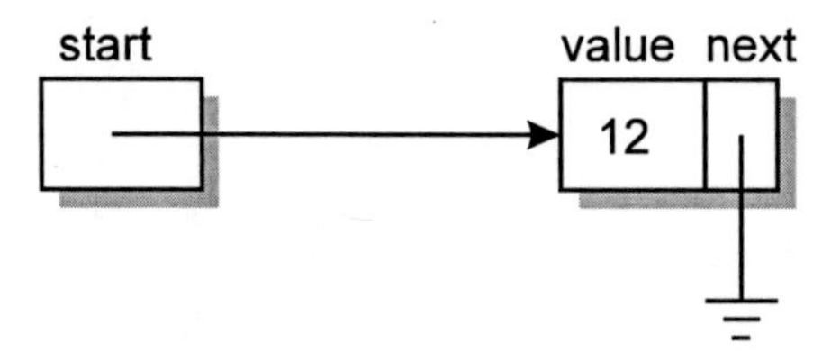

> **TASK 8.1**
>
> What expressions are required to reference the following parts of the node?
> a) *value*
> b) *next*

Notice that, as well as creating space for our data, we have also created another pointer. Now, when a second item of data needs to be stored, we can use this newly created pointer as a reference to the second data item:

```
start->next = new Node;
start->next->value.no = 53;
start->next->next = NULL;
```

This gives us the situation shown in FIG-8.3.

FIG-8.3

Pointing to the next Node

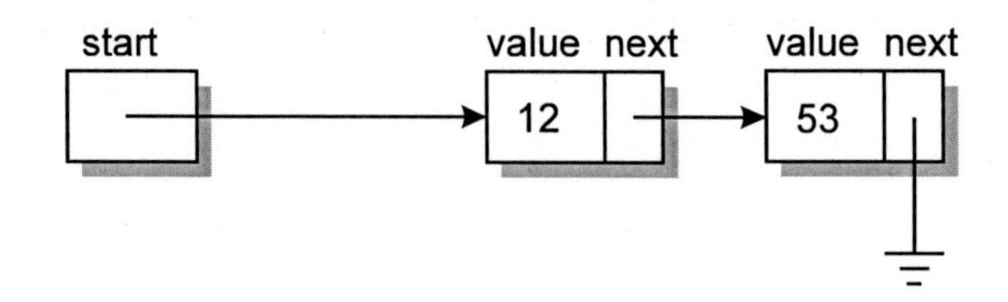

This linking together of the data components gives rise to the data structure's name: **linked list**. Continuing with this approach will allow us to create a list of any length (ignoring the fact that we may run out of memory). However, we are in danger of being overwhelmed by the syntax: to add a third node to the list the instruction would be

```
start->next->next = new Node;
```

with subsequent nodes requiring even more awkward terms.

We can solve this by introducing two additional *Node* pointers, *temp* and *current*. The first pointer, *temp*, is used when creating a new node; the second, *current*, moves along the existing list until it references the final node. We can then create a new node, insert data in the node and link it to the list using the instructions

The logic assumes there is at least one existing node in the list.

```
//*** Create node ***
temp = new Node;
//*** Place data in node ***
temp->value.no = 99;
temp->next = NULL;
//*** Find the end of the list ***
current = start;
while(current->next != NULL)
    current = current->next;
//*** Add new node to list ***
current->next = temp;
```

The steps described above are shown in FIG-8.4.

FIG-8.4

Adding a Node to the end of the List

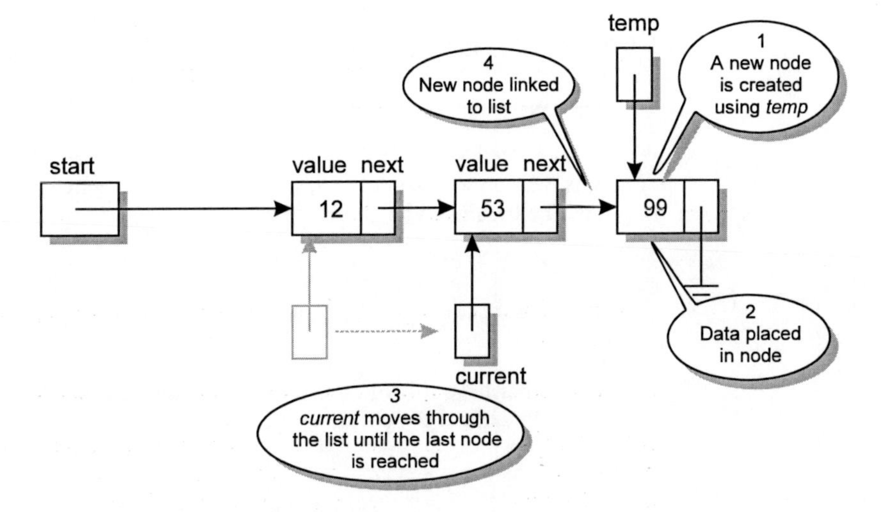

Creating a Linked List Data Structure

Now that we've examined the general approach to the problem, we need to design the components of a linked list in such a way as to allow us to go on and define variables of this type on which we can perform operations such as adding and removing data.

The Data Components

We need to begin by defining the structure of the data held in each node. For the purpose of this example, we'll keep it simple and use a single integer:

```
struct Data
{
    int     no;
};
```

Of course, the construct used will depend on the information to be held in the linked list.

TASK 8.2

Write a new declaration for *Data* which contains the following information:

```
int     idcode
char    name[30]
char    sex
int     score[6].
```

Once *Data* has been declared, we need to declare *Node* by combining the *Data* component with a pointer:

```
struct Node
{
    Data    value;
    Node    *next;
};
```

TASK 8.3

Why does the *next* pointer above reference a *Node* type rather than a *Data* type?

Finally, we need to declare the linked list structure itself. From the previous diagrams, we can see that only the *start* pointer exists when the list is empty, so we might define the linked list structure as:

```
struct List
{
    Node *start;
};
```

But, as in other lists, it is often useful to maintain a count of the number of items held, so we'll expand the declaration to include a count:

```
struct List
{
    Node *start;
    int  count;
};
```

TASK 8.4

What changes will be required to the design of *Node* and *List* to accommodate the *Data* definition produced in TASK 8.2?

The Operations Required

There are several basic operations normally used with a list of data; these are defined informally overleaf:

CreateList : Creates an empty list.

Len : Returns the number of items in the list.

IsEmpty : Returns 1 if the list is empty, otherwise returns zero.

AddAt : Adds new data at a specified point in the list.

DeleteFrom : Removes the node at a specified point in the list.

Head : Returns the first data at the front of the list. The list itself is unaffected by this operation.

Tail : Removes the first node from the list.

Display : Displays all the data in the list.

EmptyList : Removes all data from the list.

We'll now look at each of these operations in more detail.

CreateList

The list parameter used throughout these descriptions is named *seq*.

This routine simply initialises the list by setting the *start* pointer to NULL and *count* to zero (see FIG-8.5).

FIG-8.5

Initialising the List

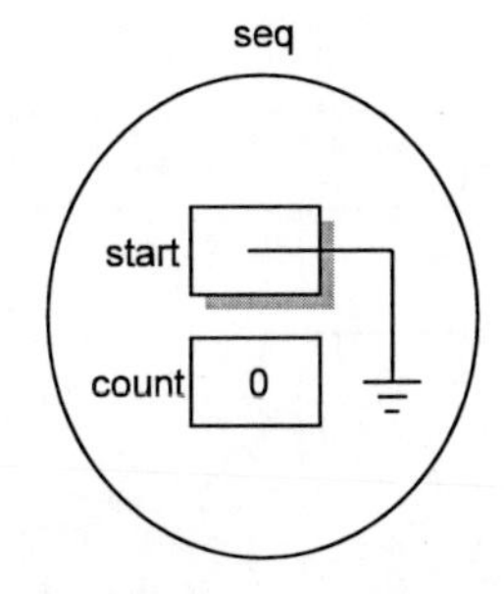

The code for this routine is

```
void CreateList(List& seq)
{
    seq.start = NULL;
    seq.count = 0;
}
```

Len

This routine returns the number of nodes in the list. All that is required is to return the value of *count*. The code is:

```
int Len(const List& seq)
{
    return seq.count;
}
```

IsEmpty

This function returns the value 1 if the list is empty, otherwise it returns zero. Code for this routine is

```
int IsEmpty(const List& seq)
{
    return(seq.count==0);
}
```

AddAt

This routine inserts a new node at a specified position. The node can be inserted anywhere in the list. For example, in a list currently containing 3 nodes, the new node can be placed at positions 1,2,3 or 4. If the position specified is outside this range then we have an invalid situation and the operation cannot be performed. One method of dealing with an error condition such as this is to return a value indicating the success or failure of the operation. Assuming the position of the new node is specified by the parameter *post*, then the code necessary to detect an invalid position is:

```
if(post<1||post>Len(seq)+1)
    return 0;
```

If the insert position is valid, we need to create a new node and transfer the new data to it. This requires the code

post is the position in the list at which the new node is to be placed.

```
temp = new Node;

temp->value = item;      //item contains the new data
temp->next=NULL;
```

FIG-8.6 shows the state of a list at this point.

FIG-8.6

Creating a New Node

Creating a New Node

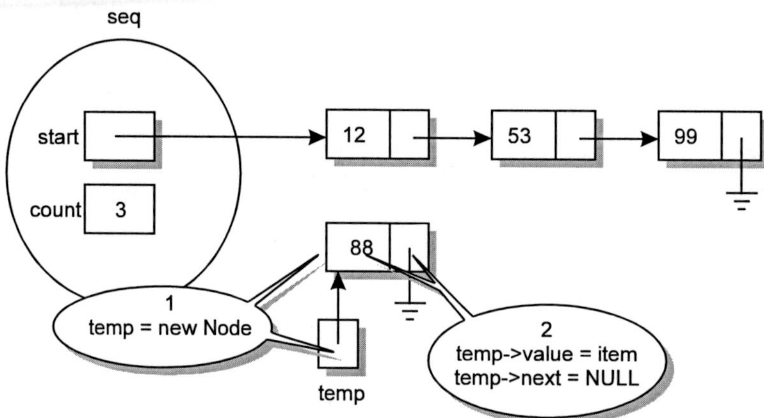

Once the new node has been created it must be inserted into the existing list. In doing this, there are two distinct circumstances which have to be dealt with:

1. If the new value is to be placed at the beginning of the list, then the value in start must be changed.

   The code for this option is:

   ```
   if(post==1)
   {
       temp->next = seq.start;
       seq.start = temp;
   }
   ```

   FIG-8.7 shows the consequences of this code.

2. If the insert point is anywhere other than the first position, we need to find the insert point in the list and adjust the pointers in the surrounding nodes to insert the new value.

FIG-8.7

Inserting at the Start of the List

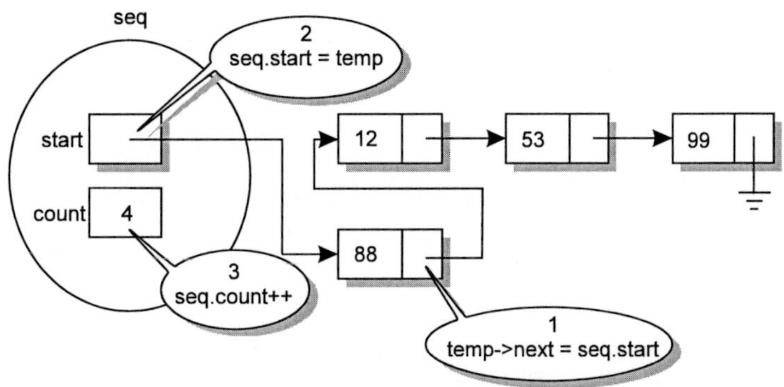

This second situation needs to be looked at in greater detail. To find the insert point for the new node we employ two pointers, *current* and *previous*, which move along the linked list until *current* references the node at the insert position and *previous*, the preceding node. The code for this is:

```
previous = NULL;
current = seq.start;
for(int c=2;c<=post;c++)
{
    previous = current;
    current = current->next;
}
```

For example, if we want to insert a new node at position 3, *current* would reference the third node and *previous* the second. Next we have to break the existing links and splice in the new node. This is done with the code

```
previous->next = temp;
temp->next = current;
```

FIG-8.8 shows the main stages in this operation.

FIG-8.8

Inserting a Node within the List

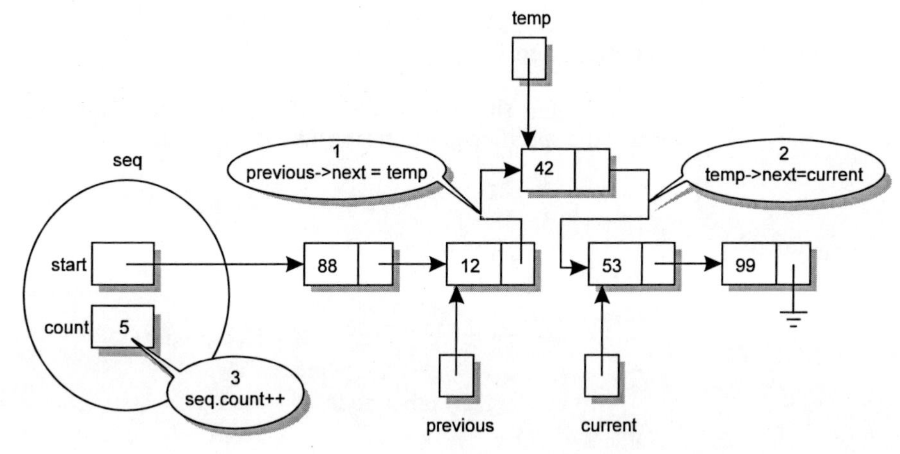

Wherever the new node is added, *count* has to be incremented:

```
seq.count++;
```

The final task is to return a value indicating the success of the operation:

```
return 1;
```

The complete code for the *InsertAt()* function is:

```
int AddAt(const Data item, int post ,List& seq)
{
    Node *current, *previous, *temp;

    //*** If an invalid position, exit routine ***
    if(post<1||post>Len(seq)+1)
        return 0;

    //*** Create space for new node ***
    temp = new Node;

    //*** Place data in node ***
    temp->value = item;
    temp->next=NULL;

    //*** If placed at start update main pointer***
    if(post==1)
    {
        temp->next = seq.start;
        seq.start = temp;
    }
    else
    //*** ELSE find insert position ***
    {
        previous = NULL;
        current = seq.start;
        for(int c=2;c<=post;c++)
        {
            previous = current;
            current = current->next;
        }
        //** Link new node into chain **
        previous->next = temp;
        temp->next = current;
    }
    //*** Add 1 to count ***
    seq.count++;
    return 1;
}
```

DeleteFrom

This routine shares some code with the previous routine: again, we need to check that the specified position is valid with the code

```
if(post<1||post>Len(seq))
    return 0;
```

and, if everything is okay, we need to distinguish between

a) deleting the first node

and

b) deleting any other node.

Removing the first node involves changing the value of *start* and deleting the node. This requires the code

```
current = seq.start;
seq.start = current->next;
delete current;
```

Deleting any other node involves referencing that node and its predecessor using the pointers *current* and *previous*. The node is then removed from the list by making the next field in the preceding node bypass it and then deleting the required node. The code for this is:

```
//*** Find required node ***
previous = NULL;
current = seq.start;
for(int c=2;c<=post;c++)
{
    previous = current;
    current = current->next;
}
//*** Adjust node pointer to bypass deleted node ***
previous->next = current->next;
//*** Delete node ***
delete current;
```

Finally, the count must be decremented.

The two situations are illustrated in FIG-8.9.

FIG-8.9

Deleting a Node

OPTION 1 : Deleting the first node

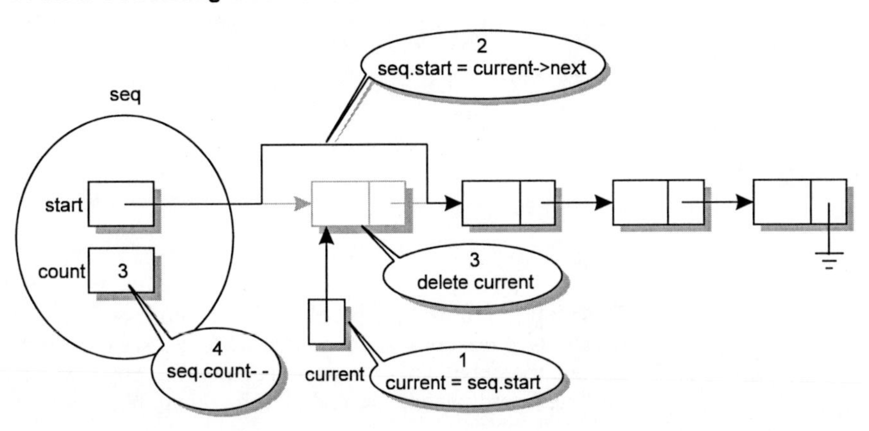

OPTION 2 - Deleting other nodes

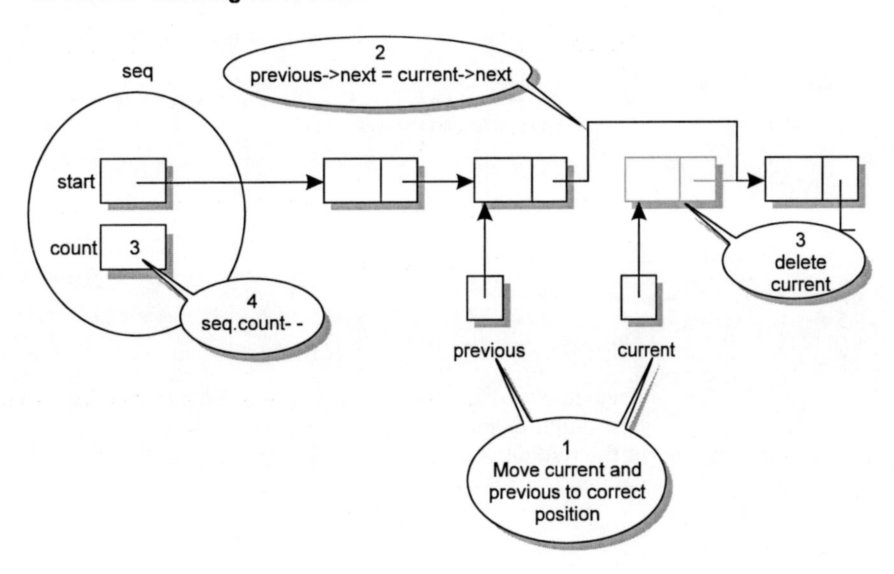

The complete code is

```
int DeleteFrom(int post, List& seq)
{
    Node *current, *previous;

    //*** If the position is invalid, exit the routine ***
    if(post<1||post>Len(seq))
        return 0;
    //*** IF first node update main pointer***
    if(post==1)
    {
        current = seq.start;
        seq.start = current->next;
        delete current;
    }
    else
    //*** ELSE find delete position ***
    {
        previous = NULL;
        current = seq.start;
        for(int c=2;c<=post;c++)
        {
            previous = current;
            current = current->next;
        }
        //** Remove node from chain **
        previous->next = current->next;
        delete current;
    }
    //*** Subtract 1 from count ***
    seq.count--;
    return 1;
}
```

Head

This routine returns the data held in the first node of the list. It can only be performed if there is at least one node in the list. Hence, we must begin by checking that the list is not empty. Where the list is empty, the program itself, rather than just this routine, is terminated. The code for the function is:

```
Data Head(const List& seq)
{
    //*** If list is empty, terminate program ***
    if(IsEmpty(seq))
    {
        cout<<"Invalid operation - Head\n";
        exit(1);
    }
    //*** Else return data in first node ***
    return seq.start->value;
}
```

The instruction `exit(1)` is responsible for ending the program. To use this function we need to include *stdlib.h* in the program.

Tail

The purpose of the operation is to remove the first node from the list. Like *Head()*, this routine cannot operate if the list is empty and needs a similar check at the start of the routine. All being well, we can remove the first node using the previously defined *DeleteFrom()* function:

```
void Tail(List& seq)
{
    //*** If list empty, terminate program ***
    if(IsEmpty(seq))
    {
        cout<<"Invalid operation - Tail\n";
        exit(1);
    }
    //*** Else delete the first node ***
    DeleteFrom(1,seq);
}
```

Display

This routine displays all the data held in the list using the code:

```
void Display(const List& seq)
{
    Node *current=seq.start;    //current node - initialised to
                                //reference first node

    //*** For each node ***
    for(int c=1;c<=Len(seq);c++)
    {
        //** Display its contents ***
        cout<<current->value.no<<endl;
        //** Move on to the next node **
        current=current->next;
    }
}
```

EmptyList

You might be tempted to think that this routine is identical to *CreateList()* and only requires the *start* pointer to be set to NULL and *count* to zero. However, if we were to do this the nodes of the list would still be allocated, and hence continue to reduce the amount of memory available. To avoid this we need to go through the list deleting each node in turn. One method of doing this is

```
void EmptyList(List& seq)
{
    while(!IsEmpty(seq))
        DeleteFrom(1,seq);
}
```

TASK 8.5

Which of the routines defined above would need to be changed if the *Data* component of a node was declared as:

```
struct Data
{
    int idcode;
    char name[30];
    char sex;
    int score[6];
};
```

A complete program using each of the operations on a list is given in LISTING-8.1.

Program Logic:

```
Create a list
REPEAT
    Display menu
    Get option
    Execute option
UNTIL option is QUIT
Empty the list
```

Program Code:

LISTING-8.1

Implementing a List Type as a Linked List

```
#include<iostream.h>
#include<conio.h>
#include<string.h>
#include<stdlib.h>

//*** Declare structure required ***
struct Data
{
  int no;
};

struct Node
{
  Data value;
  Node *next;
};

struct List
{
  Node *start;
  int count;
};

//*** Declare prototypes for list ***
void CreateList(List&);
int AddAt(const Data,int,List&);
int DeleteFrom(int,List&);
Data Head(const List&);
void Tail(List&);
int Len(const List&);
int IsEmpty(const List&);
void Display(const List&);
void EmptyList(List&);
//*** Declare other prototypes ***
int DisplayMenu(const char*);
int GetOption(int);
void ExecuteOption(int, List&);

void main()
{
  List seq;
  int option, noofoptions;

  CreateList(seq);
  do
  {
      noofoptions=DisplayMenu("1. - Create List\n2. - AddAt\n"
      "3. - DeleteFrom\n4. - Head\n5. - Tail\n6. - Length\n"
      "7. - IsEmpty\n8. - Empty\n9. - Display\n10 - QUIT\n");
      option = GetOption(noofoptions);
      ExecuteOption(option, seq);
  }
  while (option != noofoptions);
  EmptyList(seq);
  cout<<"PROGRAM TERMINATED\n";
  getch();
}
```

Continued on next page

LISTING-8.1
(continued)

Implementing a List Type as a Linked List

```
//*** Create empty list ***
void CreateList(List& seq)
{
  seq.start = NULL;
  seq.count = 0;
}



//*** Return number of items in list ***
int Len(const List& seq)
{
  return seq.count;
}



//*** Determine if list is empty ***
int IsEmpty(const List& seq)
{
  return(seq.count==0);
}



//*** Add new node ***
int AddAt(const Data item, int post ,List& seq)
{
  Node *current, *previous, *temp;

  //*** If position is invalid exit routine ***
  if(post<1||post>Len(seq)+1)
      return 0;          //Return 0 to indicate fail

  //*** Create space for new node ***
  temp = new Node;
  //*** Place data in node ***
  temp->value = item;
  temp->next=NULL;
  //*** If placed at start update list pointer***
  if(post==1)
  {
      current = seq.start;
      seq.start = temp;
      temp->next=current;
  }
  else
  //*** Else find insert position ***
  {
      previous = NULL;
      current = seq.start;
      for(int c=2;c<=post;c++)
      {
          previous = current;
          current = current->next;
      }
      //** Link new node into chain **
      previous->next = temp;
      temp->next = current;
  }
  //*** Add 1 to count ***
  seq.count++;
  return 1;              //Return 1 to indicate success
}
```

Continued on next page

LISTING-8.1
(continued)

Implementing a List Type as a Linked List

```
//*** Return first value in list ***
Data Head(const List& seq)
{
   //*** If list is empty, terminate program ***
   if(IsEmpty(seq))
   {
        cout<<"Invalid operation - Head\n";
        exit(1);
   }
   //*** Else return first value in list ***
   return seq.start->value;
}


//*** Display contents of list ***
void Display(const List& seq)
{
   Node *current=seq.start;

   //*** For each item in the list ***
   for(int c=1;c<=Len(seq);c++)
   {
        //** Display its value ***
        cout<<current->value.no<<endl;
        current=current->next;
   }
}


//*** Delete node ***
int DeleteFrom(int post, List& seq)
{
   Node *current, *previous;

   //*** If invalid position, exit routine ***
   if(post<1||post>Len(seq))
        return 0;
   //*** If first item to be deleted, update list pointer***
   if(post==1)
   {
        current = seq.start;
        seq.start = current->next;
        delete current;
   }
   else
   //*** Else find and delete node ***
   {
        //** Find node to be deleted **
        previous = NULL;
        current = seq.start;
        for(int c=2;c<=post;c++)
        {
             previous = current;
             current = current->next;
        }
        //** Remove node from chain **
        previous->next = current->next;
        delete current;
   }
   //*** Subtract 1 from count ***
   seq.count—;
   return 1;
}
```

Continued on next page

LISTING-8.1
(continued)

Implementing a List Type as a Linked List

```
//*** Remove first value from list ***
void Tail(List& seq)
{
  //*** If list is empty, terminate program ***
  if(IsEmpty(seq))
  {
      cout<<"Invalid operation - Tail\n";
      exit(1);
  }
  //*** Else delete first value ***
  DeleteFrom(1,seq);
}


//*** Remove all items from the list ***
void EmptyList(List& seq)
{
  while(!IsEmpty(seq))
      DeleteFrom(1,seq);
}



//*********************************
//* Other routines used in program *
//*********************************

//*** Display menu ***
int DisplayMenu(const char* text)
{
  //*** Display menu ***
  clrscr();
  cout<<"MENU\n\n";
  cout<<text;
  //*** Count number of options in menu ***
  for(int c=0,total=0; c<strlen(text);c++)
      if(text[c]=='\n')
          total++;
  //*** Return number of options ***
  return total;
}


//*** Get user's option ***
int GetOption(int max)
{
  int opt;
  //*** Get option ***
  cout<<"\nEnter option : ";
  cin>>opt;
  //*** Reject invalid entries and re-enter ***
  while(opt<1||opt>max)
  {
      cout<<"Invalid option\n";
      cin>>opt;
  }
  //*** Return valid option ***
  return opt;
}
```

Continued on next page

LISTING-8.1
(continued)

Implementing a List Type as a Linked List

```
//*** Execute option ***
void ExecuteOption(int opt, List& seq)
{
  Data val;
  int post;

  switch (opt)
  {
           //*** Create new list ***
      case 1:  CreateList(seq);
           break;

           //*** Add new value to list ***
      case 2:  //** Get value to be added **
           cout<<"Enter value to be added : ";
           cin >> val.no;
           //** Get insert position **
           cout<<"Add where (1 to "<<(Len(seq)+1)<<") : ";
           cin>>post;
           while(post<1||post>Len(seq)+1)
           {
               cout<<"Invalid position. Re-enter : ";
               cin>>post;
           }
           //** Add new value to list **
           AddAt(val,post,seq);
           break;

           //*** Delete item from list ***
      case 3:  //** If list isn't empty, delete item **
           if(!IsEmpty(seq))
           {
               //** Get position of item **
               cout<<"Delete from where (1 to "
                   <<Len(seq)<<") : ";
               cin>>post;
               while(post<1||post>Len(seq)+1)
               {
                   cout<<"Invalid position. Re-enter : ";
                   cin>>post;
               }
               //** Delete item **
               DeleteFrom(post,seq);
           }
           else
           //** Else issue error message **
           {
               cout<<"The list is empty\n";
               getch();
           }
           break;

           //*** Return head of list ***
      case 4:  //** If list isn't empty, return head **
           if(!IsEmpty(seq))
           {
               cout<<"First in list is : "
                   <<Head(seq).no<<endl;
               getch();
           }
           //** Else issue error message **
           else
           {
               cout<<"List is empty\n";
               getch();
           }
           break;
```

Continued on next page

LISTING-8.1
(continued)

Implementing a List Type as a Linked List

```
                    //*** Get tail of list ***
        case 5:     //** If list isn't empty, remove head **
                    if(!IsEmpty(seq))
                        Tail(seq);
                    else
                    //** Else issue error message **
                    {
                        cout<<"List is empty\n";
                        getch();
                    }
                    break;

                    //*** Display length of list ***
        case 6:     cout<<"The list contains "<<Len(seq)<<" values\n";
                    getch();
                    break;

                    //*** Determine if list is empty ***
        case 7:     if(IsEmpty(seq))
                        cout<<"List is empty\n";
                    else
                        cout<<"List is not empty\n";
                    getch();
                    break;

                    //*** Clear list ***
        case 8:     EmptyList(seq);
                    break;

                    //*** Display the contents of the list ***
        case 9:     clrscr();
                    cout<<"CONTENTS OF LIST\n";
                    Display(seq);
                    getch();
                    break;
    }
}
```

PROGRAMMING EXERCISE 8.1

1. Enter the above program and test it.

2. Add two new routines to the *List* structure:
   a) **IsAt** Returns the first position in the list of a specified value. If the value is not present, zero is returned.
   b) **Give** Returns the value at a specified position in the list. An additional value is returned to indicate the success or failure of the operation. This additional parameter returns 1 if the value at the specified position is successfully returned, zero is returned if the position specified is invalid.

Creating Other Structures - The Stack

The stack is a simplified type of list in which value can only be added and removed from the front of the list. We can compare a stack to a pile of books: additional books are placed on top of the pile, with books also being removed from the top (see FIG-8.10).

Several operations are defined for stacks:

CreateStack Creates an empty stack.

Push	Adds a value to the 'top' of the stack.
Top	Returns the value at the top of the stack. The stack itself remains unchanged. This routine should not be called if the stack is empty.
Pop	Removes the top element from the stack. No value is returned by the stack. This routine should not be called if the stack is empty.
EmptyStack	Removes all elements from an existing stack.
DisplayStack	Displays the contents of the stack.

FIG-8.10

Adding and Removing from a Stack

Rather than write the complete code for this data structure we can assemble our new data structure from our existing *List* structure. This will allow us to produce reliable software in the shortest possible time.

We begin by declaring the *Stack* structure as containing a single *List* component:

```
struct Stack
{
    List seq;
};
```

Now we can construct our new operations from existing ones. For example, *CreateStack()* can be coded as

```
void CreateStack(Stack& s)
{
    CreateList(s.seq);
}
```

and the *Push()* operation can be coded just as simply:

```
void Push(Data v,Stack& s)
{
    AddAt(v,1,s.seq);
}
```

TASK 8.6

Write the code necessary to implement *Top()* and *Pop()* operations.
HINT: These should use the *Head()* and *Tail()* functions of the *List* structure.

Using Library Files

What is a Library File?

Library files are identified by their .LIB filename extensions. These files contain semi-compiled code known as .OBJ files. A single library file can contain many such programs. In fact, Borland C++ is supplied with many such library files. Any of its .OBJ files required by your program are loaded automatically at the linkage stage of the compilation process.

As well as making use of Borland's library files we can create our own.

Why do we need Library Files?

By making use of library files we reduce the amount of code that has to appear in our source programs. In addition, we ensure that the most up-to-date version of our routines are being used.

For example, it would be inconvenient to include all of the source code for the *List* structure when writing the *Stack* program. By placing the code for our *List* structure in a library we can avoid this problem.

How do we create a Library File?

To create a library file we need to start by creating the .OBJ file(s) which we want to place in the library. This requires the following steps:

1. Create a source code file containing only the necessary `#include` statements, constants, structures, prototypes and function definitions. Typically, this will be a set of routines which have some commonality: for example, the graphics functions supplied by Borland. There should be no `main()` function.

   For example, to create an .OBJ file for the *List* structure the file would contain declarations for *Data, Node, List*; function prototypes for all routines which operate on *List* (but not additional routines such as *DisplayMenu(), GetOption()* and *ExecuteOption()*). Save this file with the normal .CPP extension.

   In addition, we need to create a header file which contains only the constants, structures and function prototypes. This file should be saved with a .H extension.

2. Use the **File|Save As** option to save this source code file (we may want to go back to it later to make changes).

3. With only this file loaded, choose the **TargetExpert** (in Borland C++ version 4.5 this is achieved by moving the mouse pointer within the code window and pressing the right mouse button and choosing **TargetExpert** in the floating menu which appears).

FIG-8.11

Choosing the Target Type

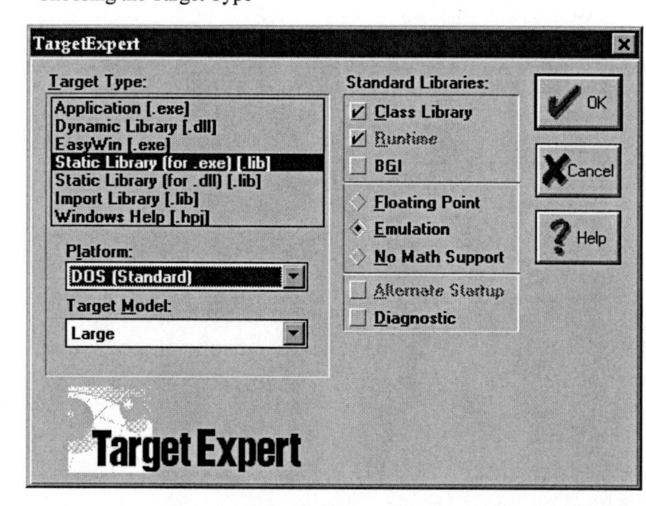

4. In the **TargetExpert** window which now appears, set **Platform:** to *DOS (standard)* and the **Target Type:** to *Static Library (for .exe) (.lib)* and click on OK. (see FIG-8.11).

5. Choose the **Project|Compile** from the main menu. An .OBJ file will now have been created. For example, if your original file was saved under the name LIST.CPP, compilation will have created the file LIST.OBJ.

We have now created the file which is to be placed in the library. We are free to place the .OBJ file in an existing library. However, this is probably not a good idea, and it would be safer to create a library file of our own.

Borland supplies a utility to deal with the work of handling library files: TLIB. TLIB is a DOS based program which allows us to add or remove .OBJ files from a library file. The steps required to add a .OBJ file are:

1. If working in Windows, create a DOS window.

2. Move to the directory in which you want to hold your library file.

3. We now type in a command of the format

This assumes the PATH information necessary to access TLIB is in place, otherwise the full path for TLIB must be specified.

TLIB name_of_library_file +name_of_OBJ_file
(e.g. `TLIB MYFILES.LIB +LIST.OBJ`)

If the library file does not exist, it will be created by this operation. To remove a file from the library we use a minus sign.
TLIB library_name - name_of_OBJ_file

To remove *list.obj* from the *myfiles* library we would enter
```
TLIB MYFILES.LIB -LIST.OBJ
```

If the original version of a source file is changed for any reason, then we must recompile it and update the library file by both removing the old version and inserting the new. To do this we use both the minus and plus sign in a single command of the form
TLIB library_name -+name_of_OBJ_file

To remove the old version of *list.obj* and replace it with the new, the command is
```
TLIB MYFILES.LIB -+LIST.OBJ
```

How do we Use a Library File?

Now that the library file has been created and the necessary .OBJ file placed within it, we can make use of the routines stored there in any future program.

A program needs to be given three main pieces of information before it can use a library file:

1. The details of any structures, constants and functions contained within any of the .OBJ files our program accesses within the library.

2. The name of the library file containing the required routines.

3. Where to find the library file.

These are achieved by the following steps (the details given here are for Borland C++ version 4.5):

1. Choose **Project|New Project** and use the following settings within **TargetExpert**:

Platform:	DOS(Standard)
Target Type:	Application (.exe)
Project Path & Name:	Any applicable name (e.g. Stack.ide)

2. Choose **File|New**, enter the code for the program which uses the library file and save it using the same filename as the project but with a .CPP extension (e.g. Stack.CPP).

   This file needs to include the header file containing the declaration of the components to be used in the program. (e.g. `#include "list.h"`).

   The header file should be enclosed in double quotes rather than the more usual angled brackets. When angled brackets are used the compiler only looks for the header files in the directories set up within the compiler (more on this later); when using quotes the compiler will look for the header file in the current directory.

3 When the project is opened, a new **Project:** window is created at the bottom of the screen (see FIG-8.12). This shows, in a tree structure, the files to be included in the project. The only file assumed to be present has the same name as the project, but with a .CPP extension.
(e.g. *Stack.cpp*)
The library file must be included in this list as follows:

   With the top name in this window highlighted, click the right mouse button and choose the **Add Node** option in the floating menu.

   In the **Add to Project** window which appears specify the drive, path and file name of the .LIB file you created previously. The project window will then have the library file added to the tree (see FIG-8.13).

The program is now ready to be compiled.

FIG-8.12 The Structure of a Project

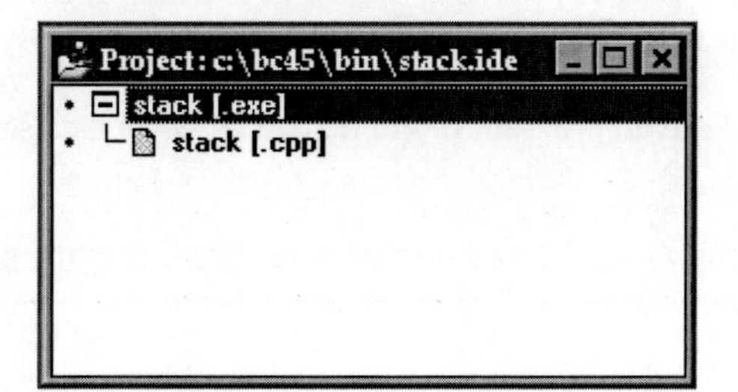

FIG-8.13 Adding a Node to a Project

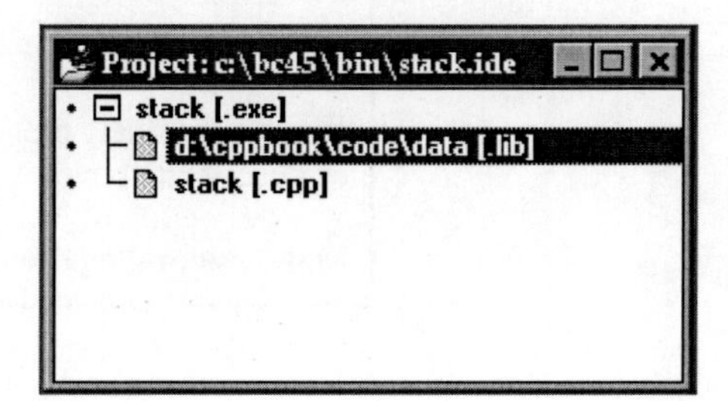

PROGRAMMING EXERCISE 8.2

1. Create .OBJ and header files for the routines in the *List* data structure. The header file should be called *list.h* and stored in your working directory; the .OBJ source file should be called *list.cpp* and inserted into a library file called *STRUCTS.LIB*.

2. Making use of the above files, create a new program in a similar style to that in LISTING-8.1 which implements a *Stack* data structure.

Creating Other Structures - The Queue

A queue is another type of restricted list. In a queue items are added at one end and deleted from the other. Queues occur all too frequently in real life: at gas stations, in the supermarket and at bus stops. The queue is often referred to as a **first in - first out** structure, since the first value placed in the queue is also the first to be removed (see FIG-8.14).

FIG-8.14

Adding and Removing from a Queue

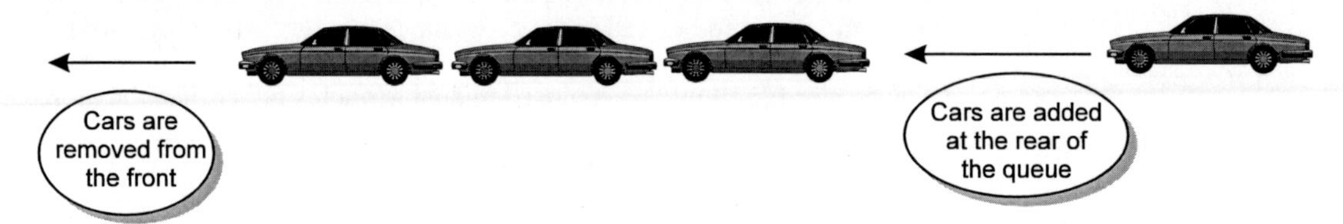
Cars are removed from the front
Cars are added at the rear of the queue

The following operations are defined for a Queue:

CreateQueue	Creates an empty queue.
Insert	Adds a value to the end of the queue.
Front	Returns the first value in the queue. The queue is unaffected by this operation.
Delete	Removes the value at the front of the queue. The queue must not be empty.
IsEmpty	Returns 1 if the queue is empty, otherwise returns zero.
Length	Returns the number of items in the queue.
EmptyQueue	Removes all entries from a queue.
Give	Returns the value held in a specified element.

PROGRAMMING EXERCISE 8.3

Write a complete menu driven program to implement a *Queue* data structure as described above.

Make use of the previously coded *List* structure when producing the program.

Summary

- A linked list is constructed from a sequence of nodes.
- A node consists of a data component and a pointer to the next node.
- Linked lists can grow and shrink as required.
- It can be useful to code routines in such a way as to return some indication of the success of the operation being performed.
- A library file contains a set of .OBJ programs.
- Library files can be created and updated using the TLIB program.
- An .OBJ file normally contains a set of related functions.
- The contents of a required .OBJ file will be extracted from a library file automatically and included in your compiled program.
- A project is a program consisting of several files.
- The name of the library file must be included in a project's file list.
- To make use of an .OBJ file a corresponding header file must be created.
- A header file should consist of constant, data types, and function declarations.
- A stack is a list in which values are added and removed at the same end.
- A queue is a list in which values are added at one end and removed from the other.

DOUBLY LINKED LISTS

What's Wrong with Linked Lists

A linked list in which each node has a single pointer to the next (or sometimes previous) node is called a **singly-linked list**. There are some things that singly-linked lists aren't very efficient at handling. For example, if we needed to display the contents of the list in reverse order we would have to use an algorithm such as:

```
FOR post := number of nodes in list DOWN TO 1 DO
    Start at the beginning of the list
    Move through the list until node at post reached
    Display value in node
ENDFOR
```

Having to move through the list for every value to be displayed is very time-consuming but cannot be avoided with the current list design.

Two-Way Nodes

By redesigning a node so that it has pointers in both directions, one to the previous node and one to the next, we get a greater flexibility in our design (see FIG-8.15).

FIG-8.15

Double Pointer Node

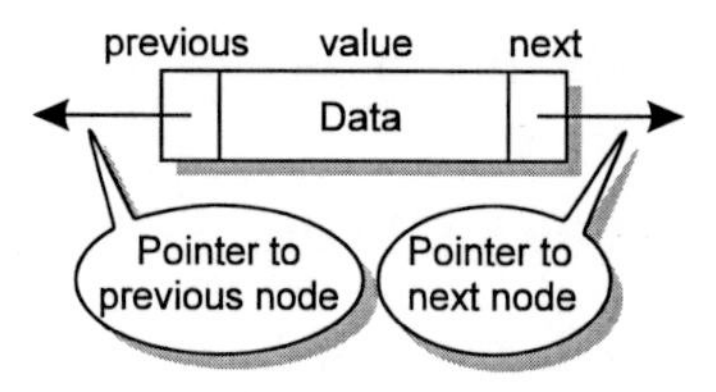

> **TASK 8.7**
>
> Rewrite the definition of the structure *Node* given previously using this new set up.

> **TASK 8.8**
>
> Draw a diagram (in the style of that given in FIG-8.3) showing a list containing three nodes of this new design.

Another aid to the efficiency of our new *List* structure is to maintain a pointer to the final node in the list. This will allow us to go directly to the last node in the list without having to start at the beginning and move through each node in turn until the end is reached. The new declaration for List would now be

```
struct List
{
    Node *start;    //Pointer to first node
    Node *end;      //Pointer to final node
    int count;      //Node counter
};
```

With the definition of *List* changed, most of the associated functions will also require modification. For example *CreateList()* will now be coded as:

```
void CreateList(List& seq)
{
    seq.start = NULL;
    seq.finish = NULL;
    seq.count = 0;
}
```

Some other routines will need even greater changes. For example, when adding a new node we may have to:

a) Change *start* and *finish* (if adding the first node)
b) Change the *start* pointer (if added at the beginning of the list)
c) Change the *finish* pointer (if added at the end of the list)
d) Change *neither* pointer (if inserting somewhere between the first and last node)

TASK 8.9

What possible modifications to *start* and *finish* exist when deleting a node?

The new code for *AddAt()* now becomes

```
int AddAt(const Data item, int post ,List& seq)
{
    Node *current, *temp; //**previous pointer removed

    //*** If position is invalid exit routine ***
    if(post<1||post>Len(seq)+1)
        return 0;        //Return 0 to indicate fail
    //*** Create space for new node ***
    temp = new Node;
    //*** Place data in node ***
    temp->value = item;
    temp->next=NULL;
    temp->previous=NULL;
    //*** If first node to be placed in list***
    if(Len(seq)==1)
    {
        seq.start = temp;
        seq.finish = temp;
    }
        //*** Else if placed at start of list ***
    else if(post==1)
    {
        current = seq.start;
        seq.start = temp;
        temp->next=current;
        current->previous = temp;
    }
        //*** Else if placed at end of list ***
    else if(post == Len(seq)+1)
    {
        current = seq.finish;
        seq.finish = temp;
        temp->previous = current;
        current->next = temp;
    }
    else
    //*** Else find insert position ***
    {
        current = seq.start;
        for(int c=2;c<=post;c++)
            current = current->next;
        //** Link new node into chain **
        current->previous->next = temp;
        temp->next = current;
    }
    //*** Add 1 to count ***
```

Modified sections of the code are shown in bold.

```
    seq.count++;
    return 1;           //Return 1 to indicate success
}
```

The four options are shown graphically in FIG-8.16 through FIG-8.19.

FIG-8.16

Add the First Node

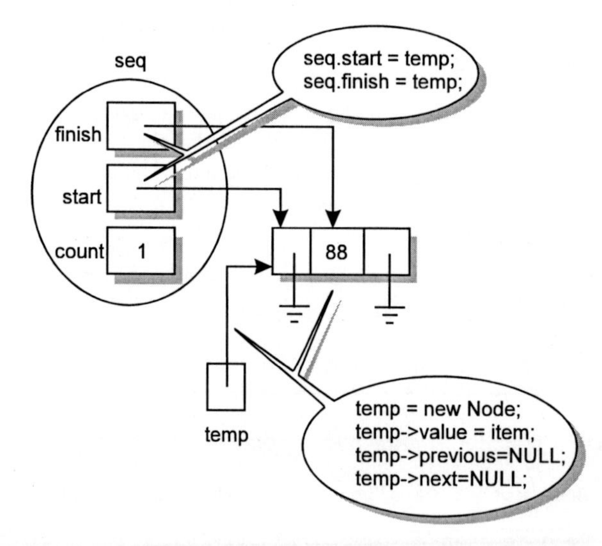

FIG-8.17

Adding a Node at the Start of the List

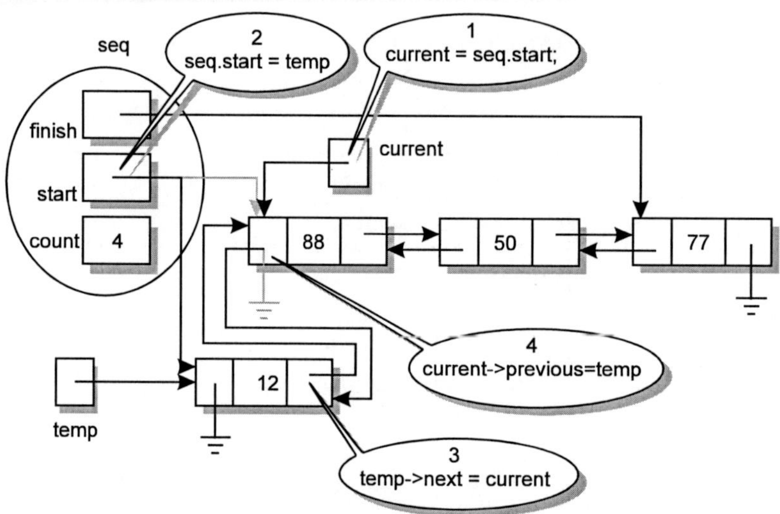

FIG-8.18

Adding a Node at the End of the List

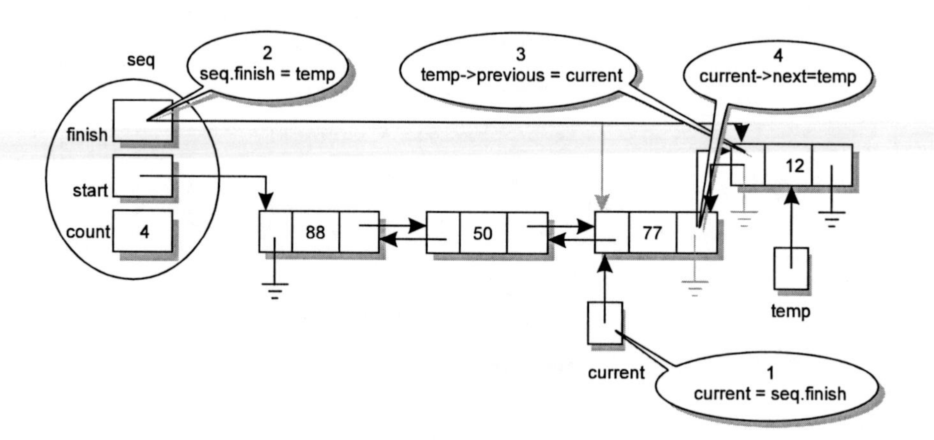

FIG-8.19

Adding a Node Within the List

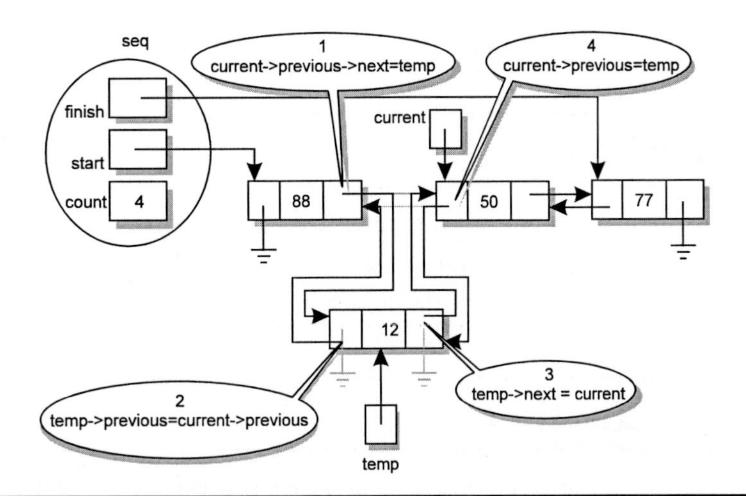

> **TASK 8.10**
>
> Write the code required for a *DeleteFrom()* operation.

> **PROGRAMMING EXERCISE 8.4**
>
> Complete the changes required to implement the List structure as a doubly linked list.

Summary

- The doubly linked list is constructed from nodes containing two pointers.
- Each node contains a pointer to the previous node and a pointer to the next node.
- Doubly linked lists allow more efficient reverse traversal of the list.
- Using a start and end pointer in a list allows quick access to the final node. This allows an efficient algorithm to be employed when adding to the end of the list.

CASE STUDY

The Problem

A program is required to convert an infix expression such as

```
(6+3)/12 - 1
```

to the postfix equivalent

```
6 3 + 12 / 1 -
```

An Explanation

We are used to writing arithmetic expressions in which the operators (+, - , * , /, etc.) are placed between the operands (6, 3, 12, etc.); this is called **infix notation**. However, calculators and computers use notation in which the operator is placed after the two operands on which it is to perform; this is known as **postfix** or **Reverse Polish notation**. Hence, whereas we would write 12 + 3 in standard infix notation, we write 12 3 + in postfix notation. Although postfix expressions may look awkward, they are in fact very efficient. For example, postfix expressions never require the use of parentheses and are evaluated on a simple left-to-right basis.

The downside of postfix notation is that we humans don't like writing in it! But this is a problem easily solved since a relatively simple algorithm can be employed to convert from infix to postfix notation.

The Algorithm

```
1.  Create an empty stack
2.  Create an empty queue
3.  Read in the infix expression to be converted
4.  Extract the left most token from the expression
5.  WHILE not at end of expression DO
6.      IF
7.          token is an operand:
8.              Add it to queue
9.          token is '(':
10.             Push it onto stack
11.         token is ')':
12.             Remove value from the stack
13.             WHILE value removed is not '(' DO
14.                 Add value removed to queue
15.                 Remove value from stack stack
16.             ENDWHILE
17.         token is an operator:
18.             REPEAT
19.                 IF stack empty OR token > top of stack THEN
20.                     Push token onto stack
21.                 ELSE
22.                     Remove value from stack
23.                     Add value removed to queue
24.             UNTIL token added to stack
25.     ENDIF
26. ENDWHILE
27. WHILE stack not empty DO
28.     Remove value from stack
29.     Add value removed to queue
30. ENDWHILE
31. Display original expression
32. Display queue
```

TASK 8.11

Using the algorithm given, convert the following expressions to postfix notation:

a) 8+3*(6-1)
b) ((1 + 2)*3/4)*(5-6)
c) 1/((2+3)*(4-5))

The Program

The program makes use of a library file called DATA.LIB containing the .OBJ files: LIST.OBJ, STACK.OBJ and QUEUE.OBJ. These files use the following declaration for the information held within a single node

```
struct Data
{
    char value[10];
};
```

and other routines have been modified, where necessary, to handle strings.

The data input should consist of numeric operands and elements of the expression must be separated by a single space character. The program also assumes that the expressions entered are syntactically correct.

LISTING-8.2

Generating Postfix Expressions

```
// *************************************************************
// * PROGRAM          : Postfixer                              *
// * AUTHOR           : Patricia Stamp                         *
// * DATE             : 21/1/1996                              *
// * VERSION          : 0.5                                    *
// * DESCRIPTION      : Creates postfix expressions from valid *
// *                     infix ones containing only integer     *
// *                     operands.                              *
// * HARDWARE         : PC Compatible                          *
// * SOURCE           : Turbo C++ v4.0                         *
// *************************************************************

#include"list.h"
#include"stack.h"
#include"queue.h"
#include<conio.h>
#include<iostream.h>
#include<string.h>
#include<stdio.h>
#include<ctype.h>

char Priority(char);


void main()
{

   Stack s;
   Queue q;
   char expression[80];  //Entered expression
   char expcopy[80];     //Copy of expression entered
   char *strptr;         //Pointer to token in expression
   Data token,value;     //Copies of tokens from expression
```

Continued on next page

LISTING-8.2
(continued)

Generating Postfix Expressions

```
//*** Initialise data structures ***
CreateStack(s);
CreateQueue(q);

//*** Get expression ***
clrscr();
cout<<"Enter expression : ";
gets(expression);

//*** Copy expression ***
strcpy(expcopy,expression);

//*** Reference first token in expression ***
strptr = strtok(expcopy," ");

//*** WHILE not at end of expression DO ***
while(strptr!=NULL)
{
    //** Copy token **
    strcpy(token.no,strptr);
    //** IF numeric, add to Queue **
    if(isdigit(token.no[0]))
    {
        Insert(token,q);
    }
    //** IF '(' , add to Stack **
    else if(!strcmp(token.no,"("))
    {
        Push(token,s);
    }
    //** IF ')'**
    else if(!strcmp(token.no,")"))
    {
        //* Get top value in stack *
        strcpy(value.no,Top(s).no);
        Pop(s);
        //* WHILE removed value not '(' DO *
        while(strcmp(value.no,"("))
        {
            // Add value to queue
            Insert(value,q);
            //Get next value from stack
            strcpy(value.no,Top(s).no);
            Pop(s);
        }
    }
    //*** IF its an operator ***
    else
    {
        int added=0;
        //** REPEAT **
        do
        {
            //*IF stack empty OR current token has a higher *
            //* priority than TOP(stack), add token to stack*
            if(IsEmptyStack(s)||
            Priority(token.no[0])>Priority(Top(s).no[0]))
            {
                Push(token,s);
                added =1;
            }
            //* ELSE remove top of stack and place in queue *
            else
            {
                strcpy(value.no,Top(s).no);
                Pop(s);
                Insert(value,q);
            }
        }
```

Continued on next page

LISTING-8.2
(continued)

Generating Postfix Expressions

```
            //** UNTIL token added to stack **
            while(!added);
        }

        //*** Reference next token in expression ***
        strptr = strtok(NULL," ");
    }

    //*** Empty stack onto queue ***
    while(!IsEmptyStack(s))
    {
        Insert(Top(s),q);
        Pop(s);
    }

    //*** Display original expression ***
    cout<<"Infix expression : "<<expression<<endl;

    //*** Display postfix expression ***
    for(int c=1;c<=Length(q);c++)
        cout<<Give(c,q).no<<' ';
    cout<<endl;

    getch();
}


//*** Give priority of token ***
char Priority(char c)
{
    const          char
oppriority[5][2]={{'*',2},{'/',2},{'+',1},{'-',1},{'(',0}};
    int post =0;
    while(oppriority[post][0]!=c)
        post++;
    return oppriority[post][1];
}
```

Solutions

TASK 8.1

```
a)  start-value
b)  start-next
```

TASK 8.2

```
struct Data
{
    int idcode;
    char name[30];
    char sex;
    int score[6];
}
```

TASK 8.3

next references another node (i.e. a structure containing both data and another pointer) rather than just data.

TASK 8.4

No changes are required.

TASK 8.5

Only the *Display()* routine needs to be modified to output the fields of *Data*.

PROGRAMMING EXERCISE 8.1

The program requires:
  Prototypes for *IsAt()* and *Give()* functions
  These options added to string parameter for *DisplayMenu()*
  Additional code in *ExecuteOption()*
and
  Definitions for *IsAt()* and *Give()*.

Code for *IsAt()*

```
int IsAt(Data d,const List& seq)
{
    Node *nptr;

    if(Len(seq)==0)
        return 0;

    int post = 1;
    nptr = seq.start;
    while (nptr != NULL
    && !strcpy(nptr->value.no,d.no))
    {
        nptr = nptr->next;
        post++;
    }
    if (nptr != NULL)
        return post;
    else
        return 0;
}
```

Code for *Give():*

```
Data Give(int post,const List& seq)
{
    if(post < 1 || post > Len(seq))
    {
        cout<<"Invalid position - Give()\n";
        exit(1);
    }
    Node  *nptr=seq.start;
    for(int c=1;c<post;c++)
        nptr = nptr->next;
    return nptr->value;
}
```

Additional code for *ExecuteOption()*:

```
case 9:
    cout<<"Enter value to be found : ";
    cin>>val.no;
    post = IsAt(val,seq);
    if(post)
        cout<<"Is at position "<<post<<endl;
    else
        cout<<"Value not found\n";
    getch();
    break;
    case 10:
        cout<<"Enter position required ( 1 to "
            <<Len(seq)<<") : ";
        cin>>post;
        if(post>=1&&post<=Len(seq))
        {
            val=Give(post,seq);
            cout<<"Position "<<post<<" contains "
                <<val.no<<endl;
        }
        else
            cout<<"Invalid position for Give()\n";
        getch();
        break;
    case 11:
        clrscr();
        cout<<"CONTENTS OF LIST\n";
        Display(seq);
        getch();
        break;
```

TASK 8.6

Code for *Top()*:

```
Data Top(Stack s)
{
    return Head(s.seq);
}
```

Code for *Pop()*:

```
void Pop(Stack& s)
{
    Tail(s.seq);
}
```

PROGRAMMING EXERCISE 8.2

1. No solution required.

2. Program code:

```
#include"list.h"
#include<conio.h>
#include<iostream.h>
#include<string.h>
void CreateStack(Stack&);
void Push(Data,Stack&);
Data Top(const Stack&);
void Pop(Stack&);
void EmptyStack(Stack&);
void Display(const Stack&);
int Length(const Stack&);

int DisplayMenu(const char*);
int GetOption(int);
void ExecuteOption(int, Stack&);

void main()
{
    Stack s;
    int opt, max;

    clrscr();
```

Continued on next page

```
    do
    {
        max = DisplayMenu("1. - CreateStack\n"
                "2. - Push\n3. - Top\n4. - Pop\n"
                "5. - Empty stack\n8. - Display\n"
                "7. - QUIT\n");
        opt= GetOption(max);
        ExecuteOption(opt,s);
    }
    while (opt != max);
    getch();
}

void CreateStack(Stack& s)
{
    CreateList(s.seq);
}

void Push(Data v,Stack& s)
{
    AddAt(v,1,s.seq);
}

Data Top(Stack s)
{
    return Head(s.seq);
}

void Pop(Stack& s)
{
    Tail(s.seq);

}

void EmptyStack(Stack& s)
{
    EmptyList(s.seq);
}

int Length(Stack s)
{
    return Len(s.seq);
}

void Display(Stack s)
{
    Display(s.seq);
}

int DisplayMenu(const char* text)
{
    clrscr();
    cout<<"MENU\n\n";
    cout<<text;

    for(int c=0,total=0; c<strlen(text);c++)
        if(text[c]=='\n')
            total++;
    return total;
}

int GetOption(int max)
{
    int opt;
    cout<<"\nEnter option : ";
    cin>>opt;
    while(opt<1||opt>max)
    {
        cout<<"Invalid option\n";
        cin>>opt;
    }
    return opt;
}

void ExecuteOption(int opt, Stack& s)
{
    Data val;
    int post;

    switch (opt)
    {
        case 1:
            CreateStack(s);
            break;
        case 2:
            cout<<"Enter value to be added : ";
            cin >> val.no;
            Push(val,s);
            break;
        case 3:
            cout<<Top(s).no<<'\n';
            getch();
            break;
        case 4:
            Pop(s);
            break;
        case 5:
            EmptyStack(s);
            break;
        case 6:
            Display(s);
            getch();
            break;
    }
}
```

PROGRAMMING EXERCISE 8.3

```
#include"list.h"
#include<conio.h>
#include<iostream.h>
#include<string.h>

struct Queue
{
    List seq;
};

void CreateQueue(Queue&);
void Insert(Data, Queue&);
Data Front(const Queue&);
void Delete(Queue&);
int IsEmpty(const Queue&);
int Length(const Queue&);
void EmptyQueue(Queue&);
void Display(const Queue&);
Data Give(int, const Queue&);

int DisplayMenu(const char*);
int GetOption(int);
void ExecuteOption(int, Queue&);

void main()
{
    Queue q;
    int option, noofoptions;

    CreateQueue(q);
    do
    {
        noofoptions=DisplayMenu("1. - Create Queue\n"
            "2. - Insert\n3. - Delete\n"
            "4. - Front\n5. - Give\n6. - Length\n"
            "7. - IsEmpty\n8. - Empty\n"
            "9. - Display\n10 - QUIT\n");
        option = GetOption(noofoptions);
        ExecuteOption(option, q);
    }
    while (option != noofoptions);
    EmptyQueue(q);
    cout<<"PROGRAM TERMINATED\n";
    getch();
}

void CreateQueue(Queue& q)
{
    CreateList(q.seq);
}

void Insert(Data v, Queue& q)
{
    AddAt(v,Length(q)+1,q.seq);
}

Data Front(const Queue& q)
{
    return Head(q.seq);
}

void Delete(Queue& q)
{
    DeleteFrom(1,q.seq);
}

int IsEmpty(const Queue& q)
{
    return IsEmpty(q.seq);
}

int Length(const Queue& q)
{
    return Len(q.seq);
}

void EmptyQueue(Queue& q)
{
    EmptyList(q.seq);
}

void Display(const Queue& p)
{
    Display(p.seq);
}
```

```
Data Give(int post, const Queue& q)
{
    return Give(post,q.seq);
}

int DisplayMenu(const char* text)
{
    clrscr();
    cout<<"MENU\n\n";
    cout<<text;

    for(int c=0,total=0; c<strlen(text);c++)
        if(text[c]=='\n')
            total++;
    return total;
}

int GetOption(int max)
{
    int opt;
    cout<<"\nEnter option : ";
    cin>>opt;
    while(opt<1||opt>max)
    {
        cout<<"Invalid option\n";
        cin>>opt;
    }
    return opt;
}

void ExecuteOption(int opt, Queue& q)
{
    Data val;
    int post;

    switch (opt)
    {
        case 1:
            CreateQueue(q);
            break;
        case 2:
            cout<<"Enter value to be added : ";
            cin >> val.no;
            Insert(val,q);
            break;
        case 3:
            if(!IsEmpty(q))
                Delete(q);
            else
            {
                cout<<"The queue is empty\n";
                getch();
            }
            break;
        case 4:
            if(!IsEmpty(q))
            {
                cout<<"First in queue is : "
                    <<Front(q).no<<endl;
                getch();
            }
            else
            {
                cout<<"Queue is empty\n";
                getch();
            }
            break;
        case 5:
            if(IsEmpty(q))
            {
                cout<<"Queue is empty\n";
                getch();
            }
            cout<<"Enter position req'd(1 to "
                <<Length(q)<<"): ";
            cin>>post;
            if(post<1||post>Length(q))
                cout<<"Invalid position\n";
            else
                cout<<" Value at position "
                    <<post<<" is "
                    <<Give(post,q).no<<endl;
            getch();
            break;
        case 6:
            cout<<"The queue contains "
                <<Length(q)<<" values\n";
            getch();
            break;
        case 7:
            if(IsEmpty(q))
                cout<<"Queue is empty\n";
            else
                cout<<"Queue is not empty\n";
            getch();
            break;
        case 8:
            EmptyQueue(q);
            break;
        case 9:
            clrscr();
            cout<<"CONTENTS OF QUEUE\n";
            Display(q);
            getch();
            break;
    }
}
```

TASK 8.7

```
struct Node
{
    Node +previous;
    Data value;
    Node *next;
};
```

TASK 8.8

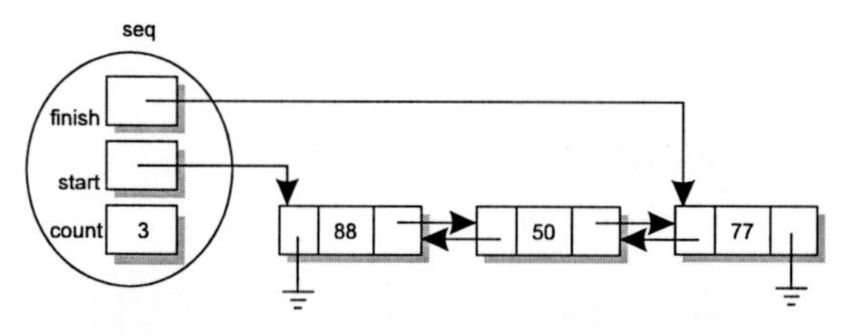

TASK 8.9

a) Change *start* and *finish* (if deleting the only node in the list)
b) Change *start* (if deleting first node)
c) Change *finish* (if deleting last node)
d) No change (if deleting other than the first or last node)

TASK 8.10

```
int DeleteFrom(int post, List& seq)
{
    Node *current, *previous;
    if(post<1||post>Len(seq))
    {
        cout<<"Invalid position\n";
        return 0;
    }
    //*** If only node change start and finish ***
    if(Len(seq)==1)
    {
        delete seq.start;
        seq.start = NULL;
        seq.finish = NULL;
    }
    //*** Else, If first node change start***
    else if(post==1)
    {
        current = seq.start;
        seq.start = current->next;
        seq.start->previous=NULL;
        delete current;
    }
    //*** Else, if last node, change finish ***
    else if(post == Len(seq))
    {
        current = seq.finish;
        seq.finish = current->previous;
        seq.finish->next = NULL;
        delete current;
    }
    else
    //*** ELSE find delete position ***
    {
        current = seq.start;
        for(int c=2;c<=post;c++)
            current = current->next;
        //** Link new node into chain **
        current->previous->next = current->next;
        current->next->previous = current->previous;
        delete current;
    }
    //*** Subtract 1 from count ***
    seq.count--;
    return 1;
}
```

PROGRAMMING EXERCISE 8.4

```
#include<iostream.h>
#include<conio.h>
#include<string.h>
#include<stdlib.h>

struct Data
{
    int no;
};

struct Node
{
    Node *previous;
    Data value;
    Node *next;
};

struct List
{
    Node *start;
    Node *finish;
    int count;
};

void CreateList(List&);
int AddAt(const Data,int,List&);
int DeleteFrom(int,List&);
Data Head(const List&);
void Tail(List&);
int Len(const List&);
int IsEmpty(const List&);
void Display(const List&);
void EmptyList(List&);
int IsAt(Data,const List&);
Data Give(int,const List&);

int DisplayMenu(const char*);
int GetOption(int);
void ExecuteOption(int, List&);

void main()
{
    List seq;
    int option, noofoptions;

    CreateList(seq);
    do
    {
        noofoptions=DisplayMenu("1. - Create List\n"
            "2. - AddAt\n3. - DeleteFrom\n"
            "4. - Head\n5. - Tail\n8. - Length\n"
            "7. - IsEmpty\n8. - Empty\n"
            "9. - Return position\n"
            "10 - Return value at position\n"
            "11 - Display\n12 - QUIT\n");
        option = GetOption(noofoptions);
        ExecuteOption(option, seq);
    }
    while (option != noofoptions);
    EmptyList(seq);
    cout<<"PROGRAM TERMINATED\n";
    getch();
}

void CreateList(List& seq)
{
    seq.start = NULL;
    seq.finish = NULL;
    seq.count = 0;
}
int AddAt(const Data item, int post ,List& seq)
{
    Node *current,*temp;
    if(post<1||post>Len(seq)+1)
    {
        cout<<"Invalid position\n";
        return 0;
    }
    //*** Create space for new node ***
    temp = new Node;
    //*** Place data in node ***
    temp->value = item;
    temp->next=NULL;
    temp->previous = NULL;

    //*** IF first node to be placed in list ***
    if(IsEmpty(seq))
    {
        seq.start = temp;
        seq.finish = temp;
    }
    else if(post==1)
    {
        current = seq.start;
        seq.start = temp;
        temp->next = current;
        current->previous = temp;
    }
    else if(post == Len(seq)+1)
    {
        current = seq.finish;
        seq.finish = temp;
        temp->previous = current;
        current->next = temp;
    }
    else
    //*** ELSE find insert position ***
    {
        current = seq.start;
        for(int c=2;c<=post;c++)
            current = current->next;
        //** Link new node into chain **
        current->previous->next = temp;
        temp->previous = current->previous;
        temp->next = current;
        current->previous = temp;
    }
    //*** Add 1 to count ***
    seq.count++;
    return 1;
}


int DeleteFrom(int post, List& seq)
{
    Node *current, *previous;
    if(post<1||post>Len(seq))
    {
        cout<<"Invalid position\n";
        return 0;
    }
    //*** If only node change start and finish ***
    if(Len(seq)==1)
    {
        delete seq.start;
        seq.start = NULL;
        seq.finish = NULL;
    }
    //*** Else, If first node change start***
    else if(post==1)
    {
        current = seq.start;
        seq.start = current->next;
        seq.start->previous=NULL;
        delete current;
    }
    //*** Else, if last node, change finish ***
    else if(post == Len(seq))
    {
        current = seq.finish;
        seq.finish = current->previous;
        seq.finish->next = NULL;
        delete current;
    }
    else
    //*** ELSE find delete position ***
    {
        current = seq.start;
        for(int c=2;c<=post;c++)
            current = current->next;
        //** Link new node into chain **
        current->previous->next = current->next;
        current->next->previous = current->previous;
        delete current;
    }
    //*** Subtract 1 from count ***
    seq.count--;
    return 1;
}

Data Head(const List& seq)
{
    if(IsEmpty(seq))
    {
        cout<<"Invalid operation - Head\n";
        exit(1);
    }
    return seq.start->value;
}

void Tail(List& seq)
{
    if(IsEmpty(seq))
    {
        cout<<"Invalid operation - Tail\n";
        exit(1);
    }
    DeleteFrom(1,seq);
}

int Len(const List& seq)
{
    return seq.count;
}
```

```
int IsEmpty(const List& seq)
{
    return(seq.count==0);
}

void Display(const List& seq)
{
    Node *current=seq.start;

    for(int c=1;c<=Len(seq);c++)
    {
        cout<<current->value.no<<endl;
        current=current->next;
    }
}

void EmptyList(List& seq)
{
    while(!IsEmpty(seq))
        DeleteFrom(1,seq);
}

int IsAt(Data d,const List& seq)
{
    Node *nptr;

    if(Len(seq)==0)
        return 0;

    int post = 1;
    nptr = seq.start;
    while (nptr != NULL && nptr->value.no != d.no)
    {
        nptr = nptr->next;
        post++;
    }
    if (nptr != NULL)
        return post;
    else
        return 0;
}
Data Give(int post,const List& seq)
{
    if(post < 1 || post > Len(seq))
    {
        cout<<"Invalid position - Give()\n";
        exit(1);
    }
    Node  *nptr=seq.start;
    for(int c=1;c<post;c++)
        nptr = nptr->next;
    return nptr->value;
}

int DisplayMenu(const char* text)
{
    clrscr();
    cout<<"MENU\n\n";
    cout<<text;
    for(int c=0,total=0; c<strlen(text);c++)
        if(text[c]=='\n')
            total++;
    return total;
}

int GetOption(int max)
{
    int opt;
    cout<<"\nEnter option : ";
    cin>>opt;
    while(opt<1||opt>max)
    {
        cout<<"Invalid option\n";
        cin>>opt;
    }
    return opt;
}

void ExecuteOption(int opt, List& seq)
{
    Data val;
    int post;

    switch (opt)
    {
        case 1:
            CreateList(seq);
            break;
        case 2:
            cout<<"Enter value to be added : ";
            cin >> val.no;
            cout<<"Add where (1 to "
                <<(Len(seq)+1)<<") : ";
            cin>>post;
            AddAt(val,post,seq);
            break;
        case 3:
            if(!IsEmpty(seq))
            {
                cout<<"Delete from where (1 to "
                    <<Len(seq)<<") :" ;
                cin>>post;
                DeleteFrom(post,seq);
            }
            else
            {
                cout<<"The list is empty\n";
                getch();
            }
            break;
        case 4:
            if(!IsEmpty(seq))
            {
                cout<<"First in list is : "
                    <<Head(seq).no<<endl;
                getch();
            }
            else
            {
                cout<<"List is empty\n";
                getch();
            }
            break;
        case 5:
            if(!IsEmpty(seq))
                Tail(seq);
            else
            {
                cout<<"List is empty\n";
                getch();
            }
            break;
        case 6:
            cout<<"The list contains "
                <<Len(seq)<<" values\n";
            getch();
            break;
        case 7: if(IsEmpty(seq))
                    cout<<"List is empty\n";
                else
                    cout<<"List is not empty\n";
                getch();
                break;
        case 8:     EmptyList(seq);
                break;
        case 9:
            cout<<"Enter value to be found : ";
            cin>>val.no;
            post = IsAt(val,seq);
            if(post)
                cout<<"Is at position "<<post<<endl;
            else
                cout<<"Value not found\n";
            getch();
            break;
        case 10:
            cout<<"Enter position required ( 1 to "
                <<Len(seq)<<") : ";
            cin>>post;
            if(post>=1&&post<=Len(seq))
            {
                val=Give(post,seq);
                cout<<"Position "<<post
                    <<" contains "<<val.no<<endl;
            }
            else
                cout<<"Invalid position "
                    <<"for Give()\n";
            getch();
            break;
        case 11:
            clrscr();
            cout<<"CONTENTS OF LIST\n";
            Display(seq);
            getch();
            break;
    }
}
```

TASK 8.11

a) 83+61-*
b) 21+3*4/56-*
c) 123+45-*/

CHAPTER 9

Advanced Data Structures

This chapter covers the following topics:

- Defining a Binary Search Tree
- Deleting from a Tree
- Directed Graphs
- Graph Terminology
- Graphs: Finding the Shortest Path
- Implementing a Binary Search Tree
- Recursive Definitions
- Recursive Routines
- Tree Terminology
- Understanding Recursion
- Undirected Graphs

RECURSION

Introduction

Recursion is a method of describing the solution to a problem in terms of the original problem. Since this explanation may not be immediately enlightening, perhaps an example is in order at this point.

In mathematics the expression 4x3x2x1 is written as 4! (called four factorial). Hence 6! is the short-hand way of writing 6x5x4x3x2x1. Mathematics states that the factorial operation may only be applied to non-negative integer values and that 0! is 1.

Given the problem of producing a solution to the term 4! we may say that the result is:

4x3x2x1 which is 24.

Alternatively, we may write that

4! = 4 x 3!

This last solution has resulted in an answer which itself involves factorials. This is an example of a recursive solution. Of course the solution gives rise to a new question: What is 3!? The answer to which can be written recursively as:

3! = 3 x 2!

We can continue in this manner

2! = 2 x 1!
1! = 1 x 0!

until we reach a point where a specific answer must be given:

0! = 1

Having reached a point where we have an exact result (0! = 1), we can now reverse our way back up through the solution:

Knowing 0! = 1, we can substitute this result in our previous equation:

1! = 1 x 0! = 1 x 1 = 1

Continuing this, we get

2! = 2 x 1! = 2 x 1 = 2
3! = 3 x 2! = 3 x 2 = 6
4! = 4 x 3! = 4 x 6 = 24

Generally, we may write that the solution to *N*! is

N x (*N*-1)!

Recursive Functions

Coding a Recursive Function

We can implement recursion within a programming language by coding a function which calls itself. For example, we can code a *Factorial()* function as simply:

```
unsigned long Factorial(unsigned n)
{
    if(n==0)
        return 1;
    else
        return (n*Factorial(n-1));
}
```

The Characteristics of a Recursive Function

All recursive functions contain three characteristics:

1. A terminating condition which gives a final, non-recursive result and stops execution of the function. For example, in *Factorial()* the terminating condition is:
   ```
   if(n==0)
       return 1;
   ```

2. A self-referencing call in which the function calls itself with a modified argument. For example:
   ```
   Factorial := n * Factorial(n-1)
   ```

3. The argument for this self-referencing call must lead towards the terminating condition being met. For example, the argument in the term *Factorial(n-1)* ensures that the condition, *n == 0* ,will eventually be met.

Length() returns the number of items in a *List* variable.

TASK 9.1

One way to determine the number of items in a list (assuming it is implemented without a *count* component) is to make use of two basic facts:

1. If the list is empty, then its length is zero.
2. If it is not empty, its length is 1 + the length of the tail of the list.

Using this information, and assuming the functions *IsEmpty()* and *Tail()* are available, write a recursive *Length()* function for a *List* type.

How Recursion Works

FIG-9.1 shows the sequence of calls to *Factorial()* using an original function argument of 3.

Once the terminating condition has been executed, the returned value is used to complete the expression evaluation in the previous call. This effect ripples back up through the sequence of calls until the result of the original function call can be determined (see FIG-9.2).

The diagrams give the impression that several copies of the function might exist within the computer's memory during execution of the function. This is not the case. In fact, the machine handles recursion by maintaining a data stack in which the parameters, local variables and return addresses for each call to the routine are held.

FIG-9.1

Recursive Calls

Phase 1: Recursive calls

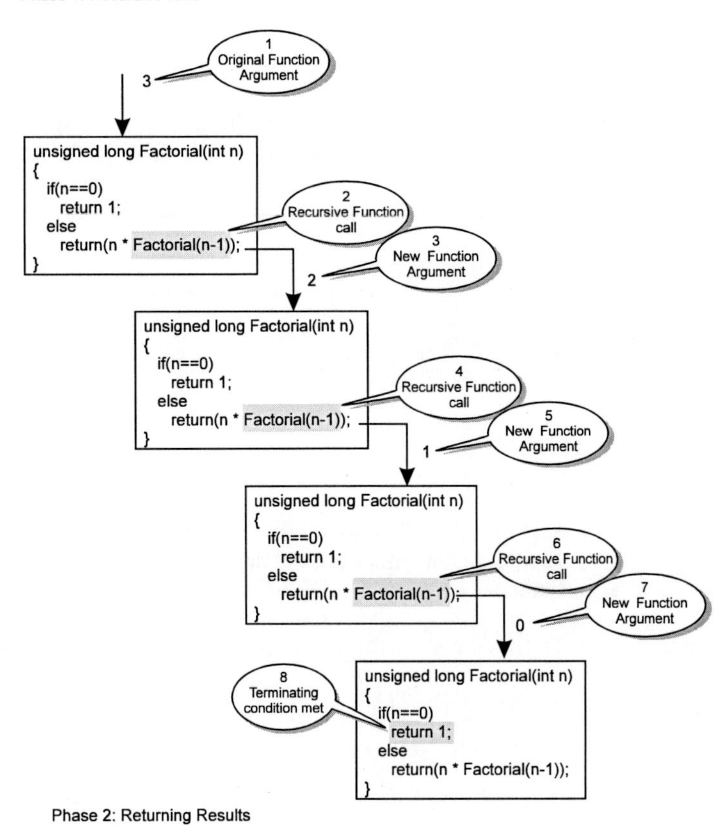

FIG-9.2

Terminating Recursive Calls

Phase 2: Returning Results

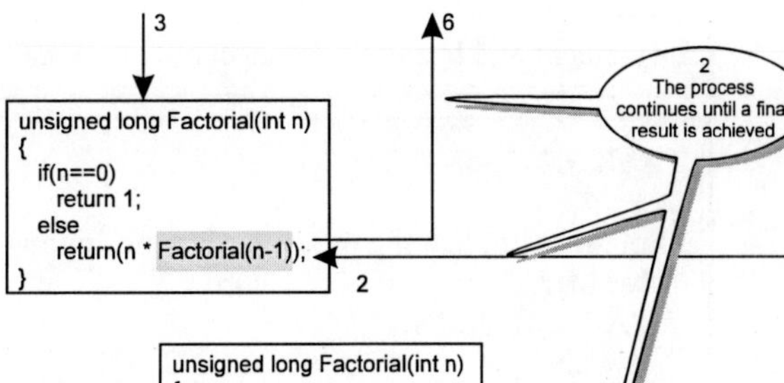

This mechanism for handling recursion can consume a great deal of memory. As a result, although recursion can result in very elegant solutions to certain problems, the overheads involved (space and time) mean that it is best avoided when implementing operations.

More Examples of Recursive Definitions

Even where we choose not to implement a routine recursively, it may still be the best method of defining the logic involved in an operation. For example, if an operation (*CountNeg*) was required to count the number of negative values in a list of integers, we might describe the logic required as:

Head() returns the front value in a *List* variable.

```
IF IsEmpty(list) THEN
    result := 0
ELSE
    IF Head(list)<0 THEN
        result := 1 + CountNeg(Tail(list))
    ELSE
        result := CountNeg(Tail(list))
    ENDIF
ENDIF
```

It's even possible to have more than one recursive call within an operation. For example, the **Fibonacci** series is a set of integers which starts with the values 1 and 1; subsequent values are obtained by summing the two previous terms. Hence the sequence continues: 2,3,5,8,13,21, etc.

To find the nth term in the series, we can define an operation, *Fibonacci*, as:

```
IF n<=2 THEN
    result := 1
ELSE
    result := Fibonacci(n-1) + Fibonacci(n-2)
ENDIF
```

PROGRAMMING EXERCISE 9.1

Implement and test the Fibonacci operation as a C++ function.

TASK 9.2

Explain in English the purpose of the following operation:

```
NAME            :  Op1
PARAMETERS
    IN          :  c : INTEGER
    OUT         :  None
    IN/OUT      :  s : LIST
PRE-CONDITION   :  None
POST-CONDITION  :  IF IsEmpty(s) THEN
                       AddAt(1,c,s)
                   ELSE
                       Op1(c,Tail(s))
                   ENDIF
```

AddAt() adds a value at a specified position in a *List* variable. Hence, *AddAt(1,c,s)* adds the value *c* at the first position in *s*.

Problems with Recursive Definitions

The main problem with recursive definitions is understanding them! And this is overcome by exposure to many examples. Some computer languages, such as Prolog and Lisp, make extensive use of recursive routines.

Another common pitfall for the unwary is creating recursive definitions which fail to terminate. For example, in the definition below, the routine will fail to terminate because the stopping condition is never met.

```
NAME            :  Sum
PARAMETERS
    IN          :  no: REAL
    OUT         :  sum: REAL
    IN/OUT      :  None
PRE-CONDITION   :  no >= 0
POST-CONDITION  :  IF no = 0 THEN
                        sum = 0
                   ELSE
                        sum = no + Sum(no/2)
```

The routine, *Sum*, is intended to sum the sequence *no + no/2 + no/4 ...+0* but the expression *no/2* although tending to zero will never reach it and hence the terminating condition, *no = 0*, is never satisfied.

So, why should we use recursion? Most importantly, recursive definitions allow a more rigorous proof of the correctness of that definition (although such proofs are beyond the scope of this text). A recursive definition also gives a short, but precise description of an operation. The argument for recursive implementation is harder to sustain since it often results in unacceptable overheads. However, even here, it sometimes offers much shorter and more easily tested code.

Summary

- A recursive operation is one which calls itself in describing the solution to that operation.
- Recursive operations have three main characteristics:

    1. A terminating condition which gives a final, non-recursive result and stops execution of the function.
    2. A self-referencing call in which the function calls itself with a modified argument.
    3. The argument for this self-referencing call must lead towards the terminating condition being met.

- The logical correctness of a recursively defined routine can be proved mathematically.
- A recursively defined routine need not be implemented recursively.
- A recursively implemented routine is usually inefficient in terms of both execution time and the amount of memory required by the routine.
- A recursive implementation is used when non-recursive methods would result in over-complicated code.

BINARY SEARCH TREES

Introduction

We have already seen that the linked list is a useful method of implementing a collection of data since it allows the structure to grow or shrink with the amount of data being held. This is a great advantage over earlier implementations using arrays which imposed a fixed size on the amount of data which could be stored. But linked lists have one great disadvantage: interrogation of the structure must be done using simple linear searching techniques. This can lead to unacceptable delays in the execution of some operations when the linked list is a long one.

For data which does not contain a key field or where the existing order of the data is important, we need to live with this problem. On the other hand, with a key field and the discretion of holding the data in any order, we are free to use a greater range of implementation methods. One structure which helps improve search times is the **binary search tree.**

The binary tree is a special form of the general tree structure.

The tree data structure is unlike any of these previous structures in that the data which it contains is organised in a hierarchical manner. Perhaps the most familiar tree structure is the family, an example of which is shown in FIG-9.3.

FIG-9.3

A Family Tree

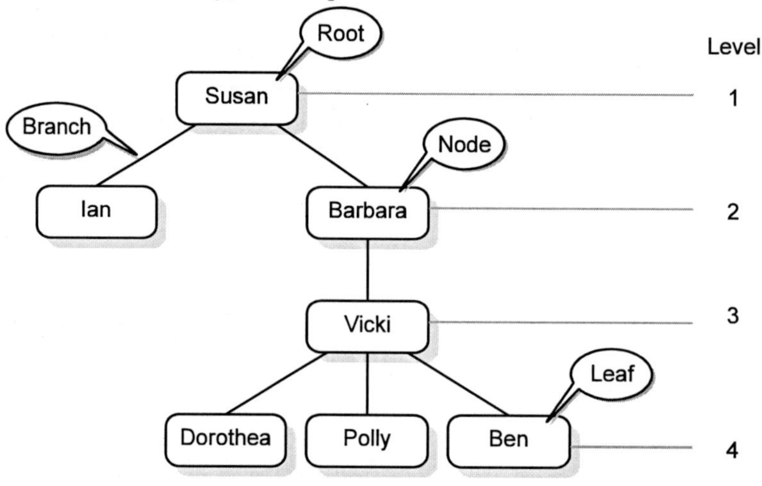

Much of the terminology used in describing tree data structures comes from the vocabulary of both botany and genealogy.

Tree Terminology

NODE A single item of data in a tree is called a node (SUSAN, IAN, POLLY are nodes from the example above).

ROOT The top-most node (SUSAN).

BRANCH A direct link between one node and another (There is a branch from SUSAN to IAN. There is no branch from BARBARA to BEN).

PARENT The immediately preceding node. All nodes, except the root, have exactly one parent (VICKI is the parent of POLLY - and also of DOROTHEA and BEN).

CHILD An immediately succeeding node. A node may have zero or more children (IAN and BARBARA are the children of SUSAN).

ANCESTOR If a node can be reached by following branches upwards through a tree, then that node is an ancestor of the node at which you started (BARBARA is an ancestor of BEN. IAN is not an ancestor of BEN).

DESCENDANT If a node can be reached by following the branches down through the tree, then that node is a descendant of the node at which you started.

SIBLING All nodes which have the same parent (IAN and BARBARA are siblings).

LEAF A node which has no children.

LEVEL The root of the tree is at level 1; its children are at level 2; its grandchildren at level 3, etc.

HEIGHT Each node is at a specific height in the tree. Leaves are at height zero; a leaf's parent has a height of 1, etc. The height of the tree is the height of the root from the lowest leaf.

DEGREE A node's degree is equal to the number of children the node has. A leaf's degree is zero.

SUBTREE A subtree is part of an existing tree. That is, if we take any node, along with its descendants, the result is another tree which is a subtree of the original tree.

FOREST A collection of separate trees is known as a forest.
A forest is very similar to a tree, since if we remove the root of a tree, the result is a forest.
A forest may also be transformed into a single tree by adding a linking root node.

Binary Trees

A binary tree is a restricted form of tree. The restriction being that no node may have more than two branches.

By definition, a binary tree may be either:

1. An empty tree (one containing no nodes)

or 2. A structure consisting of a left sub-tree (which is itself a binary tree); a root node ; and a right sub-tree (which is also a binary tree)

FIG-9.4 shows some examples of binary trees.

FIG-9.4

Examples of Binary Trees

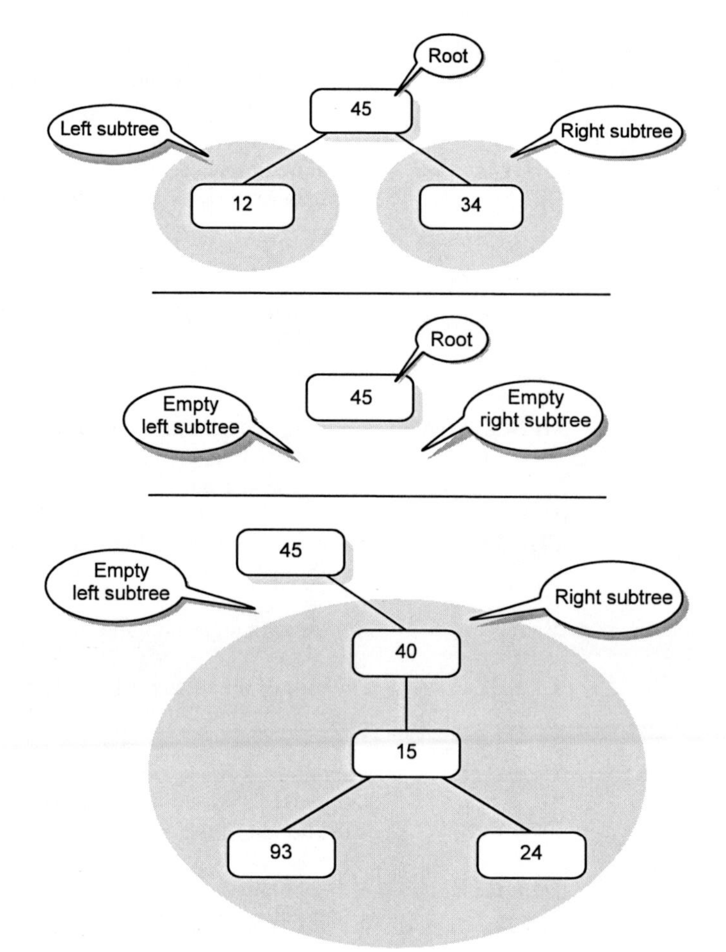

TASK 9.3

In the following binary tree

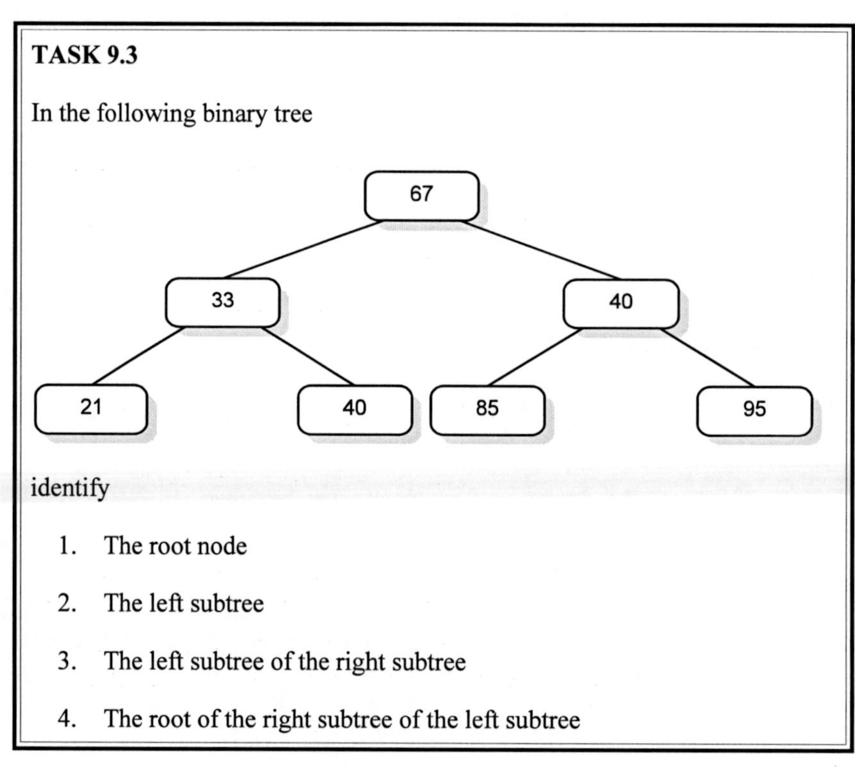

identify

1. The root node
2. The left subtree
3. The left subtree of the right subtree
4. The root of the right subtree of the left subtree

Binary Search Trees

This tree is a restricted form of binary tree in which all items in the left subtree have a value less than the root node and all values in the right subtree are greater than the root (see FIG-9.5).

FIG-9.5

A Binary Search Tree

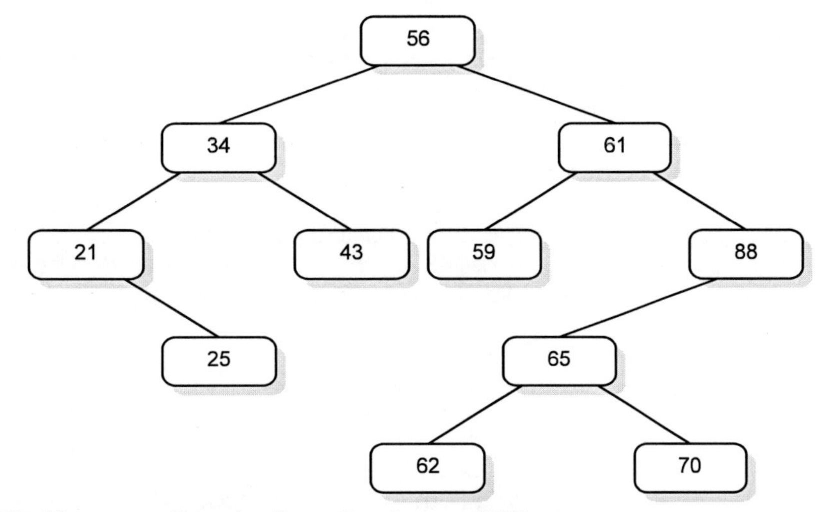

The binary search tree is often referred to as a **BSTree** .

A BSTree is defined as either

1. An empty tree

or 2. A left BSTree; a root; and a right BSTree

We can create a binary search tree from a set of values by using the following algorithm:

```
REPEAT
    IF
        the tree is empty:
            Insert new value as tree root
        value to be added < root:
            Use the left subtree for search
        value to be added > root:
            Use the right subtree for search
    ENDIF
UNTIL new value inserted
```

TASK 9.4

1. Draw a binary search tree from the following values. Assume the values are placed in the tree in the order they are given here.

   65, 12, 45, 23, 96, 44, 21, 53, 72, 88, 75, 10

2. What is the height of the tree created?

The main use of the Binary Search Tree structure is given in its name. It allows a binary search to be performed on data which is not held in physical order.

Creating a Binary Search Tree

Defining a BSTree ADT

Although we might reasonably treat a binary tree as simply a method of implementing a table, it can also be considered as a data type in its own right. The following ADT gives an informal description of such a structure.

```
ADT BSTree IS

    DATA
        Consists of a finite set of data nodes and a finite set of branches connecting pairs
        of nodes. In a non-empty BSTree, there is a single root node which is connected
        to a left BSTree and a right BSTree. All values in the left subtree are less than the
        value of  the root; all values in the right subtree are greater than the node.

    OPERATIONS
        NAME            :   CreateBSTree
        PARAMETERS
            IN          :   None
            OUT         :   t : BSTree
            IN/OUT          :   None
        PRE-CONDITION  :   None
        POST-CONDITION:   t is empty

        NAME            :   IsEmpty
        PARAMETERS
            IN          :   t : BSTree
                            result : INTEGER
            OUT         :   None
            IN/OUT      :   None
        PRE-CONDITION  :   None
        POST-CONDITION:   IF t is empty THEN
                                result =1
                            ELSE
                                result =0

        NAME            :   Add
        PARAMETERS
            IN          :   v : Item
            OUT         :   None
            IN/OUT      :   t : BSTree
        PRE-CONDITION  :   None
        POST-CONDITION:   IF t is empty THEN
                                insert v as root
                                ELSE
                                    IF key of v < key of root THEN
                                        Add(v,left subtree of t)
                                    ELSE
                                        IF key of v > key of root THEN
                                            Add(v,right subtree of t)
                                        ELSE
                                            t is unchanged
```

```
NAME              :   Root
PARAMETERS
    IN            :   t : BSTree
    OUT           :   v : Item
    IN/OUT        :   None
PRE-CONDITION     :   t not empty
POST-CONDITION    :   v holds a copy of the root of t

NAME              :   Display
PARAMETERS
    IN            :   t : BSTree
    OUT           :   None
    IN/OUT        :   None
PRE-CONDITION     :   None
POST-CONDITION    :   IF t not empty THEN
                          Display(left subtree of t)
                          Display contents of root
                          Display(right subtree of t)
END ADT
```

This time the post-conditions have been given in a much more formal manner than those in earlier chapters. This results in a less ambiguous type of description and can give the programmer a greater insight into a possible approach to implementing the new data type.

TASK 9.5

Using the ADT defined above, state:

a) What happens to the tree, *t*, when an attempt is made to add a new value whose key matches an existing entry in the tree?
b) What is the effect of trying to find the root of an empty tree?

Implementing a Binary Search Tree

Data

Although the ADT's description of the structure did not include details of the actual data stored in the tree, we'll now have to commit ourselves to what information we want to hold in our structure. For this example, we'll use the *StudentDetails* structure as the data component of a node. So, we begin with the declaration:

```
struct StudentDetails
{
    int idcode;
    char name[30];
    char sex;
    int score[6];
};
```

Next we have to declare the structure of a single node in the tree. This is constructed from a data area and two pointers. The pointers reference the left and right subtrees (see FIG-9.6).

FIG-9.6

A BSTree Node

Left subtree pointer	Data	Right subtree pointer

The declaration for a node is given as:

```
struct Node
{
    Node *left;
    Item value;
    Node *right;
};
```

The binary search tree structure is simply a pointer to a node:

```
typedef Node *BSTree;
```

Since our tree is to contain *StudentDetails* structures, we'll need to link the terms *Item* (as used within a the *Node* declaration) and *StudentDetails*. All this requires is:

```
typedef StudentDetails Item;
```

Once constructed a typical *BSTree* variable will have the form shown in FIG-9.7.

FIG-9.7

A Typical BSTree Variable

NOTE: Only the *idcode* values are shown within the nodes of the tree.

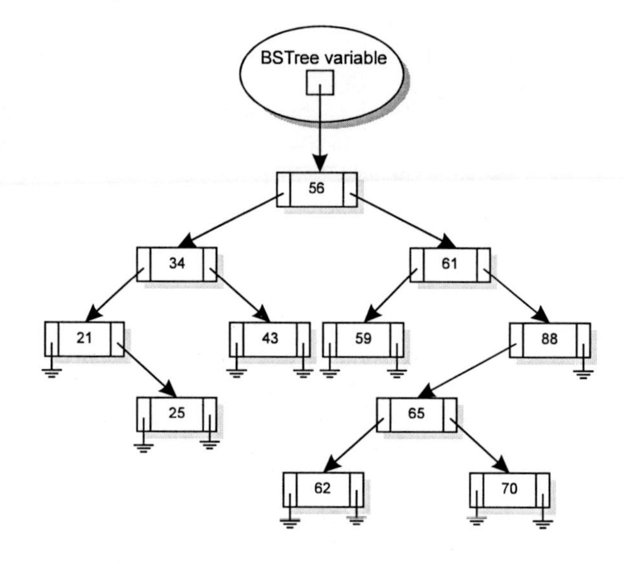

Operations

The first routine that we need to write is *CreateTree* which sets the tree pointer to NULL:

```
//*** Create an Empty Tree ***
void CreateTree(BSTree& t)
{
    //*** Set pointer to root to NULL ***
    t = NULL;
}
```

Another routine which can be easily implemented is *IsEmpty*:

```
//*** Check if tree is empty ***
int IsEmpty(const BSTree& t)
{
    //*** IF pointer to root is NULL THEN ***
    if(t==NULL)
        //*** Tree is empty ***
        return 1;
    else
        //***ELSE tree is not empty ***
        return 0;
}
```

Retrieving the root node is also relatively simple, but we need to check that its pre-condition - that the tree is not empty - is met:

```
//*** Get Root of Tree ***
Item Root(const BSTree& t)
{
    //*** IF tree is empty THEN ***
    if(IsEmpty(t))
    {
        //*** Exit program ***
        cout<<"Error cannot get root of empty tree\n";
        exit(1);
    }
    //*** ELSE Return value of root ***
    return t->value;
}
```

One possible way of implementing the *Add* operation is to use the same recursive approach suggested in the post-condition of the operation:

```
//*** Add new node to tree ***
int Add(const Item nv, BSTree& t)
{
    //*** IF tree is empty THEN ***
    if(IsEmpty(t))
    {
        //*** Create node ***
        Node *temp;
        temp = new Node;
        temp->left=NULL;
        temp->right=NULL;
        temp->value=nv;
        //*** Add node as root ***
        t=temp;
        return 1;
    }
    //*** IF root is the same as the new value THEN ***
    if(nv.idcode==Root(t).idcode)
        //*** Fail ***
        return 0;
    //*** IF new value < root THEN ***
    if(nv.idcode<Root(t).idcode)
        //*** Insert into left subtree ***
        Add(nv,t->left);
    else
        //*** Insert into right subtree ***
        Add(nv,t->right);
}
```

Now all we have to do is implement the *Display* operation which, again, follows the logic suggested by its post-condition:

This version of *Display* only outputs the *idcode* value of each node.

```
//*** Display contents of tree ***
void Display(const BSTree& t)
{
    //*** IF tree is not empty THEN ***
    if(!IsEmpty(t))
    {
        //*** Display the left subtree ***
        Display(t->left);
        //*** Display the root ***
        cout<<t->value.idcode<<endl;
        //*** Display the right subtree ***
        Display(t->right);
    }
}
```

This code is brought together in LISTING-9.1 which implements a simple tree program.

LISTING-9.1

Implementing the Binary Search Tree

```
#include <iostream.h>
#include <stdlib.h>
#include <conio.h>
#include <string.h>
#include <stdio.h>


//*************************************
// *** BSTree Data Type Declarations ***
//*************************************
//*** Data ***
struct StudentDetails
{
  int idcode;
  char name[30];
  char sex;
  int score[6];
};

typedef StudentDetails Item;struct Node
{
  Node *left;
  Item value;
  Node *right;
};

typedef Node *BSTree;


//*** Operations ***
void CreateTree(BSTree&);
int Add(const Data,BSTree&);
void Display(const BSTree&);
int IsEmpty(const BSTree&);
Item Root(const BSTree&);

//**********************************
//*** END BSTree Type Declaration ***
//**********************************


//*** Other function Prototypes ***
int DisplayMenu(char *);
int GetOption(int);
void ExecuteOption(int, BSTree&);




void main()
{
  BSTree tree;
  Item info;

  int noofopts, opt;

  CreateTree(tree);
  do
  {
      clrscr();
      noofopts=DisplayMenu("1  - Create tree\n2  - Add Node\n"
          "3  - Display\n4  - Display first value\n"
          "5  - QUIT\n");
      opt=GetOption(noofopts);
      ExecuteOption(opt,tree);
  }
  while(opt!=noofopts);
}
```

Continued on next page

LISTING-9.1
(continued)

Implementing the Binary Search Tree

```
//*******************************
//*** BSTree Type Definitions ***
//*******************************

//*** Create an Empty Tree ***
void CreateTree(BSTree& t)
{
   //*** Set pointer to root to NULL ***
   t = NULL;
}


//*** Check if tree empty ***
int IsEmpty(const BSTree& t)
{
   //*** IF pointer to root is NULL THEN ***
   if(t==NULL)
        //*** Tree is empty ***
        return 1;
   else
        //***ELSE tree is not empty ***
        return 0;
}


//*** Get Root of Tree ***
Item Root(const BSTree& t)
{
   //*** IF tree is empty THEN ***
   if(IsEmpty(t))
   {
        //*** Exit program ***
        cout<<"Error cannot get root of empty tree\n";
        exit(1);
   }
   //*** ELSE Return value of root ***
   return t->value;
}


//*** Add new node to tree ***
int Add(const Item nv, BSTree& t)
{
   //*** IF tree is empty THEN ***
   if(IsEmpty(t))
   {
        //*** Create node ***
        Node *temp;
        temp = new Node;
        temp->left=NULL;
        temp->right=NULL;
        temp->value=nv;
        //*** Add node as root ***
        t=temp;
        return 1;
   }
   //*** IF root is the same as the new value THEN ***
   if(nv.idcode==Root(t).idcode)
        //*** Fail ***
        return 0;
   //*** IF new value < root THEN ***
   if(nv.idcode<Root(t).idcode)
        //*** Insert into left subtree ***
        Add(nv,t->left);
   else
        //*** Insert into right subtree ***
        Add(nv,t->right);
}
```

Continued on next page

LISTING-9.1
(continued)

Implementing the Binary Search Tree

```
//*** Display contents of tree ***
void Display(const BSTree& t)
{
  //*** IF tree is empty THEN ***
  if(IsEmpty(t))
       //*** Exit routine ***
       return;
  //*** Display the left subtree ***
  Display(t->left);
  //*** Display the root ***
  cout<<t->value.idcode<<endl;
  //*** Display the right subtree ***
  Display(t->right);
}

//***********************************
//*** END BSTree Type Definitions ***
//***********************************


//*** Other Function Definitions ***

//*** Display menu ***
int DisplayMenu(char * m)
{
  cout<<m;
  int count=0;
  for(int c=0;c<=strlen(m);c++)
       if(m[c]=='\n')
            count++;
  return count;
}


//*** Get user option ***
int GetOption(int max)
{
  char opstr[3];
  cout<<"Enter option : ";
  gets(opstr);
  int op=atoi(opstr);
  while(op<1||op>max)
  {
       cout<<"\a?:";
       gets(opstr);
       op=atoi(opstr);
  }
  return op;
}


//*** Execute User Option ***
void ExecuteOption(int opt, BSTree& t)
{
  switch(opt)
  {
       case 1:
            CreateTree(t);
            break;
       case 2:
            cout<<"Enter value : ";
            Item st;
            cin>>st.idcode;
            Add(st,t);
            break;
       case 3:
            Display(t);
            getch();
            break;
```

Continued on next page

LISTING-9.1
(continued)

Implementing the Binary Search Tree

```
            case 4 :
                if(IsEmpty(t))
                    cout<<"Tree empty\n";
                else
                    cout<<Root(t).idcode<<endl;
                getch();
                break;
            case 5:
                cout<<"TERMINATING PROGRAM\n";
                break;
        }
    }
```

PROGRAMMING EXERCISE 9.2

1. Modify the above code to accept and display all the information for each student. Use *GetData()* to read in the information for each field.

2. Rewrite the *Add()* function using a non-recursive approach.

Deleting From a Binary Search Tree

There is one basic operation which has been omitted so far in the discussion on BSTrees and that is deletion. Unfortunately, deletion from a tree is not always a simple task. There are three distinct situations which may arise when deleting a node:

1. The Node to be Deleted has no Children (see FIG-9.8)

Deleting a leaf node is simple since it has no descendants. The node is erased by removing the branch from it to its parent. In C++, deletion of a leaf is achieved by removing the allocated node space using `delete`, and setting the left or right pointer (as appropriate) of the leaf's parent to NULL. The logic required for this operation is:

```
Find the node to be deleted and its parent
Set the parent's left or right pointer (whichever one is
    pointing to the deleted node) to NULL
Dispose of the node to be removed
```

FIG-9.8

Deleting a Leaf from a BSTree

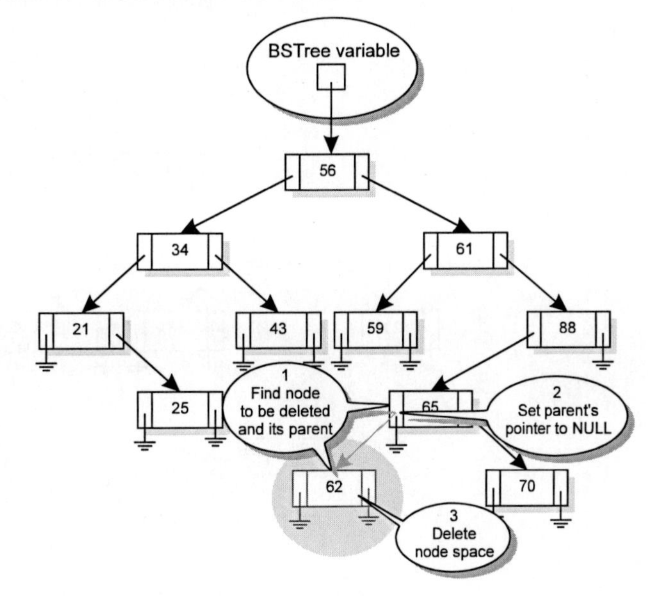

2. The Node to be Deleted has a Single Child (see FIG-9.9)

When the node to be deleted has a single branch leading from it, its child replaces the deleted item in the tree.

In C++ this is achieved by linking the parent of the node to be deleted to the child of the node to be deleted. The link is to the *left* or *right* pointer of the parent as appropriate. The logic for this operation is:

```
Find the node to be deleted and its parent
Set the parent's left or right pointer (whichever one is
    pointing to the deleted node) to point to the child of
    the deleted node
Dispose of the node to be removed
```

FIG-9.9

Deleting a Node with a Single Child

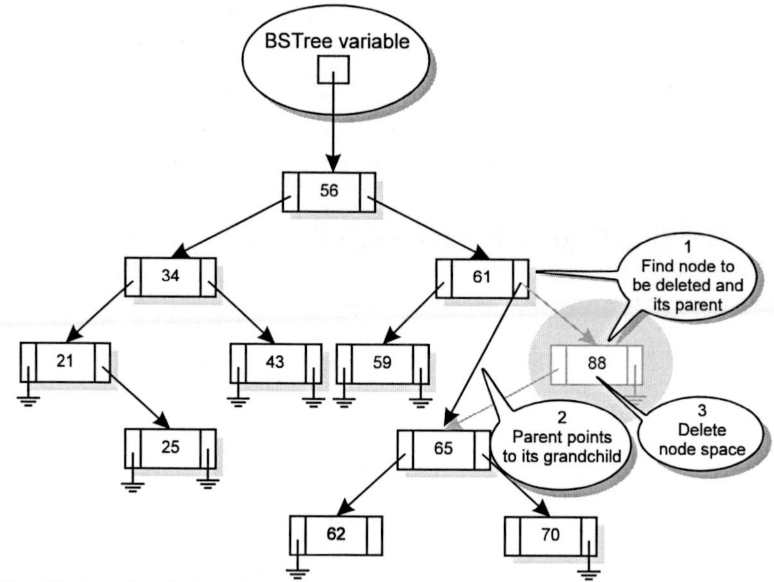

3. The Node to be Deleted has Two Children (see FIG-9.10)

This is the most complex case. Simply deleting the node will split the tree into separate parts, cutting off the descendants of the deleted node from the rest of the tree.

FIG-9.10

The Problem with Deleting a Two-Child Node

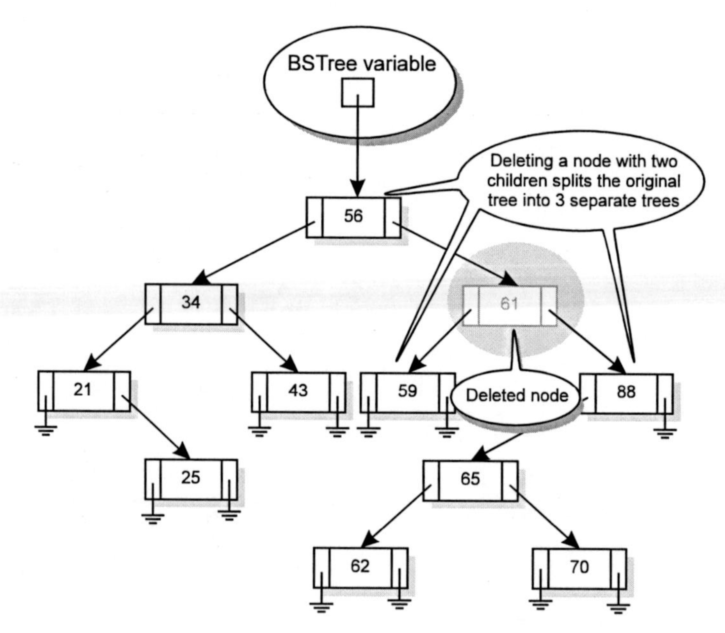

To overcome this problem we do not delete the node containing the value to be removed; we simply overwrite the contents of the node with the data of a descendant. So that the tree's structure will remain substantially the same, the new value must be close to the one just overwritten.

TASK 9.6

Which remaining value is closest to that of the deleted value in FIG-9.10 above?

In fact, although the replacement value must be close to the one being overwritten, it need not be the closest value. It is only necessary that the replacement value is such that the resulting structure still conforms to the definition of a BSTree (i.e. that all values to the left of the replacement value are less than the replacement value and that those to the right are larger).

This means that we do not have to search the tree for the nearest value to the one being deleted but need merely employ the following logic:

```
Starting with the subtree for which the value to be deleted
    is the root (we'll call this T1)
Choose the right subtree of T1 (called T2)
Go down through T2 choosing only left subtrees until the left
    subtree is empty
Make a copy of the value found
Delete the node from which the copy was made
Place the copy of the deleted node's data in the root of T1
```

FIG-9.11 gives a graphical representation of the steps involved.

FIG-9.11

Deleting a Two-Child Node

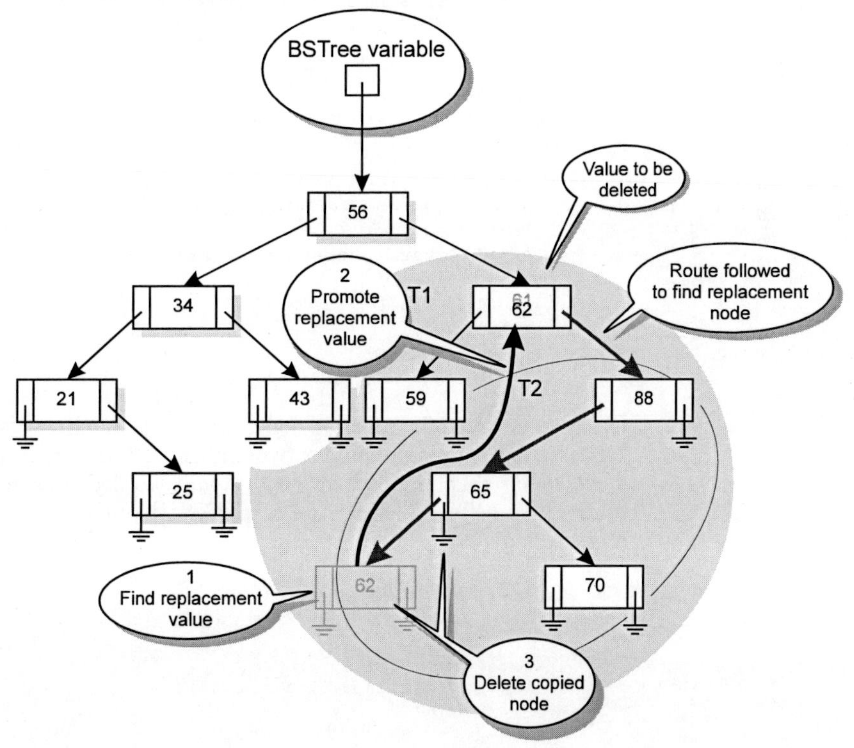

Note that the node actually deleted during this process will either be a leaf (as in FIG-9.11) or a node with a single branch. And, since we have already described how these two cases are dealt with, our approach to deleting a two-child parent is complete.

To code the *Delete* operation, we'll need to start by defining something similar to the *IsAt* operation we've used in the past. However, this time we need a routine which returns pointers to both the required node and its parent. We'll call the routine *FindParCh*. The Mini-Spec for this routine is:

NAME	:	FindParCh
PARAMETERS		
IN	:	key : INTEGER t : BSTree
OUT	:	success : INTEGER par :NODE pointer ch : NODE pointer
IN/OUT	:	None
PRE-CONDITION	:	None
POST-CONDITION	:	*success* is set to zero if *key* does not match any idcode in *t*, otherwise *success* is set to 1. If match found then *ch* holds the address of the node containing a match and *par* holds the address of its parent.

The code for this routine is:

```
int FindParCh(int key, BSTree& t, Node*& par, Node*& ch)
{
    //*** Set parent to NULL and child to root ***
    par = NULL;
    ch = t;
    //*** WHILE not end of tree AND  no match DO ***
    while(ch!=NULL&&ch->value.idcode != key)
    {
        //*** Current child becomes new parent ***
        par = ch;
        //*** Child moves down tree ***
        if(key < ch->value.idcode)
            ch = ch->left;
        else
            ch = ch->right;
    }
    //*** Return success indicator ***
    if (ch==NULL)
        return 0;
    else
        return 1;
}
```

Once we've found the required node, we need to determine what type of node it is. That is, is it a leaf, single-child or two-child node? This can be decided by examining the left and right pointers of the node. Again, we'll do this by writing another short routine, *NodeType()*, which takes a *Node* pointer and returns -1, 0, 1, or 2 representing a NULL pointer, leaf, 1-child node or 2-child node respectively.

```
int NodeType(Node* nd)
{
    if(nd==NULL)
        return -1;
    if(!(nd->left)&&!(nd->right))
        return 0;
    if(!(nd->left)||!(nd->right))
        return 1;
    else
        return 2;
}
```

> **PROGRAMMING EXERCISE 9.3**
>
> Add another user option to the program you created in Programming Exercise 9.2 which allows the user to find a match for a given key. A display of "FOUND" or "NOT FOUND" should be given as appropriate and where a match is found, its node type should be displayed as "LEAF", "1 - CHILD" or "2 - CHILDREN".

We're now ready to tackle the two simpler delete options: deleting a leaf and single-child node. In fact, these two cases can be combined into a single method: if we examine the logic for both variations (given below), we can see that the only difference lies in what value is assigned to the parent's left or right pointer.

Deleting a Leaf

```
Find the node to be deleted and its parent
Set the parent's left or right pointer (whichever one is
    pointing to the node to be deleted) to NULL
Dispose of the node to be deleted
```

Deleting a Node with a Single Child

```
Find the node to be deleted and its parent
Set the parent's left or right pointer (whichever one is
    pointing to the node to be deleted) to point to the
    child of the node to be deleted
Dispose of the node to be deleted
```

In the second case, the parent's pointer will be set to point to the child of the node to be deleted. This value will be taken from either the left or right pointer in the node to be deleted.

Where a leaf node is being deleted, the parent's appropriate pointer is set to NULL and this may simply be considered as a copy of the left or right pointer of the node to be deleted as they are both set to NULL (since we are dealing with a leaf).

We can now describe the delete strategy (first two cases only) as:

```
Find the node to be deleted and its parent
IF a match is found THEN
    Determine which type of node is to be deleted
        (zero, one or two children)
    IF node to be deleted has less than two children THEN
            Delete leaf or single child node
    ENDIF
ENDIF
```

Which is coded as:

```
int Delete(int key, BSTree& t)
{
    Node *par, *ch;

    //*** IF a match is found for key THEN ***
    if(FindParCh(key,t,par,ch))
    {
        //*** Deal with type of delete ***
        switch(NodeType(ch))
        {
            case 0: //*** Delete leaf ***
            case 1: //*** Delete 1-child node ***
                //***Determine grandchild position - ***
                //*** left, right, none             ***
            Node *grandchild;
            if(ch->left!=NULL)
                grandchild = ch->left;
            else
```

```
                grandchild = ch->right;
            //*** Link grandchild to parent ***
            //** Special case for deleting root **
            if(par==NULL)
                t=grandchild;
            else if(par->left==ch)
                par->left=grandchild;
            else
                par->right=grandchild;
            break;
        }
        //*** Deallocate node's space ***
        delete ch;
        return 1;
    }
    return 0;
}
```

Notice that the code itself is somewhat more complex than the outline logic suggests since we need to treat deletion of the root as a special case (since it has no parent), and we also need to find out if the grandchild is on the left or right side of the child node.

PROGRAMMING EXERCISE 9.4

Add this *Delete()* function to your **Trees** program.

To complete the *Delete* operation, we need to be able to handle the removal of nodes with two children. To do that, we need to find and promote a successor to the data being removed. The logic for such a process is:

```
Starting at the right subtree of the node to be deleted
Move down through the left branches of the tree until the
    end is reached
Copy data at that node to the original node
Delete the node from which the data was copied
```

The first three lines of this can be done with the code:

```
//*** Find successor ***
successor = ch->right;
par = ch;
while(successor->left!=NULL)
{
    par=successor;
    successor=successor->left;
}
//*** Copy data to original node ***
ch->value = successor->value;
```

To complete the task, we simply need to move *ch* and *par* to the promoted node and its parent and then use the previous code to delete this node. The code above already moves the *par* pointer to the correct position; all that is required to complete the job is the line:

```
ch=successor;
```

We can now complete the code for *Delete()*:

```
int Delete(int key, BSTree& t)
{
    Node *par, *ch, *successor;

    //*** IF a match is found for key THEN ***
    if(FindParCh(key,t,par,ch))
    {
```

```
        //*** Deal with type of delete ***
        switch(NodeType(ch))
        {
            case 2: //*** Two child node ***
                //*** Find successor ***
                successor = ch->right;
                par = ch;
                while(successor->left!=NULL)
                {
                    par=successor;
                    successor=successor->left;
                }
                //*** Copy data to original node ***
                ch->value = successor->value;
                //*** Now delete successor by     ***
                //*** executing next case option ***
                ch=successor;
            case 0: //*** Delete leaf ***
            case 1: //*** Delete 1-child node ***
                //***Determine grandchild position - ***
                //***left, right, none               ***
                Node *grandchild;
                if(ch->left!=NULL)
                    grandchild = ch->left;
                else
                    grandchild = ch->right;
                //*** Link grandchild to parent ***
                //** Special case for deleting root **
                if(par==NULL)
                    t=grandchild;
                else if(par->left==ch)
                    par->left=grandchild;
                else
                    par->right=grandchild;
                break;
        }
        //*** Deallocate node's space ***
        delete ch;
        return 1;
    }
    return 0;
}
```

PROGRAMMING EXERCISE 9.5

Complete the *Delete* operation in your **Trees** program.

Summary

- **A tree** is a hierarchical structure.
- **A tree is constructed** from nodes and branches.
- **The root** of a tree is the first node in the tree.
- **A leaf** is a node which has no branches.
- **A binary tree** is one in which each node has, at most, two children.
- In **a binary search tree**, all values to the left of any node are less than the value of that node and all values to the right of the node are greater than the value of the node.
- **Binary search trees are used to** allow efficient searching of a collection of data.

GRAPHS

Undirected Graphs

Introduction

A graph, like a tree, is a collection of nodes connected by lines (called **edges**). What differentiates these two structures is that a node may connect back to a previous node (something that cannot happen in a tree).

Graphs in the Real World

The map below (see FIG-9.12) shows the destinations available from ABC Airlines.

FIG-9.12

Flight Routes on a Map

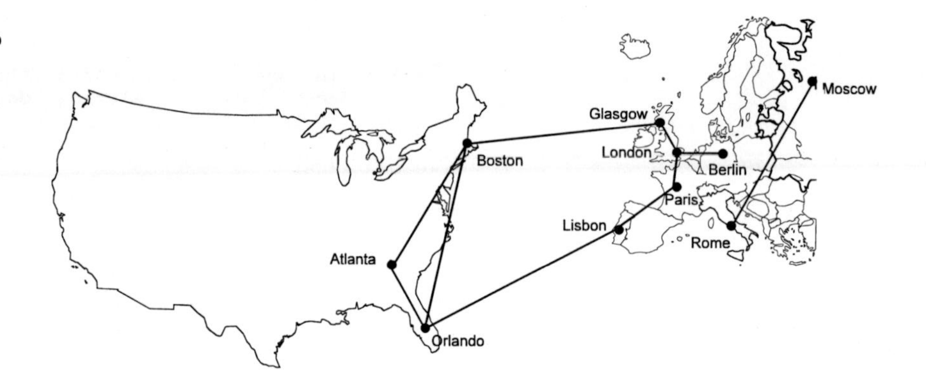

We could use this diagram to select a route from, say, Glasgow to Orlando. But we could equally well use a more abstract form of the diagram to make the same decision (see FIG-9.13).

FIG-9.13

A More Abstract Model of the Flight Routes

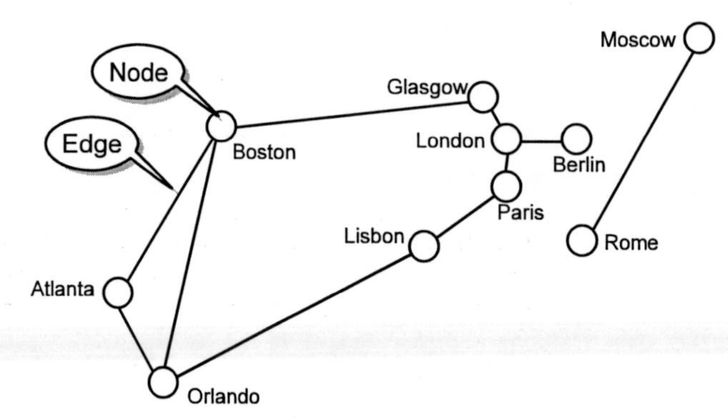

This abstract diagram is an example of a graph.

Terminology

A graph is constructed from **nodes** (also known as **vertices**) which are connected by **edges**. In the example above, the destinations (*Glasgow, Atlanta, Orlando*, etc.) are the nodes and the edges are the lines connecting the nodes. The nodes at either end are used to identify an edge; for example, one edge is (*Atlanta,Orlando*). Note that the nodes identifying an edge are enclosed in parenthesis. In this case, the order of the nodes is unimportant. Therefore the edge between *Glasgow* and *London* can be identified as (*Glasgow,London*) or (*London,Glasgow*). Later we will see examples of graphs where the order of the nodes is significant when identifying edges.

TASK 9.7

List all of the nodes and any five edges in the diagram above.

Nodes at either end of an edge are called **adjacent nodes** (*Boston* is adjacent to *Orlando*). A **path** is the list of nodes that are passed through when travelling from one node to another. One possible path from *Glasgow* to *Orlando* is (*Glasgow,Boston,Atlanta,Orlando*).

A graph is said to be **connected** if there is at least one path from each node to every other node. This is not the case in the graph on the previous page (e.g. there is no path from *Rome* to *Glasgow* - see FIG-9.13).

A **cycle** is a path of at least three different nodes that leads back to the starting node. (*Boston, Atlanta, Orlando, Boston*) is a cycle.

A connected graph that has no cycles is a **tree**. If we start with a connected graph and remove all edges that form cycles but retain connections to all nodes, then we have formed a **spanning tree** (see FIG 9.14).

FIG-9.14

Graphs and Spanning Trees

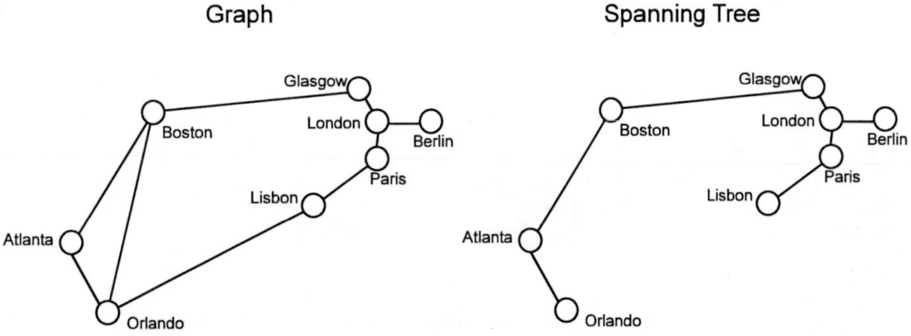

So far we have assumed that the existence of an edge allows movement in both directions between the nodes of that edge. For example, since there is an edge between *Boston* and *Glasgow* it is possible to travel both from *Glasgow* to *Boston* and *Boston* to *Glasgow*. This type of graph is known as an **undirected graph** and the edges are said to be **unordered** since the nodes used in identifying an edge can be specified in any order.

A graph can have any number of nodes but the number of edges on an undirected graph can vary from zero (where none of the nodes are connected) to a maximum value determined by the number of nodes.

In general, if a graph contains N nodes, then the maximum number of edges is given by the formula:

$N(N-1)/2$ (see FIG-9.15)

FIG-9.15

Complete Graphs

No of Nodes	Max. Edges	Diagram
2	1	
3	3	
4	6	

Where all possible edges are present in a graph, the graph is said to be **complete**. If most of the edges are present then the graph is termed **dense**, while a graph with few edges is called a **sparse graph**.

Directed Graphs

In a directed graph, edges indicate a one-way connection between nodes. This is shown graphically as an arrowed line (see FIG-9.16).

FIG-9.16

A One-way Connection in a Directed Graph

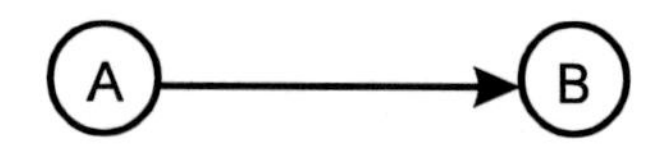

Where a connection exists in both directions between nodes then two lines are required (see FIG-9.17).

FIG-9.17

A Two-way Connection in a Directed Graph

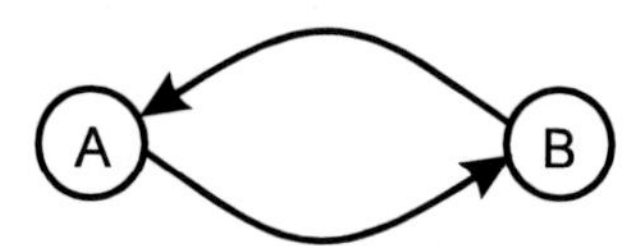

When specifying an edge between a node, A, and another node, B, then the starting node is given first. Hence the edge in FIG-9.16 is identified as (A, B), while those in FIG-9.17 are (A, B) and (B, A).

Abstract Definition of a Graph

Typical operations for a graph data type differ somewhat from other types we have created so far. As well as the usual requirements to add and remove nodes and edges, we need operations to do such things as determine which nodes are adjacent to a given node, and the shortest paths between two nodes.

```
ADT Graph is
    DATA
        A set of node identifiers and a set of edges
    OPERATIONS
        NAME            :   CreateGraph
```

PARAMETERS		
IN	:	gt : GraphType
OUT	:	g : Graph
IN/OUT	:	None
PRE-CONDITION	:	None
POST-CONDITION	:	*g* is created as an empty graph.*g t* specifies which type of graph is to be created: directed or undirected.

NAME	:	AddNode
PARAMETERS		
IN	:	n : Node
OUT	:	None
IN/OUT	:	g : Graph
PRE-CONDITION	:	None
POST-CONDITION	:	If *n* does not already exist in *g*, it is added to *g*, otherwise *g* is unchanged

NAME	:	AddEdge
PARAMETERS		
IN	:	e : Edge
OUT	:	None
IN/OUT	:	g : Graph
PRE-CONDITION	:	None
POST-CONDITION	:	If *e* does not already exist in *g*, it is added to *g*, otherwise *g* is unchanged.

NAME	:	RemoveEdge
PARAMETERS		
IN	:	e : Edge
OUT	:	None
IN/OUT	:	g : Graph
PRE-CONDITION	:	None
POST-CONDITION	:	If *e* exist in *g*, it is removed from *g*, otherwise *g* is unchanged

NAME	:	RemoveNode
PARAMETERS		
IN	:	n : Node
OUT	:	None
IN/OUT	:	g : Graph
PRE-CONDITION	:	None
POST-CONDITION	:	If *n* exists in *g*, then *n* and all edges linked to *n* are removed from *g*, otherwise *g* is unchanged

NAME	:	AdjacentNodes
PARAMETERS		
IN	:	n : Node g : Graph
OUT	:	nlist: set of Node
IN/OUT	:	None
PRE-CONDITION	:	None
POST-CONDITION	:	*nlist* contains all nodes adjacent to *n*

NAME	:	IsConnected
PARAMETERS		
IN	:	start : Node

		end : Node
		g : Graph
OUT	:	connected : INTEGER
IN/OUT	:	None
PRE-CONDITION	:	*start* and *end* must be in *g*
POST-CONDITION	:	Sets *connected* to 1 if a path exists between the two nodes *start* and *end*, otherwise *connected* is set to zero.
NAME	:	ShortestPath
PARAMETERS		
IN	:	start : Node
		end : Node
		g : Graph
OUT	:	path : Stack
IN/OUT	:	None
PRE-CONDITION	:	*start* and *end* must be in *g*
POST-CONDITION	:	*path* contains, in order, the nodes which make up the shortest path (least edges) between *start* and *end*
NAME	:	DisplayGraph
PARAMETERS		
IN	:	g : Graph
OUT	:	None
IN/OUT	:	None
PRE-CONDITION	:	None
POST-CONDITION	:	if there are any nodes in *g* then the contents of *g* are displayed else no output is produced.

END ADT

Note that there is no need to differentiate between directed and undirected graphs at this stage.

Implementing a Graph

Data

The data components of a graph consist of a set of nodes and a set of edges.

FIG-9.18

Storing Nodes

0	Glasgow
1	London
2	Boston
3	Atlanta
4	Orlando
5	Lisbon
6	Paris
7	Berlin
8	Rome
9	Moscow

The node names can be held in a string array (see FIG-9.18).

The simplest way to hold the edges of the graph is in a matrix. Each node is represented by one row and one column. Where two nodes are connected by an edge, the corresponding matrix cell holds the distance between the two nodes. For example, if we assume a distance of 3700 miles between *Glasgow* and *Boston* this connection is represented by placing this value (3700) in the corresponding cells. In an undirected graph, the value is placed in the cells representing both the (*Glasgow,Boston*) and (*Boston,Glasgow*) edges (see FIG-9.19).

TASK 9.8

How is the edge between Boston and Atlanta represented if the distance between the two nodes is 1000.

Note that the column and row numbers correspond to the position of the node name in the earlier table. Hence, row 5 and column 5 represent *Lisbon.*

FIG-9.19

Representing the Edges

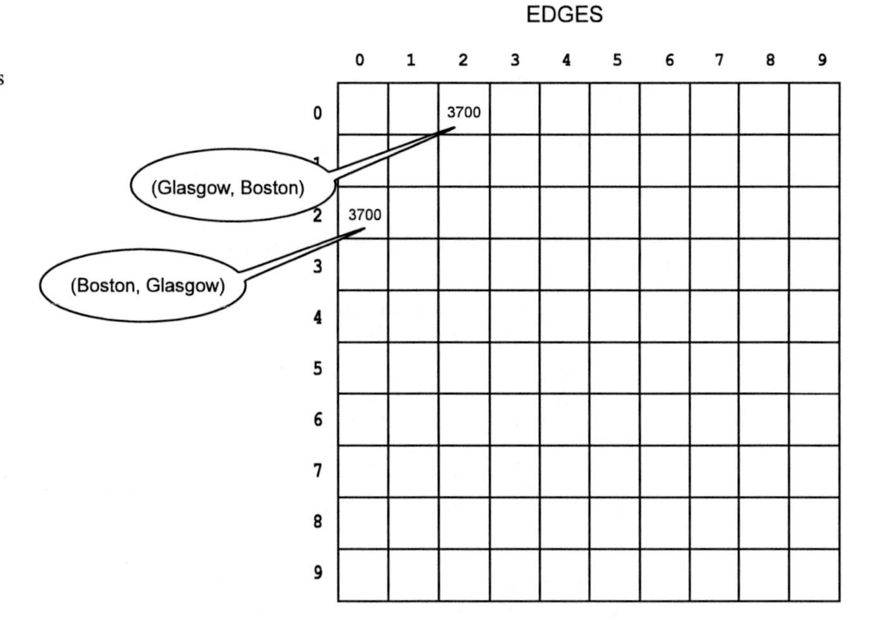

Additionally, it will be useful to maintain a count of the number of nodes in the graph and an indication of the graph type: directed or undirected. All of this can be achieved by the declarations given below.

```
const int MAXNODES = 12;   //Maximum nodes in graph

enum GraphType {directed, undirected};

struct Graph
{
    int count;                                  //No. of nodes in graph
    GraphType gtype;                            //Graph type
    char nodenames[MAXNODES][21];               //Node names
    int connections[MAXNODES][MAXNODES]; //Edges
};
```

Operations

CreateGraph

The first operation, *CreateGraph*, is only required to set the *count* and *gtype* fields of our structure:

```
//*** Create a new graph ***
void CreateGraph(GraphType gt,Graph& g)
{
    g.count=0;
    g.gtype = gt;
}
```

AddNode

This routine requires a new node name to be added to the *nodenames* array. If the name already exists, the structure is unchanged. Additionally, since we've implemented the data structure with fixed-size arrays, we'll also need to check that there is sufficient space for the new entry.

To search the existing node names list, it will be useful to create an auxiliary function, *NodeAt*, which returns the position in *nodenames* of a specified node; where the node does not exist, the function will return -1. This additional function is coded as:

```
//*** Find position of node ***
int NodeAt(char* name, const Graph& g)
{
    int post = 0;
    //*** Search for matching node name ***
    while(strcmp(g.nodenames[post],name)&&post<g.count)
        post++;
    //*** IF found THEN return its position ***
    if(!strcmp(g.nodenames[post],name))
        return post;
    //*** ELSE return -1 ***
    else
        return -1;
}
```

We're now ready to code the *AddNode* operation to which a *success* indicator has been added:

```
//*** Add a new node to graph ***
int AddNode(char *newname, Graph& g)
{
    //***IF graph full or name exists THEN exit ***
    if(g.count==MAXNODES||NodeAt(newname,g)!=-1)
        return 0;
    //*** Copy name to node names list ***
    strcpy(g.nodenames[g.count],newname);
    //*** Clear any connections ***
    for(int c=0;c<g.count;c++)
    {
        g.connections[g.count][c]=0;
        g.connections[c][g.count]=0;
    }
    //*** Increment node count***
    g.count++;
    return 1;
}
```

AddEdge

To add an edge we need to specify the two nodes which the edge is to join and the distance or cost of the edge. For example, if we wish to create an edge between *Glasgow* and *Boston*, with a distance of 3700, the routine must first check that the two nodes exist and then add the value 3700 to the appropriate cell in the connections matrix (*g.connections[0][2]*). If the graph is undirected, we need to add the corresponding edge (*Boston, Glasgow*) by placing the value 3700 in *g.connections[2][0]* (see FIG-9.19).

The code for the routine is:

```
//*** Add new edge ***
int AddEdge(char* start, char* end, int cost, Graph& g)
{
    int pstart, pend;       //*** Position of nodes in matrix

    //*** Determine position of nodes ***
    pstart=NodeAt(start,g);
    pend=NodeAt(end,g);
    //*** IF nodes not found THEN return zero ***
    if(pstart==-1||pend==-1)
        return 0;
    //*** Add edge ***
    g.connections[pstart][pend]=cost;
//*** IF undirected graph THEN add return connection ***
```

```
    if(g.gtype==undirected)
        g.connections[pend][pstart]=cost;
    return 1;
}
```

RemoveEdge

To remove an edge all that is required is to place a zero in the corresponding cell of the connections matrix. Of course, if the graph is undirected, then two cells are affected.

```
//*** Delete an Edge ***
int RemoveEdge(char* start, char* end, Graph& g)
{
    //*** Find edge's nodes ***
    int startno = NodeAt(start,g);
    int endno = NodeAt(end,g);

    //*** IF either does not exist, return zero ***
    if(startno==-1||endno==-1)
        return 0;
    //*** Change cost to zero ***
    g.connections[startno][endno]=0;
    //*** IF graph is undirected, change return edge to zero ***
    if(g.gtype==undirected)
        g.connections[endno][startno]=0;
    return 1;
}
```

RemoveNode

Removing a node is a much more complex operation since it has a widespread affect on other components in the graph as it is implemented.

For example, FIG-9.20, shows a graph with only four nodes and three connections.

FIG-9.20

The Graph before Removing a Node

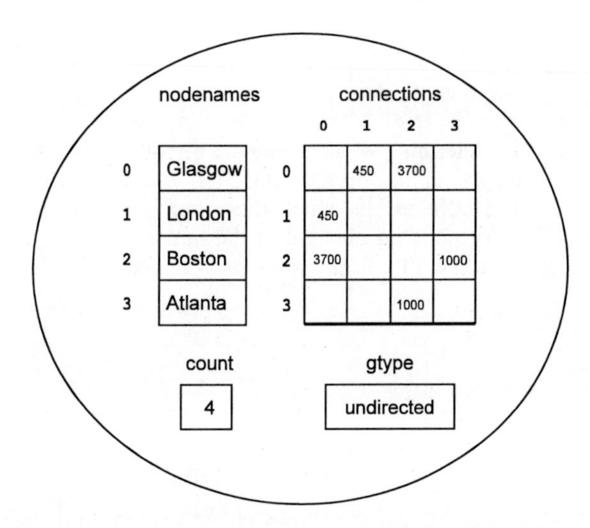

If we remove *London* from the graph, the FIG-9.21 shows what changes are required.

As you see, this requires the row and column for *London* to be removed and the contents of subsequent rows and columns to be moved.

The code required to achieve these changes is:

FIG-9.21

The Graph after a Node has been Removed

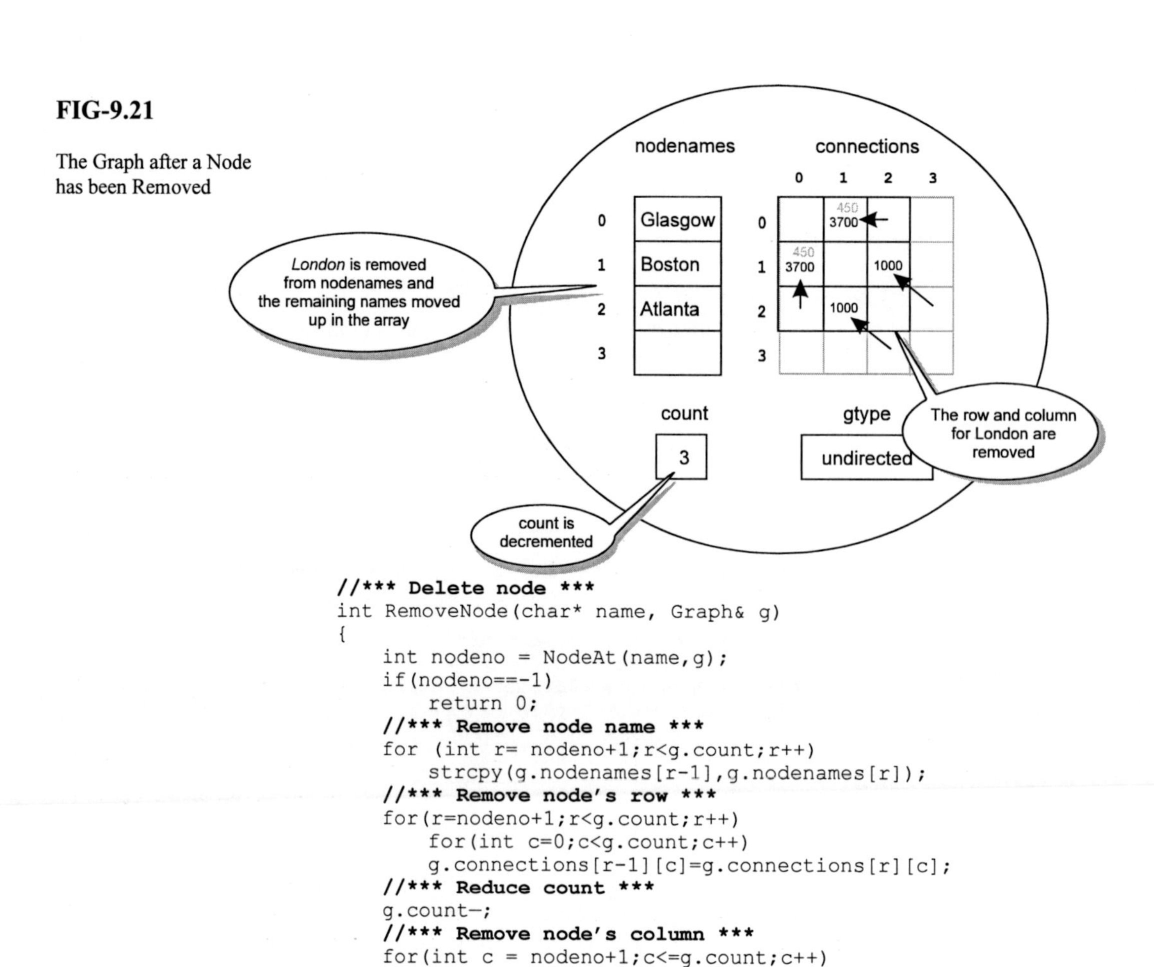


```
//*** Delete node ***
int RemoveNode(char* name, Graph& g)
{
    int nodeno = NodeAt(name,g);
    if(nodeno==-1)
        return 0;
    //*** Remove node name ***
    for (int r= nodeno+1;r<g.count;r++)
        strcpy(g.nodenames[r-1],g.nodenames[r]);
    //*** Remove node's row ***
    for(r=nodeno+1;r<g.count;r++)
        for(int c=0;c<g.count;c++)
        g.connections[r-1][c]=g.connections[r][c];
    //*** Reduce count ***
    g.count–;
    //*** Remove node's column ***
    for(int c = nodeno+1;c<=g.count;c++)
        for(r=0;r<g.count;r++)
            g.connections[r][c-1]=g.connections[r][c];
    return 1;
}
```

AdjacentNodes

To determine which nodes are directly connected to some specified node we need only scan the specified node's row in the connections matrix for non-zero values. The columns in which these non-zero values occur give us, by accessing the corresponding element in the nodenames list, the names of adjacent nodes. For example, FIG-9.22 shows the connections to *Glasgow*.

FIG-9.22

Determining Adjacent Nodes

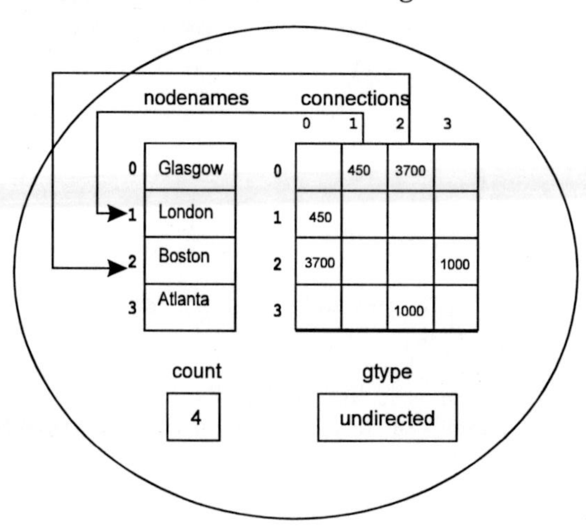

In order to return a list of such nodes a *Queue* variable is used to store the names.

```
//*** Return adjacent nodes ***
int AdjacentNodes(char* name, const Graph& g, Queue& adjnodes)
{
    int post;
    Data d;

    //*** IF the node name is invalid THEN return zero ***
    post=NodeAt(name,g);
    if(post==-1)
        return 0;
    //*** Create empty queue ***
    CreateQueue(adjnodes);
    //*** Scan node's row ***
    for(int c=0;c<g.count;c++)
        //*** IF connection found THEN add its name to queue ***
        if(g.connections[post][c]!=0)
        {
            strcpy(d.no,g.nodenames[c]);
            Insert(d,adjnodes);
        }
    return 1;
}
```

IsConnected

We need to work a bit harder to find out if two specified nodes are connected, since they may be connected indirectly through several nodes. For example, *Glasgow* and *Orlando* are connected via *Boston*.

To determine if a path exists between two nodes we need to start at the first node and move through the other connected nodes until our destination node is arrived at or there are no more nodes to visit. This is called **graph traversal**.

There are two methods of traversing a graph.

One method of visiting each node in a graph is called **depth-first** traversing. This is similar in technique to traversing a tree. Unlike a tree, a graph has no obvious beginning, so to begin a search we must specify a starting node. Let's assume we want to start traversing our graph from *Glasgow* (see FIG-9.23).

FIG-9.23

Starting a Depth-First Traversal

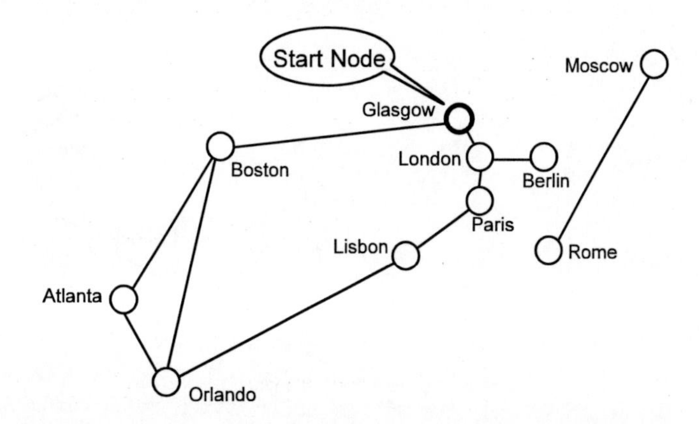

Next, a node adjacent to the first is visited. If there are several adjacent nodes any one will do.

In this case, we'll assume *Boston* is visited (see FIG-9.24).

FIG-9.24

Visit a Node Adjacent to Glasgow

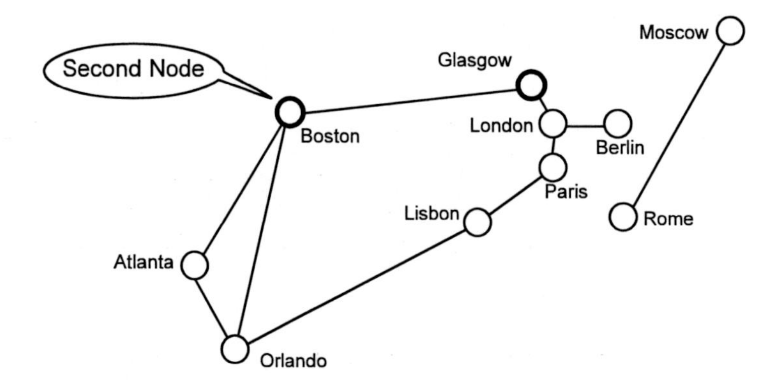

Next, we visit a node adjacent to *Boston* (see FIG-9.25).

FIG-9.25

Visit a Node Adjacent to Boston

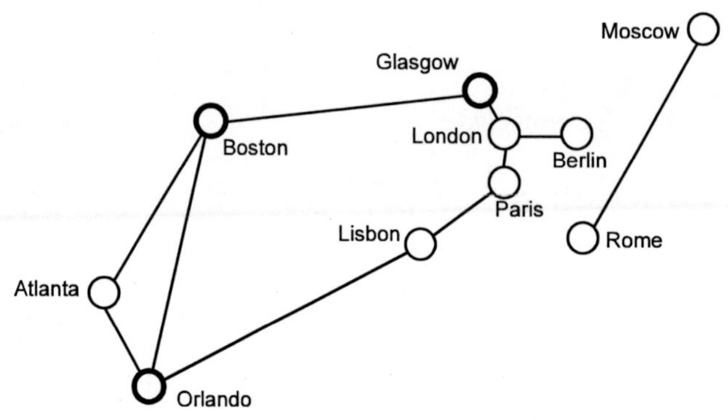

Of course, we could have revisited *Glasgow* from *Boston,* but this would be pointless so it is important to keep note of which nodes have already been visited when traversing the graph.

We now move on from *Orlando* to another adjacent node (see FIG-9.26).

FIG-9.26

Visit a Node Adjacent to Orlando

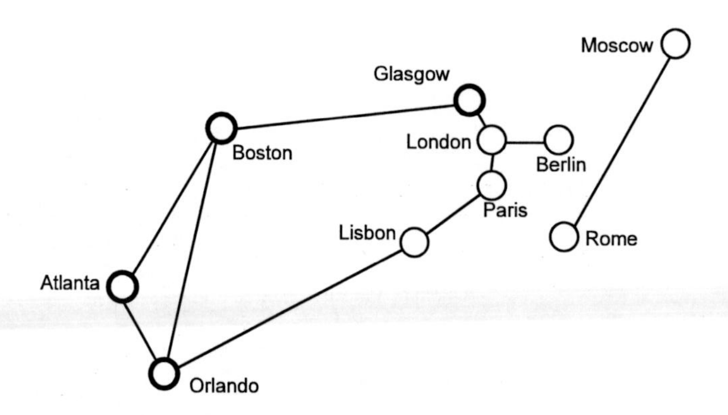

At this stage, we have reached a dead-end. There are no unvisited nodes adjacent to *Atlanta*. In this situation, we begin backtracking along the path we have taken until we find a node which has adjacent nodes which have not yet been visited. Using this strategy, we arrive back at *Orlando* and from there we can move on to *Lisbon*.

From *Lisbon* we move on through *Paris* and *London* until, finally, *Berlin* is reached.

With no further new nodes to be reached from *Berlin*, we backtrack through *London*, *Paris*, *Lisbon*, *Orlando* and *Boston* to our starting point in *Glasgow* and since none of these have any new nodes to be visited the traversal is complete.

This new routine, which we'll call *DeepSearch*, returns an array indicating which nodes have been visited. Hence, if *Lisbon* (node 5) is visited, element 5 of the array will contain a 1; array elements corresponding to nodes which have not been visited will contain a zero.

The routine parameters specify the start node, the graph to be searched, and returns an indication of the nodes visited.

```
//*** Search graph ***
void DeepSearch(int nodeno,const Graph& g, int visited[])
{
    visited[nodeno]=1;
    for(int c= 0; c<g.count; c++)
        if(g.connections[nodeno][c]!=0 && !visited[c])
            DeepSearch(c,g,visited);
};
```

This time, the routine has been coded recursively; it is equally possible to create a non-recursive version using a Stack to hold previously visited nodes.

It's now a simple matter to code *IsConnected()* by simply starting the search at the *start* parameter and checking the array returned by *DeepSearch()* to determine if the destination node (*end*) has been visited during the search.

```
//*** Check if two nodes are connected ***
int IsConnected(char* start, char* end, const Graph& g)
{
    int visited[MAXNODES]={0}; //visited nodes set to zero

    //*** Determine numeric values of start and end nodes ***
    int startno = NodeAt(start,g);
    int endno = NodeAt(end,g);
    //*** IF either node name invalid THEN return zero ***
    if(startno==-1||endno==-1)
        return 0;
    //*** Search graph ***
    DeepSearch(startno,g,visited);
    return visited[endno];
}
```

ShortestPath

Our final operation, *ShortestPath*, requires a second method of traversal known as **breadth-first** traversal. With this approach we first visit ALL of the nodes adjacent to the starting node. This means that, if we start at *Glasgow*, we visit *Boston* and *London* (see FIG-9.27).

FIG-9.27

Visit All Nodes Adjacent to Glasgow

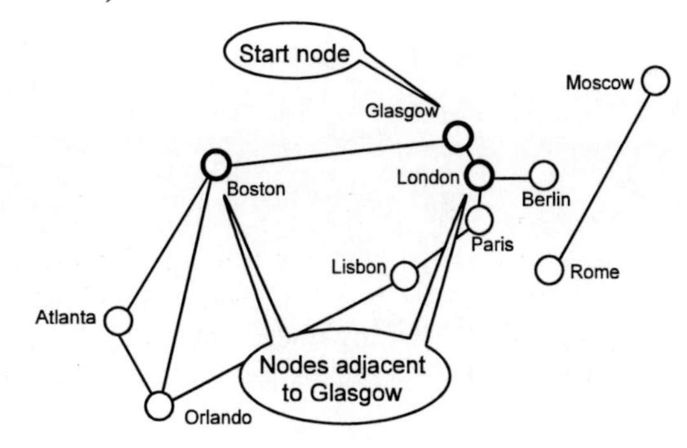

These nodes are, rather obviously, exactly one edge away from the starting node. We can say that there is a distance of one between *Glasgow* and *Boston* and between *Glasgow* and *London*.

For every node which is a distance of one away from our starting node (i.e. *Boston* and *London*) we visit ALL of their adjacent nodes. So from *Boston* we visit *Atlanta* and *Orlando* while from *London* we visit *Paris* and *Berlin* (see FIG-9.28).

FIG-9.28

Visit All Nodes at a Distance of Two from Glasgow

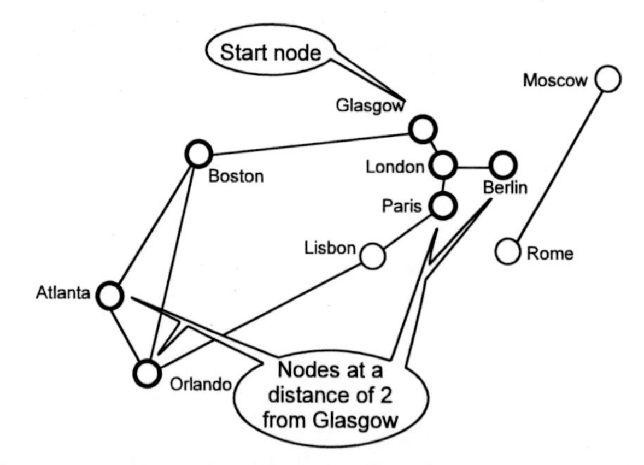

The nodes visited on this second stage (i.e. *Atlanta*, *Orlando*, *Paris* and *Berlin*) have a distance of two from our starting node.

The same strategy is repeated and we visit all unvisited nodes adjacent to *Atlanta*, *Orlando*, *Paris* and *Berlin*. This results in only one new node being visited, *Lisbon*, which has a distance of three from *Glasgow*. Since there are no unvisited nodes adjacent to *Lisbon*, the search is complete.

That is the principle behind a width-first search but in order to put the theory into practice we need to use a *Queue* data structure to hold the nodes whose adjacent nodes are still to be visited. We also need an array to hold the distance to a given node from the starting node.

We begin by creating an empty queue and setting each entry in the table of distances to -1. This value represents a non-visited node (see FIG-9.29).

FIG-9.29

Initialising a Wide Search

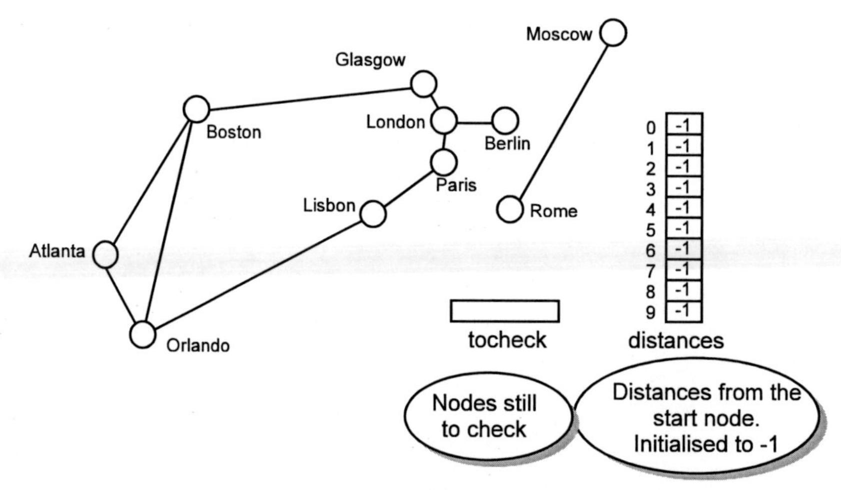

We visit the starting node; place it in the queue and set the distance to node one (*Glasgow*) to zero in the distances array (see FIG-9.30).

FIG-9.30

The Start Node

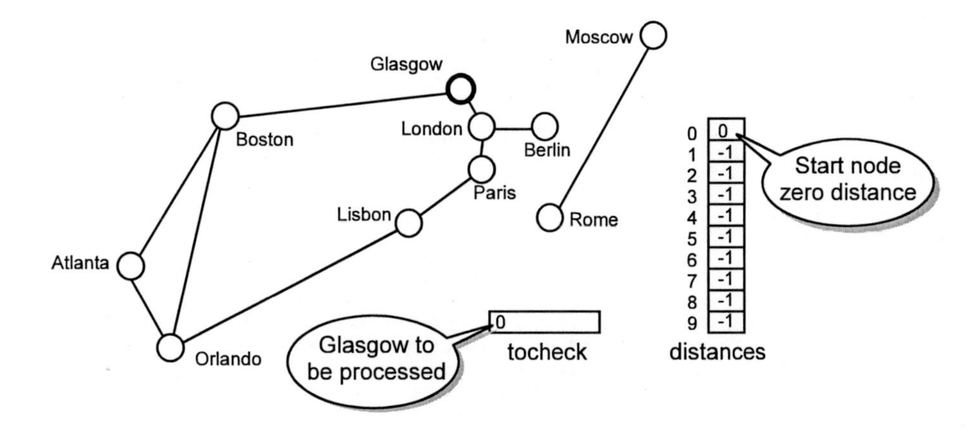

The node at the front of the queue is removed and its adjacent nodes visited. Those visited are added to the queue and their distances set to one (see FIG-9.31).

FIG-9.31

Process Nodes Adjacent to Glasgow

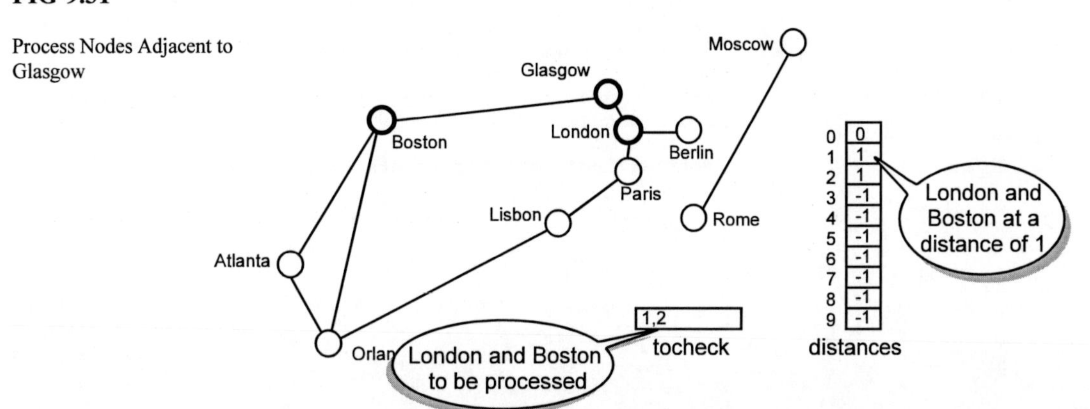

Again we remove the node at the front of the queue, check its distance from the starting node, and visit each of its adjacent nodes. Each node is placed on the queue and its distance from the starting node recorded (see FIG-9.32).

FIG-9.32

Process Nodes Adjacent to London

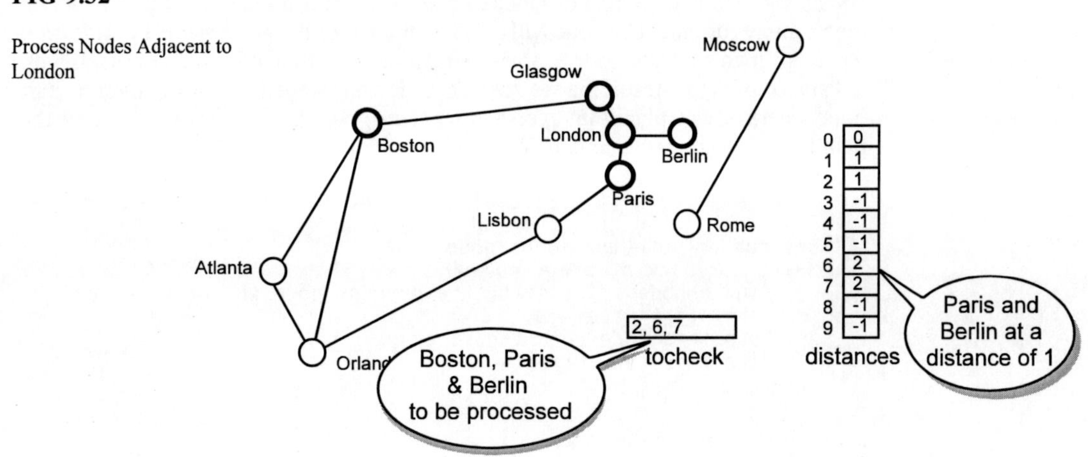

This process continues until the traversal is complete. In the case of the above example, completion of the traversal will result in the distance array containing the values:

0	1	2	3	4	5	6	7	8	9
0	1	1	2	2	3	2	2	-1	-1

The code for this search routine is given below.

```
void WideSearch(int nodeno, const Graph& g, int distance[])
{
    Queue tocheck;

    //*** Set distances to -1 ***
    for(int c=0; c<g.count;c++)
        distance[c]=-1;
    //*** Initialise queue ***
    CreateQueue(tocheck);
    //*** Set distance from start node ***
    int distanceout =-1;
    distance[nodeno]=0;
    //*** Place start node in queue ***
    Data v;
    itoa(nodeno,v.no,10);
    Insert(v,tocheck);
    //*** WHILE queue not empty DO ***
    while (!IsEmpty(tocheck))
    {
        //*** Get front of queue ***
        int currentnode = atoi(Front(tocheck).no);
        Delete(tocheck);
        //*** IF node further than previous, inc. distanceout ***
        if(distance[currentnode]>distanceout)
            distanceout++;
        //*** Set adjacent node distance and place in queue ***
        for(c=0;c<g.count;c++)
            if(g.connections[currentnode][c]!=0&&distance[c]==-1)
            {
                distance[c]=distanceout+1;
                itoa(c,v.no,10);
                Insert(v,tocheck);
            }
    }
}
```

We only require one more step to display the shortest path between two nodes. If we assume we want to travel from *Glasgow* to *Orlando* we can see from the graph that *Orlando* is a distance of two edges from *Glasgow*. But which two edges? To find out we start at *Orlando* and look for an adjacent node which is closer to *Glasgow* (i.e. a node with a distance of one). If there is more than one node which meets this requirement any one will do. Here there is only one - *Boston*. From *Boston* we look for an adjacent node nearer to *Glasgow*. This time it is *Glasgow* itself with a distance of zero. Assuming we have recorded our steps from destination to start node we merely display it in reverse order (*Glasgow, Boston, Orlando*) to give the path from *Glasgow* to *Orlando*. We can describe the logic of this routine as:

```
Determine the distance to all other nodes from the start node
Push the finish node onto an empty stack
Set currentnode to finish node
WHILE not back at start node DO
    Find a node adjacent to the current node which is nearer
     the start node
    Push this node onto the stack
    Make this the currentnode
ENDWHILE
```

From this, we derive the code:

```
//*** Get shortest path between two nodes ***
int ShortestPath(const char* start, const char* end,
    const Graph&   g, Stack& s)
{
    int visited[MAXNODES]={0};

    int startno = NodeAt(start,g);
    int endno = NodeAt(end,g);
    //*** IF nodes invalid OR not connected THEN return 0 ***
    if(startno==-1||endno==-1||!IsConnected(start,end,g))
        return 0;
    //*** Determine distances to all other connected nodes ***
    WideSearch(startno,g,visited);
    //*** Place end node on empty stack ***
    Data v;
    CreateStack(s);
    strcpy(v.no,g.nodenames[endno]);
    Push(v,s);
    int currentposition = endno;
    int currentdistance = visited[endno];
    //*** WHILE not back at start node DO ***
    while (currentposition != startno)
    {
        //*** Find closer adjacent node and place on queue ***
        Queue q;
        AdjacentNodes(g.nodenames[currentposition],g,q);
        if(visited[NodeAt(Front(q).no,g)]<currentdistance)
        {
            strcpy(v.no,Front(q).no);
            Push(v,s);
            currentposition=NodeAt(Front(q).no,g);
            currentdistance–;
        }
        else
            Delete(q);
    }
    return 1;
}
```

FIG-9.33

Shortest Path

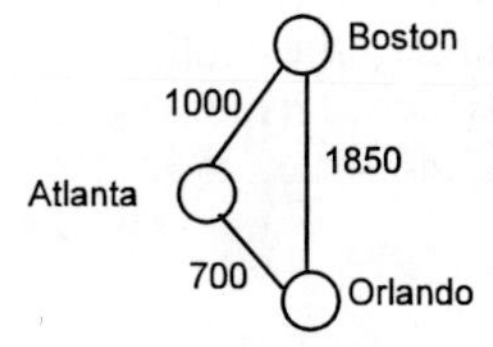

It should be emphasised that the above operation finds the route containing fewest edges between two nodes, not the shortest routine in terms of distance. Hence, for the graph shown in FIG-9.33, the route returned would be *Boston, Orlando* and not *Boston, Atlanta, Orlando* which has the shorter distance.

DisplayGraph

This routine displays the structure of the graph in the form of a matrix. For example, in the graph in FIG-9.33 above, containing only the *Atlanta*, *Boston* and *Orlando* nodes, would produce the output

```
                        GRAPH

               Atlan   Bosto   Orlan
Atlanta            0    1000     700
Boston          1000       0    1850
Orlando          700    1850       0
```

FIG-9.34

A Directed Graph

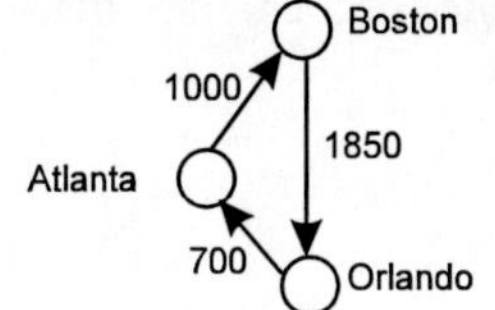

Note that the columns are identified using only the first 5 characters from the node name; this allows identical column widths in the display.

The sample output assumes an undirected graph; for a directed graph such as that in FIG-9.34, the output would be:

```
                    GRAPH

           Atlan  Bosto  Orlan
Atlanta        0   1000      0
Boston         0      0   1850
Orlando      700      0      0
```

The code required for this routine is:

```
//*** Display graph ***
void Display(Graph& g)
{
    char temp[6]="     "; //Contains part of node name

    //*** Display heading ***
    cout<<setw(42)<<"GRAPH\n\n";
    cout<<setw(22)<<' ';
    //*** Use first 5 chars of nodes as column titles ***
    for(int c=0;c<g.count;c++)
        cout<<strncpy(temp,g.nodenames[c],5)<<' ';
    cout<<endl;
    //*** Display full node names and distances in each row ***
    for(c=0;c<g.count;c++)
    {
        cout<<g.nodenames[c]<<setw(22-strlen(g.nodenames[c]))<<' ';
        for(int k=0;k<g.count;k++)
            cout<<setw(5)<<g.connections[c][k]<<' ';
        cout<<endl;
    }
}
```

The Program

At this point we're just about ready to create the complete program. However, to reduce the size of the code, it is worth starting by creating a library file containing **.obj** programs for the *List*, *Stack* and *Queue* data structures. Since we require node names to be held in these structures we'll have to define the *Data* structure as

```
struct Data
{
    char  no[21];
};
```

which will allow us node names of up to 20 characters in length.

PROGRAMMING EXERCISE 9.6

Create the required *structs.lib* file containing the necessary code for the *List, Stack* and *Queue* data structures.

In addition, create the corresponding header files.

The code that follows (see LISTING-9.2) assumes the existence of the library file created in the exercise above.

LISTING-9.2

Implementing a Graph

```
#include<iostream.h>
#include<conio.h>
#include<stdio.h>
#include<string.h>
#include<iomanip.h>
#include<stdlib.h>
#include"queue.h"
#include"stack.h"

//***********************************
//*** Graph Data Type Declarations ***
//***********************************
//*** Data ***
const int MAXNODES = 12;
enum GraphType {directed, undirected};
struct Graph
{
   int count;
   GraphType gtype;
   char nodenames[MAXNODES][21];
   int connections[MAXNODES][MAXNODES];
};

//*** Operations ***
void CreateGraph(const GraphType, Graph&);
int AddNode(const char*, Graph&);
int AddEdge(const char*,const char*,int,Graph&);
int RemoveNode(const char*, Graph&);
int RemoveEdge(const char*,const char*,Graph&);
void Display(const Graph&);
int AdjacentNodes(const char*,const Graph&,Queue&);
int IsConnected(const char*,const char*,const Graph&);
int NodeAt(const char*, const Graph&);
int ShortestPath(const char*,const char*,const Graph&,Stack&);

//*********************************
//*** END Graph Type Declaration ***
//*********************************

//*** Other function Prototypes ***
int GetData(char*, int, char*, char='L');
void ExpandString(char*);
int ReadKey();
int DisplayMenu(char*);
int GetOption(int);
void ExecuteOption(int,Graph&);


void main()
{
   Graph g;
   int opt, noofopts;

   clrscr();
   CreateGraph(undirected,g);
   clrscr();
   do
   {
       clrscr();
       noofopts = DisplayMenu("1 - CreateGraph\n2 - Add Node\n"
                "3 - Add Edge\n4 - Remove Node\n5 - Remove Edge\n"
                "6 - Test for connection\n7 - List Adjacent Nodes"
                "\n8 - Display distance between nodes\n"
                "9 - Display graph\n10- QUIT\n");
       opt = GetOption(noofopts);
       ExecuteOption(opt,g);
   }
   while(opt != noofopts);
   getch();
}
```

Continued on next page

LISTING-9.2
(continued)

Implementing a Graph

```
//*****************************
//*** Graph Type Definitions ***
//*****************************

//*** Create a new graph ***
void CreateGraph(const GraphType gt,Graph& g)
{
   g.count=0;
   g.gtype = gt;
}



//*** Find position of node ***
int NodeAt(const char* name, const Graph& g)
{
   int post = 0;
   while(strcmp(g.nodenames[post],name)&&post<g.count)
        post++;
   if(!strcmp(g.nodenames[post],name))
        return post;
   else
        return -1;
}



//*** Add a new node to graph ***
int AddNode(const char *newname, Graph& g)
{
   //***IF graph full or name exists THEN return 0 ***
   if(g.count==MAXNODES||NodeAt(newname,g)!=-1)
        return 0;
   //*** Copy name to node names list ***
   strcpy(g.nodenames[g.count],newname);
   //*** Clear any connections ***
   for(int c=0;c<g.count;c++)
   {
        g.connections[g.count][c]=0;
        g.connections[c][g.count]=0;
   }
   //*** Increment node count***
   g.count++;
   return 1;
}



//*** Add new edge ***
int AddEdge(const char* start,const char* end,int cost,
                                                   Graph& g)
{
   int pstart, pend;      //*** Position of nodes in matrix

   //*** Determine position of nodes ***
   pstart=NodeAt(start,g);
   pend=NodeAt(end,g);
   //*** IF nodes not found THEN return zero ***
   if(pstart==-1||pend==-1)
        return 0;
   //*** Add edge ***
   g.connections[pstart][pend]=cost;
   //*** IF undirected graph THEN add return connection ***
   if(g.gtype==undirected)
        g.connections[pend][pstart]=cost;
   return 1;
}
```

Continued on next page

LISTING-9.2
(continued)

Implementing a Graph

```
//*** Delete node ***
int RemoveNode(const char* name, Graph& g)
{
   //*** IF invalid node THEN return zero ***
   int nodeno = NodeAt(name,g);
   if(nodeno==-1)
       return 0;
   //*** Remove node name ***
   for (int r= nodeno+1;r<g.count;r++)
       strcpy(g.nodenames[r-1],g.nodenames[r]);
   //*** Remove node's row ***
   for(r=nodeno+1;r<g.count;r++)
       for(int c=0;c<g.count;c++)
           g.connections[r-1][c]=g.connections[r][c];
   //*** Reduce count ***
   g.count—;
   //*** Remove node's column ***
   for(int c = nodeno+1;c<=g.count;c++)
       for(r=0;r<g.count;r++)
           g.connections[r][c-1]=g.connections[r][c];
   return 1;
}


//*** Delete edge ***
int RemoveEdge(const char* start, const char* end, Graph& g)
{
   //*** IF either node name invalid THEN return zero ***
   int startno = NodeAt(start,g);
   int endno = NodeAt(end,g);
   if(startno==-1||endno==-1)
       return 0;
   //*** Set edge cost to zero ***
   g.connections[startno][endno]=0;
   //*** IF an undirected graph THEN set return edge to zero ***
   if(g.gtype==undirected)
       g.connections[endno][startno]=0;
   return 1;
}


//*** Return list of adjacent nodes ***
int AdjacentNodes(const char* name, const Graph& g,
                                             Queue& adjnodes)
{
   int post;
   Data d;

   post=NodeAt(name,g);
   //*** Empty list ***
   CreateQueue(adjnodes);
   //*** IF invalid node THEN return zero ***
   if(post==-1)
       return 0;
   //*** FOR every other node DO ***
   for(int c=0;c<g.count;c++)
       //*** IF there's a connection THEN add to list ***
       if(g.connections[post][c]!=0)
       {
           strcpy(d.no,g.nodenames[c]);
           Insert(d,adjnodes);
       }
   return 1;
}
```

Continued on next page

LISTING-9.2
(continued)

Implementing a Graph

```
//*** Depth-first search of graph ***
void DeepSearch(int nodeno,const Graph& g, int visited[])
{
    visited[nodeno]=1;
    for(int c= 0; c<g.count; c++)
        if(g.connections[nodeno][c]!=0 && !visited[c])
            DeepSearch(c,g,visited);
};


//*** Determine if two nodes are connected ***
int IsConnected(const char* start, const char* end,
                                        const Graph& g)
{
    int visited[MAXNODES]={0};

    int startno = NodeAt(start,g);
    int endno = NodeAt(end,g);
    //*** IF either node name invalid THEN return zero ***
    if(startno==-1||endno==-1)
        return 0;
    //*** Mark all adjacent nodes ***
    DeepSearch(startno,g,visited);
    //*** IF end node marked THEN return 1 ELSE return zero ***
    if(visited[endno]==1)
        return 1;
    else
        return 0;
}


//*** Width-first Search of Graph ***
void WideSearch(int nodeno, const Graph& g, int distance[])
{
    Queue tocheck;

    //*** Set distances to -1 ***
    for(int c=0; c<g.count;c++)
        distance[c]=-1;
    //*** Initialise queue and distance out from start node***
    CreateQueue(tocheck);
    int distanceout =-1;
    //*** Distance to start node is zero ***
    distance[nodeno]=0;
    //*** Place start node on queue ***
    Data v;
    itoa(nodeno,v.no,10);
    Insert(v,tocheck);
    //*** WHILE queue not empty DO ***
    while (!IsEmpty(tocheck))
    {
        //*** Get first node in queue ***
        int currentnode = atoi(Front(tocheck).no);
        Delete(tocheck);
        //*** IF this node is further out THEN incr distanceout ***
        if(distance[currentnode]>distanceout)
            distanceout++;
        //*** Add unvisited adjacent nodes to the queue ***
        //***  and record its distance out              ***
        for(c=0;c<g.count;c++)
            if(g.connections[currentnode][c]!=0&&distance[c]==-1)
            {
                distance[c]=distanceout+1;
                itoa(c,v.no,10);
                Insert(v,tocheck);
            }
    }
}
```

Continued on next page

LISTING-9.2
(continued)

Implementing a Graph

```
//*** Determine least-node path from start to end node ***
int ShortestPath(const char* start, const char* end, const
Graph& g, Stack& s)
{
    int visited[MAXNODES]={0};

    int startno = NodeAt(start,g);
    int endno = NodeAt(end,g);
    //*** IF either node invalid OR not connected THEN return 0 ***
    if(startno==-1||endno==-1||!IsConnected(start,end,g))
        return 0;
    //*** Search graph for path between nodes ***
    WideSearch(startno,g,visited);
    //*** Push the end node name onto a stack ***
    Data v;
    CreateStack(s);
    strcpy(v.no,g.nodenames[endno]);
    Push(v,s);
    //*** Set current node to the end node ***
    int currentposition = endno;
    int currentdistance = visited[endno];
    //*** WHILE not at the start node DO ***
    while (currentposition != startno)
    {
        //*** Find all nodes adjacent to the current node ***
        Queue q;
        AdjacentNodes(g.nodenames[currentposition],g,q);
        //*** IF any are closer to the start node THEN ***
        if(visited[NodeAt(Front(q).no,g)]<currentdistance)
        {
            strcpy(v.no,Front(q).no);
            //*** Push it onto the stack ***
            Push(v,s);
            //*** Make it the current node ***
            currentposition=NodeAt(Front(q).no,g);
            currentdistance—;
        }
        else
            Delete(q);
    }
    return 1;
}


//*** Display graph ***
void Display(Graph& g)
{
    char temp[6]="     ";

    //*** Display heading ***
    cout<<setw(42)<<"GRAPH\n\n";
    cout<<setw(22)<<' ';
    //*** Use first 5 chars of nodes as column titles ***
    for(int c=0;c<g.count;c++)
        cout<<strncpy(temp,g.nodenames[c],5)<<' ';
    cout<<endl;
    //*** Display full node names and distances in each row ***
    for(c=0;c<g.count;c++)
    {
        cout<<g.nodenames[c]<<setw(22-strlen(g.nodenames[c]))<<' ';
        for(int k=0;k<g.count;k++)
            cout<<setw(5)<<g.connections[c][k]<<' ';
        cout<<endl;
    }
}

//******************************
//*** END Graph Definitions ***
//******************************
```

Continued on next page

LISTING-9.2
(continued)

Implementing a Graph

```
//*** Other function Definitions ***
//*** Get data ***
int GetData(char *allowed, int max, char *result, char justify)
{
  const int ENTER=13;
  const int CURSORUP=-72;
  const int CURSORRIGHT=-77;
  const int CURSORDOWN=-80;
  const int CURSORLEFT=-75;
  const int BACKSPACE=8;

  char ch;                    //char from keyboard
  int count=0;                //chars entered
  char expandedset[256];      //allowed chars

  //*** Expanded allowed char set ***
  strcpy(expandedset,allowed);
  ExpandString(expandedset);
  //***Start with empty result***
  strcpy(result,"");
  int first=1;
  //*** Read a character ***
  ch=ReadKey();
  //*** WHILE terminating key not pressed DO ***
  while(ch!=ENTER&&ch!=CURSORLEFT&&ch!=CURSORRIGHT&&
                                  ch!=CURSORUP&&ch!=CURSORDOWN)
  {
      //*** IF allowed char & result not full THEN ***
      if(strchr(expandedset,ch)&&count<max)
      {
          //*** IF its the first character entered THEN ***
          if(first)
          {
              //*** Clear input area ***
              cout<<setw(max)<<' ';
              gotoxy(wherex()-max,wherey());
              first=0;
          }
          //*** Display char and add to result ***
          cout<<ch;
          count++;
          result[count-1]=ch;
          result[count]=0;
      }
      //*** ELSE IF delete & result not empty THEN ***
      else if(ch==BACKSPACE&&count>0)
      {
          //*** Remove last char ***
          cout<<"\b \b";
          count—;
          result[count]=0;
      }
      //*** Read another character ***
      ch=ReadKey();
  }
  //*** IF the field is to be right-justified THEN ***
  if(justify=='R'&&strlen(result)>0)
  {
      //*** Rewrite data right-justified ***
      gotoxy(wherex()-strlen(result),wherey());
      cout<<setw(max)<<' ';
      gotoxy(wherex()-max,wherey());
      cout<<setw(max)<<result;
  }
  cout<<endl;
  switch(ch)
  {
      case ENTER:
          return 0;
```

Continued on next page

LISTING-9.2
(continued)

Implementing a Graph

```
        case CURSORUP:
            return 1;
        case CURSORRIGHT:
            return 2;
        case CURSORDOWN:
            return 3;
        case CURSORLEFT:
            return 4;
    }
}



//*** Read single key press ***
int ReadKey()
{
    int ch;
    ch=getch();
    if(ch==0)
        ch=-getch();
    return ch;
}



//*** Expand string ***
void ExpandString(char *s)
{
    char temp[256]=""; //Empty temp storage

    //*** Copy the first character across ***
    temp[0]=s[0];
    //*** For all but the last 2 chars DO ***
    for(int c=1,p=1;c<=int(strlen(s))-3;c++)
    {
        //*** IF two dots THEN ***
        if(s[c]=='.'&&s[c+1]=='.')
        {
            //*** Insert range of chars implied ***
            for(char ch=s[c-1]+1;ch<=s[c+2];ch++)
                temp[p++]=ch;
            //*** Move past this part of the text ***
            c+=2;
        }
        else
            //*** Else copy char ***
            temp[p++]=s[c];
    }
    //*** Copy any remaining characters ***
    for(int k=c;k<=int(strlen(s))-1;k++,c++)
        temp[p++]=s[c];
    //*** Insert final NULL character ***
    temp[p]='\0';
    strcpy(s,temp);
}



//*** Display menu ***
int DisplayMenu(char * m)
{
    cout<<m;
    int count=0;
    for(int c=0;c<=strlen(m);c++)
        if(m[c]=='\n')
            count++;
    return count;
}
```

Continued on next page

LISTING-9.2
(continued)

Implementing a Graph

```
int GetOption(int max)
{
   char opstr[3];
   cout<<"Enter option : ";
   gets(opstr);
   int op=atoi(opstr);
   while(op<1||op>max)
   {
       cout<<"\a?:";
       gets(opstr);
       op=atoi(opstr);
   }
   return op;
}

void ExecuteOption(int opt, Graph& g)
{
   char name[21];
   char start[21],end[21];
   Queue adjnodes;
   switch(opt)
   {
       case 1:  //Create graph
            CreateGraph(undirected,g);
            break;
       case 2:  //Add Node
            cout<<"Enter node name : ";
            gets(name);
            AddNode(name,g);
            break;
       case 3:  //Add edge
            cout<<"Enter start node : ";
            gets(start);
            cout<<"Enter end node : ";
            gets(end);
            cout<<"Enter cost of edge : ";
            int cost;
            cin>>cost;
            AddEdge(start,end,cost,g);
            break;
       case 4 : //Remove node
            cout<<"Enter node to be removed : ";
            gets(name);
            RemoveNode(name,g);
            break;
       case 5:  //Remove edge
            cout<<"Enter start node : ";
            gets(start);
            cout<<"Enter end node : ";
            gets(end);
            RemoveEdge(start,end,g);
            break;
       case 6:  //Check for connection
            cout<<"Enter first node : ";
            gets(start);
            cout<<"Enter second node : ";
            gets(end);
            if(IsConnected(start,end,g))
                 cout<<"Connected\n";
            else
                 cout<<"Not connected\n";
            getch();
            break;
       case 7:  //List adjacent nodes
            cout<<"Enter node : ";
            gets(name);
            AdjacentNodes(name,g,adjnodes);
            Display(adjnodes);
            getch();
            break;
```

Continued on next page

LISTING-9.2
(continued)

Implementing a Graph

```
        case 8:
            cout<<"Enter start node : ";
            gets(start);
            cout<<"Enter finish node : ";
            gets(end);
            Stack s;
            if(ShortestPath(start,end,g,s))
                Display(s);
            else
                cout<<"Invalid nodes or not connected\n";
            getch();
            break;
        case 9:
            Display(g);
            getch();
            break;
        case 10:
            cout<<"PROGRAM TERMINATED\n";
            break;
    }
}
```

Summary

- **A graph is** constructed from nodes and edges.
- **In an undirected graph**, an edge operates in both directions.
- **In a directed graph**, an edge operates in a single direction.
- A path is the list of nodes which are passed through when travelling from one node to another.
- A connected graph is one in which a path exists between any node and every other node.

Solutions

TASK 9.1

```
int Length(List seq)
{
    if (IsEmpty(seq))
        return 0;
    else
        return 1+ Length(Tail(seq));
}
```

PROGRAMMING EXERCISE 9.1

```
#include <iostream.h>
#include<conio.h>

long Fib(int n);

void main()
{
    clrscr();
    cout<<"Which term is required? ";
    int term;
    cin>>term;
    cout<<"Term "<<term
        <<" of the Fibonacci series is "
        <<Fib(term)<<endl;
    getch();
}

long Fib(int n)
{
    if(n<=2)
        return 1;
    else
        return Fib(n-2)+Fib(n-1);
}
```

TASK 9.2

This routine adds the parameter c to the end of the List *s*.

TASK 9.3

1. Root = 67

2.

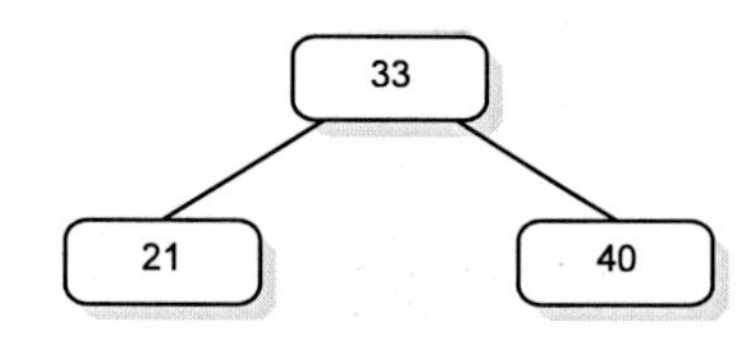

3.

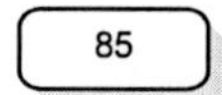

4. 40

TASK 9.4

1.

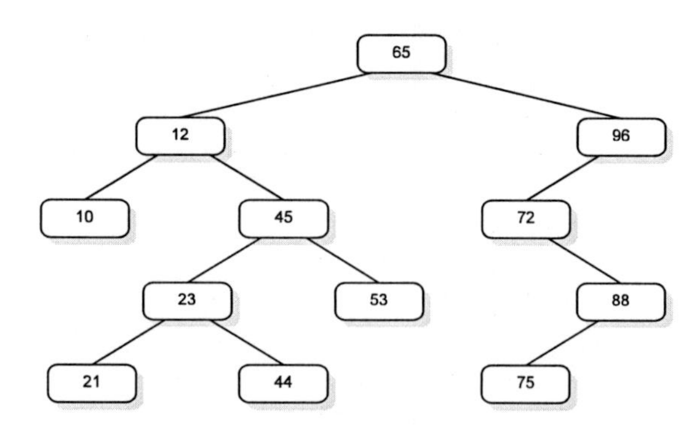

2. 4

TASK 9.5

a) *t* is unchanged

b) Attempting to find the root of an empty tree will not satisfy the pre-condition of the Root operation and hence the result is undefined (i.e. this is an illegal operation).

PROGRAMMING EXERCISE 9.2

1.

The program requires the following changes:

Additional #includes :

```
#include<ctype.h>
#include<iomanip.h>
```

Additional function prototypes:

```
void GetData(char*,int,char*);
void ExpandString(char*);
voidGetStudentDetails(StudentDetails&);
void DisplayStudentDetails(const
StudentDetails&);
```

Additional function definitions :

```
void ExpandString(char *s)
{
    char temp[256]=""; //Empty temp storage

    //*** Copy the first character across ***
    temp[0]=s[0];
    //*** For all but the last 2 chars DO ***
    for(int c=1,p=1;c<=int(strlen(s))-3;c++)
    {
        //** If two dots **
        if(s[c]=='.'&&s[c+1]=='.')
        {
            //* Insert range of chars implied *
            for(char ch=s[c-1]+1;ch<=s[c+2];ch++)
                temp[p++]=ch;
            //* Move past this part of the text *
            c+=2;
        }
        else
            //** Else copy char ***
            temp[p++]=s[c];
    }
    //*** Copy any remaining characters ***
    for(int k=c;k<=int(strlen(s))-1;k++,c++)
```

```
        temp[p++]=s[c];
    //*** Insert final NULL character ***
    temp[p]='\0';
    strcpy(s,temp);
}

void GetData(char *allowed, int max, char
*result)
{
    const int ENTER=13;
    const int BACKSPACE=8;

    char ch;                    //char from keyboard
    int count=0;                //chars entered
    char expandedset[256];      //allowed chars

    //*** Expanded allowed char set ***
    strcpy(expandedset,allowed);
    ExpandString(expandedset);
    //***Start with empty result***
    strcpy(result,"");
    //*** Read a character ***
    ch=getch();
    //*** WHILE return key not pressed ***
    while(ch!=ENTER)
    {
        //*** If allowed char & result not full ***
        if(strchr(expandedset,ch)&&count<max)
        {
            //** Display char and add to result **
            cout<<ch;
            count++;
            result[count-1]=ch;
            result[count]=0;
        }
        //*** ELSE if delete & result not empty ***
        else if(ch==BACKSPACE&&count>0)
        {
            //** Remove last char **
            cout<<"\b \b";
            count--;
            result[count]=0;
        }
        //*** Read another character ***
        ch=getch();
    }
    cout<<endl;
}


//*** Read Student  details ***
void GetStudentDetails(StudentDetails& st)
{
    char temp[30];  //Temp storage for data entered

    //*** Get idcode ***
    //** Read up to 5 digits **
    cout<<"Enter id code : ";
    GetData("0..9 ",5,temp);
    //** Convert to numeric distance **
    st.idcode=atoi(temp);
    //*** Get name ***
    cout<<"Enter name : ";
    GetData("A..Za..z . -'",29,st.name);
    //*** Get sex ***
    cout<<"Enter sex : ";
    GetData("FMfm",1,temp);
    st.sex = toupper(temp[0]);
    //*** Get six scores ***
    for(int c=0;c<6;c++)
    {
        cout<<"Enter score "<<(c+1)<<" : ";
        GetData("0..9",3,temp);
        st.score[c]=atoi(temp);
        while(st.score[c]>100)
        {
            cout<<"\a?:";
            GetData("0..9",3,temp);
            st.score[c]=atoi(temp);
        }
    }
}

//*** Display student details ***
void DisplayStudentDetails(const StudentDetails&
st)
{
    cout<<setw(6)<<st.idcode<<"  "
        <<st.name<<setw(20-strlen(st.name))<<' '
        <<setw(3)<<st.sex<<"    ";
    for(int d=0;d<6;d++)
        cout<<setw(4)<<st.score[d];
}
```

Changes to existing routines:

To *Display()*:

```
//*** Display contents of tree ***
void Display(const BSTree& t)
{
    //*** IF tree is empty THEN ***
    if(IsEmpty(t))
        //*** Exit routine ***
        return;
    //*** Display the left subtree ***
    Display(t->left);
    //*** Display the root ***
    DisplayStudentDetails(t->value);
    cout<<endl;
    //*** Displaay the right subtree ***
    Display(t->right);
}
```

To `ExecuteOption()` case 4 :

```
        case 4 :
            if(IsEmpty(t))
                cout<<"Tree empty\n";
            else
            {
                DisplayStudentDetails(Root(t));
                cout<<endl;
            }
            getch();
            break;
```

2.

```
//*** Add new node to tree ***
int Add(const Item nv, BSTree& t)
{
    Node *currentptr; //Address of current node
    Node *parentptr;  //Address of parent

    //*** Set current node to root ***
    currentptr = t;
    //*** Root has no parent ***
    parentptr = NULL;
    //*** WHILE not at bottom of tree DO ***
    while(currentptr != NULL)
    {
        //*** Save old current as new parent ***
        parentptr = currentptr;
        //*** IF new idcode < current idcode THEN
        //      go to left subtree ***
        if(nv.idcode<currentptr->value.idcode)
            currentptr = currentptr->left;
        //*** ELSE IF new idcode > current idcode
        //          THEN go to right subtree***
        else if(nv.idcode>currentptr->value.idcode)
            currentptr = currentptr->right;
        //*** ELSE no change ***
        else
            return 0;
    }
    //*** Create node ***
    Node *temp;
    temp= new Node;
    temp->left=NULL;
    temp->right=NULL;
    temp->value=nv;
    //*** Link new node to parent ***
    //*** IF tree empty THEN add node as root ***
    if(parentptr==NULL)
        t=temp;
    //*** ELSE add to left or right of parent ***
    else if(nv.idcode<parentptr->value.idcode)
        parentptr->left=temp;
    else
        parentptr->right=temp;
    return 1;
}
```

TASK 9.6

62

PROGRAMMING EXERCISE 9.3

The call to *DisplayMenu()* must be modified to add the new option to the displayed choices.

Also, an additional **case** option in *ExecuteOption()*. The code for this new option is:

```
case 5:
    Node *par, *ch;
    cout<<"Enter required key : ";
    cin>>key;
    if(FindParCh(key,t,par,ch))
        cout<<"Found\n";
    else
        cout<<"Not found\n";
    switch(NodeType(ch))
    {
        case -1:
            cout<<"Invalid node\n";
            break;
        case 0:
            cout<<"No children\n";
            break;
        case 1:
            cout<<"1 Child\n";
            break;
        case 2:
            cout<<"2 Children\n";
            break;
    }
    getch();
    break;
```

PROGRAMMING EXERCISE 9.4

No solution required.

PROGRAMMING EXERCISE 9.5

No solution required.

TASK 9.7

Nodes:
- Glasgow
- Boston
- Atlanta
- Orlando
- Lisbon
- Paris
- London
- Berlin
- Rome
- Moscow

Edges:
- (Glasgow,Boston)
- (Glasgow,London)
- (Boston,Atlanta)
- (Boston,Orlando)
- (Atlanta,Orlando)
- (Orlando,Lisbon)
- (Lisbon,Paris)
- (Paris,London)
- (London,Berlin)
- (Rome,Moscow)

TASK 9.8

The edges matrix would contain the value 1000 in the cells
(3,2) and (2,3).

CHAPTER 10

Borland Graphics

This chapter covers the following topics:

- Basic Animation
- Creating a Viewport
- Creating New Text Effects
- Filled Shape Functions
- Graphic Constants
- Line and Outline Functions
- Loading the Graphics Driver
- Pixel Functions
- Screen Coordinates
- Setting the Drawing Styles
- Text Handling Functions
- Video Display Modes

GRAPHICS OVERVIEW

The Hardware

Display Modes

Your PC compatible computer has two basic display modes: text and graphics. Normally, when operating in DOS, the computer operates in text mode. This allows only the extended set of ASCII characters to be displayed, and although these can be in various colours (if available), no true graphics, such as diagonal lines and circles, can be produced in this mode. To display pictures or drawings, the machine must be placed in graphics mode and this involves loading the appropriate software. This software is known as a **graphics driver** and is responsible for ensuring that any graphic output commands contained in your program, result in the equivalent display on your monitor.

This is not the end of the story, since most machines are capable of operating in several different graphics modes. Hence, the first requirement of any program using graphics, is to define which particular graphics mode is required. The machine will then load the appropriate graphics driver.

When working in graphics mode, the screen is organised into a grid of small rectangular cells known as **pixels** (from the term **picture elements**). The number of individual pixels which make up a single row is known as the **resolution** along the x-axis, and the pixels in a column defines the y-axis resolution. Together these define the resolution of any given graphics mode.

Early IBM compatible machines were limited to a single graphics standard called CGA (Colour Graphics Adapter). This standard allowed three graphic display modes: 350 columns by 200 rows with four colours; 350 by 200 in two colours and 350 by 400 in two colours. These resolutions are very limited and do not allow very detailed displays. CGA was soon superseded by EGA (Enhanced Graphics Adapter) which allowed improved resolutions: 320 x 200, 640 x 200 and 640 x 350 all of which can display 16 colours as well as 640 x 350 in two colours. EGA was also backward compatible with CGA resolutions. The next standard was VGA (Video Graphics Array) which , as well as allowing all previous resolutions, added several new ones: 640 x 480 in two colours, 640 x 480 in 16 colours and 350 x 200 in 256 colours. These standards are summarised in TABLE-10.1.

TABLE 10.1

Graphics Display Modes

Graphics Standard	Resolution	Colours
CGA	320 x 200	4
	320 x 200	2
	640 x 200	2
EGA	320 x 200	16
	640 x 200	16
	640 x 350	2
VGA	640 x 350	16
	640 x 480	2
	640 x 480	16
	320 x 200	256

Borland's C++ supplies drivers for each of the display standards (CGA, EGA and VGA) and for many of the resolutions available in each standard (see Table-10.2 later in this section).

There are now even higher resolutions offering up to 1280 x 1024 in 16.7 million colours. Unfortunately, Borland do not offer graphics drivers for these resolutions.

Video Adapters

All screen displays are created by a video adapter which is part of the hardware of your machine. When your program executes an instruction to display some text or graphics object on the screen the resulting output is achieved in two stages. First a representation of the item to be displayed is constructed in a special area of the main memory known as the video RAM. The information in the video RAM is then examined and converted to a video signal which is sent to the monitor and hence a visual image is created.

The amount of video RAM required to create a full screen graphics image depends on the resolution and number of colours being used. For example, when a two colour mode is being used (usually the colours black and white), then only one bit of memory is required for each pixel on the screen. A white pixel is represented by setting the bit to 1 while a black pixel is stored as zero. This means that if we are working in a 320 x 200, 2 colour mode, the total amount of video RAM required is (320 x 200) bits or (320 x 200)/8 bytes; that is, 8,000 bytes. FIG-10.1 shows the concept behind the conversion from video RAM to screen display.

FIG-10.1

Video RAM is Used to Create a Display

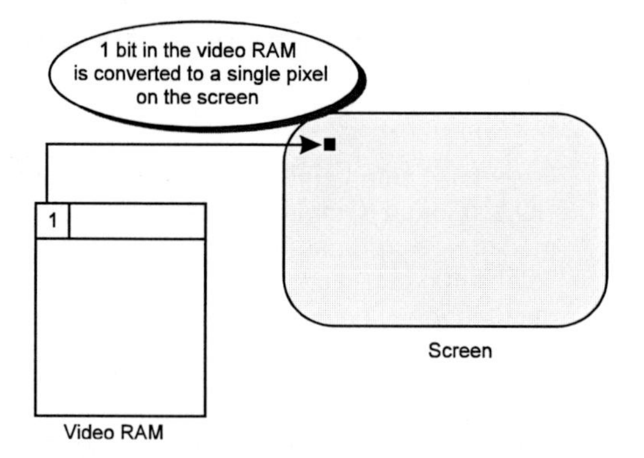

Where a resolution allowing more colours is used, then more bits are required to represent each pixel. So, for example, in a 16 colour mode 4 bits are required per pixel and a resolution of 640 x 480 requires (640 x 480)/2 bytes (153,600 bytes).

> **TASK 10.1**
>
> Using a resolution of 1280 x 1024 in 16.7 million colours how many bytes are required to:
>
> 1. Represent a single pixel?
> 2. Represent the whole screen?

The Colour Palette

All colours visible to the human eye can be represented by a combination of the primary colours: red, green and blue. Hence when the video adapter requires some non-primary colour, such as yellow, to be displayed it simply sends the appropriate signal specifying the required intensity of the red, green and blue components of that colour. This signal, known as an RGB signal, is then used by the monitor to control the output of the red, green and blue "guns" within the cathode ray tube of the display to create the desired colour.

Since we are dealing with a digital device (the computer) the strength of each colour in the RGB signal is initially represented as a binary value. In VGA display modes each colour component is represented by a single byte in which the most-significant two bits are always zero. This allows values between 0 and 63 (0000 0000 to 0011 1111) to be held for each colour. So if we want to display a yellow pixel, which is derived from full red plus full green, the complete RGB signal would be as shown in FIG-10.2.

FIG-10.2

RGB Signal Value for Yellow

RED	GREEN	BLUE
1 1 1 1 1 1 1 1	1 1 1 1 1 1 1 1	0 0 0 0 0 0 0 0

However, the above explanation seems to be at odds with the previous description of how a pixel is represented in video RAM: RAM uses at most 4 bits to represent a single pixel, while the RGB signal requires 24 bits (18 if we ignore the leading zeros in each byte). This apparent contradiction is solved using a look-up table which contains in one column the value of a colour as represented in video RAM and in the other column the corresponding RGB value required to display that colour. This table is known as the **colour palette**. Its basic format is shown in TABLE-10.2.

TABLE-10.2

The Colour Palette

Pixel Code	RGB Signal
0000	RGB value 1
0001	RGB value 2
0010	RGB value 3
0011	RGB value 4
.	.
.	.
.	.
1111	RGB value 16

With this information, we have a more accurate picture of how the data in the video RAM and a colour palette table are used to generate the correct RGB signal (see FIG-10.3).

FIG-10.3

Palette Hardware

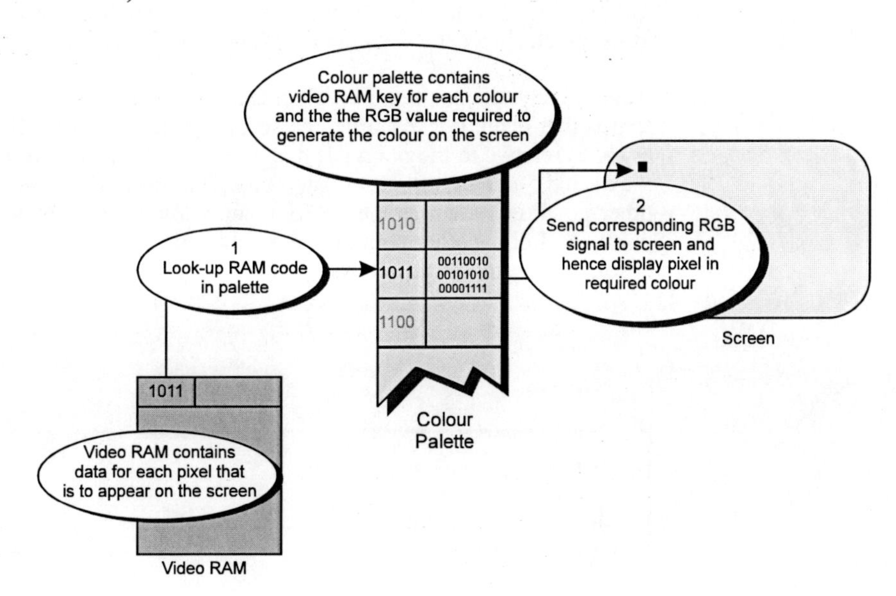

Screen Coordinates

It is possible to access and change the colour of any pixel by specifying its position on the screen. A pixel's position is defined in terms of the number of columns along and the number of rows down from the top left of the screen. In FIG-10.4 below, the pixel P1 is identified as (4,8); that is, P1 is in column 4, row 8.

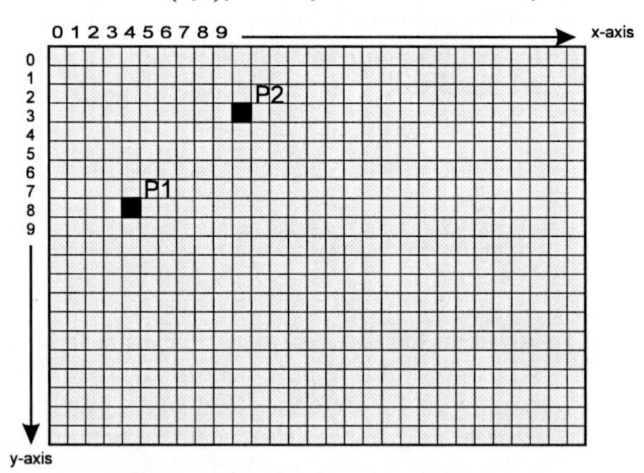

FIG-10.4

Screen Coordinates

There are two points to note:

- When giving the position of a pixel, the column position is specified before the row.
- The rows and columns start from zero, not one, so the top left pixel is identified as (0,0).

It is more usual to express a point's position, not in terms of rows and columns, but rather its position along the x-axis and y-axis. Hence we talk of the point P1 being 4 points along the x-axis and 8 points along the y-axis.

TASK 10.2
Identify the position of P2 in FIG-10.4.

The position of the pixel measured in this way is known as the **absolute coordinates** of the pixel. Hence the absolute coordinates of P1 are (4,8).

Alternatively, the position of a pixel can be specified relative to its position from some other pixel. For example, the second point P2 in FIG-10.5 can be specified as (6,-5) relative to the point P1; that is, P2 is 6 points to the right of P1 along the x-axis and 5 points further up the y-axis. The position of a pixel, relative to some other pixel, is known as the **relative coordinates**. The relative coordinates of a point, P1, from another point, P2, are obtained by calculating the difference of the absolute coordinates as follows:

$$x_{relative} = x_{P2} - x_{P1}$$

$$y_{relative} = y_{P2} - y_{P1}$$

TASK 10.3
Calculate the coordinates of P1 relative to P2.

Programming in Graphics Mode

When writing a graphics program the general strategy employed is:

```
Define the adapter standard to be used (CGA, EGA or VGA)
Define the resolution required
Attempt to load driver appropriate to your display and set video
adapter to graphics mode
IF this is not successful THEN
    terminate the program with error message
ENDIF
Produce the required graphics output
Change back to text mode
```

LISTING-10.1 below shows how this is achieved using Borland's C++.

LISTING-10.1

Using Graphics Mode

```
#include <iostream.h>
#include <conio.h>
#include <process.h>
#include <graphics.h>

void   main()
{
       int g_driver, g_mode, g_error;

       // *** Define adapter and resolution required
       g_driver = VGA;
       g_mode = VGAHI;

       // *** Load appropriate driver and switch to graphics mode
       initgraph(&g_driver,&g_mode,"D:\\BC\\BGI");

       // *** If there's problems loading the driver
       //            report this and halt
       g_error = graphresult();
       if (g_error < 0)
       {
           cout<<"Error in initialising graphics: "
               <<grapherrormsg(g_error);
           exit(1);
        }

       // *** Draw two lines
       line(0,0,639,479);
       line(639,0,0,479);

       // *** Read a key and return to text mode
       getch();
       closegraph();
}
```

An Explanation of the Code

`#include <graphics.h>` The prototypes of all the graphic routines and constants are defined in this header file. Without this, error messages would result from calls to routines such as `initgraph()`, `line()` and `closegraph()`.

`g_driver = VGA;` Specifies the graphics driver to be loaded. VGA is a constant defined within **graphics.h**

`g_mode = VGAHI;` Some graphics drivers allow several graphic sub-modes (e.g. VGA can be 640x200, 640x350 or 640x480). This specifies which mode is to be used.

VGAHI is a constant defined in **graphics.h** and sets the machine into 640 x 480 mode with 16 colours.

```
initgraph(&g_driver,&g_mode,"D:\\BC\\BGI");
```

The function `initgraph()` loads the graphics driver specified in *g_driver* and sets the system into the mode given by *g_mode*. Graphics drivers are stored on your disk with an extension of **.BGI**. The third parameter specifies the path to be used when searching for the **.BGI** file. Where the string is empty, the current directory is searched.

Note that all three parameters must be given as addresses.

```
g_error = graphresult();
```

`graphresult()` returns the error code generated by the most recently executed graphics function. In this case, that is `initgraph()` (see previous line). If `initgraph()` has been successful a value of zero will have been returned.
On the other hand, if the graphics driver was not found, then a negative value will be returned (-3 for a missing driver).
See the definition of `graphresult()` later in this chapter for other error code values.

```
if (g_error < 0)
{
    cout<<"Error in initialising graphics: "<<grapherrormsg(g_error);
    exit(1);
}
```

If an error is detected, this code prints the error message for that error code and exit the program. `grapherrormsg()` returns the text error message associated with the error code in *g_error*.

`line(0,0,639,479);` Draws a line from the screen coordinates (0,0) to (639,479). That is, from the top left of the screen to the bottom right.

`line(639,0,0,479);` Draws a line from the top right corner (639,0) to the bottom left corner (0,479).

`closegraph( )` Returns to text mode. The text screen is cleared and the cursor is placed at the top left corner of the screen.

PROGRAMMING EXERCISE 10.1

Type in and run the above program. You will have to change the path information in the `initgraph()` statement to satisfy your own system. You may also have to change the values for *g_driver* and *g_mode* if you do not have a VGA display.

The Current Position

When operating in graphics mode, the system maintains a **graphics cursor**. This is similar in function to the flashing cursor which appears when in text mode. However, the graphics cursor remains invisible at all times and is referred to in the Borland C++ manuals as the **current position** (or **CP**).

When graphics mode is first entered, CP is set to (0,0). Certain drawing commands assume that drawing is to begin at the position CP. These commands may affect the value of CP while other graphic commands do not reference CP. In the LISTING-10.2 below, there are examples of both types of commands.

LISTING-10.2

Using the Current Position

```
#include <iostream.h>
#include <graphics.h>
#include <conio.h>
#include <process.h>

void main( )
{
       int g_driver,g_mode,g_error;

       // *** Detect the best graphics mode available
       g_driver = DETECT;
       initgraph(&g_driver,&g_mode,"c:\\borlandc\\bgi");
       // *** If there's problems loading the driver
       //             report this and halt
       g_error = graphresult();
       if (g_error < 0)
       {
            cout<<"Error in initialising graphics:"
                 <<grapherrormsg(g_error);
            exit(1);
       }

       // *** Use yellow when drawing
       setcolor(YELLOW);

       // *** Draw lines on screen
       linerel(100,200);          // linerel uses CP ...
       getch();
       linerel(300,100);
       getch();
       line(0,0,200,200);         // ...line does not
       getch();
       linerel(50,-100);

       // *** wait for a key press to continue
       getch();

       // *** Restore text mode
       closegraph();
}
```

An Explanation of the Code

`setcolor(YELLOW)` Changes the current drawing colour to yellow. All subsequent graphics output will be in this colour unless another `setcolor()` command is executed. If no `setcolor()` instruction is given then the default colour, white, will be used. The colours available are determined by the graphics mode in use and the palette settings. These options will be discussed in detail later.

`linerel(100,200)`	Draws a line, starting at CP. The end of the line is 100 pixels to the right in the *x* direction and 200 pixels down in the *y* direction from the starting point. CP is changed to this new position (100,200).
`linerel(300,100)`	Draws a line from CP (i.e. from the end of the previous line) 300 to the right and 100 down. CP changes to this position where the new line terminates (400,300).
`line(0,0,200,200)`	Draws a line from the origin to (200,200). The value of CP has no effect on where this line is drawn. CP is not affected by the `line()` command.
`linerel(50,-100)`	Since CP is not effected by the previous `line()` command, this new line starts from the end of line 2 and ends 50 pixels to the left and 100 pixel up. CP is now set at (350,200).

TASK 10.4

What are the coordinates of the Current Position(CP) after line 7 of the following code has been executed? Assume CP begins at position (0,0).

```
linerel(50,300);
getch();
linerel(100,60);
getch();
line(0,0,200,200);
getch();
linerel(50,-100);
```

PROGRAMMING EXERCISE 10.2

Enter and run the above program.

If you are using monochrome output remove the `setcolor()` command from your program.

Summary

- **The computer display** can be used in either **text** or **graphics mode**.
- **Graphics mode** supports three main standards: **CGA**, **EGA** and **VGA.**
- Each standard has several **resolutions**.
- **Resolution** is measured by the number of pixels in both the horizontal and vertical directions as well as the number of simultaneous colours.
- A **pixel** is a single addressable point on the screen.
- Screen displays are created using a **video adapter**.
- **Colours are constructed** from varying strengths of the monitor's red, green and blue guns.

- **Absolute and relative coordinates** can be used when specifying screen positions.

- **graphics.h** must be included when using graphics routines.

- **initgraph()** is used to load the required graphics driver and change to graphics mode.

- **closegraph()** returns the screen to text mode.

BORLAND C++ GRAPHICS ROUTINES

This section lists most of the graphics routines and graphic constants available in Borland C++. They are introduced in the order you are most likely to require them.

Graphic Constants

Instead of having to remember the predominantly numeric arguments required by many graphic routines, Borland has thoughtfully defined many constants within **graphics.h** which allow meaningful names to be used in place of these integer values.

Graphic Adapter and Resolution Constants

When defining values for the graphics adapter (*g_driver* in the previous programs) and graphics mode (*g_mode*), the following constants (see TABLE-10.3) may be used.

TABLE-10.3

Drivers and Resolution

Driver	Mode Name	Resolution	Max. Colours
CGA	CGAC0	320 x 200	4
	CGAC1	320 x 200	4
	CGAC2	320 x 200	4
	CGAC3	320 x 200	4
	CGAHI	640 x 200	2
EGA	EGALO	640 x 200	16
	EGAHI	640 x 350	16
VGA	VGALO	640 x 200	16
	VGAMED	640 x 350	16
	VGAHI	640 x 480	16

The first four CGA modes offer different colour combinations

Since C++ is case-sensitive, mode names must be specifies in upper case

If we want to start up in EGA mode with a resolution of 640x350 in 16 colours, the driver and mode variables would be assigned using

```
g_driver    = EGA;
g_mode      = EGAHI;
```

There is one additional constant, **DETECT**, which is used when the highest graphics mode available on the machine is to be used. Using this option allows your program to interrogate the graphics card to determine the highest resolution available. This is achieved by the assignment:

```
g_driver = DETECT;
```

When this option is used there is no need to assign a value to the mode variable, hence the full code for entering graphics mode is simply:

```
g_driver = DETECT;
initgraph(&g_mode,&g_driver,"C:\\BORLANDC\\BGI");
```

Colour Constants

When creating graphics, the colour required may be specified using symbolic names (see TABLE-10.4).

TABLE-10.4

Symbolic Colour Names

Numeric Value	Symbolic Name
0	BLACK
1	BLUE
2	GREEN
3	CYAN
4	RED
5	MAGENTA
6	BROWN
7	LIGHTGRAY
8	DARKGRAY
9	LIGHTBLUE
10	LIGHTGREEN
11	LIGHTCYAN
12	LIGHTRED
13	LIGHTMAGENTA
14	YELLOW
15	WHITE

So, for example, we may use the command

```
setcolor(RED)
```

or the more cryptic

```
setcolor(4)
```

to force all subsequent graphics output to be in red.

Line Constants

Line Width

The thickness of a line can also be defined although we are limited to only two options: one pixel wide and three pixels wide. The default setting is one pixel width. Changes to the line width are reflected in any subsequent graphics output; previous output is unaffected. The settings and symbolic names are defined in TABLE-10.5. These settings are made using the `setlinestyle()` routine.

TABLE-10.5

Line Thickness

The lines shown here assume solid lines are being displayed, but both thicknesses are available with other line styles.

Numeric Value	Symbolic Name	Description
1	NORM_WIDTH	Line 1 pixel thick ———
2	THICK_WIDTH	Line 3 pixels thick ━━━

Line Style

The line style can also be specified allowing not only solid lines but dashed, dotted and other variations. The options are summarised in TABLE-10.6. These settings are are made using the `setlinestyle()` routine.

TABLE-10.6

Line Styles

Numeric Value	Symbolic Name	Description
0	SOLID_LINE	Solid line
1	DOTTED_LINE	Dotted line
2	CENTER_LINE	Dot-dash line
3	DASHED_LINE	Dashed line
4	USERBIT_LINE	User-defined (see below)

The USERBIT_LINE option allows the pattern to be defined by the binary pattern of a 16 bit word. A one in the word corresponds to a black area of the line. The line as a whole is constructed by repeating the pattern throughout its length. An example is given in FIG-10.5. See definition of `setlinestyle()` for examples.

FIG-10.5

User-Defined Line Style

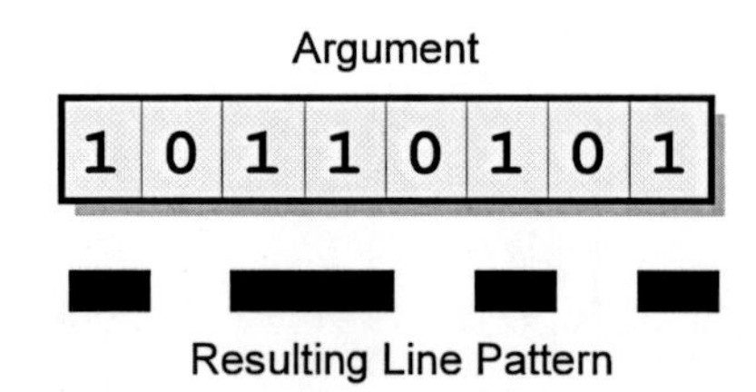

Fill Constants

Many graphic commands allow enclosed shapes, such as circles and polygons, to be filled in a specified colour. So, for example, we might fill the area enclosed within a circle in red. In addition, we may also specify the style of fill required since this need not be a solid block of colour. This is achieved by calling the routine `setfillstyle()` before calling the appropriate fill command. TABLE-10.7 lists the symbolic names available when setting the fill style:

TABLE-10.7

Fill Constants

Numeric Value	Symbolic Name	Description
0	EMPTY_FILL	Fills using background colour
1	SOLID_FILL	Solid fill in current fill colour
2	LINE_FILL	Horizontal lines
3	LTSLASH_FILL	SW-NE light lines
4	SLASH_FILL	SW-NE heavy lines
5	BKSLASH_FILL	NW-SE heavy lines
6	LTBKSLASH_FILL	NW-SE light lines
7	HATCH_FILL	Straight cross hatch
8	XHATCH_FILL	Diagonal cross hatch
9	INTERLEAVE_FILL	Interleave
10	WIDE_DOT_FILL	Wide spaced dots
11	CLOSE_DOT_FILL	Close spaced dots
12	USER_FILL	User-defined

Font Constants

There are several fonts available when displaying text in graphics mode. The font required for subsequent output is set using `settextstyle()`. There are two types of fonts: bit-mapped fonts which are held in bit-map image form and stroked fonts which are held as a set of instruction detailing how to create each letter. Bit-mapped fonts require less processing to be displayed but are rather blocky when increased in size; stroked fonts display a smother result. The font constants are given in TABLE-10.8.

TABLE-10.8

Graphic Fonts

Numeric Value	Symbolic Name	Classification
0	DEFAULT_FONT	bit-mapped
1	TRIPLEX_FONT	stroked
2	SMALL_FONT	stroked
3	SANS_SERIF_FONT	stroked
4	GOTHIC_FONT	stroked
5	SCRIPT_FONT	stroked
6	SIMPLEX_FONT	stroked
7	TRIPLEX_FONT	stroked
8	COMPLEX_FONT	stroked
9	EUROPEAN_FONT	stroked
10	BOLD_FONT	stroked

As well as choosing the font to be used, we can also specify text justification relative to the current position. Justification can be set separately for horizontal and vertical text output. This is done using `settextjustify()`. TABLE-10.9 lists the named constants available for use in this function.

TABLE-10.9

Text Justification

Numeric Value	Symbolic Name	Action
Horizontal text		
0	LEFT_TEXT	Left-justify text
1	CENTER_TEXT	Centre text
2	RIGHT_TEXT	Right-justify text
Vertical text		
0	BOTTOM_TEXT	Justify from bottom
1	CENTER_TEXT	Centre text
2	TOP_TEXT	Justify from top

Pre-defined Data Types

When creating your own graphics routines, good design normally dictates that the system should be left in the state it is found. So, for example, if a routine draws a circle with an interleaved red fill and a thick-lined perimeter, then the routine should also return the line thickness, colour and fill style to their original settings before it terminates.

To help facilitate this requirement, Borland have included several structured types which can be used when declaring variables to hold the graphics settings.

```
struct arccoordstype
{
    int x,y;
    int xstart, ystart, xend, yend;
}
```

A pointer to a variable of this type is returned by `getarccoords()` which gives the coordinates of the last call to `arc()`.

```
struct fillsettingstype
{
    int pattern;
    int color;
}
```

A pointer to a variable of this type is returned by `getfillstyle()`, which supplies details of the current colour and fill style.
pattern is set in accordance with the fill constants already specified.
color is set in accordance with the colour constants.

```
struct linesettingstype
{
    int linestyle;
    unsigned upattern;
    int thickness;
}
```

A pointer to a variable of this type is returned by `getlinestyle()` which supplies details of the current line style and thickness.
upattern and *thickness* are set in accordance with the line constants already specified.

```
structpalettetype
{
    unsigned char size;
    signed char colors[16];
}
```

A pointer to a variable of this type is returned by `getpalette()` which supplies details of the number of colours available in the current mode and the binary value of each colour available. The function `getdefaultpalette()` also returns a pointer to a variable of this type.

Details of text settings are returned by the function `gettextsettings()` which requires a pointer to a structure defined as

```
struct textsettingstype
{
    int font;
    int direction;
    int charsize;
    int horiz;
    int vert;
}
```

Although the whole screen is changed to graphics mode when `initgraph()` is called, graphical output can be restricted to one area of the screen using `setviewport()`. The settings used in the last to this function can be retrieved using `getviewsettings()` which requires a pointer to a variable of `struct viewporttype`. This is defined as

```
struct viewporttype
{
    int left,top,right,bottom;
    int clip;
}
```

Systems Control Functions

Initialising the Graphics Mode

With the driver and mode defined, we next need to call `initgraph()`, which attempts to load the appropriate driver from disk (this is a **.bgi** file) and, if successful, the screen is toggled into graphics mode.

The format of this function is:

```
initgraph(&g_driver, &g_mode,"path to required bgi file");
```

Note that it is the address of the driver and mode variables which are specified. The string argument gives details of where to find the **.bgi** files. If you have loaded Borland C++ using the default installation options, then this string will be C:\\BORLANDC\\BGI. If you've used some other directory, then you have to modify the contents of the string accordingly.

Detecting Problems in Loading the Graphics Driver

Unfortunately, your attempt at loading the **.bgi** file may not be successful: the file may be missing, or the path specified may be an invalid one. This can be checked by a call to `graphresult()` which returns an integer value indicating the nature of any problem. This integer can then be used to access a corresponding error message using `grapherrormsg()`.

Creating a Viewport

The area of the screen in which graphics output is to appear is known as the viewport. This rectangular viewport can be specified using `setviewport()`. The top left corner of the viewport is designated as position (0,0) and also subsequent output uses this point as the origin . Where the object being output falls partially or wholly outside the viewport, that portion of the output will be displayed if clipping is set to OFF, otherwise it remains hidden (see FIG-10.6).

FIG-10.6

Viewport Clipping

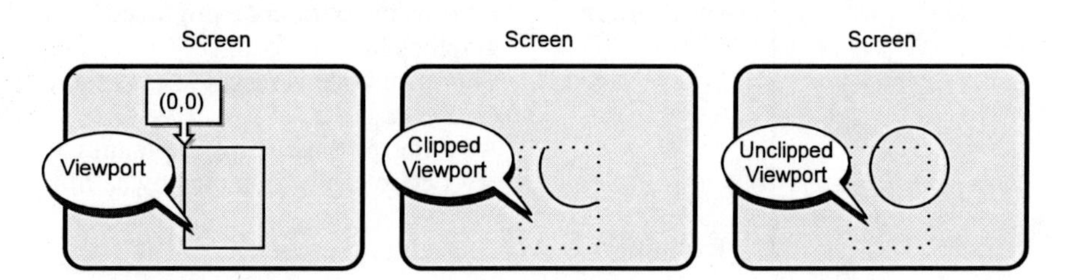

The current viewport settings can be determined using a call to `getviewsettings()`.

Restoring Text Mode

When your program is complete, or if you simply want to return to text mode, a call must be made to `closegraph()`.

It is important that this routine is called by your program, otherwise the user will be left in graphics mode when the program terminates and may have to resort to resetting the machine in order to return to text mode.

Prototype :
```
void  initgraph(int *graphdriver,
                int *graphmode, char *path);
```

Precondition : All parameters should be valid for hardware setup and directory used.

Description : Initialises the graphics system. The graphics driver is loaded and the default settings for global graphics variables are set. The screen is cleared using colour 0 and the current position (CP) is set to (0,0) at the top left of the screen.
graphdiver must contain an integer value representing the graphics driver to be used. This must be set before calling `initgraph()`. Using DETECT to set *graphdriver* assigns it the value representing the highest mode available on the hardware.
graphmode contains an integer value representing the mode to be used. If DETECT was used to set *graphdriver*, the value of this variable is set by `initgraph()`, otherwise the programmer must set it before calling `initgraph()`.
path is a string giving the directory path in which `initgraph()` searches for the required **.bgi** driver file.
If an error occurs, this can be detected using `graphresult()`.

Example :
```
int gdriver, gnode;
gdriver = DETECT;
initgraph(&gdriver,&gmode,"C:\\BORLANDC\\BGI");
```

Prototype :
```
int graphresult();
```

Precondition : Should be used immediately after a call to some other graphics function call.

Description : Returns the error code produced by the last unsuccessful graphics function call.
This error code is reset to zero as a result of a call to `graphresult()`.
An error message string explaining the meaning of the error code can be obtained by calling `grapherrormsg()`.

Example :
```
int gdriver, gmode;
int result;

gdriver = DETECT;
initgraph(&gdriver, &gmode, "Invalid path");
result=graphresult();
if (result)
    cout<<"Error load driver "<<result<<'\n';
```

Prototype : `char *grapherrormsg(int error);`

Precondition : *error* should be a value returned by a call to `graphresult()`.

Description : Returns a pointer to the text error message associated with *error*.

Example :

```
int gdriver,gmode;
int result;
gdriver = DETECT;
initgraph(&gdriver, &gmode,"Invalid path");
result=graphresult();
if (result)
    cout<<"Error load driver "
        <<grapherrormsg (result)<<'\n';
```

Prototype : `void setviewport(int x1, int y1, int x2, int y2, int clippingon);`

Precondition : (*x1,y1*) and (*x2,y2*) must be valid screen coordinates.

Description : The coordinates (*x1,y1*), (*x2,y2*) represent the top left and bottom right rectangular area of the screen in which graphical output will be produced. The top left of this area is then treated as the point (0,0) for all subsequent output.
If *clippingon* is a non-zero value, any parts of a graphics object which falls outside the viewport, will not be drawn. If *clippingon* is zero, graphical output will be displayed even when it is outside the viewport (see FIG-10.6).
The viewport area is cleared and the Current Position (CP) is moved to the top left corner (0,0).

Example : `setviewport(100,100,200,250,1);`

Prototype : `void getviewsettings(viewporttype *viewport);`

Precondition : None

Description : Returns the current viewport settings

Example :

```
viewporttype current;
getviewsettings (current);
```

Prototype : `void closegraph();`

Precondition : None

Description : Returns the screen to text mode. All memory space allocated for the graphics driver, fonts, etc., is deallocated.

Example : `closegraph();`

Positioning Functions

In graphics mode, the Current Position (CP) determines the starting point of certain draw functions. CP is set to (0,0) after a call to `initgraph()` or `setviewport()`. Its value is changed by some of the drawing functions, but it may also be altered or interrogated separately using the functions listed below. Since each graphics mode has different resolutions, it is sometimes difficult to predict, at the time of writing your code, if a coordinate is within the screen area. To determine the resolution of the screen in the x-axis use `getmaxx()` and for the y-axis use `getmaxy()`.

Moving the Current Position (CP)

Prototype : `void moveto(int x, int y);`

Precondition : (*x*,*y*) is a valid viewport coordinate.

Description : Moves the Current Position (CP) to the specified coordinate (*x*,*y*).

Example :

```
moveto(0,0);      // Move to top left of screen
moveto(newx, newy);      // Move to(newx,newy)
```

Prototype : `void moverel(int offsetx, int offsety);`

Precondition : Resulting coordinate must be a valid viewport position.

Description : Moves CP *offsetx* pixels in the x direction (positive values move CP to the right; negative values to the left), and *offsety* pixels in the y direction (positive values move down; negative values up).

Example :

```
moverel(20,-5);     // moves CP 20 pixels to the
                    // right, 5 up
```

Prototype : `int getmaxx();`

Precondition : None

Description : Returns maximum screen x-ordinate possible in the current resolution.
For example, if a 640 x 480 mode is being used, *getmaxx()* would return 639 (i.e. x-ordinate is 0 to 639).

Example : `lastx = getmaxx();`

Prototype : `int getmaxy();`

Precondition : None

Description : Returns the maximum screen y-ordinate.

Example : `lasty=getmaxy();`

Prototype	:	`int getx();`
Precondition	:	None
Description	:	Returns CP's current x-ordinate.
Example	:	`placex = getx();`

Prototype	:	`int gety();`
Precondition	:	None
Description	:	Returns CP's current y-ordinate.
Example	:	`placey=gety();`

Colour Settings Functions

Graphics output is analogous to drawing with a pen on a piece of paper. The drawing colour (pen) and background colour (paper) may be set using function calls. The drawing colour affects subsequent output but leaves existing output unchanged. However, changes to the background colour alters any previous output created in the background colour. It is also possible to interrogate the system to discover the current drawing and background colour settings.

Prototype	:	`void setcolor(int colour);`
Precondition	:	0<= *colour* <= maximum value for mode.
Description	:	Sets the drawing colour to *colour*. The colour constants defined in TABLE-10.4 or the equivalent numeric value may be used as arguments.

Example	:	`setcolor(4);`
		
		`setcolor(RED);`

Prototype	:	`void setbkcolor(int colour);`
Precondition	:	0<=*colour*<= maximum value for mode.
Description	:	Sets the background colour. This command is somewhat confusing in use since it has the effect of changing the setting for colour zero in the palette. The background colour is used when clearing the screen or if the fillstyle is set to zero. *colour* can be specified as a value (0 to 15) or by a symbolic name.
Example	:	`setbkcolor(12);`

Prototype	:	`int getcolor();`
Precondition	:	None
Description	:	Returns the current drawing colour.
Example	:	`if(getcolor()!=GREEN)` `    setcolor (GREEN)`

Prototype	:	`int getbkcolor();`
Precondition	:	None
Description	:	Returns the current background colour.
Example	:	`currentback =getbkcolor();`

Pixel Functions

The most basic drawing operation available allows a single pixel on the screen to be set to a specified colour (`putpixel()`). It is also possible to interrogate the colour of any point on the screen (`getpixel()`).

Prototype	:	`void putpixel(int x, int y  int colour);`
Precondition	:	(*x*,*y*) must be a valid viewport coordinate.
Description	:	The pixel at position (*x*,*y*) displayed in the colour specified by *colour*.
Example	:	`putpixel(200,100,YELLOW);`

Prototype	:	`int getpixel(int x, int y);`
Precondition	:	(*x*,*y*) must be a valid screen coordinate.
Description	:	Returns the colour of the pixel at viewport position (*x*,*y*).
Example	:	`colour = getpixel(200,50);`

Line and Outline Functions

Setting Line Style

The function `setlinestyle()` allow us to set the style and width of a line.

These settings affect any straight lines subsequently output. Lines may be output separately using a call to `line()` and similar functions or as part of an outline shape (e.g. as produced in a call to `rectangle()`).

Curved lines, such as those produced by `arc()` and `circle()`, although affected by the line thickness, ignore the line style, always producing solid lines.

Prototype :

```
void setlinestyle(int linestyle,
        unsigned  upattern, int  thickness);
```

Precondition : 0<=*linestyle*<=4 AND *thickness* 1 or 3.

Description : Sets the thickness and style of any subsequent lines drawn. *linestyle* may be set to one of the following values (either the integer or symbolic name may be used):

VALUE	SYMBOLIC NAME	RESULT
0	SOLID_LINE	Solid line
1	DOTTED_LINE	Dotted line□
2	CENTER_LINE	Dot-dash line
3	DASHED_LINE	Dashed line
4	USERBIT_LINE	User-defined

upattern is only significant if the linestyle is USERBIT_LINE. In this case, each bit of *upattern* which is set to 1 corresponds to a single pixel drawn in the current drawing colour. (see FIG-10.7).
If *linestyle* is set to any other value, *upattern* must still be supplied but is ignored by the routine.

thickness can be:

VALUE	SYMBOLIC NAME	RESULT
1	NORM_WIDTH	1 pixel wide
3	THICK_WIDTH	3 pixels wide.

Example :

```
//   3 pixel thick solid line
setlinestyle(SOLID_LINE,0,THICK_WIDTH);

//*** User-defined line
setlinestyle(4,0XB9,1);
```

Line Drawing Routines

Prototype :

```
void arc(int x, int y,  int sangle,
            int fangle, int rad)
```

Precondition : None

Description : Draws an arc of a circle. The arc is part of a circle centred at (*x,y*) with radius, *rad*). The arc extends from *sangle* to *fangle*. The angles are given in degrees from the horizontal in an anti-clockwise direction.
The line style is always solid; uses the current setting for line thickness.

Example :

```
arc(100,100,45,135,50);
```

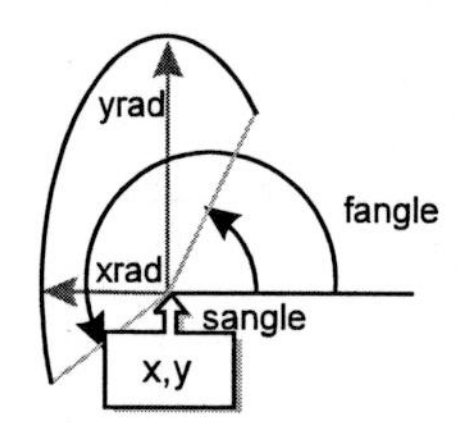

Prototype : `void ellipse(int x, int y, int sangle, int fangle, int xrad, int yrad);`

Precondition : None

Description : Draws an elliptical arc. Centred on *(x,y)* with horizontal and vertical axes *xrad* and *yrad*. The arc travels from *sangle* to *fangle*. The angles are given in degrees from horizontal in an anti-clockwise direction.
Uses the current drawing colour and line thickness.
The line style is not used: the outline is always solid.

Example :

```
ellipse(200,200,90,270,200,400);
```

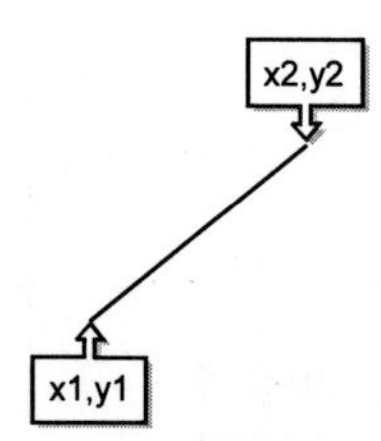

Prototype : `void line(int x1, int y1, int x2, int y2);`

Precondition : None

Description : Draws a line from *(x1,y1)* to *(x2,y2)*.
Uses the current drawing colour and line settings.
This function does not change the value of CP.

Example :

```
setcolor(RED);
setlinestyle(1,0,3);
//*** red solid line, 3 pixels wide ***
line(100,20,100,180);
```

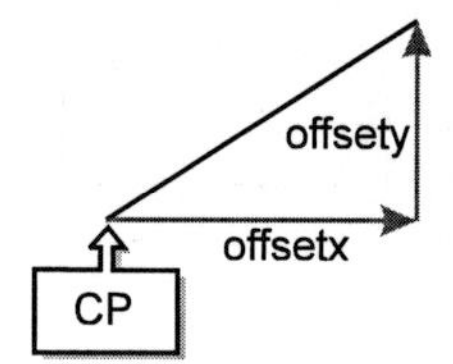

Prototype : `void linerel(int offsetx, int offsety);`

Precondition : None

Description : Draws a line from *(CP.x,CP.y)* to *(CP.x+offsetx, CP.y+offsety)*.
CP is then updated to the end of the drawn line.

Example :

```
moveto(200,50);
//***line from(200,50)to (250,40)
linerel(50,-10);
```

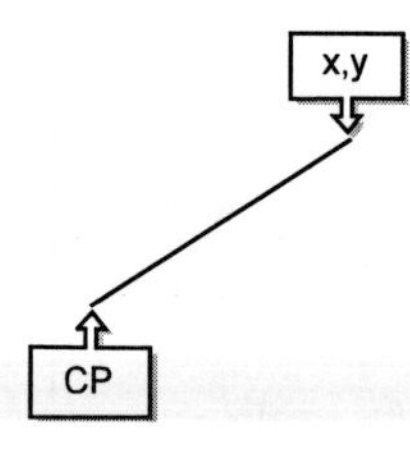

Prototype : `void lineto(int x, int y);`

Precondition : *(x,y)* must be a valid viewport coordinate.

Description : Draws a line from CP to *(x,y)*. Current Position is updated to *(x,y)*.

Example :

```
moveto(200,50);
//*** line from (200,50)  to (250,40)
lineto(250,40) ;
```

Prototype	:	`void getarccoord (arccoordstype *arccoords);`
Precondition	:	The function `arc()` should have been called previously.
Description	:	Returns details of the last call to `arc()`.

Example	:	`arccoordstype details;`
		 .
		 `arc(100,100,0,180,50);`
		 .
		 `getarccoord(details);`

Outline Drawing Routines

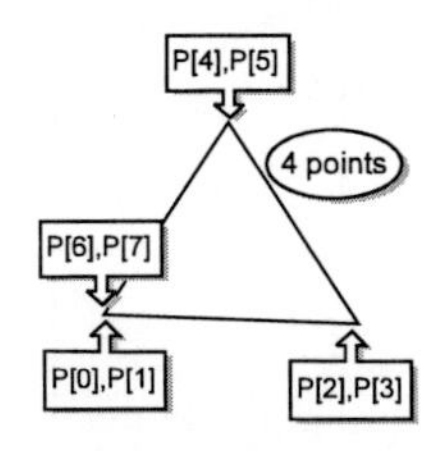

Prototype	:	`void drawpoly(int numpoints, int *polypoints);`
Precondition	:	The polypoints must reference numpoints x 2 values.
Description	:	Draws a polygon using the values referenced by *polypoints* as the coordinates of the shape's apexes. The values referenced by *polypoints* are interpreted as coordinate pairs. To create an enclosed shape, the first and last pair of values must be identical. Uses the current drawing colour and line styles.

Example	:	`// ***points for a triangle ***`
		 `int triangle[]={80,120,130,120,180,190,80,120};`
		 `drawpoly(4,triangle);`

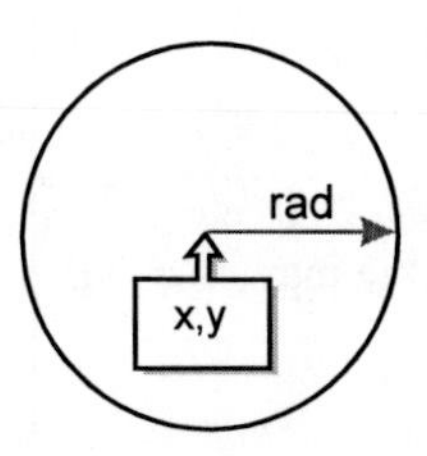

Prototype	:	`void circle(int x, int y, int rad);`
Precondition	:	*rad* must be positive.
Description	:	Draws a circle centred on (*x,y*) with radius *rad*. Uses the current drawing colour and line thickness settings. The current line style is not used, instead the line is always solid.
Example	:	`circle(200,200,50);`

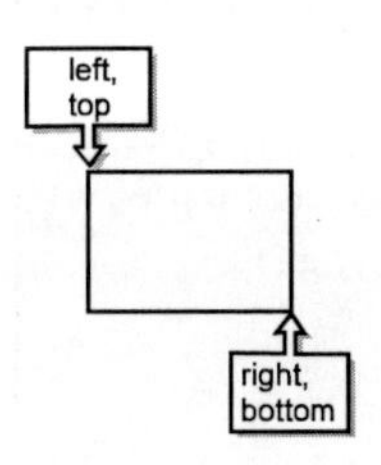

Prototype	:	`void rectangle(int left, int top, int right,int bottom);`
Precondition	:	None
Description	:	Draws a rectangle with a top left corner at (*left, top*) and bottom right corner at (*bottom, right*). Uses the current line and drawing colour settings.
Example	:	`rectangle(50,50,300,100);`

Filled Shape Functions

These routines create shapes in which the enclosed area is filled using the current fill style settings. With the exception of `bar()`, all of these functions draw a perimeter using the current drawing colour and line thickness; `bar()` has no outline. The functions which have straight line perimeters, such as `bar3d()`, use all the current line settings (colour, line style and line thickness) when drawing the outline of the shape; those with curved perimeters ignore the line style setting and always use a solid line.

Prototype : `void setfillstyle(int pattern, int colour);`

Precondition : 0 <= *pattern* <= 12 AND 0 <= *colour* <= maximum for mode.

Description : Sets the pattern and colour to be used in subsequent fill operations.
Possible values for *pattern* are :

Numeric Value	Symbolic Name	Description
0	EMPTY_FILL	Fills using background colour
1	SOLID_FILL	Solid fill in current colour
2	LINE_FILL	Horizontal lines
3	LTSLASH_FILL	SW-NE light lines
4	SLASH_FILL	SW-NE heavy lines
5	BKSLASH_FILL	NW-SE heavy lines
6	LTBKSLASH_FILL	NW-SE light lines
7	HATCH_FILL	Light cross hatch
8	XHATCH_FILL	Heavy cross hatch
9	INTERLEAVE_FILL	Interleave
10	WIDE_DOT_FILL	Wide spaced dots
11	CLOSE_DOT_FILL	Close spaced dots
12	USER_FILL	User-defined

Either the numeric value or symbolic name may be used.

colour constants are given in TABLE 10.4

Example : `setfillstyle(1,RED);`

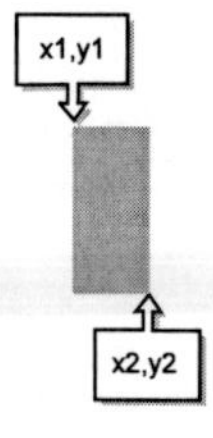

Prototype : `void bar(int x1, int y1, int x2, int y2);`

Precondition : None

Description : Draws a rectangular bar (as used in a bar graph).
Unlike `rectangle()`, this results in a filled rectangle.
The fill style is determined by `setfillstyle()`.
There is no outline.

Example : `bar(100,400,150,200);`

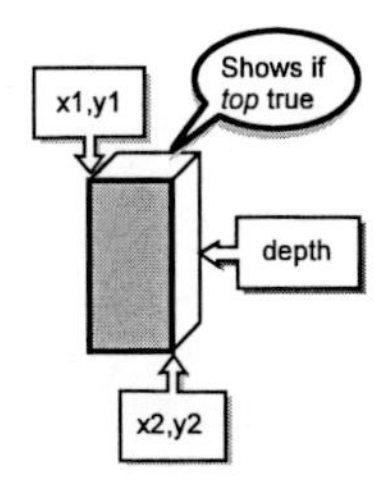

Prototype :

```
void bar3d(int x1, int y1, int x2, int y2,
                              int depth, int top);
```

Precondition : None

Description : Draws a three-dimensional bar. The coordinates *(x1,y1)* and *(x2,y2)* define the top left and bottom right corners of the basic rectangular shape.
depth specifies the depth in pixels of the third dimension of the bar.
top is used as a Boolcan to specify if the 3D effect is to be shown on the top of the bar. This may not be required if another bar is to be placed on top of it.

Example :

```
bar3d(100,400,150,200,5,1);
```

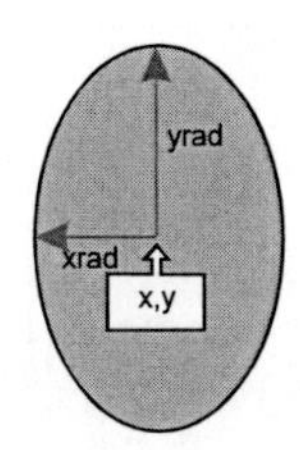

Prototype :

```
void fillellipse(int x, int y, int xrad,
                                 int yrad);
```

Precondition : None

Description : Draws a filled ellipse with centre *(x,y)* and with *xrad* and *yrad* giving the horizontal and vertical axes.
Uses the current fillstyle.
The outline is drawn using the drawing colour and line thickness.
The outline is always solid.

Example :

```
fillellipse(300,300,100,30);
```

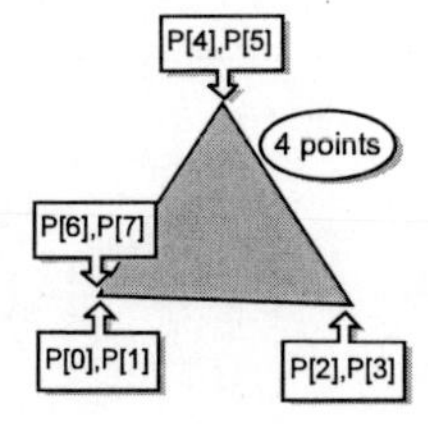

Prototype :

```
void fillpoly(int noofpoints, int *polypoints);
```

Precondition : *polypoints* must reference *noofpoints* x 2 values. The first and last pair of values referenced by polypoints must be identical to create an enclosed shape.

Description : Draws a filled polygon using the coordinates references by *polypoints*.
Uses the current fill style.
The outline is drawn using the drawing colour and line thickness.
The outline is always solid.

Example :

```
// ***points for a triangle ***
int triangle[]=(80,120,130,120,150,190,80,120);

setlinestyle(1,0,1);
setcolor (YELLOW);
setfillstyle(9,GREEN);
// *** Green interleaved triangle ***
// *** with yellow border         ***
fillpoly(4,triangle);
```

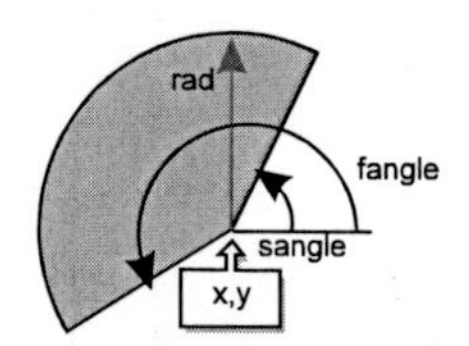

Prototype :
```
void pieslice(int x, int y, int sangle,
                             int fangle, int rad);
```

Precondition : (*x,y*) is a valid viewport coordinate.

Description : Draws a filled pie slice as used in pie charts.
The pie slice is centred on (*x,y*). The slice extends from *sangle* to *fangle* with sides of length *rad*.
Uses the current fill style.
The outline is drawn using the drawing colour and line thickness.
The outline is always solid.

Example :
```
pieslice(200,200,45,135,100);
```

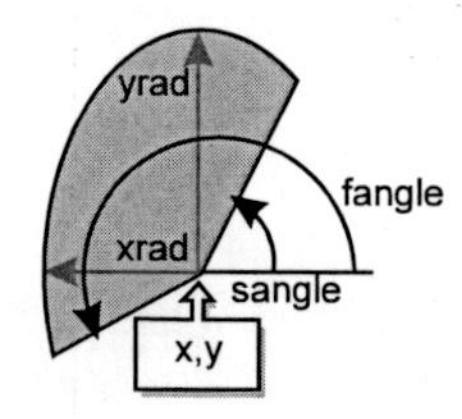

Prototype :
```
void sector(int x, int y, int sangle,
                    int fangle, int xrad, int yrad);
```

Precondition : (*x,y*) is a valid viewport coordinate.

Description : Draws a filled elliptical pie slice. The sector is centred at (*x,y*), with *xrad* and *yrad* determining the horizontal and vertical axes respectively.
The sector extends from *sangle* to *fangle*.
Uses the current fill style.
The outline is drawn using the drawing colour and line thickness.
The outline is always solid.

Example :
```
sector(300,200,300,30,50,300);
```

Text Handling Functions

The normal output routines such as `cout` and `puts` do not operate in graphics mode. String values may be output to the graphics screen using `outtext()` or `outtextxy()`. Numeric and character values cannot be output directly but must first be converted to strings.

Whereas text mode is limited to the default character style, when working in graphics mode several different text styles, sizes and widths are available. In addition, text may be displayed along either horizontal or vertical axes. These options are set using `settextstyle()`.

There are two basic classifications of fonts. **Bit-mapped** fonts contain an image of each character. When these images are enlarged, the individual pixels which make up the image also grow larger making the resulting screen output rough and unpleasing to the eye. **Stroked-fonts**, on the other hand, are defined mathematically and their general appearance is unaffected by the size being used.

The number of fonts available has increased to 10 in Version 3.1 of Borland C++.

Prototype : `void settextstyle(int font, int direction, int size);`

Precondition : None

Description : Sets the font, direction and size of any subsequent text produced using `outtext()` and `outtextxy()`.

font:

Numeric Value	Symbolic Name	Classification
0	DEFAULT_FONT	bit-mapped
1	TRIPLEX_FONT	Stroked
2	SMALL_FONT	Stroked
3	SANS_SERIF_FONT	Stroked
4	GOTHIC_FONT	Stroked
5	SCRIPT_FONT	Stroked
6	SIMPLEX_FONT	Stroked
7	TRIPLEX_SCR_FONT	Stroked
8	COMPLEX_FONT	Stroked
9	EUROPEAN_FONT	Stroked
10	BOLD_FONT	Stroked

direction:

0 - left to right horizontal.

1 - top to bottom vertical.

size:

The value given here affects the size of text shown but is not an absolute value. Hence, size 4 for font 2 is much smaller than size 4 for font 10.

Example : `settextstyle(10,0,4);`

Prototype : `void settextjustify(int horz, int vert);`

Precondition : Both parameters valued between 0 and 2.

Description : Sets the justification used on subsequent textual output. Text is justified about CP.
horz specifies the justification used on horizontal text;
vert, specifies the justification on vertical text.
See TABLE 10.9 for symbolic constants.

Example : `settextjustify(0,0);`

Prototype : `void outtext(char *string);`

Precondition : None

Description : Displays the text referenced by *string* at a position based on CP. The display will be affected by the chosen font, direction, size and justification.
If the text is horizontal and left-justified, CP is updated to the right of the last character, else CP remains unchanged.

Example : `outtext("Hello world\n");`

Prototype	:	`void outtextxy(int x, int y, char *string);`
Precondition	:	(*x,y*) should be a valid screen coordinate.
Description	:	Displays the text referenced by *string*, based on the position (x,y)
Example	:	`outtextxy(200,100,"Moved");`

Prototype	:	`void gettextsettings(textsettingstype *txtinfo);`
Precondition	:	None
Description	:	Returns information about the current text font, direction, size and justification.

Example	:	`textsettingtype data;`
		 .
		 `gettextsettings (data);`

Prototype	:	`int textwidth(char *string);`
Precondition	:	None
Description	:	Returns the length in pixels of the text referenced by *string*. In calculating this result, the font size is taken into account.
Example	:	`size = textwidth("Hello world");`

Summary

Driver & Mode Constants

Driver	Mode Name	Resolution	Maximum Colours
CGA	CGAC0	320 x 200	4
	CGAC1	320 x 200	4
	CGAC2	320 x 200	4
	CGAC3	320 x 200	4
	CGAHI	640 x 200	2
EGA	EGALO	640 x 200	16
	EGAHI	640 x 350	16
VGA	VGALO	640 x 200	16
	VGAMED	640 x 350	16
	VGAHI	640 x 480	16

Colour Constants

Numeric Value	Symbolic Name
0	BLACK
1	BLUE
2	GREEN
3	CYAN
4	RED
5	MAGENTA
6	BROWN
7	LIGHTGRAY
8	DARKGRAY
9	LIGHTBLUE
10	LIGHTGREEN
11	LIGHTCYAN
12	LIGHTRED
13	LIGHTMAGENTA
14	YELLOW
15	WHITE

Line Thickness Constants

Numeric Value	Symbolic Name	Description
1	NORM_WIDTH	Line 1 pixel wide
3	THICK_WIDTH	Line 3 pixels wide

Line Style Constants

Numeric Value	Symbolic Name	Description
0	SOLID_LINE	Solid line
1	DOTTED_LINE	Dotted-line
2	CENTER_LINE	Dot-dash line
3	DASHED_LINE	Dashed line
4	USERBIT_LINE	User-defined

Fill Constants

Numeric Value	Symbolic Name	Description
0	EMPTY_FILL	Fills using background colour
1	SOLID_FILL	Solid fill in current fill colour
2	LINE_FILL	Horizontal lines
3	LTSLASH_FILL	SW-NE light lines
4	SLASH_FILL	SW-NE heavy lines
5	BKSLASH_FILL	NW-SE heavy lines
6	LTBKSLASH_FILL	NW-SE light lines
7	HATCH_FILL	Straight cross hatch
8	XHATCH_FILL	Diagonal cross hatch
9	INTERLEAVE_FILL	Interleave
10	WIDE_DOT_FILL	Wide spaced dots
11	CLOSE_DOT_FILL	Close spaced dots
12	USER_FILL	User-defined

Font Constants

Numeric Value	Symbolic Name	Classification
0	DEFAULT_FONT	bit-mapped
1	TRIPLEX_FONT	stroked
2	SMALL_FONT	stroked
3	SANS_SERIF_FONT	stroked
4	GOTHIC_FONT	stroked
5	SCRIPT_FONT	stroked
6	SIMPLEX_FONT	stroked
7	TRIPLEX_FONT	stroked
8	COMPLEX_FONT	stroked
9	EUROPEAN_FONT	stroked
10	BOLD_FONT	stroked

Text Justification Constants

Numeric Value	Symbolic Name	Action
Horizontal text		
0	LEFT_TEXT	Left-justify text
1	CENTER_TEXT	Centre text
2	RIGHT_TEXT	Right-justify text
Vertical text		
0	BOTTOM_TEXT	Justify from bottom
1	CENTER_TEXT	Centre text
2	TOP_TEXT	Justify from top

Pre-Defined Types

```
struct arccoordstype
{
    int x,y;
    int xstart, ystart, xend, yend;
};
```

```
struct fillsettingstype
{
    int pattern;
    int color;
};
```

```
struct linesettingstype
{
    int linestyle;
    unsigned upattern;
    int thickness;
};
```

```
struct palettetype
{
    unsigned char size;
    signed char colors[16];
};


struct textsettingstype
{
    int font;
    int direction;
    int charsize;
    int horiz;
    int vert;
};


struct viewporttype
{
    int left,top,right,bottom;
    int clip;
};
```

Graphics Functions

Function Name	Return Type	Input Types	Header File	Description
System Control				
initgraph	void	int gdriver int gmode char* path	graphics.h	Sets machine into graphics mode
graphresult	int	void	graphics.h	Returns error code generated by most recent graphics function call.
grapherrormsg	char*	int error	graphics.h	Returns the message associated with error
setviewport	void	int x1 int y1 int x2 int y2 int clipon	graphics.h	Sets the area of the screen in which graphic output will occur. If clipping is on, output will be restricted to the viewport area.
getviewsettings	void	viewporttype *viewport	graphics.h	Returns details of current viewport settings in viewport
closegraph	void	void	graphics.h	Returns monitor to text mode.
Positioning				
moveto	void	int x int y	graphics.h	Moves CP to (*x*,*y*).
moverel	void	int offx int offy	graphics.h	Moves CP *offx* along the x-axis and *offy* along the y-axis.
getmaxx	int	void	graphics.h	Returns the maximum x-ordinate in the current mode.
getmaxy	int	void	graphics.h	Returns the maximum y-ordinate in the current mode.
getx	int	void	graphics.h	Returns the current x-ordinate.
gety	int	void	graphics.h	Returns the current y-ordinate.
Colour Setting				
setcolor	void	int c	graphics.h	Set current drawing colour to *c*.
setbkcolor	void	int bk	graphics.h	Sets the current background colour to *bk*.
getcolor	int	void	graphics.h	Returns the current drawing colour.
getbkcolor	int	void	graphics.h	Returns the current background colour.

Graphics Functions (continued)

Function Name	Return Type	Input Types	Header File	Description
Pixel				
putpixel	void	int x int y int colour	graphics.h	The pixel a position (*x,y*) is set to *colour.*
getpixel	int	int x int y	graphics.h	Returns the colour at position (*x,y*).
Line				
setlinestyle	void	int ls int pat int thick	graphics.h	Sets the line style to *ls*. When using a user-defined option then *pat* defines the style. *thick* can be 1 or 3.
arc	void	int x int y int sangle int fangle int rad	graphics.h	Draws arc of circle centred at (*x,y*). Starts at *sangle* degrees from the horizontal. Stops at *fangle*. Radius is given by *rad*.
ellipse	void	int x int y int sangle int fangle int xrad int yrad	graphics.h	Draws an ellipse centred at (*x,y*). Starts at *sangle* degrees from the horizontal. Stops at *fangle*. Radii is given by *xrad* and *yrad*.
line	void	int x int y int x2 int y2	graphics.h	Draws a line from (*x1,y1*) to to (*x2,y2*).
linerel	void	int offx int offy	graphics.h	Draws a line from CP to (*Cp.x+offx, CP.y+offy*)
lineto	void	int x int y	graphics.h	Draws a line from CP to to (*x,y*).
getarccoord	void	arccoords type ac	graphics.h	Returns details of last call to arc() in *ac*.
Outline				
drawpoly	void	int num int *pts	graphics.h	Draws a polygon with *num* points which are given in **pts*.
circle	void	int x int y int rad	graphics.h	Draws a circle centred at (*x,y*) with radius *rad*.
rectangle	void	int x1 int y1 int x2 int y2	graphics.h	Draws a rectangle whose top-left corner is (*x1,y1*) and (*x2,y2*) the bottom right.
Filled Shapes				
setfillstyle	void	int pat int col	graphics.h	Sets the fill pattern (*pat*) and colour (*col*) used on subsequently filled objects
bar	void	int x1 int y1 int x2 int y2	graphics.h	Draws a rectangle without outline. Corners given by (*x1,y1*),(*x2,y2*)
bar3d	void	int x1 int y1 int x2 int y2 int depth int top	graphics.h	Draws a rectangle with outline. Corners given by (*x1,y1*),(*x2,y2*). A 3D effect is achieved by giving a non-zero value for *depth*. A topped bar is given if *top* is non-zero.
fillellipse	void	int x int y int xrad int yrad	graphics.h	Draws a filled ellipse centred on (*x,y*) with radii *xrad* and *yrad*.

Graphics Functions (continued)

Function Name	Return Type	Input Types	Header File	Description
fillpoly	void	int num int *pts	graphics.h	Draws a filled polygon with *num* points held at *pts*.
pieslice	void	int x int y int sangle int fangle int rad	graphics.h	Draws a pie slice from a circle centred at (*x*,*y*) with radius *rad*. The slice is from *sangle* to *fangle*, measured anti-clockwise from the horizontal.
sector	void	int x int y int sangle int fangle int rad	graphics.h	Draws elliptical sector centred at (*x*,*y*) with radii *xrad* and *yrad*. The slice is from *sangle* to *fangle*, measured anti-clockwise from the horizontal.
Text				
settextstyle	void	int font int dir int sz	graphics.h	Sets the font, size and direction of subsequent text output.
settextjustify	void	int horz int vert	graphics.h	Sets the justification of text in both the horizontal and vertical directions.
outtext	void	char *str	graphics.h	Displays text referenced by *str*.
outtextxy	void	int x int y char *str	graphics.h	Outputs text referenced by str beginning at screen coordinates (*x*,*y*).
gettextsettings	void	text settings type ts	graphics.h	Returns details of current text settings in *ts*.
textwidth	int	char *str	graphics.h	Returns the width, in pixels, of the string referenced by *str*.

Removing Graphics from the Screen

When working in text mode it is simple enough to remove any unwanted characters from the screen: we need simply to overwrite the desired area with space characters. This approach won't work in graphics mode. For example, if we draw a red circle on a green background, the circle can be removed by redrawing the same circle using green as the drawing colour (see LISTING-10.3).

LISTING-10.3

Removing a Circle from the Screen

```
#include<graphics.h>
#include<conio.h>

void main()
{
   int gdriver, gmode;

   //***Move to graphics mode ***
   gdriver = DETECT;
   initgraph(&gdriver,&gmode,"c:\\bc45\\bgi");
   //*** Draw red circle on green background ***
   setbkcolor(GREEN);
   setcolor(RED);
   circle(100,100,80);
   getch();
   //*** Remove circle by redrawing it in background colour ***
   setcolor(getbkcolor());
   circle(100,100,80);
   getch();
   //*** Return to text mode ***
   closegraph();
}
```

A similar approach is required to remove text constants from the screen as shown in LISTING-10.4.

LISTING-10.4

Removing Text

```
#include<graphics.h>
#include<conio.h>

void main()
{
   int gdriver, gmode;

   //***Move to graphics mode ***
   gdriver = DETECT;
   initgraph(&gdriver,&gmode,"c:\\bc45\\bgi");
   //*** Draw red circle on green background ***
   setbkcolor(YELLOW);
   setcolor(RED);
   settextstyle(2,0,6);
   //*** Show text ***
   outtextxy(100,100,"Graphics text");
   getch();
   //*** Remove text ***
   setcolor(getbkcolor());
   outtextxy(100,100,"Graphics text");
   getch();
   //*** Return to text mode ***
   closegraph();
}
```

However, if we want to display and remove text entered from the keyboard, then we have a much more complex problem.

Since the normal input routines such as cin will not normally function in graphics mode, to display entered data, we need to read and display characters one at a time. This requires the logic:

```
Set required colours and font
Move CP to the required screen position
Read a key
Display it on the screen
```

The code for this would be:

```
//*** Set colours and font ***
setcolor(YELLOW);
setbkcolor(RED);
settextstyle(2,0,6);
//*** Move to required screen position ***
moveto(100,100);
char ch[2]={'\0','\0'};    //Contains key as string
//*** Read a key ***
ch[0] = getch();
//*** Display it on screen ***
outtext(ch);
```

Of course, we'll want to construct a string from the characters entered by appending each to the end of a `char` array. This will require the lines:

```
char text[21]="";      //Contains complete string entered
strcat(text,ch);
```

The most demanding task is to allow characters to be deleted using the back space character. To do this we'll need to move back over the last character and erase it from the screen. We've already seen how this is done with a string constant but the stituation is more awkward here since each character is proportionally spaced. That is, a letter such as an *i* will occupy less space than a *w*. This means that we have to determine the width in pixels of the last character displayed and move the CP back by that amount before rewriting the letter in the background colour. Luckily, the function *textwidth()* will perform exactly that function for us. All of this requires the code:

```
//*** Remove last displayed character from screen ***
ch[0] = text[strlen(text)-1]; //Put last char displayed in ch
moverel(-textwidth(ch),0);    //Move cursor back by char width
setcolor(getbkcolor());       //Change to background colour
outtext(ch);                  //Output last character
moverel(-textwidth(ch),0);    //Move the cursor back again
```

The character will also have to be removed from the string and the colour restored to its original value.

All of this requires the lines:

```
//*** Remove from string ***
text[strlen(text)-1]=0;
//*** Restore normal colour ***
setcolor(YELLOW);
```

For the final program we need to allow characters to be entered until the RETURN key is pressed. This gives us the final program which is shown in LISTING-10.5.

LISTING-10.5

Inputting Text in Graphics Mode

```
#include<graphics.h>
#include<conio.h>
#include<string.h>


void main()
{
   int gdriver, gmode;

   //***Change to graphics mode ***
   gdriver = DETECT;
   initgraph(&gdriver,&gmode,"c:\\bc45\\bgi");

   //***Set colours and font ***
   setcolor(YELLOW);
   setbkcolor(RED);
   settextstyle(2,0,6);
   //*** Move to required screen position ***
   moveto(100,100);
   //*** Set up required strings ***
   char ch[2]={'\0','\0'};      //Contains key as string
   char text[21]="";            //Contains complete string entered
   //*** Read a key ***
   ch[0] = getch();
   //*** WHILE key not RETURN DO ***
   while(ch[0]!=13)
   {
        //*** IF not backspace AND enough space THEN ***
        if(ch[0]!=8&&strlen(text)<<20)
        {
             //*** Display and add to string ***
             outtext(ch);
             strcat(text,ch);
        }
        //*** ELSE IF backspace and string not empty THEN ***
        else if(ch[0]==8&&strlen(text)>>0)
        {
             //*** Remove last character from screen ***
             ch[0] = text[strlen(text)-1];
             moverel(-textwidth(ch),0);
             setcolor(getbkcolor());
             outtext(ch);
             moverel(-textwidth(ch),0);
             //*** Remove from string ***
             text[strlen(text)-1]=0;
             //*** Restore normal colour ***
             setcolor(YELLOW);
        }
        //*** Get another character ***
        ch[0]=getch();
   }
   closegraph();
}
```

Creating Bold Text

The fonts available with the graphics drivers are neither extensive nor do they give us the ability to create italic or bold text directly. However, it is possible to create a bold font effect on screen by simply displaying an item of text twice; with the second display being output one pixel to the right of the first. Hence, the program in LISTING-10.6 gives us a bold heading at the top of the screen

LISTING-10.6

Producing Bold Text

```
#include<graphics.h>
#include<conio.h>

void main()
{
   int gdriver, gmode;

   //***Move to graphics mode ***
   gdriver = DETECT;
   initgraph(&gdriver,&gmode,"c:\\bc45\\bgi");

   //*** Set colours and font ***
   setbkcolor(BLUE);
   setcolor(RED);
   settextstyle(2,0,6);
   //*** Output text ***
   outtextxy(100,30,"This is in bold text");
   getch();
   outtextxy(101,30,"This is in bold text");
   getch();
   closegraph();
}
```

Embossed Text

Another effective use of fonts is creating embossed text. This can be done by choosing your colours carefully and displaying the text three times. The first, background, copy is printed in a dark colour (such as DARKGRAY); the next is printed in a lighter colour (here WHITE); the final copy is printed in the middle of the first two using the background colour. This gives the required effect.

The technique is demonstrated in LISTING-10.7.

LISTING-10.7

Embossed Characters

```
#include<graphics.h>
#include<conio.h>

void main()
{
   int gdriver, gmode;

   //***Move to graphics mode ***
   gdriver = DETECT;
   initgraph(&gdriver,&gmode,"c:\\bc45\\bgi");

   //*** Fill screen in LIGHTGRAY ***
   setfillstyle(1,LIGHTGRAY);
   bar(0,0,639,479);
   //*** Set style and first colour ***
   setcolor(DARKGRAY);
   settextstyle(2,0,6);
   //*** Display text ***
   outtextxy(101,30,"This is in embossed text");
   getch();
   //*** Display in highlight colour ***
   setcolor(WHITE);
   outtextxy(99,30,"This is in embossed text");
   getch();
   //*** Display in background colour ***
   setcolor(LIGHTGRAY);
   outtextxy(100,30,"This is in embossed text");
   getch();
   closegraph();
}
```

PROGRAMMING EXERCISE 10.3

Modify the program in LISTING-10.7 so that the position of the light and dark characters are reversed.

Animation

Simple animation is easily achieved by rapidly moving an image about the screen. For example, we can give the effect of a circle bouncing about the screen by moving it a few pixels at a time about the display area. This requires the basic logic:

```
WHILE no key pressed DO
    IF edge hit THEN
        Reverse direction
    ENDIF
    Display circle
    Wait for 10 milliseconds
    Hide circle
    Move to next position
ENDWHILE
```

The final program is shown in LISTING-10.8.

LISTING-10.8

Simple Animation

```
#include<graphics.h>
#include<conio.h>

void main()
{
  int gdriver, gmode;

  //***Move to graphics mode ***
  gdriver = DETECT;
  initgraph(&gdriver,&gmode,"c:\\bc45\\bgi");

  //*** Set screen background ***
  setfillstyle(1,LIGHTGRAY);
  bar(0,0,639,479);
  //*** Set start position and step size ***
  int x=100,y=100;
  int xstep=3,ystep=3;
  //*** WHILE no key pressed DO ***
  while(!kbhit())
  {
      //*** IF edge hit THEN Reverse direction ***
      if(x<<10||x>>630)
          xstep=-xstep;
      if(y<<10||y>>430)
          ystep=-ystep;
      //*** Display circle ***
      setcolor(YELLOW);
      circle(x,y,10);
      //*** Show for 10 milliseconds ***
      delay(10);
      //*** Hide circle ***
      setcolor(LIGHTGRAY);
      circle(x,y,10);
      //*** Move to next position ***
      x+=xstep;
      y+=ystep;
  }
  closegraph();
}
```

> **PROGRAMMING EXERCISE 10.4**
>
> Modify the program in LISTING-10.8 so that the the machine beeps when the circle changes direction.

Displaying BMP Images

Introduction

There are many image file formats that are widely used on computers. For example, JPEG and GIF formats are heavily used on the Internet. These files use compression techniques to minimise their size. This makes for efficient storage and transfer but the price to be paid is that these images must be uncompressed before they can be viewed.

One of the simplest image formats is Microsoft Windows BMP format which is used, amongst other things, for storing the background wallpaper images that are used to personalise many computers.

The BMP File Format

Being uncompressed, BMP files tend to be large: about 20 to 40 times larger than the same image stored in JPEG format.

BMP files can allocate 1, 4, 8 or 24 bits to each pixel in an image. This means an image can have 2, 16, 256 or 16,777,216 colours. This last option creates more colours than the human eye can distinguish and so should be more than enough for most applications.

File Format

A BMP files consists of four main sections. As well as the image itself, the file contains a header at the start of the data which contains identifying bytes and the size of the file; the image details section gives more details such as the width and height of the image; the colour palette holds the RGB settings for each colour used in the image; and finally, comes the image itself. FIG-10.7 shows the basic structure.

FIG-10.7

BMP File Structure

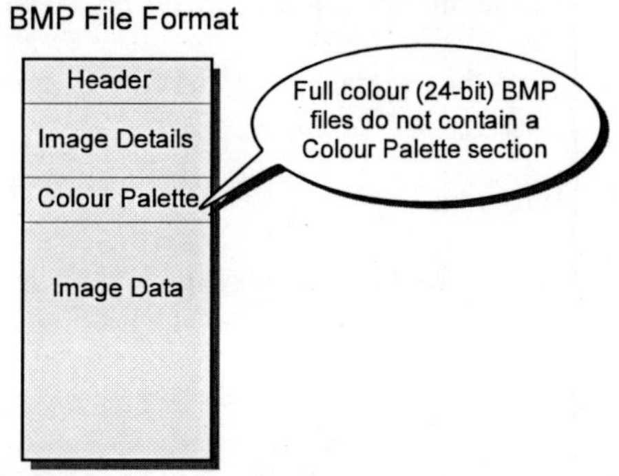

BMP File Format

Header

Image Details

Colour Palette

Image Data

Full colour (24-bit) BMP files do not contain a Colour Palette section

The Header Section

The header is 14 bytes in length. The first two bytes contain the characters BM; these are followed by 4 bytes containing the size of the file in bytes, 4 reserved bytes which are not used, and a final 4 bytes which hold offset details specifying the number of bytes between the start of the file and the image data area. All numeric values are unsigned (see FIG-10.8).

FIG-10.8

BMP Header Details

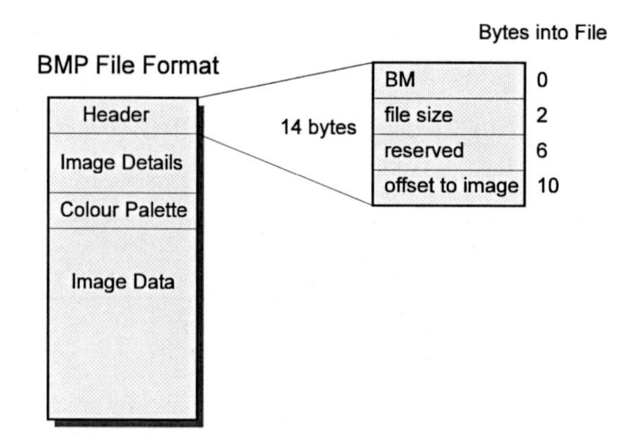

This header can be defined in the following way

```
struct BMPHeader
{
    char bm[2];                 // BM
    unsigned long size;         // File size in bytes
    unsigned long reserved;     // Reserved area
    unsigned long offset;       // Position of image data area
};
```

TASK 10.5

Use a paint package to create a BMP file containing a two-colour, single pixel. Call the file *onepixel.bmp*.

Create a second two-colour image which is 2 pixels wide and 1 pixel high. Call the file *twopixel.bmp*.

Create a third two-colour image which is 5 pixels wide and 4 pixels high. Call the file *twentypixel.bmp*.

PROGRAMMING EXERCISE 10.5

Write a C++ program (*BMPread1.cpp*) which prompts for a BMP image file name and displays the size and offset values given in the file's header.

If the file extension (*.bmp*) is not specified it should be added automatically.

Test the program using the files *onepixel.bmp, twopixel.bmp* and *twentypixel.bmp*.

Program Logic:

```
Get valid filename
WHILE filename not "END.bmp" DO
    Attempt to open file          (binary read mode)
    IF file not found THEN
        Display error message
    ELSE
        Read file header          (use fread())
        Display size and offset
        Close file
    ENDIF
    Get valid filename
ENDWHILE
```

The Image Details

The image details area is 40 bytes in length and contains details such as the image's dimensions, number of colours used, bits per pixel, and the size of the image data area. The exact format of this area can be defined as follows:

```
struct BMPDetails
{
    unsigned long detailsSize;     //Size of the image detail
                                   //area in bytes. Should be 40
    unsigned long width;           //Width of the image in pixels
    unsigned long height;          //Height of the image in pixels
    unsigned short planes;         //Number of colour planes
    unsigned short bitsPerPixel;   //Bits per pixel
    unsigned long compression;     //Compression type (always 0 )
    unsigned long imagesize;       //Image Data area's size in bytes
    unsigned long xresolution;     //Pixels per vertical metre
    unsigned long yresolution;     //Pixels per horizontal metre
    unsigned long coloursUsed;     //Number of colours used
    unsigned long importantcolours;//Important colours
}
```

See FIG-10.9 for more details.

FIG-10.9

The Image Details Area

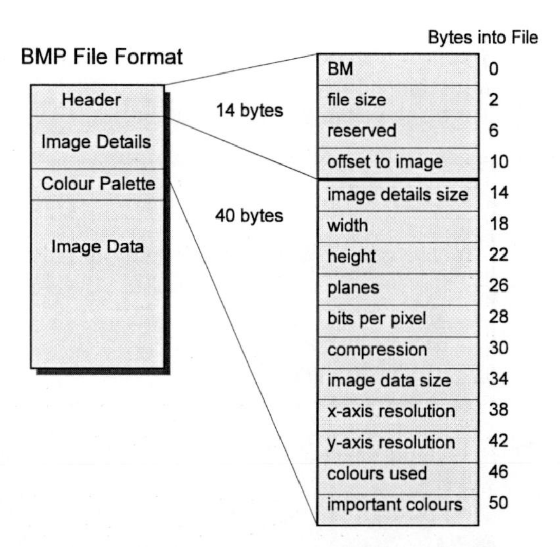

Some of the details in this section of the file are unlikely to be of use when interrogating the file. For example, *planes* is always 1; *compression* is always 0 (no compression); *xresolution* specifies the number of pixels per metre in the horizontal, while *yresolution* does the same job, but in the vertical direction. *importantcolours* states the number of frequently used colours in the image.

> **PROGRAMMING EXERCISE 10.6**
>
> Modify your last program to add a record definition which reflects the structure of the Image Details area. Save the new program as *BMPRead2.cpp*.
>
> Use a variable of this type so that *detailsSize, width, height, bitsPerPixel, imageSize* and *coloursUsed* details are displayed along with the file size and offset details already shown.
>
> Test your new program on *onepixel.bmp* and *twentypixel.bmp*.

The files *eye2.bmp* and *eye3.bmp* can be downloaded from the Digital Skills web site at

www.digital-skills.co.uk

TASK 10.6

Determine the following details about the files *eye2.bmp* and *eye3.bmp*:
width
height
number of colours used

The Colour Palette

Notice the unusual order of the colours - Blue, Green and Red - rather than the more usual Red, Green, Blue.

For 2, 16 and 256 colour images a colour palette is placed after the Image Details area. This contains one entry for every colour used in the image. Each entry is four bytes in length. The first three of these give the blue, green and red values for that colour code. For example, if a two colour image uses blue and red, then the colour palette would have the following entries:

```
FF 00 00 00
00 00 FF 00
```

In this image, any pixel coded as zero (0) would display in blue while any pixel coded as one (1) would show in red.

If your screen display mode is not in full colour, the palette data could be used to adjust any colour palette being used by the graphics card to ensure that the image was displayed in the colours intended.

TASK 10.7

What size, in bytes, would the colour palette area be in:

a) a 1-bit per pixel image
b) a 4-bits per pixel image
c) a 24-bits per pixel image

In fact, the exact length of the colour palette area in bytes can be calculated in two ways:

as

```
the number of colours used * 4 bytes
```

or as

```
offset value - (size of the header + size of the image details)
```

which is simply

```
offset - 54
```

Because of the limited scope for changing the colour palette available in Borland graphics we will not make any use of the file's palette information here.

The Image Data

The image data area contains the actual image. At its simplest - when using a two-colour image - each bit in this area represents one pixel on the screen. To display an image we might start with a program whose logic is:

```
Read file header
Read Image details
Read Image palette
FOR  row := 1 to details.height DO
    FOR column := 1 to details.width DO
        Read pixel data from file
        Display pixel on screen
    ENDFOR
ENDFOR
```

Extracting Pixel Data

It is not possible to read a single bit from a file; the minimum that can be read is a single byte.

In the case of a 2-colour image, a single byte contains the details of 8 pixels, while a byte of data from a 16 colour image contains information on 2 pixels. In the case of a 256 colour image, each byte contains details of one pixel. FIG-10.10 summarises this situation.

FIG-10.10

Pixel Data Storage

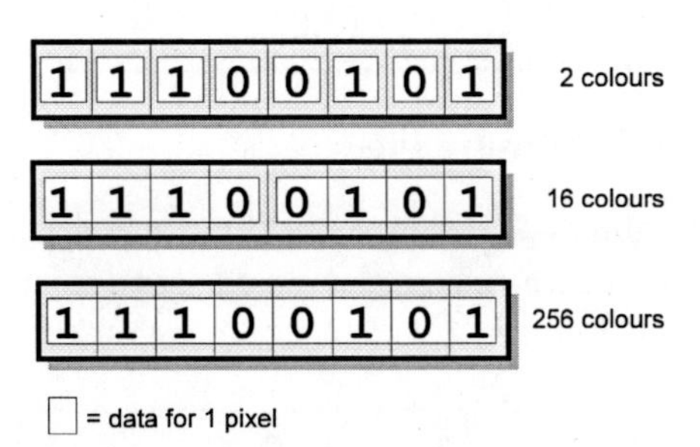

Before we start thinking about displaying an image we need to figure out how to extract pixel information from each byte read. Because of the limited number of colours available in the Borland graphics, we'll limit our investigations to 2 and 16 colour images.

From a 2 Colour Image

One possible way of extracting pixel data when dealing with a 2 colour image is to use a combination of masking and shifting. For example, using the byte value shown in FIG-10.10, the value of the first pixel (extreme left-hand bit) can be determined using the code:

```
mask = 0X80;
pixelvalue = bytevalue & mask;
pixelvalue >>= 7;
```

The effects of these statements are shown in FIG10.11.

FIG-10.11

Extracting a Single Pixel from a 2 Colour Image

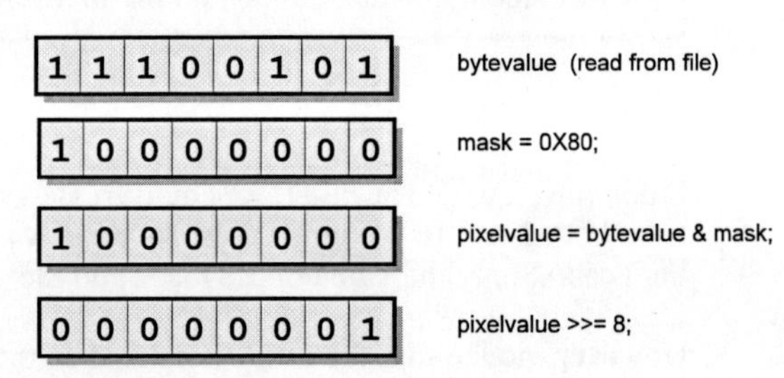

It only remains to use the pixel's value to display a single dot of the correct colour on the screen with a statement such as:

```
putpixel(x,y,pixelvalue);
```

To access the next bit in the *bytevalue* variable we need only shift the contents of the varaible one place to the left and then repeat the previous process (see FIG-10.12).

FIG-10.12

Shifting *bytevalue* to the Left

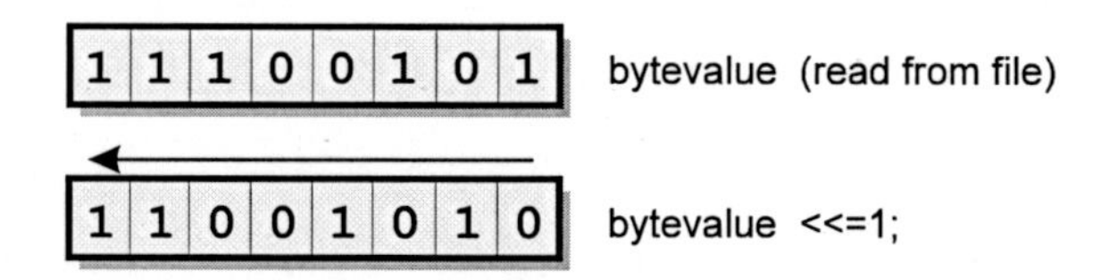

> **PROGRAMMING EXERCISE 10.7**
>
> Write a small program (*byte.cpp*) to read a single byte from the keyboard and display the contents of the byte in binary. Make use of the shift and mask methods described previously.
>
> (HINTS: Declare *bytevalue*, *mask* and *pixelvalue* as unsigned `char` types. Read the value into an `int` variable before copying it to *bytevalue.* Start with 0X to enter a hexadecimal value from the keyboard (e.g. 0X80).

From a 16 Colour Image

With images in this format we need to extract 4 bits (sometimes called a **nibble**) for each pixel. Again we can use a combination of masking and shifting as shown in FIG-10.13.

FIG-10.13

Extracting a Single Pixel from a 16 Colour Image

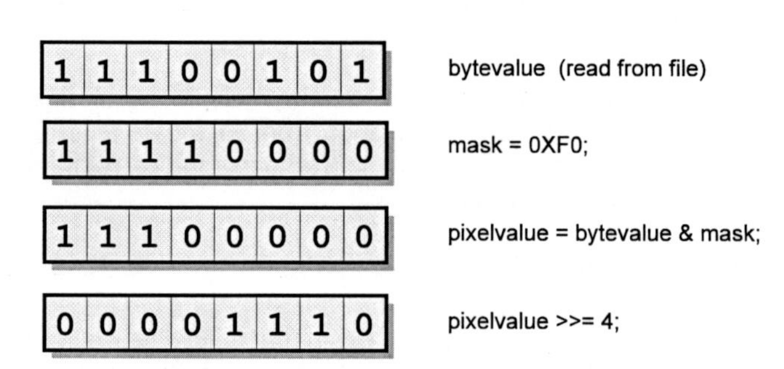

To access the second nibble in *bytevalue*, it needs to be shifted 4 places to the right before repeating the masking process.

> **PROGRAMMING EXERCISE 10.8**
>
> Write another short program (*byte2.cpp*) that uses masks and shifts to display the hexadecimal value of each nibble in a single byte.

From 2 or 16 Colour Images

If possible, it would be best if we could create a single piece of code to extract pixels from both 2 and 16 colour images. As we saw above, a similar approach is used in both cases; only the value of the mask and the shifts differ.

However, notice that the mask is related to the number of colours: in a 2 colour image the mask value is 1 shifted 7 places to the left; in a 16 colour image the mask is the value 15 shifted 4 places to the left. That is the value of the mask is one less than the number of colours. The shift required to position these values correctly within the mask is related to the number of bits per pixel and is given as:

```
maskshift = 8 - bits per pixel;
```

TASK 10.8

The shifts required in the *bytevalue* and *pixelvalue* variables also relate to the bits per pixel. Determine an expression for these two shifts.

How does the number of pixels to be extracted from each byte relate to the number of bits per pixel?

How does the number of bits per pixel relate to the number of colours?

We can now create a general algorithm for extracting pixel data from each byte:

```
Read byte
Read bitsperpixel
noofcolours = 2 to the power bitsperpixel
maskshift = 8 - bitsperpixel
mask = (numberofcolours - 1) << maskshift
bytevalueshift = bitsperpixel
pixelvalueshift = 8 - bitsperpixel
pixelsperbyte = 8 /bitsperpixel
FOR pixelsperbyte times DO
    pixelvalue = (bytevalue & mask)>>pixelvalueshift
    write pixelvalue
    bytevalue << bytevalueshift
ENDFOR
```

PROGRAMMING EXERCISE 10.9

Write a final version of the byte-displaying program. This time, as well as reading the byte value, read a value for *bitsperpixel* (1 or 4) and display the byte in binary (for 1 bit) or hexadecimal (4 bits). Assume the *bitsperpixel* value entered is valid.

We need to calculate one more piece of information before we're ready to tackle displaying an image; the number of bytes used to store a single row of the image. This can be calculated as:

```
bytesinrow = image width /pixelsperbyte
```

We should now be able to read and display 2 and 16 colour images. The overall logic of our program is as follows:

```
Open the file
Read the header
Read the Image Data
Skip the Colour Palette
Calculate the maskshift
Calculate the mask
Calculate bytevalueshift
Calculate pixelvalueshift
Calculate bytesinrow
FOR each row DO
    FOR each byteinrow DO
        Read byte
        FOR pixelsperbyte times DO
            Calculate pixelvalue
            Paint pixel on screen
            Shift bytevalue
        ENDFOR
    ENDFOR
ENDFOR
```

The FOR loops of this algorithm are coded in C++ as shown below:

```
for(int row = 0; row < details.height; row++)
{
    for(int bytecount =0; bytecount < bytesinrow; bytecount++)
    {
        unsigned char byte;
        fread(&byte,1,1,picfile);
        for(int c = 0; c<pixelsperbyte ; c++)
        {
            unsigned char digit = (byte & mask) >> digitshift;
            putpixel(bytecount*pixelsperbyte+c,row,(int)digit);
            byte<<=byteshift;
        }
    }
}
```

Notice from the code how the position of the pixel is calculated. Its x-ordinate is calculated using the expression `bytecount*pixelsperbyte+c` while the y-ordinate is simply the value of *row*.

The complete program used to display a 2 or 16 colour BMP image is shown in LISTING-10.9.

LISTING-10.9

Displaying a BMP Image - First Attempt

```
#include<iostream.h>
#include<stdlib.h>
#include<stdio.h>
#include<conio.h>
#include<string.h>
#include<graphics.h>
#include<math.h>

struct BMPHeader
{
  char bm[2];
  unsigned long size;
  unsigned long reserved;
  unsigned long offset;
};

struct BMPImageDetails
{
  unsigned long detailsSize;     // Header size in bytes
  unsigned long width,height;    // Width and height of image
  unsigned short planes;         // Number of colour planes
  unsigned short bitsPerPixel;   // Bits per pixel
  unsigned long compression;     // Compression type
  unsigned long imageSize;       // Image size in bytes
  unsigned long xresolution,yresolution; // Pixels per metre
  unsigned long coloursUsed;     // Number of colours used
  unsigned long importantColours;// Important colours
};

void getFilename(char* f);

void main()
{
  BMPHeader heading;
  BMPImageDetails details;
  FILE *picfile;
  char filename[35];

  getFilename(filename);
  int gdriver, gmode;
  gdriver = DETECT;
  initgraph(&gdriver, &gmode, "c:\\bc45\\bgi");
```

Continued on next page

LISTING-10.9
(continued)

Displaying a BMP image - First Attempt

```
   while(stricmp(filename,"end.bmp")!= 0)
   {
       picfile = fopen(filename,"rb");
       if(!picfile)
               cout<<"error opening file\n";
       else
       {
           fread(&heading,sizeof(heading),1,picfile);
           fread(&details,sizeof(details),1,picfile);
           fseek(picfile,heading.offset,0);

           int noofcolours = pow(2,details.bitsPerPixel);
           int maskshift = 8 - details.bitsPerPixel;
           int mask = (noofcolours - 1) << maskshift;
           int byteshift = details.bitsPerPixel;
           int digitshift = 8 - details.bitsPerPixel;
           int pixelsperbyte = 8 / details.bitsPerPixel;
           int bytesinrow = details.width/pixelsperbyte;

           for(int row = 0; row < details.height; row++)
           {
               for(int bytecount =0; bytecount < bytesinrow;
               bytecount++)
               {
                   unsigned char byte;
                   fread(&byte,1,1,picfile);
                   for(int c = 0; c<pixelsperbyte ; c++)
                   {
                       unsigned char digit = (byte & mask)
                       >> digitshift;
                       putpixel(bytecount*pixelsperbyte+c,row,
                       (int)digit);
                       byte<<=byteshift;
                   }
               }
           }
       }
       getFilename(filename);
   }
}


void getFilename(char* f)
{
   cout<<"Enter filename : ";
   cin>>f;
   if(strchr(f,'.')==NULL)
       strcat(f,".bmp");
}
```

REMEMBER:

You must change the target platform to DOS and select the BGI checkbox to work in graphics mode.

PROGRAMMING EXERCISE 10.10

Type in the program given in LISTING-10.9 which will display the image on the screen. Save the file as *BMPView1.cpp*.

Try displaying the 2 colour file *eye2.bmp* and the 16 colour *eye2a.bmp*.

Make sure you use *eye2.bmp* and *eye2a.bmp*; other BMP files will not operate correctly.

If your image displayed successfully, you'll see that the eye is upside down! A graphical representation of the *eye2.bmp* file is shown in FIG-10.14.

To turn the image the right way up we need to place the first pixel read from the file in the bottom-left corner rather than the top-left corner. To achieve this we need to change only the parameters for *putpixel()*.

FIG-10.14

Contents of *eye2.bmp*

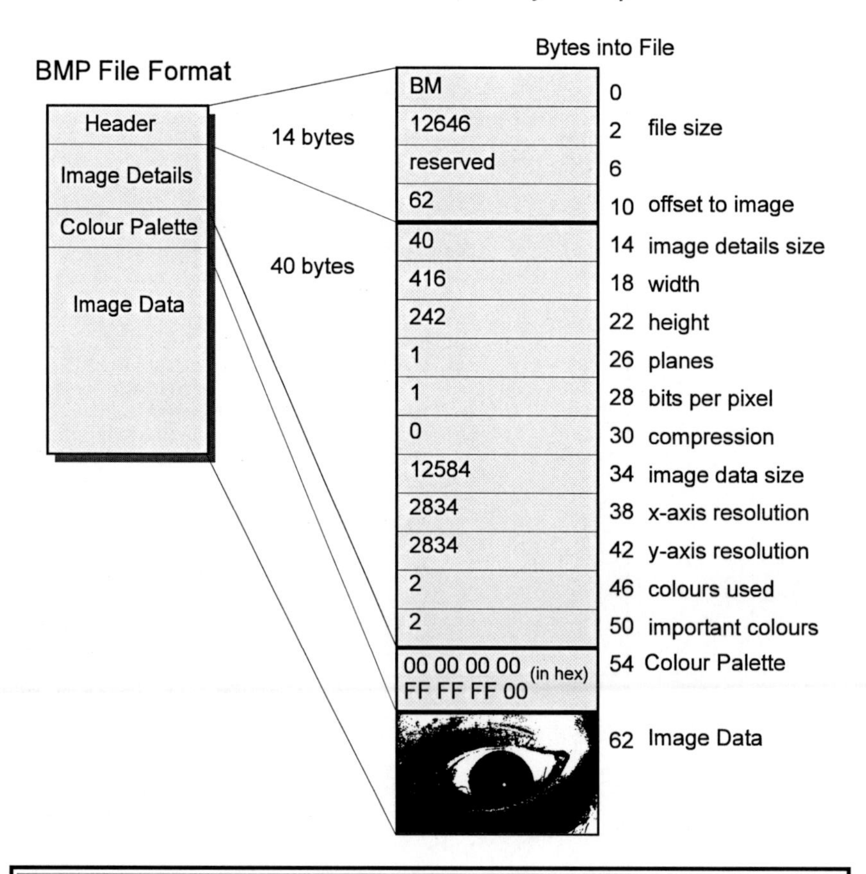

> **PROGRAMMING EXERCISE 10.11**
>
> Modify your program so that the image appears the correct way up. Name the program file *BMPView2.cpp*.

Bytes Per Line

The *eye2.bmp* is 416 pixels long and, at 1 bit per pixel, that means a single horizontal line of the image occupies 52 bytes. This is just as well since our algorithm assumes an exact number of bytes per row in the image. But if a 2 colour image was 10 pixels wide then each row would need 10 bits of storage. In this case, the remaining 6 bits of the second byte would be unused (see FIG-10.15).

FIG-10.15

Using Part of a Byte

Data for a single row
of a 2 colour, 10 pixel wide image

1	1	1	0	0	1	0	1	1	1		unused	

10 bits contain data   6 bits are unused

In fact, even this isn't the whole story: BMP files pad out the data for each row of the image to ensure it is some multiple of 4 bytes in length. So our 2 colour, 10 pixel wide image would actually store a single row as shown in FIG-10.16.

FIG-10.16

Padding at the End of a Row

Storage format for a single row
of a 2 colour, 10 pixel wide image

1	1	1	0	0	1	0	1	1	1		unused				unused					unused	

10 bits contain data   22 bits are unused

THE HENLEY COLLEGE LIBRARY

TASK 10.9

Try to display the image *eye3.bmp* using your previous program.

(Don't worry if it looks strange)

The file *eye3.bmp* is only 398 pixels wide. That is each line of the image is stored over 49 bytes and 6 bits. When the image was created an additional 2 bytes and 2 bits will have been added to pad the line out to the required multiple of 4 bytes, making it 52 bytes in length.

To display the image properly, we need to calculate three sizes:

- The whole number of bytes in the image row
- The number of pixels in a row stored over part of a byte
- The whole number of padding bytes

The first two of these values are derived as follows:

```
imagebytes   = width of image /pixels per byte
pixelsinbits = width of image %pixels per byte
```

TASK 10.10

The file *eye3a.bmp* contains a 16 colour image which is 393 pixels wide. What values would be assigned to *imagebits* and *pixelsinbits* using the formulae given above?

How many padding bytes would be required?

So, *eye3a.bmp* uses 196 bytes to store 392 pixels and an extra nibble for the last pixel in the line. This gives a total of 197 bytes containing image data. We then need 3 more bytes of padding to come to a figure that is exactly divisible by 4. To work out the padding figure we can use the following method:

This algorithm uses a mixture of pseudocode (see Chapter 1) and C++ operators (/ and %).

```
databytes := imagebytes
IF pixelsinbits > 0 THEN
    Add 1 to databytes
ENDIF
groupsoffour := databytes / 4
bytesleftover := databytes % 4
paddingbytes := 4 - bytesleftover
IF paddingbytes = 4 THEN
    paddingbytes := 0
ENDIF
```

Hopefully, this is fairly clear, but rather long-winded (we don't even need the *groupsoffour* value). However, the whole calculation can be reduced to a single line of C++ code:

```
paddingbytes = (4 - (imagebytes + (pixelsinbits > 0))%4)%4;
```

This is much more obscure in its meaning, but typical of what you might see in a C++ program written by hardened programmers.

Our algorithm for displaying an image can now be described as:

```
FOR each row DO
    FOR each imagebyte DO
        Read byte
        FOR pixelsperbyte times DO
            Calculate pixelvalue
            Paint pixel on screen
            Shift bytevalue
        ENDFOR
        IF pixelsinbits > 0 THEN
            Read byte
            FOR pixelsinbits times DO
                Calculate pixelvalue
                Paint pixel on screen
                Shift bytevalue
            ENDFOR
        ENDIF
        Skip paddingbytes in file (fseek)
    ENDFOR
ENDFOR
```

PROGRAMMING EXERCISE 10.12

Modify the program *BMPView2.cpp* to match the logic given above.

Test your program by displaying the files *eye3.bmp* and *eye3a.bmp*.

Changing the Video Display's Colour Palette

You will have noticed that the colours displayed weren't exactly realistic. Even the 2 colour image came out in black and blue rather than black and white. Of course, the colours that appear are determined by both the value given as the third parameter of *putpixel()* and by the colours defined in Borland's graphics palette. If you look back at page 583, you'll see that colour zero is black and that colour 1 is blue.

It is possible to change the actual colour assigned to each number in the palette using Borland's *setpalette()* function. This function takes two parameters, both integer. The first gives the palette entry number (0 to 15) and the second specifies the colour to be assigned to that entry in the palette. Only 64 colours are available to choose from (0 to 63). So, if we wanted our two colour pictures to display in black and white we could change the second entry in the palette from blue to white with the line

```
setpalette(1,63);
```

PROGRAMMING EXERCISE 10.13

Add the above line to your last program. Place the line immediately after the *initgraph()* call.

Attempt to display *eye2.bmp*.

To produce a more natural display from our 16 colour images we need to change the colour palette entries to match the information held in the bitmap file. Unfortunately, the Borland graphics driver only gives us a choice of 64 possible colours and this is insufficient to allow us to match the colours given in the image file.

Summary

- **To remove a graphic object,** redraw it using the background colour.
- **Removing text** requires the width of each character to be known.
- **Bold text** can be created by writing text twice, with the second copy being slightly displaced from the first.
- **Embossed text** can be achieved by displaying text three times, each in a different colour and with slight offsets.
- **Animation** is created by continually drawing, deleting and moving a still image.
- **Animation needs a delay** between each iteration to slow the process to an acceptable level.
- **BMP images** are uncompressed files containing four main sections.
- The **Header Section** specifies:

  File size
  Offset to image

- The **Image Details Section** specifies:

  Width
  Height
  Bits per pixel
  Number of colours

- The **Palette Section** specifies the colours used.
- **Each colour** is specified over 4 bytes (the last of these bytes is unused)
- **The colours are specified in the order**

  Blue
  Green
  Red

- The **Image Data Section** contains the image data.
- The **image data starts with the last row** of the image.
- **Each row's data is some multiple of 4 bytes** long.
- **Padding** is added where necessary to ensure the length of each row.

CASE STUDY

The Problem

A program is required to create a single player bat and ball game.

The aim of the game is to remove bricks from a wall by hitting them with the ball which the user must stop from disappearing off the bottom of the screen by deflecting it with the bat. The screen layout for the game is shown in FIG-10.17.

FIG-10.17

The Game Layout

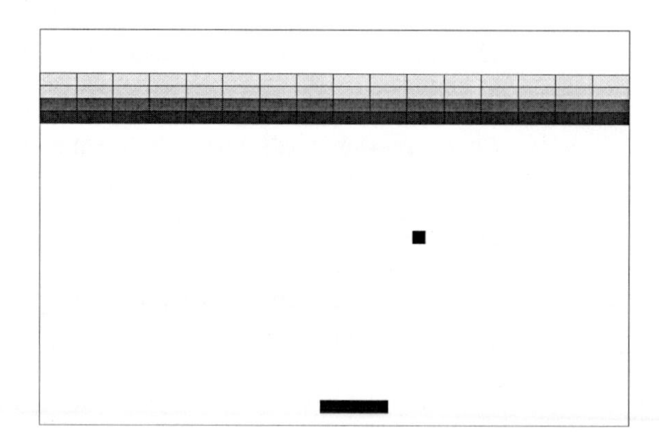

Clarification

The user is allowed three lives and scores a point for each brick removed from the first row and two points for each brick from the second etc. The final score is displayed.

The Algorithm

Program logic:

```
Initialise all variables
Draw screen setup
 REPEAT
    move ball
    IF  user request to move paddle THEN
        Move paddle as requested
    ENDIF
    IF
        brick hit:
            Remove brick
            Add to score
            Change velocity of ball
        edge hit:
            Reverse the x component of ball velocity
        top hit:
            Change velocity of ball
        bat hit:
            Change velocity of ball
        bottom hit
            Deduct 1 from lives
            Start next ball at centre of screen
    ENDIF
UNTIL lives = 0
Display score
```

Program code:

LISTING-10.10

Video Game

```
//*******************************************
//* PROGRAM        : Brickout               *
//* AUTHOR         : Patricia Stamp         *
//* DATE           : 30/1/1996              *
//* VERSION        : 0.1                    *
//* DESCRIPTION    : Plays a simple version *
//*                  of the game BrickOut   *
//* HARDWARE       : PC Compatible          *
//* SOURCE         : BorlandC++ V4.5        *
//*******************************************
#include<graphics.h>
#include<conio.h>
#include<dos.h>
#include<stdlib.h>


struct Shape
{
  int x,y;          // position of left edge
  int length;       // length
  int width;
  int colour;       // Colour
};

struct Wall
{
  Shape blocks[4][16];
};

struct Velocity
{
  int x,y;
};

struct Ball
{
  Shape b;
  Velocity v;
};

struct Screen
{
  Ball    ball;
  Shape bat;
  Wall  bricks;
};


const int colours[]={1,5,3,4};


void SetUpScreen(Screen&);
void PlaceBall(Ball&);
void PlacePaddle(Shape&);
void MovePaddleLeft(Shape&);
void MovePaddleRight(Shape&);
void MoveBall(Screen&);
void PositionBricks(Wall&);
void ShowBricks(Wall);
void RemoveBrick(Screen&);
void ChangeVelocity(Ball&,int,int);
int BrickHit(const Screen&);
int SideHit(const Ball&);
int TopHit(const Ball&);
int BottomHit(const Ball&);
int PaddleHit(const Screen&);
```

Continued on next page

LISTING-10.10
(continued)

Video Game

```
void main()
{
   Screen game
       ={{{320,230,3,3,YELLOW},{2,2}},{320,460,40,3,WHITE},{0}};
   char ch;
   randomize();
   SetUpScreen(game);
    do
   {
       MoveBall(game);
       delay(5);
       if(kbhit())
       {
           ch=getch();
           if(ch=='<'||ch==',')
               MovePaddleLeft(game.bat);
           if(ch=='>'||ch=='.')
               MovePaddleRight(game.bat);
       }
   }
   while(1);
   getch();
}


void SetUpScreen(Screen& game)
{
   int gmode, gdriver;
   gdriver=DETECT;
   initgraph(&gdriver,&gmode,"d:\\bc45\\bgi");
   setfillstyle(1,GREEN);
   bar(0,0,639,479);
   PositionBricks(game.bricks);
   ShowBricks(game.bricks);
   PlacePaddle(game.bat);
   PlaceBall(game.ball);
}


void PlacePaddle(Shape& p)
{
   setfillstyle(1,p.colour);
   bar(p.x,p.y,p.x+p.length,p.y+p.width);
}


void PlaceBall(Ball& ball)
{
   setfillstyle(1,ball.b.colour);
   bar(ball.b.x,ball.b.y,ball.b.x+ball.b.length,
                                         ball.b.y+ball.b.width);
}


void MovePaddleLeft(Shape& p)
{
   setfillstyle(1,GREEN);
   bar(p.x,p.y,p.x+p.length,p.y+p.width);
   if(p.x>5)
       p.x-=5;
   setfillstyle(1,p.colour);
   bar(p.x,p.y,p.x+p.length,p.y+p.width);
}
```

Continued on next page

LISTING-10.10
(continued)

Video Game

```
void MovePaddleRight(Shape& p)
{
   setfillstyle(1,GREEN);
   bar(p.x,p.y,p.x+p.length,p.y+p.width);
   if(p.x<675)
        p.x+=5;
   setfillstyle(1,p.colour);
   bar(p.x,p.y,p.x+p.length,p.y+p.width);
}


void ChangeVelocity (Ball& b, int addx, int addy)
{
   b.v.x+=addx;
   if(b.v.x>5)
        b.v.x=5;
   else if(b.v.x<-5)
        b.v.x=-5;
   b.v.y+=addy;
   if(b.v.y>5)
        b.v.y=5;
   else if(b.v.y<-5)
        b.v.y=-5;
   if(b.v.y==0)
        b.v.y=1;
}


void MoveBall(Screen& game)
{
   setfillstyle(1,GREEN);
   bar(game.ball.b.x,game.ball.b.y,game.ball.b.x+
            game.ball.b.length,game.ball.b.y+game.ball.b.width);
   if(BrickHit(game))
   {
        RemoveBrick(game);
        ChangeVelocity(game.ball,-(2*game.ball.v.x)+random(2),
                                 -(2*game.ball.v.y));
   }
   if(PaddleHit(game))
        ChangeVelocity(game.ball,-(2*game.ball.v.x)+random(2),
                                 -(2*game.ball.v.y));
   if(SideHit(game.ball))
        ChangeVelocity(game.ball,-(2*game.ball.v.x)+random(2),0);
   if(BottomHit(game.ball)||TopHit(game.ball))
        ChangeVelocity(game.ball,-(2*game.ball.v.x)+random(2),
                                  -(2*game.ball.v.y)+random(2));
   game.ball.b.x+=game.ball.v.x;
   game.ball.b.y+=game.ball.v.y;
   setfillstyle(1,game.ball.b.colour);
   bar(game.ball.b.x,game.ball.b.y,game.ball.b.x+
            game.ball.b.length,game.ball.b.y+game.ball.b.width);
}


int BrickHit(const Screen& game)
{
   int topleftx,toplefty,toprightx,toprighty,botleftx,botlefty,
        botrightx,botrighty;

   topleftx=botleftx=game.ball.b.x+game.ball.v.x;
   toplefty=toprighty=game.ball.b.y+game.ball.v.y;
   toprightx=botrightx=topleftx+game.ball.b.length;
   botlefty=botrighty=toplefty+game.ball.b.width;
```

Continued on next page

LISTING-10.10
(continued)

Video Game

```
    if(toplefty<130&&botlefty>50)
         if(game.ball.v.y>0)
              if((getpixel(botleftx,botlefty)!=GREEN)||
                   (getpixel(botrightx,botrighty)!=GREEN))
                   return 1;
              else
                   return 0;
         else
              if((getpixel(topleftx,toplefty)!=GREEN)||
                   (getpixel(toprightx,toprighty)!=GREEN))
                   return 1;
              else
                   return 0;
    else
        return 0;
}


int SideHit(const Ball& ball)
 {
    if(ball.b.x+ball.v.x<0||ball.b.x+ball.v.x>getmaxx()-3)
        return 1;
   else
        return 0;
}


int BottomHit(const Ball& ball)
{
   if(ball.b.y+ball.v.y>getmaxy()-3)
        return 1;
   else
        return 0;
}

int TopHit(const Ball& ball)
{
   if(ball.b.y+ball.v.y<2)
        return 1;
   else
        return 0;
}

int PaddleHit(const Screen& game)
{
   if((game.ball.b.y>400)&&(getpixel(game.ball.b.x+game.ball.v.x,
   game.ball.b.y+game.ball.v.y)==game.bat.colour||
   getpixel(game.ball.b.x+game.ball.v.x+game.ball.b.length,
   game.ball.b.y+game.ball.v.y+game.ball.b.width)==
                                              game.bat.colour))
        return 1;
   else
        return 0;
}


void PositionBricks(Wall& w)
{
   for(int row=0;row<4;row++)
        for(int col=0;col<16;col++)
        {
             w.blocks[row][col].x=col*40;
             w.blocks[row][col].y=row*20+50;
             w.blocks[row][col].length=40;
             w.blocks[row][col].width=20;
             w.blocks[row][col].colour=colours[row];
        }
}
```

Continued on next page

LISTING-10.10
(continued)

Video Game

```
void ShowBricks(Wall w)
{
   for(int row=0;row<4;row++)
       for(int col=0;col<16;col++)
       {
           setfillstyle(1,w.blocks[row][col].colour);
           bar3d(w.blocks[row][col].x,w.blocks[row][col].y,
            w.blocks[row][col].length+w.blocks[row][col].x,
            w.blocks[row][col].width+w.blocks[row][col].y,0,0);
       }
}

void RemoveBrick(Screen& s)
{
   int row, col;
   row = 3-(130-(s.ball.b.y+s.ball.v.y))/20;
   row = (row<0)?0:row;
   row = (row>3)?3:row;
   col = (s.ball.b.x+s.ball.v.x)/40;
   col = (col<0)?0:col;
   col = (col>15)?15:col;
   setfillstyle(1,GREEN);
   bar(s.bricks.blocks[row][col].x,s.bricks.blocks[row][col].y,
           s.bricks.blocks[row][col].length+
           s.bricks.blocks[row][col].x,
           s.bricks.blocks[row][col].width+
           s.bricks.blocks[row][col].y);
}
```

Solutions

TASK 10.1

1. 3 bytes (24 bits)

2. 3,932,160 bytes (almost 4Mb)

TASK 10.2

P2 is at position (10,3)

TASK 10.3

(-6,5)

TASK 10.4

(200,260)

PROGRAMMING EXERCISE 10.3

```
#include<graphics.h>
#include<conio.h>

void main()
{
    int  gdriver, gmode;

    //*** Change to graphics mode ***
    gdriver = DETECT;
    initgraph(&griver, &gmode, "c:\\bc45\\bgi");

    //*** Set colour and font ***
    setfillstyle(1,LIGHTGRAY);
    bar(0,0,639,479);
    setcolor(WHITE);
    settextstyle(2,0,6);
    outtextxy(101,30,"This is in embossed text");
    getch();
    setcolor(DARKGRAY);
    outtextxy(99,30,"This is in embossed text");
    getch();
    setcolor(LIGHTGRAY);
    outtextxy(100,30,"This is in embossed text");
    getch();
    closegraph();
}
```

PROGRAMMING EXERCISE 10.4

There are several ways in which we might introduce noise to the program.
Using a `cout<char(7);` instruction takes too long and interfers with the smooth flow of the circle.
A better approach is to make the sound during the 10 millisecond delay in which the circle is displayed.
This second approach is used here.

```
#include<graphics.h>
#include<conio.h>
#include<dos.h>
#include<iostream.h>

void main()
{
    int gdriver, gmode;

    //***Move to graphics mode ***
    gdriver = DETECT;
    initgraph(&gdriver,&gmode,"c:\\bc45\\bgi");

    //*** Set screen background ***
    setfillstyle(1,LIGHTGRAY);
    bar(0,0,639,479);
    int x = 100,y = 100;
    int xstep = 3,ystep = 3;
    int beep = 0;
    //*** WHILE no key pressed DO ***
    while(!kbhit())
    {
        //*** IF edge hit THEN Reverse ***
        if(x < 10 || x > 630)
        {
            xstep=-xstep;
            beep = 1;
        }
        if(y < 10 || y > 430)
        {
            ystep = -ystep;
            beep = 1;
        }
        //*** Display circle ***
        setcolor(YELLOW);
        circle(x,y,10);
        //*** Show for 10 milliseconds ***
        if(beep)
        {
            sound(1000);
            delay(10);
            nosound();
            beep = 0;
        }
        else
            delay(10);
        //*** Hide circle ***
        setcolor(LIGHTGRAY);
        circle(x,y,10);
        x += xstep;
        y += ystep;
    }
    closegraph();
}
```

TASK 10.5

No solution required.

PROGRAMMING EXERCISE 10.5

```
#include<iostream.h>
#include<stdio.h>
#include<string.h>

//*** Define BMP File header ***
struct BMPHeader
{
    char bm[2];
    unsigned long size;
    unsigned long reserved;
    unsigned long offset;
};


//*** Function prototype ***
void getFilename(char*);


void main()
{
    BMPHeader heading;  //file header
    FILE *picfile;      //File handle
    char filename[35];  //Name of file

    //*** Get name of file to be opened ***
    getFilename(filename);
    //*** WHILE name not end.bmp DO
    while(stricmp(filename,"end.bmp")!= 0)
    {
        //*** Open file ***
        picfile = fopen(filename,"rb");
        //*** IF not found THEN error message ***
        if(!picfile)
            cout<<"error opening file\n";
        else
        {
            //*** ELSE Read file header ***
            fread(&heading,sizeof(heading),1
            ,picfile);
            //*** Display header details ***
            cout<<"\nSize : "<<heading.size
                <<"\nOffset : "<<heading.offset
                <<endl;
        }
        //*** Get name of next file ***
        getFilename(filename);
```

```
    }
    cout<<"Program terminated\n";
}

//*** Get valid file name ***
void getFilename(char* f)
{
//*** Read file name ***
cout<<"Enter filename : ";
cin>>f;
//*** Add file extension if required ***
if(strchr(f,'.')==NULL)
    strcat(f,".bmp");
}
```

PROGRAMMING EXERCISE 10.6

```
    #include<iostream.h>
    #include<stdlib.h>
    #include<stdio.h>
    #include<conio.h>
    #include<string.h>

//*** Define BMP File header ***
struct BMPHeader
{
    char bm[2];
    unsigned long size;
    unsigned short reserved[2];
    unsigned long offset;
};

//*** Define BMP Image Details ***
struct BMPImageDetails
{
    unsigned long size; //Header size in bytes
    long width,height;  //Width & height of image
    unsigned short planes; //No. of colour planes
    unsigned short bitsperpixel;//Bits per pixel
    unsigned long compression; //Compression type
    unsigned long imagesize;//Image size in bytes
    long xresolution,yresolution;//Pixels/metre
    unsigned long coloursused;//No. of colours used
    unsigned long importantcolours;//Imp. colours
};

//*** Function prototype ***
void getFilename(char*);

void main()
{
    BMPHeader heading;
    BMPImageDetails details;
    FILE *picfile;
    char filename[35];
    //*** Get name of file to be opened ***
    getFilename(filename);
    //*** WHILE name not end.bmp DO
    while(stricmp(filename,"end.bmp")!= 0)
    {
        //*** Open file ***
        picfile = fopen(filename,"rb");
        //*** IF not found THEN error message ***
        if(!picfile)
            cout<<"error opening file\n";
        else
        {
            //*** ELSE Read Header & Details ***
            fread(&heading,sizeof(heading),1,picfile);
            fread(&details,sizeof(details),1,picfile);
            //*** Display details ***
            cout<<"\nSize           : "
                <<heading.size
                <<"\nOffset         : "
                <<heading.offset<<endl;
            cout<<"Image width    : "
                <<details.width
                <<"\nImage height   : "
                <<details.height
                <<"\nBits per pixel : "
                <<details.bitsperpixel
                <<"\nColours used   : "
                <<details.coloursused
                <<"\n\n\n"<<endl;
        }
        //*** Get name of next file ***
        getFilename(filename);
    }
    cout<<"Program terminated\n";
}

//*** Get valid file name ***
void getFilename(char* f)
{
    //*** Read file name ***
    cout<<"Enter filename : ";
    cin>>f;
    //*** Add file extension if required ***
    if(strchr(f,'.')==NULL)
        strcat(f,".bmp");
}
```

TASK 10.6

TASK 10.7

1 bit / pixel	requires 8 byte palette
4 bits / pixel	requires 64 byte palette
24 bits / pixel	no palette is used

PROGRAMMING EXERCISE 10.7

```
#include<iostream.h>

void main()
{
    int value;
    unsigned char byte;
    unsigned char mask = 0XF0;
    unsigned char digit;

    cout<<"Enter number (0 to 255) : ";
    cin >> value;
    byte = value;

    for(int c = 0; c<2 ; c++)
    {
        digit = (byte & mask) >>4;
        cout<<(int)digit;
        byte<<=4;
    }
}
```

PROGRAMMING EXERCISE 10.8

```
#include<iostream.h>

void main()
{
    int value;
    unsigned char bytevalue;
    unsigned char nib1mask = 0XF0;
    unsigned char nib2mask = 0X0F;
    unsigned char pixel1value, pixel2value;

    cout<<"Enter number (0 to 255) : ";
    cin >> value;
    bytevalue = value;
    pixel1value = (bytevalue & nib1mask)>>4;
    pixel2value = bytevalue & nib2mask;
    cout<<"Contents of left nibble  : "
        <<(int)pixel1value<<endl;
    cout<<"Contents of right nibble : "
        <<(int)pixel2value<<endl;
}
```

TASK 10.8

bytevalue shift = bits per pixel
pixelvalue shift = 8 - bits per pixel
pixels per byte = 8 /bits per pixel
number of colours = 2 to the power bits per pixel

PROGRAMMING EXERCISE 10.9

```
#include<iostream.h>
#include<math.h>

void main()
{
    int value;
    int bitsperpixel;
```

```
    unsigned char byte;
    int byteshift;
    int maskshift;
    int digitshift;
    int pixelsperbyte;
    int noofcolours;
    unsigned char mask;
    unsigned char digit;

    cout<<"Enter number (0 to 255) : ";
    cin >> value;
    byte = value;
    cout<<"Enter bits per pixel (1 or 4) : ";
    cin>>bitsperpixel;

    noofcolours = pow(2,bitsperpixel);
    maskshift = 8 - bitsperpixel;
    mask = noofcolours-1 << maskshift;
    byteshift = bitsperpixel;
    digitshift = 8 - bitsperpixel;
    pixelsperbyte = 8/bitsperpixel;
    for(int c = 0; c<pixelsperbyte ; c++)
    {
        digit = (byte & mask) >>digitshift;
        cout<<hex<<(int)digit;
        byte<<=byteshift;
    }
}
```

PROGRAMMING EXERCISE 10.10

No solution required.

PROGRAMMING EXERCISE 10.11

Change the *putpixel()* call line to read:

```
putpixel(bytecount*pixelsperbyte+c,
        details.height-row,(int)digit);
```

TASK 10.9

No solution required.

TASK 10.10

16 colours requires 4 bits per pixel and hence is stored 2 pixels to a byte.

Therefore:

imagebytes	= 393 / 2	=	196
pixelsinbits	= 393 % 2	=	1
padding bytes		=	3

PROGRAMMING EXERCISE 10.12

```
#include<iostream.h>
#include<stdlib.h>
#include<stdio.h>
#include<conio.h>
#include<string.h>
#include<graphics.h>
#include<math.h>

struct BMPHeader
{
    char bm[2];
    unsigned long size;
    unsigned long reserved;
    unsigned long offset;
};

struct BMPImageDetails
{
    unsigned long detailsSize;
    unsigned long width,height;
    unsigned short planes;
    unsigned short bitsPerPixel;
    unsigned long compression;
    unsigned long imageSize;
    unsigned long xresolution,yresolution;
    long coloursUsed;
    unsigned long importantColours;
};

void getFilename(char* f);
void main()
{
    BMPHeader heading;
    BMPImageDetails details;
    FILE *picfile;
    char filename[35];
        clrscr();
    getFilename(filename);
    int gdriver, gmode;
    gdriver = DETECT;
    initgraph(&gdriver, &gmode, "c:\\bc45\\bgi");
    while(stricmp(filename,"end.bmp")!= 0)
    {
        picfile = fopen(filename,"rb");
        if(!picfile)
            cout<<"error opening file\n";
        else
        {
            fread(&heading,sizeof(heading),1,picfile);
            fread(&details,sizeof(details),1,picfile);
            fseek(picfile,heading.offset,0);
            int noofcolours=pow(2,details.bitsPerPixel);
            int maskshift=8-details.bitsPerPixel;
            int mask =(noofcolours - 1)<<maskshift;
            int byteshift=details.bitsPerPixel;
            int digitshift=8-details.bitsPerPixel;
            int pixelsperbyte=8/details.bitsPerPixel;
            int imagebytes=details.width/pixelsperbyte;
            int pixelsinbits=details.width%pixelsperbyte;
            int paddingbytes=(4-(imagebytes
                    +(pixelsinbits > 0))%4)%4;
            for(int row=0;row<details.height;row++)
            {
                for(int bytecount=0;
                bytecount<imagebytes; bytecount++)
                {
                    unsigned char byte;
                    fread(&byte,1,1,picfile);
                    for(int c=0;c<pixelsperbyte;c++)
                    {
                        unsigned char digit=
                        (byte & mask)>>digitshift;
                        putpixel(bytecount*
                         pixelsperbyte+c,
                         details.height-row,
                         int)digit);
                        byte<<=byteshift;
                    }
                }
                if (pixelsinbits > 0)
                {
                    unsigned char byte;
                    fread(&byte,1,1,picfile);
                    for(int c=0;c<pixelsinbits;c++)
                    {
                        unsigned char digit =
                        (byte & mask)>>digitshift;
                        putpixel(bytecount*
                         pixelsperbyte+c,
                         details.height-row,
                         (int)digit);
                            byte<<=byteshift;
                    }
                }
                fseek(picfile,paddingbytes,1);
            }
        }
        getFilename(filename);
    }
    cout<<"Program terminated\n";
    getch();
}

void getFilename(char* f)
{
    cout<<"Enter filename : ";
    cin>>f;
    if(strchr(f,'.')==NULL)
        strcat(f,".bmp");
}
```

PROGRAMMING EXERCISE 10.13

No solution required.

CHAPTER 11

Classes and Objects

This chapter covers the following topics:

Constructors

Copy Constructor

Defining an Object

Destructors

Friends

Inline Methods

Operator Overloading

`private`, `public` and `protected` Class Methods

`this` Pointer

Typecasting Classes

Types of Objects

Understanding Classes

CLASSES AND OBJECTS

Introduction

So far we've looked at the various instructions available in C++. In many ways these are not dissimilar to those of previous programming languages such as Pascal and Basic. However, the most fundamental aspect of C++ is that, unlike Pascal and Basic, it is an object-oriented programming language.

Although object-oriented programming has been with us for over 30 years, it is still an unfamiliar concept to many - even to those who have been programming professionally for a number of years. In this chapter we'll explore the concepts of object-oriented programming and how C++ implements these ideas.

What is an Object?

Real World Objects

Our lives are populated with objects: *computers, books, clouds, words, customers,* etc. Some objects have a physical existence such as *computers* and *books*; others represent roles people or things play such as *customers* or *guard dogs*; yet other objects are incidents, such as *a traffic jam* or *enrollment in a class*.

One way to describe an object is to list its characteristics and the operations which can be performed by or on the object. For example, a beach ball is round, has a diameter and colour; it can be inflated, deflated, rolled, bounced, kicked, thrown and burst.

More abstract objects, such as roles and incidents, may be defined in terms of the information required for their description and the operations which can be performed on that information. For example, a bank account might be described in terms of the *name* and *address* of the account holder and the *current balance,* while the operations likely to be performed are *make deposit*, *make withdrawal*, *change address*, and *add interest*.

TASK 11.1

List the characteristics and operations which could be used in describing:

1. a pencil
2. a date on the calendar

Object Classes

We also need to differentiate between a general description of all objects of the same type and specific objects. Hence, *beach ball* is a general term for all beach balls and *Elizabeth's beach ball* refers to one specific beach ball. When we identify the attributes and operations of an item, this represents a description of all items of that type. This grouping is known as an **object class** or simply a **class**. An individual item from such a class is called an **object** or an **instance** of that class.

TASK 11.2

Identify each of the following as either a class or an object.

1. Dogs
2. Lassie
3. Galaxy class starships
4. The USS Enterprise NCC-1701-D
5. Integers
6. The value 26

Programming Objects

An object-oriented approach to software analysis and design views a system as a collection of objects and interactions between those objects. In addition, the software itself may introduce the need for additional objects which arise through implementation requirements. For example, we may need to define such objects as *drop-down menus*, *option buttons* and *scrollable data lists*.

Once the objects required in the system have been identified, the relevant characteristics and operations of the classes to which these objects belong are defined.

In the world of object-oriented design, a class's characteristics are known as its **attributes**, while the tasks it can perform are known as its **operations**. Generally, an operation within a class will modify or make use of one or more attributes defined within that class.

Collectively, the attributes and operations are known as the **features** or **members** of the class. For example, if a system requires an imperial weight given in pounds and ounces, the corresponding imperial weight class could be defined as in FIG-11.1.

FIG-11.1

Weight Class

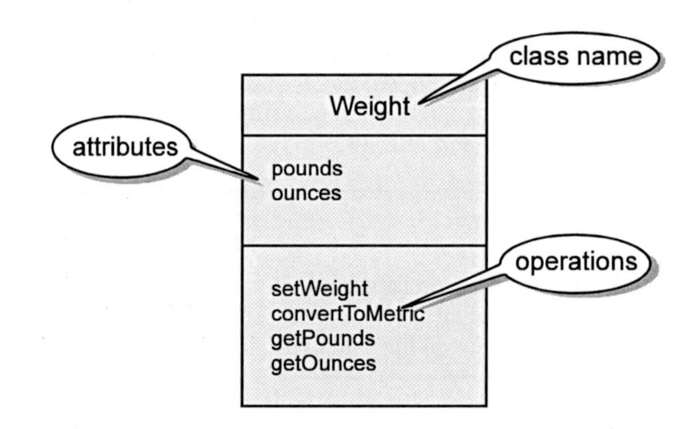

The diagrams in this text conform to the Unified Modelling Language (UML) standard.

This class definition specifies the name of the class along with its attributes and operations.

C++ has no specific standards for naming functions. The convention used here has been borrowed from Java. Where a name is derived by linking several words, the first word is in lower case and subsequent words are capitalised.

FIG-11.1 states that a class *Weight* contains two attributes: *pounds* and *ounces*, and four operations: *setWeight*, *convertToMetric, getPounds* and *getOunces*.

Each operation requires an explanation and this can be documented in normal Mini-Spec format. Informally, the operations for the *Weight* class are:

setWeight : Sets the attributes *pounds* and *ounces* to specified values.

Notice how each operation makes use of the attributes defined within the class.

convertToMetric: Converts the imperial weight held in the attributes *pounds* and *ounces* to the metric equivalent in kilograms.

getPounds : Returns a copy of the value held in the *pounds* attribute.

getOunces : Returns a copy of the value held in the *ounces* attribute.

The class definition will be expanded as the design becomes more detailed to include the attribute types and the parameters of the operations. For example, the operation *setWeight()* requires, as parameters, the new values to be allocated to the class attributes, *pounds* and *ounces*. Hence the *setWeight()* function heading would be written as:

Since this is a design specification, language-specific terms such as `int` and `double` are not used when referring to data types.

```
setWeight(newlbs, newoz : INTEGER)
```

The operation *convertToMetric*, on the other hand, has no IN parameters but does return a result and is declared as:

```
convertToMetric():REAL
```

Note that the parentheses are retained to emphasize that there are no IN parameters. These are followed by a colon and the type of value returned by the operation.

When defining operation parameters, the attributes of the class are not included since all operations of a class have automatic access to the attributes of that class (see Class Scope later in this chapter).

The more detailed definition of *Weight* class is given in FIG-11.2.

FIG-11.2

Defining a Class

Weight
pounds : INTEGER ounces : INTEGER
setWeight(newlbs, newoz : INTEGER) convertToMetric():REAL getPounds():INTEGER getOunces():INTEGER

TASK 11.3

Using the box notation shown above, create a definition for a *Distance* class (attributes: *yards, feet* and *inches*) with operations *setDistance, getYards, getFeet, getInches* and *convertToMetric*.

Classes and Objects in C++

In C++, an object class is defined within the `class` statement. A class is a blueprint for the structure of objects yet to be defined. Think of a class definition as being equivalent to the design plans a company would create for a new car before going on to build many cars based on that design.

Notice that this is a similar idea to record structures. We define the format of a record in a `struct` statement and later create variables of that structure. One of the things that makes classes different from a record is that a class contains operations as well as data within its definition.

A first attempt at a C++ definition of the *Weight* class we designed earlier might be as given below.

```
class Weight
{
    public:
        int pounds;
        int ounces;

        void setWeight(int,int);
        double convertToMetric();
        int getPounds();
        int getOunces()
};
```

An Explanation of the Code

`class Weight`	This declares a new class called *Weight*. In some respects this statement is similar to `struct` in that it marks the beginning of a set of grouped items. By convention, class names are always capitalised.
`public:`	The items that follow this keyword can be accessed by any program creating objects of this class.
`int pounds;` `int ounces;`	The attributes of the class are defined.

`void setWeight(int, int);`
`double convertToMetric();`
`int getPounds();`
`int getOunces();`
	The prototypes of each operation.
	The actual code for each operation is given later.
	C++ does not have any strong naming conventions for operations. Here the Java format is used with the first word of the name in lower case while subsequent words are capitalised.

PROGRAMMING EXERCISE 11.1

Write a class definition for the *Distance* class you defined in TASK 11.3.

Save the file as *Distance.cpp*.

The class definition is followed by the code for each of the operations within the class. The complete code for the *Weight* class is given in LISTING-11.1.

LISTING-11.1

The *Weight* Class

```
class Weight
{
  public:
      int pounds;
      int ounces;

      void setWeight(int,int);
      double convertToMetric();
      int getPounds();
      int getOunces();
};

void Weight::setWeight(int lbs, int oz)
{
  if(lbs < 0 || oz < 0 || oz > 15)
      return;
  pounds = lbs;
  ounces = oz;
}

double Weight::convertToMetric()
{
  return (pounds * 16 + ounces)*0.0283495;
}

int Weight::getPounds()
{
  return pounds;
}

int Weight::getOunces()
{
  return ounces;
}
```

NOTE: Once coded, we refer to the operations as the **methods** of the class.

The code is the method by which the operation is implemented.

An Explanation of the Code

Although similar to normal function definitions, a class's methods are prefaced by the class name and a **scope resolution operator** (::). This allows the compiler to link the code to function names defined in the class and overcomes any problems that might occur should another class have methods of the same name.

The methods make reference to the attributes without requiring them to be passed as parameters. This is because the attributes of a class can be accessed by any method in that class. The attributes are said to have **class scope**.

Note that the *setWeight()* method checks that the parameters (*lbs* and *oz*) are valid before assigning them to the attributes *pounds* and *ounces.*

PROGRAMMING EXERCISE 11.2

Type in the code given in LISTING-11.1 and save the file as *Weight.cpp*.

PROGRAMMING EXERCISE 11.3

Add the code for the operations in the *Distance* class to your *Distance.cpp* file.
(1 inch = 0.0254 metres)

At this point, our task as a programmer might be over. Often classes are designed by one group of programmers and used by another. We can identify these groups as the **class designers** and the **application programmers**. It is the application programmer who is going to create and use class objects.

In our previous program we created variables to help in the solution to our problems. Hence, to store someone's age we created an `int` variable, and to hold a name we created an array of type `char`. So, if an application programmer requires to store an imperial weight for some reason, his program can create an object of the class *Weight.*

Normally, the application programmer would not have access to the class's source code and would use the `#include` command and libraries to gain access to a class. However, for the moment, we'll keep things simple and place the *main()* method into the same file as the class code.

In the next program we will create a *Weight* object, set it to some user specified value and display the result in both imperial and metric values.

The code for *main()* begins with the lines

```
void main()
{
    Weight w1;
```

This creates an object named *w1*. An object is often referred to as an **instance** of its class. Hence, *w1* is an instance of the *Weight* class. We may think of the object as containing an exact copy of everything defined within the *Weight* class (see FIG-11.3).

FIG-11.3

The *Weight* Class Object *w1*

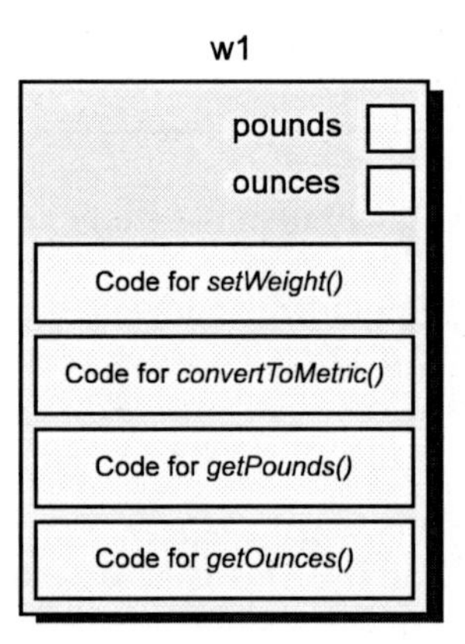

Finally, the program needs to use the *Weight* variable, *w1*, to access the features of the object that has been created. The syntax for this takes the form:

```
object name . feature to be accessed
```

In this program we only have one object, *w1*, so the first part of this expression must be:

```
w1.
```

Since we'll want to start by assigning a value to our *Weight* object, the first feature we want to access is *setWeight()*. So to assign the value 7 pounds 9 ounces, we use the expression:

Again, the approach is similar to that used when accessing a field within a record variable.

```
w1.setWeight(7,9)
```

TASK 11.4

What expression should we use in the code discussed above to determine the value of our weight (*w1*) in kilogrammes?

We're now ready to attempt a complete program using an object of the *Weight* class. The program in LISTING-11.2 employs the following logic:

```
Create Weight object
Read in the required weight value
Assign the value to the Weight object
Display the weight's value in pounds and ounces
Display the weight's value in kilogrammes
```

LISTING-11.2

An Application Using a Weight Object

The class designer would supply his software in the form of a compiled library file and separate header file.

```
#include <iostream.h>

//***Code for the Weight class (see LISTING-11.1) goes here***

void main()
{
   //*** Create the Weight object ***
   Weight w1;
   //*** Read values for weight ***
   cout<<"Enter pounds: ";
   int lbs;
   cin>>lbs;
   cout<<"Enter ounces: ";
   int oz;
   cin>>oz;
   //*** Assign value to weight object ***
   w1.setWeight(lbs, oz);
   //*** Display the weight in pounds and ounces ***
   cout << "The weight entered was " << w1.getPounds() <<
        " lbs " << w1.getOunces() << " oz" << endl;
   //*** Display the weight in kilos ***
   cout<<"This is " << w1.convertToMetric() << " kilos" <<endl;
}
```

PROGRAMMING EXERCISE 11.4

Add the code given in LISTING-11.2 to your program *Weight.cpp*.

Run the program and check that it operates correctly by entering the values 7 and 3 for the pounds and ounces values.

What happens if you enter the values 7 and 23?

When an object is created, its attributes' contents are undefined. Because the value 23 cannot be assigned to the *ounces* attribute, the values in *pounds* and *ounces* remain unchanged. In this case, that means that *pounds* and *ounces* will continue to have undefined values.

PROGRAMMING EXERCISE 11.5

Add a *main()* function to your *Distance.cpp* file. *main()* should perform the following logic:

Create a distance object (*d1*)
Read in a value to be assigned to *d1*
Call *d1*'s *setDistance()* method to assign the value read to the object
Display the distance held in both imperial and metric format

Encapsulation

As you've experienced, there are two phases to using objects; first we design and code the class and then we (or others) create objects of that class.

Those two stages may be done separately with one person or company creating the class (the class designers) and another making use of objects of that class to produce applications (the application programmer).

These two groups may never meet or have any contact with each other. All that is required of class creators is that they produce sufficient documentation to allow the second group to manipulate the objects they wish to create.

For example, if the class designer creates the *Weight* class, then they would have to produce documentation stating the name, parameters and purpose of each operation defined for the class; the application programmer would then be in a position to make use of *Weight* objects.

You may have noticed that when designing the *setWeight()* method, pre-condition checks have been made on the parameters. If the value to be assigned to *pounds* or *ounces* is invalid then no change is made to the object's attributes, and the routine exits.

This stops the group using *Weight* objects from creating corrupted data should they accidentally type a line such as

```
w1.setWeight(4,29);
```

because the pre-condition check will cause the *setWeight()* routine to be exited without the *pounds* and *ounces* attributes of *w1* being changed.

However, there's a problem. What if the application programmer writes lines such as

```
w1.pounds = 4;
w1.ounces = 29;
```

Because they have assigned values directly to *pounds* and *ounces* rather than used *setWeight()*, no checks are carried out and the meaningless value of 29 will be assigned to the *ounces* attribute *(pounds* is also assigned the value 4).

PROGRAMMING EXERCISE 11.6

In the file *Weight.cpp*, replace the line

```
w1.setWeight(lbs, oz);
```

with

```
w1.pounds = lbs;
w1.ounces = oz;
```

Run the program again entering 4 and 29.

This time the display reads 4 lbs 29 oz. The invalid value has been assigned.

Obviously, it would be useful if there was some way to eliminate the possibility of the application programmer making such a mistake. In fact, that's exactly what C++ allows us to do by modifying how the *Weight* class is defined.

By inserting the word `private` and moving the word `public` so that our code now reads

```
class Weight
{
    private:
        int pounds;
        int ounces;
    public :
        void setWeight(int,int);
        double convertToMetric();
        int getPounds();
        int getOunces();
};
```

The attributes are marked as private
The methods are marked as public

This restricts the application programmer's access to the *pounds* and *ounces* attributes of any *Weight* object.

PROGRAMMING EXERCISE 11.7

Modify the code of the *Weight* class, adding the keyword **`private`** to the *pounds* and *ounces* attributes and moving the **`public`** keyword as shown above.

Attempt to recompile the *Weight.cpp*, making sure it still contains the lines

```
w1.pounds = lbs;
w1.ounces = oz;
```

Remove the lines above and return to using `w1.setWeight(lbs,oz);` in *main()*.

The compilation error message

Weight::pounds is not accessible in function main()

that you should have seen when completing PROGRAMMING EXERCISE 11.7 demonstrates the effect of marking an attribute as `private` within a class. The application programmer can no longer access the *pounds* and *ounces* attributes of any *Weight* object directly. Instead, he must adjust the value of those two attributes by using *setWeight()* and hence, we ensure that only valid values can be assigned.

We can therefore make the statement that:

Features marked as `private` *within a class definition cannot be directly accessed in objects of that class.*

It is equally important to realise that adding `private` to the declaration of the *pounds* and *ounces* attributes has no effect on the ability of the code within the *Weight* class itself to access those attributes. Hence, *setWeight()* still contains the lines

```
pounds = lbs;
ounces = oz;
```

without causing any complaint from the compiler.

Not only has using the term `private` deprived the application programmer of the opportunity to change the value in *pounds* or *ounces*, he can't even find out what value is currently held in those attributes. For example, if *main()* contained the line

```
cout<<w1.pounds;
```

the same compilation error as we saw earlier would be displayed.

Marking an attribute as `private` cuts all direct access to that attribute. Instead, the application programmer must rely on the *getPounds()* method (which is `public`) to find out what value is held in the *pounds* attribute:

```
cout << w1.getPounds();
```

Access Modifiers

In fact, any feature within a class can be marked as either

```
    private
or  public
```

The term `public` has the opposite effect from `private` and allows full access to that feature within any objects that are created in subsequent programs.

As a general rule, the class designer will want to stop the application programmer from gaining direct access to the attributes of an object and so these will be defined as `private`. On the other hand, the methods within the class are designed to allow the application programmer access to those attributes in a controlled and organised way, and so are marked as `public`.

A guideline for class definitions is shown in FIG-11.4 below. Although this diagram does not reflect all possible options within a class definition, it is a good starting point for most simple classes.

FIG-11.4

Class Declaration Syntax

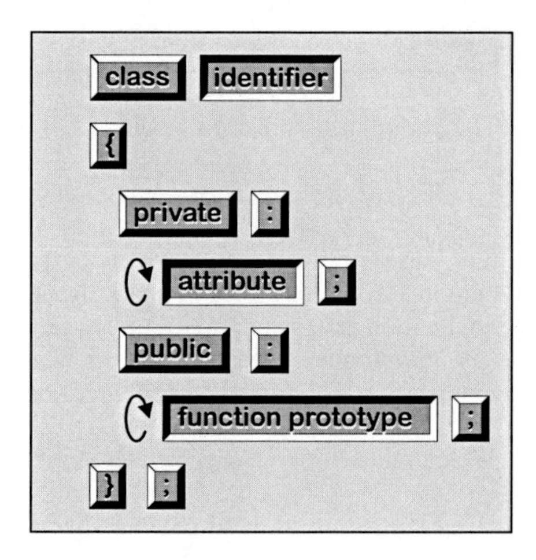

Information Hiding

The inability to access the private members of a class is the first of many advantages of an object-oriented approach to programming.

We've seen that making an attribute private forces the application programmer to use only recognised methods of access to the private attributes. However, there's another equally important reason for keeping attributes private.

Let's assume that the class designer has decided to make the attributes of the *Weight* class public since he knows that the application programmer never makes mistakes!

The application programmer can now create *Weight* objects and write statements such as

```
Weight w1;
w1.pounds = 8;
w1.ounces = 4;
```

Later, the class programmer has a flash of inspiration and decides that a weight can be stored as a single real value in which the ounces component is stored as a fraction of a pound. Hence, the weight 4 lbs 8 oz would be stored as 4.5.

Using this approach the attributes of the *Weight* class can be rewritten as:

```
class Weight
{
    public:
         double value;
```

Keen to distribute the new and improved version of the code, the class designer now sends his new implementation of the *Weight* class to the application programmer in a new version of the *Weight.class* file. The application programmer is now in big trouble! The next time he tries to compile his program containing the assignment statements

```
w1.pounds = 4;
w1.ounces = 8;
```

these will no longer be valid since the *pounds* and *ounces* attributes no longer exist within the *Weight* class. But, by marking the attributes as private, and forcing the application programmer to write

```
w1.setPounds(4,8);
```

the application program will compile correctly with either version of the *Weight* class. This alternative version of the *Weight* class is given in LISTING-11.3.

LISTING-11.3

A new Version of the *Weight* Class

```
class Weight
{
  private:
       double value;
  public:
       void setWeight(int,int);
       double convertToMetric();
       int getPounds();
       int getOunces();
};

void Weight::setWeight(int lbs, int oz)
{
  if(lbs < 0 || oz < 0 || oz > 15)
       return;
  value = lbs + oz/16.0;
}

double Weight::convertToMetric()
{
  return (value*16*0.0283495);
}

int Weight::getPounds()
{
  return (int)value;
}

int Weight::getOunces()
{
  return (int)((value - getPounds()+0.0001)*16);
}
```

The only constraint on the class designer is that the names and parameters of the public operations must not be changed when new versions of a class are produced.

By following these rules, the application programmer will be unaware of the actual changes implemented between one version of an object class and the next.

> **PROGRAMMING EXERCISE 11.8**
>
> Create a new file named *Weight2.cpp*.
>
> In the file enter the code for this new version of the *Weight* class, but use the same version of *main()* as in the previous program.
>
> Compile and run *Weight2.cpp.*

As a result of PROGRAMMING EXERCISE 11.8 you can see that *main()* continues to execute correctly without any changes, even though an entirely new implementation of the *Weight* class is now being used.

This ability to conceal the details of a class implementation is known as **information hiding**. To achieve information hiding we need to restrict access to the attributes, allowing access to them through the operations of the class only. This linking of data and related operations is known as **encapsulation** (see FIG-11.5).

FIG-11.5

Encapsulation Concepts

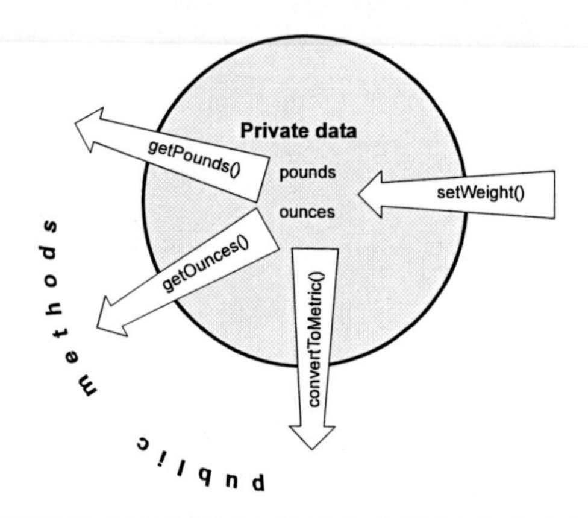

> **PROGRAMMING EXERCISE 11.9**
>
> Make the attributes of the *Distance* class private.

Class Scope

The attributes and methods of a class belong to that class's **scope**. This means that the member functions can access any other feature of the class, `private` or `public`, directly, without the need to specify them as parameters. Outside the class's scope (i.e. in application programs containing objects of this class), `public` members of the class can be accessed via the objects of that class; `private` members cannot.

Multiple Objects

Just as we might need several integer variables when writing a program, so it is likely that we will need more than a single object when creating applications.

For example, let's assume we need a program to read in two weights and determine which is the larger. Our program could follow the logic:

```
Read in first weight
Read in second weight
IF first weight > second weight THEN
    Display first weight
ELSE
    Display second weight
ENDIF
```

The coding for *main()* in this program is given in LISTING-11.4.

LISTING-11.4

More than One Object

```
void main()
{
  Weight w1;
  Weight w2;

  //*** Read in First Weight ***
  cout << "Enter pounds: ";
  int lbs;
  cin >> lbs;
  cout << "Enter ounces: ";
  int oz;
  cin >> oz;
  w1.setWeight(lbs, oz);
  //*** Read in second Weight ***
  cout << "Enter pounds: ";
  cin >> lbs;
  cout << "Enter ounces: ";
  cin >> oz;
  w2.setWeight(lbs, oz);
  //*** Display larger weight ***
  if(w1.convertToMetric() > w2.convertToMetric())
      cout << "Larger weight is " << w1.getPounds() << " lbs "
      << w1.getOunces() << " oz";
  else
      cout << "Larger weight is " << w2.getPounds()<< " lbs "
      << w2.getOunces() << " oz";
}
```

A graphical representation of the objects created by the program above is shown in FIG-11.6.

FIG-11.6

Creating Multiple Objects

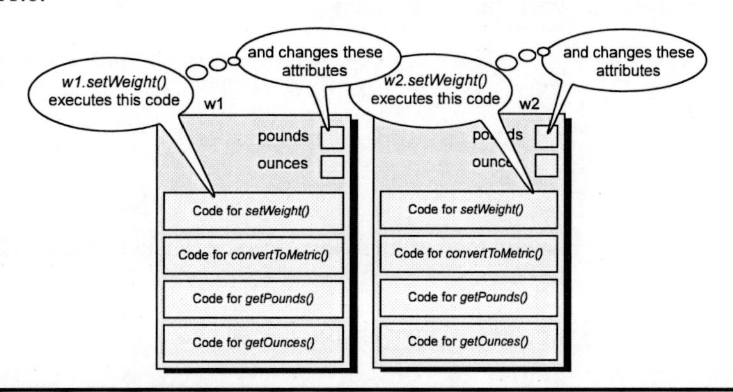

PROGRAMMING EXERCISE 11.10

Type in and run the program given in LISTING-11.4. Use the original version of the *Weight* class (as defined in *Weight.cpp*) in your program.

Does the program produce the correct result?

PROGRAMMING EXERCISE 11.11

Write a program, similar to that in LISTING-11.4, which displays the longer of two distances.

Check the program operates correctly using the distances, 3yds 2ft 8in and 1 yd 2ft 11in.

When a program is executing a method within an object, that object is known as the **current object**. Hence, during execution of the line

```
w1.setWeight(7,3);
```

w1 is the current object.

TASK 11.5

What is the current object during execution of the line

```
w2.getPounds();
```

Designing a Class

The class designer has a difficult task on his hands. In creating a new class he has to attempt to predict what uses the application programmer is likely to require from the objects created in the application program. If the class designer doesn't build the correct features into the original class, then the application programmer may find it difficult or impossible to achieve the effects required.

For example, let's say the application programmer, having assigned values to two *Weight* objects (*w1* and *w2*), wishes to add *w2* to *w1*; how is this going to be achieved?

It is possible, but creates a rather complex piece of code.

We could try the line

```
w1.setWeight(w1.getPounds()+w2.getPounds(),
             w1.getOunces()+w2.getOunces());
```

but this won't work if the expression

```
w1.getOunces()+w2.getOunces()
```

gives a total of more than 15 ounces and hence supplies an invalid parameter to *setWeight()*.

A more foolproof approach would be

```
int carrypounds = (w1.getOunces()+w2.getOunces())/16;
w1.setWeight(w1.getPounds()+w2.getPounds()+carrypounds,
(w1.getOunces()+w2.getOunces())%16);
```

As you can see, the limited operations of the *Weight* class are making the application programmer's job difficult.

As a starting point, the class designer will often create *set* (also known as **mutator methods**) and *get* (also called **accessor methods**) methods for each attribute in a class. We already have *getPounds()* and *getOunces()* in the *Weight* class.

Occasionally, a single operation will set more than one attribute if those attributes are closely linked. For example, the *Weight* class uses *setWeight()* to set both the *pounds* and *ounces* attributes, rather than separate *setPounds()* and *setOunces()* operations. The reasoning behind this being that in most cases the application programmer will want to set both values *(pounds* and *ounces*) at the same time.

However, if a *Customer* class contained both *name* and *address* as attributes, the class designer would create separate *set* methods for each of these attributes (*setName()* and *setAddress()*) since the two attributes are not closely linked.

In the next section of this chapter we'll add more functions to the *Weight* and *Distance* classes to make them more useful to the application programmer.

Summary

- **A class is the blueprint** for a structure containing data and functions designed to operate on that data.
- **Using Unified Modelling Language**(UML) a class is shown in the form of a diagram.
- An **object** is an **instance** of a class.
- In C++ classes are defined in a **class** statement.
- **To create an object** in C++ use the following format:

```
class_name object_name;
```

- A class normally has both **private** and **public** members.
- When an object is created, private members of that object can only be accessed through public functions; public members can be accessed freely.
- **Access to public members** takes the form

```
object_name.public_member_name
```

- All members of a class have **class scope**. This means all members can be accessed freely within the code defining the methods of the class.
- **As a general rule**, classes should contain methods to set and get each of its attributes.
- Classes should be designed with the possible requirements of the end-user in mind.

OTHER CLASS OPTIONS

Member Functions Variations

Various categories of functions arise when writing the methods of a class. Examples of these are described below.

Inline Methods

In a previous chapter we introduced the idea of inline functions. Inline methods can also be defined within a class.

The simplest way of creating an inline method is to include the code for the routine involved within the class definition. Hence, in the *Weight* class, we could change the *convertToMetric()* method to an inline function by rewriting the *Weight* class definition to read:

```
class Weight
{
    private:
        int pounds;
        int ounces;
    public:
        void setWeight(int,int);
        double convertToMetric()
        {
            return (pounds * 16 + ounces) *0.283495;
        }
        int getPounds();
        int getOunces();
};
```

An alternative way of creating an inline function is to add the term `inline` to the method declaration and definition shown in the code below:

```
class Weight
{
    private:
        int pounds;
        int ounces;
    public:
        void setWeight(int,int);
        inline double convertToMetric();
        int getPounds();
        int getOunces();
};


inline double Weight::convertToMetric()
{
    return (pounds * 16 + ounces) *0.0283495;
}
```

Note that by using the first approach there is no requirement to use the term `inline` at any point. As with other inline functions, actually implementing the routine as inline is at the compiler's discretion.

Inline is best applied to small, frequently used routines.

PROGRAMMING EXERCISE 11.12

In the *Weight* class, make *convertToMetric()* an inline function.

In the *Distance* class, make *converToMetric()* and inline function.

A Class as a Parameter Type

As we saw previously, adding one weight to another is rather difficult using the methods currently available in the *Weight* class. We can make the application programmer's job easier by adding a new method to the *Weight* class which is specifically designed to do this.

The function will take a *Weight* object as an argument and add this to the current *Weight* object.

The new method (*addToWeight()*) is coded as part of the *Weight* class:

Note that the normally private attributes of object *w* can be accessed in this method because we are within a *Weight* class method and w is an instance of that class.

```
void Weight::addToWeight(Weight w)
{
    int totaloz;

    totaloz = (pounds+w.pounds)*16+ounces+w.ounces;
    pounds = totaloz/16;
    ounces = totaloz%16;
};
```

The application programmer can now use this new method to add *w2* to *w1* with the statement:

```
w1.addToWeight(w2); //*** Add w2 to w1 ***
```

PROGRAMMING EXERCISE 11.13

Add the method given above to the *Weight* class.

Modify your previous version of *main()* to perform the following logic:

```
Read in values for two weights
Display the values of both weights
Add the second weight's value to the first weight
Display the value of the first weight
```

PROGRAMMING EXERCISE 11.14

Create an *addToDistance()* method for the *Distance* class. This new method should take a *Distance* object as a parameter and add that parameter's value to the current *Distance* object.

Test your new method by writing a version of *main()* that follows logic similar to that given in PROGRAMMING EXERCISE 11.13.

Overloading a Method

We already have a method, *setWeight()*, for assigning a value to a *Weight* object. However, that operation takes two integer values, but it would be useful to have a second *setWeight()* operation that takes a real value as a parameter. For example, we might want to set a *Weight* object to 4 lbs 8 oz using the real value 4.5.

C++ is quite happy to allow two or more methods to have the same name as long as their parameters differ in type, order, or number. However, two functions cannot share the same name if they differ only by the type of value returned.

Creating multiple functions with the same name is called **function overloading**.

TASK 11.6

Which of the following overloads for a function *f()* would cause a conflict?

```
void f()                    void f(int, int)
void f(int)                 void f(float)
void f(int, char)           void f(long)
void f(char, int)           int f(float)
```

In the *Weight* class we can overload the *setWeight()* method with the following code:

The *Weight* class declaration also requires to be changed by adding the line

```
void setWeight(double);
```

```
public void setWeight(double v)
{
    if (v < 0)
        return;
    pounds = (int)v;
    ounces = (int)((v - int(v))*16+0.5);
}
```

When an overloaded method is called, C++ determines which version of the method is to be executed by examining the parameters of the call. In the case of *setWeight()*, if two integer parameters are specified, then the original version of the routine is executed; where the parameter is a `double` value, the new version of *setWeight()* is run. Now we can copy 4.5 to *w1* with the statement:

```
w1.setWeight(4.5);
```

PROGRAMMING EXERCISE 11.15

Add a new *setDistance(double v)* method to your *Distance* class which allows the value in a `double` to be copied to a *Distance* class object.

Test your code with a *main()* function which executes the following logic:

```
Read in real value
Copy the real value into Distance object d1
Display the contents of d1
```

The Assignment Operator and Objects

The assignment operator (=) can be used to assign the values held in the attributes of one object to the corresponding attributes of a second object of the same class. Hence, we can write:

```
w2 = w1;
```

which will copy the values in *w1.pounds* and *w1.ounces* to *w2.pounds* and *w2.ounces* (see FIG-11.7).

FIG-11.7

Copying from One Object to Another

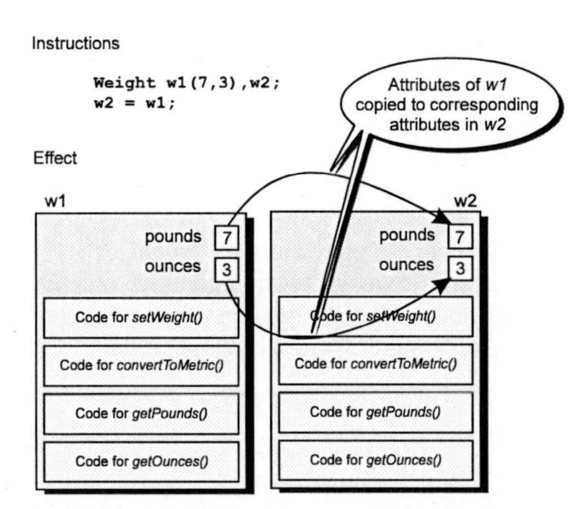

The copying of each attribute from one object to another is known as **member-wise assignment**.

Returning a Class Value from a Function

Another requirement which arises in most programs is to add two values and store the result in a third variable. This situation is reflected in the statement:

```
no3 = no1 + no2;
```

Although we can add one weight to another using *addToWeight()*, we have no way of adding two weights and storing the result in a third weight. To achieve this we need to add yet another new method to the *Weight* class. This method adds the two weights and returns their sum as another *Weight* value. The method, which we will call *sumWeights()*, is coded as shown below:

```
public Weight Weight::sumWeights(Weight w)
{
    Weight ans;    //Stores result
    int temp = (pounds+w.pounds)*16 + ounces + w.ounces;
    ans.pounds = temp/16;
    ans.ounces = temp%16;
    return ans;
}
```

We also need to add the line

```
Weight sumWeights(Weight);
```

to the `public` section of the *Weight* class definition. Now the sum of *w1* and *w2* can be stored in *w3* using the statement:

```
w3 = w1.sumWeights(w2);
```

Alternatively, we could write

```
w3 = w2.sumWeights(w1);
```

PROGRAMMING EXERCISE 11.16

Add a *sumDistances()* method (which returns the sum of two distances) to the *Distance* class.

Test your routine by storing the sum of *d1* and *d2* in a third *Distance* object, *d3*, and displaying *d3*'s contents.

Comparing Objects

With normal variables (`int`, `float`, `char`, etc) we can compare two values with statements such as:

```
if (no1 == no2)
```

However, relation operators (such as `==`) can only operate on the standard variable types, so if we want to compare two *Weight* objects, we will need to add appropriate methods to the *Weight* class. For example, we could test if two *Weight* objects are equal by adding the following method to the *Weight* class:

```
int Weight::same(Weight w)
{
    if (pounds == w.pounds && ounces == w.ounces)
        return 1;
    else
        return 0;
}
```

This allows application programmers using *Weight* objects to write code such as:

```
if(w1.same(w2))
    cout << "The weights are equal";
else
    cout << "The weights are different";
```

PROGRAMMING EXERCISE 11.17

Add an *isLarger()* method to the *Distance* class, allowing two distances to be compared. The routine should return 1 if the current *Distance* object is longer than the parameter object, otherwise 0 should be returned.

Using this routine, write a version of *main()* that reads in two weights and displays the larger of the two.

The `this` Pointer

If we stop to take a deeper look at how objects work, we're going to discover a problem. So far we've given the impression that every object created has its own copy of all the features designed for its class (see FIG-11.16). But the truth is that this would be an unacceptably inefficient way of going about things. Of course, each object needs its own copy of any attributes specified for the class, but creating duplicates of each method serves no useful purpose and would occupy an excessive amount of memory. Although we can continue to think of each object in this theoretical manner, the reality is that each method defined within a class is held only once and each object created employs a reference-type value to locate each of its methods. The setup is shown in FIG-11.8.

FIG-11.8

Each Object References its Methods

For simplicity, only the original set of methods are shown.

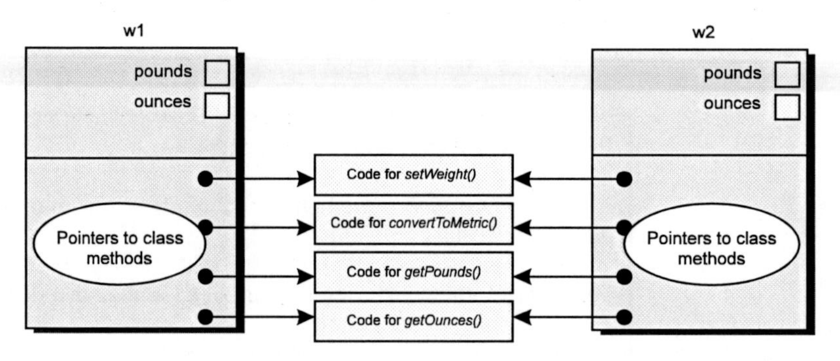

This raises a question about how a method is executed. If all objects from a given class share a common set of routines, how can the program tell which object's attributes are to be accessed?

For example, the line

```
pounds = lbs;
```

appears in the *setWeight()* method. When this line is executed, how does the program know which object to access? Should it be *w1.pounds* that is assigned the value or *w2.pounds*?

You might be tempted to think that the line that calls the routine, such as

```
w1.setWeight(12,8);
```

supplies this information. But the object doing the calling (*w1*) isn't one of the parameters to *setWeight()* so that information doesn't appear to be passed to the method.

In fact, C++ adds a hidden parameter to every method in a class. This hidden parameter is a reference variable, specifying which object actually called the routine. The hidden parameter is called `this` and can be accessed by any of the class methods to access the calling object.

So, although a method may start with the line

```
void Weight::setWeight(int lbs, int oz)
```

in fact, C++ effectively modifies this to become

```
void Weight::setWeight(int lbs, int oz, Weight& this)
```

In addition, any line within a method of the class that makes reference to an attribute as in the line

```
pounds = lbs;
```

has the term `this->` inserted before the attribute name. Hence, the line becomes

```
this->pounds = lbs;
```

So, when an application program contains the line

```
w1.setWeight(7,3);
```

`this` will contain the address of *w1*.

It is possible to explicitly access `this` within your program code. For example, if a method was coded as

```
void Weight::setWeight(int pounds, int ounces)
{
    if (pounds < 0 || ounces < 0 || ounces > 15)
        return;
    pounds = pounds;
    ounces = ounces;
}
```

most of its lines would be ambiguous, since it is not clear if *pounds* and *ounces* refer to the parameters or the attributes. However, this is cleared up using the `this` term:

```
void Weight::setWeight(int pounds, int ounces)
{
    if (pounds < 0 || ounces < 0 || ounces > 15)
        return;
    this->pounds = pounds;
    this->ounces = ounces;
}
```

It is also necessary to make use of `this` when you need to refer to the current object when writing methods within the object's class. For example, let's assume we need another method in the *Weight* class which returns the smaller of two weights. Such a routine would employ the following logic:

```
IF the current weight is less than the parameter weight THEN
    return the current weight
ELSE
    return the parameter weight
ENDIF
```

This can be coded as:

```
public Weight Weight::smaller(Weight w)
{
    if ((pounds * 16 + ounces) < (w.pounds * 16 + w.ounces))
        return *this;
    else
        return w;
}
```

Notice how `this` is used to return the current weight.

> **PROGRAMMING EXERCISE 11.18**
>
> Write a *smaller()* method for the *Distance* class which returns the shorter of two distances.
>
> Using this method, write a *main()* function which reads in two distances and assigns the smaller of the two to a third *Distance* object.

Private Methods

Some of the methods of *Weight* class make use of the expression `pounds*16+ounces;` which calculates the total number of ounces in a weight. It may be useful to create a method, *toOunces()*, to perform this operation. Yet, *toOunces()* is not a basic operation of the class, rather it is a subsidiary function which comes in useful in coding the main methods of the class. As such, we would not want the application programmer to have access to the *toOunces()* function.

To ensure *toOunces()* is not available to the application programmer, we declare *toOunces()* as a `private` method of *Weight*. This prevents programmers using *Weight* objects from accessing the routine, yet still allows it to be used in coding other methods in the *Weight* class. Because the function requires little in the way of code and could be used by many other routines in the class, it could be useful to make *toOunces()* an inline method. The definition for the *Weight* class now becomes

```
class Weight
{
    private:
        int pounds;
        int ounces;
        inline int toOunces();
    public:
```

```
        void setWeight(int,int);
        void setWeight(double);
        inline double convertToMetric();
        int getPounds();
        int getOunces();
        void addToWeight(Weight);
        Weight sumWeights(Weight);
        int same(Weight);
};
```

and the new method is coded as:

```
inline int Weight::toOunces()
{
    return pounds * 16 + ounces;
}
```

We can now use the function in the definition of the other *Weight* methods. For example, *convertToMetric()* could now be coded as:

```
double Weight::convertToMetric()
{
    return toOunces()*0.0283495;
};
```

The code for the *addToWeight()* operation would become:

```
void Weight::addToWeight(Weight w)
{
    int temp = toOunces() + w.toOunces();
    pounds = temp / 16;
    ounces = temp % 16;
}
```

PROGRAMMING EXERCISE 11.19

Create a private *toInches()* method for the *Distance* class which converts the distance held within the object from yards, feet, and inches to inches.

Using this new method, update the *addToDistance(Distance d)* method for the *Distance.*

Constructors

If we were to call the *getPounds()* for some object before using its *setWeight()* method, we would get an undefined value returned. This is because the attributes, *pounds* and *ounces,* are assigned space when a *Weight* object is created, but that space continues to hold any random 1s and 0s that were already in the allocated space.

Although this may not present a problem, there will be times when the application programmer will want to create an object with known start-up values assigned to that object's attributes.

Let's assume we want to be able to specify the initial value of all *Weight* objects.

Unfortunately, C++ does not allow attributes of a class to be declared with an initial value. Therefore, being a class definition with lines such as

```
class Weight
{
    private:
```

```
int pounds = 0;     //Invalid
int ounces = 0;     //Invalid
```

are illegal and will result in syntax error messages when you attempt a compilation.

To achieve the results we require, we have to add a new type of method, known as a **constructor**, to our class.

Unlike other methods, a constructor is executed by the program at the instant an object variable's space is allocated.

A constructor method is used to initialise class objects. A constructor always has the same name as the class itself. Although a constructor can have any number of parameters, it cannot return a value; even the term `void` is not allowed as a return type. Instead any mention of a return type is omitted.

To create a constructor, we begin by adding the constructor method to the class declaration:

A constructor never has a return type

Constructors have the same name as the class

```
class Weight
{
    private:
        int pounds;
        int ounces;
        inline int [illegible]unces();
    public:
        Weight(int,int);
        void setWeight(int,int);
        void setWeight(Weight);
        inline double convertToMetric();
        int getPounds();
        int getOunces();
        void addToWeight(Weight);
        Weight sumWeights(Weight);
        int same(Weight);
};
```

This is followed by the constructor's code:

We need to specify a default value for the attributes should the parameters be invalid. Without this the attributes would start up with undefined values, just as before.

```
Weight::Weight(int lbs, int oz)
{
    if (lbs < 0 || oz < 0 || oz > 15)
    {
        pounds = 0;
        ounces = 0;
    }
    else
    {
        pounds = lbs;
        ounces = oz;
    }
};
```

Objects of the class can now be declared with statements such as

```
Weight w1(5,0);
```

which sets *w1* to 5 lbs 0 oz.

Of course, we won't want to initialise every variable to a specific value, and so we might still want to use statements such as:

```
Weight totalweight;
```

It will, therefore, come as a bit of a shock to discover that this no longer works! Instead, we get the error message:

```
Could not find a match for "Weight::Weight()" in function main()
```

The Default Constructor

Why did this work fine before we added a constructor? The truth is that the C++ always calls a constructor when a class object is defined. Where no constructor has been defined explicitly within the class, the compiler generates a default constructor with no parameters and this is called at the start of the class object's lifetime. Although this default constructor performs no useful task, it satisfies the requirement that a constructor should be called every time a new object is created.

ans and *w1* are assumed to be instances of *Weight* class

When a constructor is defined by the programmer, no default constructor is created. In the case of *Weight* class, this means that we now have only one constructor (as defined above) which requires two `int` parameters and it is not possible to define an object of class *Weight* without supplying the parameters required by that constructor.

Overloading the Constructor

To overcome this problem, we need to overload the constructor with a second version which requires no parameters. The class definition would then contain the line

```
class Weight
{
    private :
        int pounds;
        int pounds;
        int ounces;
        inline int toOunces();
    public:
        Weight();
        Weight(int,int);
```

and this second constructor would be coded as:

```
Weight::Weight()
{
    pounds = 0;
    ounces = 0;
};
```

Now, creating objects with or without parameters is acceptable:

```
Weight w1;          //OK - uses the zero-argument constructor
Weight w2(3,10);    //OK - uses the two-argument constructor
```

Constructors and Default Parameter Values

It is perfectly valid to define a constructor (or any other method in a class) with default values in its parameter list. For example, we could replace the line in the *Weight* class which defines the two-argument constructor to read:

```
class Weight
    {
        private :
            int pounds;
            int pounds;
            int ounces;
            inline int toOunces();
        public:
            Weight(int=0,int=0);
```

There is no need to change the code of the constructor function. This change now allows us three ways of creating a *Weight* object:

```
Weight w1(4,9);
Weight w2(7);
Weight w3;
```

TASK 11.7

What values would be assigned to the *pounds* and *ounces* attributes for objects *w1, w2* and *w3* created in the lines above?

In fact, by using default values in the parameter list we've eliminated the need for the second constructor definition, since our updated constructor now performs the same task. The compiler would also object to the ambiguity caused by the two versions of the constructor if we were to leave the zero-argument constructor in place.

TASK 11.8

Write (as a paper only exercise) a new constructor for the *Weight* class that takes a single `double` value. Hence, if we declare an object with the line

```
Weight v(7.5);
```

the result would be that *v.pounds* = 7 and *v.ounces* = 8.

PROGRAMMING EXERCISE 11.20

Write two constructors for the *Distance* class.

The first should take three integer parameters and use these to set the value of yards, feet and inches. If any of the parameters are invalid, all attributes should be set to zero. Parameters, if omitted when the constructor is called, should all default to zero. The second constructor should accept a `double` value, with the integral part being assigned to the yards attribute, while the fraction makes up the feet and inches.

The Copy Constructor

Another important form of the constructor is one which takes an existing object of the same class and copies its values to the object being created. For example, if we begin by creating a *Weight* object *w1* in the usual way:

```
Weight w1(7,3);
```

we can then create a second *Weight* object with the same attribute settings as *w1*:

```
Weight w2(w1);
```

For this last line to be valid, the *Weight* class would need to contain a constructor of the form:

```
Weight::Weight(const Weight& w)
{
    pounds = w.pounds;
    ounces = w.ounces;
}
```

In fact, C++ also adds this constructor for you automatically. And, unlike the zero-argument, default constructor, this one is not removed as soon as you create a constructor of your own. This constructor, known as the **copy constructor**, will only be removed if you write your own copy constructor with exactly the same parameters as the default one. This may be necessary if your class contains any pointer attributes.

> **PROGRAMMING EXERCISE 11.21**
>
> Check out the operation of the copy constructor in your *Distance* class by writing a program which sets one *Distance* object to 3 yds 2 ft 10 in and then creates a second object containing the same value.
>
> Display the contents of this second object.

Typecasting and Constructors

As we saw in an earlier chapter, C++ offers us automatic typecasting between data types inherent to the language. Hence, we may write

```
int no = 'A'
```

with impunity knowing that the capital A will be stored as the value 65 in the variable *no*.

This feature would be useful if it could be extended to cover classes, allowing us to write statements such as :

```
Weight w1, w2, w3;

w1 = 7;                 //w1 = 7 lbs 0 oz
w2 = 8.25;              //w2 = 8 lbs 4 oz
w3 = Weight(5,7);       //w3 = 5 lbs 7 oz
```

All of this is, in fact, possible - but only if we have included the appropriate constructors in the *Weight* class. When we attempt to assign a value of one type to an object of another, C++ examines the constructors defined for the receiving object's class and, where it finds a match for the type to be cast, it uses the information in that constructor to perform a type conversion. Hence, assuming the *Weight* class contains a constructor with the signature `Weight(double);` (as you produced in TASK 11.7) and another with the signature `Weight(int=0, int=0)`, all three conversions required in the code above can be handled.

In the first line (`w1 = 7;`) C++ converts 7 to a *Weight* object by using the `Weight(int=0,int=0)` constructor. The first value is assumed to be 7 and the second zero, giving a weight of 7 lbs 0 oz which is copied into *w1*. The second line uses the `Weight(double)` constructor to convert 8.25 to a weight of 8 lbs 4 oz. In the final line, involving two values (5 and 7), we need to use the `Weight(int,int)` constructor directly to create a *Weight* object which is then copied to *w3*.

Destructors

At the start of an object's life its constructor is called and at the end of its life (when its space is deallocated), its **destructor** is executed.

Like the constructor, C++ will provide a default destructor method if none is explicitly defined in the class. The default version of this method doesn't actually do anything, so a class needs to override it in order to do something useful. When the class designer decides to include a destructor in the design of a class, that destructor's name must start with a tilde (~) followed by the class name. For example, if we were to add a destructor to the *Weight* class it would be called `~Weight()`. There are other restrictions on the destructor's definition: it must not return a value, cannot take parameters and must not be overloaded.

The commonest reason for including a destructor in a class is to deallocate any dynamic space reserved by an object. This might occur if the object has a pointer as one of its attributes and that pointer is used to reference dynamically allocated space. However, there are other reasons why a destructor might be required. For example, if a class was designed to communicate via a modem, it might be necessary to create a class destructor which transmitted appropriate signals to indicate termination of the communication link.

The program code below adds a trivial destructor to the *Weight* class causing the message "Weight object destroyed" to be displayed whenever a *Weight* object reaches the end of its life.

```
class Weight
{
    private :
        int pounds;
        int pounds;
        int ounces;
        inline int toOunces();
    public:
        Weight(int=0,int=0);
        ~Weight();
```

The destructor is coded as:

```
Weight::~Weight()
{
    cout<<"Weight object destroyed"<<endl;
}
```

This new code can be tested with a *main()* function such as:

Use of the *getch()* function requires a `#include<conio.h>` statement at the start of the program.

```
void main()
{
    Weight w1(7,3);
    {
        Weight w2(7.5)
        getch();
    }
    getch();
}
```

w2 destructor executed here

w1 destructor executed here

w2 will be destroyed when execution reaches the end of the inner block. At that point we should see the message *Weight object destroyed* appear on the screen. As the program terminates, *w1* will be destroyed and the message should appear for a second time.

PROGRAMMING EXERCISE 11.22

Create a destructor for the *Distance* class which displays the message "Distance object destroyed".
Test the operation of the destructor in a *main()* function, similar to the example given above.

More Class Features

Constants

For some classes there are certain fixed values that it seems sensible to associate with that class. For example, if we implemented a *Date* class we might want to associate the term *NewYear* with 1st of January; in the *Math* class the term *pi* is associated with the value 3.14159265 (but to more decimal places).

We can set up such constants as class attributes by preceding them with the usual term, `const`. For example, if we had designed the *Weight* class for a program involving postage, we might want to set the various weight limits on letters, and parcels.

This can be done as shown below:

```
class Weight
{
    public:
        //*** Maximum weights in ounces for each type ***
        const int letter;
        const int parcel;

    private:
        int pounds;
        int ounces;
        .
        .
```

Notice that we have not specified the values of the constants. Attempting to write

```
const int letter = 21;
```

as part of the *Weight* class definition would produce a compilation error. Instead, we need to initialise the constants in the class constructor. But even this has a strange syntax with the constant's value being given between the constructor heading and the body of the constructor as shown below:

```
Weight::Weight(int lbs, int oz)
:letter(21),parcel(7055)
{
    if(lbs < 0 || oz < 0 || oz > 15)
    {
        pounds = 0;
        ounces = 0;
    }
    else
    {
        pounds = lbs;
        ounces = oz;
    }
}
```

The exact syntax for initialising constants is shown in FIG-11.9.

FIG-11.9

Initialising Constant Attributes

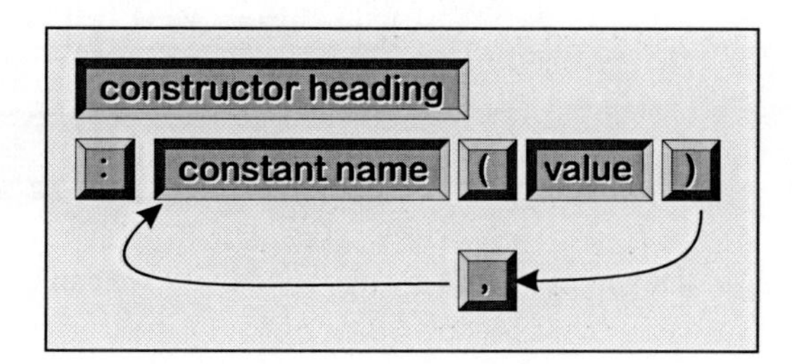

It is possible to initialise constants to a different value in each of the objects created. This is done by using a variable or expression within the parentheses. A trivial example of this might be

```
Weight::Weight(int lbs, int oz)
:letter(lbs*2),parcel(7055)
```

where *letter* is set to twice the value of the parameter *lbs*.

More usefully, we might introduce additional parameters to the constructor with the intention of using these to initialise the constants:

```
Weight::Weight(int lbs, int oz, int a, int b)
:letter(a),parcel(b)
```

This would also require the prototype within the *Weight* class to be changed to:

```
Weight(int,int,int,int);
```

However, the most likely scenario is to initialise the constants to identical values in every object that is created.

Any feature of a class that uses the term `const` cannot have its value modified once the object has been created. So, although we have defined *letter* and *parcel* as `public`, there is no danger of the application programmer modifying their values.

These constants can be used anywhere in the methods of the class or in any other code where objects of the *Weight* class are used. Hence, *main()* might contain the line:

```
cout<<"Upper limit for 21p letters is "<<w1.letter<<" ounces";
```

There is one aspect of this feature that has to be questioned - *if the value held in a constant is fixed and every object assigns the same value to that constant, why do we need a copy of that value in every single object that is created when one copy would be sufficient?*

The answer is - we don't. But as things stand, any attribute defined within a class is duplicated in every object of that class. (see FIG-11.10)

FIG-11.10

Duplicated Constants

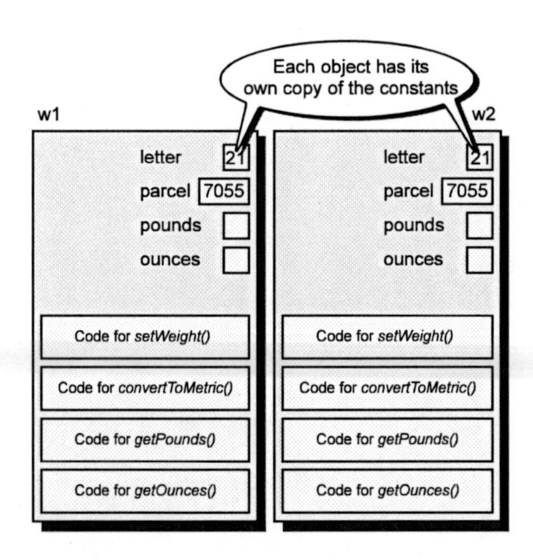

However, there's a way round that - we can declare an attribute as `static`.

Static Attributes

If we use the term `static` beside any feature of a class it means that only a single copy of that feature is ever allocated space and that all objects of the class access that single copy. Therefore, by changing the definition of the *Weight* constants to

```
class Weight
{
    public:
        static const int letter;
        static const int parcel;
```

there is now only a single copy of each attribute (see FIG-11.11).

FIG-11.11

Sharing Static Attributes

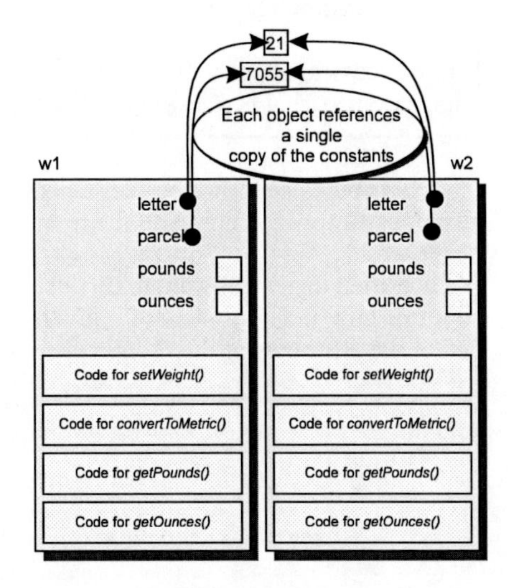

However, we need to use a different method of initialisation when dealing with `static` constants. Rather than initialise the constants at the beginning of the class's constructors, the lines

```
const int Weight::letter=21;
const int Weight::parcel=7055;
```

should be inserted after the class definition as shown below:

```
class Weight
{
    public :
        static const int letter;
        static const int parcel;
    private:
        int pounds;
        int ounces;
        int toOunces();
    public:
        Weight(int=0,int=0);
            .
            .
};
const int Weight::letter=21;
const int Weight::parcel=7055;
```

Another characteristic of a `static` feature is that those features exist even when no objects of that class have been created. When you want to access `static` attributes before any objects are created, you need to use the class name and scope resolution operator. Hence, we can access the constant *letter* with the term

```
Weight::letter
```

allowing statements such as:

```
cout<<"Upper limit for 21p letters is "<<Weight::letter<<" oz";
```

Of course, it is also still possible to access the constants through any objects that are created, so we can still write *w1.letter* within our code after *w1* has been defined.

PROGRAMMING EXERCISE 11.23

Add two `static` constants to the *Distance* class:

metre = 39
centimetre = 0.3937

Test accessing these values by using both the class name and object name approaches. That is, *Distance::metre* and *d1.centimetre.*

Static attributes need not be constants. It is also possible to create static variable attributes simply by including the term `static`.

It's not often that we'll want to do this, but one simple example might be to keep a count of how many objects of a given class are in existence. For example, if we define the attributes of the *Weight* class as

```
class Weight
{
    public:
        static const int letter;
        static const int parcel;
        static int count;
    private:
        int pounds;
        int ounces;
            .
            .
```

with the intention of incrementing the static attribute *count* each time an object is created (by adding the appropriate statement to each constructor), then we must start by ensuring *count* is initialised to zero at the start of the program by using the statement

```
int Weight::count = 0;
```

immediately after the class declarations.

Next we need to make sure *count* is incremented each time an object is created. This is achieved by adding the line

```
count++;
```

to each of the constructors as shown below:

```
Weight::Weight(int lbs, int oz)
{
    if (lbs < 0 || oz < 0 || oz > 15)
    {
        pounds = 0;
        ounces = 0;
    }
    else
    {
        pounds = lbs;
        ounces = oz;
```

```
    }
    count++;
}


Weight::Weight (double v)
{
    if (v < 0)
    {
        pounds = 0;
        ounces = 0;
    }
    else
    {
        pounds = (int)v;
        ounces = (int)((v - (int)v)*16);
    }
    count++;
}
```

then we can find out how many objects are in existence at any time by accessing *count:*

```
void main()
{
    cout<<"There are "<<Weight::count<<" Weight objects\n";
    Weight w1(4,2);
    cout<<"There are "<<Weight::count<<" Weight objects\n";
    Weight w2(11.8);
    cout<<"There are "<<Weight::count<<" Weight objects\n";
}
```

PROGRAMMING EXERCISE 11.24

Add a static *count* attribute to the *Distance* class. Initialise *count* to zero and increment it each time a *Distance* object is created.

Test your program to ensure that count increments correctly.

To differentiate between attributes which are created in every object of a given class and those that are created only once and shared between the objects, the terms **instance attribute** (occurs in every object) and **class attribute** (shared by objects) are used. Hence, *pounds* is a instance attribute of the *Weight* class, while *letter* is a class attribute.

Class Methods

It's not only attributes that can be declared static, methods can also be static. Such routines are known as **class methods** or **static methods**. And, as with attributes, class methods are available even when an object of the class has not yet been defined.

There are two main reasons for having static methods.

You'll see in the example above that *count* has been declared as `public`. If it were `private` the statement

```
cout<<"There are "<<Weight::count<<" Weight objects\n";
```

would produce an error message, since we cannot access `private` methods of a class - even if they are static.

But we also know it's good policy to keep attributes private, for as things stand, it is possible for the application programmer to write

```
Weight::count = 23;
```

inside *main()* and destroy the purpose of *count.*

However, if we make *count* `private`, we are going to have to write a new method, *getCount(),* in order to access the *count* attribute.

Now, although we declare these methods like any others, that would mean the methods can't be accessed until an object of the *Weight* class is declared. This leads to the situation where, when no *Weight* objects have been defined, *count* exists but it cannot be accessed. However, if we declare a method to be `static` it will exist independently of objects of the class and therefore can accessed at any time.

To summarise, it is best to make methods which are designed solely to access static attributes static themselves. The relevant code for the *Weight* class is given below:

```
class Weight
{
    public:
        static const int letter;
        static const int parcel;
    private:
        static int count;
        int pounds;
        int ounces;
        int toOunces();
    public:
        static int getCount();
                 .
                 .
};
```

The new routine codes as:

```
int Weight::getCount()
{
    return count;
}
```

Notice that the term `static` is not repeated in the method's definition

> **PROGRAMMING EXERCISE 11.25**
>
> Make a similar change to the *Distance* class, so that its *count* property is private and accessed through a static *getCount()* method.
>
> Modify the destructor of the *Distance* class so that it decrements *count.*
>
> Write a version of *main()* which checks that *count* functions correctly as *Distance* objects are created and destroyed.

A second reason for creating class methods is when a set of methods have a tight commonality but do not require specific objects. A good example of this is Java's *Math* class which contains class methods such as *sqrt(), sin(), cos(),* etc.

These routines obviously belong together since they are all of a mathematical nature and yet do not involve *Math* objects in their results. Rather, the results of these functions will tend to be of type `double` or `int`.

By including related functions in a single class, the application programmer can write statements such as

```
double x = Math::sin(1.3);
```

calling up the class method at any time without the need to create objects of that class.

Items of a class which are declared as `static` are usually referred to as **class** features. Hence, *letter* is a **class constant**, *count* is a **class variable**, and *getCount()* is a **class method**.

Overloading Operators

When using standard variables, we can write expressions such as

```
no1 += no;
```

but if we wanted to perform a similar instruction using two *Weight* objects we would have to write

```
w1.addToWeight(w2);
```

and attempting to write

```
w1 += w2;
```

would fail because C++ would not know how to apply the += operator to two *Weight* objects (*w1* and *w2*).

However, C++ allows us to link a sequence of instructions to operators such as +, *, +=, etc. We already know how to overload a function by defining alternative versions of the function with differing parameters, but we are free to do the same with operators such as +=, *, /, etc.

To overload the += operator so that it can handle *Weight* objects we need to make changes to the *Weight* class declaration to include the line:

```
void operator +=(Weight);
```

This new line states that the *Weight* class contains a method for the += operator and that this method takes a *Weight* object argument but returns no result. If we think of the term `operator +=` as a function name, we can see that the syntax for this new method is no different from the other methods in the class.

The new method is then coded as:

```
void Weight::operator +=(Weight w)
{
    int totaloz = toOunces() + w.toOunces();
    pounds = totaloz / 16;
    ounces = totaloz % 16;
}
```

If we continue to think of operator += as the function's name, then it follows that the application programmer, having created two *Weight* objects, *w1* and *w2*, can add the *Weight* in *w2* to that already held in *w1* with the statement:

```
w1.operator+=(w2);
```

In fact, this is perfectly valid C++ and can be used, but since we are defining an operator, this syntax can be relaxed and the more familiar form can be used:

```
w1 += w2;
```

Despite its more relaxed format, you should be aware that this second form is still a request to execute the *operator+=()* method defined in object *w1*.

By defining a += operation for the *Weight* class we have eliminated the need for the *addToWeight()* method (which contains exactly the same code).

Relational Operators

Relational operators such as <, ==, >=, !=, etc. can also be defined as methods within a class. Knowing this we can rename *Weight*'s *same()* method as *operator ==()* which allows the application programmer to replace a statement such as

```
if(w1.same(w2))
```

with

```
if(w1 == w2)
```

An updated version of the *Weight* class with operators replacing more traditionally named methods is shown in LISTING-11.5 (not all features given in the previous pages are shown in the class).

LISTING-11.5

Overloading Operators

```
class Weight
{
  private:
       int pounds;
       int ounces;
       int toOunces();
  public:
       Weight(int=0,int=0);
       Weight(double);
       void setWeight(int,int);
       inline double convertToMetric();
       int getPounds();
       int getOunces();
       void operator +=(Weight);
       Weight operator +(Weight);
       int operator ==(Weight);
       Weight smaller(Weight w);
};

int Weight::toOunces()
{
  return (pounds*16 + ounces)*0.283495;
}

Weight::Weight(int lbs, int oz)
{
  if(lbs < 0 || oz < 0 || oz > 15)
  {
       pounds = 0;
       ounces = 0;
  }
  else
  {
       pounds = lbs;
       ounces = oz;
  }
}
```

continued on next page

LISTING-11.5
(continued)

Overloading Operators

```
Weight::Weight(double v)
{
   if (v < 0)
   }
         pounds = 0;
         ounces = 0;
   }
   else
   {
         pounds = (int)v;
         ounces = (int)((v-(int)v)*16+0.5)
   }

void Weight::setWeight(int lbs, int oz)
{
   if(lbs < 0 || oz < 0 || oz > 15)
         return;
   pounds = lbs;
   ounces = oz;
}

inline double Weight::convertToMetric()
{
   return (pounds * 16 + ounces)*0.0283495;
}

int Weight::getPounds()
{
   return pounds;
}

int Weight::getOunces()
{
   return ounces;
}

void Weight::operator+=(Weight w)
{
   int totaloz;

   totaloz = toOunces() + w.toOunces();
   pounds = totaloz/16;
   ounces = totaloz%16;
};

Weight Weight::operator +(Weight w)
{
   Weight ans;
   int temp = toOunces() + w.toOunces();
   ans.pounds = temp / 16;
   ans.ounces = temp % 16;
   return ans;
}

int Weight::operator ==(Weight w)
{
   if (toOunces()==w.toOunces())
         return 1;
   else
         return 0;
}

Weight Weight::smaller(Weight w)
{
   if(toOunces() < w.toOunces())
         return *this;
   else
         return w;
}
```

PROGRAMMING EXERCISE 11.26

In the *Distance* class, rename *isLarger()* so that the method overloads the > operator. Also change *sumDistances()* to overload + and *addToDistance()* to implement +=.

Finally, add an equality (==) method to the *Distance* class.

Check that your modifications function correctly by producing a *main()* function that performs the following logic:

w1, w2, w3 and *w4* are *Weight* objects.

```
Read in w1
Read in w2
Read in w3
Double the value in w1
Set w4 to the sum of w2 and w3
IF w1 > w4 THEN
    Display w1
ELSE
    IF w1 = w4 THEN
        Display "Weights are equal"
    ENDIF
ENDIF
```

Overloading the Increment and Decrement Operators

The increment (++) and decrement (--) operators can be used either before or after the variable being changed (prefix or postfix). For example:

```
++count ; //Prefix
count++ ; //Postfix
```

C++ requires that, when overloading these operators, the prefix and postfix versions be overloaded separately.

For example, let's assume we want to overload the ++ operator in the *Weight* class to add 1 ounce to the current weight. This will require two methods to be added to the *Weight* class. One of these will have the prototype:

```
void operator ++();
```

and this represents the prefix version of the operator. The postfix version must have a different prototype and this is:

```
void operator ++(int);
```

The `int` parameter is included only to distinguish the postfix version of the operation from the prefix version and serves no other purpose. It is not used in the coding of the routine.

The *Weight* class declaration now becomes:

```
class Weight
{
    private:
        int pounds;
        int ounces;
        int toOunces();
    public:
        Weight(int=0,int=0);
```

```
        Weight(double);
        void setWeight(int,int);
        inline double convertToMetric();
        int getPounds();
        int getOunces();
        void operator +=(Weight);
        Weight operator +(Weight);
        int operator ==(Weight);
        void operator ++();
        void operator ++(int);
        Weight smaller(Weight w);
};
```

The two routines are then coded as:

```
void Weight::operator ++()
{
    int totaloz;

    totaloz = toOunces() + 1;
    pounds = totaloz / 16;
    ounces = totaloz % 16;
}

void Weight::operator ++(int)
{
    int totaloz;

    totaloz = toOunces() + 1;
    pounds = totaloz / 16;
    ounces = totaloz % 16;
}
```

Notice that the `int` parameter is totally ignored when writing the method's code.

Actually, the code for these overloaded operators isn't quite right. They will work happily enough in stand-alone situations such as

```
w1++;
```

or

```
++w2;
```

but, should we attempt a statement like

```
w1 = ++w2;
```

then there will be a problem. What that problem is should be clearer if we rewrite the above statement as

```
w1 = w2.operator++();
```

which is a valid alternative. Now we can see that a function is being called and that we are assigning the value returned by that function to the object *w1*. Unfortunately, our ++ operations do not return any values.

We need to rewrite these functions so that a *Weight* value is returned by each. The updated versions are shown below:

```
Weight Weight::operator ++()
{
    int totaloz;
    Weight ans;

    totaloz = toOunces() + 1;
    ans.pounds = pounds = totaloz / 16;
    ans.ounces = ounces = totaloz % 16;
    return ans;
}
```

```
Weight Weight::operator ++(int)
    {
        int totaloz;

        totaloz = toOunces() + 1;
        pounds = totaloz / 16;
        ounces = totaloz % 16;
        return this;
    }
```

PROGRAMMING EXERCISES 11.27

Add the ++ and -- operations to the *Distance* class. Each should operation adjust the value held by 1 inch.

Overloading the Extraction and Insertion Operators

So far we have managed, by overloading operators, to allow objects of our *Weight* and *Distance* classes to use basic operations such as +=, =, <, etc. in much the same way as these operators are used on built-in data types such as `int` and `double`. It would be useful to extend the similarity so that we could use the extraction operator (>>) and insertion operator (<<) to read and write our objects. This would allow the application programmer to replace statements such as

```
cout <<w1.getPounds()<<" lbs "<<w1.getOunces()<<" oz";
```

with the statement

```
cout << w1;
```

Unfortunately, overloading these operators isn't quite as straight-forward as the others. If you take a second look at the statement above you'll see what the problem is.

Since the << operator appears before the object name, *w1*, the operator is not a method of object *w1* (it would have to appear after *w1* for that to be the case).

In fact, the << operator belongs to the term `cout`. So far we've always thought of `cout` as just another keyword in C++ (like `if` or `for`), but it is, in fact, an object from a class called `ostream` which is an integral part of the C++ language.

In that class the << operator is overloaded to output the contents of the basic C++ types (`int`, `double`, `char`, etc.) so perhaps we could modify the `ostream` class and add in code to output the attributes of a *Weight* object.

Even if we had access to the source code for the `ostream` class, this is not a good idea; we can't just tamper with other people's carefully designed classes - it's just not good programming practice!

What's needed is a good old-fashioned stand-alone function which takes `ostream` and *Weight* parameters The routine would pass the attributes of the *Weight* object to the `ostream` object which would then output these to the screen. The code for the routine is:

```
void operator << (ostream& cc, Weight w)
{
    cc << w.getPounds()<<" lbs "<<w.getOunces()<<" oz";
}
```

Once this function has been included in the application program, the contents of a *Weight* object can be displayed with a statement such as:

```
cout << w1;
```

A simple example of a *main()* function using this approach is shown in LISTING-11.6.

LISTING-11.6

Using the Overloaded Insertion Operator to Output a *Weight* Object

```
void main()
{
   //*** Create the Weight object ***
   Weight w1;

   //*** Read values for weight ***
   cout<<"Enter pounds: ";
   int lbs;
   cin>>lbs;
   cout<<"Enter ounces: ";
   int oz;
   cin>>oz;
   //*** Assign values to weight ***
   w1.setWeight(lbs, oz);
   //*** Display the weight ***
   cout << w1;
}
```

PROGRAMMING EXERCISE 11.28

Load up your *Weight* class program.

Add the code for the *operator <<()* function given earlier.

Modify your *main()* function to match that given above.

Notice that, again, the function is called in an unusual way. Normally, if we have a function *f()* which takes two parameters (*a* and *b*), we would call the function using the term

```
f(a,b)
```

but because this is an operator being overloaded, the call has changed to:

```
cout << w1;
```

However, this does not mean that we cannot use the more traditional style. Hence it is quite valid to write

```
operator<<(cout,w1)
```

and achieve the same effect.

PROGRAMMING EXERCISE 11.29

Modify the last statement in your previous program to use this alternative layout.

Does the program still work correctly?

Like the ++ operator previously, there's a problem with this first attempt at writing the *operator<<()* function. Imagine we want to display the contents of two *Weight* objects, *w1* and *w2*.

We could write

```
cout << w1 << w2;
```

and this would appear to be fine, but if we rewrite the statement with the alternative layout

```
operator<<(operator<<(cout,w1),w2);
```

we might begin to see that there's a problem. Output of more than one item is produced by nesting calls to the function. Notice how the result returned by the inner function call becomes the first parameter of the outer function call.

Since our function doesn't actually return a value, we're going to get a compilation error when we try to display more than one value in a single `cout` statement.

To correct this we need to make sure our function returns a reference to our `ostream` object. This gives us the following new code:

```
ostream& operator << (ostream& cc, Weight w)
{
    cc << w.getPounds()<<" lbs "<<w.getOunces()<<" oz";
    return cc;
}
```

PROGRAMMING EXERCISE 11.30

Update your own version of the *operator<<()* function.

Test it by creating a second *Weight* object (*w2*) in *main()* and displaying the contents of both *w1* and *w2* in a single `cout` statement.

PROGRAMMING EXERCISE 11.31

Add a << operator to your *Distance* class so that *Distance* objects are displayed in the style:

3 yds 2ft 1 in

The overloaded extraction operator reads a *Weight* value from the keyboard. It is coded in a similar fashion.

This time the parameters are an object from the `istream` class (`cin` being an instance of that class) and a *Weight* object. To cope with multiple inputs, the function must return an `istream` object address, but also needs to return the *Weight* object whose values have been read from the keyboard.

A simple version of the routine (with minimal error-checking) is given below:

```
istream& operator>>(istream& ci, Weight& w)
{
    int lbs, oz;
    cout << " Enter pounds : ";
    ci >> lbs;
    while (lbs < 0)
    {
        cout << " Pounds must be greater than zero. Re-enter ";
        ci >> lbs;
    }
    cout << " Enter ounces : ";
    ci >> oz;
```

```
    while (oz < 0 || oz > 15)
    {
        cout << " Ounces must be between 0 to 15. Re-enter ";
        ci >> oz;
    }
    w.setWeight(lbs, oz);
    return ci;
}
```

To read a value into a *Weight* object, we can now use a statement such as:

```
cin >> w1;
```

> **PROGRAMMING EXERCISE 11.32**
>
> Add the *operator>>()* function to your own *Weight* application.
>
> Test the statement by reading in values for both *w1* and *w2* in a single `cin` statement.

> **PROGRAMMING EXERCISE 11.33**
>
> Add a >>operator to your *Distance* class so that *Distance* objects can be read in using a statement such as:
>
> ```
> cin >> d1;
> ```

Since the *operator <<()* and *operator >>()* functions are not part of the *Weight* class they cannot access the attributes of the *Weight,* hence we have to write

```
cc << w.getPounds()<<" lbs "<<w.getOunces()<<" oz";
```

rather than

```
cc << w.pounds<<" lbs "<<w.ounces<<" oz";
```

Friends

It is possible to give a standard function full access to a class by making that function a **friend** of that class.

Friend functions have full access to a class's private attributes without actually being a method in that class. To make a function a friend of a given class we need to modify the source code of that class and to add the prototype of the function to the class declaration, prefixing it with the keyword `friend`. Therefore, if we change the definition of the *Weight* class to begin

```
class Weight
{
    private:
        int pounds;
        int ounces;
        int toOunces();
    public:
        friend ostream& operator<<(ostream& Weight);
        Weight(int=0,int=0);
```

we could then code the *operator<<()* function as:

```
ostream& operator << (ostream& cc, Weight w)
{
    cc << w.pounds<<" lbs "<<w.ounces<<" oz";
```

```
        return cc;
    }
```

As a general rule, using friend functions is considered bad programming style and should probably be avoided. Also, in order to use them, you'll need access to the class's source code and would be violating the original design of the class by making changes to it.

Other Ways to Create Objects

Arrays of Objects

As well as creating individual objects, it is also possible to create arrays of objects. For example, we can create an array of three *Weight* objects using the statement:

```
Weight list[3];
```

Each object will be created using the zero-argument constructor for the class.

If you want to use a different version of the constructor in order to initialise the objects to some start-up value, we can use the following style:

```
Weight list[3]={Weight(2,3),Weight(1,1),Weight(5,10)};
```

To access the features of the objects held in the array, we need to use a combination of array access notation and object method access. For example, to find out the kilogram equivalent of the second weight in the array, we would use the expression:

```
list[1].convertToMetric()
```

The following code would display the metric equivalent for all three weights:

```
for(int c = 0; c < 3; c++)
    cout<<list[c].convertToMetric()<<endl;
```

PROGRAMMING EXERCISE 11.34

Write a program which uses an array containing 4 *Distance* objects.
Read in a value for each object and display each distance in metres.

Dynamic Objects

It is possible to create a pointer to an object by using a statement such as

```
Weight *wghtptr;
```

in *main()*.

We can then make this pointer contain the address of an existing *Weight* object by adding a line such as:

```
wghtptr = & w1;     //This assumes w1 has previously been
                    //declared as a Weight object.
```

Alternatively, we could use the pointer to reference a dynamically allocated object:

```
wghtptr = new Weight;
```

If the object constructor requires arguments, these can be specified as part of the instruction:

```
wghtptr = new Weight(2,3);
```

The effect of this statement is shown in FIG-11.12.

FIG-11.12

Using a Class Object Pointer

Not all features of the current version of the *Weight* class are shown.

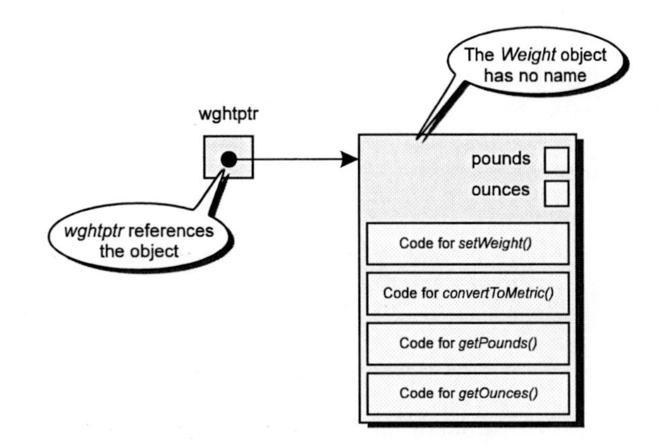

To access the features of the *Weight* object, we just dereference the pointer in the same way as we did when using a pointer to a record structure. Hence, we may write either

```
(wghtptr*).setWeight(5,9);
```

or

```
wghtptr->setWeight(5,9);
```

to execute the *setWeight()* method of the object referenced by *wghtptr*.

Objects allocated in this way need to be deallocated using the normal `delete` command:

```
delete  wghtptr;
```

This will result in the class destructor (if it has one) being executed immediately prior to the object's space being freed.

PROGRAMMING EXERCISE 11.35

Write a program that it implements the following logic:

Create a *Distance* object pointer call *distptr*.
Dynamically, create a *Distance* object (referenced by *distptr*) with it's initial value set to 3 yds 0 ft 11 in.
Display the contents of the *Distance* object.

Arrays of Dynamic Objects

By creating an array of object pointers with a statement such as

```
Weight *ptrs[5];
```

we can dynamically create a group of objects:

```
for(int c = 0; c < 5; c++)
    ptrs[c] = new Weight;
```

and access these objects in any order by dereferencing the pointers in the array:

```
for(c=0; c < 5; c++)
    cout<<ptrs[c]->getPounds()<<" lbs "<<ptrs[c]->getOunces
        <<" oz\n";
```

Constant Objects

Not only can we declare basic-type constants with statements such as

```
const double pi=3.14159;
```

but we can also declare object constants. For example, an application which dealt with mail might define an upper weight limit for first-class letter post using a *Weight* constant:

```
const Weight  firstclasslimit(2,5);
```

However, this can cause unforeseen problems. If the application programmer wants to check a package's weight against this upper limit, he might write code such as:

This code assumes *package* has been declared as a *Weight* object and that the *Weight* class has defined a method for the < operator.

```
if(firstclasslimit < package)
    cout<<"Package is too heavy\n";
```

In fact, the compiler will throw up an error message in response to this code.

When an object is declared as a constant, C++ bars us from changing any attribute values in that object. This is as we might expect. But we are also barred from calling any of the object's methods as well, since these might attempt to change the value of one or more attributes. Hence, the expression

```
firstclasslimit < package
```

which calls the < method of the *firstclasslimit* object, is illegal and causes a compilation error.

To get round this problem, we can tell the compiler that certain methods in a class do not attempt to change any attributes and therefore are safe to use even when the object involved has been declared as a constant. We do this by declaring those methods to be **constant member functions**.

We declare a method to be a constant member function by adding the word `const` to the end of the prototype and at the end of the first line of the function definition. For example, to make the < method in the *Weight* class a constant member function, the following changes would be required:

```
class Weight
{
    private:
          .
        public:
          .
        int operator<(Weight)const;
          .
};

int Weight::operator<(Weight w)const
{
          .

}
```

TASK 11.9

Which methods of the *Distance* class can be declared as constant member functions?

If the application program creates a function in which an object parameter is defined using the `const` term as in the line

```
void myfunction (const Weight w)
```

the same limitations will apply to parameter *w* within that function, with only calls to constant member functions being valid.

Summary

- **A class object may appear as a parameter** to a function.
- **A class object may be returned** by a function.
- **Methods may be private,** in which case they can only be called from within other member methods of the class.
- A **constructor** is a method which is called automatically when a class object is created.
- If no constructor is created by the programmer, a **default constructor** is created automatically.
- A **constructor** must have the same name as the class and may return no value.
- **Constructors** can be overloaded.
- **Only a single copy of static data members is created** no matter how many objects from that class exist.
- A static, variable, data item is often known as a **class variable**.
- Each object accesses the same copy of the **static item**.
- **Static items exist even when no object of that class exists.**
- **To access a public static attribute** when no object exists, use the format:

  ```
  Class-name::static-data-name
  ```

- **To access a private static attribute** when no object exists, a public class method is required

  ```
  public static return-type function-name(parameter list);
  ```

  to declare the function.
- **Static members of a class exist** even before any objects from that class are created.

DESIGNING CLASSES

Introduction

At the beginning of this chapter we saw that one tool for helping with the design of an object-oriented system is the Unified Modelling Language (UML). The complete UML system and object-oriented design as a whole is outside the scope of this text. However, it will be useful to explore UML class diagrams in some more detail by showing how the *Weight* class would be represented in this system.

We've already seen that the basic diagram is a rectangle split into three areas. These areas contain:

the class name
the attributes of the class
the operations of the class

In addition, the access modifier information can be added to the diagram: private items are started with a minus (-) sign; public features begin with a plus (+) sign.

The modified version of the *Weight* class is shown in FIG-11.13.

FIG-11.13

A More Detailed UML Class Diagram

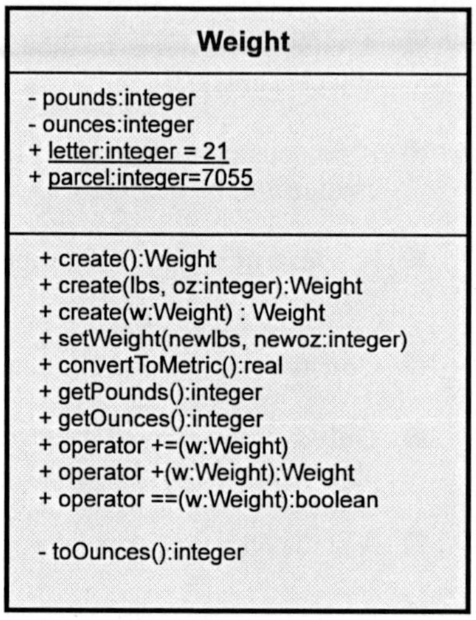

```
Weight
-----------------------------------------
- pounds:integer
- ounces:integer
+ letter:integer = 21
+ parcel:integer=7055
-----------------------------------------
+ create():Weight
+ create(lbs, oz:integer):Weight
+ create(w:Weight) : Weight
+ setWeight(newlbs, newoz:integer)
+ convertToMetric():real
+ getPounds():integer
+ getOunces():integer
+ operator +=(w:Weight)
+ operator +(w:Weight):Weight
+ operator ==(w:Weight):boolean

- toOunces():integer
```

Notice that constructor operations are named *create* and return an object of the class being defined. This is a useful convention to follow with all classes. Of course, in the implementation, C++ requires that the constructors are named after the class, but this is not true of all object-oriented languages.

Any class attributes or methods (only the constant class attributes *letter* and *parcel* are shown above) are underlined.

The initial value of an attribute is shown by adding an equals sign followed by the required initial value, but there is no specific method for signifying a constant attribute.

Other documentation in the form of mini-specs will be required for each operation. In addition to the information given in previously discussed mini-specs, we'll need to add access details and which attributes are accessed by an operation. For example, the mini-spec for `setWeight(newlbs, newoz : integer)` would be as shown overleaf:

Operation	:	setWeight
Access	:	public
Parameters		
In	:	newlbs : integer newoz : integer
Out	:	None
In/Out	:	None
Attributes Accessed		
read	:	None
written	:	pounds ounces
Pre-condition	:	newlbs >= 0 AND newoz >= 0 AND newoz <= 15
Post-condition	:	pounds = newlbs AND ounces = newoz
Description	:	*newlbs* copied to *pounds* and *newoz* copied to *ounces.*
Outline Logic	:	`Set pounds to newlbs` `Set ounces to newoz`

PROGRAMMING EXERCISE 11.36

Create and test new classes for each of the following:

1.
Clock : Objects of this class are set to a specific time and made to increment by one second each time the *tick()* method is executed.

Attributes:

hours : integer
minutes : integer
seconds : integer

Operations:

create()
Creates a *Clock* object with the time set to midnight (0,0,0)

create(h,m,s:integer)
Creates a *Clock* object set to time *h:m:s*. If the parameters are invalid, the time is set to midnight.

setTime(h,m,s:integer)
Sets time to *h:m:s*. If the parameters are invalid, the time is unchanged.

tick()
Adds one second to the current time.

getHours():integer
Returns a copy of the *hours* attribute.

getMinutes():integer
Returns a copy of the *minutes* attribute.

getSeconds():integer
Returns a copy of the *seconds* attribute.

toString():string
Returns the current time as a string in the form
hh:mm:ss

runClock(v:integer)
Displays the time on screen as the clock ticks through *v* seconds.

In C++, use a `char*` type to return a string.

The time should be displayed with a slight delay between each update. This can be achieved using a `for` loop which performs CPU intensive calculations.

continued on next page

PROGRAMMING EXERCISE 11.36 (continued)

2.

ChangeDispenser: This represents the type of mechanism found inside a drinks machine. Money is added to its store and change is returned. This class will accept the price of an item, insertion of coins and return a set of coins as change.

Attributes:

coins[2][5] : integer = {5,10,20,50,100} {3,3,3,3,0}
-coin values:no. of coins in machine
moneyinserted : integer - all values are in pence
costofitem : integer

Operations:

create()
Creates an object with default number of coins(as shown above); *moneyinserted* = 0 and *costofitem*=0.

create(coincount[5]:integer)
Creates an object with number of coins specified by *coincount[]* parameter. If the parameter is invalid, then the default number of coins is used.

setCostOfItem(cost:integer)
Sets *costofitem* to *cost*. If *cost* is invalid no change is made.(0 to 500 and some multiple of the coin values)

addMoney(coin:integer)
Adds *coin* to *moneyinserted*. Adds 1 to appropriate element of *coins[][]*. If parameter does not match known coin values then exit routine.

refund():integer[]
Returns a set of coins to the value of *moneyinserted. moneyinserted* is reset to zero. Appropriate elements of *coins[1][]* are decremented to reflect the coins returned.

buy():integer[]
Returns change due after purchase. If *moneyinserted* is less than *costofitem* or *costofitem* is zero, then coins to the value of *moneyinserted* are returned.

isSufficient():boolean
Returns *true* if *moneyinserted* > *costofitem*, otherwise *false* is returned.

empty():integer[]
Returns the coins held in the machine. *coins[1][0..4]* are set to zero.

addChange(cash:integer[])
adds set of coins specified in *cash[]* to *coins[1][]*. If any elements of cash are invalid no coins of that particular value are added.

getCoins():integer[]
Returns the number of coins of each denomination held. The contents of *coins[][]* are unchanged.

getCoinValues:integer[]
Returns the denomination of each coin type.

getMoneyInserted():integer
Returns the value of *moneyinserted.*

getCostOfItem():integer
Returns the value of *costofitem.*

Summary

UML

- Private features are marked with a minus sign.
- Public features are marked with a plus sign.
- Class features are shown using an underline.
- The initial value of items can be shown in the diagram.
- Array attributes or parameters should be shown with square brackets and where appropriate these should enclose the number of elements.

Mini-specs

- Should include access modifier details.
- Should identify which attributes are accessed by the method.
- Attributes that will be changed should be marked as written.
- Attributes that are not changed should be marked as read.

CASE STUDY

The Problem

Strings in C++ are awkward to use. To declare a string we need to set up an array of characters:

```
char words[25];
```

or use dynamic allocation:

```
char *ptr = new char[25];
```

Reading a string from the keyboard requires a different function, *gets()*, and there is no guarantee that the characters entered will not overflow the allocated space. Also comparisons and assignments are awkward:

```
if(!strcmp(s1,s2))
    strcpy(s3,"End");
```

One way to overcome this is to create our own *String* class. The case study that follows shows how such a class might be defined.

Clarification

Rather than have to declare strings using pointers and use string functions to assign a value to a string, join strings, and compare them, a more natural approach would allow us to use statements such as:

```
String t1,t2,t3;          //*** Declare string variables

t1 = "Fred" ;             //*** Assign a value to variable
t2 = "Bloggs";
t3 = t1 + t2;             //*** Join two strings to form a third
if(t3 == "Fred Bloggs")   //*** Compare two strings
    cout << "Hello Fred\n";
```

It would also be useful if various input options were available to restrict the number and set of characters allowed.

The set of operations required by this is:

create() — Creates an empty string.

create(s : char)* — Creates a string containing the characters in *s*.

create(s : String) — Creates a string which is an exact copy of *s*.

readString(acceptable : char)*
Reads a string from the keyboard.

readString(acceptable:char, max:integer)*
Reads a string from the keyboard. Only characters from *acceptable* are to be accepted. The string may be contain no more than *max* characters.

readString(acceptable:char, min:integer, max:integer)*
Reads a string from the keyboard. Only characters from *acceptable* are to be accepted. The string may be contain between *min* and *max* characters.

setString(s : String)	Sets the current *String* object to *s*.
setString(s : char)*	Sets the current *String* object to *s*.
equals(s :String)	Returns 1 if both strings are equal, otherwise returns 0.
equals(s :char)*	Returns 1 if both strings are equal, otherwise returns 0.
notEquals(s :String)	Returns 1 if both strings are not equal, otherwise returns 0.
notEquals(s :char)*	Returns 1 if both strings are not equal, otherwise returns 0.
concate(s : String)	Joins *s* to the end of the current string.
concate(s : char)*	Joins *s* to the end of the current string.
length():integer	Returns the number of characters, excluding the terminating NULL character, in the current *String* object.
display()	Displays the contents of a string on the screen.

The Strategy

Strings vary in size, hence the space allocated to a string needs to be created dynamically. There is no escaping the approach used by C++ itself, but, by encapsulating the details of implementation within a class, we can protect the user from the complexities involved.

No attempt is being made to write a total replacement for the strings used within C++, rather a flavour of the approach is given by a limited number of operations.

Attributes of the Class

The only attribute required by the *String* class is a `char` pointer. Space for any text placed within the *String* object can then be dynamically allocated and referenced using this pointer:

```
private:
    char * cptr;
```

String Constructors

There are three constructors mentioned in the design. The first two of these are coded below:

```
//*** Create an empty string ***
String::String()
{
```

```
        cptr = new char;
        *cptr = '\0';
    }

    //*** Construct string from C++ string ***
    String::String(char *s)
    {
        cptr = new char [strlen(s)+1];
        strcpy(cptr, s);
    }
```

The third constructor is the copy constructor. The version of this created automatically by C++ does not produce the required results, making the new object's pointer reference the same memory space as the original *String* object. For example, if *main()* contained the following code

```
    Weight w1("abcd");
    Weight w2(w1);
```

the default copy constructor, executed when *w2* is created, would produce the results shown on the left of FIG-11.14 whereas we want the results shown on the right of the figure.

FIG-11.14

Problems when Using the Default Copy Constructor

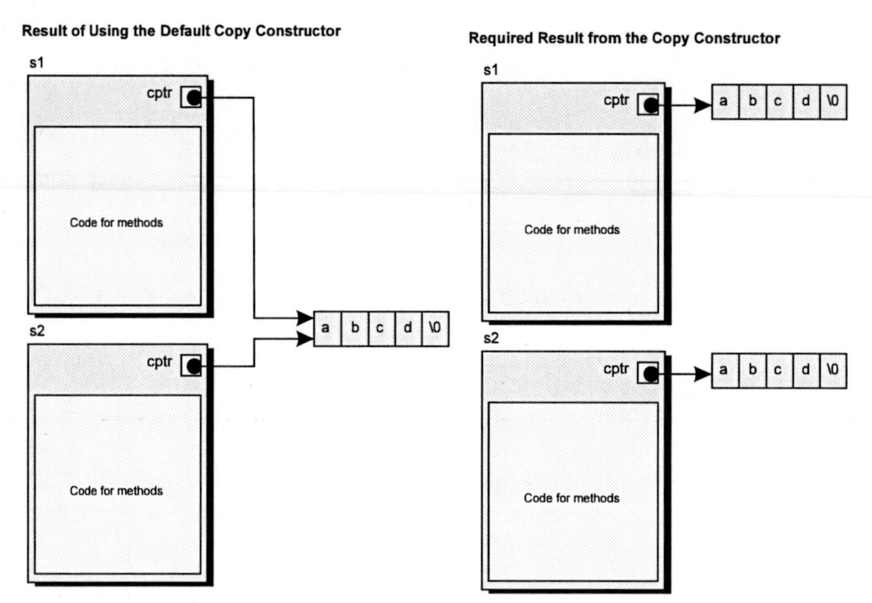

To correct this problem, the copy constructor needs to create a new copy of the referenced character array. This is done using the following code:

```
    //*** Copy Constructor ***
    String::String(String& s)
    {
        cptr = new char [strlen(s.cptr) + 1];
        strcpy(cptr, s.cptr);
    }
```

The assignment operator (=) also needs to be defined explicitly otherwise the same problem will arise. How this is to be done needs careful consideration.

Assume *main()* contains the following code:

```
    String s1("Hello"), s2("Goodbye");
    s1 = s2;
```

To achieve the desired effect, the steps shown in FIG-11.15 are required.

FIG-11.15

Copying a String

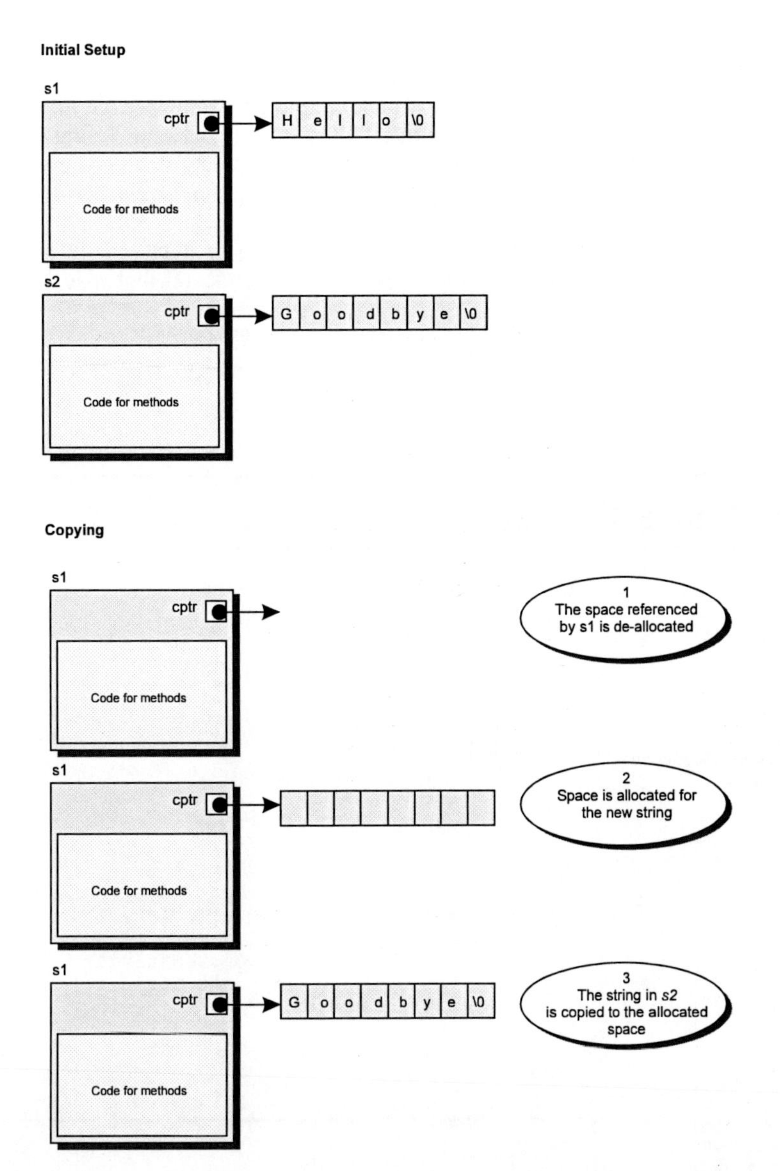

There is, however, one trap for the unwary: any attempt to perform self-assignment as in

```
s1 = s1;
```

would begin by de-allocating the space reserved for *s1* and hence lead to disaster. To safeguard against this, the situation must be tested for and, if detected, the string left untouched.

The code required to perform this logic is:

```
void String::operator = (const String &s)
{
    //*** IF self-copy THEN return ***
    if (&s == this)
        return;
    //*** Delete old allocated space ***
    delete [] cptr;
    //*** Allocate new space and copy ***
    cptr = new char[strlen(s.cptr)+1];
    strcpy(cptr,s.cptr);
}
```

When defining the set of acceptable characters to be used with the *readString()* methods, it is rather long-winded to have parameters such as "0123456789" so a short-hand method of defining a long sequence would be desirable. Hence we might write "0..9" to indicate all characters between '0' and '9'. This short-hand will have to be interpreted and expanded into the full character set it represents and this will be performed by an additional function, *expandString()*.

Since, the *String* class makes use of dynamically allocated space, we'll need a destructor for the class which de-allocates that space. This is coded as:

```
//*** Deallocate string space ***
String::~String()
{
    delete [] cptr;
}
```

The Class Declaration

The *String* class declaration is coded as:

We have already created the *expandString()* function in Chapter 5.

```
class String
{
    private:
        char *cptr;
        char *expandString(char*);
    public:
        String();
        String(char*);
        String(String&);
        ~String();
        void readString(char*);
        void readString(char*, int);
        void readString(char*, int, int);
        void operator = (const String&);
        int operator ==(const String&);
        int operator !=(const String&);
        String operator +(const String&);
        int length();
        void display();
};
```

TASK 11.10

Notice that methods such as *operator =()* have not been overloaded as might be implied by the original definition of the *String* class. Why is this?

The mini-specs for each method to be implemented are shown over the next few pages:

Operation	:	expandString
Access	:	private
Parameters		
In	:	shortallow : char*
Out	:	longallow : char*
In/Out	:	None
Attributes Accessed		
Read	:	None
Written	:	None
Pre-condition	:	*shortallow* must not start with ".."
Post-condition	:	*longallow* contains the expanded version of *shortallow*.
Description	:	Expands abbreviated character strings used to specify which characters are to be allowed when entering a string. See *readString()* . For example, expands "0..9" to "0123456789".

Outline Logic :

```
Set longallow to empty string
FOR each character in shortallow DO
    IF at least 2 characters from the
        end AND current and next
        character are '.'
    THEN
        Skip past double dots
        Insert in longallow all
        characters between last character
        placed in longallow and next
        character in shortallow
    ELSE
        Insert character from shortallow
        in longallow
    DIF
ENDFOR
Insert NULL character in longallow
```

Operation : readString
Access : public

Parameters
In : allow : char*
min : INTEGER
max : INTEGER
Out : None
In/Out : None

Attributes Accessed
Read : None
Written : cptr : char*

Pre-condition : *allow* must not begin with ".."
min >= 0
max >= min
Post-condition : *cptr* references the block of characters read from the keyboard.

Description : Reads at least *min* and up to *max* characters from the keyboard, and creates a string of these characters which is referenced by *cptr*.
Only characters from the set *allow* are accepted.

Outline Logic :

```
Set temp to empty string
Set count to zero
Expand allow using expandString()
Read a key
WHILE key is not ENTER OR count < min DO
    IF key part of allow AND count<<max
    THEN
        Display key
        Add key to temp
        Add NULL to temp
        Add 1 to count
    ELSE
        IF key is BACKSPACE AND
            count > 0
        THEN
            Delete last character from
            screen
            Replace last character in
            temp with NULL
            Subtract 1 from count
        ENDIF
    ENDIF
    Read a key
ENDWHILE
Delete previously allocated space
Create space equivalent to size of
temp + 1 referenced by cptr
Copy temp to this space
```

Operation	:	readString
Access	:	public
Parameters		
In	:	allow : char*
Out	:	None
In/Out	:	None
Attributes Accessed		
Read	:	None
Written	:	cptr : char*
Pre-condition	:	*allow* must not begin with "..".
Post-condition	:	*cptr* references the block of characters read from the keyboard.
Description	:	Reads up to 120 characters from the keyboard, and creates a string of these characters which is referenced by *cptr*. Only characters from the set *allow* are accepted.
Outline Logic	:	`readString(allow,0,120)`

Operation	:	readString
Access	:	public
Parameters		
In	:	allow : char* max : INTEGER
Out	:	None
In/Out	:	None
Attributes Accessed		
Read	:	None
Written	:	cptr : char*
Pre-condition	:	*allow* must not begin with "..". *max* >= 0
Post-condition	:	*cptr* references the block of characters read from the keyboard.
Description	:	Reads up to *max* characters from the keyboard, and creates a string of these characters which is referenced by *cptr*. Only characters from the set *allow* are accepted.
Outline Logic	:	`readString(allow,0,max)`

Operation	:	operator =	
Access	:	public	
Parameters			
In	:	s	: String class
Out	:	None	
In/Out	:	None	
Attributes Accessed			
Read	:	None	
Written	:	cptr	: char*
Pre-condition	:	*s* not the same object as the current object.	
Post-condition	:	*cptr* references a sequence of characters identical to that referenced by *s*.	
Description	:	Copies the contents of *s* to the area referenced by *cptr*.	

Outline Logic	:	`Delete area currently referenced by cptr`
		`Create new area referenced by cptr`
		`Copy s to cptr area.`	

Operation	:	operator ==	
Access	:	public	
Parameters			
In	:	s	: String class
Out	:	b	: INTEGER
Attributes Accessed			
Read	:	cptr	: char*
Written	:	None	
Pre-condition	:	None	
Post-condition	:	*b* is 1 if the current string contains exactly the same sequence of characters as *s*, otherwise *b* is zero.	
Description	:	Compares *s* with value referenced by *cptr*. Returns 1 if the values are the same, otherwise returns zero.	
Outline Logic	:	see below	

```
IF s = *cptr THEN
    b = 1
ELSE
    b = 0
ENDIF
```

Operation	:	operator !=
Access	:	public
Parameters		
In	:	s : String class
Out	:	b : INTEGER
Attributes Accessed		
Read	:	cptr : char*
Written	:	None
Pre-condition	:	None
Post-condition	:	*b* is 1 if the current string is not an exact match for *s*, otherwise *b* is zero.
Description	:	Compares *s* with value referenced by *cptr*. Returns 1 if the values are different, otherwise returns zero.
Outline Logic	:	`IF s <> *cptr THEN` `b = 1` `ELSE` `b = 0` `ENDIF`

```
IF s <> *cptr THEN
    b = 1
ELSE
    b = 0
ENDIF
```

Operation	:	operator +
Access	:	public
Parameters		
In	:	s : String class
Out	:	temp : String class
In/Out	:	None
Attributes Accessed		
Read	:	None
Written	:	cptr : char*
Pre-condition	:	None
Post-condition	:	*temp* is set to a string which is equal to *s* appended to the current string.
Description	:	Joins *s* to the end of the string referenced by *cptr*.
Outline Logic	:	see below

```
Create space for result, referenced by
temp
Copy original string at cptr and s
into area at temp
return temp
```

Operation	:	length
Access	:	public
Parameters		
In	:	None
Out	:	size : INTEGER
Attributes Accessed		
Read	:	cptr : char*
Written	:	None
Pre-condition	:	None
Post-condition	:	*size* is equal to the number of characters in the current string.
Description	:	Returns the number of characters at *cptr*. The result excludes the terminating NULL character.
.Outline Logic	:	`Return length of string at cptr`

Operation	:	display
Access	:	public
Parameters		
In	:	None
Out	:	size : INTEGER
Attributes Accessed		
Read	:	cptr : char*
Written	:	None
Pre-condition	:	None
Post-condition	:	Contents of the current string are displayed.
Description	:	Displays the string at *cptr*.
Outline Logic	:	`Display string referenced by cptr`

LISTING-11.7

The String Class

```
#include <conio.h>
#include <iostream.h>
#include <string.h>

//*********************************
//*   String Class Declaration    *
//*********************************
class String
{
  private:
       char *cptr;
       char *ExpandString(char*);
  public:
       String();
       String(char*);
       String(String&);
       ~String();
       void readString(char*);
       void readString(char*, int);
       void readString(char*, int, int);
       void operator = (const String&);
       int operator ==(const String&);
       int operator !=(const String&);
       String operator +(const String&);
       int length();
       void display();
};

//********************************
//*   String Class Definitions   *
//********************************
//*** Auxiliary Functions ***
int ReadKey()
{
  int ch;

  ch=getch();
  if(ch==0)
       ch=-getch();
  return ch;
}

//****** PRIVATE METHODS ******

//*** Expand allowed string ***
char* String::ExpandString(char *allowed)
{
  char temp[256]="";//Holds expanded string
  //Copy the first character across ***
  temp[0]=allowed[0];
  //***FOR all but last two chars in compressed string DO ***
  for(int c=1,p=1; c<int(strlen(allowed))-3;c++)
  {
       //*** IF two periods THEN ***
       if(allowed[c]=='.'&&allowed[c+1]=='.')
       {
            //*** Insert range of characters implied ***
            for(char ch=allowed[c-1]; ch<=allowed[c+2];ch++)
                 temp[p++]=ch;
            //*** Move past this part of compressed string ***
            c+=2;
       }
       //*** ELSE if not two dots ***
       else
            temp[p++]=allowed[c];
  }
  //*** Copy any remaining characters ***
  for(int k=c;k<=strlen(allowed)-1;k++,c++)
```

Continued on next page

LISTING-11.7
(continued)

The String Class

```
        temp[p++]=allowed[c];
    //*** Insert final NULL character ***
    temp[p]='\0';
    //*** Return expanded string ***
    return temp;
}


//****** PUBLIC METHODS ******

//*** Read string from keyboard ***
void String::readString(char *allowed, int min,int max)
{
    //*** Declare named constants ***
    const int ENTER = 13;
    const int BACKSPACE = 8;
    const int ESCAPE = 27;

    int ch;               //Holds current key press
    int count = 0;        //Holds no. of chars in entered string
    char temp[200];       //Holds entered string
    char tempallow[256];  //Holds allowed char set

    //*** Expanded allowed string ***
    strcpy(tempallow,ExpandString(allowed));
    //*** Empty entered string ***
    strcpy(temp, "");
    //*** Read a key ***
    ch=ReadKey();
    //*** WHILE not ESCAPE AND ((not ENTER and not control
            key)OR(no. of char not reached minimum)) DO
    while(ch!=ESCAPE&&((ch!=ENTER&&ch>=0)||count<min))
    {
        //*** IF allowed char and space in entered string THEN **
        if(strchr(tempallow, ch) && count<max)
        {
            //*** Display char ***
            cout<<char(ch);
            //*** Add char to entered string and inc count ***
            temp[count++]=ch;
            //*** Terminate entered string ***
            temp[count]='\0';
        }
        //*** ELSE ***
        else
            //*** IF it's a valid backspace THEN ***
            if(ch==BACKSPACE&&count>0)
            {
                //*** Remove last char from screen ***
                cout<<"\b \b";
                //*** and entered string; dec count ***
                temp[--count]='\0';
            }
        //*** Read another char ***
        ch=ReadKey();
    }
    //*** IF didn't end with escape THEN ***
    if(ch!=ESCAPE)
    {
        //*** Delete old allocated space ***
        delete cptr;
        //*** Allocate new space ***
        cptr=new char[strlen(temp)+1];
        //*** Copy entered string into object ***
        strcpy(cptr, temp);
    }
}
```

Continued on next page

LISTING-11.7
(continued)

The String Class

```
void String::readString(char *allowed)
{
   readString(allowed,0,120);
}


void String::readString(char *allowed, int max)
{
   readString(allowed,0,max);
}


//*** Construct empty string ***
String::String()
{
   cptr = new char;
   *cptr = '\0';
}


//*** Construct string from C++ string ***
String::String(char *s)
{
   cptr = new char [strlen(s)+1];
   strcpy(cptr, s);
}


//*** Copy Constructor ***
String::String(String& s)
{
   cptr = new char [strlen(s.cptr) + 1];
   strcpy(cptr, s.cptr);
}


//*** Deallocate string space ***
String::~String()
{
   delete [] cptr;
}


//*** String assignment ***
void String::operator = (const String &s)
{
   //*** IF self-copy THEN return ***
   if (&s == this)
        return;
   //*** Delete old allocated space ***
   delete [] cptr;
   //*** Allocate new space and copy ***
   cptr = new char[strlen(s.cptr)+1];
   strcpy(cptr,s.cptr);
}


//*** Equality operator ***
int String::operator==(const String &s)
{
   //*** IF strings equal THEN ***
   if (!strcmp(cptr,s.cptr))
        //*** Return 1 ***
        return 1;
   else
   //*** ELSE return zero ***
        return 0;
}
```

Continued on next page

LISTING-11.7
(continued)

The String Class

```
//*** Inequality Operator ***
int String::operator !=(const String &s)
{
   //*** IF strings not equal THEN return 1 ***
   if (strcmp(cptr, s.cptr))
        return 1;
   else
   //*** ELSE return zero ***
        return 0;
}


//*** Concatenate strings ***
String String::operator +(const String &s)
{
   String temp; //Temp object for result

   //*** Allocate space for result ***
   temp.cptr = new char[strlen(cptr)+strlen(s.cptr)+1];
   //*** Copy both strings into space ***
   strcpy(temp.cptr,cptr);
   strcat(temp.cptr,s.cptr);
   //*** Return the result ***
   return temp;
}


//*** Return length of string ***
int String::length()
{
   return strlen(cptr);
}


//*** Display string object ***
void String::display()
{
   cout<<cptr;
}

//*************************************
//*** End of String Class Definition ***
//*************************************




//*************************************
//***        Test String class        ***
//*************************************
void main()
{
   String s1("hello"),s2(s1),s3,s4;
   s3 = s1+s2;
   s1 = s1 + " again";
   s1.display();
   s4.readString("a..o ",11,11);
   if (s1 == s4)
   {
        cout<<'\n';
        s2.display();
        cout<<'\n'<<s1.length()<<endl;
   }
}
```

Solutions

TASK 11.1

1. Characteristics
   - Length
   - Diameter
   - Colour of lead

   Operations
   - Write
   - Sharpen

2. Characteristics
   - Day
   - Month
   - Year

   Operations
   - SetDate
   - calculate Day of Week
   - Display
   - Is Leap Year

TASK 11.2

1. class
2. object
3. class
4. object
5. class
6. object

TASK 11.3

Distance
yards : INTEGER feet : INTEGER inches : INTEGER
setDistance(y,f,i : INTEGER) convertToMetric():REAL getYards() :INTEGER getFeet() :INTEGER getInches() :INTEGER

PROGRAMMING EXERCISE 11.1

```
class Distance
{
    public:
    int yards;
    int feet;
    int inches;
    void setDistance(int,int,int);
    double convertToMetric();
    int getYards();
    int getFeet();
    int getInches();
};
```

PROGRAMMING EXERCISE 11.2

No solution required.

PROGRAMMING EXERCISE 11.3

```
class Distance
{
    public:
        int yards;
        int feet;
        int inches;
        void setDistance(int,int,int);
        double convertToMetric();
        int getYards();
        int getFeet();
        int getInches();
};

void Distance::setDistance(int newyds,
            int newft, int newin)
{
    if(newyds<0 || newft<0 || newft>2 || newin<0
    || newin>11)
        return;
    yards = newyds;
    feet = newft;
    inches = newin;
}

double Distance::convertToMetric()
{
    return (yards*36+feet*12+inches)*0.0254;
}

int Distance::getYards()
{
    return yards;
}

int Distance::getFeet()
{
    return feet;
}

int Distance::getInches()
{
    return inches;
}
```

TASK 11.4

```
w1.convertToMetric()
```

PROGRAMMING EXERCISE 11.4

Attempting to enter 23 for the *ounces* value is invalid (*setWeight()* checks that the second parameter is in the range 0 to 15) and will therefore be rejected and the contents of the *Weight* object will be unchanged.

PROGRAMMING EXERCISE 11.5

```
#include <iostream.h>

class Distance
{
    public:
        int yards;
        int feet;
        int inches;

        void setDistance(int,int,int);
        double convertToMetric();
        int getYards();
        int getFeet();
        int getInches();
};

void Distance::setDistance(int newyds,
            int newft, int newin)
{
    if(newyds<0 || newft<0 || newft>2 || newin<0
    || newin>11)
        return;
    yards = newyds;
    feet = newft;
    inches = newin;
}

double Distance::convertToMetric()
{
    return (yards*36+feet*12+inches)*0.0254;
}

int Distance::getYards()
{
    return yards;
}
```

```
int Distance::getFeet()
{
    return feet;
}

int Distance::getInches()
{
    return inches;
}

void main()
{
    //*** Create Distance object ***
    Distance d1;
    //*** Read values for distance ***
    cout<< "Enter yards: ";
    int yds;
    cin >> yds;
    cout<< "Enter feet: ";
    int ft;
    cin >> ft;
    cout<< "Enter inches: ";
    int in;
    cin > in;
    //*** Assign values to Distance object ***
    d1.setDistance(yds,ft,in);
    //*** Display in yards, feet & inches ***
    cout << "The distance entered was "
        <<d1.getYards()<<" yds "<<d1.getFeet()
        <<" ft "<<d1.getInches()<<" in"<<endl;
    //*** Display distance in metres ***
    cout<<"This is "<<d1.convertToMetric()
        <<" metres"<<endl;
}
```

PROGRAMMING EXERCISE 11.6

No solution required.

PROGRAMMING EXERCISE 11.7

No solution required.

PROGRAMMING EXERCISE 11.8

The program should run exactly as before.

PROGRAMMING EXERCISE 11.9

The *Distance* class declaration should now read

```
class Distance
{
    private:
        int yards;
        int feet;
        int inches;
    public:
        void setDistance(int,int,int);
        double convertToMetric();
        int getYards();
        int getFeet();
        int getInches();
};
```

PROGRAMMING EXERCISE 11.10

The program should perform as expected.

PROGRAMMING EXERCISE 11.11

```
void main()
{
    //*** Create Distance objects ***
    Distance d1 ,d2;
    //*** Read values for first distance ***
    cout<< "Enter yards: ";
    int yds;
    cin >> yds;
    cout<< "Enter feet: ";
    int ft;
    cin >> ft;
    cout << "Enter inches: ";
    int in;
    cin >> in;
    //*** Assign value to 1st Distance object ***
    d1.setDistance(yds,ft,in);
    //*** Read values for second distance ***
    cout<< "Enter yards: ";
    cin >> yds;
    cout << "Enter feet: ";
    cin >> ft;
    cout << "Enter inches: ";
    cin >> in;
    //*** Assign value to 2nd Distance object ***
    d2.setDistance(yds,ft,in);
    //*** Display  larger distance ***
    if (d1.convertToMetric() > d2.convertToMetric())
        cout << "Larger distance is "
            <<d1.getYards()<<" yds "
            <<d1.getFeet()<<" ft "
            <<d1.getInches()<<" in"<<endl;
    else
        cout << "Larger distance is "
            <<d2.getYards()<<" yds "
            <<d2.getFeet()<<" ft "
            <<d2.getInches()<<" in"<<endl;
}
```

TASK 11.5

The current object is *w2*

PROGRAMMING EXERCISE 11.12

The new declaration for the *Weight* class is

```
class Weight
{
    private:
        int pounds;
        int ounces;
    public:
        void setWeight(int,int);
        inline double convertToMetric();
        int getPounds();
        int getOunces();
};
```

with *convertToMetric()* now being coded as

```
inline double Weight::convertToMetric()
{
    return (pounds * 16 + ounces)*0.0283495;
}
```

The *Distance* class declaration is:

```
class Distance
{
    private:
        int yards;
        int feet;
        int inches;
    public:
        void setDistance(int,int,int);
        inline double convertToMetric();
        int getYards();
        int getFeet();
        int getInches();
};
```

with *convertToMetric()* being coded as:

```
inline double Distance::convertToMetric()
{
    return (yards*36+feet*12+inches)*0.0254;
}
```

PROGRAMMING EXERCISE 11.13

```
#include<iostream.h>

class Weight
{
    private:
```

```
        int pounds;
        int ounces;
        int toOunces();
    public:
        void setWeight(int,int);
        inline double convertToMetric();
        int getPounds();
        int getOunces();
        void addToWeight(Weight);
};

void Weight::setWeight(int lbs, int oz)
{
    if(lbs < 0 || oz < 0 || oz > 15)
        return;
    pounds = lbs;
    ounces = oz;
}

inline double Weight::convertToMetric()
{
    return (pounds * 16 + ounces)*0.0283495;
}

int Weight::getPounds()
{
    return pounds;
}

int Weight::getOunces()
{
    return ounces;
}

void Weight::addToWeight(Weight w)
{
    int totaloz;

    totaloz = (pounds+w.pounds)*16
              +ounces+w.ounces;
    pounds = totaloz/16;
    ounces = totaloz%16;
};


void main()
{
    Weight w1;
    Weight w2;
    //*** Read in First Weight ***
    cout<< "Enter pounds: ";
    int lbs;
    cin >> lbs;
    cout << "Enter ounces: ";
    int oz;
    cin >> oz;
    w1.setWeight(lbs, oz);
    //*** Read in second Weight ***
    cout<< "Enter pounds: ";
    cin >> lbs;
    cout << "Enter ounces: ";
    cin >> oz;
    w2.setWeight(lbs, oz);
    //*** Add w2 to w1 ***
    w1.addToWeight(w2);
    //*** Display larger weight ***
    cout<<"Weight w1 is "<<w1.getPounds()<<" lbs "
        <<w1.getOunces()<<" oz\n";
}
```

PROGRAMMING EXERCISE 11.14

```
#include <iostream.h>

class Distance
{
    private:
        int yards;
         int feet;
         int inches;
    public:
        void setDistance(int,int,int);
        inline double convertToMetric();
        int getYards();
        int getFeet();
        int getInches();
        void addToDistance(Distance);
};

void Distance::setDistance(int newyds,
                int newft, int newin)
{
    if(newyds<0 || newft<0 || newft>2 || newin<0
    || newin>11)
     return;
    yards = newyds;
    feet = newft;
    inches = newin;
}

inline double Distance::convertToMetric()
{
    return (yards*36+feet*12+inches)*0.0254;
}

int Distance::getYards()
{
    return yards;
}

int Distance::getFeet()
{
    return feet;
}

int Distance::getInches()
{
    return inches;
}

void Distance::addToDistance(Distance d)
{
    int totalinches;

    totalinches = (yards+d.yards)*36
              +(feet+d.feet)*12
              + inches + d.inches;
    yards = totalinches / 36;
    feet = totalinches%36/12;
    inches = totalinches%12;
}


void main()
{
    //*** Create Distance objects ***
    Distance d1 ,d2;
    //*** Read values for first distance ***
    cout << "Enter yards: ";
    int yds;
    cin >> yds;
    cout << "Enter feet: ";
    int ft;
    cin >> ft;
    cout << "Enter inches: ";
    int in;
    cin >> in;
    //*** Assign value to 1st Distance object ***
    d1.setDistance(yds,ft,in);
    //*** Read values for second distance ***
    cout << "Enter yards: ";
    cin >> yds;
    cout << "Enter feet: ";
    cin >> ft;
    cout << "Enter inches: ";
    cin >> in;

    //*** Assign value to 2nd Distance object ***
    d2.setDistance(yds,ft,in);
    //*** Display  both distances ***
    cout<<"d1 is "<<d1.getYards()<<" yds "
        <<d1.getFeet()<<" ft "<<d1.getInches()
        <<" in"<<endl;
    cout<<"d2 is "<<d2.getYards()<<" yds "
        <<d2.getFeet()<<" ft "<<d2.getInches()
        <<" in"<<endl;
    //** Add second distance to first ***
    d1.addToDistance(d2);
    //*** Display first distance ***
    cout<<"d1 is "<<d1.getYards()<<" yds "
    <<d1.getFeet()<<" ft "<<d1.getInches()
    <<" in"<<endl;
}
```

TASK 11.6

The function prototypes

void f(float) and *int f(float)*

do not differ in their parameter lists and therefore would not compile if used in the same program.

PROGRAMMING EXERCISE 11.15

Updated parts of the *Distance* class are shown below:

```
#include<iostream.h>

class Distance
{
    private:
        int yards;
        int feet;
        int inches;
    public:
        void setDistance(int,int,int);
        inline double convertToMetric();
        int getYards();
        int getFeet();
        int getInches();
        void addToDistance(Distance);
        void setDistance(double);
};

void Distance::setDistance(double v)
{
    if (v<0)
        return;
    int totalinches = (int)(v*36+0.5);
    yards = totalinches/36;
    feet = totalinches%36/12;
    inches = totalinches%12;
}
```

The *main()* function should be coded as:

```
void main()
{
    //*** Create Distance object ***
    Distance d1;
    //*** Read real value ***
    cout<<"number: ";
    double value;
    cin>>value;
    //*** Assign value to Distance object ***
    d1.setDistance(value);

    //*** Display  distance ***
    cout<<"d1 is "<<d1.getYards()<<" yds "
        <<d1.getFeet()<<" ft "<<d1.getInches()
        <<" in"<<endl;
}
```

PROGRAMMING EXERCISE 11.16

Updated parts of the *Distance* class are shown below:

```
#include <iostream.h>

class Distance
{
    private:
        int yards;
        int feet;
        int inches;
    public:
        void setDistance(int,int,int);
        void setDistance(double);
        inline double convertToMetric();
        int getYards();
        int getFeet();
        int getInches();
        void addToDistance(Distance);
        Distance sumDistances(Distance d);
};


Distance Distance::sumDistances(Distance d)
{
    Distance ans;
    int temp = (yards+d.yards)*36
               +(feet+d.feet)*12
               +inches + d.inches;
    ans.yards = temp/36;
    ans.feet = temp%36/12;
    ans.inches = temp%12;
    return ans;
}
```

The *main()* function should be coded as:

```
void main()
{
    //*** Create Distance objects ***
    Distance d1, d2, d3;
    //*** Read values for first distance ***
    cout<<"Enter yards: ";
    int yds;
    cin>>yds;
    cout<<"Enter feet: ";
    int ft;
    cin>>ft;
    cout<<"Enter inches: ";
    int in;
    cin>>in;
    //*** Assign value to 1st Distance object ***
    d1.setDistance(yds,ft,in);
    //*** Read values for 2nd distance ***
    cout<<"Enter yards: ";
    cin>>yds;
    cout<<"Enter feet: ";
    cin>>ft;
    cout<<"Enter inches: ";
    cin>>in;
    //*** Assign value to 2nd Distance object ***
    d2.setDistance(yds,ft,in);
    //*** Sum the two distances ***
    d3 = d1.sumDistances(d2);
    //*** Display  distance ***
    cout<<"d3 is "<<d3.getYards()<<" yds "
        <<d3.getFeet()<<" ft "<<d3.getInches()
        <<" in"<<endl;
}
```

PROGRAMMING EXERCISE 11.17

Updated parts of the *Distance* class are shown below:

```
#include <iostream.h>

class Distance
{
    private:
        int yards;
        int feet;
        int inches;
    public:
        void setDistance(int,int,int);
        inline double convertToMetric();
        int getYards();
        int getFeet();
        int getInches();
        void addToDistance(Distance);
        void setDistance(double);
        Distance sumDistances(Distance d);
        int isLarger(Distance);
};

int Distance::isLarger(Distance d)
{
    if (convertToMetric()  d.convertToMetric())
    tab return 1;
    else
    tab return 0;
}
```

The *main()* function should be coded as:

```
void main()
{
    //*** Create Distance objects ***
    Distance d1, d2, d3;
    //*** Read values for first distance ***
    cout<<"Enter yards: ";
    int yds;
    cin>>yds;
    cout<<"Enter feet: ";
    int ft;
    cin>>ft;
    cout<<"Enter inches: ";
    int in;
    cin>>in;
    //*** Assign value to 1st Distance object ***
    d1.setDistance(yds,ft,in);
    //*** Read values for second distance ***
    cout<<"Enter yards: ";
    cin>>yds;
    cout<<"Enter feet: ";
    cin>>ft;
    cout<<"Enter inches: ";
    cin>>in;
    //*** Assign value to 2nd Distance object ***
    d2.setDistance(yds,ft,in);
    if (d1.isLarger(d2))
```

```
        cout<<"Larger is d1 at "<<d1.getYards()
            <<" yds "<<d1.getFeet()<<" ft "
            <<d1.getInches()<<" in"<<endl;
    else
        cout<<"Larger is d2 at "<<d2.getYards()
            <<" yds "<<d2.getFeet()<<" ft "
            <<d2.getInches()<<" in"<<endl;
}
```

PROGRAMMING EXERCISE 11.18

Updated parts of the *Distance* class are shown below:

```
#include<iostream.h>

class Distance
{
    private:
        int yards;
        int feet;
        int inches;
    public:
        void setDistance(int,int,int);
        inline double convertToMetric();
        int getYards();
        int getFeet();
        int getInches();
        void addToDistance(Distance);
        void setDistance(double);
        Distance sumDistances(Distance d);
        int isLarger(Distance);
        Distance smaller(Distance);
};


Distance Distance::smaller(Distance d)
{
    if (convertToMetric()<d.convertToMetric())
        return *this;
    else
        return d;
}
```

The *main()* function should be coded as:

```
void main()
{
    //*** Create Distance objects ***
    Distance d1, d2, d3;
    //*** Read values for first distance ***
    cout<<"Enter yards: ";
    int yds;
    cin>>yds;
    cout<<"Enter feet: ";
    int ft;
    cin>>ft;
    cout<<"Enter inches: ";
    int in;
    cin>>in;

    //*** Assign value to 1st Distance object ***
    d1.setDistance(yds,ft,in);
    //*** Read values for second distance ***
    cout<<"Enter yards: ";
    cin>>yds;
    cout<<"Enter feet: ";
    cin>>ft;
    cout<<"Enter inches: ";
    cin>>in;
    //*** Assign value to 2nd Distance object ***
    d2.setDistance(yds,ft,in);
    d3 = d1.smaller(d2);
    cout<<"smaller value is "<<d3.getYards()
        <<" yds "<<d3.getFeet()<<" ft "
        <<d3.getInches()<<" in"<<endl;
}
```

PROGRAMMING EXERCISE 11.19

Updated parts of the *Distance* class are shown below:

```
class Distance

{
    private:
        int yards;
        int feet;
        int inches;
        int toInches();
    public:
        void setDistance(int,int,int);
        inline double convertToMetric();
        int getYards();
        int getFeet();
        int getInches();
        void addToDistance(Distance);
        void setDistance(double);
        Distance sumDistances(Distance d);
        int isLarger(Distance);
        Distance smaller(Distance);
};

int Distance::toInches()
{
    return yards*36 + feet*12 + inches;
}


void Distance::addToDistance(Distance d)
{
    int totalinches;

    totalinches = toInches() + d.toInches();
    yards = totalinches / 36;
    feet = totalinches%36/12;
    inches = totalinches%12;
}
```

TASK 11.7

w1 = 4 lbs 9 oz
w2 = 7 lbs 0 oz
w3 = 0 lbs 0 oz

TASK 11.8

```
Weight::Weight(double v)
{
    if (v<0)
    {
        pounds = 0;
        ounces = 0;
    }
    else
    {
        pounds = (int)v;
        ounces = (int)((v-int(v))*16+0.5)/16);
    }
}
```

PROGRAMMING EXERCISE 11.20

Updated parts of the *Distance* class are shown below:

```
class Distance
{
    private:
        int yards;
        int feet;
        int inches;
        int toInches();
    public:
        Distance(int=0, int=0, int=0);
        Distance(double);
        void setDistance(int,int,int);
        inline double convertToMetric();
        int getYards()
        int getFeet();
        int getInches();
        void addToDistance(Distance);
        void setDistance(double);
        Distance sumDistances(Distance d);
        int isLarger(Distance);
        Distance smaller(Distance);
};

Distance::Distance(int y, int f, int i)
{
    if(y<0 || f<0 || f>2 || i<0 || i>11)
    {
        yards = 0;
        feet = 0;
        inches = 0;
    else
    {
        yards = y;
        feet = f;
        inches = i;
    }
}
```

```
Distance::Distance(double v)
{
    if (v 0)
    {
        yards = 0;
        feet = 0;
        inches = 0;
    }
    else
    {
        int totalinches = (int)(v*36+0.5);
        yards = totalinches / 36;
        feet = totalinches %36 / 12;
        inches = totalinches % 12;
    }
}
```

A *main()* function to test the constructors is given below:

```
void main()
{
    //*** Create Distance objects ***
    Distance d1(1,2,3), d2(4.5);
    //*** Display Distance objects ***
    cout<<"d1 is "<<d1.getYards()<<" yds "
        <<d1.getFeet()<<" ft "<<d1.getInches()
        <<" in"<<endl;
    cout<<"d2 is "<<d2.getYards()<<" yds "
        <<d2.getFeet()<<" ft "<<d2.getInches()
        <<" in"<<endl;
}
```

PROGRAMMING EXERCISE 11.21

```
void main()
{
    //*** Create 1st Distance object ***
    Distance d1(3,2,10);
    //*** Create 2nd Distance object ***
    Distance d2(d1);
    //*** Display Distance object d2 ***
    cout<<"d2 is "<<d2.getYards()<<" yds "
        <<d2.getFeet()<<" ft "<<d2.getInches()
        <<" in"<<endl;
}
```

PROGRAMMING EXERCISE 11.22

Updated parts of the *Distance* class are shown below:

```
#include<iostream.h>

class Distance
{
    private:
        int yards;
        int feet;
        int inches;
        int toInches();
    public:
        Distance(int=0, int=0, int=0);
        Distance(double);
        ~Distance();
        void setDistance(int,int,int);
        inline double convertToMetric();
        int getYards()
        int getFeet();
        int getInches();
        void addToDistance(Distance);
        void setDistance(double);
        Distance sumDistances(Distance d);
        int isLarger(Distance);
        Distance smaller(Distance);
};

Distance::~Distance()
{
    cout<<"Distance object destroyed\n";
}
```

A *main()* function to test the destructor is given below:

```
void main()
{
    //*** Create Distance objects ***
    Distance d1(3,2,10);
    {
        Distance d2(3.7);
        getch();
    }
    getch();
}
```

PROGRAMMING EXERCISE 11.23

```
class Distance
{
    private:
        int yards;
        int feet;
        int inches;
        int toInches();
    public:
        static const int metre;
        static const double centimetre;
        Distance(int=0, int=0, int=0);
        Distance(double);
        ~Distance();
        void setDistance(int,int,int);
        inline double convertToMetric();
        int getYards()
        int getFeet();
        int getInches();
        void addToDistance(Distance);
        void setDistance(double);
        Distance sumDistances(Distance d);
        int isLarger(Distance);
        Distance smaller(Distance);
};
const int Distance::metre=39;
const double Distance::centimetre=0.3937;
```

No other changes are required to the code for *Distance.*

main() is coded as:

```
void main()
{
    //*** Create Distance object ***
    Distance d1(3,2,10);
    //*** Display Distance constants ***
    cout<<"1 metre is "<<Distance::metre
        <<" inches\n1 centimetre is "
        <<d1.centimetre<<" inches\n";
}
```

PROGRAMMING EXERCISE 11.24

The *Distance* class is now declared as:

```
class Distance
{
    private:
        int yards;
        int feet;
        int inches;
        int toInches();
    public:
        static const int metre;
        static const double centimetre;
        static int count;
        Distance(int=0, int=0, int=0);
        Distance(double);
        void setDistance(int,int,int);
        inline double convertToMetric();
        int getYards()
        int getFeet();
        int getInches();
        void addToDistance(Distance);
        void setDistance(double);
        Distance sumDistances(Distance d);
        int isLarger(Distance);
        Distance smaller(Distance);
};
const int Distance::metre=39;
const double Distance::centimetre=0.3937;
int Distance::count = 0;

Distance::Distance(int y, int f, int i)
{
    if(y<0 || f<0 || f>2 || i<0 || i>11)
    {
        yards = 0;
        feet = 0;
        inches = 0;
    else
    {
        yards = y;
```

```
        feet = f;
        inches = i;
    }
    count++;
}

Distance::Distance(double v)
{
    if (v 0)
    {
        yards = 0;
        feet = 0;
        inches = 0;
    }
    else
    {
        int totalinches = (int)(v*36+0.5);
        yards = totalinches / 36;
        feet = totalinches %36 / 12;
        inches = totalinches % 12;
    }
    count++;
}
```

One possible coding of *main()* which shows the *count* increasing as objects are created is:

```
void main()
{
    //*** Display number of Distance objects ***
    cout<<"There are "<<Distance::count
        <<" Distance objects\n";
    //*** Create first Distance object ***
    Distance d1(3,2,10);
    //*** Display number of Distance objects ***
    cout<<"There are "<<Distance::count
        <<" Distance objects\n";
    //*** Create second Distance object ***
    Distance d2(12.6);
    //*** Display number of Distance objects ***
    cout<<"There are "<<Distance::count
        <<" Distance objects\n";
}
```

PROGRAMMING EXERCISE 11.25

count becomes private, *getCount()* is added and the class destructor decrements *count*:

```
class Distance
{
    private:
        int yards;
        int feet;
        int inches;
        int toInches();
        static int count;
    public:
        static const int metre;
        static const double centimetre;
        static int getCount();
        Distance(int=0, int=0, int=0);
        Distance(double);
        ~Distance();
        void setDistance(int,int,int);
        inline double convertToMetric();
        int getYards()
        int getFeet();
        int getInches();
        void addToDistance(Distance);
        void setDistance(double);
        Distance sumDistances(Distance d);
        int isLarger(Distance);
        Distance smaller(Distance);
};
const int Distance::metre=39;
const double Distance::centimetre=0.3937;
int Distance::count = 0;
```

The new methods are coded as follows:

```
int Distance::getCount()
{
     return count;
}

Distance::~Distance()
{
    count--;
}
```

The effect of these changes is highlighted in the following version of *main()*:

```
void main()
{
    //*** Display no. of Distance objects ***
    cout<<"There are "<<Distance::getCount()
        <<" Distance objects\n";
    {
        //*** Create first Distance object ***
        Distance d1(3,2,10);
        //*** Display no. of Distance objects ***
        cout<<"There are "<<Distance::getCount()
            <<" Distance objects\n";
        //*** d1 destroyed here ***
    }
    //*** Display no. of Distance objects ***
    cout<<"There are "<<Distance::getCount()
        <<" Distance objects\n";
    //*** Create second Distance object ***
    Distance d2(12.6);
    //*** Display no. of Distance objects ***
    cout<<"There are "<<Distance::getCount()
        <<" Distance objects\n";
}
```

PROGRAMMING EXERCISE 11.26

Class declaration:

```
class Distance
{
    private:
        int yards;
        int feet;
        int inches;
        int toInches();
        static int count;
    public:
        static const int metre;
        static const double centimetre;
        static int getCount();
        Distance(int=0, int=0, int=0);
        Distance(double);
        ~Distance();
        void setDistance(int,int,int);
        void setDistance(double);
        inline double convertToMetric();
        int getYards()
        int getFeet();
        int getInches();
        void operator+=(Distance);
        Distance operator+(Distance d);
        int operator>(Distance);
        int operator==(Distance);
        Distance smaller(Distance);
};
const int Distance::metre=39;
const double Distance::centimetre=0.3937;
int Distance::count = 0;
```

Changed and new methods:

```
void Distance::operator+=(Distance d)
{
    int totalinches;

    totalinches = toInches() + d.toInches();
    yards = totalinches/36;
    feet = totalinches%36/12;
    inches = totalinches%12;
}

Distance Distance::operator+(Distance d)
{
    Distance ans;
    int temp = (yards+d.yards)*36
               +(feet+d.feet)*12
               +inches + d.inches;
    ans.yards = temp/36;
    ans.feet = temp%36/12;
    ans.inches = temp%12;
    return ans;
}

int Distance::operator>(Distance d)
{
    if (convertToMetric()>d.convertToMetric())
        return 1;
    else
```

```
        return 0;
}

int Distance::operator==(Distance d)
{
    if (toInches() == d.toInches())
        return 1;
    else
        return 0;
}
```

main() coded as:

```
void main()
{
    Distance d1,d2,d3,d4;
    int y,f,i;

    //*** Get first distance ***
    cout<<"Distance 1\n";
    cout<<"Enter yards : ";
    cin>>y;
    cout<<"Enter feet : ";
    cin>>f;
    cout<<"Enter inches : ";
    cin>>i;
    d1.setDistance(y,f,i);
    //*** Get second distance ***
    cout<<"Distance 2\n";
    cout<<"Enter yards : ";
    cin>>y;
    cout<<"Enter feet : ";
    cin>>f;
    cout<<"Enter inches : ";
    cin>>i;
    d2.setDistance(y,f,i);
    //*** Get third distance ***
    cout<<"Distance 3\n";
    cout<<"Enter yards : ";
    cin>>y;
    cout<<"Enter feet : ";
    cin>>f;
    cout<<"Enter inches : ";
    cin>>i;
    d3.setDistance(y,f,i);
    //*** Double d1 **
    d1 += d1;
    //*** Set d4 to d1 + d2 ***
    d4 = d1 + d2;
    //*** Choose output message ***
    if (d1 >d4)
        cout<<"d1 is "<<d1.getYards()<<" yds "
            <<d1.getFeet()<<" ft "<<d1.getInches()
            <<" in\n";
    else
        if (d1 == d4)
            cout<<"Distances are equal\n";
        else
            cout<<"d4 is "<<d4.getYards()
                <<" yds "<<d4.getFeet()<<" ft "
                <<d4.getInches()<<" in\n";
}
```

PROGRAMMING EXERCISE 11.27

Distance class declaration:

```
class Distance
{
    private:
        int yards;
        int feet;
        int inches;
        int toInches();
        static int count;
    public:
        static const int metre;
        static const double centimetre;
        static int getCount();
        Distance(int=0, int=0, int=0);
        Distance(double);
        ~Distance();
        void setDistance(int,int,int);
        void setDistance(double);
        inline double convertToMetric();
        int getYards()
        int getFeet();
        int getInches();
        void operator+=(Distance);
        Distance operator+(Distance d);
        int operator>(Distance);
        int operator==(Distance);
        Distance operator ++();
        Distance operator ++(int);
        Distance operator --();
        Distance operator --(int);
        Distance smaller(Distance);
};
const int Distance::metre=39;
const double Distance::centimetre=0.3937;
int Distance::count = 0;
```

Code for ++ and -- operators

```
Distance Distance::operator++()
{
    int totalinches;

    totalinches = toInches()+1;
    yards = totalinches/36;
    feet = totalinches%36/12;
    inches = totalinches%12;
    return *this;
}

Distance Distance::operator++(int)
{
    int totalinches;
    Distance ans;

    ans = *this;
    totalinches = toInches()+1;
    yards = totalinches/36;
    feet = totalinches%36/12;
    inches = totalinches%12;
    return ans;
}

Distance Distance::operator--()
{
    int totalinches;

    totalinches = toInches()-1;
    if (totalinches<0)
        totalinches = 0;
    yards = totalinches/36;
    feet = totalinches%36/12;
    inches = totalinches%12;
    return *this;
}

Distance Distance::operator--(int)
{
    int totalinches;
    Distance ans;

    ans = *this;
    totalinches = toInches()-1;
    if (totalinches<0)
        totalinches = 0;
    yards = totalinches/36;
    feet = totalinches%36/12;
    inches = totalinches%12;
    return ans;
}
```

Possible *main()* function:

```
void main()
{
    Distance d1,d2,d3,d4;
    int y,f,i;

    //*** Get first distance ***
    cout<<"Distance 1\n";
    cout<<"Enter yards : ";
    cin>>y;
    cout<<"Enter feet : ";
    cin>>f;
    cout<<"Enter inches : ";
    cin>>i;
    d1.setDistance(y,f,i);
    d2 = d1++;
    cout<<"d1 = "<<d1.getYards()<<" yds "
        <<d1.getFeet()<<" ft "<<d1.getInches()
        <<" in\n";
    cout<<"d2 = "<<d2.getYards()<<" yds "
        <<d2.getFeet()<<" ft "<<d2.getInches()
        <<" in\n";
    d3 = (++d1)+(d2--);
    cout<<"\nd1 = "<<d1.getYards()<<" yds "
        <<d1.getFeet()<<" ft "<d1.getInches()
        <<" in\n";
    cout<<"d2 = "<<d2.getYards()<<" yds "
        <<d2.getFeet()<<" ft "<<d2.getInches()
        <<" in\n";
    cout<<"d3 = "<<d3.getYards()<<" yds "
        <<d3.getFeet()<<" ft "<<d3.getInches()
        <<" in\n";
```

```
        d4 = (--d1)+(++d2);
        cout<<"\nd1 = "<<d1.getYards()<<" yds "
            <<d1.getFeet()<<" ft "<d1.getInches()
            <<" in\n";
        cout<<"d2 = "<<d2.getYards()<<" yds "
            <<d2.getFeet()<<" ft "<<d2.getInches()
            <<" in\n";
        cout<<"d4 = "<<d4.getYards()<<" yds "
            <<d4.getFeet()<<" ft "<<d4.getInches()
            <<" in\n";
}
```

PROGRAMMING EXERCISE 11.28

No solution required.

PROGRAMMING EXERCISE 11.29

The program should still operate correctly.

PROGRAMMING EXERCISE 11.30

No solution required.

PROGRAMMING EXERCISE 11.31

No change is required to the *Distance* class itself. A new function is added as shown below:

```
ostream& operator<<(ostream& cc, Distance d)
{
    cc<<d.getYards()<<" yds "<<d.getFeet()
        <<" ft "<<d.getInches()<<" in";
    return cc;
}
```

This is tested in the *main()* that follows:

```
void main()
{
    Distance d1;
    int y,f,i;

    //*** Get distance ***
    cout<<"Enter yards : ";
    cin>>y;
    cout<<"Enter feet : ";
    cin>>f;
    cout<<"Enter inches : ";
    cin>>i;
    d1.setDistance(y,f,i);
    cout<<"d1 = "<<d1<<endl;
}
```

PROGRAMMING EXERCISE 11.32

No solution required.

PROGRAMMING EXERCISE 11.33

```
istream& operator>>(istream& ci, Distance& d)
{
    int y, f, i;

    cout<" Enter yards : ";
    ci>>y;
    while (y<0)
    {
        cout<<"Yards must be greater than zero.
            Re-enter ";
        ci>>y;
    }
    cout<<"Enter feet : ";
    ci>>f;
    while (f<0||f>2)
    {
        cout<<"Feet must lie between 0 and 2.
                Re-enter ";
        ci>>f;
    }
    cout<<"Enter inches : ";
    ci>>i;
    while (f<0||f>11)
    {
        cout<<"Inches must lie between 0 and 1.
                Re-enter ";
        ci>>I;
    }
    d.setDistance(y,f,i);
    return ci;
}

void main()
{
    Distance d1;

    //*** Get distance ***
    cin>>d1;
    cout<<"d1 = "<<d1<<endl;
}
```

PROGRAMMING EXERCISE 11.34

```
#include<iostream.h>

//Distance class code goes here

void main()
{
    Distance list[4];

    for(int c=0; c<3;c++)
    {
        cout<<"Enter distance : ";
        cin>>list[c];
    }

    for(c=0;c<4;c++)
        cout<<list[c]<<" is "
            <<list[c].convertToMetric()
            <<" metres\n";
}
```

PROGRAMMING EXERCISE 11.35

```
void main()
{
    Distance *distptr;
    distptr = new Distance(3,0,11);
    cout<<"distance = "<<*distptr<<endl;
}
```

PROGRAMMING EXERCISE 11.36

```
1.

#include <stdlib.h>
#include <string.h>
#include<iostream.h>
#include<math.h>

class Clock
{
    private:
        int hours;
        int minutes;
        int seconds;

    public:
        Clock();
        Clock(int,int,int);
        void setTime(int,int,int);
        int getHours();
        int getMinutes();
        int getSeconds();
        void tick();
        char* toString();
        void runClock(int);
};

Clock::Clock()
{
    hours = 0;
    minutes = 0;
    seconds = 0;
}
```

```
Clock::Clock(int h, int m, int s)
{
    if(h < 0 || h > 23 || m < 0 || m > 59
    || s < 0 || s > 59)
    {
        hours = 0;
        minutes = 0;
        seconds = 0;
    }
    else
    {
        hours = h;
        minutes = m;
        seconds = s;
    }
}

void Clock::setTime(int h, int m, int s)
{
    if(h > 23 || h < 0 || m < 0 || m > 59
    || s < 0 || s > 59)
        return;
    hours = h;
    minutes = m;
    seconds = s;
}

int Clock::getHours()
{
    return hours;
}

int Clock::getMinutes()
{
    return minutes;
}

int Clock::getSeconds()
{
    return seconds;
}

void Clock::tick()
{
    long totalsecs = hours *3600L + minutes * 60
                        + seconds + 1;
    hours = (totalsecs/3600)%24;
    minutes = (totalsecs%3600/60);
    seconds = totalsecs%60;
}

char* Clock::toString()
{
    char h[3],m[3],s[3], result[9]="";
    strcpy(result,itoa(hours,h,10));
    strcat(result,":");
    strcat(result,itoa(minutes,m,10));
    strcat(result,":");
    strcat(result,itoa(seconds,s,10));
    return result;
}

void Clock::runClock(int secs)
{
    for(int c = 1; c <= secs; c++)
    {
        cout<<"              \r"<<toString()<<'\r';
        tick();
        for(long k =0; k <900000;k++)
            double x = sin(k/1000);
    }
}


void main()
{
    Clock cl(23,59,54);
    cl.runClock(10);
}
```

2.

```
#include<iostream.h>
#include<string.h>

class ChangeDispenser
{
    private:
        int coins[5][5];
        int moneyinserted;
        int costofitem;
    public:
        ChangeDispenser();
        ChangeDispenser(int[]);
        void setCostOfItem(int);
        int matchCoin(int);
        void addMoney(int);
        int* refund();
        int* buy();
        int isSufficient();
        int* empty();
        void addChange(int[]);
        int* getCoins();
        int* getCoinValues();
        int getMoneyInserted();
        int getCostOfItem();
};

ChangeDispenser::ChangeDispenser()
{
    const int values[5][5]={{5,10,20,50,100},
                            {3,3,3,3,0}};
    for(int r=0; r < 2; r++)
        for(int p = 0; p < 5; p++)
            coins[r][p] = values[r][p];
    moneyinserted = 0;
    costofitem = 0;
}

ChangeDispenser::ChangeDispenser(int coincount[])
{
    const int values[]={5,10,20,50,100};
    for(int p = 0; p < 5; p++)
        coins[0][p] = values[p];
    for(int c = 0; c < 5; c++)
        coins[1][c]=coincount[c];
    moneyinserted = 0;
    costofitem = 0;
}

void ChangeDispenser::setCostOfItem(int cost)
{
    if(cost<0||cost>500||cost%coins[0][0]!=0)
        return;
    costofitem = cost;
}

int ChangeDispenser::matchCoin(int coin)
{
    for(int c = 0; c < 5; c++)
        if (coin == coins[0][c])
            return c;
    return -1;
}

void ChangeDispenser::addMoney(int coin)
{
    int foundat = matchCoin(coin);
    if (foundat == -1)
        return;
    coins[1][foundat]++;
    moneyinserted+=coin;
}

int* ChangeDispenser::refund()
{
    int *moneyreturned = new int[5];
    for(int c = 0; c < 5; c++)
        moneyreturned[c]=0;
    int insertedcopy = moneyinserted;
    int position = 4;
    while (insertedcopy != 0 && position >= 0)
    {
        moneyreturned[position] =
                insertedcopy / coins[0][position];
        if (coins[1][position] <
        moneyreturned[position])
            moneyreturned[position] =
                            coins[1][position];
        insertedcopy -= moneyreturned[position]
                            *coins[0][position];
        coins[1][position] -=
                        moneyreturned[position];
        position--;
    }
    moneyinserted = 0;
    return moneyreturned;
}

int* ChangeDispenser::buy()
{
    if(!isSufficient())
        return refund();
    moneyinserted -=costofitem;
    int *result= refund();
    moneyinserted = 0;
    return result;
}

int ChangeDispenser::isSufficient()
{
    return (moneyinserted >= costofitem);
}

int* ChangeDispenser::empty()
{
    int *copy = new int[5];
```

```
    for(int c = 0; c < 5; c++)
    {
        copy[c] = coins[1][c];
        coins[1][c]=0;
    }
    return copy;
}

void ChangeDispenser::addChange(int cash[])
{
    for(int c = 0; c < 5; c++)
        coins[1][c]+=cash[c];
}

int* ChangeDispenser::getCoins()
{
    int *coinscopy = new int[5];
    for(int c = 0; c < 5; c++)
        coinscopy[c] = coins[1][c];
    return coinscopy;
}

int* ChangeDispenser::getCoinValues()
{
    int *coinscopy = new int[5];
    for(int c = 0; c < 5; c++)
        coinscopy[c] = coins[0][c];
    return coinscopy;
}

int ChangeDispenser::getMoneyInserted()
{
    return moneyinserted;
}

int ChangeDispenser::getCostOfItem()
{
    return costofitem;
}

//*** Function prototypes ***
int DisplayMenu(char*);
int GetOption(int);
void ExecuteOption(int,ChangeDispenser&);

void main()
{
    ChangeDispenser cd;
    int option, noofoptions;

    do
    {
        noofoptions=DisplayMenu(
            "1. - setCostOfItem()\n
            2. - addMoney()\n
            3. - refund()\n4. - buy()\n
            5. - empty()\n6. - addChange()\n
            7. - getCoins()\n8. - QUIT\n");
        option = GetOption(noofoptions);
        ExecuteOption(option, cd);
    }
    while (option != noofoptions);
    cout<<"PROGRAM TERMINATED\n";
}


int DisplayMenu(char* m)
{
    cout<<m;
    for(int c=0, count=0; c<strlen(m);c++)
        if(m[c]=='\n')
            count++;
    return count;
}

int GetOption(int max)
{
    int opt;
    cout<<"\nEnter option : ";
    cin>>opt;
    while(opt<1||opt>max)
    {
        cout<<"Invalid option\n";
        cin>>opt;
    }
    return opt;
}

void ExecuteOption(int opt, ChangeDispenser& cd)
{

    int post,c;
    int cost, coin;
    int *money, *denom;
    switch (opt)
    {
        case 1:
            cout<<"Enter cost of item : ";
            cin>>cost;
            cd.setCostOfItem(cost);
            break;
        case 2:
            cout<<"Insert coins (enter values
                    in pence)\n";
            cout<<"Enter -1 after last coin\n";
            cout<<"Enter coin value: ";
            cin>>coin;
            while(coin!=-1)
            {
                cd.addMoney(coin);
                cout<<"Enter coin value: ";
                cin>>coin;
            }
            break;
        case 3:
            cout<<"Your refund is "
                <<cd.getMoneyInserted()<<"p\n";
            cout<<"Coins returned :\n";
            money = cd.refund();
            denom = cd.getCoinValues();
            for(c = 0; c < 5; c++)
                if(money[c] > 0)
                    cout<<money[c]<<"  "<<denom[c]
                        <<"p coins\n";
            cout<<"\n\n";
            delete [] money;
            delete [] denom;
            break;
        case 4:
            cout<<"Your item cost "
                <<cd.getCostOfItem()<<"p\n";
            cout<<"You inserted "
                <<cd.getMoneyInserted()<<"p\n";
            money = cd.buy();
            denom=cd.getCoinValues();
            cout<<"Coins returned : ";
            for(c=0; c<5; c++)
                if(money[c] > 0)
                    cout<<money[c]<<"  "<<denom[c]
                        <<"p coins\n";
            cout<<"\n\n";
            delete [] money;
            delete [] denom;
            break;
        case 5:
            cout<<"The machine contained : \n";
            money = cd.empty();
            denom = cd.getCoinValues();
            for(c=0; c<5; c++)
                cout<<money[c]<<"  "<<denom[c]
                    <<"p coins\n";
            cout<<"\n\n";
            delete [] money;
            delete [] denom;
            break;
        case 6:
            denom=cd.getCoinValues();
            money=new int[5];
            for(c=0;c<5;c++)
            {
                cout<<"How many "<<denom[c]
                    <<"p coins? ";
                cin>>money[c];
            };
            cd.addChange(money);
            delete [] money;
            delete [] denom;
            break;
        case 7:
            cout<<"The machine contains :\n";
            money = cd.getCoins();
            denom=cd.getCoinValues();
            for(c=0; c<5; c++)
                cout<<money[c]<<"  "<<denom[c]
                    <<"p coins\n";
            cout<<"\n\n";
            delete [] money;
            delete [] denom;
            break;
    }
}
```

Chapter 12
Class Relationships

This chapter covers the following topics:

Abstract Classes

Aggregate Classes

Class Relationships and Pointers

Class Templates

Container Classes

Delegation

Function Templates

Multiple Inheritance

Polymorphism

Single Inheritance

Static Attributes and Derived Classes

Virtual Base Classes

INHERITANCE

Relationships

Introduction

We all have ancestors. From these ancestors we have inherited our features and basic abilities through our DNA. Although this DNA comes from both our parents, in asexual species the DNA is an exact copy of the parent. Nevertheless, even asexual species can adapt and modify inherited traits from generation to generation.

Inheriting what has gone before and adapting it to the current environment is not limited to the animal kingdom; for example, widescreen high-definition stereo television also has an ancestry which can be traced through radio; black-and-white TV; colour TV; stereo, colour TV; and 16:9 widescreen TV. At each step in the process the features of its immediate predecessor were incorporated in the latest advance, but these were then added to and modified where necessary to create the new product.

This approach of building on what has gone before is one of the main goals of object-oriented programming. By adopting this technique it is hoped that classes can be reused in other applications, or modified to create new classes with a minimum amount of development time and a reduction in errors.

Class Relationships

If we were to create UML class diagrams for radio and black-and-white television, we might come up with the diagrams shown in FIG-12.1

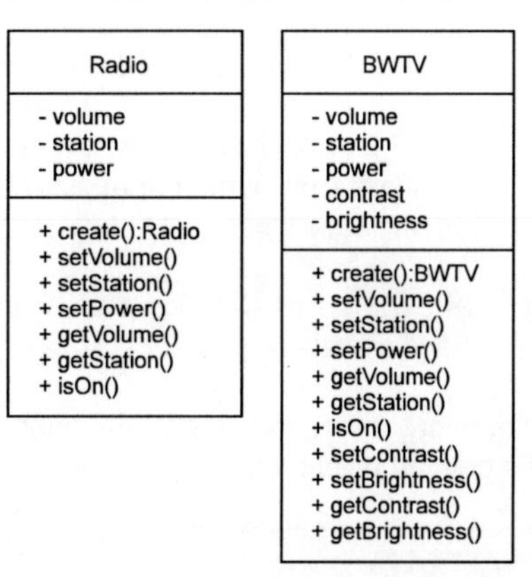

FIG-12.1

Radio and BWTV Classes

We can see that the television class (*BWTV*) is simply an extension of the *Radio* class with extra attributes and operations. That isn't surprising since, as we have already inferred, television is simply a radio with pictures.

UML uses a diagram somewhat akin to a family tree to represent this relationship (see FIG-12.2).

The diagram with the arrowed line shows that *BWTV* is a class which is descended from the *Radio* class. Notice also that only the features new to the *BWTV* class are included in its rectangle. This is because, in object-oriented design, any new class is automatically assumed to have inherited all its parent's features. The new class can then have additional features added and only these new features are shown in the diagram.

FIG-12.2

A Class Relationship Diagram

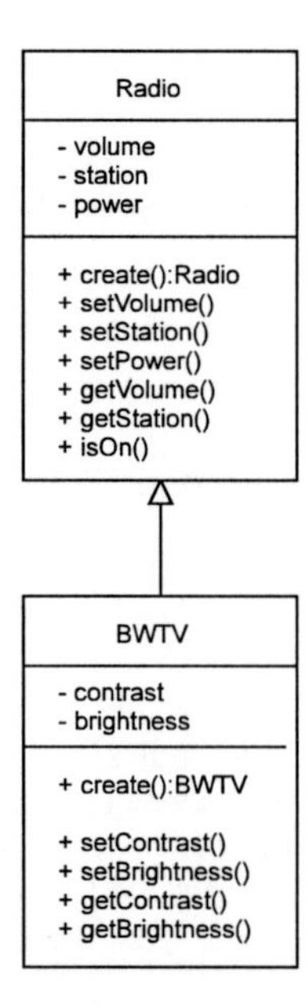

If these two classes were to become part of a computer program (perhaps as part of a simulation game), then the traditional program approach would require each to be coded separately. Since both items have many things in common, the resulting code would contain a great deal of duplication. However, using an object-oriented approach, this duplication can be avoided.

> **TASK 12.1**
>
> From the diagram above, list the attributes of the *BWTV* class.

FIG-12.2 introduces the need for a few new terms:

- The terms **base class**, **superclass** or **parent class** are used to describe the class from which another class is derived. In the diagram above, *Radio* is the base class.
- The terms **derived class**, **subclass** or **child class** are used to describe a derived class.

There are no restrictions on the number of generations of derived classes that may be created or the number of child classes that can be derived from a single class.

> **TASK 12.2**
>
> Draw the UML diagram above.
>
> Add a new class, *ColourTV*, which is derived from *BWTV* class.
>
> The new class has the attributes:
> *volume, station, power, contrast, brightness,* and *colour intensity*
>
> It has the same operations as the *BWTV* class but adds *setColourIntensity()* and *getColourIntensity()* operations.

> **TASK 12.3**
>
> Add a fourth class to your diagram: *StereoRadio*. This class is derived from the *Radio* class but has an additional *balance* attribute and *setBalance()* and *getBalance()* methods.

Implementing Derived Classes

The *Clock* Class

In the previous chapter we created a *Clock* class. The code for the class is given below:

```
class Clock
{
    private:
        int hours;
        int minutes;
        int seconds;

    public:
        Clock();
        Clock(int,int,int);
        void setTime(int,int,int);
        int getHours();
        int getMinutes();
        int getSeconds();
        void tick();
        char* toString();
};
Clock::Clock()
{
    hours = 0;
    minutes = 0;
    seconds = 0;
}
Clock::Clock(int h, int m, int s)
{
    if(h < 0 || h > 23 || m < 0 || m > 59 || s < 0 || s > 59)
    {
        hours = 0;
        minutes = 0;
        seconds = 0;
    }
    else
    {
        hours = h;
        minutes = m;
        seconds = s;
    }
}
void Clock::setTime(int h, int m, int s)
{
    if(h > 23 || h < 0 || m < 0 || m > 59 || s < 0 || s > 59)
        return;
    hours = h;
    minutes = m;
    seconds = s;
}
int Clock::getHours()
{
    return hours;
}
int Clock::getMinutes()
{
    return minutes;
}
```

```
int Clock::getSeconds()
{
    return seconds;
}
void Clock::tick()
{
    long totalsecs = hours *3600L + minutes * 60 + seconds + 1;
    hours = (totalsecs /3600)%24;
    minutes = (totalsecs % 3600 / 60);
    seconds = totalsecs % 60;
}
char* Clock::toString()
{
    char h[3],m[3],s[3], result[9]="";
    strcpy(result,itoa(hours,h,10));
    strcat(result,":");
    strcat(result,itoa(minutes,m,10));
    strcat(result,":");
    strcat(result,itoa(seconds,s,10));
    return result;
}
void Clock::runClock(int secs)
{
    for(int c = 1; c <= secs; c++)
    {
        cout<<"              \r"<<toString()<<'\r';
        tick();
        for(long k =0; k <900000;k++)
            double x = sin(k/1000);
    }
}
```

The *AlarmClock* Class

An alarm clock has all the same features as a clock, but with additional abilities; not only does it display the current time, but also triggers an alarm at a specific time of day. To program an alarm clock we need to create a new class (*AlarmClock*). Since an alarm clock has all the features of a normal clock, the *AlarmClock* class should be a descendant of the original *Clock* class. But, in addition, the new class needs attributes to hold the time at which the alarm is to go off and operations to set and get this alarm time. Finally, we need an operation to check if the current time equals the alarm time. All of this information is given in the UML diagram in FIG-12.3.

FIG-12.3

The *Clock* and *AlarmClock* Classes

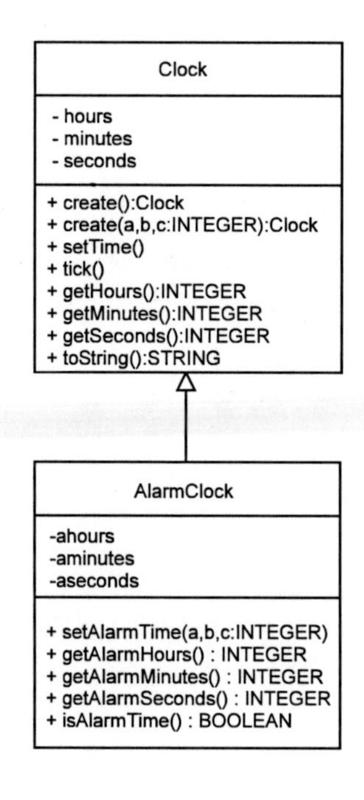

No constructor operations have been included in the *AlarmClock* class at this point.

When we come to code the *AlarmClock* class in C++, we can show that the new class is derived from the *Clock* class by starting the class declaration with the line

```
class AlarmClock : public Clock
```

By adding the expression `: public Clock` we tell the compiler that our new *AlarmClock* class is a descendant of the *Clock* class.

As a subclass of *Clock, AlarmClock* inherits all the features of *Clock*. This means our code only requires to specify the additional features of the new class. We need new attributes to record the time at which the alarm is to go off:

```
class AlarmClock : public Clock
{
    private:
        int ahours;
        int aminutes;
        int aseconds;
```

We also need new methods to set and get these new attributes:

```
public:
    void setAlarmTime(int, int, int);
    int getAlarmHours();
    int getAlarmMinutes();
    int getAlarmSeconds();
```

Since C++ does not implement a Boolean type, the final operation, *isAlarmTime()*, is coded with an `int` return type:

```
int isAlarmTime();
```

So, our final *AlarmClock* declaration is coded as:

```
class AlarmClock : public Clock
{
    private:
        int ahours;
        int aminutes;
        int aseconds;
    public:
        void setAlarmTime(int, int, int);
        int getAlarmHours();
        int getAlarmMinutes();
        int getAlarmSeconds();
        int isAlarmTime();
};
```

This is followed by the code for each of the methods declared:

```
void AlarmClock::setAlarmTime(int h, int m, int s)
{
    if(h < 0 || h > 23 || m < 0 || m > 59 || s < 0 || s > 59)
        return;
    ahours = h;
    aminutes = m;
    aseconds = s;
}

int AlarmClock::getAlarmHours()
{
    return ahours;
}

int AlarmClock::getAlarmMinutes()
{
    return aminutes;
}
```

```
int AlarmClock::getAlarmSeconds()
{
    return aseconds;
}

int AlarmClock::isAlarmTime()
{
    if(hours==ahours && minutes==aminutes && seconds==aseconds)
        return 1;
    else
        return 0;
}
```

> **PROGRAMMING EXERCISE 12.1**
>
> Add the code for the *AlarmClock* class to the C++ file containing your *Clock* class. The new code should be placed immediately before *main()*.
>
> Attempt to compile the updated file.

If we try compiling this, we'll get error messages such as:

```
Clock::hours is not accessible in function AlarmClock::isAlarmTime()
```

The reason for this is that *hours, minutes* and *seconds* are declared as private within the superclass, *Clock*. We've already seen that an attribute that is declared as private cannot be accessed by an application program which defines objects of that class. Now, a further restriction has become apparent: private attributes inherited by a descendent class cannot be accessed from the methods added in that new class. Hence, the private attributes *hours*, *minutes*, and *seconds* inherited from the *Clock* class cannot be accessed by the *isAlarmTime()* in the descendant *AlarmClock* class.

To get round this we could rewrite *isAlarmTime()* using *getHours(), getMinutes()* and *getSeconds():*

```
int AlarmClock::isAlarmTime()
{
    if(getHours() == ahours && getMinutes() == aminutes
    ↳&& getSeconds() == aseconds)
        return 1;
    else
        return 0;
}
```

Protected Attributes

Alternatively, since we have access to the *Clock* source code, we could replace the term `private` with the keyword `protected`.

An attribute labelled as `protected` is still inaccessible to the application programs that create objects of that class, but descendent classes have free access. Hence, if we re-code the *Clock* class to begin

```
class Clock
{
    protected:
        int hours;
        int minutes;
        int seconds;
                    .
```

we can use our original version *isAlarmTime()*.

PROGRAMMING EXERCISE 12.2

Change the attributes of the *Clock* and *AlarmClock* classes from `private` to `protected`.

In *main()* define *cl* as a *AlarmClock* object. Execute the object's *tick()* method and display the time.

Does the program execute correctly?

Constructors in Descendant Classes

The one feature that a class does not inherit from its parent class is its constructor. After all, a constructor must have the same name as the class to which it belongs, so it would not be appropriate for *AlarmClock* to inherit a constructor called *Clock()*.

So, we could include a constructor for *AlarmClock* which sets both the current time and the alarm time:

```
public AlarmClock(int h, int m, int s, int ah, int am, int as)
{
    if(h<0||h>23||m<0||m>59||s<0||s>59||ah<0||ah>23||am<0
    ↳||am>59||as<0||as>59)
    {
        hours = 0;
        minutes = 0;
        seconds = 0;
        ahours = 0;
        aminutes = 0;
        aseconds = 0;
    }
    else
    {
        hours = h;
        minutes = m;
        seconds = s;
        ahours = ah;
        aminutes = am;
        aseconds = as;
    }
}
```

Calling the Base Class Constructor

If you compare the code for the *Clock* class constructor with that of the *AlarmClock*'s constructor, you'll see that both contain similar code for assigning values to *hours, minutes* and *seconds.*

We can save many lines of coding within the *AlarmClock* constructor by getting it to execute the code of the *Clock* constructor. Luckily, this is possible. A descendant class can execute its parent's constructor within its own constructor by adding the an expression of the form

```
: superclass-name(parameters for superclass's constructor)
```

between the end of the constructor heading and the opening brace enclosing the constructor's code. More specifically, the *AlarmClock* class's constructor can call the *Clock* class's constructor by starting with the code:

```
AlarmClock::AlarmClock(int h, int m, int s, int ah, int am, int as)
:Clock(h,m,s)
```

So we can rewrite the *AlarmClock* constructor as:

```
AlarmClock::AlarmClock(int h, int m, int s, int ah, int am, int as)
:Clock(h,m,s)
    {
        if(ah<0||ah>23||am<0||am>59||as<0||as>59)
        {
            ahours = 0;
            aminutes = 0;
            aseconds = 0;
        }
        else
        {
            ahours = ah;
            aminutes = am;
            aseconds = as;
        }
    }
```

In fact, the constructor of a new class MUST call the constructor of its parent class. Where the parent class has a zero-argument constructor, that constructor will be called automatically, but when this is not the case, there must be an explicit call (as shown above) to the parent constructor as the first line in the constructor of the new class.

PROGRAMMING EXERCISE 12.3

Add the constructor given above to the *AlarmClock* class and recompile your file.

Write an application program which uses the following logic:

```
Create an alarm clock set to 12:29:59
Set the alarmTime to 12:30:00
Add 1 second to the time (Using tick())
IF alarm time reached THEN
    Display "Time to get up "
ENDIF
```

Overriding Methods

Of course, there will be times when an inherited method is not appropriate for a new class. For example, looking at the code for *tick()*:

```
void Clock::tick()
{
    long totalsecs = hours *3600L + minutes * 60 + seconds + 1;
    hours = (totalsecs /3600)%24;
    minutes = (totalsecs % 3600 / 60);
    seconds = totalsecs % 60;
}
```

We can see that it does not react to reaching the specified alarm time. Because of this, the solution to PROGRAMMING EXERCISE 12.3 contained code such as:

```
al.tick();
if (al.isAlarmTime())
    cout<<"Time to get up\n";
```

However, it might suit our purposes if this alarm message was displayed by *tick()* itself when the appropriate time was reached.

To achieve this, the *AlarmClock* class needs a new version of the *tick()* method. To create the new routine, we simply include the code for the new method within the *AlarmClock* class.

This is known as **overriding** the inherited method. To overwrite an inherited method the new version must have the same name and parameters as the original inherited method.

So, to make the *tick()* method of the *AlarmClock* class produce a message when the current time is equal to the alarm time, we use the following code:

```
void AlarmClock::tick()
{
    long totalsecs = hours *3600L + minutes * 60 + seconds + 1;
    hours = (totalsecs / 3600) % 24;
    minutes = (totalsecs % 3600 / 60);
    seconds = totalsecs % 60;
    if (isAlarmTime())
        cout<<"Time to get up!\n";
}
```

Notice, as in the constructor, we're using code that duplicates all the lines given in the original version of *tick()*. Again, we can get the new routine to call the old one and save the extra typing and testing. This time, however, the line required to do this is

```
Clock::tick();
```

which executes the *tick()* method used in the superclass.

This gives us the final code for the new version of *tick()* in the *AlarmClock* class:

```
void AlarmClock::tick()
{
    Clock::tick();
    if(isAlarmTime())
        cout<<"Time to get up!\n";
}
```

PROGRAMMING EXERCISE 12.4

Add the overridden version of *tick()* to *AlarmClock* and test the class.

Test that the new method is executed correctly by modifying *main()* to perform the following:

```
Create an AlarmClock object with the time set to 12:0:0 and
the alarm time set to 12:0:1.
Execute the object's tick() method
```

Did the "Time to get up" message appear?

If the parameters of the new method were different, then the method would have been overloaded, giving multiple versions of *tick()* within the *AlarmClock* class. So, the *AlarmClock* version of *tick()* is coded as

```
void AlarmClock::tick(String s)
{
    Clock::tick();
    if(isAlarmTime())
        cout<<s<<endl;
}
```

which allows the message displayed to be passed as a parameter, then we would have two versions of *tick()* within the *AlarmClock* class; the one inherited from *Clock* (which takes no parameters) and this new one defined within *AlarmClock* (which takes a *char** parameter*)*.

> **PROGRAMMING EXERCISE 12.5**
>
> Create a new class, *CountdownClock*, which is a descendant of the *Clock* class, but differs from that class in that the *tick()* method reduces the time by one second.
>
> Add a constructor to the class. This should have three parameters representing the time (hours, minutes and seconds) to which the clock is to be set. Define the constructor to use default values of 0,0,0.
>
> Create an object of this class in *main()*, setting its time to 0:0:10. Display the time both before and after execution of the object's *tick()* method.
>
> Did the clock's time move back 1 second?
>
> Try running the program again with the initial time set to midnight (0:0:0).

Polymorphism

Introduction

> **PROGRAMMING EXERCISE 12.6**
>
> Create an application program containing both a *Clock* object and a *CountdownClock* object.
>
> Set both objects to the time 12:00:00.
>
> Execute the *tick()* methods of both objects and display the time of each.

From the results of PROGRAMMING EXERCISE 12.6 we can see that each object executes its own version of *tick()*. So the *Clock* object moves on to 12:00:01 while the *CountdownClock* object moves back to 11:59:59. This ability to execute the version of a routine appropriate to the type of object involved is known as **polymorphism** and, as we will see, is a cornerstone of object-oriented programming.

With Inherited Routines

If you have another look at the *runClock()* method defined in the *Clock* class, you'll see that the routine calls *tick()*. Now, if we create a *Clock* class object in our program, when *main()* contains the lines

```
Clock time(1,2,3);
time.runClock(20);
```

we should see the clock count though the time interval 1:2:3 to 1:2:22.

> **PROGRAMMING EXERCISE 12.7**
>
> Change *main()* in your last program and declare a *Clock* object called *time*. Set *time* to 1:30:00 and call *runClock()* to display for 20 seconds.
>
> Now, change *time* to a *CountdownClock* object and execute the program again.
>
> What effect does this have on the statement:
> `time.runClock(20);` ?

Although we created a *CountdownClock* object, the time moved forward rather than backwards!

To understand why this has happened we need to know something of how the C++ compiler operates. You already know that the basic concept behind a compiler is to change the source language (C++ in this case) to the object language (Intel machine code). Normally, this is done before execution of the program begins.

If the source code contains a call to another function, this is translated into machine call as a jump to the start address of that routine (see FIG-12.4).

This means the machine code for *runClock()* is committed to executing the version

FIG-12.4

Jumping to a Subroutine

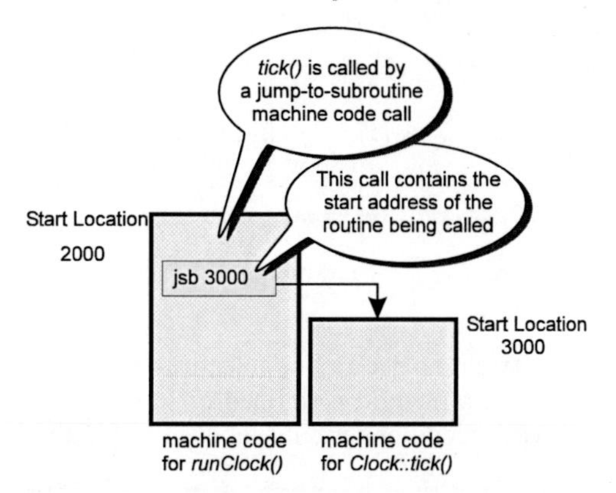

of *tick()* defined within the *Clock* class : the same class that *runClock()* itself is defined in.

Unfortunately, this isn't what we want. We'd like *runClock()* to execute the version of *tick()* defined within the object which is executing *runClock()*. That is to say, if a *CountdownClock* object calls *runClock()* then we want *runClock()* to execute *tick()* as defined within the *CountdownClock* class, but *runClock()* executed by an *AlarmClock* object should execute the version of *tick()* defined in the *AlarmClock* class.

This can only be achieved if we can delay the decision on what address is to be used by the jump-to-subroutine instruction in the machine code until the program is actually running. At that point we can determine what type of object is executing *runClock()* and insert the address for the appropriate version of *tick()* (see FIG-12.5).

Deciding on the address of a routine at compile time is known as **early binding**. Waiting until the program is running, when the appropriate version of the routine can be called, is known as **late binding**.

FIG-12.5

The Effect of Late Binding

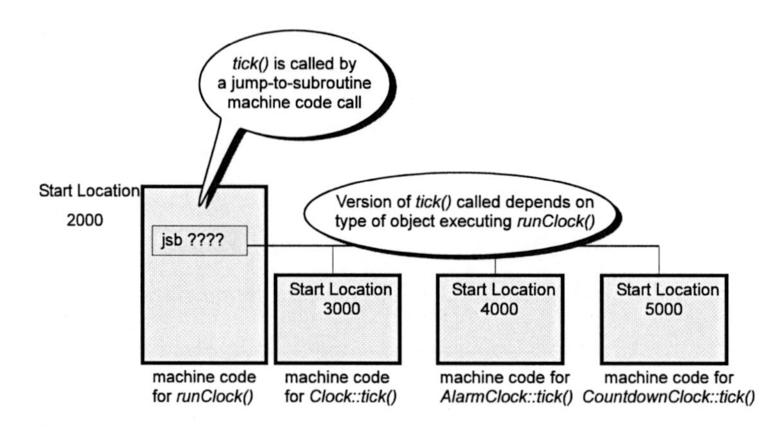

By default, C++ uses early binding when deciding on which version of a routine is to be called. To force late binding, the routine in question should use the keyword **virtual** in its prototype. In our example we want to force late binding on the *tick()* method, so we change the *Clock* class definition to read:

```
class Clock
{
    protected:
        int hours;
        int minutes;
        int seconds;

    public:
        Clock();
        Clock(int,int,int);
        void setTime(int,int,int);
        int getHours();
        int getMinutes();
        int getSeconds();
        virtual void tick();
        char* toString();
        void runClock(int);
};
```

There is no need to include the term **virtual** in any later versions of the *tick()* class. Once a method is defined as `virtual` all overriding methods in later classes are assumed to be virtual (i.e. use late binding) too.

PROGRAMMING EXERCISE 12.8

Add the term `virtual` to the prototype for *tick()* in the *Clock* class.

Re-run your program.

Does the *CountdownClock* object tick backwards?

Object Pointers and Descendant Classes

We saw in the last chapter that a pointer could be used to reference a dynamically allocated object. Hence, the statement

```
Clock  *ckptr = new Clock(1,2,3);
```

causes *ckptr* to reference a *Clock* object.

But we can use that same *Clock* pointer variable to reference an object of any descendant class. This means it is also valid to write

```
Clock *ckptr = new AlarmClock(1,2,3,1,2,4);
```

and *ckptr* will quite happily reference an *AlarmClock* object, since the *AlarmClock* class is a descendant of the *Clock* class.

TASK 12.4

Which of the following statements are also valid?

a) `Clock *ckptr = new CountdownClock(1,2,3);`
b) `Clock *ckptr = new Distance(1,2,3);`
c) `Clock *ckptr = new Weight(2,3);`
d) `AlarmClock *ckptr = new Clock();`

What's more, if we use a statement such as

```
ckptr->tick();
```

C++ will execute the version of *tick()* appropriate to the actual class of object that *ckptr* is referencing, as long as that function has been declared as `virtual`. Hence, the combination

```
Clock *ckptr = new Clock(1,2,3);
ckptr->tick();
```

will execute the code

```
void Clock::tick()
{
    long totalsecs = hours *3600L + minutes * 60 + seconds + 1;
    hours = (totalsecs /3600)%24;
    minutes = (totalsecs % 3600 / 60);
    seconds = totalsecs % 60;
}
```

while the lines

```
Clock *ckptr = new AlarmClock(1,2,3,1,2,4);
ckptr->tick();
```

will execute

```
void AlarmClock::tick()
{
    Clock::tick();
    if (isAlarmTime())
        cout<<"Time to get up\n";
}
```

PROGRAMMING EXERCISE 12.9

Create a new test program for the *Clock* classes. Within *main()* begin with the line

```
    Clock *time;
```

and then make this variable reference an AlarmClock object

```
    time = new AlarmClock(1,2,3,1,2,4);
```

and check that the *AlarmClock* version of *tick()* is executed by the statement:

```
    time->tick()
```

Modify the program to check that the *CountdownClock* version of *tick()* is executed when *time* references a *CountdownClock* object.

TASK 12.5

Class *A* defines a method *f()*. Class *B* is a descendant of class *A*. Class *B* overrides method *f()*. If *main()* contains the following lines:

```
A *ptr = new B();
ptr->f();
```

which version of *f()* will be executed *A::f()* or *B::f()*?

Limitations

However, there are limitations in making an object pointer reference a descendant class; methods not named in the original class cannot be accessed directly.

Hence, having written

```
Clock *ckptr = new AlarmClock(1,2,3,1,2,4);
```

the term

```
cl->getAlarmHours();
```

is invalid because *getAlarmHours()* is not defined in the *Clock* class which *ckptr* is primarily designed to reference (see FIG-12.6).

FIG-12.6

Limited Access to Derived Class Objects

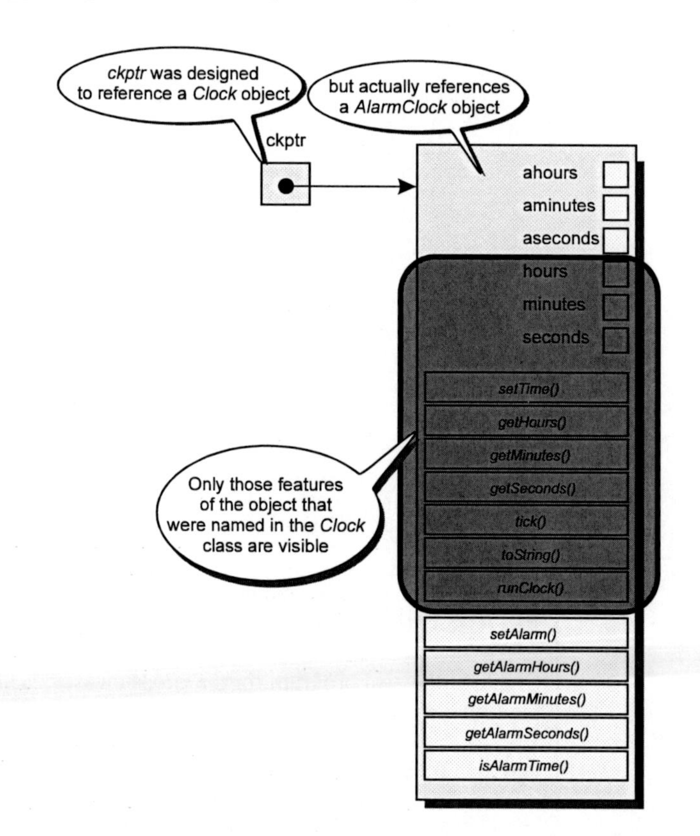

To access methods named for the first time in the *AlarmClock* class, we need to cast *ckptr* to an *AlarmClock* pointer type using the expression

```
((AlarmClock*)cl)->getAlarmHours()
```

This allows code such as:

```
cout<<"Alarm hour is"<<((AlarmClock*)cl)->getAlarmHours();
```

TASK 12.6

If a program contains the line

```
Clock *ckptr = new CountdownClock(1,2,3);
```

what methods of the *CountdownClock* class would necessitate the casting of *ckptr* to a *CountdownClock* object?

There are some situations where the programmer might not know the type of object that is being referenced. For example, *main()* in LISTING-12.1 has the following logic:

```
Ask user what type of clock is to be created
Create requested clock type
Display time
Make clock tick for 1 second
Display clock time
```

LISTING-12.1

Referencing Descendant Class Objects

```
void main()
{
  Clock *c1=NULL;
  cout << "Which type of clock?\n";
  cout << "1 - Clock\n";
  cout << "2 - AlarmClock\n";
  cout << "3 - CountdownClock\n";
  cout << "Enter choice (1,2,3): ";
  int choice;
  cin >> choice;
  switch(choice)
  {
      case 1:
          c1 = new Clock(1,2,3);
          break;
      case 2:
          c1 = new AlarmClock(1,2,3,1,2,4);
          break;
      case 3:
          c1 = new CountdownClock(1,2,3);
          break;
  }
  cout<<c1->toString()<<endl;
  c1->tick();
  cout<<c1->toString()<<endl;
}
```

PROGRAMMING EXERCISE 12.10

Modify your program containing the *Clock, AlarmClock* and *CountdownClock* classes to use the version of *main()* given in LISTING-12.1.

Check that each type of object is created successfully and that the correct version of *tick()* is executed.

As you can see, the programmer cannot know which type of object will be created. For the most part, that doesn't matter since the correct version of *tick()* will be automatically chosen and executed as long as the original version of *tick()*, in the *Clock* class, has been declared using the keyword `virtual`.

The *typeid* Keyword

But what if we wanted to allow the user to set the alarm time when an *AlarmClock* object is created? Since *setAlarm()* is a method only defined within the *AlarmClock* class, we need to add the following logic to our program:

```
IF object created is an alarm clock THEN
    Set Alarm time
ENDIF
```

C++ allows us to find out exactly the type of object referenced by using the keyword:

```
typeid
```

This acts much like a function call, taking an object or a class name as an argument and returning details of the argument's class.

The *typeinfo* Class

The `typeid` keyword actually returns an object of the class *typeinfo*. This is a simple class with the following methods:

`const char* name()`
Returns the name of the class given as an argument to `typeid`.
Typical usage:
```
cout << typeid(c1).name();
```

`int before(const typeinfo& t)const`
Returns 1 if the current *typeinfo* object's *name()* method returns a string which is less than *t.name()*, otherwise 0 is returned.
Typical usage:
```
if (typeid(c1).before(typeid(c2))
```

`int operator==(const typeinfo& t)const`
Returns 1 if the current *typeinfo* object's *name()* returns the same value as *t.name()*, otherwise 0 is returned.
Typical usage:
```
if(typeid(c1) == typeid(Clock))
```

`int operator!=(const typeinfo& t)const`
Returns 1 if the current *typeinfo* object's *name()* returns a different value from *t.name()*, otherwise 0 is returned.
Typical usage:
```
if (typeid(c1) != typeid(c2))
```

To make use of the *typeinfo* object returned by `typeid`, you need to add the line

```
#include<typeinfo.h>
```

at the start of your program.

The *typeinfo* class has a private constructor, so you can't create objects of this class with statements such as

```
typeinfo ti;
```

but you can make use of the *typeinfo* object returned by *typeid* to check if an object is of a given class with a statement such as:

```
if(typeid(*c1) == typeid(AlarmClock))
    cout << "c1 references an AlarmClock object\n";
```

PROGRAMMING EXERCISE 12.11

Modify the program you created in PROGRAMMING EXERCISE 12.10 so that the user can choose the alarm time if an alarm clock is created.

Insert your code after the end of the `switch` statement and make use of the `typeid` keyword.

Where else in *main()* could the alarm time be set without having to make use of `typeid`?

The `typeid` test will give a compilation error if you use a class pointer with a value of NULL For example, if *c1* is originally defined as

```
Clock *c1 = NULL;
if(typeid(*c1) == typeid(AlarmClock))
    cout << "You are using an AlarmClock object\n"
```

the program will give a runtime error. You can avoid this problem by checking for the NULL value first:

```
if(c1 != NULL && typeid(*c1) == typeid(AlarmClock))
    cout << "You are using an AlarmClock object\n"
```

The `typeid` keyword can also be used on basic C++ type. Hence, we could check that variable *x* is of type `int` with the statement:

```
if(typeid(x) == typeid(int))
```

Parameters and Descendant Classes

As demonstrated earlier, we can create a reference variable designed to contain the address of an object of one class and end up using it to reference an object of a descendant class. The same rules apply to function parameters.

Let's assume that the application programmer wants to display the time as a number of seconds since midnight. Since there is no method in the *Clock* class that allows him to do this, he could write a traditional function to perform the task. This would be coded as:

```
long toSeconds(Clock c)
{
    return (c.getHours()*3600+c.getMinutes()*60+c.getSeconds());
}
```

The routine can be called using a *Clock* object as the actual parameter or an object from any descendant class. For example, assuming the declarations

```
Clock c1 = new Clock(1,2,3);
CountdownClock c2 = new CountdownClock(1,2,3);
AlarmClock c3 = new AlarmClock(1,2,3,4,5,6);
```

each of the following statements would be valid:

```
cout << toSeconds(c1);
cout << toSeconds(c2);
cout << toSeconds(c3);
```

Within the routine itself, the `idtype` keyword could be used, where necessary, to discover the type of object actually passed. An example of this is shown in the routine below which returns the parameter's class name:

```
char* getClassName(Clock *c)
{
    char *name = new char[15];
    if (typeid(*c) == typeid(CountdownClock))
        strcpy(name,"CountdownClock");
    else if (typeid(*c) == typeid(AlarmClock))
        strcpy(name,"AlarmClock");
    else if(typeid(*c) == typeid(Clock))
        strcpy(name,"Clock");
    return name;
}
```

PROGRAMMING EXERCISE 12.12

Modify your previous program so that it displays the class name of the object created by the user. Make use of the *getClassName()* function defined above.

Input and Output Operations

The exception is the *runClock()* method defined in the *Clock* class.

You may have noticed that, with one exception, none of the classes we have created contain operations to read information from the keyboard or display information on the screen. The reason for this is simply that such routines are of very limited use. If we add a *readWeight()* method to the *Weight* class that reads the value for pounds and ounces from the keyboard, it will be of little use to the application programmer if he needs to read the information from a disk file or from an item selected in a menu. An output method that displays on the screen is no use if we want to output to a printer or a file.

So our alternative, as the class designer, is to produce *set* and *get* methods which the application programmer can use as required.

Of course, there are exceptions to this rule. For example, a set of graphics classes designed to create circles, polygons, lines etc. will require a method to display the shape on the screen.

Static Attributes and Derived Classes

We already know that a `static` attribute of a class has only one occurrence, irrespective of the number of objects of that class that are created.

This rule extends to classes derived from a class containing a `static` attribute. Hence, if *Clock* were to contain a `static` attribute, there would only be one occurrence of this attribute, no matter how many *Clock, AlarmClock* or *CountdownClock* objects are defined.

Abstract Classes

Dogs, cats and mice are different, but we can link them by saying that they are all types of mammal. We can make use of this idea to link seemingly incompatible classes in an object-oriented system.

Imagine a computerised wages system in which we want to create the classes shown in FIG-12.7.

FIG-12.7

Types of Employees

PartTimeWorker	FullTimeWorker	ContractWorker
name address salary hoursthisweek	name address salary pensioncontr	name address salary contractperiod
setName() setAddress() setSalary() setHours() getName() getAddress() getSalary() getHours()	setName() setAddress() setSalary() setPension() getName() getAddress() getSalary() getPension()	setName() setAddress() setSalary() setContract() getName() getAddress() getSalary() getContract()

Each is a different class and yet they are related in that all three are types of worker.

We can emphasis this relationship by creating a *Worker* class using those features that are common to the three original classes. The original classes can now be defined as descendants of this *Worker* class (see FIG-12.8).

FIG-12.8

Designing an Abstract Class

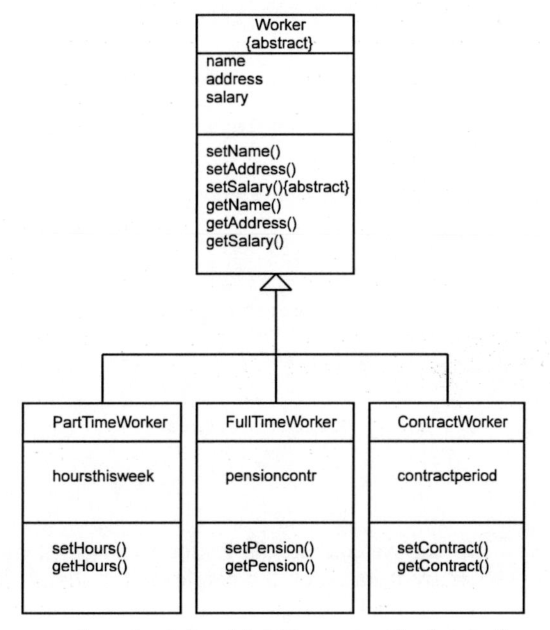

What advantages are there in doing this? To start with, the attributes and methods common to all three of the original classes need only be defined once - in the *Worker* class; these will then be inherited by the descendant classes where only new and updated features need be coded.

Creating an Abstract *Worker* Class

Of course, defining the *Worker* class is only a ploy to connect the other three classes together. When the application programmer creates objects using these classes, none of those objects will be of type *Worker*, but of one of its descendant classes. In the same way, no animal can be described solely as a mammal, but is always one of the descendant types (cat, dog or mice, etc.)

When we define a class like the *Worker* class, where we have no intention of creating an actual object of that class, but simply employ the class as a common ancestor to more practical classes, that class is known as an **abstract class**. Normal classes - those from which we can create objects - are known as **concrete classes**.

To define an abstract class in C++ we begin in the same way as any other class: declaring the features of the class. Hence, the *Worker* class's code would begin with:

For any routine that might be overridden in descendant classes we should also add the term `virtual` to that routine's prototype.

```
class Worker
{
    protected:
        char name[31];
        char address[91];
        float salary;
    public:
        void setName(char*);
        void setAddress(char*);
        void setSalary(int);
        char* getName();
        char* getAddress();
        float getSalary();
};
```

If the code for any of the routines named is identical in two or more of the descendant classes, then we can also add the code for those routines to the abstract class:

```
void Worker::setName(char* s)
{
    strcpy(name,s);
}

void Worker::setAddress(char* s)
{
    strcpy(address,s);
}

char* Worker::getName()
{
    return name;
}

char* Worker::getAddress()
{
    return address;
}

float Worker::getSalary()
{
    return salary;
}
```

In this system, the salaries for each type of employee is calculated differently. The salary is based on the employee's grade, which is the parameter to the *setSalary* operation. For a full-time employee, the salary is set to the figure set for the specified grade; for the contract worker, the salary is set to twice the figure for that grade; and for the part-time worker, the salary is set to 75% of the figure for the specified grade. There are ten possible grades (1 to 10).

Because the method for calculating salary is different for each type of employee, we cannot code the *setSalary()* method in the *Worker* class. Since the method will be overridden in derived classes, the *setSalary()* method should also be declared as `virtual`:

```
class Worker
    {
        protected:
            char name[31];
            char address[91];
            float salary;
        public:
            void setName(char*);
            void setAddress(char*);
            virtual void setSalary(int);
            char* getName();
            char* getAddress();
            float getSalary();
    };
```

However, we have not yet created an abstract class, which is to say, the application programmer could still create an object of the *Worker* class with a statement such as:

```
Worker emp1;
```

A class is abstract (i.e. one for which no objects can be created) when at least one of the virtual functions in that class is a **pure virtual function**.

To create a pure virtual function, a function prototype must:

- Be declared as a virtual function
- Include the initialiser `=0` after the parameter list

Using these rules, we can make the *setSalary()* method a pure virtual function by changing the function prototype in the *Worker* class to read:

The compiler does not expect any code to be associated with a pure virtual function.

```
virtual void setSalary(int)=0;
```

Now, any attempt to create an object of this class will result in a compilation error.

The *PartTimeWorker* Class

We can then go on and define the descendant classes. It is possible, in a complex situation, that some of these descendant classes could themselves be abstract. But, more often, we will create concrete descendant classes. These concrete sub-classes must include code for any methods defined as abstract within the parent. The *PartTimeWorker* class, being derived from the *Worker* class, must contain code for the *setSalary()* method.

Of course, new methods can be added as required in the descendant class.

The code for the *PartTimeWorker* class is:

```
//*** PartTimeWorker Class          ***
class PartTimeWorker : public Worker
{
    protected:
        float hoursthisweek;
    public:
        void setSalary(int);
        void setHours(float);
        float getHours();
};

//*************************************
//*** PartTimeWorker Class Methods  ***
//*************************************
void PartTimeWorker::setSalary(int grade)
```

```
{
    const long salaries[]={0,15000,20000,23000,29000,31000,
    35000L,40000L,45000L,50000L,60000L};
    if (grade < 1 || grade > 10)
        salary = 0;
    else
        salary = salaries[grade]*0.75;
}

void PartTimeWorker::setHours(float h)
{
    if(h < 0 || h > 168)
    return;
    hoursthisweek = h;
}

float PartTimeWorker::getHours()
{
    return hoursthisweek;
}
```

TASK 12.7

Write code for the *ContractWorker* class.

This requires the code for the following:

Attributes:

contractperiod : INTEGER

Methods:

setSalary(grade : INTEGER)-	Sets the salary to double the normal salary associated with the specified grade. *grade* must be in the range 1 to 10.
setContract(w : INTEGER) -	which sets *contractperiod* to *w* weeks. *w* must lie in the range 1 to 156.
getContract():INTEGER -	which returns the value held in *contractperiod*.

Pointers to Abstract Classes

Although the application programmer cannot create an object of class *Worker*, he may create a *Worker* class pointer with a line such as:

```
Worker *Wptr;
```

This does not violate the rule since only a pointer has been created - not an object.

The pointer can now be used to reference an object of a concrete class derived from the *Worker* class. For example:

```
Wptr = new ContractWorker();
```

Arrays of Abstract Class Pointers

By creating an array of such pointers

```
Worker *employees[3];
```

we can make these pointers reference objects of differing, but descendant, classes:

```
employee[0] = new PartTimeWorker();
employee[1] = new FullTimeWorker();
employee[2] = new ContractWorker();
```

The program in LISTING-12.2 gives a full definition of all the *Worker*-based classes and demonstrates the use of a pointer array to store and display salary details of each worker.

LISTING-12.2

Working with an Abstract Class

```
#include<string.h>
#include<iostream.h>

//************************************
//***      Class Declarations      ***
//************************************

//*** Worker Class (abstract)       ***
class Worker
{
  protected:
      char name[31];
      char address[91];
      float salary;
  public:
   void setName(char*);
   void setAddress(char*);
   virtual void setSalary(int)=0;  //This makes class abstract
   char* getName();
   char* getAddress();
   float getSalary();
};

//*** FullTimeWorker Class         ***
class FullTimeWorker : public Worker
{
  protected:
      float pensioncontr;

  public:
      void setSalary(int);
      void setPension(float);
      float getPension();
};

//*** PartTimeWorker Class         ***
class PartTimeWorker : public Worker
{
  protected:
      float hoursthisweek;

  public:
      void setSalary(int);
      void setHours(float);
      float getHours();
};

//*** ContractWorker Class        ***
class ContractWorker : public Worker
{
  protected:
      int contractperiod;

  public:
      void setSalary(int);
      void setContract(int);
      float getContract();
};
```

Continued on next page

LISTING-12.2
(continued)

Working with an Abstract Class

```
//***********************************
//***      Worker Class Methods     ***
//***********************************

void Worker::setName(char* s)
{
  strcpy(name,s);
}
void Worker::setAddress(char* s)
{
  strcpy(address,s);
}

char* Worker::getName()
{
  return name;
}

char* Worker::getAddress()
{
  return address;
}

float Worker::getSalary()
{
  return salary;
}


//***********************************
//*** FullTimeWorker Class Methods  ***
//***********************************

void FullTimeWorker::setSalary(int grade)
{
  const long salaries[]={0,15000,20000,23000,29000,31000,
                      35000L,40000L,45000L,50000L,60000L};
  if (grade < 1 || grade > 10)
      salary = 0;
  else
      salary = salaries[grade];
}

void FullTimeWorker::setPension(float v)
{
  if (v < 0 || v > salary * 0.15)
      return;
  pensioncontr = v;
}

float FullTimeWorker::getPension()
{
  return pensioncontr;
}

//***********************************
//*** PartTimeWorker Class Methods  ***
//***********************************

void PartTimeWorker::setSalary(int grade)
{
  const long salaries[]={0,15000,20000,23000,29000,31000,
                      35000L,40000L,45000L,50000L,60000L};
  if (grade < 1 || grade > 10)
      salary = 0;
  else
      salary = salaries[grade]*0.75;
}
```

Continued on next page

LISTING-12.2
(continued)

Working with an Abstract Class

```
void PartTimeWorker::setHours(float h)
{
  if(h < 0 || h > 168)
      return;
  hoursthisweek = h;
}

float PartTimeWorker::getHours()
{
  return hoursthisweek;
}


//************************************
//*** ContractWorker Class Methods  ***
//************************************

void ContractWorker::setSalary(int grade)
{
  const long salaries[]={0,15000,20000,23000,29000,31000,
                         35000L,40000L,45000L,50000,60000L};
  if (grade < 1 || grade > 10)
      salary = 0;
  else
      salary = salaries[grade]*2;
}


void ContractWorker::setContract(int w)
{
  if(w < 1 || w > 156)
      return;
  contractperiod = w;
}

float ContractWorker::getContract()
{
  return contractperiod;
}



void main()
{
  Worker *employees[3];
  employees[0] = new FullTimeWorker();
  employees[1] = new PartTimeWorker();
  employees[2] = new ContractWorker();
  for(int c = 0; c < 3; c++)
      employees[c]->setSalary(5);
  for(c=0; c<3; c++)
      cout << "£"<<employees[c]->getSalary()<<".00\n";
}
```

PROGRAMMING EXERCISE 12.13

Type in and run the program given in LISTING-12.2.

Change the salary values (held in the *salaries* array) so that it is a static, protected class constant.

Add a fourth concrete class called *AgencyWorker* which sets salary at 1.2 times the scale amount. There are no other additional features in this class.

Aggregate Classes

Design

The classes we have encountered up to this point have been created to demonstrate basic aspects of C++ programming. However, when you come to design and implement a real system, many classes will almost certainly be required. Sometimes one class will be part of another class. For example, in a system designed to computerise horse racing, we might identify *Race* as one of the main classes of the system. But a race involves horses, so we identify *Horse* as another class. Since horses are part of what makes up a race, UML shows this association between the two classes by the use of a diamond symbol as shown in FIG-12.9.

FIG-12.9

An Aggregate Class

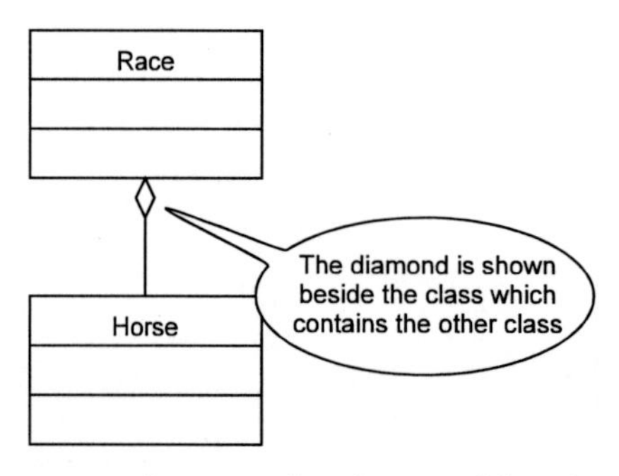

This is known as an **aggregation**: one class is part of the other. Here, *Horse* is part of *Race.*

Since a race is always run over a specified distance, and assuming we have defined a *Distance* class in our system, we could say that *Distance* is also part of *Race*. This changes our diagram to that shown in FIG-12.10.

FIG-12.10

An Aggregate Class Linked to Multiple Classes

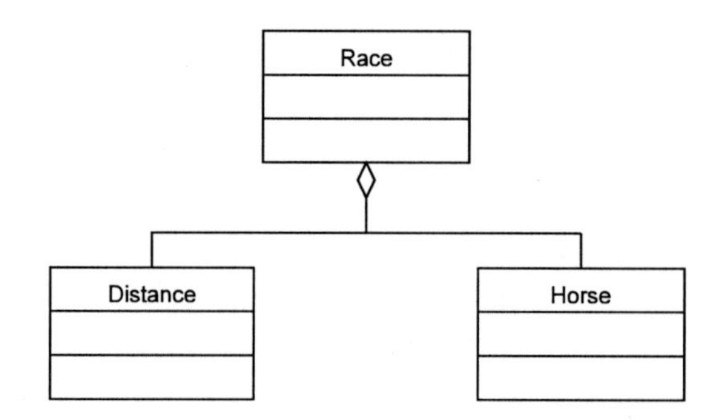

TASK 12.8

When creating a Graphical User Interface, a designer identifies the need for the following classes: Button, Label, EditBox, Menu and Window. Buttons, labels, edit boxes and a menu always appear as part of a window.

Draw a UML diagram to show the aggregation of these classes.

Implementation

To illustrate how an aggregate class is programmed, let's assume that the *Horse* class mentioned above containing the name of the horse, handicap weight carried and winning distance of the horse's last successful race. The UML diagram for setup is shown in FIG-12.11.

FIG-12.11

An Aggregate Horse Class

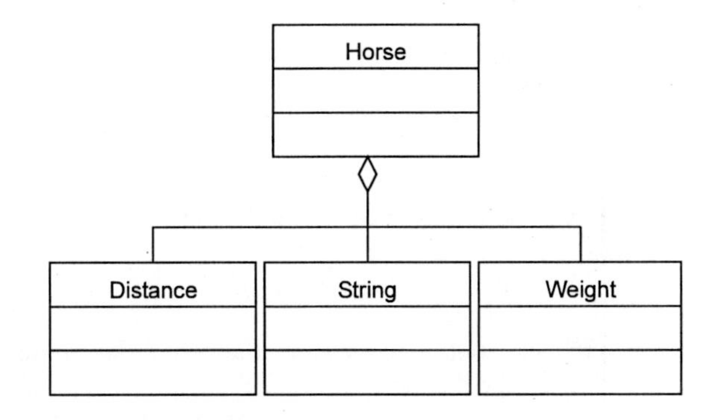

We could declare the features of such a class as

```
class Horse
{
    private:
        String name;
        Weight handicap;
        Distance wonby;
    public:
        Horse(String, Weight, Distance);
        void setName(String);
        void setWinningDistance(Distance);
        void setHandicap(Weight);
        String getName();
        Distance getWinningDistance();
        Weight getHandicap();
};
```

the methods code being:

```
Horse::Horse(String n, Weight h, Distance w)
{
    name = n;
    handicap = h;
    wonby = w;
}

void Horse::setName(String n)
{
    name = n;
}

void Horse::setHandicap(Weight h)
{
    handicap = h;
}
void Horse::setWinningDistance(Distance w)
{
    wonby = w;
}

String Horse::getName()
{
    return name;
}

Weight Horse::getHandicap()
{
    return handicap;
}

Distance Horse::getWinningDistance()
{
    return wonby;
}
```

PROGRAMMING EXERCISE 12.14

Create a new file containing the code for the *String*, *Distance* and *Weight* classes.

Add functions to overload the output operator (<<) for each of these classes.

Add the *Horse* class to the file.

Create a *main()* function which creates a *Horse* object, using the constructor to set the attributes to "Red Rum", 20 lbs 0 oz, 1 yd 2 ft 0 in.

Use the `cout` to display the name, handicap and winning distance of the horse.

Container Classes

As well as creating objects capable of holding a single item, we can create classes which contain a collection of similar items. Such a class is known as a **container class**.

We've already met this idea in Chapter 8 when we created various data structures such as Lists, Stacks, Queues etc. Here we'll revisit the List structure, this time implementing it as a container class.

The operations required of a List are repeated below:

A few minor changes have been made to List operations.

Empty has been renamed *create* and will become the class constructor.

All operation names now start with a lowercase letter

create	-	which creates an empty list.
addAt	-	which adds a new value at a specified position in the list.
deleteFrom	-	which deletes a value from a specified position in the list.
head	-	which returns the first value in the list.
tail	-	which removes the first item from the list
len	-	which returns the number of entries in the list.
isEmpty	-	which returns 1 if the list is empty, otherwise zero is returned.
display	-	which displays the complete sequence.

We need to begin by declaring two auxiliary structures:

```
struct Data
{
    int no;
};

struct Node
{
    Data value;
    Node *next;
};
```

The *List* class itself is then declared as:

```
class List
{
    protected:
        Node *start;
        int count;
    public:
```

```
        List();
        int addAt(const Data, int);
        int deleteFrom(int);
        Data head();
        void tail();
        int len();
        int isEmpty();
        void display();
};
```

The code for each class method closely reflects that produced in Chapter 8, but with the list variable missing from the function parameters (since the methods of the class have automatic access to the attributes of the class).

The code for the constructor and *addAt()* is given below:

```
List::List()
{
    start = NULL;
    count = 0;
}

int List::addAt(const Data item, int post)
{
    Node *current, *previous, *temp;
    //*** IF attempting to insert at invalid position, exit ***
    if(post<1||post>len()+1)
        return 0;
    //*** Create space for new node ***
    temp = new Node;
    //*** Place data in node ***
    temp->value = item;
    temp->next=NULL;
    //*** IF placed at start update main pointer***
    if(post==1)
    {
        current = start;
        start = temp;
        temp->next=current;
    }
    else
    //*** ELSE find insert position ***
    {
        previous = NULL;
        current = start;
        for(int c=2;c<=post;c++)
        {
            previous = current;
            current = current->next;
        }
        //** Link new node into chain **
        previous->next = temp;
        temp->next = current;
    }
    //*** Add 1 to count ***
    count++;
    //*** Return indication of success ***
    return 1;
}
```

TASK 12.9

Write the code required for the *len()* method of the *List* class.

The program in LISTING-12.3 gives the full definition of the *List* class and a menu-driven application program allowing each of the operations to be tested.

LISTING-12.3

The *List* Container Class

```
#include<iostream.h>
#include<conio.h>
#include<string.h>
#include<stdlib.h>

//*** Type Declarations ***
struct Data
{
  int  no;
};

struct Node
{
  Data value;
  Node *next;
};

//*** List class Declaration ***
class List
{
  protected:
       Node *start;
       int count;
  public:
       List();
       int addAt(const Data, int);
       int deleteFrom(int);
       Data head();
       void tail();
       int len();
       int isEmpty();
       void display();
};

//*** Function Prototypes ***
int DisplayMenu(const char*);
int GetOption(int);
void ExecuteOption(int, List&);


//*** List class Methods ***

  List::List()
  {
       start = NULL;
       count = 0;
  }

int List::addAt(const Data item, int post)
{
  Node *current, *previous, *temp;
  if(post<1||post>len()+1)
       return 0;
  //*** Create space for new node ***
  temp = new Node;
  //*** Place data in node ***
  temp->value = item;
  temp->next=NULL;

  //*** IF placed at start update main pointer***
  if(post==1)
  {
       current = start;
       start = temp;
       temp->next=current;
  }
  else
  //*** ELSE find insert position ***
  {
```

Continued on next page

LISTING-12.3
(continued)

The *List* Container Class

```
        previous = NULL;
        current = start;
        for(int c=2;c<=post;c++)
        {
            previous = current;
            current = current->next;
        }
        //** Link new node into chain **
        previous->next = temp;
        temp->next = current;
    }
    //*** Add 1 to count ***
    count++;
    return 1;
}

int List::deleteFrom(int post)
{
    Node *current, *previous;
    if(post<1||post>len())
    {
        cout<<"Invalid position\n";
        return 0;
    }
    //*** IF first node update main pointer***
    if(post==1)
    {
        current = start;
        start = current->next;
        delete current;
    }
    else
    //*** ELSE find delete position ***
    {
        previous = NULL;
        current = start;
        for(int c=2;c<=post;c++)
        {
            previous = current;
            current = current->next;
        }
        //** Remove node from chain **
        previous->next = current->next;
        delete current;
    }
    //*** Subtract 1 from count ***
    count--;
    return 1;
}

Data List::head()
{
    if(isEmpty())
    {
        cout<<"Invalid operation - Head\n";
        exit(1);
    }
    return start->value;
}

void List::tail()
{
    if(isEmpty())
    {
        cout<<"Invalid operation - Tail\n";
        exit(1);
    }
    deleteFrom(1);
}
```

Continued on next page

LISTING-12.3
(continued)

The *List* Container Class

```
int List::len()
{
  return count;
}

int List::isEmpty()
{
  return(count==0);
}

void List::display()
{
  Node *current=start;

  for(int c=1;c<=len();c++)
  {
      cout<<current->value.no<<endl;
      current=current->next;
  }
}


void main()
{
  List seq;
  int option, noofoptions;

  do
  {
      noofoptions=DisplayMenu("1. - addAt\n2. - deleteFrom\n"
      "3. - head\n4. - tail\n5. - len\n6. - isEmpty\n"
      "7. - display\n8. - QUIT\n");
      option = GetOption(noofoptions);
      ExecuteOption(option, seq);
  }
  while (option != noofoptions);
  cout<<"PROGRAM TERMINATED\n";
  getch();
}


//*** Other routines ***
int DisplayMenu(const char* text)
{
  clrscr();
  cout<<"MENU\n\n";
  cout<<text;

  for(int c=0,total=0; c<strlen(text);c++)
      if(text[c]=='\n')
          total++;
  return total;
}

int GetOption(int max)
{
  int opt;
  cout<<"\nEnter option : ";
  cin>>opt;
  while(opt<1||opt>max)
  {
      cout<<"Invalid option\n";
      cin>>opt;
  }
  return opt;
}
```

Continued on next page

LISTING-12.3
(continued)

The *List* Container Class

```
void ExecuteOption(int opt, List& seq)
{
   Data val;
   int post;

   switch (opt)
   {
         case 1:
                   cout<<"Enter value to be added : ";
                   cin >> val.no;
                   cout<<"Add where (1 to "<<(seq.len()+1)<<") : ";
                   cin>>post;
                   seq.addAt(val,post);
                   break;
         case 2:
                   if(!seq.isEmpty())
                   {
                        cout<<"Delete from where (1 to "
                             <<seq.len()<<") : ";
                        cin>>post;
                        seq.deleteFrom(post);
                   }
                   else
                   {
                        cout<<"The list is empty\n";
                        getch();
                   }
                   break;
         case 3:
                   if(!seq.isEmpty())
                   {
                        cout<<"First in list is : "
                             <<seq.head().no<<endl;
                        getch();
                   }
                   else
                   {
                        cout<<"List is empty\n";
                        getch();
                   }
                   break;
         case 4:
                   if(!seq.isEmpty())
                        seq.tail();
                   else
                   {
                        cout<<"List is empty\n";
                        getch();
                   }
                   break;
         case 5:
                   cout<<"The list contains "<<seq.len()<<" values\n";
                   getch();
                   break;
         case 6:
                   if(seq.isEmpty())
                        cout<<"List is empty\n";
                   else
                        cout<<"List is not empty\n";
                   getch();
                   break;
         case 7:
                   clrscr();
                   cout<<"CONTENTS OF LIST\n";
                   seq.display();
                   getch();
                   break;
   }
}
```

PROGRAMMING EXERCISE 12.15

Implement the *Stack* structure (as defined in Chapter 8) as a class using an `int` array to store the contents of the stack.

Include a *main()* method similar to that in LISTING-12.3 to test your code.

Delegation

There are occasions when a new class needs less facilities than an existing one. For example, a stack is a type of list where values can only be added and removed from the head of the sequence. If we create a *Stack* class derived from the *List* class, the new class will inherit methods, such as *addAt()*, which are not appropriate.

Rather than use inheritance, we can create the new class with an object of the existing, more powerful class, as an attribute. For example:

```
class Stack
{
    private:
        List seq;
```

The operations of a stack are defined informally as:

Empty	-	creates an empty stack.
Push	-	adds a value to the top (front) of the stack.
Top	-	returns the top element in the stack.
Pop	-	removes the top element in the stack.
IsEmpty	-	returns 1 if the stack is empty else zero.
Len	-	returns the number of values in the stack.
Display	-	displays the contents of the stack.

The *List* object, *seq*, will contain the values added to the stack. Hence, we could write *Stack*'s *Push* operation as

```
void Stack::push(Data v)
{
    seq.addAt(v,1);
}
```

making use of the *List* object's more powerful *addAt()* operation to implement the *Stack*'s operation.

A program using this technique to implement the *Stack* class is given in LISTING-12.4.

LISTING-12.4

Using Delegation to Implement the *Stack* Class

```
#include<iostream.h>
#include<conio.h>
#include<string.h>
#include<stdlib.h>

//*** Type Declarations ***
struct Data
{
int no;
};
```

Continued on next page

LISTING-12.4
(continued)

Using Delegation to Implement the *Stack* Class

```
struct Node
{
  Data value;
  Node *next;
};


//*******************************
//***  List class source code  ***
//***  should be placed here   ***
//*******************************


//*** Stack class Declaration ***
class Stack
{
  protected:
       List seq;
  public:
       void push(Data);
       void pop();
       Data top();
       void empty();
       int isEmpty();
       int len();
       void display();
};

void Stack::push(Data v)
{
  seq.addAt(v,1);
}

void Stack::Pop()
{
  seq.tail();
}

Data Stack::top()
{
  return seq.head();
}

void Stack::empty()
{
  seq.empty();
}

int Stack::isEmpty()
{
  return seq.isEmpty();
}

int Stack::len()
{
  return seq.len();
}

void Stack::display()
{
  seq.display();
}

//*** Other Function Prototypes ***
int DisplayMenu(const char*);
int GetOption(int);
void ExecuteOption(int, Stack&);
```

Continued on next page

LISTING-12.4
(continued)

Using Delegation to Implement the *Stack* Class

```
void main()
{
  Stack s;
  int option, noofoptions;

  do
  {
      noofoptions=DisplayMenu(
          "1. - Create Stack\n2. - Push\n3. - Pop\n"
          "4. - Top\n5. - Pop\n6. - Length\n7. - IsEmpty\n"
          "8. - Empty\n9. - Display\n10 - QUIT\n");
      option = GetOption(noofoptions);
      ExecuteOption(option, s);
  }
  while (option != noofoptions);
  s.empty();
  cout<<"PROGRAM TERMINATED\n";
  getch();
}

int DisplayMenu(const char* text)
{
  clrscr();
  cout<<"MENU\n\n";
  cout<<text;

  for(int c=0,total=0; c<strlen(text);c++)
      if(text[c]=='\n')
          total++;
  return total;
}

int GetOption(int max)
{
  int opt;
  cout<<"\nEnter option : ";
  cin>>opt;
  while(opt<1||opt>max)
  {
      cout<<"Invalid option\n";
      cin>>opt;
  }
  return opt;
}

void ExecuteOption(int opt, Stack& s)
{
  Data val;
  int post;

  switch (opt)
  {
      case 1:
          s.empty();
          break;
      case 2:
          cout<<"Enter value to be added : ";
          cin >> val.no;
          s.push(val);
          break;
      case 3:
          if(!s.isEmpty())
              s.pop();
          else
          {
              cout<<"The stack is empty\n";
              getch();
          }
          break;
```

Continued on next page

LISTING-12.4
(continued)

Using Delegation to Implement the *Stack* Class

```
        case 4:
            if(!s.isEmpty())
            {
                cout<<"Top of stack is : "<<s.top().no<<endl;
                getch();
            }
            else
            {
                cout<<"Stack is empty\n";
                getch();
            }
            break;
        case 5:
            if(!s.isEmpty())
                s.pop();
            else
            {
                cout<<"Stack is empty\n";
                getch();
            }
            break;
        case 6:
            cout<<"The stack contains "<<s.len()<<" values\n";
            getch();
            break;
        case 7:
            if(s.isEmpty())
                cout<<"Stack is empty\n";
            else
                cout<<"Stack is not empty\n";
            getch();
            break;
        case 8:
            s.empty();
            break;
        case 9:
            clrscr();
            cout<<"CONTENTS OF STACK\n";
            s.display();
            getch();
            break;
    }
}
```

Multiple Inheritance

It is possible for a new class to have more than one super class from which it inherits its features. This is known as **multiple inheritance**.

For example, we could create a class, Multi, which inherits the features of both the *Distance* and *Weight* classes by starting with the line:

```
class Multi : public Distance, public Weight
```

The new class would then contain the following attributes:

```
int yards;
int feet;
int inches;
int pounds;
int ounces;
```

These are inherited from the two parent classes.

All of the methods (except the constructors) of the parent classes would also be inherited.

Because our new class has two parents, its constructor must execute the constructors of both parent classes. This will be done automatically if the parent classes contain zero-argument constructors, but if explicit calls to the parents' constructors were necessary, then the new class's constructor would take the form:

```
Multi::Multi(int a, int b, int c, int d, int e)
:Weight(a,b),Distance(c,d,e)
{
    // more code
}
```

The application programmer can create objects of the new class in the usual manner

```
Multi myobj(1,2,3,2,10);
```

and call any public methods of the class:

```
cout<<myobj.getPounds()<<endl;
```

However, there can be a problem if both parent classes contain routines of the same name. In our case, both the *Weight* and *Distance* classes contain a method named *convertToMetric()*. Our new class inherits both of these routines and, when the application programmer needs to call one of these methods, he is required to include the name of the class from which the routine has been inherited to avoid any ambiguity:

```
cout<<myobj.Distance::convertToMetric();
```

As a general rule, multiple inheritance causes more problems than it solves and should be avoided.

Summary

- **New classes can be created as descendants** of existing classes.
- **Superclass** is the term used for the parent class.
- **Subclass** is the term used for the descendant class.
- **A subclass inherits** all the features of its superclass.
- **Only constructors are not inherited**
- **Private features of the superclass** cannot be accessed in the subclass.
- **Protected features of a superclass** can be accessed in the subclass.
- **Constructors in the subclass** must call the constructor of the superclass.
- **Superclass constructor calls are automatic** if the superclass's constructor has no arguments.
- **Inherited methods can be overridden** in the subclass.
- **Overridden methods** must have the same heading as the original, inherited method.

- Methods which may be overridden should be declared as **virtual**.
- **Virtual functions** use late-binding to ensure that the correct version of the method is executed.
- **A pointer variable** can hold the address of an object from the specified class or any descendant class.
- **When a pointer variable contains the address of a descendant class object**, only methods named in the original class can be accessed.
- **When referencing a subclass**, methods not named in the reference variable's class can be accessed by casting the reference variable to the appropriate class.
- **The actual parameter to a routine** can be of the class specified or any descendant class.
- **Input and output operations should usually be avoided** when defining the operations of a class.
- **Any static feature** in an ancestral class has only a single occurrence irrespective of the number of objects or their classes.

TEMPLATES

Function Templates

Often we have to rewrite a function simply to handle a different data type. For example, a trivial function to return the smallest of a list of `int` values could be coded:

```
int Minimum(int list[],int size)
{
    int smallest=list[0];
    for(int c = 1; c << size-1;c++)
        if(list[c] << smallest)
            smallest = list[c];
    return smallest;
}
```

If we later required a routine to determine the minimum in a list of `char` values we would need to rewrite the function as:

```
char Minimum(char list[], int size)
{
    char smallest = list[0];
    for(int c = 1; c << size-1;c++)
        if(list[c] << smallest)
            smallest = list[c];
    return smallest;
}
```

The two routines differ only in the parameter and local variable types (as highlighted).

To avoid this repetitive effort, we need to be able to create generic functions. That is, functions which can be defined without specifying the type of any parameters or returned values.

This is exactly what function templates allow us to do. Instead of specifying the parameter type, we begin the function with the statement

```
template<class T>
```

and then write the function as normal but using the term **T** wherever the parameter types may be changed:

```
T Minimum(T list[], int size)
{
    T smallest = list[0];
    for(int c = 1;c << size-1;c++)
        if(list[c] << smallest)
            smallest = list[c];
    return smallest;
}
```

To use our new routine within a program we can use an explicit template function declaration by including a prototype of the function with the actual types to be used, as in LISTING 12.5.

LISTING-12.5

Function Templates

```
#include<iostream.h>
//*** Explicit casting for prototype function ***
int Minimum(int[],int);
char Minimum(char[],int);

void main()
{
  //*** Define lists to be searched ***
  char letters[] = {"HELLO"};
  int  numbers[] = {42,89,12,8,99,7};
  //*** Define result variables ***
  int ans1;
  char ans2;
  //***Determine and display results ***
  ans1 = Minimum(numbers,6);
  ans2 = Minimum(letters,5);
  cout << "Min number = " << ans1 << " Min letter = " << ans2
       << endl;
}

//*** Function Definition ***
template<class T>
T Minimum(T list[], int size)
{
  T smallest=list[0];
  for(int c = 1;c < size;c++)
       if(list[c] < smallest)
            smallest = list[c];
  return smallest;
}
```

Alternatively, we may omit the explicit template function prototypes, in which case the compiler works out the type required when executing the function. But, assuming the function definition is placed after *main()*, we must include the template function prototype:

```
template<class T>
T Minimum(T[],int);
```

PROGRAMMING EXERCISE 12.16

1. Write a program using *Minimum()* as defined above, to return the smallest of a list of distances.
   (Make sure your *Distance* class contains code for operators << and <<)

2. Write a template function which returns the greater of two values.
   Test your routine using `char`, `int`, *Weight* and *Distance* classes.

We can extend this use of templates to include any number of generic types in a single function. For example, the next program (see LISTING-12.6) contains a function, *Difference()*, which returns the difference between two values. The value returned is defined as a different type from those passed into the routine, since the difference between two values may not be of the same type as the values themselves (e.g. the difference between two dates is an integer value).

LISTING-12.6

Implicit Template Function Casting

```
#include<conio.h>
#include<iostream.h>

template<class T1, class T2>
void Difference(T1 , T1 , T2&);
```

Continued on next page

LISTING-12.6
(continued)

Implicit Template Function Casting

```
void main()
{
   int no1 = 8, no2 = 2,no3;
   float r1 = 12.653, r2 = 12.99, r3;

   Difference(no1,no2,no3);
   Difference(r1,r2,r3);
   cout << no3 << ' ' << r3 < endl;
}

template<class T1, class T2>
void Difference(T1 a, T1 b, T2& c)
{
   if(a < b)
        c = b-a;
   else
        c = a-b;
}
```

There are limitations when it comes to using templates. Hence, in the function *Difference()* given above, we could not have written the result as a return type

```
template<class T1, class T2>
T2 Difference(T1 a, T1 b)
```

since the types to be replaced must occur in the function argument list.

Class Templates

Container classes are quite straight-forward but suffer from a lack of flexibility. For example, LISTING-12.7 contains a simple class (*Container*) which is used to hold 10 integer values. If we needed to store double values we'd need to write an entirely new class, even though the new class would differ very slightly from our existing one.

LISTING-12.7

A Traditional Container Class

```
#include<iostream.h>

class Container
{
   private:
        int list[10];
        int count;
   public:
        Container();
        void add(int);
        void display();
};

Container::Container()
{
   count = 0;
}

void Container::add(int v)
{
     if(count < 10)
        list[count++]=v;
}
```

Continued on next page

LISTING-12.7
(continued)

A Traditional Container Class

```
void Container::display()
{
  for(int c = 0; c < count; c++)
      cout<<list[c]<<endl;
}


void main()
{
  Container con;
  int opt;

  cout<<"1 - add\n2 - display\n3 - QUIT\n";
  cin >> opt;
  while (opt != 3)
  {
      switch(opt)
      {
          case 1:
              int v;
              cout<<"Enter value to be added : ";
              cin>>v;
              con.add(v);
              break;
          case 2:
              con.display();
              break;
      }
      cout<<"1 - add\n2 - display\n3 - QUIT\n";
      cin >> opt;
  }
  cout<<"PROGRAM TERMINATED\n";
}
```

We can eliminate this problem using a template to avoid specifying the data types used in class attributes and operations. LISTING-12.8 shows the same *Container* class defined using templating. Changes to the code have been highlighted.

LISTING-12.8

Defining a Template Container Class

```
template <class T>
class Container
{
  private:
      T list[10];
      int count;
  public:
      Container();
      void add(T);
      void display();
};
template <class T>
Container<T>::Container()
{
  count = 0;
}
template <class T>
void Container<T>::add(T v)
{
    if(count < 10)
      list[count++]=v;
}
template <class T>
void Container<T>::display()
{
  for(int c = 0; c < count; c++)
      cout<<list[c]<<endl;
}
```

The changes to the code have been highlighted in the listing. Notice that the class and each operation need to be preceded by the line

```
template <class T>
```

and that each operation definition has had the term `<T>` added after the class name as in

```
void Container<T>::display()
```

Finally, any attributes, parameters, or return values which would vary when using *Container* objects to store various items have been replaced by the term `T` as in

```
T list[10]
```

and

```
void Container::add(T v);
```

The application program now has to specify what type of value is to be stored when declaring a *Container* class object. To create a *Container* object for storing double values we would use the line:

```
Container<double> con;
```

LISTING-12.9 demonstrates the use of a *Container* object to store strings.

LISTING-12.9

Using a Template Container

```
#include<iostream.h>

void main()
{
  Container<char*> con;
  int opt;

  cout<<"1 - add\n2 - display\n3 - QUIT\n";
  cin >> opt;
  while (opt != 3)
  {
      switch(opt)
      {
          case 1:
              char v[21];
              cout<<"Enter value to be added : ";
              cin>>v;
              con.add(v);
              break;
          case 2:
              con.display();
              break;
      }
      cout<<"1 - add\n2 - display\n3 - QUIT\n";
      cin >> opt;
  }
  cout<<"PROGRAM TERMINATED\n";
}
```

PROGRAMMING EXERCISE 12.17

Create a program which uses a *Container* object to store *Distance* objects. (You will have to copy your *Distance* class source code into the *Container* class file.)

Summary

Aggregate Classes

- An aggregate class is one in which some or all of the attributes are themselves classes.
- Default and zero-argument constructors of the attributes of an aggregate class are executed automatically.
- Other attribute constructors must be called from within the aggregate class constructor.
- Only public features of the attribute objects can be accessed within an aggregate class.

Container Classes

- A container class is designed to hold several objects of a given class or family of classes.

Delegation

- Delegation allows access to the methods of an existing class to be restricted by enclosing the existing class in a new one.

Templates

- Function templates allow the parameter types of a function to be omitted from the function definition.
- Any function parameter type may be specified using templates.
- The return type and local variables may also use templates, only if these match one or more templated parameter types.
- Executable function code will be generated from the templates by explicitly defining the function prototypes. Alternatively, the code is generated automatically by the compiler when a function call is encountered in the code.

Solutions

TASK 12.1

Attributes of the *BWTV* class are:

volume
station
power
contrast
brightness

the first 3 being inherited from the *Radio* class.

TASK 12.2

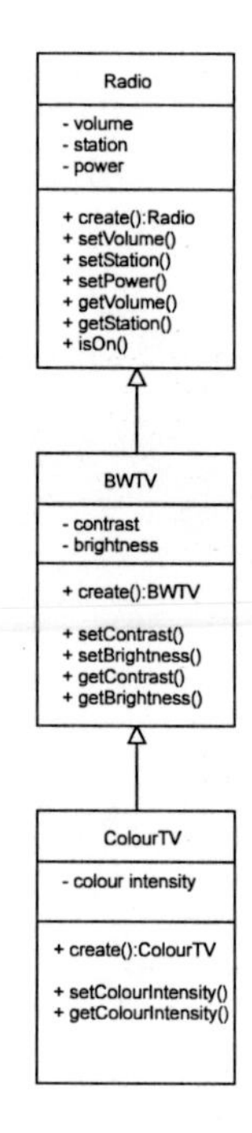

TASK 12.3

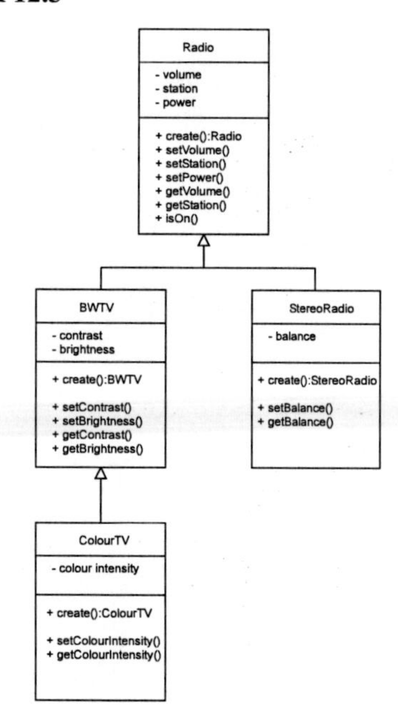

PROGRAMMING EXERCISE 12.1

```
#include<stdlib.h>
#include<string.h>
#include<iostream.h>
#include<math.h>

class Clock
{
    private:
        int hours;
        int minutes;
        int seconds;
    public:
        Clock();
        Clock(int,int,int);
        void setTime(int,int,int);
        int getHours();
        int getMinutes();
        int getSeconds();
        void tick();
        char* toString();
        void runClock(int);
};

Clock::Clock()
{
    hours = 0;
    minutes = 0;
    seconds = 0;
}

Clock::Clock(int h, int m, int s)
{
    if(h < 0 || h > 23 || m < 0 || m > 59
    || s < 0 || s > 59)
    {
        hours = 0;
        minutes = 0;
        seconds = 0;
    }
    else
    {
        hours = h;
        minutes = m;
        seconds = s;
    }
}

void Clock::setTime(int h, int m, int s)
{
    if(h > 23 || h < 0 || m < 0 || m > 59
    || s < 0 || s > 59)
        return;
    hours = h;
    minutes = m;
    seconds = s;
}

int Clock::getHours()
{
    return hours;
}

int Clock::getMinutes()
{
    return minutes;
}

int Clock::getSeconds()
{
    return seconds;
}

void Clock::tick()
{
    long totalsecs = hours *3600L + minutes * 60
    + seconds + 1;
    hours = (totalsecs /3600)%24;
    minutes = (totalsecs % 3600 / 60);
    seconds = totalsecs % 60;
}

char* Clock::toString()
{
    char h[3],m[3],s[3], result[9]="";
    strcpy(result,itoa(hours,h,10));
    strcat(result,":");
    strcat(result,itoa(minutes,m,10));
    strcat(result,":");
    strcat(result,itoa(seconds,s,10));
    return result;
}
```

Continued on next page

```
void Clock::runClock(int secs)
{
    for(int c = 1; c <= secs; c++)
    {
        cout<<"             \r"<<toString()<<'\r';
        tick();
        for(long k =0; k <900000;k++)
            double x = sin(k/1000);
    }
}

class AlarmClock : public Clock
{
    private:
        int ahours;
        int aminutes;
        int aseconds;

    public:
        void setAlarmTime(int, int, int);
        int getAlarmHours();
        int getAlarmMinutes();
        int getAlarmSeconds();
        int isAlarmTime();
};

void AlarmClock::setAlarmTime(int h, int m,
                    int s)
{
    if(h<0||h>23||m<0||m>59||s<0||s>59)
        return;
    ahours = h;
    aminutes = m;
    aseconds = s;
}

int AlarmClock::getAlarmHours()
{
    return ahours;
}

int AlarmClock::getAlarmMinutes()
{
    return aminutes;
}

int AlarmClock::getAlarmSeconds()
{
    return aseconds;
}

int AlarmClock::isAlarmTime()
{
    if(hours==ahours && minutes==aminutes &&
seconds==aseconds)
        return 1;
    else
        return 0;
}
```

The program will NOT compile.

PROGRAMMING EXERCISE 12.2

The changes required to the *Clock* class are:

```
class Clock
{
    protected:
        int hours;
        int minutes;
        int seconds;
    public:
        Clock();
        Clock(int,int,int);
        void setTime(int,int,int);
        int getHours();
        int getMinutes();
        int getSeconds();
        void tick();
        char* toString();
        void runClock(int);
};
```

The changes required to the *AlarmClock* class are:

```
class AlarmClock : public Clock
{
    protected:
        int ahours;
        int aminutes;
        int aseconds;
    public:
        void setAlarm(int, int, int);
        int getAlarmHours();
        int getAlarmMinutes();
        int getAlarmSeconds();
        int isAlarmTime();
};
```

main() is coded as:

```
void main()
{
    AlarmClock cl(23,59,54,0,0,0);
    cl.tick();
    cout<<cl.toString()<<endl;
}
```

PROGRAMMING EXERCISE 12.3

The changes to the *AlarmClock* class are shown below:

```
class AlarmClock : public Clock
{
    protected:
        int ahours;
        int aminutes;
        int aseconds;
    public:
        AlarmClock(int,int,int,int,int,int);
        void setAlarmTime(int, int, int);
        int getAlarmHours();
        int getAlarmMinutes();
        int getAlarmSeconds();
        int isAlarmTime();
};

AlarmClock::AlarmClock(int h, int m, int s, int
ah, int am, int as)
{
    if(h<0||h>23||m<0||m>59||s<0||s>59||ah<0||
    ah>23||am<0||am>59||as<0||as>59)
    {
        hours = 0;
        minutes = 0;
        seconds = 0;
        ahours = 0;
        aminutes = 0;
        aseconds = 0;
    }
    else
    {
        hours = h;
        minutes = m;
        seconds = s;
        ahours = ah;
        aminutes = am;
        aseconds = as;
    }
}
```

The *main()* function is coded as:

```
void main()
{
    AlarmClock cl(12,29,59,12,30,0);
    cl.tick();
    if (cl.isAlarmTime())
        cout<<"Time to get up";
}
```

PROGRAMMING EXERCISE 12.4

AlarmClock declaration changes to:

```
class AlarmClock : public Clock
{
    protected:
        int ahours;
        int aminutes;
        int aseconds;
    public:
        AlarmClock(int,int,int,int,int,int);
        void setAlarmTime(int, int, int);
        int getAlarmHours();
        int getAlarmMinutes();
        int getAlarmSeconds();
        int isAlarmTime();
        void    void tick();
};
```

Continued on next page

```
void AlarmClock::tick()
{
    long totalsecs = hours *3600L + minutes*60
                    + seconds + 1;
    Clock::tick();
    if(isAlarmTime())
        cout<<"Time to get up\n";
}
```

main() coded as:

```
void main()
{
    AlarmClock cl(12,0,0,12,0,1);
    cl.tick();
}
```

The message does appear.

PROGRAMMING EXERCISE 12.5

The code for the *CountdownClock* is:

```
class CountdownClock : public Clock
{
    public:
        CountdownClock(int=0,int=0,int=0);
        void tick();
};

CountdownClock::CountdownClock(int h, int m,
int s)
:Clock(h,m,s)
{}

void CountdownClock::tick()
{
    long totalsecs = (hours * 3600L)
        +(minutes*60)+seconds + 86399L;
    hours = (totalsecs /3600)%24;
    minutes = (totalsecs % 3600 / 60);
    seconds = totalsecs % 60;
}
```

main() coded as:

```
void main()
{
    CountdownClock cdc(0,0,10);
    cdc.tick();
    cout<<cdc.toString();
}
```

The clock's time does move back 1 second.

When starting at 0:0:0, *tick()* causes the clock to go back to 23:59:59.

PROGRAMMING EXERCISE 12.6

```
void main()
{
    Clock cl(12,0,0);
    CountdownClock cdc(12,0,0);
    cl.tick();
    cdc.tick();
    cout<<"Clock's time          : "
        <<cl.toString()<<endl;
    cout<<"CountdownClock's time: "
        <<cdc.toString()<<endl;
}
```

PROGRAMMING EXERCISE 12.7

main() using a *Clock* object::

```
void main()
{
    Clock time(1,30,0);
    time.runClock(20);
}
```

The clock runs correctly from 1:30:00 to 1:30:19

main() using a *CountdownClock* object:

```
void main()
{
    CountdownClock time(1,30,0);
    time.runClock(20);
}
```

The time runs forwards rather than backwards.

PROGRAMMING EXERCISE 12.8

The *CountdownClock* class should now be declared as:

```
class CountdownClock : public Clock
{
    public:
        CountdownClock(int=0,int=0,int=0);
        virtual void tick();
};
```

The *CountdownClock* object now ticks backwards.

TASK 12.4

a) Valid.
b) Invalid. *Distance* is not a descendant of *Clock.*
c) Invalid. *Weight* is not a descendant of *Clock.*
d) Invalid. *Clock* is not a descendant of *AlarmClock.*

PROGRAMMING EXERCISE 12.9

The appropriate version of *tick()* is executed in each case.

TASK 12.5

If function *f()* has been declared in class A as virtual, then *B::f()* will be executed.

If *f()* is not virtual, then *A::f()* will be executed.

TASK 12.6

No methods require the pointer to be cast to a *CountdownClock* type since the *CountdownClock* class contains no methods not already named in the *Clock* class.

PROGRAMMING EXERCISE 12.10

No solution required.

PROGRAMMING EXERCISE 12.11

The program should add the line

```
#include<typeinfo.h>
```

main() should be coded as:

```
void main()
{
    Clock *cl=NULL;
    cout << "Which type of clock?\n";
    cout << "1 - Clock\n";
    cout << "2 - AlarmClock\n";
    cout << "3 - CountdownClock\n";
    cout << "Enter choice (1,2,3): ";
    int choice;
    cin >> choice;
    switch(choice)
```

Continued on next page

```
    {
        case 1:
            c1 = new Clock(1,2,3);
            break;
        case 2:
            c1 = new AlarmClock(1,2,3,1,2,4);
            break;
        case 3:
            c1 = new CountdownClock(1,2,3);
            break;
    }
    if(typeid(*c1) == typeid(AlarmClock))
    {
        int h,m,s;
        cout<<"What time is the alarm to be
            set for?\n";
        cout<<"Hour : ";
        cin>>h;
        cout<<"Minute : ";
        cin>>m;
        cout<<"Second : ";
        cin>>s;
        ((AlarmClock*)c1)->setAlarmTime(h,m,s);
    }
    cout<<c1->toString()<<endl;
    c1->tick();
    cout<<c1->toString()<<endl;
}
```

The code asking for the alarm time can also be placed in the `case 3:` part of the switch statement. This would eliminate the need for the `if` statement.

PROGRAMMING EXERCISE 12.12

```
void main()
{
    Clock *c1=NULL;
    cout << "Which type of clock?\n";
    cout << "1 - Clock\n";
    cout << "2 - AlarmClock\n";
    cout << "3 - CountdownClock\n";
    cout << "Enter choice (1,2,3): ";
    int choice;
    cin >> choice;
    switch(choice)
    {
        case 1:
            c1 = new Clock(1,2,3);
            break;
        case 2:
            c1 = new AlarmClock(1,2,3,1,2,4);
            break;
        case 3:
            c1 = new CountdownClock(1,2,3);
            break;
    };
    if(typeid(*c1) == typeid(AlarmClock))
    {
        int h,m,s;
        cout<<"What time is the alarm to be
            set for?\n";
        cout<<"Hour : ";
        cin>>h;
        cout<<"Minute : ";
        cin>>m;
        cout<<"Second : ";
        cin>>s;
        ((AlarmClock*)c1)->setAlarmTime(h,m,s);
    };
    cout<<c1->toString()<<endl;
    c1->tick();
    cout<<c1->toString()<<endl;
    cout<<"You created a "<<getClassName(c1)
        <<" object\n";
}
```

TASK 12.7

The *ContractWorker* class is declared as:

```
class ContractWorker : public Worker
{
    protected:
        int contractperiod;
    public:
        void setSalary(int);
        void setContract(int);
        float getContract();
};
```

The methods are coded as:

```
void ContractWorker::setSalary(int grade)
{
    const long
salaries[]={0,15000,20000,23000,29000,31000,35000L
,40000L,45000L,50000L,60000L};
    if (grade < 1 || grade > 10)
        salary = 0;
    else
        salary = salaries[grade]*2;
}

void ContractWorker::setContract(int w)
{
    if(w < 1 || w > 156)
        return;
    contractperiod = w;
}

float ContractWorker::getContract()
{
    return contractperiod;
}
```

PROGRAMMING EXERCISE 12.13

The *Worker* class should now be declared as:

```
//*** Worker Class (abstract)        ***
class Worker
{
    protected:
        static const long salaries[11];
        char name[31];
        char address[91];
        float salary;
    public:
        void setName(char*);
        void setAddress(char*);
        virtual void setSalary(int)=0;
        char* getName();
        char* getAddress();
        float getSalary();
};
const long Worker::salaries[]={0,15000,20000
        ,23000,29000,31000,35000L,40000L,45000L
        ,50000L,60000L};
```

The *setSalary()* methods can have the `const` declaration removed. For example:

```
void PartTimeWorker::setSalary(int grade)
{
    if (grade < 1 || grade > 10)
        salary = 0;
    else
        salary = salaries[grade]*0.75;
}
```

The new *AgencyWorker* class is declared as:

```
class AgencyWorker : public Worker
{
    public:
        void setSalary(int);
};

void AgencyWorker::setSalary(int grade)
{
    if (grade < 1 || grade > 10)
        salary = 0;
    else
        salary = salaries[grade]*1.2;
}
```

TASK 12.8

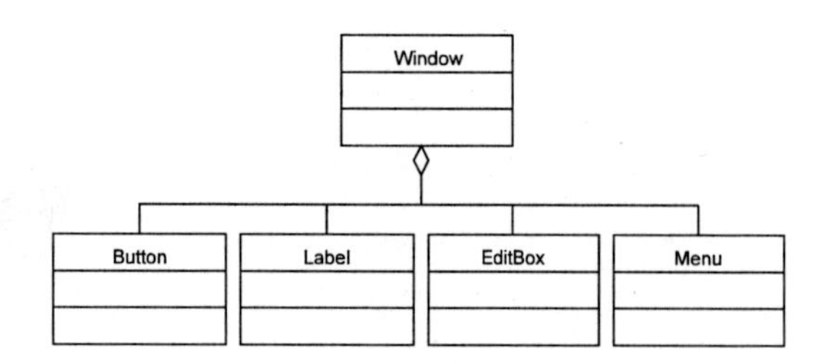

PROGRAMMING EXERCISE 12.14

```
#include <iostream.h>
#include <conio.h>
#include <string.h>

//****************************************
//***        Class Declarations        ***
//****************************************
//*** Distance Class ***
class Distance
{
    private:
        int yards;
        int feet;
        int inches;
    public:
        Distance(int=0,int=0,int=0);
        void setDistance(int,int,int);
        double convertToMetric();
        int getYards();
        int getFeet();
        int getInches();
};

//*** Weight Class ***
class Weight
{
    private:
        int pounds;
        int ounces;
        int toOunces();
    public:
        Weight(int=0,int=0);
        Weight(float);
        void setWeight(int,int);

        inline double convertToMetric();
        int getPounds();
        int getOunces();
        void operator +=(Weight);
        Weight operator +(Weight);
        int operator ==(Weight);
        Weight smaller(Weight w);
};

//*** String Class ***
class String
{
    private:
        char *cptr;
        char *ExpandString(char*);
    public:
        String();
        String(char*);
        String(String&);
        ~String();
        int ReadIn(char*, int, int=0);
        void operator = (const String&);
        int operator ==(const String&) const;
        int operator !=(const String&) const;
        String operator +(const String&) const;
        int Length()const;
        friend ostream& operator<<(ostream&,
        const String&);
};

//*** Horse Class ***
class Horse
{
    private:
        String name;
        Weight handicap;
        Distance wonby;
    public:
        Horse(String, Weight, Distance);
        void setName(String);
        void setWinningDistance(Distance);
        void setHandicap(Weight);
        String getName();
        Distance getWinningDistance();
        Weight getHandicap();
};

//****************************************
//***  Distance Class Methods          ***
//****************************************
Distance::Distance(int y,int f,int i)
{
    yards = y;
    feet = f;

    inches = i;

}

void Distance::setDistance(int newyds, int
newft, int newin)
{
    if(newyds < 0 || newft < 0 || newft > 2
    || newin < 0 || newin > 11)
        return;
    yards = newyds;
    feet = newft;
    inches = newin;
}

double Distance::convertToMetric()
{
    return (yards*36+feet*12+inches)*0.0254;
}

int Distance::getYards()
{
    return yards;
}

int Distance::getFeet()
{
    return feet;
}

int Distance::getInches()
{
    return inches;
}

//*** Display Distance object ***
ostream& operator<<(ostream& co, const Distance&
d)
{
    co<<d.getYards()<<" yds "<< d.getFeet()
        <<" ft "<<d.getInches()<<" in";
    return co;
}

//****************************************
//***    Weight Class Methods          ***
//****************************************
int Weight::toOunces()
{
    return (pounds*16 + ounces)*0.283495;
}

Weight::Weight(int lbs, int oz)
{
    if(lbs < 0 || oz < 0 || oz > 15)
    {
        pounds = 0;
        ounces = 0;
    }
    else
    {
        pounds = lbs;
        ounces = oz;
    }
}

Weight::Weight(float v)
{
    Weight(5, 4);
}

void Weight::setWeight(int lbs, int oz)
{
    if(lbs < 0 || oz < 0 || oz > 15)
        return;
    pounds = lbs;
    ounces = oz;
```

```
}

inline double Weight::convertToMetric()
{
    return (pounds * 16 + ounces)*0.0283495;
}

int Weight::getPounds()
{
    return pounds;
}

int Weight::getOunces()
{
    return ounces;
}

void Weight::operator+=(Weight w)
{
    int totaloz;

    totaloz = (pounds+w.pounds)*16+ounces+w.ounces;
    pounds = totaloz/16;
    ounces = totaloz%16;
};

Weight Weight::operator +(Weight w)
{
    Weight ans;
    int temp = toOunces() + w.toOunces();
    ans.pounds = temp / 16;
    ans.ounces = temp % 16;
    return ans;
}

int Weight::operator ==(Weight w)
{
    if (toOunces()==w.toOunces())
        return 1;
    else
        return 0;

}

Weight Weight::smaller(Weight w)
{
    if(toOunces() < w.toOunces())

        return *this;

    else

        return w;

}

//*** Display Weight object ***
ostream& operator<<(ostream& co, const Weight& w)

{
    co<<w.getPounds()<<" lbs "<< w.getOunces()
        <<" oz";
    return co;
}

//**************************
//*** Auxilary Functions ***
//**************************
inline int ReadKey()
{
    int ch;

    ch=getch();
    if(ch==0)
        ch=-getch();
    return ch;
}

//********************************
//*     String Class Methods     *
//********************************
//****** PRIVATE METHODS ******

//*** Expand allowed string ***
char* String::ExpandString(char *allowed)
{
    char temp[256]="";//Holds expanded string

    //Copy the first character across ***
    temp[0]=allowed[0];
    //***FOR all-2 chars in compressed string DO ***
    for(int c=1,p=1; c<int(strlen(allowed))-3;c++)
    {
        //*** IF two periods THEN ***
        if(allowed[c]=='.'&&allowed[c+1]=='.')
        {
            //***Add range of chars implied ***
            for(char ch=allowed[c-1];
            ch<=allowed[c+2];ch++)
                temp[p++]=ch;
            //*** Move past this part of string ***
            c+=2;
        }
        //*** ELSE if not two dots, copy char ***
        else
            temp[p++]=allowed[c];
    }
    //*** Copy any remaining characters ***
    for(int k=c;k<=strlen(allowed)-1;k++,c++)
        temp[p++]=allowed[c];
    //*** Insert final NULL character ***
    temp[p]='\0';
    //*** Return expanded string ***
    return temp;
}

//****** PUBLIC METHODS ******

//*** Read string from keyboard ***
int String::ReadIn(char *allowed, int max,
        int min)
{
    //*** Declare named constants ***
    const int ENTER = 13;
    const int BACKSPACE = 8;
    const int ESCAPE = 27;

    int ch;          //Holds current key press
    int count = 0;  //Holds no. of chars entered
    char temp[200];      //Holds entered string
    char tempallow[256];//Holds allowed char set
    //*** Expanded allowed string ***
    strcpy(tempallow,ExpandString(allowed));
    //*** Empty entered string ***
    strcpy(temp, "");
    //*** Read a key ***
    ch=ReadKey();
    //*** WHILE not ESCAPE AND ((not ENTER and
    not control key)OR(no.of char not reached
    minimum)) DO ***
    while(ch!=ESCAPE&&((ch!=ENTER&&ch>=0)
    ||count<min))
    {
        //*** IF allowed char & space remains THEN **
        if(strchr(tempallow, ch) && count<max)
        {
            //*** Display char ***
            cout<<char(ch);
            //*** Add char to string & inc. count ***
            temp[count++]=ch;
            //*** Terminate entered string ***
            temp[count]='\0';
        }
        //*** ELSE ***
        else
            //*** IF it's a valid backspace THEN ***
            if(ch==BACKSPACE&&count>0)
            {
                //*** Remove last from screen ***
                cout<<"\b \b";
                //*** & string; dec count ***
                temp[--count]='\0';
            }
        //*** Read another char ***
        ch=ReadKey();
    }
    //*** IF didn't end with escape THEN ***
    if(ch!=ESCAPE)
    {
        //*** Delete old allocated space ***
        delete cptr;
        //*** Allocate new space ***
        cptr=new char[strlen(temp)+1];
        //*** Copy entered string into object ***
        strcpy(cptr, temp);
    }
    //*** Return last character ***
    return ch;
}

//*** Construct empty string ***
String::String()
{
    cptr = new char;
    *cptr = '\0';
}

//*** Construct string from C++ string ***
String::String(char *s)
{
    cptr = new char [strlen(s)+1];
    strcpy(cptr, s);
}

//*** Copy Constructor ***
String::String(String& s)
{
    cptr = new char [strlen(s.cptr) + 1];
```

```
    strcpy(cptr, s.cptr);
}

//*** Deallocate string space ***
String::~String()
{
    delete [] cptr;
}

//*** String assignment ***
void String::operator = (const String &s)
{
    //*** IF self-copy THEN return ***
    if (&s == this)
        return;
    //*** Delete old allocated space ***
    delete [] cptr;
    //*** Allocate new space and copy ***
    cptr = new char[strlen(s.cptr)+1];
    strcpy(cptr,s.cptr);
}

//*** Equality operator ***
int String::operator==(const String &s)const
{
    //*** IF strings equal THEN ***
    if (!strcmp(cptr,s.cptr))
        //*** Return 1 ***
        return 1;
    else
    //*** ELSE return zero ***
        return 0;
}

//*** Inequality Operator ***
int String::operator !=(const String &s)const
{
    //*** IF strings not equal THEN return 1 ***
    if (strcmp(cptr, s.cptr))
        return 1;
    else
    //*** ELSE return zero ***
        return 0;
}

//*** Concatenate strings ***
String String::operator +(const String &s)const
{
    String temp; //Temp object for result

    //*** Allocate space for result ***
    temp.cptr = new char[strlen(cptr)
                +strlen(s.cptr)+1];
    //*** Copy both strings into space ***
    strcpy(temp.cptr,cptr);
    strcat(temp.cptr,s.cptr);
    //*** Return the result ***
    return temp;
}

//*** Return length of string ***
int String::Length()const
{
    return strlen(cptr);
}

//*** Display string object ***
ostream& operator<<(ostream& co, const String& s)
{
    co<<s.cptr;
    return co;
}

//***************************************
//***  Horse Class Methods          ***
//***************************************
Horse::Horse(String n, Weight h, Distance w)
{
    name = n;
    handicap = h;
    wonby = w;
}

void Horse::setName(String n)
{
    name = n;
}

void Horse::setHandicap(Weight h)
{
    handicap = h;
}

void Horse::setWinningDistance(Distance w)
{
    wonby = w;
}

String Horse::getName()
{
    return name;
}

Weight Horse::getHandicap()
{
    return handicap;
}

Distance Horse::getWinningDistance()
{
    return wonby;
}



//***    Main Program ***

void main()
{
    Horse h1("Red Rum",
Weight(10,0),Distance(0,0,0));

    cout<<"Horse's name           :
"<<h1.getName()<<"\nHandicap carried       :
"<<h1.getHandicap()<<"\nLast winning distance :
"<<h1.getWinningDistance()<<endl;
}
```

TASK 12.9

```
int List::len()
{
    return count;
}
```

PROGRAMMING EXERCISE 12.15

```
#include <stdio.h>
#include<iostream.h>
#include<stdlib.h>
#include<conio.h>
#include<string.h>

class Stack
{
    private:
        int data [10];
        int count;
    public:
        Stack();
        void push(int v);
        void pop();
        int top();
        int len();
        int isEmpty();
        void display();
};

Stack::Stack()
{
    count = 0;
}

void Stack::push(int v)
{
    if (len() == 10)
        return;
    data[count++] = v;
}

void Stack::pop()
{
    if(isEmpty())
        return;
    --count;
}

int Stack::top()
{
    if (isEmpty())
        exit(1);
    return data[count-1];
}

int Stack::len()
{
    return count;
}
```

```
int Stack::isEmpty()
{
    return (count==0);
}


void Stack::display()
{
    for(int c = len()-1; c >= 0; c--)
        cout << data[c]<<endl;
}


//*** Function Prototypes ***
int DisplayMenu(const char*);
int GetOption(int);
void ExecuteOption(int, Stack&);


void main()
{
    Stack s;
    int option, noofoptions;

    do
    {
        noofoptions=DisplayMenu("1. - Push\n
            "2. - Pop\n3 - Top\n4. - Pop\n"
            "5. - Length\n6. - IsEmpty\n"
            "7. - Display\n8 - QUIT\n");
        option = GetOption(noofoptions);
        ExecuteOption(option, s);
    }
    while (option != noofoptions);
    cout<<"PROGRAM TERMINATED\n";
    getch();
}

int DisplayMenu(const char* text)
{
    clrscr();
    cout<<"MENU\n\n";
    cout<<text;

    for(int c=0,total=0; c<strlen(text);c++)
        if(text[c]=='\n')
            total++;
    return total;
}

int GetOption(int max)
{
    int opt;
    cout<<"\nEnter option : ";
    cin>>opt;
    while(opt<1||opt>max)
    {
        cout<<"Invalid option\n";
        cin>>opt;
    }
    return opt;
}

void ExecuteOption(int opt, Stack& s)
{
    int val;

    switch (opt)
    {
        case 1:
            cout<<"Enter value to be added : ";
            cin >> val;
            s.push(val);
            break;
        case 2:
            if(!s.isEmpty())
                s.pop();
            else
            {
                cout<<"The stack is empty\n";
                getch();
            }
            break;
        case 3:
            if(!s.isEmpty()
            {
                cout<<"Top of stack is : "
                    <<s.top()<<endl;
                getch();
            }
            else
            {
                cout<<"Stack is empty\n";
                getch();
            }
            break;
        case 4:
            if(!s.isEmpty())
                s.pop();
            else
            {
                cout<<"Stack is empty\n";
                getch();
            }
            break;
        case 5:
            cout<<"The stack contains "<<s.len()
                <<" values\n";
            getch();
            break;
        case 6:
            if(s.isEmpty())
                cout<<"Stack is empty\n";
            else
                cout<<"Stack is not empty\n";
            getch();
            break;
        case 7:
            clrscr();
            cout<<"CONTENTS OF STACK\n";
            s.display();
            getch();
            break;
    }
}
```

PROGRAMMING EXERCISE 12.16

```
#include<iostream.h>
#include <iostream.h>
#include<conio.h>

class Distance
{
    private:
        int yards;
        int feet;
        int inches;
        int toInches();
        static int count;
    public:
        static const int metre;
        static const double centimetre;
        static int getCount();
        Distance(int=0, int=0, int=0);
        Distance(double);
        ~Distance();
        void setDistance(int,int,int);
        void setDistance(double);
        inline double convertToMetric();
        int getYards();
        int getFeet();
        int getInches();
        void operator+=(Distance);
        Distance operator+(Distance d);
        int operator>(Distance);
        int operator< (Distance);
        int operator==(Distance);
        Distance operator ++();

        Distance operator ++(int);

        Distance operator --();

        Distance operator --(int);

        Distance smaller(Distance);

};

const int Distance::metre=39;
const double Distance::centimetre=0.3937;
int Distance::count = 0;

int Distance::getCount()
{
     return count;
}

Distance::Distance(int y, int f, int i)
{
    if(y < 0 || f < 0 || f > 2 || i < 0 || i > 11)
    {
        yards = 0;
        feet = 0;
        inches = 0;
    }
    else
```

```
   {
       yards = y;
       feet = f;
       inches = i;
   }
   count ++;
}

Distance::Distance(double v)
{
   if (v < 0)
   {
       yards = 0;
       feet = 0;
       inches = 0;
   }
   else
   {
       int totalinches = (int)(v*36+0.5);
       yards = totalinches / 36;
       feet = totalinches %36 / 12;
       inches = totalinches % 12;
   }
   count++;
}

Distance::~Distance()
{
   count--;
}

int Distance::toInches()
{
   return yards*36 + feet*12 + inches;
}

void Distance::setDistance(int newyds, int
newft, int newin)
{
   if(newyds < 0 || newft < 0 || newft > 2
   || newin < 0 || newin > 11)
       return;
   yards = newyds;
   feet = newft;
   inches = newin;
}

inline double Distance::convertToMetric()
{
   return (yards*36+feet*12+inches)*0.0254;
}

int Distance::getYards()
{
   return yards;
}

int Distance::getFeet()
{
   return feet;
}

int Distance::getInches()
{
   return inches;
}

void Distance::operator+=(Distance d)
{
   int totalinches;

   totalinches = toInches() + d.toInches();
   yards = totalinches / 36;
   feet = totalinches%36/12;
   inches = totalinches%12;
}

void Distance::setDistance(double v)
{
   if (v < 0)
       return;
   int totalinches = (int)(v*36+0.5);
   yards = totalinches / 36;
   feet = totalinches %36 / 12;
   inches = totalinches % 12;
}

Distance Distance::operator+(Distance d)
{
   Distance ans;
   int temp = (yards+d.yards)*36
              +(feet+d.feet)*12
              +inches + d.inches;
   ans.yards = temp / 36;
   ans.feet = temp%36/12;
   ans.inches = temp%12;
   return ans;
}

int Distance::operator>(Distance d)
{
   if (convertToMetric() > d.convertToMetric())
       return 1;
   else
       return 0;
}

int Distance::operator<(Distance d)
{
   if (convertToMetric() < d.convertToMetric())
       return 1;
   else
       return 0;
}

int Distance::operator==(Distance d)
{
   if (toInches() == d.toInches())
       return 1;
   else
       return 0;
}

Distance Distance::operator++()
{
   int totalinches;

   totalinches = toInches()+1;
   yards = totalinches / 36;
   feet = totalinches%36/12;
   inches = totalinches %12;
   return *this;
}

Distance Distance::operator++(int)
{
   int totalinches;
   Distance ans;
   ans = *this;
   totalinches = toInches()+1;
   yards = totalinches / 36;
   feet = totalinches%36/12;
   inches = totalinches %12;
   return ans;
}

Distance Distance::operator--()
{
   int totalinches;

   totalinches = toInches()-1;
   if (totalinches < 0)
       totalinches = 0;
   yards = totalinches / 36;
   feet = totalinches%36/12;
   inches = totalinches %12;
   return *this;
}

Distance Distance::operator--(int)
{
   int totalinches;
   Distance ans;
   ans = *this;
   totalinches = toInches()-1;
   if (totalinches < 0)
       totalinches = 0;
   yards = totalinches / 36;
   feet = totalinches%36/12;
   inches = totalinches %12;
   return ans;
}

Distance Distance::smaller(Distance d)
{

   if (convertToMetric() < d.convertToMetric())
       return *this;
   else
       return d;
}

ostream& operator<<(ostream& cc, Distance d)
{
   cc<<d.getYards()<<" yds "<<d.getFeet()<<" ft "
       <<d.getInches()<<" in";
   return cc;
}

istream& operator>>(istream& ci, Distance& d)
{
   int y, f, i;

   cout<<" Enter yards : ";
   ci>>y;
   while (y < 0)
   {
```

```
        cout << "Must be > 0. Re-enter ";
        ci >> y;
    }
    cout << "Enter feet : ";
    ci >> f;
    while (f < 0||f > 2)
    {
        cout << "Must be 0 to 2. Re-enter ";
        ci >> f;
    }
    cout << "Enter inches : ";
    ci >> i;
    while (f < 0||f > 11)
    {
        cout << "Must be 0 to 11. Re-enter ";
        ci >> i;
    }
    d.setDistance(y,f,i);
    return ci;
}

//*** Explicit casting for prototype function ***
Distance Minimum(Distance[],int);

void main()
{
    //*** Define lists to be searched ***

    Distance list[]={Distance(1,2,3),
Distance(1,0,0), Distance(2,1,10)};
    //*** Define result variable ***
    Distance ans;
    //***Determine and display results ***
    ans = Minimum(list,3);
    cout << "Min distance = " << ans << endl;
}

//*** Function Definition ***
template<class T>T Minimum(T list[], int size)
{
    T smallest=list[0];
    for(int c = 1;c < size;c++)
        if(list[c] < smallest)
            smallest = list[c];
    return smallest;
}
```

PROGRAMMING EXERCISE 12.17

```
#include<iostream.h>
#include <iostream.h>
#include<conio.h>


//*****************************************
//*** Code for Distance class goes here ***
//*****************************************


template <class T>
class Container
{
    private:
        T list[10];
        int count;
    public:
        Container();
        void add(T);
        void display();
};
template <class T>
Container<T>::Container()
{
    count = 0;
}
template <class T>
void Container<T>::add(T v)
{
      if(count < 10)
        list[count++]=v;
}

template <class T>
void Container<T>::display()
{
    for(int c = 0; c < count; c++)
        cout<<list[c]<<endl;
}

void main()
{
    Container<Distance> con;
    int opt;

    cout<<"1 - add\n2 - display\n3 - QUIT\n";
    cin >> opt;
    while (opt != 3)
    {
        Distance v;
        switch(opt)
        {
            case 1:
                cout<<"Enter value to be added :\n";
                cin>>v;
                con.add(v);
                break;
            case 2:
                con.display();
                break;
        }
        cout<<"1 - add\n2 - display\n3 - QUIT\n";
        cin >> opt;
    }
    cout<<"PROGRAM TERMINATED\n";
}
```

Chapter 13

I/O Streams

This chapter covers the following topics:

- Checking I/O Success
- Format Flags
- fstream Class
- ifstream Class
- I/O Buffering
- ios Class
- istream Class
- ofstream Class
- ostream Class
- Printer Output
- Redirection
- Text and Binary Files

INPUT/OUTPUT STREAMS

Introduction

We've already seen in Chapter 6 that C++ treats an I/O device or data file as a stream of bytes to which data can be sent or from which data can be extracted. The file handling techniques shown in that chapter were inherited from C and are retained for backward compatibility with that earlier language. However, C++ also offers a class-based approach to handling both input and output streams.

The classes *istream* (input) and *ostream* (output) are used for handling basic I/O, normally via the keyboard and screen respectively. Derived classes, *ifstream* (file input) and *ofstream* (file output), define features for disk file handling. Where a single object requires the ability to perform both input and output, an *istream* object is used for basic I/O while an *fstream* object is used for file I/O . All of these structures are related. This relationship is shown in FIG-13.1.

FIG-13.1

I/O Stream Classes

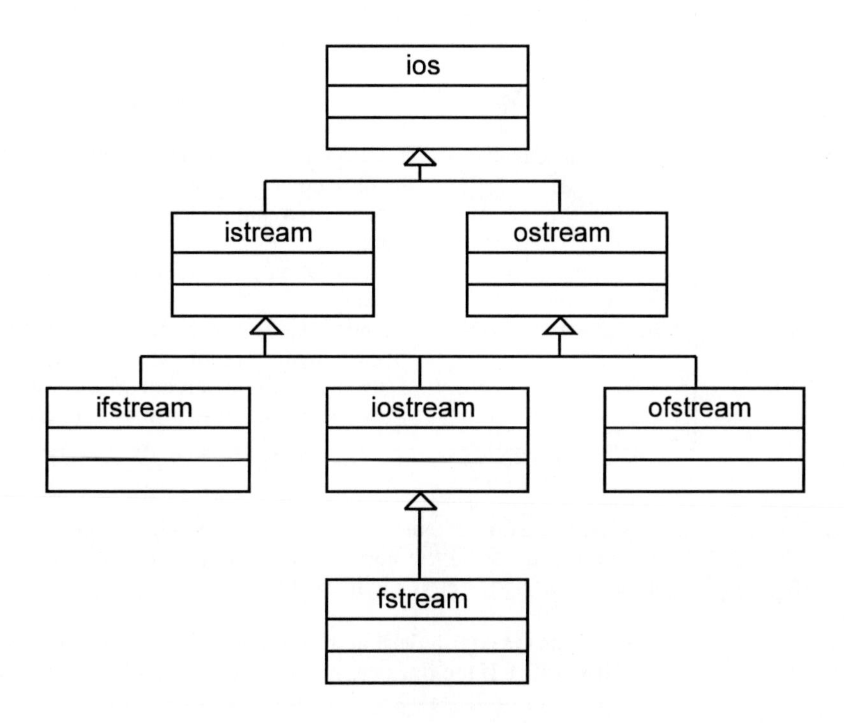

The objects from the classes *istream* and *ostream* are used in almost every program since `cin` is an *istream* object and `cout` is an *ostream* object. These objects are created automatically in every C++ program. Two additional *ostream* objects, `cerr` and `clog`, are also created in every program. These can be used in the same manner as we use `cout` and normally direct their output to the screen.

The *ios* Class

Both *istream* and *ostream* are derived from the abstract *ios* class from which they inherit several attributes and methods. These inherited features provide formatting, error checking and status information. Some of these features are appropriate only to outputting (i.e. in *ostream* objects); others deal exclusively with input; while a few affect both input and output.

The *ios* class defines flags which affect the layout produced on screen and how the data in the input stream is to be treated. The format flags affecting output are listed in TABLE-13.1.

TABLE-13.1

Format Flags

Flag	Purpose
`skipws`	Ignores whitespace characters on input streams if set.
`left`	Specifies left justified output.
`right`	Specifies right justified output.
`internal`	Specifies that a numbers sign should be left-justified. and the value right justified.
`dec`	Specifies that the values which follow should be treated as decimal.
`oct`	Specifies that the values which follow should be treated as octal.
`hex`	Specifies that the values which follow should be treated as hexadecimal.
`showbase`	Forces the base of a numeric value to be output.
`showpoint`	Forces floating-point values to be output with a decimal point and trailing zeros.
`uppercase`	Forces the output to use an uppercase X when displaying hexadecimal numbers and uppercase E when displaying floating-point values in scientific notation.
`showpos`	Forces the output to display a + sign on positive values.
`scientific`	Shows floating-point values in scientific notation.
`fixed`	Shows floating-point values in fixed notation.
`unitbuf`	Flushes the output stream after an output operation.
`stdio`	Flushes the output stream after every character.

The flags are implemented as single bits in a long int class attribute. By setting the required flags to 1, the corresponding output format feature is activated, while resetting a flag to zero deactivates that option.

These flags are adjusted using the methods *flag()* and *unsetf()* described below (see TABLE-13.2). If the flags are untouched the default formats are used.

TABLE-13.2

Output methods in *ios*

Method	Purpose
`char fill();`	Returns the character used to fill output to the required screen output width.
`char fill(char c);`	Sets the pad character to *c* and returns the previous pad character.
`long flags();`	Returns the status of flags.
`long flags(long f)`	Sets the format flags to the desired options.
`long setf(long f);`	Returns the old flag status and sets the flags corresponding to those marked in *f*. Other flags are unchanged.
`ostream* tie()`	Returns 'tied' stream details.

Continued on next page

TABLE-13.2
(continued)

Output methods in *ios*

Method	Purpose
`ostream* tie (ostream* s)`	Ties an output stream to an input stream.
`long unsetf(long f);`	Unsets the flags corresponding to those in *f* Returns the old flag status.
`int width();`	Returns the current width setting used when displaying values.
`int width(int w);`	Sets the width used on subsequent output and returns the old setting.
`int precision()`	Returns the precision used when displaying real numbers.
`int precision(int)`	Sets the precision used when displaying real numbers.

Other flags and operations are declared within the `ios` class. These are described later within the classes in which they are used.

The *ostream* Class

The *ostream* class inherits most of its features from the *ios* class but includes three additional methods:

```
<<
put(char)
write(char*, int)
```

For example,

```
cout << 'a';
```

is equivalent to

```
cout.put('a');
```

The `write()` method allows strings to be written. Hence,

```
cout.write("Hello",5);
```

is similar to

```
cout << "Hello";
```

Inherited Methods

With the inherited methods from the `ios`, we can manipulate the output format.

`width()`

This method allows us to set the display field size. For example, to set the display size to five characters we use the code:

```
cout.width(5);
cout << 17 << endl;
```

This gives us an output of:

```
∇∇∇17
```

The width setting applies to the next output only and must be repeated if required for several values:

```
cout.width(5);
cout << 17 << endl;
cout.width(5);
cout << 121 << endl;
```

Since this is rather inelegant, an alternative approach is to use the `setw()` manipulator:

```
cout<<setw(5)<<17<<endl<<setw(5)<<121<<endl;
```

However, this requires the inclusion of the **iomanip.h** header file in your program.

We can discover the current width setting using the zero parameters version of the function. For example, the code:

```
int w,wid;

cout << "Enter field width : ";
cin >> w;
cout.width(w);
wid = cout.width();
cout << 17 << endl;
cout << "width used on output was " << wid << endl;
cout << "width now " << cout.width() << endl;
```

will, for an input of 8, produce the output

```
∇∇∇∇∇∇17
width used on output was 8
width now 0
```

fill()

The `fill()` method is designed to allow characters other than a space to occupy the unused positions in a display field. Hence, if we write

```
cout.fill('*');
cout.width(5);
cout << 17 << endl;
```

we get the output

```
***17
```

The fill character is set until explicitly changed. We can determine its current setting by using the second version of the `fill()` method. Hence, adding the line

```
cout << "The fill character is << cout.fill() << endl;
```

to our previous code will produce the result

```
The fill character is *
```

`flags()`

For other output formats we need to modify the format flags defined in TABLE-13.1. This can be done using the `flags()` method.

First, we can discover the current flag settings using the statement:

```
cout<<hex<<cout.flags()<<endl;
```

This will produce the output

```
2001
```

Since the flags are stored in a 16 bit integer (see FIG-13.2), we only need to map the hexadecimal number shown to the corresponding flags.

FIG-13.2

The I/O Format Flags

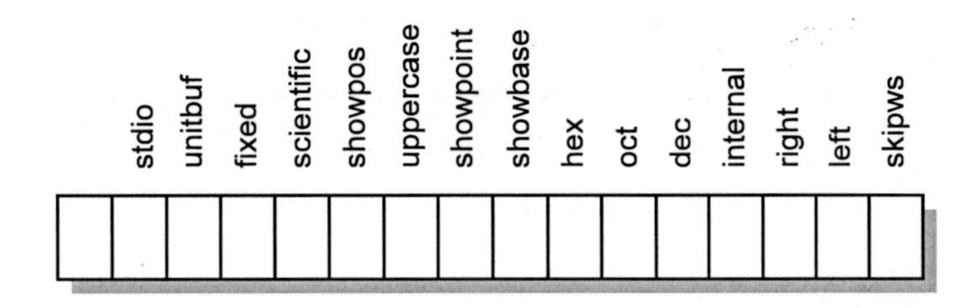

From this we can see that the program begins with the *skipws* and *unitbuf* flags set.

> **PROGRAMMING EXERCISE 13.1**
>
> Use the *Binary()* function developed in PROGRAMMING EXERCISE 5.19 to display the flags' settings in binary.

We can change a format feature by setting its flag. For example, to show the number base when displaying numeric values we use the statement:

```
cout.flags(ios::showbase);
```

We are allowed to use the flag names as constants since these are declared in an enumerated type within the `ios` class.

To set more than one flag, for example, to show the number base and the letters of hexadecimal values in upper case we use the statement:

```
cout.flags(ios::showbase|ios::uppercase);
```

The bitwise OR operator is used because each flag is stored as a single bit. The effect of ORing is to set the bits corresponding to the required flags.

The `flags()` operation sets only the flags specified; all other flags are reset to zero. This means that, if we execute the statement

```
cout.flags(ios::showbase|ios::uppercase);
```

at the start of a program, the *skipws* and *unitbuf* flags will be switched off. To prevent this happening we need to specify all of the flags that are to be set. We could do this using

```
cout.flags(ios::skipws|ios::unitbuf|ios::showbase|ios::uppercase);
```

but this implies that we know exactly which flags should be on at any point in our program. A more flexible approach is to use the statement

```
cout.flags(cout.flags()|ios::showbase|ios::uppercase);
```

which captures the current state of the flags as part of the argument when resetting them.

setf()

An alternative to `flags()` is `setf()` which allows us to set specific flags without affecting the current state of other flags. Hence we may set the *showbase* and *uppercase* flags without changing *skipws* and *unitbuf* with the statement:

```
cout.setf(ios::showbase|ios::uppercase);
```

You may have noticed that some of the flags must be mutually exclusive. For example, it makes no sense to have both the *hex* and *oct* flags set at the same time.

Each group of mutually exclusive flags are named:

```
adjustfield
               left
               right
               internal
basefield
               dec
               oct
               hex
floatfield
               scientific
               fixed
```

In these groups, setting one flag implies that the others should be reset. All of this can be handled automatically using an extended version of `setf()` which takes two arguments. The first of these is the flag to be set; the second is the group involved. Hence, we may set the *hex* flag using the command:

```
cout.setf(ios::hex, ios::basefield);
```

If the *dec* or *oct* flag had previously been set, it would have been reset by this command.

PROGRAMMING EXERCISE 13.2

Write a program to demonstrate the use of the *left, internal, oct, hex* and *scientific* flags.

unsetf()

This method allows us to reset a flag. For example, we might reset the *showbase* flag (assuming it was currently set) using the statement:

```
cout.unsetf(ios::showbase);
```

precision()

Using this allows us to set the number of numeric digits to be displayed with real values. The code

```
cout.precision(3);
cout << 3.1415967;
```

results in the display

```
3.14
```

while the lines

```
cout.precision(3);
cout << 43.1415967;
```

gives an output of

```
43.1
```

As you can see from the examples, `precision()` specifies the total number of digits used, not the number after the decimal point.

If the number of characters specified is too small for the integer part of the value, the result is given in scientific notation. For example:

```
cout.precision(1);
cout << 43.1415967;
```

displays

```
4e01
```

Without a parameter, `precision()` returns the current precision setting.

Stream Buffers

flush()

When we output data to an `ostream` object, we are, in fact, sending the information to an area in memory associated with that object. This is the **stream buffer**. It is only when the contents of the buffer is emptied (or **flushed**) that we see the output on the screen.

When examining the I/O format flags, we saw that the flag *unitbuf* was set. This flag has the effect of flushing the associated object's buffer every time data is sent to it. This results in any screen output appearing immediately. However, if we were to turn this flag off, we would get a delay in the output.

PROGRAMMING EXERCISE 13.3

Enter and run the following program, observing the results.

```
#include<iostream.h>
#include<conio.h>

void main()
(
    cout.unsetf(ios::unitbuf);
    cout << "Hello\n";
    getch();
}
```

You'll notice that the output didn't appear until the program terminated. Without the instruction to flush the buffer area associated with `cout`, its contents will only appear on the screen when the buffer is full, or the program terminates.

Alternatively, we may add another method belonging to the `ostream` class, `flush()`, which allows us to empty the contents of the buffer area:

```
cout << "Hello\n";
cout.flush();
```

Now, the output will appear before the key press.

This leads us to a subtle difference between `'\n'` and `endl`. The latter not only forces the carriage return, linefeed combination, but also flushes the buffer. Hence, by writing

```
cout << "Hello"<<endl;
```

there is no need to use the `flush()` method on that line of output.

The *istream* Class

The methods defined in `istream` are listed in TABLE-13.3.

The extraction or input operator is overloaded to allow input to any predefined type such as `int, float`, etc.

get(char&)

The simplest form of `get()` accepts a single character from the input stream. This allows statements such as

```
cin.get(ch);
```

which is equivalent to

```
ch = getch();
```

TABLE-13.3

`istream` Methods

Method	Purpose
`int gcount();`	Returns the number of characters read by the last input operation.
`istream& get(char& c);`	Reads a single character from the input stream.
`istream& get(char* s, int n, char d='\n');`	Reads up to *n* characters into *s* and adds a terminating NULL character to *s*. Reading stops early if character *d* is encountered. Character *d*, if encountered, is not extracted from the input stream.
`istream& getline (char* s,int n, char d='\n');`	As *get()* above, but the *d* is extracted.
`istream& ignore (int n=1,int d=EOF);`	Discards the next *n* characters from the stream but stops early if *d* encountered. Character *d* is removed.
`int peek();`	Returns the next character in the stream without removing it. Returns EOF if no characters in the stream.
`istream& putback (char c);`	Places *c* onto the start of the input stream.
`istream& read(char*s, int no);`	Reads *no* characters into *s*. Terminates early if EOF encountered.
`>>`	Extraction operator.

`get(char*, int, char='\n')`

Previously, we have used `gets()` to read a string since a simple `cin>>name` will take any whitespace character as the string terminating character. Using `get(char*,int, char='\n')` solves this problem. The statement

```
cin.get(name,80);
```

will read up to 80 characters from the standard input stream, terminating only when a return character (the default value for the third parameter) is entered or all 80 characters have been read. A NULL character ('\0') will be inserted at the end of the data transferred to *name*.

By changing the default value we can even accept a string which normally is typed over several lines, such as an address. For example, using the statement

```
cin.get(address,120,'*');
```

will allow us to enter data such as

```
14 High Street
Glasgow
G2*
```

which would result in *address* containing the value

```
14 High Street\nGlasgow\nG2\0
```

Using this version of `get()` always leaves the terminating character at the head of the input stream and this will be read as the next character should another input method be used. To get round this we need only follow up with a character `get()`. For example:

```
cin.get(address,120,'*'); //*** Read address - * left in stream
cin.get(ch);              //*** Remove * from input stream
```

`getline()`

The method `getline()` is identical to the above form of `get()` in all respects other than the fact that it removes the terminating character from the input stream. Hence

```
cin.getline(address,120,'*');
```

not only assigns a value to *address,* but also removes the asterisk from the input stream. The extracted terminating character is discarded.

`read()`

Using this we can read an exact number of characters from the input stream into a string. For example, the code

```
char name[51];
cin.read(name,20);
```

will read exactly 20 characters into *name*. The operation will wait until all 20 characters have been entered. The only way to satisfy the statement with less than 20 characters is to enter the EOF character (Ctrl-Z).

`gcount()`

We can use this function to return the number of characters read from the input stream by a previous `get()`, `getline()` or `read()` statement. For example, the program in LISTING-13.1 will display the message

```
the number of characters read was 14
```

if we enter the text *Patricia Stamp* after the prompt.

LISTING-13.1

Counting the Characters Read

```
#include<iostream.h>

void main()
{
   char name[51];

   cout << "Enter name : ";
   //*** Read up to 20 characters ***
   cin.get(name,20);
   //*** Display number of characters read ***
   cout << "the number of characters read was "<< cin.gcount()
        << endl;
}
```

peek()

This operation allows us to examine the first character on the input buffer without actually removing it. It is similar in operation to a stack's *Top()* operation we encountered earlier in Chapter 8. For example, if we want to extract only the numeric digits from an input string such as

```
B7HD13X1
```

then we could use `peek()` to see what the next character will be without actually removing it from the input stream. LISTING-13.2 uses this technique to create a string containing only the numeric digits of an input string.

LISTING-13.2

Using peek()

```
#include<iostream.h>
#include<ctype.h>
void main()
{
  char ch;
  char numstring[51]="";
  int c = 0;

  cout << "Enter string : ";
  //*** REPEAT ***
  do
  {
      //*** Look at next character in cin buffer ***
      ch = cin.peek();
      //*** IF it's numeric THEN add to string ***
      if(isdigit(ch))
          numstring[c++] = ch;
      //*** Now actually remove character from buffer ***
      cin.get();
  }
  //*** UNTIL EOF ***
  while(ch != EOF);
  //*** Add terminator to string ***
  numstring[c] = '\0';
  //*** Display string ***
  cout << endl << numstring << endl;
}
```

putback()

The method allows us to place a character in the input buffer. The character is placed at the front of the input buffer and hence will be the first character extracted. For example, in LISTING-13.3, if "FRED" is entered at the keyboard, the value displayed will be XFRED.

LISTING-13.3

Using putback()

```
#include<iostream.h>

void main()
{
  char name[51];

  cout << "Enter text : ";
  //*** Add X to text in buffer ***
  cin.putback('X');
  //*** Read text ***
  cin.getline(name,10);
  //*** Display text ***
  cout << name << endl;
}
```

Inherited Characteristics

tie()

We saw earlier that if we reset the *unitbuf* flag, cout's buffer is not sent to the screen as soon as we send data to it. Because of this, we might reasonably expect the program in LISTING-13.4 to display the prompt message after the data is accepted from the keyboard.

LISTING-13.4

Tied streams

```
#include<iostream.h>

void main()
{
    int no;

    //*** Switch off flush buffer flag ***
    cout.unsetf(ios::unitbuf);
    //*** Issue prompt ***
    cout << "Please enter value : ";
    //*** Read input ***
    cin >> no;
    //*** Display results ***
    cout << "The value entered was " << no << endl;
}
```

However, this is not the case. When the program is executed, the reset unitbuf appears to have no effect. The reason for this is that cout has been **tied** to cin. When input is requested from an input object tied to an output object, the output object's buffer is flushed before the input statement is executed.

To untie objects we call the tie() method with an argument of zero. Hence, by adding the line

```
cin.tie(0);
```

we will get the out-of-sync effect we had been expecting in the first place.

PROGRAMMING EXERCISE 13.4

Modify the program in LISTING-13.4 to include the above tie() statement and observe the effects.

We can reconnect the two streams using the instruction

```
cin.tie(&cout);
```

Stream Redirection

Although cin and cout normally use the keyboard and screen respectively, it is possible to link these streams to other files. In this way, cin may accept data from, say, a disk file, while cout can send its information to a printer. This ability to change the source and destination of a stream is known as **redirection**.

To achieve redirection we need to be able to tell the program at run time the name of the alternative files to be used when reading and writing. For example, the program in LISTING-13.5 reads a series of strings until an empty string is entered.

LISTING-13.5

Normal I/O

```
#include<iostream.h>
#include<string.h>
#include<iomanip.h>
void main()
{
    char text[81];

    //*** Read line of text ***
    cin.getline(text,80);
    int count = 0;
    //*** WHILE not blank string ***
    while(strcmp(text,""))
    {
        //*** Increment count ***
        count++;
        //*** Display count and text ***
        cout << setw(3) << count << ' ' << text << endl;
        //*** Get next line ***
        cin.getline(text,80);
    }
}
```

Whereas, under normal circumstances input will be from the keyboard and output to the screen, we may modify this behaviour by running the program with redirection instructions. There are two ways to achieve this: from the DOS command line and from the Borland IDE.

To use the DOS approach we must first compile our program to create an .EXE file. If we assume our program creates a file called REDIRECT.EXE and that the input data is held in a file called IN.DAT, then we can redirect `cin` by entering the command:

```
REDIRECT<IN.DAT
```

Executing this line will produce screen output without any requirement to enter text at the keyboard. This is a very powerful, not to say, useful ability. For example, it allows us to set up the test data of a program in a text file and saves us the time and bother of having to type it in each time we test our code, since we need only redirect our input stream to that file.

It's equally possible to redirect output to a file. Hence the command

REDIRECT.EXE must be compiled as a DOS program.
The command assumes REDIRECT.EXE and IN.DAT are both in the current directory. Where this is not the case, path information must also be entered.

```
REDIRECT>OUT.DAT
```

will send all the results to OUT.DAT. The file will be created if it does not already exist.

By entering

```
REDIRECT<IN.DAT>OUT.DAT
```

both input and output are directed to disk files.

To send the output to the printer, redirect your output to **prn**.

PROGRAMMING EXERCISE 13.5

Create a text file to be used as redirected input.
Using the program in LISTING-13.5 with redirection from your file and to the printer.

An alternative way of redirecting I/O without entering the DOS environment is to set up the details in the RUN|Arguments option.

`eof()`

The program in LISTING-13.5 used a blank line to terminate data input, but it is equally possible to use the end-of-file indicator for this purpose. This is done using the `eof()` operation. For example, the following program, (LISTING-13.6), terminates the reading of text lines using this approach.

LISTING-13.6

Redirection and *eof()*

```
#include<iostream.h>
#include<string.h>
#include<iomanip.h>

void main()
{
   char text[81];

   //*** Read a line of text ***
   cin.getline(text,80);
   int count = 0;
   //*** WHILE not EOF DO ***
   while(!cin.eof())
   {
        //*** Increment count ***
        count++;
        //*** Display count and text ***
        cout << setw(3) << count << ' ' << text<<endl;
        //*** Read next line of text ***
        cin.getline(text,80);
   }
}
```

If the program is run without redirection, as many lines as required may be entered at the keyboard - use Ctrl-Z to act as the end of file.

`ignore()`

When data comes from an existing source (e.g. a text file) there's always the possibility that we may want only part of the data. For example, if a file contains the following personnel records

```
Deans,Tracey        F    5
Heron,Liz           F   35
Hutton,Jack         M   58
```

and we wish to extract only the *age* components of each record, then we can use the `ignore()` function to skip the unwanted characters in each record. Assuming the age field begins at character position 31, we can tell the program to ignore the first 30 characters with the instruction

```
cin.ignore(30);
```

LISTING-13.7 uses this technique to display only the *age* component of each record.

LISTING-13.7

Using ignore()

Notice it is necessary to skip 31 characters after the first record. This removes the return characters at the end of each line.

```
#include<iostream.h>
#include<string.h>
#include<iomanip.h>
void main()
{
   int no;

   //*** Skip start of record ***
   cin.ignore(30);
   //*** Read age ***
   cin >> no;
   //*** WHILE not EOF DO ***
   while(!cin.eof())
   {
       //*** Output age ***
       cout << no << endl;
       //*** Skip to next age ***
       cin.ignore(31);
       //*** Read age ***
       cin >> no;
   }
}
```

What about coping with unformatted data where each field can vary in size? For example our three previous records might be stored as:

```
Deans,Tracey|F|5
Heron,Liz|F|35
Hutton,Jack|M|58
```

We can handle this with an extended version of `ignore()` which allows us to specify a terminating character. Hence, if we write

```
ignore(50,'|');
```

the first 50 characters will be skipped unless a '|' character is encountered in which case skipping stops at the first character after the terminating symbol. LISTING-13.8 shows this technique in action.

LISTING-13.8

Using *ignore()* with a Character terminator

```
#include<iostream.h>
#include<string.h>
#include<iomanip.h>
void main()
{
   int no;

   //*** Skip first two '|' ***
   cin.ignore(50,'|');
   cin.ignore(50,'|');
   //*** Read age ***
   cin >> no;
   //*** WHILE not EOF DO
   while(!cin.eof())
   {
       //*** Display value read ***
       cout << no << endl;
       //*** Skip next two '|' ***
       cin.ignore(50,'|');
       cin.ignore(50,'|');
       //*** Read age ***
       cin >> no;
   }
}
```

Checking the Success of I/O Operations

There's not much to go wrong when reading from the keyboard and writing to the screen. However, if streams are redirected things may be different: the file to be read may not exist, or we might attempt to output to a write protected disk.

The success or failure of any I/O operation is recorded in the I/O state flags (see TABLE-13.4) and these can be interrogated using the I/O state methods (see TABLE-13.5). These attributes are inherited from the `ios` class.

TABLE-13.4

I/O State Flags in *ios*

Flag	Purpose
`goodbit`	Set if the last I/O operation was successful.
`eofbit`	Set if a read operation detects the end of file.
`failbit`	Set if the last I/O operation failed.
`badbit`	Set if the stream data is corrupt.

TABLE-13.5

I/O State Methods in *ios*

Method	Purpose
`int bad()`	Returns 1 if badbit set.
`int eof()`	Returns 1 if eofbit set.
`int fail()`	Returns 1 if failbit set.
`int good()`	Returns 1 if goodbit set.
`int rdstate()`	Returns the set of I/O state flags.

The program in LISTING-13.9 is a modification of the earlier LISTING-13.7. However, on this occasion, the number of characters to be ignored is more than the size of the file.

LISTING-13.9

Checking the Success of Input

```
#include<iostream.h>
#include<string.h>
#include<iomanip.h>
#include<stdlib.h>
void main()
{
    int no;

    //*** Ignore too many characters ***
    cin.ignore(3000);
    //*** IF ignore operation unsuccessful THEN***
    if(!cin.good())
    {
        //*** Display error message and exit program ***
        cout << "Error on ignore\n";
        exit(1);
    }
    cin >> no;
    while(!cin.eof())
    {
        cout << no << endl;
        cin.ignore(31);
        cin >> no;
    }
}
```

Running the program will result in the output

```
Error on ignore
```

since the end-of-file is encountered.

If we add a check for end-of-file within the earlier check giving the code segment

```
if(!cin.good())
{
    cout << "Error on ignore\n";
    if(cin.eof())
        cout << "End-of-file detected\n";
    exit(1);
}
```

we will produce an output of

```
Error on ignore
End-of-file detected
```

Although the flag *goodbit* is not set when the end-of-file is encountered, this is not considered to be an error and hence the *failbit* is not set in these circumstances. Hence, if we were to change the check to

```
if(cin.fail())
{
    cout << "Error on ignore\n";
    exit(1);
}
```

no error would be detected.

However, the same is not true of the next `cin` statement in the program, `cin>>no;` which would fail because it would be attempting to read past the end-of-file. A new version of the program with complete error check on all input operations is shown in LISTING-13.10.

LISTING-13.10

Complete Checking on Input

```
#include<iostream.h>
#include<string.h>
#include<iomanip.h>
#include<stdlib.h>
void main()
{
  int no;

  cin.ignore(30);
  if(!cin.good())
  {
      cout << "Error on ignore\n";
      if(cin.eof())
          cout << "End of file detected\n";
      exit(1);
  }
  cin >> no;
  if(cin.fail())
  {
      cout << "Fail on reading\n";
      exit(2);
  }
  while(!cin.eof())
  {
      cout << no << endl;
```

Continued on next page

LISTING-13.10
(continued)

Complete Checking on Input

```
            cin.ignore(31);
            if(!cin.good())
            {
                cout << "Fail on subsequent skipping\n";
                exit(3);
            }
            cin >> no;
            if(cin.fail())
            {
                cout << "Fail on subsequent reading\n";
                exit(4);
            }
        }
}
```

We still might run into a few problems with the program above. For instance, if we were to redirect the output, any error messages would be redirected as well!

To stop the error messages being redirected we need to use another `ostream` object created automatically by every program - `cerr`. So if we rewrite our error message with statements such as

```
    if(!cin.good())
    {
        cerr << "Fail on subsequent skipping\n";
        exit(3);
    }
```

any redirection of `cout` will have no effect on the display of error messages.

If we're going to add checks on input, we should be including the same sort of safeguards for any output. Hence, we may modify our write statements to:

```
    if(cout.fail())
    {
        cerr << "Fail on writing\n";
        exit(5);
    }
```

Since such testing may be extensive, a shorter version of the `fail()` test can be used:

`if(!cin)`	is equivalent to	`if(cin.fail())`
`if(!cout)`	is equivalent to	`if(cout.fail())`

It is possible to determine the state of all the I/O state flags using the `rdstate()` operation:

```
    int iostate = cin.rdstate();
```

An I/O stream's error flag remains set until it's cleared using the `clear()` function:

```
    if(!cout)
    {
        cerr << "An error has occurred\n";
        cout.clear();
    }
```

The *ofstream* and *ifstream* Classes

Most data needs to be recorded on a semi-permanent or permanent basis. To do this we need to be able to store this data on disk in much the same fashion as we record the programs themselves.

There are many ways of organising data on disk. One is to treat the disk as we would the screen and simply write the information one character after the other into the file. This is often referred to as **unformatted data**. We begin by looking at this file structure.

Opening an Output File

The easiest way to produce a disk file for writing is to define an *ofstream* object :

NOTE: To use objects from these classes you must add

```
#include<fstream.h>
```

to your program.

```
ofstream myfile;
```

This needs to be opened and the associated DOS filename specified:

```
myfile.open("A:\\text.dat");
```

Now we can write to the file in exactly the same way as we write to the screen. Hence, to output the string *"test data\n"* to *myfile* we simply write:

```
myfile << "test data\n";
```

Once all the data has been output, the file should be closed:

```
myfile.close();
```

When outputting data using this method, the file is treated in much the same way as the screen. No additional characters are added to the file to mark the end of each data item; it is therefore important that we insert newline or space characters between each value written to the file so that it may be easily read later.

The following program (LISTING-13.11) outputs a student's details to a DOS file named *"student.dat"* on drive A. Note that any type of value may be output to the file. All data is held in the file in character format, hence these are often referred to as **text files**.

LISTING-13.11

Writing to a Text File

```
#include<fstream.h>

void main()
{
  ofstream myfile;

  //*** Open output file ***
  myfile.open("A:\\student.dat");
  //*** Write data to file ***
  myfile << "Jane Smith\nHNDCompStudies\nF\n";
  myfile << "12 13 10 11 11 9 \n";
  //*** Close file ***
  myfile.close();
}
```

It is possible to use an alternative constructor when declaring an *ofstream* object which performs the `open()` function automatically:

```
ofstream myfile("A:\\student.dat");
```

When a file is opened for writing, the actual disk file is automatically created if it does not already exist. Where it does exist, the contents of the file is overwritten by the new data. However, there are occasions where these actions may be unwanted. For example, it may be that we don't want the file to be created if it doesn't exist, or maybe we want to add data to the existing information in a file.

To control how a file is opened, a second parameter may be added to the *ostream* constructor. This second parameter specifies one or more status flags inherited from the `ios` class. For example, to add new data at the end of existing data, rather than overwriting the old information, we define the file object using the statement:

```
ofstream myfile("A:\\student.dat",ios::app);
```

The following program (LISTING-13.12) adds another record to our file *student.dat*.

LISTING-13.12

Appending a Record to an Existing File

```
#include<fstream.h>

void main()
{
  //*** Open file for appending ***
  ofstream myfile("A:\\student.dat",ios::app);

  //*** Add new record at the end of the file ***
  myfile << "Liz Heron\nHD Applic Maths\nF\n";
  myfile << "20 19 17 20 15 18\n";
  //*** Close file ***
  myfile.close();

}
```

The other options available when opening a file (all of which are inherited from the `ios` class) for output are given in TABLE-13.6.

TABLE-13.6

File Open Options

Open Mode	Purpose
`app`	Adds new data at the end of current data.
`out`	Opens a file for output. This is the default.
`nocreate`	Opens a file for output. If the file does not already exist no attempt is made to create one and the operation fails.
`noreplace`	Attempts to create a new file for output. However, if the file already exists the operation fails.
`binary`	Opens a file for binary read and write operations.

Inherited methods can be used to check that the file operation has been successful. For example, we might check that a file has been opened successfully by using the inherited `fail()` method:

```
ofstream myfile("A:\\student.dat");

if(myfile.fail())
{
    cout << "Could not create file\n";
    exit(1);
}
```

Opening a File for Input

To read from an existing disk file we need to define an object from the `ifstream` class and link it to a DOS file:

```
ifstream  readfile;
readfile.open("A:\\student.dat");
```

This may be combined into the single statement:

```
ifstream readfile("A:\\student.dat");
```

Normally, we start at the beginning of the file and keep reading data until we reach the end of the data. When the end of the file is reached the method `eof()` will return a **true** (non-zero) value.

In a similar way, the following program, LISTING-13.13, reads and displays the file's contents.

LISTING-13.13

Reading an Unformatted File

`input.fail()`

can be shortened to

`!input`

```
#include<fstream.h>
#include<stdlib.h>
#include<conio.h>

void main()
{
  char line[81];
  int count = 0;
  //*** Open the file ***
  ifstream input("A:\\student.dat");
  //*** Display error message if open fails ***
  if(input.fail())
  {
      cerr << "Error opening the file:\n";
      exit(1);
  }
  //*** WHILE not EOF DO ***
  while (!input.eof())
  {
      //*** Read a line of text from the file ***
      input.getline(line, 80);
      //*** Display the line read ***
      cout << line << '\n';
      getch();
  }
  //*** Close the file ***
  input.close();
}
```

PROGRAMMING EXERCISE 13.6

Write a program to make a copy of a text file by reading the original one line at time and writing it to the second file.

Include error checks for the success of each I/O operation.

Binary Files

By default, file stream operations are performed in text mode but it is also possible to read and write binary files.

Binary files differ from text files in several important aspects. These differences are shown in TABLE-13.7.

TABLE-13.7

The Differences between Text and Binary Files

Text Files	Binary Files
Numeric values are written in text format.	Numeric values are written using the same format used for variables.
The NEWLINE character is written as RETURN NEWLINE ($0D_{16}0A_{16}$).	NEWLINE is written as a single character ($0A_{16}$).
The RETURN/NEWLINE combination is read as a single NEWLINE character.	RETURN/NEWLINE combination is read as two separate bytes.
$1A_{16}$ if read, is taken as an end-of-file indicator.	$1A_{16}$ has no special significance.

For a program to read .EXE, .COM and bit-map picture files it is necessary to define such files as binary files so that their contents will be correctly interpreted.

To open an input file in binary mode we write statements such as:

```
ifstream input("A:mypic.BMP", ios::binary);
```

Binary file I/O uses the inherited `read()` and `write()` methods. The format for these commands are:

```
inputfileobject.read(char* s,int n);
outputfileobject.write(char* s,int n);
```

where

`...fileobject`	is an *istream/ostream* class object.
`s`	is the address of the variable whose value is to be written to/read from the file.
`n`	is the number of bytes to be read from/written to the file.

The program in LISTING-13.14 writes the contents of *StudentDetails* records to a binary file.

LISTING-13.14

Writing to a Binary File

```
#include<iostream.h>
#include<fstream.h>
#include<conio.h>

struct StudentDetails
{
   int id;
   char name[30];
   char sex;
   int score[6];
};
```

Continued on next page

LISTING-13.14
(continued)

Writing to a Binary File

```
void main()
{
  StudentDetails s;      //Contains student's details
  ofstream output("C:\\STUDENT.DAT",ios::binary);
                                    //Holds students' records

  //*** REPEAT ***
  do
  {
      //*** Read student's id ***
      cout << "Enter student's id  : ";
      cin >> s.id;
      //*** IF zero THEN exit loop ***
      if(s.id == 0)
          break;
      //*** Remove RETURN char from cin buffer ***
      cin.get();
      //*** Read rest of student's details ***
      cout << "Enter student's name: ";
      cin.get(s.name,29);
      cout << "Enter student's sex : ";
      cin >> s.sex;
      for(int c = 0;c < 6;c++)
      {
          cout << "Enter score " << (c+1) << ' ';
          cin >> s.score[c];
      }
      //*** Write record to file ***
      output.write((char*)&s,sizeof(s));
  }
  //*** UNTIL forever ***
  while(1);
  //*** Close file ***
  output.close();
  cout << "PROGRAM TERMINATED\n";
}
```

The program uses the inherited `write()` function which takes as parameters the address and size of the data being written to the file:

```
output.write((char*) &s, sizeof (s));
```

Since `write()` expects a `char*` parameter, we need to cast the address of *s* to that type. We also need to specify the number of bytes to be written to the file and this is done using the `sizeof()` function.

The program in LISTING-13.15 reads back the above file and displays its contents.

LISTING-13.15

Reading from a Binary File

```
#include<iostream.h>
#include<fstream.h>
#include<conio.h>

struct StudentDetails
{
  int id;
  char name[30];
  char sex;
  int score[6];
};
```

Continued on next page

LISTING-13.15 (continued)

Reading from a Binary File

```
void main()
{
  StudentDetails s;                    //Contains student's details
  ifstream input("C:\\STUDENT.DAT",ios::binary);
                                       //Holds students' records

  //*** Read first record ***
  input.read((char*)&s,sizeof(s));
  //*** WHILE not EOF DO ***
  while(!input.eof())
  {
      //*** Display record ***
      cout << s.id << ' ' << s.name << ' '<< s.sex << ' ';
      for(int c = 0;c < 6;c++)
          cout << s.score[c] << ' ';
      //*** Wait for key press ***
      cin.get();
      //*** Read next record ***
      input.read((char*)&s,sizeof(s));
  }
  //*** Close file ***
  input.close();
  cout << "PROGRAM TERMINATED\n";
}
```

The *fstream* Class

Often we'll want to both read and write to a single file. For this we need to define an object from the `fstream` class. Such files can be open in *read*, *write* or *read/write* mode. To choose which we require, we set the appropriate flag(s) in the constructor call. Hence, to open *studentbase* in *read/write* mode we would use the statement:

```
fstream studentbase("C:\\STUDENT.DAT", ios::in | ios::out);
```

Because we can both read and write to such a file, the system maintains two file indicators. The first holds the position in the file from which the next read operation will begin (this is called the *get* pointer); the other holds the start position for any write operation (the *put* pointer). The positions are given in the number of bytes from the start of the file.

When a file is first opened, both the *get* and *put* pointers reference the start position in the file; that is, they will contain the value zero.

To move the position of the *get* pointer we use the `seekg()` member function. This comes in two versions: the first takes a single parameter specifying which byte in the file the *get* pointer is to be moved to. Hence, the statement

```
stfile.seekg(0);
```

moves the *get* pointer to the beginning of the file. If we wanted to move to the position of the first character in the student's name of the first record in the file, we'd write

```
stfile.seekg(2);
```

The *id* field of the first student's record will occupy bytes 0 and 1 of *stfile*. Hence, the first character of the *name* field is in byte 2.

A second format for the function allows us a relative move. Hence, we may move a specified number of bytes from the beginning, end, or current position in the file. This form of `seekg()` requires two parameters: the first is the offset in bytes and the second the position from which this offset is to be measured. To move 2 bytes in from the start of the file we write:

```
stfile.seekg(2,ios::beg);
```

As you can see, moving relative to the start of the file gives us the same result as the earlier version of the function. However, if we wanted to move to the second last byte in the file the instruction would be:

```
stfile.seekg(-1,ios::end);
```

The last option is to move from the current position. Hence,

```
stfile.seekg(10,ios::cur);
```

moves the *get* pointer 10 bytes on from its current position.

The starting point for relative movements through a file are shown in TABLE-13.8.

TABLE-13.8

Relative Movement Start Positions

Enumerated Value	File Position
ios::beg	From the beginning of the file.
ios::cur	From the current file pointer position.
ios::end	From the end of the file.

The program in LISTING-13.16 demonstrates how we may read from a specific point in a file.

LISTING-13.16

Moving the *get* Pointer

```
#include<fstream.h>

void main()
{
  char name[30];
  fstream stfile("C:\\STUDENT.DAT",ios::in|ios::binary);
  //*** Position get pointer at start of first student's name ***
  stfile.seekg(2);
  //*** Read name from file ***
  stfile.getline(name,29);
  //*** Display name read ***
  cout << name << endl;
  //*** Close file ***
  stfile.close();
}
```

We can move the *put* pointer in the same manner using the `seekp()` function. Again, this comes in two forms allowing us to specify an absolute or relative position in the file.

```
seekp(10);
```

moves to the 11th byte in the file, while the statement

```
seekp(6,ios::cur);
```

moves 6 bytes on from the current position of *get*.

We can use a similar approach to modify the contents of the file. LISTING-13.17 changes the first student's name to *David Deans*.

LISTING-13.17

Modifying Specific Parts of a File

```
#include<fstream.h>

void main()
{
   char name[30] = "David Deans";
   fstream stfile("C:\\STUDENT.DAT",ios::out|ios::in|ios::binary);

   //*** Move to start of name ***
   stfile.seekp(2);
   //*** Write new name ***
   stfile.write(name,sizeof(name));
   //*** Close file ***
   stfile.close();
}
```

Creating Random Access Files

Using the *get* and *put* pointers allows us to create random access files in which we can move to any record position within a file. For example, the program in LISTING-13.18 writes a set of *StudentDetails* records out to a file or allows us to read back any specific record by giving its record position in the file.

LISTING-13.18

Creating Random Access Files

```
#include<fstream.h>
#include<conio.h>
struct StudentDetails
{
   int id;
   char name[30];
   char sex;
   int score[6];
};
void ReadRecs(fstream&);
void WriteRecs(fstream&);
void main()
{
   int choice;
   fstream stfile("C:\\STUDENT.DAT",ios::in|ios::out|ios::binary);
   clrscr();
   //*** Display menu ***
   cout << "1 Write recs\n2 Read recs\n3 EXIT\n";
   do
   {
       //*** Get choice ***
       cin >> choice;
       //*** Execute option ***
       switch(choice)
       {
           case 1:  //Write records
               stfile.seekp(0,ios::beg);
               WriteRecs(stfile);
               break;
           case 2:  //Read records
               ReadRecs(stfile);
               break;
           case 3:  //Terminate program
               cout << "PROGRAM TERMINATED\n";
       }
   }
   while(choice != 3);
   //*** Close file ***
   stfile.close();
}
```

Continued on next page

LISTING-13.18
(continued)

Creating Random Access Files

```
//*** Read details and write to disk ***
void WriteRecs(fstream& stfile)
{
  StudentDetails s;
  clrscr();
  do
  {
      cout << "Enter id :";
      cin >> s.id;
      if(s.id == 0)
          break;
      cin.get();
      cout << "Enter name : ";
      cin.getline(s.name,29);
      cout << "Enter sex  : ";
      cin >> s.sex;
      for(int c = 0; c < 6;c++)
      {
          cout << "Enter score " << (c+1) << " : ";
          cin >> s.score[c];
      }
      stfile.write((char*)&s,sizeof(s));
  }
  while(1);
}


//*** Read and display specified record ***
void ReadRecs(fstream& stfile)
{
  StudentDetails s;
  clrscr();

  do
  {
      cout << "Enter rec position :";
      int post;
      cin >> post;
      if(post == 0)
          break;
      stfile.seekg((post-1)*sizeof(s));
      stfile.read((char*)&s,sizeof(s));
      cout << s.id << s.name << s.sex;
      for(int c = 0; c < 6; c++)
          cout << s.score[c] << ' ';
      cout << endl;
  }
  while(1);
}
```

Since we are able to move the *get* and *put* indicators, we may well need to find out where these pointers are at any point in our program. This can be discovered using the inherited `tellg()` and `tellp()` methods which have the format:

```
file_name.tellg();
file_name.tellp();
```

Performing Printer Output

We've already seen that we can send output to the printer using redirection, but we may also create a printer file. Sending data to this file will result in that information being printed.

This is achieved by opening an output file using the device name **prn** as in the statement:

```
ofstream printer ( "prn");
```

For example, the following program, LISTING-13.19, prints the file *C:\student.dat.*

LISTING-13.19

Outputting to the Printer

```
#include<iostream.h>
#include<fstream.h>
#include<conio.h>
#include<stdlib.h>

struct StudentDetails
{
  int id;
  char name[30];
  char sex;
  int score[6];
};

void main()
{
  StudentDetails s;                //Contains student's details
  ifstream input("C:\\STUDENT.DAT",ios::binary);
                                   //Holds students' records
  ofstream print("prn");
  if(!print)
  {
      cerr << "Could not open printer\n";
      getch();
      exit(1);
  }

  //*** Read first record ***
  input.read((char*)&s,sizeof(s));
  //*** WHILE not EOF DO ***
  while(!input.eof())
  {
      //*** Print record ***
      print << s.id << ' ' << s.name << ' ' << s.sex << ' ';
      for(int c = 0;c < 6;c++)
          print << s.score[c] << ' ';
      print << endl;
      //*** Read next record ***

      input.read((char*)&s,sizeof(s));
  }
  //*** Close files ***
  input.close();
  print.close();
  cout << "PROGRAM TERMINATED\n";
}
```

Summary

The summary lists the main attributes of each class.

ios

This is the abstract base class for all other I/O classes.

Protected Data Members

x_fill	Padding character
x_flags	Format bit flags
x_precision	Floating point output precision
**x_tie*	Pointer to tied `ostream`
x_width	Width field on output

Public Data Members

enum *seek_dir*	Seek direction.
beg=0	
cur=1	
end=2	
enum *open_mode*	File open mode.
app	Append data at end of file.
ate	Move to end of file.
in	Open for input (default for `ifstreams`).
out	Open for output (default for `ofstreams`).
binary	Open file in binary mode.
trunc	Overwrite file if it exists. This is the default if *out* is specified and neither *ate* nor *app* is specified).
nocreate	Will not create an output file. Hence, if the file does not exist, open fails.
noreplace	Will not overwrite a file. If the file exists, open for output will fail unless *ate* or *app* is set.
adjustfield	Use this with `setf()` to control padding to the left, right, or for internal fill.
basefield	Use this with `setf()` to set the notation to a decimal, octal, or hexadecimal base.
floatfield	Use this with `setf()` to set the floating-point notation to scientific or fixed.

Public Member Functions

`int bad()`	Returns non-zero if error occurred by checking *ios::badbit* and *ios::hardfail* in *ios::state*.
`void clear(int=0)`	Sets the stream state to the given value by setting *ios::state* to the given value. The constants of the *io_state* enumeration in class *ios* are normally used as the parameter. The values of *io_state* can be ORed together to set more than one bit in state.
`int eof()`	Returns non-zero when the end of file is encountered by checking the *ios::eofbit* in *ios::state*.
`int fail()`	Returns non-zero if an I/I/O operation causes the *ios::failbit*, *ios::badbit*, or *ios::hardfail* bits in *ios::state* to be set.
`char fill()`	Returns the current fill character.
`char fill(char)`	Resets the fill character and returns the previous one.
`long flags()`	Returns the current format flags. The format flags can be compared to the values in the formatting flags enumeration of class *ios*. *flags(0)* resets the formatting flags to the default value.
`long flags(long)`	Sets the format flags to be identical to the given long. The flags of the long are set using the values in the formatting flags enumeration in class *ios*. It returns the previous flags. *flags(0)* resets to the default format.
`int good()`	Returns non-zero if the *ios::failbit*, *ios::badbit*, and *ios::hardfail* bits in *ios::state* are all set to zero.
`int precision(int)`	Sets the floating-point precision, and returns the previous setting. This must be reset for each data item being output.
`int precision()`	Returns the current floating-point precision.
`int rdstate()`	Returns the stream state by returning the value of the data member state of class *ios*.

`long setf(long setbits, long fld)`
fld should have the value *adjustfield, basefield* or *floatfield*. Clears the *x_flags* bits corresponding to those in *fld* and then resets those marked in *setbits*. *setbits* can be specified by using the constants in the format flags. Enumeration of class *ios*.

`long setf(long f)` Sets the flags in *x_flags* corresponding to the set bits in *f*.
f can be specified by using the constants in the formatting flags enumeration of class *ios*.
Returns the previous settings.

`ostream* tie()` Returns the tied stream, or zero if no stream is tied.

`ostream* tie(ostream* is)`
Ties *is* to calling stream and returns the previously tied stream, if any.
By default, *cin, cerr* and *clog* are tied to *cout*.

`long unsetf(long f)` Clears the bits corresponding to those marked in *f*.
Returns the previous settings.

`int width()` Returns the current width setting.

`int width(int)` Sets the width, and returns the previous width.
Must be respecified for each data item.

istream

Public Member Functions

`>>` Overloaded for inputting all fundamental types.

`int gcount()` Returns the number of characters last extracted using *get(), getline(),* or *read()*.

`istream& get(char*)` Extracts the next character or EOF.

`istream& get(char* str, int len, char del= '\n')`
Extracts characters into *str* until the *del* or end-of-file is encountered, or until (*len* - 1) bytes are read.
A terminating null is placed in *str*. The *del* character is not extracted from the input stream.
Fails if no characters were extracted.

`stream& getline(char* str, int, char del='\n')`
Extracts up to the *del* character, puts the characters in str and removes the *del* from the input stream.

`istream& ignore(int n = 1, int del = EOF)`
Up to *n* characters in the input stream are skipped.
Stops sooner if *del* is encountered. In this case, *del* is extracted from the stream.

`int peek()` Returns the next character without extraction.

`istream& putback(char ch)`
Pushes *ch* onto the stream.

`istream& read(char* str, int)`
Extracts a given number of characters into str.

`istream& seekg(streampos pos)`
Moves to an absolute position.

`istream& seekg(streamoff off, seek_dir dir)`
Moves the *get* indicator *off* number of bytes relative to *dir*. *dir* is given as *beg, cur,* or *end.*

`long tellg()` Returns the value of the *get* indicator.

ostream

Member Functions

`<<` Overloaded for outputting all fundamental types.

`ostream& flush()` This member function flushes the stream.

`ostream& put(char ch)`
The *put()* member function inserts the character *ch*.

`ostream& seekp(streampos)`
Moves to an absolute position (as returned from *tellp()*).

`ostream& seekp(streamoff, seek_dir)`
Moves to a position relative to the current position, following the definition: `enum seek_dir` *beg, cur, end.*

`streampos tellp()` The *tellp()* member function returns the current stream position.

`ostream& write(const char*, int n)`
The write member function inserts *n* characters (nulls included).

ifstream

Member Functions

`void open(const char *name, int mode,int prot=filebuf::openprot)`
Opens a file for the specific class object.
The *mode* parameter can be set using the *open_mode* enumeration defined in class *ios.*

ofstream

Member Functions

`void open(const char *name, int mode,int prot=filebuf::openprot)`
Opens a file for the specific class object.
The *mode* parameter can be set using the *open_mode* enumeration defined in class *ios.*

fstream

Input and output are initiated using the functions of the base classes *istream* and *ostream*. For example, *fstream* can use the function *istream::getline()* to extract characters from the file.

Member Functions

`void open(const char *name, int mode,int prot=filebuf::openprot)`
Opens a file for the specific class object.
The *mode* parameter can be set using the *open_mode* enumeration defined in class *ios.*

Solutions

PROGRAMMING EXERCISE 13.1

```
#include<iostream.h>

void Binary(int);
void main()
{
    Binary(cout.flags());
}

void Binary(int no)
{
    for(int c=1;c<=sizeof(int)*8;c++)
    {
        if(no<0)
            cout<<1;
        else
            cout<<0;
        no<<=1;
    }
}
```

PROGRAMMING EXERCISE 13.2

```
#include<iostream.h>

void main()
{
    cout<<"LEFT JUSTIFIED FIELD\n";
    cout.setf(ios::left,ios::adjustfield);
    cout.width(10);
    cout<<-23<<'['<<endl;
    cout<<"INTERNAL FIELD\n";
    cout.setf(ios::internal,ios::adjustfield);
    cout.width(10);
    cout<<-23<<'['<<endl;
    cout.setf(ios::showbase|ios::uppercase);
    cout<<"OCTAL VALUE\n";
    cout.setf(ios::oct,ios::basefield);
    cout<<23<<endl;
    cout<<"HEXADECIMAL VALUE\n";
    cout.setf(ios::hex,ios::basefield);
    cout<<23<<endl;
    cout<<"SCIENTIFIC NOTATION\n";
    cout.setf(ios::scientific,ios::floatfield);
    cout<<23.9781<<endl;
}
```

PROGRAMMING EXERCISE 13.3

No solution required

PROGRAMMING EXERCISE 13.4

```
#include<iostream.h>

void main()
{
    int no;

    //*** Switch off flush buffer flag ***
    cout.unsetf(ios::unitbuf);
    //*** Untie cout/cin ***
    cin.tie(0);
    //*** Issue prompt ***
    cout<<"Please enter value : ";
    //*** Read input ***
    cin>>no;
    //*** Display results ***
    cout<<"The value entered was "<<no<<endl;
}
```

PROGRAMMING EXERCISE 13.5

Assuming the file created is called MYDATA.DAT then the statement required for redirection is

```
REDIRECT<MYDATA.DAT>PRN
```

PROGRAMMING EXERCISE 13.6

```
#include<fstream.h>
#include<stdlib.h>
#include<conio.h>

void main()
{
    char source[21];
    char destination[21];
    //*** Get file names ***
    clrscr();
    cout<<"Enter name of source file : ";
    cin.getline(source,20);
    cout<<"Enter name of destination file : ";
    cin.getline(destination,20);
    //*** Open files ***
    ifstream in(source);
    if(!in)
    {
        cerr<<"File not found\nPress any key\n";
        getch();
        exit(1);
    }
    ofstream out(destination);
    if(!out)
    {
        cerr<<"Destination file could not be"
            "created\nPress any key\n";
        getch();
        exit(2);
    }
    //*** Read a line of text from source ***
    char line[301];
    int c=1;
    in.getline(line,300);
    if(!in&&!in.eof())
    {
        cerr<<"Fail on first file read\n"
            "Press any key\n";
        getch();
        exit(3);
    }
    //*** WHILE not EOF DO ***
    while(!in.eof())
    {
        //*** Write to output file ***
        out<<line<<'\n';
        if(!out)
        {
            cerr<<"Fail on file write\n"
                "Press any key\n";
            getch();
            exit(4);
        }
        //*** Read a line of text from source ***
        c++;
        in.getline(line,300);
        if(!in&&!in.eof())
        {
            cerr<<"Fail on file read "<<c
                <<"\nPress any key\n";
            getch();
            exit(3);
        }
    }
    //*** Display completed message ***
    cout<<"Copy complete\n";
    //*** Close files ***
    in.close();
    out.close();
}
```

CHAPTER 14
Handling Errors

This chapter covers the following topics:

assert()

catch

Error Classes

Handling Resources

Replacing terminate()

Replacing unexpected()

throw

Traditional Error Handling Methods

try

Unhandled Exceptions

Universal Handlers

Using Error Flags

TRADITIONAL ERROR HANDLING

Introduction

Every line of code we write introduces the possibility of error. Some errors are due to incorrect syntax, others to faulty or incomplete logic, yet others may be caused by accepting invalid input. While it may not be possible to eliminate all errors from a program, if we are to be taken seriously as software engineers, this is a task we must attempt.

Some errors, such as syntax errors are easily detected by the compiler, while the more trivial logic errors are often highlighted using black and white box testing methods. However, some error situations may arise infrequently and be more difficult to detect. For example, we might run into insufficient storage space problems when attempting to store a large number of records in a dynamically created linked list or on a disk file. Such a problem is less likely to be detected during program testing.

By necessity, the amount of error detection included in the examples in this text has been limited. If this had not been the case, the methods and techniques being demonstrated would have been obscured under a blanket of error detection code. However, we have already covered the main traditional methods of error detection:

- **User input validation.** By replacing the use of `cin>>` with programmer-defined routines such as *GetData()* we have reduced the likelihood of accepting invalid data values from the user.

- **Function pre-conditions.** Placing a pre-condition check at the start of every applicable function has ensured that the parameters supplied to the function are within an acceptable range.

- **Function result indicators.** By returning a result indicator from a function, we have allowed the function user to check on the success or failure of calls to a routine.

This last approach is used by almost all traditional C functions. Typically, zero was returned to indicate the success of a function's operation while some non-zero value gave coded details of what had gone wrong. For example, the syntax for `fseek()` is

```
int fseek(FILE *stream, long offs, int start);
```

in which the returned `int` is set to zero if the seek operation is successful, and non-zero if an error occurs.

Other Options

`assert()`

The `assert()` function returns 1 if its argument evaluates to **true**, otherwise it returns zero. When the function returns a zero, the program will terminate detailing the assertion statement which has failed. The program in LISTING-14.1 shows how `assert()` may be used to check for an attempt to divide by zero.

LISTING-14.1

Using `assert()`

```
#include<iostream.h>
#include<assert.h>
void main()
{
   float no1,no2,ans;

   //*** Read in two values ***
   cout << "Enter two numbers ";
   cin >> no1 >> no2;
   //*** Assert that the second value is not zero ***
   assert(no2! = 0);
   //*** Perform division ***
   ans = no1/no2;
   //*** Display result ***
   cout << no1 << '/' << no2 << '=' << ans << endl;
   getch();
}
```

Note, that we must use `#include<assert.h>` in order to make use of the `assert()` routine.

Now, when we execute the program in LISTING-14.1 with input data such as 4 and 0, making the value for *no2* zero, the program terminates since the `assert()` function returns a zero value. This produces the following screen message:

```
Assertion failed: no2!=0, file ..\..\CPPCODE\ASSERT01.CPP, line 9
Abnormal program termination
```

As you can see, the condition which failed, the file name, and the line at which termination occurred is given in the display.

It's useful to add such `assert()` calls in appropriate parts of your code to check

a) Any necessary condition is met before executing the next part of the program.

b) Any statements just executed have produced an acceptable result.

TASK 14.1

Add `assert()` calls to the following instructions:

1.
```
int *ptr;
ptr = new int[500];
```

2.
```
cin>>x>>y;
gotoxy(x,y);    //Assume 80 by 25 screen size
```

The `assert()` statement is only of limited use in a final program, since the user is unlikely to react well to programs which handle errors in such a brutal way. However, often `assert()` calls are used during the debugging phase of implementation and removed later once testing is complete.

Rather than use the editor to physically remove these `assert()` calls, we may insert the line

```
#define NDEBUG
```

at the start of our program. This causes the compiler to ignore all `assert()` calls when compiling the source code.

> **PROGRAMMING EXERCISE 14.1**
>
> Add the `#define NDEBUG` to the program in LISTING-14.1 and find how this effects execution of the program.

Maintaining an Error Flag

As already stated, a function often returns an `int` (or other type) to indicate how successful it has been. Sometimes, however, it is not possible to do this. For example, when overloading C++ operators such as + or ==, it's not going to be possible to return an error indicator. An alternative approach is to create an error status attribute within your `struct` or `class` declaration:

```
class myclass
{
    private:
        int errorstatus;    //Used as an error indicator
```

This can then be set and interrogated by the various class methods to indicate their success or failure.

This is exactly the approach used in the `iostream` class which maintains a *status* field whose bits can be interrogated with methods such as `bad()`, `good()`, `eof()`, etc.

The main disadvantage of this approach is that it depends on the user interrogating the error status attribute to determine a previous operation's success. As we saw in the previous chapter, it's tempting to miss out such checks. On the other hand, if error checking is comprehensive, the resulting code can be difficult to read, obscuring the underlying logic of what your program is attempting to do.

Summary

- **Error checking** attempts to catch errors which may occur in an executing program and handle them in an organised manner.
- **Input validation**. Controlling the input of data can significantly reduce the potential for errors in a program.
- **Adding a pre-condition** check at the start of a function ensures that the parameters are within a specified range of values.
- **Returning an error indicator** from a function allows the calling code to check the success of the function.
- Where it is not possible to return a value from a function, **error status fields** may be maintained when struct and class variables are involved.
- **The `assert()` function** can be used to check for error causing situations during the debugging stage.
- The `assert()` function calls are disabled using **`#define NDEBUG`** at the start of a program.

EXCEPTION HANDLING

Introduction

The latest version of C++ added a new way of handling certain types of error conditions. Generally, it is used by functions to allow them to terminate early and return an indication of the error which has occurred; this error is then handled by a section of of code in the routine which called the offending function.

Typical errors which might be detected in this way are such conditions as running out of memory, an out-of-bounds array subscript error, or failing the pre-condition of a function.

Using this approach, when a function detects an error it is unable to handle it **throws** (or **raises**) an **exception**. This should then be received and dealt with by an **exception handler**. If no appropriate exception handler exists the program terminates.

This approach is so different to anything that's gone before that it's probably easiest to start with an example (see LISTING-14.2).

LISTING-14.2

Introducing Exceptions

```
#include<iostream.h>
#include<math.h>

void main()
{
   double no;

   //*** Read a number ***
   cout << "Enter number : ";
   cin >> no;
   //*** Try to execute some code ***
   try
   {
       //*** IF there's a problem THEN throw an exception ***
       if(no < 0)
           throw -1;
       //*** Otherwise display results ***
       cout << "Square root is " << sqrt(no) << endl;
   }
   //*** Any exception throwing an int value comes here ***
   catch(int)
   {
       cerr << "Exception thrown" << endl;
   }
   //*** Display terminating message ***
   cout << "PROGRAM TERMINATED\n";
}
```

An Explanation of the Code

The program reads in a number with the intention of calculating its square root. The section of the code in which we suspect an error could occur is enclosed in a `try` block.

Only within a `try` block will thrown exceptions be recognised for what they are and handled correctly.

If the number entered is invalid (i.e. negative), an exception is thrown. If this happens the remainder of the `try` block is skipped and control moves to the first `catch` block specifying the same type as that of the thrown exception (in this case an `int` value).

```
try
{
    .
}
```

This block of code contains the instruction which may throw an exception.

```
if(no < 0)
    throw -1;
```

If the condition *no<0* is true, then an exception is thrown. This means that the remainder of the `try` block will be bypassed and control jumps the succeeding `catch` block whose argument type matches that of the value throw.

```
cout<<"Square root is " << sqrt(no) << endl;
```

This line will be executed if no exception is thrown by the previous `if` statement.

```
.
catch(int)
{
    .
}
```

This block of code will be executed if:

a) an exception is thrown by the previous try block

and b) the exception value is of the same type as this block's argument

Where no exception has been thrown, this block will be bypassed.

```
cout << "PROGRAM TERMINATED\n";
```

Since this line comes after the `catch` block, it will be executed unconditionally whether or not an exception is thrown.

PROGRAMMING EXERCISE 14.2

Write a similar program to the one in LISTING-14.2 which reads in two integer values (*no1* and *no2*) and throws an exception if the second of two numbers input is a zero. Where no exception is thrown, the program should calculate and display the result of *no1/no2*.

Throwing an Exception from a Function

Although an exception can be thrown directly by code in the `try` block, this is not how the structure was designed to be used. The most likely practice is to throw an exception from within a function.

When an exception is thrown from within a function, several things happen:

1) The remainder of the function is bypassed.
2) All variables created within the function are destroyed. Where objects are involved, their destructors will be executed.
3) Control will return to the code responsible for calling the function.

The program in LISTING-14.3 shows the square root error being thrown from within a function.

LISTING-14.3

Throwing Exceptions from a Function

```
#include<iostream.h>
#include<math.h>

double CalcSqrt(double);


void main()
{
  double no;

  cout << "Enter number : ";
  cin >> no;
  try
  {
       float result = CalcSqrt(no);
       cout << "Square root is " << result << endl;
  }
  catch(int)
  {
       cerr << "Exception thrown"<<endl;
  }
  cout << "PROGRAM TERMINATED\n";
}


//*** Square root function ***
double CalcSqrt(double v)
{
  //*** Throw an exception if the parameter's invalid ***
  if(v < 0)
       throw -1;
  return sqrt(v);
}
```

PROGRAMMING EXERCISE 14.3

1. Modify your last program (from PROGRAMMING EXERCISE 14.2) so that the division is performed within a routine. The routine should throw an exception if the divisor is zero.

2. Single step your way through your program, entering 9 and 0 as the data values.

Exceptions in Lower Functions

We've seen that if a function called within a `try` block throws an exception that it is caught and dealt with by an appropriate `catch` block.

This is also the case where the function throwing the exception is not called directly by the `try` block. Hence, if the `try` block calls *DisplaySquareRoot()*, which itself calls *CalcSqrt()*, then any exception thrown by *CalcSqrt()* will be caught by the `try` block.

To do this correctly, not only does *CalcSqrt()* terminate as soon as the exception is thrown, but the routine which called it, must also be terminated without executing any more of its statements.

LISTING-14.4 shows the code involved.

LISTING-14.4

Exceptions from a Lower Level

```
#include<iostream.h>
#include<math.h>

double CalcSqrt(double);
void DisplaySquareRoot(double);


void main()
{
   double no;

   cout << "Enter number : ";
   cin >> no;
   try
  {
   //*** The called routine does not throw an exception      ***
   //*** but one called by this routine does                 ***
   //*** When thrown this try block will still be terminated ***
   DisplaySquareRoot(no);

   }
   //*** And the catch block will be executed ***
   catch(int)
   {
        cerr << "Exception thrown" << endl;
   }
   cout<<"PROGRAM TERMINATED\n";
}



//*** This routine does not throw an exception ***
void DisplaySquareRoot(double v)
{
   double result;
   result = CalcSqrt(v);
   cout << "Square root is " << result << endl;
}



//*** But this one does ***
double CalcSqrt(double v)
{
   if(v < 0)
        throw -1;
   return sqrt(v);
}
```

As each of the earlier routines are exited, they too have any local variables deallocated. Since, the local variables created in a function are held on to a stack, the deallocation of these variables is termed **unwinding the stack** (see FIG-14.1).

FIG-14.1

Unwinding the Stack

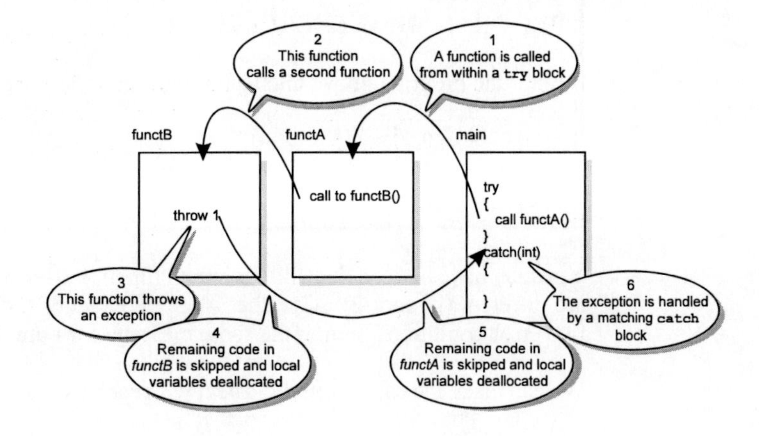

Handling Several Potential Exceptions

What if the `try` block contains calls to many functions, several of which are capable of throwing an exception?

If all the exceptions which might be thrown are of the same type (i.e. `int`) then a single `catch` block will intercept them all. Hence, in LISTING-14.5, where both *CalcSqrt()* and *CalcDiv()* throw an `int` value, only one `catch` block is used.

LISTING-14.5

Catching Several Exceptions

```
#include<iostream.h>
#include<math.h>

double CalcSqrt(double);
double CalcDiv(double,double);

void main()
{
   double no1,no2;
   cout << "Enter two numbers : ";
   cin >> no1 >> no2;
   try
   {
       //*** If either routine called here throws an exception ***
       cout << "Square roots are " << CalcSqrt(no1) << ' '
           << CalcSqrt(no2) << endl;
       cout << no1 << '/' << no2 << '=' << CalcDiv(no1,no2);
   }
   //*** it will be caught here ***
   catch(int)
   {
       cerr << "Exception thrown"<<endl;
   }
   cout << "PROGRAM TERMINATED\n";
}


double CalcSqrt(double v)
{
   if(v < 0)
       throw -1;
   return sqrt(v);
}

double CalcDiv(double n1, double n2)
{
   if(n2 == 0)
       throw -2;
   return n1/n2;
}
```

PROGRAMMING EXERCISE 14.4

Enter the program above and test it with the following values:

a) 9 4
b) 9 -8
c) -9 8
d) 7 0

You may have noticed that although both functions throw `int` values, these values are different (-1 and -2). Also, the `catch` block does not differentiate between the two error conditions, giving the same message for both.

We can make the catch command deal with each exception differently in two ways:

Using a `catch` Variable

We are at liberty to give a variable name to the type specified in the `catch` parameter:

```
catch(int value)
```

When this is done, the value thrown by the exception can now be referenced in the `catch` block:

```
catch(int value)
{
    cout << "Exception thrown : " << value << endl;
}
```

> **PROGRAMMING EXERCISE 14.5**
>
> Modify your program from PROGRAMMING EXERCISE 14.4 to display either *"Error performing the square root operation"* or *"Error performing division operation"* as appropriate when an exception is thrown.
> This should be done by using a `switch` statement in the `catch` block.

Throwing Different Types

An alternative approach to separating the handling of different exceptions is to make the exception throw different value types. Hence, we might rewrite our *CalcDiv()* function to be:

```
double CalcDiv(double n1, double n2)
{
    if(n2 == 0)
        throw "Division error";
    return n1/n2;
}
```

Of course, this exception will not be caught by our previous `catch` block which only receives `int` exception, so a new `catch` block is required to catch the `char*` type thrown by *CalcDiv()*. LISTING-14.6.

LISTING-14.6

Throwing Different Exception Types

```
#include<iostream.h>
#include<math.h>

double CalcSqrt(double);
double CalcDiv(double,double);

void main()
{
  double no1,no2;

  cout << "Enter two numbers : ";
  cin >> no1 >> no2;
  try
  {
      cout << "Square roots are " << CalcSqrt(no1) << ' '
           << CalcSqrt(no2)<<endl;
      cout << no1 << '/' << no2 << '=' << CalcDiv(no1,no2);
  }
```

Continued on next page

LISTING-14.6
(continued)

Throwing Different Exception Types

```
    //*** Two catch options ***

    //*** Catches int exceptions ***
    catch(int)
    {
        cerr << "Program failed performing square root operation\n";
    }
    //*** Catches char* exceptions ***
    catch(char*)
    {
        cerr<< "Program failed performing division operation\n";
    }

    //*** Executed unconditionally ***
    cout << "PROGRAM TERMINATED\n";
}


double CalcSqrt(double v)
{
    if(v < 0)
        throw -1;
    return sqrt(v);
}


double CalcDiv(double n1, double n2)
{
    if(n2 == 0)
        throw "Division error";
    return n1/n2;
}
```

Where several `catch` blocks are defined, only the first one which matches the type thrown will be executed, all others will be ignored.

Often the `catch` block will need to terminate execution of the program since the exception caught indicates a fault too serious to continue. To achieve this we need simply add an `exit()` call within the catch block:

```
catch(char*)
{
    cerr << "Program failed performing division operation\n";
    exit(1);
}
```

Dealing with Unhandled Exceptions

When writing a function we are at liberty to specify which type of exceptions that function is capable of throwing as part of the function prototype. Hence we could write

```
double CalcSqrt(double)          throw(int);
double CalcDiv(double,double)    throw(char*);
```

to document the type of exceptions these functions are capable of throwing.

It is possible that a complex routine may have several `throw` statements within it. If each of these threw different types, then the prototype would list those types. Hence, if *myfunct()* contained code to throw `int, float` and `char` exceptions, the prototype for the function would be:

```
float myfunct(int) throw(int,float,char);
```

Where a function contains no throws, this can also be declared explicitly within the function prototype by adding the term `throw()`. Hence, the prototype

```
int next(int) throw();
```

states that the function *next()* throws no exceptions.

Without a statement of what a function throws, it may throw any exceptions it wishes.

If stated in the prototype, the `throw()` descriptions must also be given in the function definition.

There are two likely programming errors which may occur when dealing with exceptions:

1) Where a list of possible exception types is included in a function's prototype, an exception of a type not stated may be thrown.
2) An exception may be thrown for which no handler (i.e. `catch` block) exists.

In the first case, the exception is handled by an automatic call to a predefined function called `unexpected()`. This, in turn, calls `terminate()`, which then calls `abort()`. This final routine terminates the program with an error message.

In the second case, where no handler exists for an exception, `terminate()` is called.

PROGRAMMING EXERCISE 14.6

1. Enter and run the program in LISTING-14.6. Test it by creating error conditions for both exceptions.

2. Change the type caught by the second exception to an `int` and re-run the program, causing a divide error. (This causes the `unexpected()` function to be called).

3. Change the prototype of *CalcSqrt()* to
   ```
   double CalcSqrt(double) throw();
   ```
   making the first line of the definition
   ```
   double CalcSqrt(double v) throw();
   ```
   Re-run the program and cause an error by entering a negative value.

Replacing `unexpected()` and `terminate()`

It is possible to write our own version of the `unexpected()` function. To do this we need to:

1) Add a `#include<except.h>` statement to the start of our program.
2) Write a function to replace `unexpected()`. This function must return no value and take no parameters.
3) Call `set_unexpected()` giving the address of our replacement function as its argument.

The `terminate()` function can be replaced in a similar way using `set_terminate()` to give the address of the replacement routine.

The program in LISTING-14.7 demonstrate the use of these techniques.

LISTING-14.7

Replacing *unexpected()* and *terminate()*

```
#include<iostream.h>
#include<math.h>
#include<except.h>

double CalcSqrt(double)throw();  //*** No throws from CalcSqrt()
double CalcDiv(double,double);
//***Prototypes for unexpected() & terminate() replacements***
void HandleInvalidThrow();
void HandleUncaughtThrow();


void main()
{
    double no1,no2;

    //*** Set new addresses for replacements ***
    set_unexpected(HandleInvalidThrow);
    set_terminate(HandleUncaughtThrow);

    cout << "Enter two numbers : ";
    cin >> no1 >> no2;
    try
    {
        cout << "Square roots are " << CalcSqrt(no1) << ' '
            << CalcSqrt(no2) << endl;
        cout << no1 << '/' << no2 << '=' << CalcDiv(no1,no2);
    }
    catch(int)
    {
        cerr << "Program failed performing square root operation\n";
    }
    catch(char*)
    {
        cerr << "Program failed performing division operation\n";
    }
    cout << "PROGRAM TERMINATED\n";
}

//*** State types thrown (none) ***
double CalcSqrt(double v) throw()
{
    if(v < 0)
        throw 2.5;    //*** But does perform an unstated throw ***
    return sqrt(v);
}


double CalcDiv(double n1, double n2)
{
    if(n2 == 0)
        throw 2.5;    //*** Performs a throw which has no handler
    return n1/n2;
}

//*** Replacement for unexpected() ***
void HandleInvalidThrow()
{
    cerr << "Routine threw undeclared type\n";
    exit(1);
}

//*** Replacement for terminate() ***
void HandleUncaughtThrow()
{
    cerr << "There was no catch for this throw \n";
    exit(2);
}
```

PROGRAMMING EXERCISE 14.7

Enter and run the program in LISTING-14.7, causing both error conditions to be created.

A Universal Handler

Instead of creating a replacement for `terminate()`, it is possible to create a `catch` block which will handle any exception by replacing the parameter type with an ellipsis:

```
catch(...)
{
    //*** All exceptions will be caught by this block ***
    //*** unless already handled by an earlier catch block ***
}
```

Since, when an exception is thrown, only the first matching `catch` block is executed, the catch-all method above must appear as the last `catch` option otherwise it will handle exceptions intended for other `catch` blocks.

Throwing Class Objects

If functions are going to throw exceptions using only the standard types (`int`, `float`, `char`, etc.) we are soon going to run out of options. We may also discover that library functions are throwing the same exception types as our own routines - something which might cause some confusion in our programs.

This problem can be solved by creating and throwing our own error class objects. The program in LISTING-14.8 shows how this is done.

LISTING-14.8

Throwing Classes

```
#include<iostream.h>
#include<math.h>

//*** Declare error classes ***
class SqrtErr{};
class DivErr{};
double CalcSqrt(double);
double CalcDiv(double,double);

void main()
{
  double no1,no2;

  cout << "Enter two numbers : ";
  cin >> no1 >> no2;
  try
  {
      cout << "Square roots are " << CalcSqrt(no1) << ' '
          << CalcSqrt(no2) << endl;
      cout << no1 << '/' << no2 << '=' << CalcDiv(no1,no2);
  }
  //*** Catch SqrtErr class ***
  catch(SqrtErr)
  {
      cerr << "Program failed performing square root operation\n";
  }
```

Continued on next page

LISTING-14.8
(continued)

Throwing Classes

```
    //*** Catch DivErr class ***
    catch(DivErr)
    {
        cerr << "Program failed performing division operation\n";
    }
    cout << "PROGRAM TERMINATED\n";
}


double CalcSqrt(double v)
{
    if(v < 0)
        //*** Throw a SqrtErr object ***
        throw SqrtErr();
    return sqrt(v);
}

double CalcDiv(double n1, double n2)
{
    if(n2 == 0)
        //*** Throw a DivErr object ***
        throw DivErr();
    return n1/n2;
}
```

Points to Note

The program declares two classes at the start of the code. These are like no classes we've come across before since they contain no characteristics. However, this is all that's needed in this case:

```
class SqrtErr{};
class DivErr{};
```

The class names can now be treated as new types, capable of being specified in a `catch()` block header:

```
catch(SqrtErr)
```

To throw an object of these types we need to specify the class name and the arguments required by the constructor; this creates an object constant:

```
throw DivErr();
```

If it suits our purposes, we may declare and throw more complex class objects. Hence, if we wanted our *SqrtErr* class to contain a message, we could write:

```
class SqrtErr
{
    private:
        char message[31];
    public:
        SqrtErr(char*);
        void Display();
};
SqrtErr::SqrtErr(char* m)
{
    strcpy(message,m);
};
void SqrtErr::Display()
{
    cout << message << endl;
};
```

This gives us the necessary attributes and methods to set and display a message.

When we throw an object of this class, its constructor must be called with an appropriate string:

```
double CalcSqrt(double v)
{
    if(v < 0)
        throw SqrtErr("Square Root Error");
    return sqrt(v);
}
```

If this is then caught as a named object, we can access the string field to display the message received from the function.

```
catch(SqrtErr se)
{
    se.Display();
}
```

PROGRAMMING EXERCISE 14.8

Using the *SqrtErr* class described above, and a similarly expanded *DivErr* class, update the program in LISTING-14.8 to display the messages returned by the exceptions thrown.

Error Class Hierarchies

It is possible to create a hierarchy of error classes. For example, let's assume that we are about to write the *list, queue* and *stack* structures as a set of classes which might throw *listerr, queueerr* or *stackerr* exceptions respectively. It is possible to create a relation between our error classes:

```
class listerr
{
    //class details go here
};

class queueerr: public listerr
{
    // new class details go here
};

class stackerr: public listerr
{
    // new class details go here
};
```

Now, since *queueerr* and *stackerr* are descendants of *listerr*, a *listerr* handler will catch any of the three classes. If we want the exception classes handled separately, we must ensure that the base class handler (i.e. the `catch` block for *listerr*) appears last.

Handling Resources

If a routine makes use of a file, the file must be closed when it is no longer required; if a block of memory is dynamically allocated, it should be deallocated when no longer required. However, there are situations where this may not happen. For example, consider the outline function below:

```
void myfunct1( )
{
    int *ptr;
    ptr = new int[4000];
```

```
        myfunct2();
        delete[] ptr;
}

void myfunct2()
{

    //IF some error THEN
    //    throw an int exception
}
```

If *myfunct2()* throws an exception, the remaining code in *myfunct1()* will be bypassed which will result in the dynamically allocated space not being freed.

Of course, we could get round this by placing a `try` block and handler in *myfunct1()*:

```
void myfunct1()
{
    int *ptr;
    ptr = new int [4000];
    try
    {
        myfunct2();
    }
    catch(int)
    {
        delete [] ptr;
        throw;
    }
    delete[] ptr;
}
```

Notice, the catch block contains another throw without a value. This allows the exception to be thrown to a higher level `try` block, probably in the routine calling *myfunct1()*.

This method works, but is messy, since we end up duplicating the `delete` instruction.

An alternative is to perform the task of allocating and deallocating memory within a class of its own:

```
class MemBlock
{
    private:
        int *ptr;
    public:
        MemBlock(int);//Allocate memory block
        ~MemBlock();    //Deallocates memory block;
};
```

Now we can write *myfunct1()* as:

```
void myfunct1()
{
    MemBlock ptr(4000);
    myfunct2();
}
```

The need to worry about deallocation has gone completely. Why? Because, the *MemBlock* class destructor will be called on normal exit from *myfunct1()* and also if *myfunct2()* throws an exception (remember, local variables and objects are automatically deallocated and any associated destructor executed).

Summary

■ **An exception** is an error indicator thrown by a section of code to indicate some error or unexpected condition has occurred.

■ **Typical uses of an exception**: Invalid function parameters, array subscripts out of bounds, division by zero, etc. where error handling is to be dealt with in another function from the one in which the error was detected.

■ **Exceptions should not be used** where normal error handling methods are sufficient.

■ **The format for a `throw` statement is**:

```
throw value;
```

■ **An exception can be thrown from**:

a) code within a try block
b) a function called directly by the try block
c) a function called indirectly from the try block

■ **Once thrown, an exception causes** the remaining code in its function to be ignored. Any local variables are deallocated; any local objects are destroyed using their destructor.

■ **The remainder of the `try` block is bypassed** when an exception is thrown.

■ **The general format for an exception handler is**:

```
try
{
    actions
}
catch( type [name] )
{
    actions
}
```

There may be many `catch` blocks.

■ **Where a name is given in the `catch` block parameter**, this may be used within the `try` block to reference the value thrown.

■ **A `catch` block which catches all exceptions has the format:**

```
catch(...)
{
    actions
}
```

■ **The first `catch` block matching the type thrown** will be executed; all other `catch` blocks are ignored.

■ **A class object may be thrown** by an exception.

■ **When an object is thrown**, the first `catch` specifying that class or an ancestor of that class is executed; other `catch` blocks are ignored.

- **A function's prototype** and definition may specify the type of exceptions thrown by that function.
- When a function throws an exception type not specified in this list, the function `unexpected()` is executed.
- `unexpected()` defaults to executing `terminate()`, which calls `abort()` to stop execution of the program.
- **If an exception is thrown for which there is no `catch` block,** `terminate()` is executed.
- **Alternative routines** may be defined for `unexpected()` and `terminate()` using `set_unexpected()` and `set_terminate()`.
- **Allocated resources** (e.g. files or dynamically allocated memory) should be deallocated before exiting a routine throwing an exception.

Solutions

TASK 14.1

```
1.
int *ptr;
ptr = new int [500];
assert(ptr!=0);

2.
cin>>x>>y;
assert(x>=1&&x<=80&&y>=1&&y<=25);
gotoxy(x.y);
```

PROGRAMMING EXERCISE 14.1

```
#define NDEBUG
#include<iostream.h>
#include<assert.h>

void main()
{
    float no1,no2,ans;
    cout<<"Enter two numbers ";
    cin>>no1>>no2;
    assert(no2!=0);
    ans = no1/no2;
    cout<<no1<<'/'<<no2<<'='<<ans<<endl;
}
```

The program now displays a *Floating point: Divide by zero error* message.

PROGRAMMING EXERCISE 14.2

```
#include<iostream.h>
#include<math.h>
void main()
{
    double no1,no2;

    cout<<"Enter two numbers : ";
    cin>>no1>>no2;
    try
    {
        if(no2==0)
            throw 1;
        cout<<no1<<'/'<<no2<<'='<<(no1/no2)<<endl;
    }
    catch(int)
    {
        cout<<"Exception thrown"<<endl;
    }
}
```

PROGRAMMING EXERCISE 14.3

```
#include<iostream.h>
#include<math.h>

double CalcDiv(double,double);
void main()
{
    double no1,no2;
    cout<<"Enter two numbers : ";
    cin>>no1>>no2;
    try
    {
        cout<<no1<<'/'<<no2<<'='
            <<CalcDiv(no1,no2)<<endl;
    }
    catch(int)
    {
        cout<<"Exception thrown"<<endl;
    }
    cout<<"PROGRAM TERMINATED\n";
}

double CalcDiv(double n1, double n2)
{
    if(n2==0)
        throw 1;
    return n1/n2;
}
```

PROGRAMMING EXERCISE 14.4

No solution required.

PROGRAMMING EXERCISE 14.5

```
#include<iostream.h>
#include<math.h>

double CalcSqrt(double);
double CalcDiv(double,double);

void main()
{
    double no1,no2;

    cout<<"Enter two numbers : ";
    cin>>no1>>no2;
    try
    {
        cout<<"Square roots are "<<CalcSqrt(no1)
            <<' '<<CalcSqrt(no2)<<endl;
        cout<<no1<<'/'<<no2<<'='<<CalcDiv(no1,no2);
    }
    catch(int value)
    {
        switch(value)
        {
            case -1:
                cerr<<"Error performing the"
                    " square root operation\n";
                break;
            case -2:
                cerr<<"Error performing division"
                    " operation\n";
        }
    }
    cout<<"PROGRAM TERMINATED\n";
}


double CalcSqrt(double v)
{
    if(v<0)
        throw -1;
    return sqrt(v);
}

double CalcDiv(double n1, double n2)
{
    if(n2==0)
        throw -2;
    return n1/n2;
}
```

PROGRAMMING EXERCISE 14.6

No solution required.

PROGRAMMING EXERCISE 14.7

No solution required.

PROGRAMMING EXERCISE 14.8

The new class is coded as:

```
class DivErr
{
    private:
        char mesage[31];
    public:
        void Display();
};
void DivErr::Display()
{
    cout<<message<<endl;
};
```

This allows us to use the code

```
double CalcDiv(double n1, double n2)
{
    if(n2==0)
        throw DivErr("Divisor zero error");
    return n1/n2;
}
```

to throw the error.

Catching the exception then requires:

```
catch(DivErr se)
{
    se.Display();
}
```

Appendix A ASCII Character Set

Dec	Hex	Char
00	00	nul
01	01	soh
02	02	stx
03	03	etx
04	04	eot
05	05	enq
06	06	ack
07	07	bel
08	08	bs
09	09	ht
10	0A	nl
11	0B	vt
12	0C	ff
13	0D	cr
14	0E	so
15	0F	si
16	10	dle
17	11	dcl
18	12	dc2
19	13	dc3
20	14	dc4
21	15	nak
22	16	syn
23	17	etb
24	18	can
25	19	em
26	1A	sub
27	1B	esc
28	1C	fs
29	1D	gs
30	1E	rs
31	1F	us
32	20	space
33	21	!
34	22	"
35	23	#
36	24	$
37	25	%
38	26	&
39	27	'
40	28	(
41	29	)
42	2A	*
43	2B	+
44	2C	,
45	2D	-
46	2E	.
47	2F	/
48	30	0
49	31	1
50	32	2
51	33	3
52	34	4
53	35	5
54	36	6
55	37	7
56	38	8
57	39	9
58	3A	:
59	3B	;
60	3C	<
61	3D	=
62	3E	>
63	úF	?
64	40	@
65	41	A
66	42	B
67	43	C
68	44	D
69	45	E
70	46	F
71	47	G
72	48	H
73	49	I
74	4A	J
75	4B	K
76	4C	L
77	4D	M
78	4E	N
79	4F	O
80	50	P
81	51	Q
82	52	R
83	53	S
84	54	T
85	55	U
86	56	V
87	57	W
88	58	X
89	59	Y
90	5A	Z
91	5B	[
92	5C	\
93	5D	]
94	5E	^
95	5F	_
96	60	`
97	61	a
98	62	b
99	63	c
100	64	d
101	65	e
102	66	f
103	67	g
104	68	h
105	69	i
106	6A	j
107	6B	k
108	6C	l
109	6D	m
110	6E	n
111	6F	o
112	70	p
113	71	q
114	72	r
115	73	s
116	74	t
117	75	u
118	76	v
119	77	w
120	78	x
121	79	y
122	7A	z
123	7B	{
124	7C	|
125	7D	}
126	7E	~
127	7F	del

Appendix B Operator Precedence

RANK	OPERATOR	MEANING
1	::	Scope resolution
	::	Global variable access
	[]	Array subscript
	()	Function call
	()	Enclosed expression
	.	Member selection (object)
	->	Member selection (pointer)
2	++	Increment
	--	Decrement
	new	Allocate space
	delete	Delete space
	*	Dereference
	&	Address of
	+	Unary plus
	-	Unary minus
	!	Not
	~	Bitwise complement
	sizeof	Size of type
	(type)	Typecast
	.*	Apply pointer to class member
	->*	Dereference pointer to class
3	*	Multiplication
	/	Division
	%	Remainder
4	+	Addition
	-	Subtraction
5	<<	Shift left
	>>	Shift right
6	<	Less than
	<=	Less than or equal to
	>	Greater than
	>=	Greater than or equal to
7	==	Equal to
	!=	Not equal to
8	&	Bitwise AND
9	^	Bitwise Exclusive OR
10	|	Bitwise OR
11	&&	AND
12	||	OR
13	? :	Conditional assignment
14	=	Assignment
	*=	Multiplication assignment
	/=	Division assignment
	%=	Remainder assignment
	+=	Addition assignment
	-=	Subtraction assignment
	<<=	Shift left assignment
	>>=	Shift right assignment
	&=	Bitwise AND assignment
	|=	Bitwise OR assignment
	^=	Bitwise Exclusive OR assignment
15	,	Comma

Index

C

D

E

F

G

H

I

K

L

M

N

O